The Perfection of Freedom

VERITAS

Series Introduction

"... the truth will set you free." (John 8:32)

In much contemporary discourse, Pilate's question has been taken to mark the absolute boundary of human thought. Beyond this boundary, it is often suggested, is an intellectual hinterland into which we must not venture. This terrain is an agnosticism of thought: because truth cannot be possessed, it must not be spoken. Thus, it is argued that the defenders of "truth" in our day are often traffickers in ideology, merchants of counterfeits, or anti-liberal. They are, because it is somewhat taken for granted that Nietzsche's word is final: truth is the domain of tyranny.

Is this indeed the case, or might another vision of truth offer itself? The ancient Greeks named the love of wisdom as *philia*, or friendship. The one who would become wise, they argued, would be a "friend of truth." For both philosophy and theology might be conceived as schools in the friendship of truth, as a kind of relation. For like friendship, truth is as much discovered as it is made. If truth is then so elusive, if its domain is *terra incognita*, perhaps this is because it arrives to us—unannounced—as gift, as a person, and not some thing.

The aim of the Veritas book series is to publish incisive and original current scholarly work that inhabits "the between" and "the beyond" of theology and philosophy. These volumes will all share a common aspiration to transcend the institutional divorce in which these two disciplines often find themselves, and to engage questions of pressing concern to both philosophers and theologians in such a way as to reinvigorate both disciples with a kind of interdisciplinary desire, often so absent in contemporary academe. In a word, these volumes represent collective efforts in the befriending of truth, doing so beyond the simulacra of pretend tolerance, the violent, yet insipid reasoning of liberalism that asks with Pilate, "What is truth?"—expecting a consensus of non-commitment; one that encourages the commodification of the mind, now sedated by the civil service of career, ministered by the frightened patrons of position.

The series will therefore consist of two "wings": (1) original monographs; and (2) essay collections on a range of topics in theology and philosophy. The latter will principally by the products of the annual conferences of the Centre of Theology and Philosophy (www.theologyphilosophycentre.co.uk).

Conor Cunningham
Peter Candler
Series editors

The Perfection of Freedom

Schiller, Schelling, and Hegel
between the Ancients and the Moderns

D. C. SCHINDLER

CASCADE *Books* • Eugene, Oregon

THE PERFECTION OF FREEDOM
Schiller, Schelling, and Hegel between the Ancients and the Moderns

Veritas 8

Copyright © 2012 D. C. Schindler. All rights reserved. Except for brief quotations in critical publications or reviews, no part of this book may be reproduced in any manner without prior written permission from the publisher. Write: Permissions, Wipf and Stock Publishers, 199 W. 8th Ave., Suite 3, Eugene, OR 97401.

Cascade Books
A Division of Wipf and Stock Publishers
199 W. 8th Ave., Suite 3
Eugene, OR 97401

www.wipfandstock.com

ISBN 13: 978-1-62032-182-9

Cataloging-in-Publication data:

    Schindler, D. C.

    The perfection of freedom : Schiller, Schelling, and Hegel between the ancients and the moderns / D. C. Schindler.

    Veritas 8

    xxvi + 414 p. ; 23 cm. Includes bibliographical references and index.

    ISBN 13: 978-1-62032-182-9

    1. Schiller, Friedrich, 1759–1805. 2. Schelling, Friedrich Wilhem Joseph von, 1775–1854. 3. Hegel, Georg Wilhelm Friedrich, 1770–1831. 4. Liberty—Philosophy. 5. Metaphysics. I. Title. II. Series.

B2898 S35 2012

Manufactured in the U.S.A.

For **Davy**, who was born the week I put pen to paper;
John, who was born the month I finished the first draft;
and **Eva**, who was born the month I completed the book.

L'ordre, et l'ordre seul, fait en définitive la liberté.
Le désordre fait la servitude.

—Charles Péguy

Wer Großes will, muß sich zusammenraffen;
In der Beschränkung zeigt sich erst der Meister,
Und das Gesetz nur kann uns Freiheit geben.

—Goethe

Contents

Acknowledgments ix
Abbreviations x

Introduction: On the German Contribution:
Giving Form to Freedom xiii

1. **Friedrich Schiller's Dramatic Philosophy: Freedom in Form** 1
   I. On the Significance of Style 1
   II. Biographical Background 4
   III. Nature Speaks to Nature 9
   IV. Writing as a Free Gift 16
   V. Meaning in Motion 22
   VI. Elements of the Dramatic 28
   VII. Freestyle 38
   VIII. Poet or Philosopher? 41

2. **An Aesthetics of Freedom: Schiller and the Living Gestalt** 49
   I. Introduction: Schiller's Breakthrough 49
   II. The Analogy of Form 51
   III. Form Overcoming Form 55
   IV. Manifest Freedom in Nature 60
   V. Heautonomy and Heteronomy 71
   VI. Freedom and Human Nature 76
   VII. Living Gestalt and Human Wholeness 85
   VIII. The Seriousness of Play 91
   IX. A Criticism and the Question of Contradiction 98
   X. Nobility or Bourgeois Aestheticism? 109

3. **The Dark Roots of Life: Organic Form as a Symbol of Freedom in Schelling's *Naturphilosophie*** 111
   I. The Philosophy of the Future 111
   II. The Origins of Schelling's *Naturphilosophie* 117

Contents

- III. The Impoverishment of Nature 120
- IV. The Impoverishment of Spirit 132
- V. *Naturphilosophie* and the Place of the Organism 143
- VI. Natural Freedom 159
- VII. Freedom or Form? 164

4. **From Organism to Incarnation: The Fall and Redemption of Finite Form in Schelling's Late Philosophy** 171
   - I. Ontological Freedom 171
   - II. The Fate of the Real in the Early Systems 177
   - III. The Positivity of Finite Freedom 188
   - IV. The Actuality of Evil and Love in History 197
   - V. Creation as Theogony 207
   - VI. Love, Nature, and Freedom: A Final Assessment 226

5. **Freedom as the Concrete Form of Reason in Hegel's *Philosophy of Right*** 238
   - I. Introduction: Hegel's Uniqueness 238
   - II. Preliminary Considerations 242
   - III. Rational Politics 248
   - IV. Political Reason 255
   - V. On the Meaning of Actuality 261
   - VI. Philosophical Sources 266
   - VII. The Importance of Being Finite 277
   - VIII. The Will as Concrete Freedom 283
   - IX. Conclusion 295

6. **"The 'I' That Is 'We' and the 'We' That Is 'I'": On the Sociality of Freedom in Hegel and Its Excesses** 301
   - I. The Controversy Surrounding Hegel's Conception of the State 301
   - II. Communal Spirit 305
   - III. *Sittlichkeit* as Social Form 320
   - IV. Freedom and Absolute Spirit 357

7. **A Dramatic Conclusion: Opening Up Actual Possibility** 373

Bibliography 385
Index 401

Acknowledgments

MOST OF THE RESEARCH and reflection for this book, and a large part of the writing of the initial draft, took place in Munich from the summer of 2007 to the summer of 2008. That year was made possible by a generous grant from the Alexander von Humboldt foundation, as well as by a sabbatical provided by Villanova University. A number of people made the time especially fruitful and offered all manner of help to me, my wife, Jeanne, and eventually our first son, during our time abroad. I would like, first of all, to thank Thomas Buchheim and his wife, Iris, for so generously hosting us. Thomas was unstinting in his willingness to help me puzzle through one point or another in Schelling's late works, and find my way to various academic resources. I also wish to express gratitude to the following people for their friendship, conversation, and hospitality while we were in Munich: Marie-Elisabeth Hoyos, Rocio Daga, Erika and Sebastian Hügel, Nicoletta Lotti, Fr. Stefan Oster, Ferdinand Ulrich, Stefan and Susanne Rugel, Mette Lebech, Asa and Sabine McWilliams, Rémi Brague, Martin Groos, Axel Hütter, and Ana Álvarez. My colleagues in the Humanities Department at Villanova offered helpful suggestions for the introduction and conclusion. I wish to thank Conor Cunningham for finding a fitting home for this book, Robin Parry and Heather Carraher for their gracious and efficient help seeing the manuscript through the editorial process, and Michael Camacho for his careful work proofreading and preparing the index. I owe a special debt, moreover, to two professors I was fortunate to have in graduate school: Richard Vekley, who first introduced me to Schelling, and Riccardo Pozzo, who opened up dimensions of Hegel that I had never considered before. Finally, I am immeasurably grateful to my wife and our three children, to whom this book is dedicated.

The Irish Philosophical Society has kindly granted permission to reprint, in chapter 2 of the present book, material that originally appeared as "An Aesthetics of Freedom: Friedrich Schiller's Breakthrough Beyond Subjectivity," *Yearbook of the Irish Philosophical Society* (2008) 84–109.

Abbreviations

1802 System	Schelling's *On the Relation of Natural Philosophy to Philosophy in General*
1804 System	Schelling's *System of Philosophy in General and of the Philosophy of Nature in Particular*
A	Anmerkung, i.e., 'Remark,' after section numbers in texts by Hegel.
AEM	Schiller's *Letters on the Aesthetic Education of Man*
Anti-Fichte	Schelling's *Exposition of the True Relationship of the Philosophy of Nature to the Improved Version of Fichte's Teaching*
Aph	Schelling's *Aphorisms on the Philosophy of Nature*
AS	Schelling's *Lectures on the Method of Academic Study*
B	The critical edition of Schelling's *Freiheitsschrift*, edited by Thomas Buchheim
Bruno	Schelling's *Bruno, or On the Natural and the Divine Principle of Things*
CJ	Kant's *Critique of Judgment*
CPR	Kant's *Critique of Pure Reason*
CPrR	Kant's *Critique of Practical Reason*
DK	Diels' and Kranz's edition of the fragments of the Presocratic philosophers
DS	Hegel's *The Difference between Fichte's and Schelling's System of Philosophy*
E (1817), (1827), (1830)	Hegel's *Encyclopedia*, first, second, and third editions
EE	Schelling's *First Sketch of a System of Naturphilosophie*
EEE	Schelling's *Introduction to the First Sketch of a System of Naturphilosophie*

Abbreviations

Freedom	Schelling's *Philosophical Investigations into the Essence of Human Freedom*
Further Expositions	Schelling's *Further Expositions of My System of Philosophy*
GL	Hegel's *"Greater Logic"*
GPP	Schelling's *Grounding of the Positive Philosophy*
Grace	Schiller's *On Grace and Dignity*
GW	Hegel's *Gesammelte Werke*
Hist of Phil	Hegel's *Lectures on the History of Philosophy*
HK	Hermann Klenner's edition of Hegel's *Grundlinien der Philosophies des Rechts*
HMP	Schelling's *On the History of Modern Philosophy*
Ideas	Schelling's *Ideas for a Philosophy of Nature*
Intro to Aph	Schelling's *Introduction to the Aphorisms on the Philosophy of Nature*
Intro to PH	Hegel's *Introduction to the Philosophy of History*
JA	The *"Jubiläumsausgabe"* of Hegel's collected works
KA	The critical edition of Schelling's complete works
Kallias	Schiller's *Kalliasbriefe*
Kemp Smith	Norman Kemp-Smith's translation of Kant's *Critique of Pure Reason.*
LPR	Hegel's *Lectures on the Philosophy of Religion*
Meta.	Aristotle's *Metaphysics*
My System	Schelling's *Exposition of My System of Philosophy*
NLB	Schiller's *On the Necessary Limits of the Beautiful*
PandR	Schelling's *Philosophy and Religion*
Phen	Hegel's *Phenomenology of Spirit*
Phil Letters	Schelling's *The Philosophical Letters*
Phil of Art	Schelling's *Philosophy of Art*
Plastic	Schelling's *On the Relationship of the Plastic Arts to Nature*
Pluhar	Werner S. Pluhar's translation of Kant's *Critique of Judgment.*
PM	Schelling's *Historical-Critical Introduction to the Philosophy of Mythology*
PO	Schelling's *Philosophie der Offenbarung*
PR	Hegel's *Philosophy of Right*
Rev	Schelling's *Philosophy of Revelation*, as published in the complete works
SS	Schelling's *Stuttgart Seminars*
ST	Aquinas's *Summa Theologiae*

Abbreviations

STI	Schelling's *System of Transcendental Idealism*
SW	Schiller's *Sämmtliche Werke*
UD	Schelling's *Universal Deduction of the Dynamic Process*
V	Hegel's *Vorlesungen*
W	Schelling's *Werke* (Schröter edition)
WA (1811), (1813), (1815)	Schelling's various drafts of the *Ages of the World*
WA (1827)	Schelling's *System der Weltalter* (Munich Lectures of 1827)
WS	Schelling's *On the World Soul*
WW	Wilkinson and Willhoughby's edition of Schiller's *On the Aesthetic Education of Man*
Z	Zusatz, i.e., 'Addition,' after section numbers in texts by Hegel.

INTRODUCTION

On the German Contribution: Giving Form to Freedom

BECAUSE THIS BOOK TAKES an unusual approach to the philosophy of freedom, it is appropriate to preface it with some explanation of why it was written, what it aims to accomplish, and how it proposes to accomplish it.

The reason for the book can be stated simply: it was written out of a conviction that our current conception of freedom is deeply problematic. Although we cannot enter here into a full exploration of the current conception and its implications,[1] it is important to say enough to orient the reader to the study of Schiller, Schelling, and Hegel that follows. On the one hand, there is a general recognition—regardless of where one falls in the political spectrum—of freedom as a great human good, something worth promoting and protecting even at the cost of sacrificing other goods; on the other hand, there has been an impoverishment of our understanding of the notion, so that freedom has come to represent little more in the popular imagination than the power to choose. What is problematic about this understanding is not simply that it fails to do justice to the reality that originally warranted recognition as a great human good. What we wish to suggest is that this reduction actively undermines the *good-character* of freedom. In other words, our claim is that there is something essentially self-destructive in the contemporary relationship to freedom; the nature

---

1. Problems with the conventional view have been raised from a variety of different perspectives, for example: Murdoch, *The Sovereignty of Good*; Pinckaers, *The Sources of Christian Ethics*; MacIntyre, *After Virtue: A Study in Moral Theory*; Sandel, *Democracy's Discontent: America in Search of a Public Philosophy*; Taylor, *Ethics of Authenticity*; Hart, *Atheist Delusions: The Christian Revolution and Its Fashionable Enemies*. We have worked out some of the problematic implications in "Freedom Beyond Our Choosing: Augustine on the Will and Its Objects," in *Augustine and Politics*, 67–96, esp. 68–75.

Introduction—On the German Contribution

of what we pursue erodes the very thing we wish to affirm and cultivate. The problem, in a nutshell, is that we think of freedom as an end but define it as a means, and so we treat a *bonum utile* as if it were a *bonum honestum*. But this is not a mere problem of logic or classification. Instead, this confusion has far-reaching philosophical and cultural implications. To put the problem in its starkest terms, instrumental goods can only ever be good in a derivative sense; a means can be, not just an instrument, but an instrumental *good*, only through a relationship to an end to which it is subordinate. If we make a means an end in itself, we do two things at once: we both eliminate its goodness and we elevate its status; we transform the absence of goodness into a purpose. Inside of this confusion of ends and means is therefore what we could justifiably call a kind of nihilism. To the extent that we exclude those features of freedom that would qualify it as an end, and at the same time continue to promote it as such even in this reduced form, our notion of freedom becomes a source of nihilism.

The difficulty seems to stem from the conception of freedom in terms of possibility or potency: it is the *power* to choose or the *ability* to do X, Y, or Z. While this view of freedom—which we will henceforward refer to as the "possibilistic" conception—is quite obvious in the popular definition of freedom as indeterminate choice; it also lies in the highest-level articulations of the dominant political theory of contemporary English-speaking society. According to John Rawls, for example, to be free means two things: "First, citizens are free in that they conceive of themselves and of one another as having the moral power to have a conception of the good."[2] He goes on to specify this as the "moral power to form, to revise, and rationally to pursue a conception of the good," and to include in the meaning of this power the right of citizens "to view their persons as independent from and not identified with any particular conception of the good."[3] Second, it means that free persons "regard themselves as self-authenticating sources of valid claims," which means they regard themselves "as being entitled to make claims on their institutions so as to advance their conceptions of the good."[4] Now, it is not the place here to enter into a discussion of Rawls' theory in all its detail; we wish only to point out the identification of freedom with *power* that lies at the foundation of this theory. It is a power that he characterizes as standing *over* the good, insofar as the power determines the good (i.e., the means determine the

---

2. Rawls, *Justice as Fairness: A Restatement*, 21.
3. Ibid.
4. Ibid., 23.

Introduction—On the German Contribution

end) rather than the other way around. This power is absolute in the sense that it stands *outside of* and *above* any context (it is "independent from and not identified with any particular conception of the good"), and in the sense that it is, therefore, essentially "self-authenticating," which means its goodness, its justification, does not derive from anything outside of itself. The social expression of freedom, according to Rawls' view, is the radiation of the power from individual agents into the public sphere; it is, so to speak, the force of this power felt by institutions. It may be the case, in reality, that people cannot help but be determined to some extent by the institutions—culture, family, tradition, and so forth—in which they live, but this means only that people are not perfectly free. To be free is to have *power over* these institutions. Rawls' description of freedom is a paradigm of the "possibilistic" conception that we have suggested bears within itself a latent nihilism.

As Steven Smith has observed, "[i]t is now virtually a commonplace that as a theory of politics, not to mention human personality, liberalism is seriously impoverished."[5] But the greater part of the discussions of freedom in the English-speaking world tend to take for granted some version of the possibilistic conception of freedom as the starting point of the conversation rather than the very thing that requires scrutiny. So, for example, in the political arena, the discussion generally concerns how best to protect and promote the ability to choose, and where exactly to place the boundary that marks the point at which this ability must subordinate itself to the order imposed by law, or the point at which rights get trumped by duties. The conversation appears to penetrate more deeply when one introduces Isaiah Berlin's classic distinction between negative and positive freedom, or as some put it, "freedom *from*" and "freedom *to* or *for*." Along these lines, a fairly recent book has attempted to get to the root of the contemporary problem of freedom by contrasting two nineteenth-century theorists of liberalism, John Stuart Mill and Lord Acton (John Emirich Dalberg-Acton).[6] While the former conceived of freedom simply as the ability to do what one wants, the latter insisted that true freedom requires a recognition of the ends proper to man, and a directing of our choices to those ends. Genuine liberty is thus "ordered liberty," which means freedom that is limited by reason, nature, law, or some other determining principle that lends meaning by providing an orienting context. This subordination of freedom to other goods might appear to overcome the

---

5. Smith, *Hegel's Critique of Liberalism: Rights in Context*, 232.
6. Gregg, *On Ordered Liberty: A Treatise on the Free Society*.

problematic character of the current notion we have been describing insofar as it resists absolutizing a power, and, indeed, this approach does seem to recover the "goodness" of freedom that the absolutizing of instrumentality surrenders. But we suggest that the approach remains inadequate for two reasons: first, it fails to do justice to the deep intuition we have that freedom is more than merely an instrumental good—that it makes sense, in other words, to say, without qualification, "I desire to be free,"[7] and that St. Paul, for example, is not spinning a vicious circle when he speaks of our being set free "for freedom" (Gal 5:1). Second, insofar as this approach concedes the definition of freedom in terms of power, and then insists that this power be exercised according to certain limits, it does not reach the heart of the matter. Instead, it only contains, rather than resolves, the problem. It is not ultimately a critique of the conception of freedom so much as a critique of the use to which it is put; it is, in other words, an essentially *moral* rather than a substantial response. And because this is the case, it arguably tends to reinforce the nihilism we mentioned above even in its efforts to combat it.

The more abstract or theoretical discussions of freedom in philosophy, for all the scrutiny they give to various dimensions of the issue, operate for the most part with the same basic assumption regarding its nature. They are largely concerned with the mechanics of the exercise of free will, understood as a power, and with the conditions and implications of this exercise.[8] Indeed, there is a boundless array of philosophically interesting questions and problems surrounding free will and the act of choosing proper to it. What makes a choice free? Can the freedom of choice be reconciled with determinisms of various sorts? With causal necessity? With logical necessity? With moral or rational necessity? Can we be free in the context of physical coercion—i.e., while sitting, like Socrates, in a jail cell? Can we be free in the absence of physical restraints, but in the presence

---

7. It is not intelligible, by contrast, to say without either explicit or implicit qualification, "I desire to be able."

8. This is not to suggest that all contemporary philosophers assume that freedom equals the ability to choose between alternatives without any necessity or coercion, i.e., the notion of freedom as unfettered choice. In fact, this—still fairly common—philosophical view is beginning to be challenged in a variety of ways (see, e.g., Kane, "Some Neglected Pathways in the Free Will Labyrinth," in *Oxford Handbook on Free Will*, 406–37. I am grateful to my colleague, Jesse Couenhoven, for drawing my attention to this interesting text). Instead, our claim is that even these challenges reflect on freedom as in some sense a *power* of the will, something the will exercises in discrete acts, however this power may otherwise be qualified so as to be compatible with various external or internal determinations.

Introduction—On the German Contribution

of psychological ones, perhaps even of our own making—i.e., addictions and the like? Do we need knowledge to be free or does knowledge curtail freedom? Do we need to be able to choose even that which motivates any particular choice in order to be free? What boundaries can we legitimately set to freedom? Are we responsible for only those actions we have done freely? Are we free in all those actions for which we can be held responsible? These philosophical discussions, by their nature, reach something more essential than engagements with the question that remain within the sphere of politics, but it should be evident that they generally occur within the same horizon of what we have been calling the "possibilistic" conception of freedom, no matter how opposed the responses may be to the sorts of questions just raised: they take for granted that a philosophical exploration of the nature of freedom (*libertas*) is essentially an investigation of the faculty of choice (*liberum arbitrium*)—its conditions of possibility, its necessary features, or even its existence *simpliciter*. While these discussions may address certain problems involved in the question of freedom, they do not touch the one that prompts this book most directly: the instrumentalizing of freedom.

The conviction behind the present book is that a full response to the problematic notion requires getting beyond a "possibilistic" conception. The book thus aims to retrieve a genuine alternative to this conception, to articulate at least some features of freedom as a kind of *actuality*, and therefore not as a mere (possibilizing) instrument, but as a true end in itself, as a perfection that thereby does not require something else for its justification. There would be many ways to proceed in the pursuit of this aim; the present book does not at all claim to be definitive, but seeks in the first place to begin a new conversation.[9] It is meant, in this sense, to have a sort of "experimental" character: What would be entailed in a conception of freedom as actuality, and what would follow from such a conception? Where is such a conception of freedom to be found? To this end, the book focuses on just one aspect of the issue, namely, the *relationship between freedom and form*—which is a primary locus of actuality in classical philosophy—and explores this relationship in three thinkers, Johann Christoph Friedrich von Schiller (1759–1805), Friedrich Wilhelm Joseph von Schelling (1775–1854), and Georg Wilhelm Friedrich Hegel (1770–1831). To oversimplify a bit for the purposes of basic orientation, we may say that

---

9. If circumstances permit, this book will be followed up with one that pursues the same end on the basis of the classical philosophical and Christian intellectual traditions, and will engage in a more systematic critique of the conventional notion of freedom and the things associated with it.

Introduction—On the German Contribution

the term "form" in this context generally means what would be understood in the time period under discussion by the word "Gestalt," namely, a complex, structured whole. It should be noted, however, that this definition will have to be fleshed out more concretely as we proceed. To think of freedom in terms of form means to conceive freedom in the first place as denoting a kind of completion or ontological perfection, to conceive it not simply as a quality of agency or action, but more fundamentally as a *mode of being*—which will, of course, subsequently bear on the way one acts and the manner of choice. Because the conventional view defines itself as possibility, it contrasts itself with actuality, and therefore with limit and everything that would entail limitation. As a result, the conventional view tends toward a kind of atomistic abstraction, and thus sets in motion a series of oppositions: between individuals, between the individual and the community, between freedom and nature, freedom and reason, freedom and law, freedom and desire, and so forth. Thinking of freedom in the first place, not as opposed to limit, but precisely as integrated with form and so realized *in* (and indeed not only compatible with but essentially defined by) limitation, therefore promises to avoid these problems, which are increasingly being attributed to the conventional view. But our principal interest here will lie in the extent to which this way of thinking about freedom helps close the gap between our explanations and the rich reality of our experience of freedom. The aim, in other words, is, not to say everything that needs to be said about freedom, but nevertheless to say something essential, to disclose something of freedom *in its truth*, however incomplete the endeavor will inevitably turn out to be.

Why these particular authors? In his famous speech, delivered at the Athénée Royal in Paris in 1819, Benjamin Constant introduces the substance of his presentation with the following question: "First ask yourselves, Gentlemen, what an Englishman, a Frenchman, and a citizen of the United States of America understand today by the word 'liberty.'"[10] He then contrasts this understanding—which he labels the "modern" conception—to the "ancient" view of freedom professed by the classical tradition, explaining that we have tended to fall into confusion because we use the same word for something significantly different, if not altogether opposed.[11] There are a number of things about Constant's articulation of

---

10. Benjamin Constant, "The Liberty of the Ancients Compared with that of the Moderns," in *Political Writings*, 310.

11. Constant ultimately identifies the modern conception of freedom with "the enjoyment of security in private pleasures." An argument would be necessary to show how this view is "possibilistic" in the sense we have been using the term, or how it

Introduction—On the German Contribution

the issue that are interesting for our purposes. First, he groups the French together with the English and Americans as sharing the same concept of freedom, and contrasts it only with the "ancient" view. He thus leaves out other conceptions of freedom, among them the notion of freedom being developed by thinkers in Germany at this time. Setting aside whatever historical grounds there may be for this omission,[12] it is interesting to consider its implications. The omission is significant above all, not only because Germany was in the midst of a period of almost unparalleled philosophical creativity, but also because this creative work took place to a great extent—and much more explicitly even than in France and England—under the banner of freedom.[13] The text that has come to be known as the "Oldest Systematic Program of German Idealism" claims as its goal to rethink every aspect of philosophy in relation to the sole legitimate absolute, namely, freedom. There is, then, not just the "modern"—i.e., French and Anglo-American—and the "ancient" view, but also the *German* conception of freedom.[14]

This leads to another point. While the three thinkers we explore in this book understood themselves to be developing a "modern" conception of freedom, they did not in the least think of their conception as something opposed to the classical notion. To the contrary, they sought

---

relates to the conventional view of freedom as the ability to choose. There is no place for such an argument here, since our aim is not to analyze Constant's particular understanding of freedom. Nevertheless, it ought to be pointed out that he himself describes what he means by the modern view of freedom in terms of the right to choose and express one's opinions, one's labor, one's comings and goings, one's religion, and so forth ("Liberty," 310–11). Moreover, he understands this as *essentially* individualistic. Insofar as this implies a rejection of any primacy accorded to the whole of which the individual is a part; insofar as a whole represents completion; and insofar as completion is actuality, then an individualistic notion of freedom is a possibilistic one.

12. Constant was more familiar with German literature than he was with philosophy. He did, however, know both Goethe and Schiller well, and discussed Schelling's philosophy with them on occasion. He does not seem to have had any contact, however, with Hegel.

13. In his early text, *The German Constitution*, Hegel claims that it is precisely the "desire for freedom" that represents the fame of the Germans in history: *Political Writings*, 10 (GW.5.58).

14. In his first publication, Hegel identified modern fragmentation geographically with the Northwest—i.e., England and France—which places Germany, and Swabia in particular (the homeland of all three figures we treat in this book), directly between the modern world and the ancient world of the Southeast, i.e., Greece and Rome: Hegel, DS, 91 (esp. fn 10) (GW.4.14). Domenico Losurdo cites a number of authors who place the Germans outside of the Western spirit altogether: see *Hegel and the Freedom of the Moderns*, 268–72.

to articulate a view ample enough to hold together *both* the "ancient" view *and* the various insights gained in modern thinking on the matter. This point is even more significant for our general project than might initially appear, since it sets into relief what is essentially inadequate about any "polarized" thinking. To set up opposed notions, as Constant did, is plausible to the extent that there is at least something compelling about each side. And yet to present the two as mutually exclusive opposites is to force a person to reject one to the extent that he embraces the other. There is, in other words, something essentially fragmentary about this way of thinking, which begins within a horizon that precludes from the outset the possibility of a genuinely comprehensive perspective: it leaves out, in its very terms, the unity that necessarily precedes the opposition. In this respect, any polarized approach to freedom, which would simply pit a modern conception against the ancient one, or positive freedom against negative freedom, or even "freedom" against "liberty," is locked in fragmentation from the start.[15] If part of the impoverishment of the current view of freedom is due to its reductionist character and its isolation from the classical tradition, then a perspective, like that of the Germans, that embraces the modern without abandoning the ancient, will be especially promising.

More needs to be said, however, about our particular selection of authors. In addition to the three here, there are other German thinkers who made freedom central to their philosophical reflection, not only the most obvious ones, Kant and Fichte, but also less prominent figures in histories of philosophy, such as Jacobi and the Romantics. The reason we have focused on Schiller, Schelling, and Hegel is that these three represent, to our mind, particularly fruitful resources specifically for an integration of freedom and form. The other thinkers we mentioned, while they introduce essential insights into the nature of freedom, nevertheless adopt, in our judgment, some version of a "possibilistic" view, and so do not represent as distinct an alternative to the conventional understanding of

---

15. Someone might argue that we are *also* engaged in polarized thinking by pitting the German "against" the French/Anglo-American conception, or a holistic conception "against" a possibilistic one: but our argument is that a conception is good, "adequate," to the extent that it can show it includes whatever is positive in the view it rejects, and so does not oppose itself to anything that would ultimately be compelling in itself. In other words, in a paradoxical way, it is polarized, if you will, but only in relation to polarization in itself. Incidentally, it is worth noting that the sort of comprehensive approach we are pleading for here is different from what we would call a "bipartisan" approach in the political sphere, which means striking a compromise that is equally acceptable to all sides (which remain opposed). Instead, it aims at genuinely integrating whatever is good within a unified view.

Introduction—On the German Contribution

freedom as do these others. Schiller conceives of freedom as *aesthetic form*, Schelling—at least in his early thought—thinks of it as *organic form*, and Hegel as *social form*. Schiller aimed at overcoming the division between human subjectivity and the objectivity of the world that Charles Taylor has identified as the central philosophical problem of the age,[16] and did so by conceiving a notion of phenomenal form that was adequate to the infinite ideality of spirit. This he called the manifestation of freedom in the *lebende Gestalt*, the living form, which Hegel subsequently took to be the necessary breakthrough beyond the subjectivizing tendencies in Kant and Fichte.[17] This view of form, then, became a model for both Schelling and Hegel: for Schelling, in his lifelong endeavor to unify "freedom and system," and for Hegel in his interpretation of the highest achievement of the human spirit in the objective order, that is, the social sphere. In their developments, as we will see, Schelling and Hegel save Schiller's notion from its temptation to collapse into bourgeois aestheticism, but they also restrict some of the richness of Schiller's notion, which leads to fundamental problems in both cases. We will suggest, in our conclusion, how a retrieval of this richness would allow one in principle to reconcile the notorious differences between Schelling and Hegel while also preserving the particular achievements of each.

From this brief description, it should be clear that this study is not primarily historical. Though Schelling and Hegel were contemporaries, and even, for a time, friends, and though they were quite familiar with Schiller's work, both poetic and philosophical, we will not be exploring their historical points of contact and the significance this contact may have had on the development of their own thought on freedom.[18] Instead, our interest is decidedly philosophical, and, indeed, we approach the work of these thinkers against the backdrop of a specific contemporary philosophical interest, namely, an enrichment of our conception of freedom, the articulation of a genuine alternative to the possibilistic notion that dominates most English-language discussions. Our basic aim is thus, in

---

16. Taylor, *Hegel*, 3.

17. Ernst Cassirer observes that Kant resolves the dichotomy between freedom and form by reducing form to freedom, that is, to the subject's spontaneous self-positing. The same could be said even more directly regarding Fichte. See *Freiheit und Form*, in Cassirer, *Gesammelte Werke*, vol. 7, 176–80.

18. On Schiller's importance for both Schelling and Hegel, see Cassirer, *Idee und Gestalt*, in *Gesammelte Werke*, vol. 7, 344–45; on Schiller's significance for Hegel specifically, see Walter Kaufmann, *Hegel: A Reinterpretation*, 46–58, and Kelly, *Hegel's Retreat from Eleusis: Studies in Political Thought*, 55–89.

Introduction—On the German Contribution

each case, to give an "internal" philosophical interpretation of the ideas of the particular thinker, which means above all to attempt to articulate the unity that can account for the variety of claims the thinker makes on the particular topic. Historical detail may be illuminating in this regard, and receives mention when it is, but it is not made an object of exploration for its own sake. We reflect on their integration of freedom and form against the backdrop of their philosophies more generally, which requires somewhat different approaches in each case. Because Schiller is not as well known specifically in philosophy as the other two, we spend more time giving a general presentation of his style of philosophy before explaining, specifically, his particular notion of freedom in form. Similarly, we expound at some length aspects of Schelling's philosophy of nature, on the one hand, and his late philosophy of revelation, on the other, because these aspects of his thought are not as well represented in English-language scholarship as some others. The treatment of Hegel is much more directly focused on his philosophy of freedom because there is no shortage of books and essays written about every aspect, not only of his thought but also of his life more generally.

It is our hope, moreover, that this focus on the integration of freedom and form casts these thinkers in a relatively new light. In the intellectual history of this period in Germany, it has been observed that the figures of Kant and Goethe stand as antipodes of a sort, representing in each case a different ethos, a different basic stance toward reality:[19] Kant represents, we might say, the philosophy of spirit, the unconditionality of moral freedom, and so the transcendence of the material world—in a word, the "modern." Goethe, by contrast, represents the holism of nature, the harmony between spirit and the objective world of matter—i.e., the "classical."[20] Now, as one would no doubt expect, most philosophical treatments of the three authors in this book interpret them in relation to Kant: Hegel and Schelling thus appear as figures along the line of "German Idealism" that extends from Kant and through Fichte, while Schiller is essentially taken to be a Kantian thinker who seeks to extend—successfully or not—some of Kant's thinking in a new aesthetically-grounded direction. One of the

---

19. See Kuno Fischer's characterization, for example, in *Schiller als Philosoph*, 8.

20. This is, of course, an oversimplification. While there is some legitimacy to associating Kant with the "modern," Goethe is a broader figure, who stood at the origin of many of the modern movements in German literature (*Sturm und Drang*, romanticism), but was also taken as a representative of classicism. That is in part the point we wish to make: the spirit of Goethe can include the spirit of Kant, while one cannot make the converse claim so readily.

Introduction—On the German Contribution

more general ways of characterizing the peculiar approach adopted here would be to say that, as the prominence of "form" probably already suggests, this book reads these three thinkers primarily in the spirit of Goethe, even if the relation to Goethe is only occasionally made explicit. Schiller, of course, was a great friend of Goethe's, and this friendship proved to be a wholesome light that brought many of Schiller's native thoughts to blossom. Schelling, who received much support from Goethe in his early period, shared with this latter a conviction regarding the one-sidedness of the Fichtean notion of subjectivity, and so, like Goethe, sought to enrich our understanding of the "objective" world of nature. Hegel remained a devoted lifelong admirer of Goethe, and even conceived of his work as a transposition of Goethe's vision of the world into the conceptual terms of philosophy.[21] When read with Goethe in mind, aspects of the meaning of freedom and its relation to form, which would otherwise be eclipsed by more familiar Kantian themes, stand out in sharp relief. Needless to say, however, bringing out the "Goethean" side of these thinkers is not meant to exclude the evident Kantian themes in a new polarization. Rather, as we will see, all three of these thinkers seek to do justice to the Kantian revolution in philosophy even while rethinking the themes of that revolution from within the more concrete and holistic perspective that stands under the sign of Goethe.

If reading these thinkers in the spirit of Goethe casts them in an unfamiliar light, we wish to suggest that this light does not distort them, but rather illuminates something central in their thought. While this claim can be justified only through the more detailed expositions that will follow, it may be helpful to state very briefly how the approach in this book compares with current general trends in English-language scholarship. Schiller has often been taken to be a philosophical dilettante, if he is read as a philosopher at all. While new attention has been given to the work he did, especially in the philosophy of freedom,[22] this book argues that his most essential contribution will be overlooked to the extent that we think of him as an idiosyncratic Kantian. Schiller in fact seeks to articulate and practice a significantly different *approach* to philosophy, which follows from his interpretation of freedom in terms of form, and vice versa. Only in light of this philosophy of freedom do the apparent inconsistencies and contradictions that have frustrated so many scholars fall away.

---

21. According to Kaufmann, "Hegel is closer to Goethe than to Kant" (*Hegel*, 45).
22. See, for example, Beiser, *Schiller as Philosopher: A Reexamination*.

Moreover, the light of his particular integration of freedom and form sets in relief a new profile of the notions of freedom developed by Schelling and Hegel. Regarding Schelling, he is coming more and more in English-language scholarship to stand, above all, as the philosophical pioneer of the irrational, largely, it appears, because of the work of Slavoj Žižek, who reads Schelling as a precursor to Jacques Lacan.[23] But this line of interpretation, however brilliant it may be, isolates one evident stream in Schelling's philosophy over against the rest, and as a result significantly distorts his thought. While it is true that Schelling endeavored to open philosophy to the essential surprise, the "Unvordenklichkeit" (literally, the "unprethinkability"), of the real, and harshly criticized his former seminary roommate Hegel for imprisoning the life of the world in rational concepts, he nevertheless never desired to downplay the ultimate intelligible order of the world. Contrary to claims in recent scholarship, Schelling did not, even at the end, aim to explode the system for the sake of freedom,[24] but always sought to reconcile the two, however opposed they may appear or even be in principle.

Finally, with respect to Hegel, the integration of freedom and form allows us to make some sense of the notion of objective spirit, which has been an especially elusive one for the broad "anti-metaphysical" stream in English-language scholarship: the essence of spirit is freedom and its objectivity is the actualized form that freedom takes in the world. Unless we come to terms with this peculiar mode of spirit, we will fail to grasp what is most *Hegelian* in Hegel's political thought, namely, the concept of *Sittlichkeit* (usually translated as "ethical life" or "ethical substance"), and instead tend to reduce his notion of freedom to something more familiar to the Anglo-American tradition, whether that be freedom as self-determination, as pure negativity (i.e., pure possibility), or as a form of Rousseau self-realization. We will discuss all of these at greater length in due course.

To conclude, it bears remarking once again that this book contains little that one generally would expect from a philosophical treatment of freedom: almost nothing is said about the question of choice and the

---

23. Žižek, *The Indivisible Remainder: Essays on Schelling and Related Matters*; and his essay in *The Abyss of Freedom/Ages of the World*.

24. Jason Wirth, for example, defines freedom, in Schelling's sense, as "an *infinite lack* that is, as such, the infinite power otherwise than every beginning and ending but given within and thereby dis-completing every beginning and ending": see his "Foreword" to Schelling's *Historical-Critical Introduction to the Philosophy of Mythology*, x.

Introduction—On the German Contribution

problem of determinism; almost nothing about agency and responsibility; almost nothing about equality, rights and duties, political power, and law. Instead, the book tries to show that, taken most concretely, the question of freedom is inextricably bound up with a series of other questions, which at first glance seem to have no more to do with the nature of freedom than they do with one another. But they seem that way only to a mind wed to a possibilistic conception of freedom, and which therefore cannot imagine what relationship freedom might have with form. Some examples of claims made here: the question of freedom is essentially connected to architecture, the quality of marriage, the way one takes one's meals, one's relationship to one's work, methodology in science, one's conception of the church, the nature of light, what is distinctive about the organism, what counts as good poetic style, the notion of God and creation, and the relationship that exists among the various academic disciplines. This may seem to be an impossibly eclectic list (and it is by no means exhaustive). The point in all of this, as we will elaborate over the course of the book, is that freedom cannot properly be understood primarily as an instrumental *power*, but rather as an *actual, and so formed, reality*, which one first enjoys and only in a secondary sense uses or directs to some further end. The enjoyment of a mere power is the essence of perversion: it is, as Plato so insightfully perceived, a kind of *incurvatio in se*, in which there is, finally, no real self into which to be absorbed: a self-less selfishness. But to say this does not mean that power—as *potentia* or *dynamis*—has no place in freedom properly conceived. Instead, the argument will be that potency is liberated by form: as objective, complete, and real, form *elevates* the subject, makes the subject more "able," which will mean in fact more fruitful of form. In other words, the achievement of form is the achievement of freedom. The argument of the book is that, properly understood—and indeed contrary to what one might call the entire liberal tradition—form and freedom coincide. As our title has it, form represents "the perfection of freedom."

But the book is not intended primarily as a polemic and will make such observations incidentally in trying to bring out what is unique in the thinker in question. One of the many things that stands out about these three great figures, and it can be said about many of the thinkers of the *Goethezeit*, is that they recognized that the essential philosophical questions, in whatever area they arise, cannot be separated from one another. The fruitfulness of this period is no doubt due in part to this habit of "synopsis," which the Germans shared with the original philosophers in ancient Greece. In any event, it has helped give rise to an understanding, which—such is our hope—at least does more justice than the conventional notion to the deep sense we have of freedom as a great human good.

1

Friedrich Schiller's Dramatic Philosophy: Freedom in Form

I. On the Significance of Style

IT IS OUR AIM to study Schiller's philosophy of freedom, but to do so we must first assure ourselves that he in fact *has* one. That freedom was a notion of great importance for him, there can be no doubt. Indeed, it is arguably the central theme of both his life and his work, appearing as an ideal not only in his poetry and drama, but also in his writings on history and aesthetics. He became known in nineteenth-century America as "the Poet of Freedom," and was named an "honorary citizen" of France by the revolutionaries.[1] Goethe once said, in a reflection on his close collaborator and friend, that Schiller "preached the gospel of freedom,"[2] that freedom was the idea that animated all of his work, from first to last,[3] and this judgment has been echoed up through the most recent studies on Schiller's thought.[4] What is less obvious is the question whether Schiller has indeed

---

1. Of course, when he learned of the honor, he had quite lost his enthusiasm for the revolutionaries; he explained that the message regarding his citizenship came from the "kingdom of the dead," and even contemplated traveling to France to come to the defense of Louis XVI who was under arrest. See Wilkinson and Willoughby, *Models of Wholeness*, 55.
2. Goethe, *Scientific Studies*, 30.
3. January 18, 1827. See *Gespräche mit Goethe*, 171.
4. See Beiser, *Schiller as Philosopher*, 212: "Freedom is indeed the central theme

a *philosophy* of freedom, in the sense of a coherent body of thought on the matter, rather than mere flashes of brilliant intuitions scattered throughout his writings on aesthetics, intuitions that are unsystematic at best and self-contradictory at worst. To be able to make this judgment, before we inspect the various ideas about freedom he records, we have to come to terms with his particular *way* of philosophizing. Our first task will thus be to reflect on Schiller's philosophical style.

According to the scholastic dictum, the object determines the method. The unreflective imposition of what Hegel would call an "abstract" method—i.e., one that bears only an incidental relation to its subject matter—threatens to set aside a priori what is most proper to its object, and so to undercut its most basic aim: to understand. While this dictum holds for any significant figure in philosophy, it is especially important for the study of Friedrich Schiller's philosophical thought for three reasons. In the first place, his philosophical writings seem at first glance to be burdened by inconsistency and contradiction—an observation made regularly by those who study them.[5] Before we conclude that Schiller was simply clumsy in a field that he never really appropriated,[6] or that his changing ideas and new influences passed over into his writings undigested,[7] we ought to consider the possibility that the apparent contradictions are not mistakes betraying confusion but are a *deliberate* feature of Schiller's style that holds philo-

---

behind all Schiller's writing." Cf., Miller, *Schiller and the Ideal of Freedom*, 19; Wilkinson and Willhoughby, "Introduction," in WW, xxxii; Cassirer, *Freiheit und Form*, 180, 306; Kaiser, *Vergötterung und Tod*, 18; Lindner, "Zur philosophischen Leistung Friedrich Schillers," 865–73, here: 866.

5. See the references to Schiller's critics on this score made by Muehleck-Müller, *Schönheit als Freiheit*, ii–iii; Pugh, *Dialectic of Love*, 64; Sharpe, *Friedrich Schiller*, 138; Kontje, *Constructing Reality*, 121; Hamburger, "Schillers Fragment 'Der Menschenfeind'" 367–400.

6. John M. Ellis, for example, presents Schiller as introducing logical concepts that he is never able to master: *Schiller's Kalliasbriefe*. To be sure, Schiller himself makes a confession of this sort, namely, that he is a novice in philosophy who flew before learning to walk: see his letter to Christian Gottfried Schütz, June 20, 1793.

7. The classic statement of the "incoherence" of Schiller's anthropology because of his inability to integrate the influence of Kant with his own, more holistic views, is Lutz, *Schillers Anschauungen von Kultur und Natur*. According to Lutz, Schiller's AEM betray two different layers of argumentation with virtually no connection between them: 221–24. Lutz's claim is repeated (without citation) in Snell, "Introduction," 14–16. The very first substantial philosophical presentation of Schiller's thought, in fact, portrayed him as developing successively over time, moving from a more strictly Kantian position (aesthetics subordinated to morality) through a balance (aesthetics on par with morality) to a more strictly Goethian position (aesthetics superior to morality): see Fischer, *Friedrich Schiller als Philosoph*.

Friedrich Schiller's Dramatic Philosophy

sophical significance. What seems to conflict, in other words, might reveal at a deeper level something essential. This possibility acquires prima facie plausibility when we consider how explicitly and emphatically Schiller states what is evidently contradictory,[8] and his constant observation in his letters of the unity, soundness, simplicity, rigor, and inner consistency of his highest philosophical achievement, the *Letters on the Aesthetic Education of Man*.[9] Significantly, the scholars who discern a unity amidst the various tensions among Schiller's statements are typically those who attend directly to what might be called the "rhetorical" aspect of Schiller's thought.[10]

Second, by his own admission, Schiller does not fall clearly into standard categories of genre, but writes essays that, like some of Kierkegaard's, are "too rigorous to be edifying and too edifying to have the rigour of scholarship."[11] Although trained to be a medical doctor and officially employed as a professor of history, Schiller thought of himself as a dramatic poet with a strong philosophical bent. While he would complain in moments of frustration that the poet in him prevented him from ever being a true philosopher, and the philosopher in him would always intrude

---

8. For an example, consider the passage from XVIII 18 of the AEM: "Beauty . . . unites two conditions *which are diametrically opposed* and can never become One. . . . In the second place, . . . beauty *unites* these two opposed conditions and thus destroys the opposition," 123 (SW.8.363). To point to a passage such as this as evidence that Schiller contradicts himself is to betray contempt for his intelligence. Another example would be the classic one, namely, that he makes the aesthetic condition both an end in itself and a means to morality; we will discuss this in the following chapter.

9. See Wilkinson and Willoughby's discussion of this point, with reference to several letters: WW, xlviii.

10. See, for example, Curran, "Schiller's Essay 'Über Anmut und Würde' as Rhetorical Philosophy," 21–36; Wilkinson, *Schiller: Poet or Philosopher?*, 18–19; and WW more generally. Wilkinson and Willoughby are no doubt too extreme in their efforts to justify every inconsistency, as some have judged (see, e.g., Sharpe, *Schiller's Aesthetic Essays*, 64–65). One can quite easily find "slips": to take an immediate example, in his list of the philosophical accounts of beauty on offer in the *Kallias* letter 25 January, 1793, Schiller presents three possibilities, and then presents a fourth as his own. He goes on to claim that each of the other three grasps part of the truth. The problem is that the Kantian, which he lists second, is the direct opposite of what he claims as his own. If the Kantian view contains a partial truth, then that truth is missing from his own account. Nevertheless, what we wish to challenge is the claim that Schiller is contradictory precisely when he carefully articulates paradoxes, which would present him as confused at the very moment, in our view, he is at his best. Such approaches tend to count Schiller's philosophical contribution as meager, and affirm it only when he is repeating something someone else said.

11. *Sickness Unto Death*, 35.

whenever he would try to write poetry,[12] at bottom, he presents a rare synthesis of the two. To the extent that this synthesis in fact succeeds, the most promising approach to Schiller's philosophy will be to observe it, as it were, in its natural habitat, to try to interpret it, as far as possible, in the light of what his friend Wilhelm von Humboldt called its "original unity" with poetry,[13] the meaning of which we will discuss at the end of this chapter. Among other things, this approach entails an attention to the aesthetic dimension of his philosophical writing.[14]

Third, a basic principle in Schiller's writing, and indeed in his sense of being in general, is the ideal of inseparable unity between form and content—a unity, as we will eventually see, that he *identifies* with freedom. If this principle implies that content cannot be abstracted from its form without significant loss, a certain sterility and superficiality will characterize any study of Schiller's thought that does not reflect at the same time on his style. While we thus have another reason to begin our study of Schiller's philosophy of freedom by investigating his mode of expression, this principle also presents an important difficulty: if form and content are inseparable, then we will be unable fully to understand the significance of Schiller's style until we grasp the *substance* of what he says about freedom. In this respect, the reflections in this first chapter ought to be taken as merely preliminary; they wait upon the study of the second chapter to flesh out their significance. The first two chapters of this book are meant to be read in light of one another.

In what follows, we will take a brief look at his biographical connection to philosophy, and then turn our attention to an essay he wrote on the significance of style in the expression of ideas before returning at the end to face the question directly in what sense Schiller offers a *philosophy of freedom*.

II. Biographical Background

There are three things in Schiller's youth and education we wish to highlight in relation to our theme:[15] his generous idealism, his association of

---

12. See his well-known observation in a letter to Goethe, August 31, 1794. Cf., also December 1, 1788.

13. Humboldt, *Über Schiller*, 27.

14. Not to judge its beauty, but to judge the philosophical meaning of the way it presents itself.

15. For a good recent biography that attends especially to the Schiller's involvement

freedom with drama and poetry, and the rigorous intellectual training he received, which was centered on what we could call philosophical anthropology. The idealism that characterizes Schiller's mature work was present from the beginning. He seems to have been deeply inspired by the learned pastor in Lorch, Pfarrer Moser, with whom he began to study Latin at the ripe age of six. To the regular consternation of his parents, he took the pastor's lessons to heart and would secretly give away his books and clothes to those he thought needed them more than he. Once he even snuck out the sheets from the beds in his house to help a beggar on the street keep warm.

When it came time to start his higher education, it was his wish to become a pastor himself. This desire was quite directly frustrated, however. The duke of Württenburg, Karl Eugen, had at that time founded an experimental new institution of education that came to be known as the "Karlsschule," with the intention of producing an elite military by means of a systematically ordered curriculum coupled with intensive physical training and discipline. One of the most distinguishing features of this school was its aim to approach every subject from a rigorous philosophical perspective, and its emphasis, in pursuing this aim, on contemporary sources.[16] Promising young men from the area were essentially drafted into the school and destined for one profession or another according to the duke's determination of aptitude and need. When Schiller proved to be too poor and inconsistent a student to pursue law, his initial "Fach," it was decided that he would train to become a doctor. He was thus redirected to the study of what was called at the school "philosophical medicine."[17] This change, incidentally, pleased him greatly, insofar as he considered medicine "more closely connected to poetry" than all the others subjects, presumably because of the philosophical approach the teachers at the Karlsschule adopted.[18] After his graduation on December 14, 1780, he was incorporated with his other classmates into the duke's regiment. Notably, Schiller's favorite professor while a student there was Jacob Friedrich Abel, the philosophy professor who was responsible for the central role of that discipline in the curriculum. It happened to be Abel who also first introduced Schiller to Shakespeare.

---

with philosophy, see Safranski, *Schiller*. The best classic presentation of his life and thought, in our estimation, is the two-volume work published by Benno von Wiese on the bicentenary of Schiller's birth: *Friedrich Schiller*.

16. See Riedel, *Jacob Friedrich Abel*.

17. See Beiser, *Friedrich Schiller*, 16; cf., Riedel, *Die Anthropologie des jungen Schiller*, 11–37.

18. Quoted in Burschell, *Friedrich Schiller*, 19.

The Perfection of Freedom

The pain of being torn from home against his and his parents' will and forced to conform to a rigid discipline that ran contrary to his nature was a suffering that stamped his character and stayed with him his life long. Nevertheless, this discipline was the continuation of an experience he had from the start: when he wrote, later, of his "spirit- and heartless education," he meant the strict household that his father ran and the demanding schools to which he was sent as a boy.[19] It seems to be the writing of poetry, which he first began to dabble in at thirteen, and his playing theater, which started even earlier, that provided Schiller with a sense of freedom in the midst of this imposed order. Significantly, the drama that made him famous, *The Robbers*, a play of tragic rebellion that he wrote secretly on the side of his studies at the Karlsschule, proved to occasion the break from the path into which he had been forced. He stole away to watch the extraordinarily successful opening of his play in Mannheim on January 13, 1782.[20] When the duke later learned of Schiller's absence without leave, he had him arrested and made him pledge that he would never write poetry and drama again. This threat to prevent Schiller from entering a land he had just discovered, as it were, provoked a permanent desertion of the Karlsschule, by means of an elaborate scheme aided by friends, so that he could devote himself to what he had now come to see as his vocation. Like a character in one of his plays, Schiller spent the next two years in hiding, pouring himself into his writing while living incognito in a modest farmhouse near Mannheim until he had assurances that Karl Eugen had finally resigned himself to letting Schiller go.

His desire for liberation, however, was not a drive to throw off the shackles of authority, but from first to last a passion to integrate freedom and order, to affirm the integrity of the self with dependence on laws in both the natural and the social order.[21] And he sought not only to achieve this integration, but to *understand* it and give it expression. This aspiration appears in his earliest writing. His very first extant text is a speech he gave at the Karlsschule on "the question whether excessive goodness, affability,

19. Ibid., 12.

20. According to reports, the play was received like no other before or since: though it began in silence, by the third act the audience started to erupt in applause, which became increasingly intense as the play reached its climax, and was accompanied by cries, pumping fists, and fainting.

21. A great deal has been written on this topic, at the center of which lies an interpretation of Schiller's attitude toward the French revolution, which he seemed to support initially and then later criticized. One's interpretation of Schiller's relationship to the French Revolution depends in large part on how one understands what he means by freedom.

and great liberality belong in the strict sense to virtue," in which he insists that free generosity (love) has to be united with the lawfulness of reason (wisdom).[22] The main problem that occupied him in his advanced studies was how to reconcile human freedom and the realities of genuine human experience, with a scientific view of nature. This problem appears both in his rejected thesis, "Philosophy of Physiology," as well as in the work that found approval by the faculty and was officially published, namely, the "Essay on the Connection of Man's Animal with His Spiritual Nature." His aim in this essay, as in that of his later philosophical writings, was to articulate a unity, a true whole, that does full justice to the individuality of the constitutive elements of human nature.[23] Though he abandoned Karl Eugen's regiment, he did not abandon the philosophical interests he had developed at the Karlsschule, and continued to write essays—typically in the "dialogical" form of conversations, letters, or public address—alongside his poetry and drama, and eventually his historical studies.[24] The problems of the early writings were largely "existential," that of his later writings generally connected with aesthetics, though always within an ethical and anthropological context. The greatest stimulus to his philosophical development was no doubt his reading of Kant's *Critique of Judgment* in 1791–92,[25] though that stimulus was soon counterbalanced by the decisive friendship that arose between Schiller and Goethe in 1794. Schiller's most mature philosophical works were published during this period. Of these, the three works typically considered his most significant are *On Grace and Dignity* (an essay on moral and aesthetic freedom) (1793), his masterpiece the *Letters on the Aesthetic Education of Man* (1793; 1795),[26]

22. SW.8.7–13.

23. See Wilcox, *Anmut und Würde*, 21–23; cf., 129.

24. His first published philosophical piece, after his student thesis, called *Der Spaziergang unter den Linden* (1782), dramatizes the problem of the relationship between spirit and matter that he had addressed in his dissertation (and in fact takes over passages, word for word, from that work) in the light of questions concerning "the last things." Interestingly for our purposes, he presents two opposed perspectives in this text and leaves them unreconciled. Before he began publishing his studies on aesthetics, Schiller wrote a second dialogue on questions of ultimate meaning (*Der Jüngling und der Greis*, 1782), a speech on the benefits brought by drama (*Was kann eine gute stehende Schaubühne eigentlich wirken?*, delivered in 1784), and, perhaps most significant, a set of letters on themes similar to those treated in the dialogues (*Philosophische Briefe*, 1786).

25. A succinct account of Schiller's study of Kant can be found in Höffe, "'Gerne dien ich den Freunden,'" 1–20, here: 2.

26. In correspondence with his publisher Cotta, January 9, 1795, Schiller claims that the *Letters* are "the best thing that I have ever done and indeed the best that I

and the essay *On Naive and Sentimental Poetry* (1795–96). We ought to include in this list the series of letters he wrote to his friend Körner in 1793, in which he tried to work out his own theory of beauty in the wake of his reading of Kant. Though these letters, which have come to be known as the "Kalliasbriefe," were never published as a finished work, they continued to hold importance for Schiller,[27] and provide an important background for his published writings, especially the AEM, which address similar themes.

So Schiller did indeed write properly philosophical texts, even if they were few and not particularly comprehensive in scope and size. But to what extent they are *successful* as philosophy is a question we must still consider. Their reception was quite mixed,[28] and the relatively few philosophical studies of Schiller that exist regularly observe that he has not yet been given his due in this regard.[29] As we explained at the outset, it appears to be the case that his *style* presents the first obstacle. One of the more direct objections on this score came from Fichte, who attacked Schiller after the latter rejected an essay Fichte had written for Schiller's journal in 1794, under the title, "On the Spirit and Letter in Philosophy." The reason Schiller gave for his disinclination to include the essay concerned above all Fichte's style. Fichte responded with a complaint about Schiller's philo-

---

will ever be able to produce," and believed they, more than anything else he had written, would bring him "immortality." The dates of the AEM are significant. Schiller originally wrote a series of letters on this theme in 1793 to a Danish Prince, Friedrich Christian of Schlesweg-Holstein-Augustenburg, in part in gratitude for a gift of a three-year stipend that the prince made to him when he learned that the poet was seriously ill and in financial straights. It is not clear whether these letters were intended for publication. In any event, the original letters were destroyed in a fire (though some copies ultimately survived: see SW.8.673–728) in the palace in 1794. Schiller rewrote them for publication in his journal *Die Horen* in three installments in 1795, making very substantial revisions. In between the first and second writing was the event of his friendship with Goethe. Schiller wrote to his wife in September 12, 1794, that what he learned from his conversations with Goethe inspired him to rework the *Letters*. The notion of the *lebende Gestalt*, which plays such a key role in the final form of the *Letters* but was absent in the first series, was no doubt due to Goethe's influence (see Fischer, *Schiller als Philosoph*, 77).

27. Schiller sent Goethe a copy of his central letter from this series, February 23, 1793, as a follow-up to the point they had argued about at their first real encounter. Goethe's brief essay, "The Extent to Which the Idea 'Beauty Is Perfection in Combination with Freedom' May Be Applied to Living Organisms," which he presented to his new friend, seems to have been inspired by the letter.

28. Lesley Sharpe presents a general review of the *Rezepzionsgeschichte* of Schiller's philosophy in *Two Centuries*.

29. See, for example, Lindner, "Zur philosophischen Leistung Friedrich Schillers," 865.

sophical essays, saying that he could find no parallel to Schiller's style in either classical or contemporary writers, and that the texts were confusing in the demands Schiller put on the imagination. Partly as an answer to this charge, Schiller proceeded to publish a text that he had been working on, off and on, for several years, entitled, "On the Necessary Limits of the Beautiful."[30] Though it is a minor essay, it is valuable insofar as it is the sole work in which Schiller reflects at length on the ideal approach he aimed at in his own writing. It thus merits a careful consideration before we turn explicitly once again to the question of Schiller's philosophical status at the end of this chapter.

III. Nature Speaks to Nature

Schiller's essay, published in *Die Horen* three months after the appearance of the last of three parts of the AEM, purports, in the spirit of critical philosophy, to set "limits" to the use of beauty in order to preserve the purity of philosophical truth. The essay thus treats the effects of taste on man's spiritual and intellectual powers, the relationship between the understanding and the imagination, and the corresponding relationship between concepts and images, intellectual content and outward form. Prompted to some extent by Fichte's complaints, and aware of the importance of his ideas on the subject, Schiller uses the occasion to work out in more detail than ever before what he considered to be an ideal form of writing. The essay thus articulates a much more sophisticated vision than one might expect given the fairly straightforward problematic, and ranges well beyond the theme stated in the title. Let us, then, explore the text more closely.

Instead of resting on a simplistic dichotomy between a more popular, rhetorical presentation, on the one hand, and the intellectual rigor of systematic philosophy on the other, Schiller presents three distinct ways

---

30. The composition of this text occurred in fits and starts. He first mentions it as something he has completed in October 1793, but appears to have revised it several times before publishing it. It appeared first in the ninth issue of *Die Horen*, 1795, and was followed in the eleventh issue with a second text on a related theme, which he called "On the Danger of Aesthetic Morals." Schiller combined these two texts into a single essay with the title, "On the Necessary Limits in the Use of Beautiful Forms," which he published in a volume called *Kleinere prosaische Schriften*. Schiller's work on this text, then, essentially accompanies his writing of his most accomplished philosophical text, the AEM; the text may thus be taken to represent his mature thought on the topic.

of communicating ideas.[31] The first he calls "scientific" (*wissenschaftlich*), in the broad German sense of the term, which denotes in Schiller's time a systematic method, whether in the natural sciences or in the humanities.[32] This approach, Schiller explains, follows the strict necessity of logic and avoids the use of examples as far as possible. In this respect, it appeals in a more or less exclusive way to the intellect. The second is the "popular" presentation, which is *didactic* in the sense that it appeals to the passive imagination, providing examples that directly express the lesson the audience is meant to receive. The third approach has no single name; Schiller refers to it variously as the "free presentation" (*freie Darstellung*), the "organic" presentation, the "beautiful style" (*schöne Schreibart*) or the "beautiful diction," the "expressive" (*darstellend*) style, and sometimes simply as "eloquence." The fact that he does not devise a unique technical term for this mode suggests he thought of himself more as recovering the general classical rhetorical tradition than introducing something simply new, which would require the coining of a title, though his emphasis on *freedom* in the interpretation of beauty is surely a novelty with respect to the tradition. If the first approach seeks constancy in addressing itself solely to the mind, and the second seeks variety in consort with the imagination, the third aims at the union of opposites: it appeals to both the mind and the sensual imagination simultaneously, and thus exhibits multiplicity without surrendering unity.

What Schiller proposes here could easily seem banal if we allow ourselves to interpret it in the most obvious way. He is not calling for a simple balancing of aspects, so that one would have to alternate between offering an abstract, conceptual exposition and then "applying" these ideas to several concrete examples "on the ground" before returning again to the thin air of abstraction. No, Schiller intends a genuine synthesis, a unity that integrates even while preserving—indeed, even *enhancing*—the distinctiveness of the opposed parts:

> The truly beautiful is founded on the strictest determinateness, the most precise separation, and the highest inner necessity; only in this case the determinateness must allow itself to be discovered rather than forcefully imposing itself on the reader. The highest lawfulness must be present, but it must appear as nature. A product of this sort will perfectly satisfy the understanding, as

---

31. NLB (SW.8.411, 416).

32. And, we should point out, this was the central term for Fichte, which designated the ideal form of thinking, namely, the unifying of a body of thought on the basis of a first principle.

soon as it is studied, but precisely because it is truly beautiful, it does not force its lawfulness on the reader, it does not address itself to his understanding *exclusively*, but rather speaks as pure unity to the harmonizing whole of the person, as nature to nature.[33]

What is being communicated in this third approach is not simply *truth* in an abstract sense,[34] but the "truly beautiful"—the word "truly," "*wahrhaft*," which he uses twice here, ought to be read in the literal sense of "containing truth," and thus as beauty which preserves truth in its integrity within itself. On the one hand, the truly beautiful is "completely determined and necessary"; it is, then, no less necessary than scientific exposition, which means that the synthesis Schiller pursues does not compromise what it unites. At the same time, however, this necessity does not impose itself on the reader, but allows itself to be discovered through the reader's own free engagement.

What is it that keeps this necessity from imposing itself forcefully? The mediation of appearance or manifestation (*Erscheinung*). The beautiful style, Schiller says, subsists in a "happy relation between external freedom and inner necessity."[35] The reader receives the determinate idea not abstractly in itself, but, as it were, *through* freedom. To understand why this relation is "happy," we have to avoid reading this distinction between the external and the internal as if it were comparable to the Kantian distinction between phenomena and noumena (we will discuss the important question of Schiller's relation to Kant later), which would leave them simply separate from one another. Schiller seeks to unite these two spheres without confusing them. The possibility of such a unity lies in the significance of the adjectives: the necessity in the beautiful style is not external but *internal*. This, rather than any difference in rigor, seems to be what distinguishes the beautiful from the scientific approach, which so to speak spells out that necessity by presenting each of the logical steps from the beginning to the end. As Schiller puts it, the scientific approach is concerned above all with *understanding*, and so it does not content itself with presenting results, but requires the steps by which the result was achieved;

---

33. NLB (SW.8.419).

34. It is interesting to compare Schiller's essay to the one by Fichte that was published in the first issue of *Die Horen* (January, 1795): "Über Belebung und Erhörung des reinen Interesse für Wahrheit," in which Fichte strives to separate man's spiritual nature from what is merely animal in him. Schiller is not simply opposed to this aim, but it represents nevertheless only half of the complete picture, as we shall see.

35. NLB (SW.8.415).

it provides the roots *as well as* the fruits.[36] Indeed, the capacity to reproduce such arguments from start to finish is the only *sure* sign that one has understood the matter being presented.[37] In the scientific style, as we see, the necessity is not internal, i.e., implicit, but has been made explicit; the logical connections between the various propositions are presented, as it were, directly on the surface.

Similarly, the *popular* mode of presentation is also explicit, even if it is not concerned with providing arguments. Like the beautiful style, it depends on concrete examples to communicate an idea. But it differs from the beautiful style by engaging only the reproductive imagination, and neglecting the productive one: "The imagination in the popular mode of presentation is thus brought much more into play [than in the scientific mode], but it is always only the *reproductive* imagination (which re-produces [*erneuern*] images it has received) and not the *productive* imagination (which demonstrates its own capacity to form images)."[38] The cause of this difference is the nature of the examples used: the examples in the popular style present the idea in a *direct* fashion, they communicate their content, we could say, wholly *literally*, so that their message can be read right off the surface. This means that the form itself, the mode of appearing, turns into a mere vehicle for delivering the content: "Each of the individual cases or intuitions is much too precisely calculated for the present goal and much too specifically arranged for the use that is meant to be made of it for the imagination to be able to overlook the fact that it acts wholly in *the service of the understanding*."[39] In both the scientific and the popular presentation, then, what is most significant is made explicit, though in different ways.

But the beautiful style retains necessity *inwardly*; the conceptual determination is not obvious even though it is really present. Because it does not lie on the surface, the reader must actually *enter into* the text in order to find it, the meaning is not externally imposed on him, but he is instead invited into it. As Schiller puts it, this determination "has to allow itself to be discovered." This difference entails a unique relationship between the writer, the reader, and the truth that is being communicated. All three styles communicate an idea, Schiller writes, and in this respect they all may work with principally the same content. The scientific

36. NLB (SW.8.417).
37. NLB (SW.8.419, 421).
38. NLB (SW.8.413).
39. Ibid.

approach presents that content in its *necessity*; the popular approach presents it in its *actuality*; and the beautiful style presents it as possible and at the same time as desirable.[40] The first two are similar in that the meaning they communicate is offered as already complete in itself, and therefore as something to which the reader relates as something external to him. In the third case, by contrast, the content calls on the reader: in its desirability it draws him inwardly in (rather than externally coercing him), and in its possibility it demands his participation to come to completion. The adequate reader, in this case, must ap-propriate the idea—not (passively) take in and so reproduce in himself what was initially already outside, but creatively *pro*-duce it from himself, to make it be as if he himself were its author. In the first version of the AEM, addressed to Augustenburg, Schiller contrasts the poet with not only the teacher who introduces truth into the student, but even with the one who elicits it *from* the student: "The *dogmatic* teacher, one could say, imposes his concepts on us; the *Socratic* teacher lures them out of us, the rhetor and poet gives us the opportunity to produce them out of ourselves with apparent freedom."[41] The difference between the Socratic teacher and the poet turns on the *originality* of the role the student plays in the reality of the idea. The significance Schiller accords to the productive imagination is a genuine novelty with respect to the classical tradition, and, as the passage just quoted indicates, that significance is connected with Schiller's particular understanding of freedom, which we will unfold below.

Schiller observes that, while it is rare to find a reader who thinks (the sort of reader demanded by scientific exposition), it is even rarer to find one who can think in an expressive way (*darstellend denken können*).[42] This is admittedly a peculiar expression, and it should cause us to forestall our expectations. Schiller does not explain it or present an elaborate argument in the text regarding its nature, so we must reflect on it ourselves in relation to the larger argument he is making. We would normally envision the author as active and the reader as receptive, and would assume that the most successful communication would occur, the unity of the author's determinate idea would best be preserved in the reader's mind, if the reader were to re-produce without adding anything of his own, so to speak, to what the author originally produced. But in fact a mere reproduction is

---

40. NLB (SW.8.416).
41. Nov 21, 1793 (SW, 8, 714). See also Meyer, "Schillers philosophische Rhetorik," 371.
42. NLB (SW.8.420).

not a genuine unity but simply a doubling of the same. The reader who *co-generates*, by contrast, joins with the author in one and the same idea, which is not present as complete in the text but rather comes to be in the encounter.[43] The productivity of the imagination, as Schiller understands it, does not make interpretation *arbitrary*, which is evident in the fact that he insists on the strict *determinateness* of the concept, but rather implies a particular relationship of the reader *to* the idea in its determinateness. We need to unfold the insight further in order to see how this is so.

"Productive" reading such as this, of course, presupposes a reader who has both a mature formation and a natural affinity. For this reason, Schiller insists that the beautiful style is inappropriate for teaching in the typical sense of the word: namely, for introducing a notion to someone who is simply ignorant of it. Teaching, thus understood, assumes an incapacity in the recipient and so must offer what is ready-made. It is certainly easiest to reproduce intuitions and tangible examples, which is why the didactic mode is appropriate for a large audience; Schiller observes that the popular style does not need to be met with any interest at all to be able to communicate. The scientific approach, on the other hand, is quite demanding, since it does not supply any intuitional aids but requires the reader to think the logical connections themselves and to do so *for* himself. A reader will have the energy for this only if he already has a great interest. But what this approach offers is already complete, which is why it is fitting for instruction, even if for more advanced and engaged students. Indeed, it is an indispensable means of instruction, because truth *qua* truth requires the mind's active work for its communication. Necessity is an essential property of truth, and thus if a person cannot demonstrate the necessity of an idea by reproducing arguments for it, he is not master of its truth, as Schiller puts it.[44]

It is crucial not to overlook the significance of the scientific approach in the formation of the human being for Schiller, because doing so would lead us to see contradiction where Schiller is in reality presenting a complex, but integrated, whole. We will flesh out that whole in detail next chapter, but we need to see here the importance Schiller places on the adequate *distinction* between reason and all that pertains to man's life of the body: the senses, feeling, imagination, and intuition. Whether it be in the sphere of truth, goodness, or beauty, reason's proper object transcends the

---

43. It is, of course, Hans-Georg Gadamer who spells out this notion of "artistic truth" most systematically: "all encounter with the language of art is an encounter with an unfinished event and is itself part of this event," *Truth and Method*, 99.

44. NLB (SW.8.421).

physical realm;⁴⁵ reason aims at an ideal that, however much it illuminates experience and provides its meaning, is never captured fully and without remainder by any particular experience. Precisely herein lies the danger of beautiful forms: beauty, as Schiller understands it, concerns the *unity* of reason and the senses, and the taste that discerns beauty seeks a meaning, so to speak, not in its conceptual abstraction, but in its outward manifestation, it seeks internal content in external form. A student formed only in taste, who is presented with nothing but beauty (and that, moreover, of a particular, superficial sort) will not enjoy the *unity* of his reason and senses (because unity implies the joining of what is different) but merely their indistinct *"Verschmolzung,"* their confused running together.⁴⁶ "The understanding in reading of this sort"—Schiller means here the reading of texts that are "merely" beautiful in a superficial way—"is always exercised merely in harmony with the imagination, and thus never learns to distinguish the form from the material and thus to act as a pure faculty."⁴⁷ Such an education produces a "spirit of superficiality and frivolity," even in the circles of the highest sophistication. The student receives ideas, to be sure, but because they are not distinct from their form, they are simply swallowed whole, with relish of course because the beautiful cannot help but arouse interest, but without genuine benefit. The understanding recognizes, he says, only where it distinguishes, and we never really take hold of something except by means of the understanding. If the mind is simply passive, it receives without acquiring; it *feels* rich but lacks the capacity to show what it has. As Schiller puts it, using a decidedly Platonic image, such a soul possesses only the shadows of things. For this reason, the sheer work of thinking without the respite of sensual enjoyment is a *"Hauptmoment bei dem Jugenduntericht,"* that is, a crucial stage in the education of youth.⁴⁸

To say that it is a *"Hauptmoment,"* however, is not to identify it with education *tout court*. If "merely" aesthetic formation offers only the "shadow of a possession," mere intellectual work, intercourse with abstract contents alone, is likewise deficient: "Matter without form, to be sure, is only a half possession: For the most glorious notions lie in a head that lacks the ability to give them form, like dead treasures buried in the

---

45. See AEM I, 5 (SW.8.307).

46. In a letter to Goethe, 9 February, 1798, Schiller criticizes the confusion of those who reject analysis and distinction altogether in an ill-conceived defense of wholeness.

47. NLB (SW.8.418).

48. Ibid.

earth."⁴⁹ The goal of education is the formation of the *whole* human being, which includes both the adequate distinction of the component aspects of humanity *and* their real unity. There is a connection between being a whole human being in this sense and being capable of relating to, and taking possession of, reality as a whole. A superficial person, he says, remains indifferent to reality and sets value on external form alone; an intellectual without taste would perceive the real only in fragmented bits of content. A genuine relation to reality requires the ability both to understand, and to create:

> Whoever transmits his knowledge to me in a scholastic [*schulgerechter*] form convinces me, to be sure, that he grasps that knowledge correctly and can make his claim; but the one who at the same time is capable of communicating that knowledge in a beautiful form, he proves not only that he is made to extend this knowledge, he also proves that he has taken it into his nature, and is capable of expressing it in his action. There is no other passage for the results of thinking into the will and life than through imagination that is capable of acting on its own. Nothing can become a living deed outside of us unless it is already a living deed within us, and what holds for organic formations is equally true of the creations of the spirit: the fruit comes forth only by way of the blossom.⁵⁰

As we saw above, there is no opposition in principle for Schiller between spontaneity and receptivity. To the contrary, it is only the properly spontaneous reader—that is, the one who can think in an expressive way and who can give thoughts beautiful outward form as a fruit—that truly receives. He alone takes hold of more than a half-possession or the shadow of a whole, and he does so because he engages more than half or the shadow of himself.

IV. Writing as a Free Gift

The beautiful style, in its most ideal form, occurs as a reciprocal event or encounter, which requires an understanding of one of Schiller's central intuitions if we are to make sense of it. As we observed above, this essay expresses in a more complete form what Schiller had initially attempted

---

49. NLB (SW.8.424–25).
50. NLB (SW.8.421).

to explain to Fichte in a private letter.[51] In the letter, Schiller endeavors to distinguish his own approach to philosophy by saying he places his whole soul into the hands of his readers when he writes, because he desires to affect not just their minds, but *themselves*.[52] The beautiful style, then, is not simply a rhetorical mode, or a description of the extrinsic *"Einkleidung"* that an author happens to impose on thoughts that could have worn clothes of some other fashion. Rather, in the first place, it is a *way of being*—specifically, being in the mode of *gift*. It is a "being for," or the offering of oneself in a comprehensive way. This is why he explains the particularity of his style in terms of his inner "subjective" act, as it were, rather than the way he arranges what he writes. The devotion Schiller gives to his writing, the single-mindedness of his daily work, his fidelity to his vocation, are what character-ize his writing, what stamp it with its distinctive form. The beautiful style, as Schiller means the phrase, can only be a natural fruit of an integral and integrated life: one cannot write in this way, say, by the sheer potency of talent, if one is distracted in a basic way or one is instrumentalizing the writing for the sake of some end foreign to it.[53] In that case, one is not in fact—and in spite of one's intentions, whatever they may be—putting one's "whole soul" into one's work and therefore into the hands of one's readers. Such a thing is possible only if the soul is indeed *whole* to begin with. It is necessary to emphasize this point, because it runs so contrary to our typical assumptions regarding rhetoric as nothing more than a technique, a simple skill to be learned in fundamental indifference to the quality of one's life or one's mode of being. (As we will see shortly, such an assumption, along with its implications, represents a radical betrayal of freedom as Schiller understands it.) A living deed outside us—which is how Schiller describes the beautiful style—necessarily implies a living deed *within* us, which means it depends on a proper integration in the person. If one can give one's thoughts a beautiful form, one shows that

51. Only drafts (dated 3 and 4 August 1795) exist, but there is a consistency of content in them all; apparently, the many drafts are due, not to indecision about what to say, but about how precisely to say it.

52. Cited in Wilkinson, *Schiller: Poet or Philosopher?*, 16.

53. See Otfried Höffe's observation that the highest level of play in Schiller's thought is to devote one's entire life, body and soul, to a *"zweckfreien Sache,"* "Gerne dien ich den Freunden," 14. Jacques Maritain describes the sort of asceticism required to foster artistic creativity as a selfless attentiveness to what he calls "poetic intuition," which is undermined if it gets subordinated to something other than itself. See *Creative Intuition*, 102–3. Incidentally, the paradoxical notion at the center of Maritain's book, creative intuition, reflects the very same simultaneity of pure receptivity and spontaneity that we have seen in Schiller.

one has taken them *into one's nature*. And if they have penetrated into one's nature, one can produce them, rather than merely *re*-produce them, only *out* of one's nature, that is, through a whole gift of self. It is for this reason that Schiller claims that the beautiful style does not simply address the reader's mind, but "speaks as pure unity to the harmonizing whole of man, as nature to nature."[54] As he says in "Naive and Sentimental Poetry," the perception of beauty requires the *free* engagement of the whole human being.[55]

The reality of devotion that lies behind Schiller's writing serves to bring into greater clarity a point we made about the beautiful style above, and resonates with the spontaneous generosity that we noted at the outset in our biographical sketch. Schiller affirms that the beautiful style consists of the unity of internal necessity and outward freedom. There is an unconstrained, spontaneous variety that is presented to the senses and thereby offered to the imagination. To say that it is unconstrained, or "free," means that these outward forms are not logically derived from the idea "behind them," as it were, which is what distinguishes the style, on the one hand, from the explicit connections in the scientific approach, and, on the other hand, from the instrumentalization of the outward form, which utterly reduces it to the idea, in the didactic mode. But to call it thus free is not to make it haphazard or arbitrary. There *is* necessity present, but it is of an *internal* kind. Specifically, it is internal to the externally free forms. An arbitrary form would be one that possesses no intrinsic relationship to the idea it expresses. The didactic style is essentially arbitrary in this sense, insofar as the forms are just accidental vehicles for delivering the idea, and so could be substituted *ad libitum* for others as long as they make the same point (and dispensed with altogether once the point is made). To say that free external forms bear an intrinsic relationship to a determinate idea, which is their internal necessity, means that one sees why "It must be so!" precisely to the extent that one freely enters *into* the appearances; there is a direct, rather than inverse, relationship once again between the reader's spontaneous giving of himself (i.e., in the productive imagination) and his being inwardly compelled by what he reads, his receiving its internal necessity.

But the realization that "It must be so!" is not the transformation of an inner necessity into an external one, which means that this realization does not coincide with the claim, "It could not be otherwise!" This is a

---

54. NLB (SW.8.419).
55. See "Naive and Sentimental Poetry," 245 (SW.8.506–7).

difficult, but crucial point. To see that a free external form possesses an internal necessity is not identical to an insight into how the form, taken as an idea, can be logically derived from the preceding one. It may be the case that a logical relationship can be demonstrated; if there were nothing more than this, however, that relationship would not represent the *whole* of the phenomenon, but only an aspect of it, regardless of how indispensable that aspect might be. If it *were* the whole, the demonstration would capture, as it were, all that needs to be said. Schiller is clear, however, that the ability to give an argument for a matter indicates that one has grasped it, but not yet that one has appropriated it as a living whole, and if the matter is itself a living whole, and not a mere idea, then one has in this case not *really* grasped it. What is determinate is the idea, which thus imposes itself only from the inside; one sees the necessity when one stands as it were *with* the idea, and sees the form arise spontaneously (i.e., not forced by something extrinsic), as the necessary fruit of the idea's determination, its inner completeness—though, as we saw above, this does not exclude the reader's involvement, but in fact demands it. In this respect, the outward form is free *precisely because* the inner idea is determined. There is a perfect coincidence of freedom and necessity. If an extrinsic necessity governed the relationship between the idea and the form, both the idea and the form would be bound to one another and so there would be no spontaneity. The spontaneity of the outward form arises from the fact that it owes itself, so to speak, wholly to the idea; it is not an arbitrary addition to it or an extrinsic imposition. But the idea can thus produce the form only if it is perfectly inwardly determinate, wholly complete in itself. This inner completion of the idea is both what *separates* it from any particular expression and enables it to *be* expressed, to produce images in a "natural" and spontaneous way. The importance of this point for understanding Schiller's philosophical insight in general cannot be overstated, and we will return to it at the end of the next chapter.

At the same time, though the outward forms owe themselves wholly to the idea, they nevertheless remain *free* forms: the fact that they are not simply *deduced* from the idea means that they cannot simply be *reduced* back to it in turn. The outward expression is not meant to be merely a passageway to the meaning but a reality in itself, a true object of contemplation and not a mere instrument. In the beautiful style, the images have a *life of their own*. Schiller draws an interesting contrast between the scientific approach, which gives rise to a mechanical order in which the "various parts, lifeless in themselves, give artificial life to the whole through their fitting together"—i.e., in which the parts are simply instruments of the whole—and the beautiful style in which the parts not only give rise to the life of the whole but at the very same time possess life in themselves, so much so that they could, in a certain respect, simply stand on their own.[56] Indeed, Schiller explains in other contexts that expressiveness can be so complete that the sense world is transformed into a realm of freedom,[57] i.e., the image *becomes* itself intellectual as it were. In his essay on "Naive and Sentimental Poetry," Schiller writes:

> While the sign always remains different from and alien to what is signified in the case of scholastic understanding, the language of genius springs from thought as by an inner necessity and is so one with it that even concealed by the body the spirit appears as though exposed. This manner of expression, where the sign completely disappears in what is signified, and where language, as it were, leaves naked the thought it expresses while someone else can never present that thought without at the same time concealing it, this above all is what people call ingeniousness and esprit in the style of writing.[58]

The disappearance of the sign into the signified, or the image into the concept, is the "flip side" of the concept's pouring itself out unreservedly, as it were, into the image, to enter so completely into it that the two become, at least in one respect, indistinguishable from one another. A fascinating analogy thus emerges between the author who places his "whole soul" in his writing, and thus ensouls or animates it, making it a "living deed outside us," and the concept that, moved "as by an inner necessity," empties itself into the image and so gives it a kind of independent life of its own. A free author produces a free text; a free concept gives rise to a free form.

We should note here that this paradox creates an ambiguity. Earlier, we said that what distinguishes the beautiful style in particular is that its meaning, its conceptual necessity, is *internal*, while in the other styles the meaning can be read "right off the surface." Now we see, however, that the unity between the internal necessity and free external form is such that the meaning is no longer simply internal *as opposed to* external. Rather, the content appears *in* the form; it is fully expressed. This is, we recall, the very reason Schiller flags the potential danger of beauty: the force of the expression can lead one to substitute it for what is expressed. But it would

---

56. NLB (SW.8.416).
57. Grace, 131 (SW.8.178).
58. Schiller, *Essays*, 190–91 (SW.8.445–46).

be short-sighted therefore to eliminate the expression in order to avoid the danger. What is needed is a capacious ability to read—namely, the "free engagement" we saw above—that both affirms the completeness of the image and at the very same time perceives the conceptual meaning that remains wholly distinct from it. The reader has to see both at once, and yet see each in its irreducibly distinct and asymmetrically related role. In one of the drafts of his rejection letter to Fichte, Schiller insists on a "reciprocal causality between image and concept, but not a confusion of the one for the other as is often the case in your letters."[59] For all of the freedom in Schiller's writing, it is clear that the preservation of order is of the highest importance to him.

There is a kind of vulnerability in the "self-gift" that Schiller describes, in two respects. On the one hand, and most obviously, the inner idea is, as Schiller puts it, "exposed" or made naked in the expression. It lies, as it were, directly on the surface, so that it can be "consumed" without being received or registered: "One gulps down such writing . . . the concepts drive into the soul *en masse*."[60] On the other hand, the beautiful style is vulnerable precisely because it does not impose its meaning in an extrinsic way, as we have observed. The meaning is freely offered, we could say, and so can be properly received only in freedom. It is important to see, however, that the freedom meant here is not merely an unconstrained act of the will in the sense that one receives the expression if one deliberately decides to do so. Instead, it indicates a quality of being that implies in turn a capacity to perceive: one must *be* a living whole in order to *perceive* a living whole, and, as we will elaborate below, this wholeness is a significant aspect of Schiller's understanding of freedom. What he contrasts to the *free* human being, in this sense, is on the one hand what he calls the "vulgar judge," which is a person with intelligence but not taste.[61] On the other hand, however, would be the mere aesthete whose taste is superficial and therefore empty: this one swallows wholes without judgment, and so without making the careful distinctions in the absence of which one fails to grasp what is being communicated. There is thus a risky subtlety in the beautiful style, because it contains both beautiful form and rich content, each of which depends upon the other—which is why Schiller uses the term "*Wechselwirkung*," reciprocal causality, in speaking of their relationship—but each of which remains at the same time irreducibly different

---

59. 23 June, 1795. Text quoted in Meyer, "Schillers philosophische Rhetorik," 382.
60. NLB (SW.8.419).
61. NLB (SW.8.420).

from the other. Those who think abstractly will find in this style, he says, the satisfaction that they seek for their understanding, even as they reject the demand made on them "*lebendig zu bilden*," to give form to things in a living way. Those who only feel will delight in the varied and free wealth of images, even as they withdraw from the "bitter work of thinking." The difficulty is that both can claim with (only relative) justice that they understand the text, though they will at the same time claim in different ways that it is imperfect.

When one surveys the discussion of Schiller's philosophical writings, one sees how prophetic Schiller was. The two approaches are partially right, and can even justify their particular interpretation at length, but they in fact miss what is for Schiller the essential: "Because, however, both are merely very imperfect representatives of general and genuine humanity, which demands the complete harmony of both occupations, the fact that they contradict each other means nothing; quite the contrary, they confirm to the author that he has attained what he sought."[62]

V. Meaning in Motion

Taking a step back, let us note how this demand for totality affects the form of the present essay, and why it can so easily give the impression of contradiction. Schiller insists on the isolation of the spirit from the senses, but then defends their essential unity; he begins by denigrating the clothing of thoughts in beautiful forms, but then cries that all is lost if we fail to do so; he bemoans the tendency to emphasize taste, but then argues for its supreme importance. It is not a surprise that scholars find him frustrating. It often happens that one begins to feel that one understands a key concept in his texts, and subsequently one discovers that he turns left, as it were, the moment one expects him to turn right, which then demands a reconsideration of what one thought one understood. The temptation is to pull passages out of context when they confirm one's expectations, and account the rest philosophical amateurishness. But while proof-texting is problematic in reading any genuine thinkers, it is fatal with Schiller. The reason for this is that the organic presentation that Schiller aspires to, the living whole constituted by living parts, the unity in difference and the difference in unity, makes every aspect we might say *essentially and deliberately* ambiguous.[63] It is the case, for example, that the parts, insofar as they

---

62. NLB (SW.8.420).

63. Wilcox cites critics who worry about the ambiguities and equivocities: *Die*

are alive, as he puts it, can and must stand on their own, and in this sense they *can*, in fact, be separated from their context. But it is also the case that they serve the life of the whole, and indeed only *have* their own life *because* they serve it. It is true that, in the beautiful style, the necessity of the idea remains *inward* or implicit, but it is nevertheless true that this idea lies on the surface, exposed. This ambiguity is in fact razor sharp: being implicit or being explicit are not simply two separate properties juxtaposed to one another. Instead, as we saw above, at the deepest level they share an identity; they are mutually implicatory aspects of a single phenomenon. The external form is a spontaneous "fruit" of the idea, which, because it is impelled by an inward necessity, pours itself without remainder into the form, which is for that reason perfectly one with the thought. But this spontaneity is a result of the idea's internal completion, i.e., of its utter independence from the form. We could say that the perfect unity between the concept and the form is the same as their absolute and irreducible distinction from one another. The matter, to say it again, is ambiguous in an essential way. Fichte had complained specifically that Schiller made the imagination think by forcing images to *stand for* concepts, rather than placing them before or after as illustrations. But they can stand for concepts, even in their freedom, because the concepts are so fully expressed in them that the two are one.

The ambiguity is not, however, a simple contradiction, once again because of the living or organic character of the whole. Contradiction occurs when opposites are affirmed of one and the same thing at the same time and in the same respect. The reason Schiller's ambiguities are at least in principle not contradictions is that the *Darstellung* he offers does not fall into a monotonous simplicity or a single point in time (which is not to say, please note, that it lacks simplicity or dissolves into an endless "becoming," a permanent flux without distinct form). As Elizabeth Wilkinson, among others, has observed, Schiller's philosophical style is essentially *temporal*.[64] Organic wholeness, she explains, implies a free responsiveness to concrete situations, a moment-by-moment adaptability that results in the constant inversion of hierarchies and thus the reciprocal subordination of parts.[65]

Dialektik der menschlichen Vollendung, 17. Some others defend this phenomenon: see Curran, "Schiller's Essay," 29 and Wilkinson, *Schiller: Poet or Philosopher?*, 18–19. For a general discussion of this issue in Schiller, see Sayce, "Das Problem der Vieldeutigkeit," 149–77.

64. Wilkinson, *Schiller: Poet or Philosopher?*, 18.

65. Ibid., 14. Schiller himself observes that "movement is the only change an object can undergo without altering its identity," Grace, 125 (SW.8.171).

The Perfection of Freedom

Benno von Wiese speaks of the "process-like nature of his philosophizing" (*das Prozeßhafte dieses Philosophierens*), the acknowledgment of which allows us to reconcile affirmations that would seem to be mutually exclusive.[66] In reference to Schiller's claim in "Anmut und Würde" that the ideal human being has *both* dignity (his mind and will are detached from the senses) and grace (he is an inseparably integrated whole), von Wiese claims that these affirmations would come into conflict only if we thought of the human being "as a statue," that is, abstracted from the concrete life in time; if we understand that the object Schiller intends, by contrast, is the human being as he exists concretely then it is easy to see how these two attributes may inhere in a single person, for situations demand the display of one or the other, and only a full human being in Schiller's sense is capable of both.

Recognition of the temporality of Schiller's style and the "situational" character it implies sheds light on the essay we have been discussing. Schiller criticizes beauty, for instance, because the formation of taste in the wrong person at the wrong time can prevent a student from ever learning to think in a strong and unimpeded way; it can turn him, in fact, into a slave of the senses and the material world. But pure intellectual training without a context of taste will produce what Schiller calls in the *Letters on Aesthetic Education* a "barbarian." In this case, beauty is essential for integration. One might complain that Schiller does not always make the context sufficiently explicit to help prevent possible confusions, and the most basic terms in his philosophical writing are notoriously elusive of attempts to make them univocal. The same word—"nature," "form," or "freedom," for example—can stand for more or less opposed things,[67] and most often

---

66. Von Wiese, *Friedrich Schiller*, 466.

67. On the tensions in Schiller's use of the term "nature," see Potyka, *Naturvorstellungen*. On "form," see von Wiese, *Friedrich Schiller*, 491; and Taminiaux, *La nostalgie de la Grèce*, 80–81. A perusal of the glossary Wilkinson and Wilhoughby provided in their translation of the *Letters* quickly brings to light the unusual amount of tension in Schiller's vocabulary. This glossary is quite helpful in coming to an understanding of Schiller's philosophy. One ought to keep in mind, however, the philosophical sterility of any list of definitions, because the variety of meanings that play off of one another in different contexts can set up what Charles Kahn has called "linguistic density" and "resonance." See his comments in *The Art and Thought of Heraclitus*, 87–95, in which he explains: "By *linguistic density* I mean the phenomenon by which a multiplicity of ideas are expressed in a single word or phrase. By *resonance* I mean a relationship between fragments by which a single verbal theme or image is echoed from one text to another in such a way that the meaning of each is enriched when they are understood together," ibid., 89. It may seem peculiar to refer to Heraclitus when speaking of Schiller, but there is hardly any philosopher one could name between the two so intent in

does not give any clear indication of which he intends. The classic example of essential ambiguity is Schiller's use of the term *"Aufhebung,"* which was to have a great career in the work of another thinker.[68] In the present essay, he occasionally specifies a distinction between *true* beauty and the "common" sort, but for the most part he simply requires the reader to discern the context and to interpret the praise or censure. As confusing as this may be, it is important to see that ambiguity of a certain type is essential to the beautiful style he has been elaborating. The determinateness of concepts coincides with a freedom in the outer form: in this case, words are the outer forms of concepts, and thus exhibit freedom in their use. A direct, one-to-one correspondence between word and thought—the ideal sought in all technical vocabulary—would certainly be useful in the "scientific" approach, but is inappropriate in the beautiful style. Schiller is similar in this respect to Plato, who was critical of the sophists' predilection for technical terminology and claimed that it is vulgar to insist on the precise meaning of terms.

Tracking the movement of context is essential in determining the proper note of the terms "beauty" and "rhetoric" as Schiller uses the terms in the present essay. Beauty will corrupt as a substitute for truth, but is essential for the *whole* truth, as it were. Similarly, though he had distinguished three different approaches to the communication of ideas at the outset, he often contrasts just two, that of the rhetor and that of the scientific speaker. It is easy, therefore, to overlook in his explanation the integrating third, and envision instead a simple dualism. In fact, both the popular writer and the "free" one present beauty, in the reception of which the reader's reason and senses enjoy a harmony. Is this to be criticized or lauded? The answer, of course, depends on the context, on the nature of the speaker and on the nature of the audience. It is problematic insofar as it encourages confusion and it is necessary insofar as it leads to integration. The original unity must be challenged, then, by the work of separating reason from the senses, even while this challenge ought not to be absolutized. What emerges here, to say it again, is an ideal that contains within it three distinct moments. It is important to *begin* with beauty, both

---

the use of chiasms as a means of generating meaning.

68. See AEM XVIII, 124–25 (SW.8.363). Reginald Snell believes this is the first time in German thought that the term is used in this technical sense requiring the ambiguity: see Snell, "Introduction," 88–89, fn. He also speculates that Hegel discovered the possibilities of this term through his reading of Schiller, a judgment echoed by Wilkinson and Willoughby: WW, 304–5.

because, as Schiller observes in other contexts,[69] the human being is in the first place an animal, so that education must start with the senses, and also that what starts as simply separate may be brought together but can never be truly united. Moreover, beauty is necessary for awakening interest, and the second moment, the "scientific" training of reason, presupposes a high level of interest in the student that it cannot itself provide. If it is indeed present, the second moment strengthens the intelligence and allows the grasp of the idea in its truth. And the third moment represents, then, the "recovery" of wholeness. Beauty is, so to speak, the crowning of the education; it puts the "form" in the formation. As the text moves from one perspective to the other, and then circles back, setting up contrasts, replacing them, and immediately initiating new ones, an idea begins to emerge that reflects an internal light from many different facets.[70] If the reader attends to only the parts in their distinction—like the "vulgar" judge who sees only the pillars in St. Peter's[71]—he won't understand properly even the parts. A genuine reading demands an intellectual agility, as well as *taste*, to move *with* the author, and to follow the shifts and turns of the text—and indeed not simply to follow in a passive way, but to anticipate actively like a good dance partner, to use a favorite example.[72] What Schiller calls the beautiful style is, in this respect, not just one among many styles, but a whole that includes the others and unfolds them as is fitting, in a pedagogically sensitive manner.

This last point requires emphasis if we are to avoid what would be an easy mistake to make here. It is true that there is an essential temporality to Schiller's style, and this means, as we pointed out, that it constantly inverts hierarchies and adapts to situations. But this is only partly true. It is in fact only by changing in a particular respect that an ideal can remain *constant*

---

69. See AEM III, 10-15 (SW.8.309-12).

70. In notes Schiller made on the margin of his friend Wilhelm von Humboldt's essay, "On the Study of the Ancients, and of the Greeks in Particular," Schiller listed the three essential moments in the development of a human culture, a triad that reflects his approach to philosophical problems generally, and which we see reappear with some modification in Hegel (see Safranski, *Schiller*, 418): "1. The object stands before us as a whole, but confused and fluid. 2. We separate particular characteristics and distinguish; our knowledge is now *distinct*, but isolated and limited. 3. We unite what we have separated, and the whole stands before us again, no longer confused, however, but illuminated from all sides," cited in WW, 234.

71. NLB (SW.8.420).

72. See the *Kallias* letter from 23 February, 1793 for a description of dance as the ideal illustration of the proper relation between two freedoms. Schiller was so struck by the fittingness of this image that he wrote a poem about it, *Der Tanz*.

Friedrich Schiller's Dramatic Philosophy

in time. As Schiller writes in his poem, *Der Tanz*, "*Der Ruhe besteht in der bewegten Gestalt*," in the moving form lies rest. External variety in time is the expression of an internal unity beyond time. Schiller's style is essentially temporal, but it also, albeit in a different respect, aspires to a timeless ideal in which it is likewise grounded. There is, to be sure, a *process* character to his writing, but it is not an unceasing evolution, as some have thought who point to new developments that appear inconsistent with earlier insights. Instead, it is the free unfolding of a stable, determinate concept. Schiller claims that what characterizes temporality is the succession of mutually exclusive moments;[73] a *merely* temporal style would lack all capacity to integrate. There is something *absolute* in the concept the beautiful style discloses, something that transcends context. What Schiller seeks to present is the *whole*, which includes *both* trans-temporal simplicity *and* temporal complexity, and includes them *both* as irreducibly different from one another *and* as inseparably one. Wilkinson is correct to say that, in this aspiration to totality rather than to mere individuality, Schiller ought to be interpreted as classical rather than romantic.[74] If we neglect this unifying idea, we will see only a confused pastiche, an episodic succession of intuitions and insights with neither connection nor destination. However much such a scene might feed the imagination, it fails to nourish the intelligence, and so betrays the reading desired by the beautiful style. Grasping the whole, by contrast, requires a deeper penetration into the text. It is not enough, in other words, to affirm the importance of reason, and then after that to emphasize the senses; it is not enough to understand the concepts, and after that to enjoy its outward expression in the form. What we would have in this case is an aggregate, but no whole. To see the whole, one must grasp the parts all at once. One must see them *in* their complex "*Wechselwirkung*" as internally connected to and so reciprocally dependent on one another. To affirm *each*, in succession, is to leave the parts extrinsically related to one another, which is closer to the "artificial life" of a mechanical whole than to the organic totality of the beautiful style. What characterizes an organic whole, once again, is the *life* of the individual parts, a life that they possess because of their intrinsic participation in one another and so in the whole. If A cannot be understood in a complete and living way without B, and B cannot be understood without A, then we understand neither unless we understand them both *at once* in both their tension and their unity. What gives the whole its organic life,

---

73. AEM XXII, 79 (SW.8.340–41).
74. Wilkinson, *Poet or Philosopher?*, 5–6.

namely, the specifically internal necessity, is exactly what makes it hidden and so places such a special demand on the reader.

At one point in the essay, Schiller characterizes a particular way of failing to meet this special demand by making direct reference to a comment Augustenburg had made regarding his AEM:

> The vulgar judge, to be sure, who, lacking any sense for harmony, always drives on to individual details, who would indeed seek out in St. Peter's Basilica only the pillars that support that artful firmament, . . . will first have to translate [beautiful writing] if he wants to understand it, just like the merely naked understanding that, deprived of any capacity for illustrative expression, must first translate the beautiful and harmonious, whether in nature or art, into its own language and separate out its elements, in brief, just like the student who has to spell things out in order to read.[75]

The "all at once" character of the perception reveals yet again the necessity of a gift of the self in both the author and the reader. The paradoxical simultaneity of motion and rest, of the succession of parts and the constancy of unity, demands the same simultaneity from the perceiver. It is not enough to alternate the powers, for the cumulative sum of parts is not the same as the whole. The reader must involve himself in a total way; his attention has to arise from within his *nature*, from within the core of his being, if he is to be able to perceive the whole as an *organic* reality that preserves the integrity of each part. Allusion to the total engagement of the personality brings us, then, to the realm of the dramatic, which according to Schiller occupies "all the powers of the soul, of the mind, and of the heart."[76]

VI. Elements of the Dramatic

The notion of *drama* is in fact helpful in bringing a great deal of insight into the particularity of Schiller's style. Schiller is best known, certainly, as a dramatist; it was his play *The Robbers*, completed when he was only twenty-one, that first brought him, so to speak, onto the public stage, and it was to drama that he devoted his energies at the very end of his life.[77] At

---

75. NLB (SW.8.420).

76. SW.8.85.

77. When he died on May 8, 1805, he was revising his play *Demetrius*, sketching out a new drama called "Agrippina," trying to improve a translation he had made of

Friedrich Schiller's Dramatic Philosophy

the bloom of his life, he and Goethe collaborated in directing the important stage in Weimar. A spirit of drama is pervasive in Schiller; in its most literal sense, the phenomenon of drama was a constant preoccupation—not only did he compose plays of course, but he often wrote on the nature and significance of drama, the role of the theater, and aspects and objects of the tragic art[78]—but more generally drama best describes his sense of being itself. It is arguably this sense that prompted him to write tragedies. The stage represents, for Schiller, not simply an occasion for diversion, but the privileged place wherein the meaning of existence reveals itself.[79] This sense is so basic in Schiller it comes to expression in both the content and the form of his philosophical writing. Though, given the evident significance of drama for Schiller, we would expect to find it alluded to more frequently in discussions of his thought, nevertheless, it has received some mention in a few important studies. The great mid-nineteenth century historian of philosophy, Kuno Fischer, observes that Schiller's philosophizing was not *epic*, in the sense of a detached survey of ideas already complete, but *dramatic*, because of the actuality of the author's involvement.[80] Benno von Wiese explains that the dramatist and the philosopher in Schiller operate in the same way, namely, that they follow out a process into a tension between extreme situations and equally extreme decisions.[81] Ernst Cassirer describes Schiller's method as dramatic, which includes he says a dialogic that represents a precursor to dialectic.[82] This particular kind of dialectic, in fact, springs in the first place directly from Schiller's own life.[83] In the English-language realm, although not specifically using the term, S. S. Kerry describes Schiller's "personalizing" of principles that makes their interaction analogous to the event of an encounter between freedoms,[84] and Elizabeth Wilkinson speaks of the hallmark of Schiller's

---

Othello, and working on an adaptation of Racine's *Phaedra* for the German stage.

78. In 1785, he gave a speech entitled "Was kann eine gute stehende Schaubühne eigentlich wirken?" The writings of his mature period contained many reflections on the nature and phenomena of tragedy, the manifestation of beauty and the sublime in theater, and the distinguishing features of drama in relation to other arts.

79. See SW.8.92 and 94.

80. Fischer, *Schiller als Philosoph*, 79. Fischer was no doubt alluding to the distinction that Schiller and Goethe made between epic and dramatic poetry: SW.8.738–45.

81. Von Wiese, *Friedrich Schiller*, 466.

82. Cassirer, *Idee und Gestalt*, 337. We will discuss the relationship between the dramatic and dialectic later.

83. Ibid., 344.

84. Kerry, *Schiller's Writings on Aesthetics*, esp. 92–99.

style as the non-reductive synthesis of opposites in terms reminiscent of drama.[85]

It would be good, here, to specify what we mean to speak of a philosophical style as *dramatic*; as we will see, the term serves to gather up into a unity many of the observations we have been making along the way regarding the particularities of Schiller's approach to truth, and thus puts us in a good position to address the controverted question whether he is a philosopher or poet in the end. What will become evident is that the tendency toward a dramatic form is, in part, a result of Schiller's deep interest in freedom, and in turn reveals something essential about his understanding of the notion. In other words, it is not an accident that the "Poet of Freedom" was a dramatic poet, or indeed a dramatic philosopher, but follows naturally from his particular understanding of freedom.

The first and most fundamental feature of the dramatic philosophical style is what some refer to as Schiller's tendency toward synthesis and the unity of opposites—though, in fact, it would do more justice to his approach to say he both sharpens and reconciles opposition. The mere effort to overcome all difference would result in an essentially non-dramatic unity, and is in any event patently not how Schiller proceeds. As we saw above, a truly *living* whole arises from parts that have life in themselves, and in fact brings about that life. In this respect, it is not the case that the differences between the parts begin to fade to the extent that the unity of the whole shines forth, or that the distinctive individuality of the parts grows blunt the more they join harmoniously with one another. Quite to the contrary: there is a *direct* relationship between the unity and the difference, which is why the phenomenon of drama is so radiant and fruitful.

We can contemplate the relation between the opposition of difference and the reconciliation of unity in terms of the unfolding of the "argument" of a plot and the role that characters play therein. If one aims above

---

85. Wilkinson, *Poet or Philosopher?*, 9, 14–16. Interestingly, rather than reflecting on the significance of drama as a philosophical method, Wilkinson illuminates Schiller's uniqueness by reference to Eastern patterns of thought. While the allusion is intriguing, it is somewhat artificial, and in any event anachronistic (insofar as an interest in the East was awakened most significantly in the generation after Schiller). Behind this appeal to the East is the assumption that the West is bound to what she calls "linear" thinking. This, however, is only one current in Western thought, however prominent it may be in certain epochs. Plato and Neoplatonism, for example, hardly marginal to the West, are not examples of "linear" thinking. Moreover, *drama* is another "non-linear" form that is not only fundamental to the West, but so obviously the natural mode for Schiller. Wilkinson, interestingly, confesses little appreciation for Schiller's drama (ibid., 29).

Friedrich Schiller's Dramatic Philosophy

all at what Schiller referred to as a "mechanical unity," one seeks to make the destination as clear as possible at the outset, and one introduces and elaborates each point just so far as it enables progress down the established path. In a drama, if the outcome is already clear before the action begins, and the successive scenes do not offer anything new, but only rush, as it were, to catch up with what one already knows, the play will be a failure. A good drama contains characters that are more than mere tokens of the plot, even while they do indeed serve it. They arrive on the scene, and find themselves enmeshed within complex situations and woven into relationships with other characters. There is a clear *"Wechselwirkung"* here: the situations and relationships determine the meaning of the characters, in the sense that the characters do not possess their identities somehow in isolation from them, while at the same time the characters determine the meaning of the situations and relationships, both through their identities and through the decisions they make. They are called on to make a decision, upon which the meaning of the whole turns, even while the constellation of actions and characters provide the context in which the decision *has* meaning. Drama, then, consists of characters that reveal who they are through the extremities of action and thereby reveal the meaning of the whole in which they participate with the other characters. The occasion for the revelation is conflict, which lies at the base of all drama, and the revelation brings about a *resolution*, whatever form it may take.[86] In the best cases, the resolution does nothing to compromise the individuality of the characters, but, to the contrary, stamps them for all time in the collective memory of man.

Schiller's philosophical approach bears an analogy to this. Schiller does not prematurely synthesize opposites; he first celebrates their opposition. The principles he expounds often seem to follow their own inner impulse, out of the author's control. Cassirer remarks on the *dynamic* quality of Schiller's thinking, pointing out that, rather than speak of principles, Schiller more often uses the term *"Triebe,"* drives.[87] Rather than reel them in, Schiller gives them free reign and allows them to follow the inner

---

86. It may be objected that modernist and postmodernist drama has gotten beyond the need for resolution, but it ought to be specified that modern and postmodern drama of this sort dispense only with simplistic resolutions. The most successful forms of modernist and postmodernist drama invariably offer the lack of resolution, for example, as a final statement that serves to illuminate, if not explain, the action of the whole. Such an ending, in other words, remains a revelation of meaning, even if that meaning is, paradoxically, that there is no meaning.

87. Cassirer, *Idee und Gestalt*, 337.

promptings of their own nature to the end, so that the principles can give full expression to what they mean, even if that expression seems to run at cross-purposes with other principles. Conflict inevitably occurs in this, but rather than steer away from it to the extent possible or to soften it if not, Schiller seems to strengthen it, to give it as much force as he can. Why would he do such a thing? Our first thought might be that he is, at bottom, a *dualist*, that he is simply giving expression to what remains unresolved in his own understanding of the world because of the philosophical tradition he inherited,[88] or perhaps that he finds unity empty, if not dead. But we would be forced to dismiss a great deal of evidence to the contrary to draw such conclusions. If anything, Schiller has a higher regard for unity than difference, although we must keep in mind that these do not stand in competition with one another for him. No, the better inference to make—and it is impossible to overemphasize this point—is the following: Schiller's constant instigating to conflict, his almost "obsessive" use of chiasms, as Paul de Man observes,[89] his tendency to make points always by sharp contrast with others, his tightening of oppositions, arises in the end from a *great confidence in the ultimacy of unity*. He can allow free reign to principles, not only because he knows that they will eventually return, as it were, of their own accord, but even more so because the unity will be superficial, it will be false, precisely insofar as the reconciliation is imposed simply from the outside. As he says in *On Grace and Dignity*, an enemy that has merely been vanquished always threatens to rebel; one that has been reconciled has truly and reliably been made one.[90] And such reconciliation demands that the other join of its *own* accord. There is room for *reversal* in this dramatic approach to philosophy, where such room is lacking in straightforward logical argumentation. Schiller has no fear of allowing his principles to be in some cases even *hostile* to one another, to strive against one another as enemies; once again, not because his sense of unity is so weak, but because it is indomitable. His is not a romantic, but a classical aesthetics in the end. Recognizing the essentially dramatic character of Schiller's philosophizing shows us how indispensable it is not to abstract his ideas from the whole in which they participate. The conflict he expresses at one time may turn out to lead to a more comprehensive

---

88. This is the thesis of David Pugh, which will discuss in the next chapter. It is also a position argued by Sharpe, *Drama, Thought and Politics*.

89. Paul de Man, *Aesthetic Ideology*, 135–37.

90. See Grace, 150 (SW.8.200).

unity than one anticipated, a unity that casts the conflict in a wholly new light: we have simply to watch the drama unfold.

The particular sense of unity in Schiller, which both reconciles opposites and enhances their difference, is the basis for the other features of the dramatic style. The second is the "personification" of principles that we mentioned in reference to Kerry. What does it mean, in this context, to "personify"? Kerry explains that Schiller had a tendency to see "Personen" in nature,[91] and to project a kind of *freedom* into objects,[92] which Kerry says breaks all the rules of philosophy, though he should have specified, of *Kantian* philosophy.[93] As we will explore more thoroughly in the next chapter, what Schiller intends to do by this is to indicate an irreducible self-identity that is not one of the qualities a thing has, or even all of its qualities together, but instead indicates the particular *way* it possesses the qualities that constitute the thing; it is not a content but a form. This "self-possession" is another way of describing the fact that the parts of a living whole have a life *of their own*. To affirm this is to say that they are not a mere means to the end, which is the whole, but are at the same time reciprocally and asymmetrically an end in relation to which the whole is itself a means. It follows that they possess an end in themselves, which would make them an *entelecheia* in the sense that Aristotle ascribes to living things. Though Kerry unnecessarily takes this as the triumph of metaphor over thought and thus of rhetoric over philosophy, he offers some insightful observations that are rich with philosophical implication. Because Schiller's principles are not mere functions but are analogous to persons, they can "exchange" functions in a certain respect with their opposites,[94] which is another way of saying they bear an *intrinsic* relation to one another, wherein each participates in what characterizes the other without in any sense forfeiting what identifies it, rather than relating merely externally, which would make their difference inversely proportional to their unity. As Kerry puts it, they are not merely functions, but something like "persons having functions," which allows them to participate in one another.[95] It is this "person-like" character that makes their reconciliation

---

91. Kerry, *Schiller's Writings*, 8, 11. See *Kallias*, 163.

92. Kerry, *Schiller's Writings*, 57.

93. The properties that Schiller means to attribute to things by thinking of them analogously as "persons" possessing "freedom," as we will see, are those that attend a fairly traditional "substance" metaphysics, in Aristotle and in scholastic thought.

94. Ibid., 79–80.

95. Ibid., 98–99.

a "quasi-social event,"[96]—in other words, makes it analogous to drama. However peculiar this use of the term "person" may seem, it in fact resonates with the most decisive moments in the early history of the word: its first root was in theater, as the name for the mask that both represented the character and allowed the actor to project his voice; it was then used as a technical term in Roman law to designate the legal agent, i.e., the bearer of certain properties; and finally it was taken over and developed in the christological controversies over the relation between divine and human natures in Jesus, wherein a distinction was drawn between nature, as faculties, and *person*, the *one* who has a nature.[97]

The next feature is the intersection that we touched on above between the temporal and the timeless, or "eternal."[98] It is helpful to see how this, too, is characteristic of drama. There is a kind of "actuality" in drama that distinguishes it from all other genres. In a short piece that Schiller wrote with Goethe called "Über epische und dramatische Dichtung," the authors claim that, while the epic poet presents the event he relates as "perfectly past," the dramatist shows it as "perfectly present,"[99] as taking place right in this moment. The "now-ness" of moving time belongs more to drama than perhaps any other art form. Schiller had earlier written that "all that is dramatic makes the past present."[100] A plot *unfolds*, which means that it progresses through time, and that the meaning of things changes over the course of the progression. Indeed, if it is a good drama, the changes that occur are truly significant, which means not only that they introduce something new, but also that this novelty serves to reconfigure what has gone before. The significance is not relative simply to the *particular* change that takes place, but relative to everything before and after, which gives it an absolute character of sorts. For this very reason, however, the meaning of the particular event is not wholly circumscribed by the moment in which it occurs, but in fact transcends that moment insofar as it gathers up into the unity of its *own* meaning the meaning of the moments that both precede and follow. In this respect, the end is already present at the

---

96. Ibid., 92.

97. For a brief, but rich, account of the history of the notion of the person, see Schmitz, "The Geography of the Human Person," 27–48.

98. The word "eternal" in this context means simply the quality of being irreducible to time and the constant change it implies (see AEM, 78–83). Typically, the word conjures up supernatural entities floating in space, as most people envision the Platonic forms; but this is not how Schiller means it.

99. SW.8.831.

100. "Über die tragische Kunst," SW.8.159.

beginning: not in an *explicit* way, for that would not only deprive it of its dramatic quality, but would also make it a beginning rather than allow it to be an *end*. A dramatic ending must surprise and fulfill at the same time: *surprise* in the sense that it is the introduction of something genuinely new; and *fulfill* in the sense that it resolves, i.e., it brings an adequate response to, the expectations that were awakened at the outset. To do both there has to be a unity that governs the whole from first to last and so transcends all the particular moments as they unfold, but that does so both implicitly and in a way that creatively liberates all that happens in the uniqueness of its individuality. In other words, we need precisely the coincidence of the strict lawfulness and internal (eternal) necessity of the idea and the freedom of external (temporal) forms, wherein these forms are not mere ornamentation but the creative expression of the ideas—which is just how Schiller describes the beautiful style. There is no drama where there is no author guiding the action "from above," but there is no real drama if he does so intrusively. The best dramatists are surprised by their own characters. We may explain drama, then, as a kind of *Wechselwirkung* of the eternal and temporal: each is not only distinguishable from the other but in some respect opposed, and yet at the same time, each depends on the other. The internal necessity, and the supra-temporal identity, of the idea expresses itself *only in* the moving forms in time, and those forms are not expressions of themselves but of what transcends them. In drama that is *free* and *beautiful* in Schiller's sense of the terms, these opposites are perfectly one: the sensible realm is so transparent that it becomes the idea, it is meaning made not only visible but also temporal, and the *"bewegte Gestalt"* shows itself to *be* (supra-temporal) rest.

In part because of this intersection of time and the timeless, drama has an essentially *revelatory* character. The identity of the characters is not merely given at the outset, but is disclosed through the action and through the decisions they make. The characters not only *say* who they are, but also *show* it (through time). At the same time, the full meaning of the situation rarely remains the same, but more often unveils itself gradually over the course of the action. Similarly, in Schiller's philosophical writing, the differentiation of principles occurs progressively, and their reconciliation takes place as an event, a moment toward which the thoughts in the essay were progressing, and in this event the full significance of the interrelated aspects becomes for the first time clear. The revelatory character of the communication is due to the tension created through the internal relationship of the parts in the whole. None of the parts has its meaning simply in itself, but depends in a basic way on the meaning of its opposite, even while this meaning in turn depends on the first. It is not sufficient, then, simply to explain one aspect first, and then move on to the next. Instead, one must begin with one and develop it until it reaches a critical point, and then to develop the other until it demands the first. The full meaning of each will come to be, then, at the moment when the synthesis is found in which they can both be disclosed at once, each bringing out what lies hidden in the other. Schiller's description of the conflicting drives that constitute human existence in the AEM, for example, comes as a kind of dramatic climax: "We have now been led to the notion of a reciprocal action between the two drives, reciprocal action of such a kind that the activity of the one both gives rise to, and sets limits to, the activity of the other, and in which each in itself achieves its highest manifestation precisely by reason of the other being active."[101] The word Schiller uses here, in fact, is the more active one *"Verkündigung"—annunciation*: each *announces* what it is, reveals itself, by virtue of its oppositional relation to the other.

In the essay we have been discussing, we see this broadly in the way in which the presentation of the beautiful rises as a crescendo after the building up of contrasts of the popular and scientific styles, the language increasing in ardor as it describes the unity, and at the same time finding itself drawn to concrete images. But we see smaller examples of it in Schiller's relentless use of chiasms and his coupling of opposites in a single sentence: the tension created between the items coupled makes the meaning they communicate a revelatory act, insofar as their reciprocal dependence in difference brings to light a unity that could be expressed the same way neither in being simply stated in itself, nor through the successive elaboration of each distinct part. Consider the phrases Schiller uses to describe the genial artist in the last paragraph of the essay on style: "He studies . . . the human form under the anatomist's knife, delves into the deepest depths, in order to be true on the surface, and inquires into the whole race in order to do justice to the individual. . . . [W]hen possessed by the most burning feeling for the whole, he retains a coolness and persevering patience for the individual, and in order not to truncate perfection (*Vollkommenheit*) prefers to sacrifice the enjoyment of completion (*Vollendung*)."[102] The need of depth for the truth of the surface, the demand of the whole for the individual and the individual for the whole,

101. AEM XIV, 95 (SW.8.348).
102. NLB (SW.8.426).

manifests itself immediately here; the reciprocal dependence is revealed in a single, complex expression. The inward necessity of the idea that forms the content in Schiller's beautiful style would lose its inwardness if it were simply *stated*. It has to be *revealed* instead, because such a mode allows it to remain inward even in its manifestation, which is the condition of possibility for complex wholeness. There is some anticipation here of Hegel's insistence that the true is never simply result, but is *both* the result *and* the process that leads up to it.

The final feature we will mention here is somewhat different from the others since it concerns not the relationships between the various elements *within* the text but rather the relationship between the author and reader that is mediated by the text. This relationship, too, such as we have described it, is essentially dramatic in Schiller. The disclosure of self through the extremities of action describes not only the characters Schiller created but also his own act of creating them. As he wrote to Fichte, and as his friends testify, he poured himself into his work, he was driven to it by what Humboldt described as a need and task that arose "from his innermost nature,"[103] so that he could not rest until he accomplished it, and so his writing arose from the core of his being. As we suggested earlier, it is this self-gift that grants his writing an animating center, it is why it calls, in turn, on the whole of the reader, so that he attend to what is being communicated from the core of his being, and thus engage all of his powers at once. It is for this reason that the beautiful style does not simply implant ideas or draw them out ready-made, but in fact beckons the reader to give rise to them from out of himself through a reciprocating gift of self. It demands, we have said, a properly *productive* imagination. A kind of *Wechselwirkung* obtains in the relationship between author and reader, which makes this encounter itself a dramatic event. There is, to be sure, a certain sense in which the author has no dependence on his audience: as Schiller insists, the genuine author pursues the ideal without looking over his shoulder to see if others are following; he exhibits a sovereign indifference to the question of success.[104] This is just like the inner completion of the concept that gives it the "freedom," so to speak, to enter wholly into the outer form. Similarly, in spite of, or even because of, the author's sovereign indifference, it remains the case that the event of communication consists of the intertwined contributions of both subject and object, wherein the

---

103. Humboldt, *Über Schiller*, 51; cf., Kerry, *Schiller's Writings*, 1; Ellis, *Schiller's Kalliasbriefe*, 13.

104. NLB (SW.8.420).

two work together in concert, precisely because it is not an agent working on a patient, but rather an inter-action, an event that occurs between two fully engaged agencies. Thus, when Schiller finishes a passage criticizing a merely aesthetic style, he explains that the criticism was directed simultaneously to the style and its recipient: "This holds, incidentally, only for beauty of a vulgar sort, and for the vulgar way of perceiving beauty."[105] "Vulgar," we recall, is an adjective indicating a merely *partial* engagement of the self, specifically, a superficial engagement, the involvement of one's "surface" alone, so that one's inner being remains unmoved. In this respect, a "merely" aesthetic communication is not an event or an encounter; the meaning expressed is not "perfectly present" to the reader, because the reader is not "perfectly present" to the meaning. The dramatic mode of communication occurs when nature speaks directly to nature.

VII. Freestyle

While we have been referring to Schiller's style as dramatic, and more generally as simply "beautiful," before we conclude with a discussion of Schiller's status in philosophy and the status of philosophy in Schiller, we need to reflect for a brief moment on why Schiller describes this style at the same time as essentially *free*. What does "free" mean in this context? We will explore Schiller's view of freedom more thoroughly in the next chapter. Our concern here is to open up the question of the connection between freedom and order specifically in relation to style.

In hearing that a style is essentially free, one's first thought is that it possesses no recognizable form. But that is quite clearly *not* what is meant here. Poetry is, for Schiller, an excellent example of genuinely free expression, not because it lacks order, but *precisely because* it possesses order—of a particular sort: "the beauty of poetic depiction is: '*free self-activity of nature in the chains* of language.'"[106] Similarly, dance, with the beautiful whole that arises from the ordered motions of independent individuals, is an example of genuinely free movement. Early on in the essay, Schiller links freedom and form in a phrase: "The content must recommend itself directly to the understanding by means of itself alone, while the beautiful form speaks to the imagination and smiles at it with the appearance (*Schein*) of freedom."[107] Rather than read the ambiguous

---

105. NLB (SW.8.419).
106. This is the last line of Schiller's *Kalliasbriefe*, 183 (SW.8.673).
107. NLB (SW.8.410).

word *"Schein"* here in the negative sense as "unreal semblance," we ought to understand it in the positive sense as "manifestation," that is, as revelation or communication (a reading supported by the verbs associated with it in this passage, "to speak" and "to smile"). There is a coincidence, here, between the beautiful form—which, we might add, is presented here not as a static "thing" in the world, but as an event, an expressive act—and the "smile" of freedom. This coincidence recalls the famous definition that Schiller had formulated in the lectures he gave on aesthetics at Jena, and which he had articulated in the so-called *Kallias* letters, written to his friend Körner two years earlier: beauty is the appearance of freedom.[108] As we will study in depth next chapter, beauty is more than simply the indifferently exchangeable accident of form but in fact represents the ideal "form of form."[109] Given this explanation, we may infer that *form* is the appearance, i.e., the manifestation or revelation of freedom. Genuine form is, in other words, free expression. Schiller explains directly what exactly makes an expression free: "The expression is *free* if the understanding does indeed determine the connection between the ideas, but does so with such a hidden law (*Gesetzmäßigkeit*) that the imagination appears in all this to operate in a wholly arbitrary way, and to follow nothing but the accident of temporal connection."[110] Freedom is not simply identified here with arbitrariness, though this arbitrariness can be an expression of freedom if it is guided by a hidden law.

We are reminded of the passage we discussed at length concerning the coincidence of internal necessity and outward freedom. In this case, something is free if it has its ground i.e., that which determines it, *within* itself. If appearances are without any reason, if they are arbitrary in the sense of being wholly indeterminate, then they are not free, because they are not the expression of anything, they lack beauty, which is to say, they lack genuine form. But if appearances are determined by what lies *outside* of them, as in the case of the scientific mode in which the parts are mere steps for the whole, there is of course reason and determination, but no freedom. Appearances are *free* only if the determination lies *within* them, if it, so to speak, *belongs* to them. In this case, the determination is not a limit imposed on the appearance, but is its own "work," its own doing, so that we could say that the determinateness coincides with *determinability*, that is, the ability to determine itself and so receive determination.

108. 8 Feb, 1793, 151 (SW.8.638).
109. 25 Jan, 1793, 147 (SW.8.632).
110. NLB (SW.8.414).

The Perfection of Freedom

In the other two cases, we see that determinateness and determinability are opposed in the sense that an increase of the one means a decrease of the other. Here, they are united in the same. Unless we understand this identity, Schiller's description of freedom in the beautiful style would seem like incoherence itself: "The eloquent writer thus creates for himself the most glorious order out of anarchy itself, and erects an unshakeable building on a constantly shifting foundation, on the ever-flowing stream of the imagination."[111] Again, it is not that the author is able to get control of the movement, to stop up the flow of the imagination, by imposing determination on it. Schiller is instead insisting that the movement and the order are simultaneous, that the closedness of determination is one with the openness of determinability; in short, that form and freedom coincide. Benno von Wiese insightfully observes that Schiller's description of Wilhelm Meister captures the ideal that he strove after himself: "he achieves determinateness without losing beautiful determinability, he learns to limit himself, but precisely in this limitation, and by way of form, he rediscovers the passageway to the infinite."[112] This passage captures with admirable succinctness the meaning of freedom that informs the text we have been studying. Beauty, once again, is determinable *in* its determination, and the limit of form is opening to infinite freedom. It is this mystery we will explore more fully in the next chapter, and indeed over the course of the present book.

But the unity is complex, and it is necessary to consider the different elements that constitute it in order to get the complete picture of freedom that lies in Schiller's style. In the first place, the inner concept is perfectly determined in itself, which means that it is wholly self-contained. In other words, it has no *dependence* on sensibility, it is not confused with outward appearances, or, as Schiller says, it is perfectly separate from them. Schiller speaks at the outset of being "free from every influence of sensuality"[113] in the pure operation of the understanding, and what he means by this is analogous to the inward simplicity of the idea that separates it from the appearance. Second, this perfect separation is precisely what allows the expression to be free in the sense of being internally rather than externally determinate, or, in other words, to have real independence. Third, this independence is paradoxically the result of its perfect subordination to the concept, as the pure expression thereof, even while at the same time

---

111. NLB (SW.8.416).
112. Quoted in von Wiese, *Friedrich Schiller*, 550.
113. NLB (SW.8.409).

the concept expresses its sovereignty over the outward form only by disappearing behind the image, as it were, and thus "hiding" its governing law. Looking at this relationship from the side of the subject, Schiller writes that in the beautiful style the imagination "is permitted momentarily to forget her subordinate role and to behave like a master of herself and of her own will (*eine willkürliche Selbstherrscherin*), because sufficient care has been taken, through a tight inner bond, that she can never wholly flee the reigns of the understanding."[114] Finally, this reciprocal but asymmetrical subordination, this *"Wechselwirkung,"* between concept and image, understanding and senses, soul and body, requires the total engagement of the self as a whole, because the phenomenon would collapse with the mere succession of parts. The self-gift that we spoke of earlier is therefore an indispensable condition for the full concept of freedom, for it allows a genuine unity that strengthens and clarifies the individual distinctiveness of its elements, which means that it allows for the emergence of a truly dramatic whole, a "living deed outside of us." Freedom, as appearance, entails a dramatic form.

VIII. Poet or Philosopher?

We are now in position to address the question of Schiller's status as a philosopher with regard to the theme of freedom. It cannot be denied that Schiller thought of himself, and has generally been thought by others, as first and foremost a dramatic poet, and that the mature writing he did in philosophy generally remained within the field of interest determined by that primary vocation, namely, aesthetics. Indeed, he wrote no *book* of philosophy, but only a few essays. Since the resurgence of interest in Schiller's philosophy after WWII, he has most often been read as a Kantian who attempted to translate the new critical philosophy into new areas, with more or less success.[115] To be sure, after an initial neglect of his work when it first appeared, Schiller did receive some philosophical attention: Hegel considered him to be of great philosophical importance,[116] and wrote of his frustration with the lack of philosophical recognition of Schiller to his

---

114. NLB (SW.8.415).

115. See Sharpe's account of these studies: Sharpe, *Two Centuries*, 75–86.

116. In his *Lectures on Aesthetics* (JA.12.96), Hegel presents Schiller as being the one who broke through Kantian subjectivity and abstract thinking, and penetrated into the nature of beauty, an achievement significant not only for art but for philosophy in general. We will explore Hegel's judgment at length in the next chapter.

friend Schelling.¹¹⁷ Perhaps because the tendency toward specialization had not yet fixed the boundaries between disciplines so rigidly, there were a handful of philosophical treatments of Schiller in the late nineteenth and early twentieth centuries.¹¹⁸ But since then there has been relatively little published work.¹¹⁹ The most significant recent books on Schiller's philosophy in English are no doubt David Pugh's *Platonism in Schiller's Aesthetics* and Friedrich Beiser's *Schiller as Philosopher: A Re-Examination*. We will discuss Pugh's book in the next chapter. Beiser's book is important, in this context, not only because it is the most recent, but also because it offers what may be the strongest argument on behalf of Schiller's *philosophical* contribution to date. And it is arguably the most thorough exposition of Schiller's philosophical thought in any language.¹²⁰ Beiser confronts many of the "myths and legends" regarding Schiller's philosophy by offering a careful exposition of his early philosophy and by tracing the development of his mature thought, in particular the AEM, with chapters on Schiller's relationship to Kant and the Enlightenment, and specifically on his philosophy of freedom. Although he is forthright about his criticisms of Schiller's work, he shows that there is much more philosophical substance in Schiller than has generally been appreciated.

But there is an important sense in which the book threatens to mislead as to what is truly unique in Schiller's philosophical work. We can set this sense into relief by considering Beiser's own assessment of poetry and philosophy in the book's first appendix, in which he offers an interpretation of the essay we have been discussing here. According to Beiser, "[o]ne of the greatest obstacles to the philosophical appreciation of Schiller's aesthetic writings has been the recent—and growing—emphasis on their rhetorical dimension."¹²¹ The problem with this emphasis, he explains, is that it takes the ambiguities and inconsistencies in Schiller's thought as deliberate and essential, and thereby discourages a rigorous

---

117. See his 30 Aug, 1795, letter, in which Hegel groups Schiller together with Fichte, lamenting "their treatment by would-be philosophers. My God, what pedants and slaves are among them!" Cited in Kaufmann, *Hegel*, 304.

118. Heidegger, for example, held a seminar on Schiller's AEM in the Winter semester of 1936–37: *Übungen für Anfänger*.

119. See Beiser's account of the scholarship in German and English on Schiller's *philosophy*: Beiser, *Schiller*, 7–10.

120. Beiser confesses, however, the book's inadequacy in two key respects: He does not treat Schiller's essay *On Naive and Sentimental Poetry*, and he "gives scant attention to [Schiller's] poems or dramatic works," which Beiser claims would be necessary for a complete look at his philosophy (*Schiller*, 10).

121. Ibid., 263.

philosophical examination of his texts. In Beiser's opinion, a rhetorical approach, of this sort, would view Schiller too much through the distorting lens of his "romantic progeny," and overlook the constant demand Schiller makes for clarity, rigor, and system (in the specific sense of relating parts to a founding first principle).[122]

To demonstrate his point, Beiser explains that we need to investigate the very essay we have studied at length here, "Über die nothwendigen Grenzen beim Gebrauch schöner Formen." In this essay, Schiller sketches out three kinds of exposition, the 'popular', the 'scientific' or 'philosophical', and the 'aesthetic' or 'beautiful.' Beiser then raises the question, which style does Schiller use in his own work? While we might expect, given his high regard for the beautiful, that he would indicate the third style as his own, Beiser claims that Schiller means to argue for his aesthetic writings as *philosophical*—even if it is "not in the conventional sense Fichte had in mind."[123] Beiser bases his claim on the fact that Schiller evidently *does* use conceptual rigor in his aesthetic writings, and, moreover, is explicit in his rejection of the conflation of form and substance that would arise if one were to allow rhetoric simply to substitute for philosophy, which is what those who would read him as a Romantic inevitably do. What distinguishes him from, say, Fichte, however, is that he "also goes a step further by making the abstract concrete, by attempting to fuse analyzed terms into a single whole," and thus he recovers a sense of philosophy that goes back to Plato.[124]

The most immediate problem with Beiser's interpretation is that it makes Schiller's essay into a confused jumble. Schiller describes three different approaches. Beiser suggests that Schiller's writing on aesthetics comes closest to the second (the scientific-philosophical), but that, in addition to conceptual clarity, he proceeds to make his thoughts concrete by integrating them into a single whole. The question that arises here is whether the approach Beiser is describing represents a fourth mode, not mentioned in Schiller's list, or whether it is simply not in any substantial sense different, in the end, from the "philosophical" style—that it is, in other words, philosophical argumentation, which has *then*, secondarily, been clothed in concrete images. Beiser seems to opt for both. On the one hand, he characterizes this ornamentation as a "further step" in which the (previously) analyzed concepts are fused into a whole. On the other hand,

122. Ibid., 264.
123. Ibid., 264.
124. Ibid., 265–66.

he claims that this simultaneous engagement of the understanding and imagination does not have a specific name of its own (i.e., is not one of the styles Schiller had named), but Schiller simply refers to it as the style of the *"darstellende Schriftsteller."*[125] But we have seen that Schiller *does* in fact have a specific mode in mind. He explicitly calls the style that integrates the conceptual and the imaginative dimensions without compromise of either the "truly beautiful" style.[126] It thus characterizes the ideal meaning of the third of the types he had listed at the outset of his essay. When Schiller criticizes the attempt to make content conform to form, which is the only text from the essay Beiser quotes in making his case that Schiller intends to be strictly philosophical in his own writing, Schiller is describing the confusion of concepts and images that occurs when one tries to *mix* the philosophical and the popular styles. It is just this that Schiller accuses Fichte of doing in the extant drafts of the (no longer existing) rejection letter he wrote to him. This confusion is *not* typical of the beautiful style, as Beiser implies, because this style consists *precisely* in preserving a perfect difference between form and content, which turns out in fact to be the precondition for their genuine unity, as we have seen. Schiller had written to Fichte that he (Schiller) placed the whole of himself in his writing, so that, not just the mind, but the whole reader would be moved in all of his faculties. Because of this particular way of writing, Schiller tells Fichte his writing may not be compared to other philosophical essays without confusion, but requires "a wholly different perspective" (*einen ganz anderen Standpunkt*).[127] What he writes in the essay about the truly beautiful style echoes the description he gives of his own writing: it "does not address the understanding *in particular*, but speaks as pure unity to the harmonizing whole of man."[128] There can be no doubt that Schiller took the beautiful style as the ideal he sought in his own work on aesthetics, which is what was under discussion between him and Fichte.

A deeper problem with Beiser's interpretation is that it rests on a simple either-or between rhetoric and philosophy. He identifies rhetoric, on the one hand, with the absence of intellectual rigor, and thus with the ultimately irrational embrace of ambiguity and inconsistency; philosophy, by contrast, stands for the logical clarity that eschews ambiguity and inconsistency as far as possible. But this judgment is not only an inadequate

---

125. Ibid., 266.
126. NLB (SW.8.419).
127. 3 August 1795, first draft.
128. NLB (SW.8.419).

Friedrich Schiller's Dramatic Philosophy

characterization of *both* rhetoric *and* philosophy, it directly undermines the integration that Schiller so persistently pursued. Rhetoric in the classical tradition that began with Isocrates among the ancient Greeks and the Romans Quintilian and Cicero—rhetoricians whom Schiller admired[129]—is not the cultivation of external adornment and strategies of persuasion at the expense of substance, but the engagement of the whole person. As Quintilian most famously expressed it, the aim of education in rhetoric is the fashioning of a "good person who speaks well," and thus aims at both being *and* appearance. In striving after the wholeness of beauty, it seeks not *less* than the mind, but the mind and more. As Vico expressed it, classical rhetoric deals *"non cum mente, sed cum anima tota"*[130]—though, of course, we need to add that the whole soul *includes* the mind. It is true that romantic versions of rhetoric often consider the injury of intellectual integrity a virtue, and imply that the more the mind is subdued, the more feeling is set free. Beiser's book provides an indispensable corrective to the tendency to romanticize Schiller in this way, to isolate aspects or passages in his work that, though crucial, are not meant to stand alone, and thereby to make him an anti-intellectual. The passage that Beiser cites from Schiller's letter to Goethe harshly censuring those who would allow the senses to do the work of reason is particularly illuminating in this regard.[131] But in rejecting this trivializing of beauty, one ought not to reject what Schiller calls the "truly beautiful" (*wahrhaft schön*), the beauty that *contains* (philosophical) truth in itself, or simply allow it as secondary while conceding its trivialized form. One ought not, in other words, to reject the classical rhetorical tradition in which Schiller stands, which at least intends to do full justice to conceptual rigor. Moreover, the aspiration to exclude all ambiguity from thinking and in the articulation of one's thoughts may belong to certain schools of philosophy, the Anglo-American school of analytic philosophy most prominent among them, but does not belong to philosophy *as such*. The affirmation and positive use of textures and layers of meaning embedded in words, the resonance that multiplies implications and sometimes creates surprisingly fruitful tensions in "staged" opposition, characterize the work of many respected philosophers. We need not only look, for example, to Schiller's countrymen Hegel or Nietzsche, but should also consider the great thinkers at the origin of philosophy,

---

129. WW, lxxiii, fn2.

130. See Borchmeyer's essay, "Rhetorische und ästhetische Revolutionsdialektik," 56.

131. 9 Feb, 1798. See Beiser, *Schiller*, 264.

Heraclitus, Parmenides, Empedocles, Plato. As we have seen in our analysis, ambiguity need not compromise intellectual clarity in the least, but its affirmation can indeed coincide with strict conceptual rigor. The assumption that ambiguous expression necessarily implies confused thinking is itself a confusion.

Schiller was clearly not content to be merely a poet or merely a philosopher, but sought some particular combination of *both* in his activity. Even the question of whether Schiller was a poet or philosopher must thus be answered dramatically. In one respect, the poet and the philosopher represent polar opposites: and yet for that very reason, Schiller's ideal embraces both.[132] Schiller aimed at a "synthesis" of the two—and thus we find scholars speaking of both his "rhetorical philosophy" and his "philosophical rhetoric"[133]—but one that does not simply resolve the tension between them. According to his friend Wilhelm von Humboldt, Schiller's creative energy arose from an original unity between poetry and philosophy, the basic feature of which is the human wholeness that engages all the soul's power in their absolute freedom.[134] Schiller's complaints that the one interfered with the other in his work need to be read, in this light, not as a definitive statement of their incompatibility, but as a strengthening of the tension between them that allows their reconciliation to be a dramatic event, the achievement of a living whole. To take for granted their incompatibility is to dismiss at the outset what lies at the center for Schiller.

This leads to the deepest problem with Beiser's interpretation. The dramatic integration of poetry and philosophy in Schiller's writing is not a mere issue of style, but has implications for the substance of what he says. For Beiser, synthesis comes *after* the analysis of the parts in themselves. As we have seen, however, this approach both makes the parts only *accidentally* related to one another, insofar as it implies that each of the parts does not enter in a significant way into the meaning proper to the others, and it makes impossible any sense of a concrete whole other than a mere aggregate. Schiller insists, by contrast, on wholeness both preceding and following analysis, so that distinction always occurs within a prior unity that it then recapitulates and so reinforces. In this case, the beauty implied by integration is not a subsequent, and so purely external, adornment of an otherwise "rigorously logical" conceptual argument, but bears in fact

---

132. See Humboldt, *Über Schiller*, 27.

133. See Curran's essay, "Schiller's Essay," and that of Meyer, "Schillers philosophische Rhetorik."

134. Humboldt, *Über Schiller*, 19.

on the *truth* of the content. In other words, the dramatic form in which Schiller synthesizes his apparently unruly insights has genuine philosophical significance. To affirm this is not to confuse poetry and philosophy: we can still describe them as polar opposites, each possessing a basically different formal object, and a correspondingly different means of attaining it. Nevertheless, polar opposition does not mean simple dualism; it does not require us to see the two as merely extrinsically related to one another. Rather, we can say that philosophical writing means to communicate ideas and uses logical argumentation as its primary instrument in doing so. And we can nevertheless add that the *form* of that communication makes a profound difference to the meaning it expresses. It is not the *same* thing to be a philosophical poet and to be a poetic philosopher, but even if he is arguably more centrally the first than the second, Friedrich Schiller is both.[135]

To judge the significance of Schiller's philosophical insights into freedom awaits our more substantial discussion in the following chapter, but we may conclude with three remarks regarding the nature of his contribution. First, in his thinking about freedom from an aesthetic perspective, he links it with expressive form and thereby opens the notion up in a decisive way beyond subjectivistic reductions of the notion to deliberate and discreet acts of individual will, as we shall see. In this way, the notion of freedom acquires a depth that allows, in principle, a connection to that to which it often gets opposed, namely, to nature, on the one hand, and to the social order with its objective institutions, on the other.[136] We will follow out the implications in these two directions in our study of Schelling and Hegel, respectively.

---

135. Wilhelm von Humboldt wrote to Schiller on August 4, 1795: "Both directions [i.e., poetry and metaphysics] spring from a single source in you and what specifically characterizes your genius is precisely that it possesses both of these, but also that it would be utterly unable to possess just one. When I observe something similar elsewhere, it is always a poet who is philosophizing or a philosopher who is writing poetry. In you, these are absolutely united, but this is admittedly why both your poetry and your philosophy are quite different from what one normally encounters, and the latter especially will confuse one-sided minds for a good long while. One could say that there is in both more, and a higher, truth than one typically has a sense for, in poetry there is more necessity of the ideal, in philosophy, there is more nature and essence, insofar as it stands over against the mere form, the system. . . . That which otherwise so wholly separates the poet and the philosopher—the great difference between the truth of reality, of perfect individuality, and the truth of the idea, of simple necessity—this difference simply disappears for you, as it were."

136. See Lindner, "Zur philosophischen Leistung Friedrich Schillers," 871.

Second, because his thinking about freedom arises from an original and integral human core, the core from which so much genuine human creativity stems, that thinking possesses the power to renew. Though Schiller's insights into freedom remained to a certain extent like yet-closed buds in his work, without the space in which to develop and unfold in their full philosophical significance, and though Schiller did not elaborate his thoughts in direct relation to the philosophical tradition, his writings promise not just some new philosophical ideas about freedom, but a new impulse for philosophical thinking in general.[137] However modest this impulse may be, Schiller's contribution in this regard is *basic*, and it shows its fruitfulness in both Schelling and Hegel.

Finally, by integrating philosophical thinking within a beautiful form—"veiling" truth within beauty, and the philosopher within the poet, as Kuno Fischer put it[138]—Schiller's philosophy turns out to be "of freedom" in both the objective and the subjective sense of the genitive. As part of an integral human whole, the "shape" of his thought is trans-formed. Indeed, it is *given form*: namely, the form of freedom. This, then, is Schiller's contribution: not just a philosophy of freedom, but a model of free philosophy.

---

137. In this respect, Safranski is right to call him the "inventor of German idealism," which is the title of his philosophical biography of Schiller.

138. Fischer, *Schiller als Philosoph*, 36–37.

2

An Aesthetics of Freedom: Schiller and the Living Gestalt

I. Introduction: Schiller's Breakthrough

WE ARE ACCUSTOMED TO think about freedom primarily in terms of possibility: freedom is the *power* to choose and act, the *ability* to attain certain ends. While possibility is undeniably an essential part of the meaning of freedom, if we make it the whole, we separate freedom at one stroke from the real world. Freedom, then, gets threatened by any particular, definite realization, and, conversely, everything actual comes to be seen as "freedom-less," as simply "there" without any depth, anything new to offer, anything worthy of wonder. One of the surest signs of a loss of a sense for what Gabriel Marcel referred to as the "ontological mystery" is a "subjectivizing" of freedom.

Hegel, as is well known, took Kant to be a representative of the "subjectification" of freedom, and he pointed to Friedrich Schiller as the one who first managed to break open a path beyond this subjectivism to the possibility of a new understanding of spirit.[1] Though Hegel does not elaborate in much detail *how* Schiller achieved this, he links it to Schiller's interpretation of *beauty*. As Hegel sees it, the aim of beauty in Schiller's

---

1. On Schiller's place in the development of German Idealism, see Lindner, "Zur philosophischen Leistung Friedrich Schillers," 831. Cf., Kroner, *Von Kant bis Hegel*, vol. 2, 45–47; Cassirer, *Idee und Gestalt*, 344–34
5; Safranski, *Schiller*.

understanding is "to form inclination, sensuality, drive and temperament [*Gemüt*] in such a way that they become rational in themselves, and therefore so that reason, freedom, and the reality of spirit [*Geistigkeit*] emerge from their abstraction and take on flesh and blood in union with the natural side that has thus become rational. The beautiful is thus the unification [*Ineinsbildung*, literally, the *form*-ing into one] of the rational and sensual, and this unification is expressed as the truly real."[2] Hegel was indeed correct that beauty represented for Schiller, not a mere "aesthetic" phenomenon, but a reality with ontological significance. Indeed, the philosopher-poet presented his theory to Goethe in a letter as a "metaphysics of beauty."[3] Schiller was driven his life long to reconcile in a non-reductivistic way the ideal and real, spirit and matter, the absolute demands of the spirit and the limited condition of the realm of the body, and the notion he developed of beauty was the culmination of these efforts.[4]

Moreover, the notion of beauty was, for Schiller, indissolubly wed to that of freedom. Schiller calls freedom the *sole ground* of beauty,[5] he defines beauty as "freedom in appearance" (which may better be translated as "manifest freedom"),[6] he claims that only the genuine experience of genuine beauty can bestow freedom,[7] and says that what offers a true formation in freedom is nothing other than an *aesthetic* education. Our aim in the present chapter is to work out an understanding of Schiller's notion of freedom, in the light of Hegel's claims, through an interpretation of the notion in the so-called *Kalliasbriefe*, where the famous definition of beauty first appears, and then of the *Letters on the Aesthetic Education of Man*, Schiller's main philosophical work. The study of the *Kalliasbriefe* will provide us with an understanding of *form* and *nature*, two notions essentially related to freedom in Schiller's thinking, which will then provide a helpful way into the AEM. We will see, in the end, that freedom is connected, not principally with possibility alone, for Schiller, but in the first place with *human wholeness*, which is an actuality full of potential. Such a

---

2. Hegel, *Lectures on Aesthetics* (JA.12.96f.).

3. See the letter dated 7 January, 1795: "I certainly do not have to assure you that I am quite anxious to know what you think of my metaphysics of beauty. Just as beauty itself is drawn from the whole of man, so is my analysis of it drawn from the whole of my humanity, and it cannot but concern me greatly to know how it corresponds to yours."

4. See Wilcox, *Die Dialektik der menschlichen Vollendung*, 129.

5. 23 Feb, 1793, 168 (SW.8.658).

6. 8 Feb, 1793, 152 (SW.8.638).

7. AEM, II, 9 (SW.8.309).

view of freedom is a key one for the project of the present book in general; it sets the stage for our further studies of Schelling and Hegel, who developed their own views of freedom in the wake of Schiller's "breakthrough."

II. The Analogy of Form

The name *"Kalliasbriefe"* refers to a series of letters that Schiller wrote to his most constant correspondent, Christian Gottfried Körner, from January to March 1793, in which Schiller sought among other things to clarify for himself insights he had into the nature of beauty that struck him in his study of Kant's *Critique of Judgment*.[8] It was also a time in which Schiller lectured on aesthetics at the university in Jena and had gathered and sorted through a variety of materials to this end.[9] The series of letters to Augustenburg, which would eventually be revised as the famous AEM, were announced in February of this year, even if they were not begun in earnest until July.[10] Thus, the beginning of the AEM overlap with the end of Schiller's first sketch,[11] and they indeed make use of the concept Schiller developed in the earlier letters, namely, the account of beauty as the manifestation of freedom.[12] Though he was inspired by Kant in a decisive

---

8. Schiller had written to Körner on December 21 of the previous year about his desire to write a dialogue on beauty that he would call "Kallias." (Körner incidentally responded on December 27 that Schiller was just the person to write this important work specifically because of his dramatic talent.) Schiller never carried out this project, but because he expounded his aesthetic theory to Körner in letters that began to acquire the form of a treatise, the letters he wrote to Körner during these months were published in 1847, and repeatedly since, as an independent, though incomplete, work and given the name *Kalliasbriefe*. This was never a name, however, that Schiller himself gave to them. We use it nonetheless for the sake of convenience.

9. Schiller lectured on aesthetics in the winter semester 92/93, and presented in these lectures his theory of beauty as "Freiheit in der Erscheinung," in relation to other proposals being made in the eighteenth century. See SW.8.622.

10. For a thorough presentation of the history of the two series and their relation to one another, see WW, 334–37, and especially SW.8.880–93.

11. See Muehleck-Müller, *Schönheit und Freiheit*, 125.

12. Because the AEM do not elaborate the same theory as the *Kalliasbriefe* in the same detail, some believe that Schiller considered that earlier attempt a failure and so abandoned it. But in fact the letters mention the theory in passing as a more or less established fact. The passage from the footnote to XXIII, 167fn (SW.8.383fn): "Schönheit aber ist der einzig mögliche Ausdruck der Freiheit in der Erscheinung," is not only a direct citation of this theory but a confident emphasis of his discovery. The reason he does not elaborate this theory in the AEM is simply because they represent a further development of this theory in a new sphere, rather than a retracing of the same ground.

way, one of the things that prompted his writing of these letters was a conviction that he had discovered something that Kant had missed, namely, the objective ground of beauty, a ground that would both enable a more philosophically systematic account and also do more justice to the phenomenon in its richness.[13]

Let us begin our analysis of Schiller's interpretation simply by laying out some of his affirmations regarding form, nature, freedom, and beauty next to one another, and then endeavor to unfold what they mean in their interconnection. As we shall see, the discussion of "free style" in the previous chapter offers an indispensable perspective for interpreting these

---

13. See his letter to Johann Heinrich Ramberg, 7 March, 1793: "A great deal of light has gone on for me regarding the nature of beauty, so that I believe I will win you over to my theory. I believe I have discovered the objective concept of beauty, which also qualifies *eo ipso* as an objective principle of taste, which is a possibility Kant had doubted." Many scholars believe that the *Kalliasbriefe* represent a *failure* to find such an objective ground. Beiser, for example, points to Schiller's apparent confession of his difficulties in another letter to Körner in October of 1794, and thus later than this letter to Ramberg (*Schiller*, 75). It should be noted, however, that Schiller persists even in this later letter in calling the concept *objective*, and simply states that it cannot be *proven empirically*. But this is precisely how he describes the situation to Körner in his very first letter in the series, 25 January, 1793, which means the later letter does not represent a change in view. Beiser's judgment ultimately rests on a claim we intend to dispute, namely, that Schiller held an ultimately Kantian view of nature as determined from first to last by external causes. Though there is some ambiguity on this point in the *Kalliasbriefe*, even here Schiller is clearly moving in a different direction. Beiser's claim would hold only if Schiller became a more convinced Kantian on this point the further he moved from Kant's influence and the closer to Goethe's, which is not plausible. The direction Schiller takes is evident in the major philosophical essay Schiller wrote that Beiser did not discuss in his book, namely, *On Naive and Sentimental Poetry*, in which he observes in the opening pages: the things of nature "act serenely on their own, being there according to their own laws; we cherish that inner necessity, that eternal oneness with themselves," ibid., 180 (SW.8.434). Even here, Schiller tries to move Kant himself in a Goethean direction, as it were (see his footnote on this same page).

There are others who affirm the success of Schiller's attempt to discover an objective concept of beauty, and see the AEM as a fulfillment of his theory; in fact, this was the first position taken in print (see Danzel, *Schillers Briefwechsel mit Körner*, 1–25) and even more strongly argued by Berger, *Die Entwicklung von Schillers Ästhetik*. For more recent arguments for the success of the *Kalliasbriefe*, see Römpp, "Schönheit als Erfahrung der Freiheit," 428–45, and a more qualified expression in Wilcox, *Dialektik der menschlichen Vollendung*, 36. Although we cannot enter into the dispute surrounding that question, our own position is that the matter would have to remain for Schiller ambiguous, insofar as the locus of beauty, namely, *appearance*, is necessarily both subjective and objective at once. Nevertheless, we take the aesthetic theory articulated here to be a successful one in principle, even if it eludes the attempt to deduce it transcendentally or demonstrate it empirically.

complex notions. According to Schiller, beauty is freedom in appearance, which is another way of saying that freedom is the ground of beauty. Schiller also defines beauty as the form of perfection, or the form of form,[14] and claims that we perceive something as beautiful when the *mass* of that thing is "completely dominated by form."[15] Freedom, for its part, is defined as *autonomy*,[16] which Schiller explains as a thing's determining itself from within itself.[17] This latter affirmation is explained further as a thing's existing "out of pure form,"[18] and acting solely on the basis of its nature.[19] Schiller defines nature here as "the inner principle of the existence of a thing, which can be at the same time seen as the ground of its form: *the inner necessity of form.*"[20] Schiller then goes on to specify *aesthetic* autonomy as *heautonomy*.[21] And finally he elaborates freedom in a broader sense as the coordination of parts within a whole, a coordination that both gives rise to genuine unity and at the same time preserves the irreducible uniqueness of all the parts.[22] It is clear, here, that to understand freedom we need to understand the role that form plays as a constitutive ontological principle in Schiller's thought, the connection it therefore has with nature, and then, finally, the implication of this view of form for the part-whole relationship. How do the various affirmations Schiller makes here fit together?

Schiller's use of the term "Form" or "Gestalt" reflects much of the ambiguity it has within the Platonic and Aristotelian traditions. While some commentators discern two different meanings in the term,[23] there seem

14. 25 Jan, 1793, 147 (SW.8.632).
15. 23 Feb, 1793, 164 (SW.8.653).
16. 8 Feb, 1793, 151 (SW.8.637).
17. 18 Feb, 1793, 153 (SW.8.640).
18. Ibid.
19. 23 Feb, 1793, 163 (SW.8.652).
20. Ibid.
21. Ibid.
22. See ibid., 171–72 (SW.8.662).
23. See von Wiese, *Friedrich Schiller*, 491, who distinguishes between a rational and an aesthetic sense of form. Cf., Taminiaux, *La nostalgie de la Grèce*, 80–81, who focuses on the tension between nature and subjectivity in German Idealism which he claims comes to expression in Schiller's thought. Taminiaux discerns two conceptions of form in Schiller, one that emerges from the existence of a thing (nature) and one that the understanding imposes on it (subjectivity). Wilkinson and Willoughby distinguish essentially between rational form and the *Gestalt* that represents the concretely existing thing, though they mention in passing the "non-technical" sense of *Gestalt* as "outward appearance" (WW, 308–10). Admittedly, they are focusing primarily on the AEM, where these two senses are arguably the most important. They, and von

in fact to be four, which we can express as a pair of polarities. First, form can be the intelligible aspect of a thing in contrast to its matter, the aspect to which the logical concept we form of things refers (compare Plato's use of *eidos*). Secondly, form can mean the concretely and individually existing thing itself, as for example we would in English speak of a "lifeform" (compare Aristotle's use of *morphē*). In Schiller's AEM, this latter usage is often taken over by the native word *Gestalt*—which we may attribute, at least in part, to Goethe's influence, since the term, which plays such a fundamental role in the final version, scarcely appears in the extant letters from 1793. Nevertheless, the word "form" *includes* within its semantic scope what is contained in *Gestalt*, even if the reverse is not always true: Form can always be used in place of *Gestalt*, but not vice versa.[24] Third, within a formed whole, form can be the internal organizing principle of the thing that makes it in fact *be* a whole (once again, *morphē*). Finally, form can mean the outward appearance of a thing, the structure that gives it the character that identifies it as what it is: *eidos* similarly is cognate with both "to know" and "to see," and means not only the "idea" of a thing, but also the "look" that it has.

The great richness of the term implies a certain ambiguity, but this ambiguity in Schiller's vocabulary ought not to be taken as a sign of philosophical amateurishness—unless we would wish to call Aristotle, for example, an amateur. Instead, the previous chapter has instructed us to see ambiguity as an important dimension of the complex phenomenon Schiller wishes to elucidate; problems arise in our interpretation if we reduce it. There is a great tension in the term, to be sure, insofar as form, for example, can identify precisely what is *abstracted* from the whole, and at the same time stand for the whole precisely in its concreteness. Moreover, form can be the "inner principle" of the thing, and at the same time the outward appearance of it. But it is important to see how the various meanings do not conflict in principle, but in a certain sense depend on one another. It is presumably this inner richness of the term that has always made it difficult to limit to any single definition. What *identifies* a thing, and so allows us to form a logical concept of it, is the same "thing" that organizes it into what it is. The principle of its organization is, in turn, what makes an independently existing whole, a structured entity. And it is likewise

---

Wiese, miss however the "internal principle" that Taminiaux sees, while for his part Taminiaux forces Schiller into an over-simplified dualism precisely, as we shall see, because he misses the aesthetic meaning of form that mediates between the objectivity of nature and the subjectivity of the human cognitive faculties.

24. WW, 308–9.

what gives a thing the particular *look* that it has. The outward appearance, then, though in one respect clearly and importantly *different* from its inner being, nonetheless reflects or manifests nothing *other than* that internal being, so that we would fail to see the outward appearance if we saw it as something else, or indeed as an independently existing "thing" in its own right—that is, if we were to "reify" appearance. To interpret Schiller properly requires us *both* to recognize the distinction of meanings *and* to hold them at the same time together in a reciprocally illuminating unity.

In other words, it requires us to read Schiller "dramatically," in the sense argued for in chapter 1. A dramatic reading would formulate the analogy of form, not just by affirming one aspect "and also" the other in the polarity, but by grasping the *whole*, which means the one, the other, and the movement between them. Fischer wrote that, in Schiller, if beauty is veiled truth,[25] the poet is the veiled philosopher;[26] to grasp the whole phenomenon in Schiller, however, we would have to say that this veil must be both *kept in place* and in a certain respect *lifted*. The whole form, similarly, is the embrace of the partial meaning by the more comprehensive one. More specifically, we could say that form in the concrete sense *contains* form as abstraction, without eliminating its relative autonomy, and form as appearance *contains* the inner principle, while allowing it to remain internal. The key to this "analogicity" of form is the point we discovered in the previous chapter, indicating its capital importance for understanding everything else in Schiller's philosophical work: the inner completion of the concept is what allows it, as it were, the freedom to be wholly present in the expression, so that form is simultaneously inner principle and external appearance, and it is so without compromising the difference between these aspects.

III. Form Overcoming Form

With this complex unity as a guiding background, we can explore the work the term does for Schiller in the *Kalliasbriefe*. In the letter of January 25, Schiller compares his aesthetic interpretation of form to Kant's. Kant insisted on a *separation* of beautiful form from logical concept, according to Schiller, for the good reason that we can experience something

---

25. He is no doubt making allusion to Schiller's poem, *Das verschleierte Bild zu Sais*.
26. See Fischer, *Schiller als Philosoph*, 37.

as beautiful without understanding what it is.[27] This separation has two immediate implications, however, that Schiller finds problematic. In the first place, it removes the beautiful from the sphere of objectivity, and so renders it impossible to discover an objective principle of taste. Second, it leads to the formalism that would rank the abstract pattern of an arabesque a higher beauty than that of a perfect human form, which represents for Schiller (as for the Greeks he admired) the "highest beauty." At the same time, however, he finds the motivation for the separation compelling. How does Schiller account for the experience without being forced to follow Kant in making the separation? He makes a distinction, as it were, *within* form, which allows beautiful form to be distinct from the logical concept without being separated from it, and this entails a "dramatic" view of the matter: "beauty presents itself in its greatest splendor only once it has overcome the *logical* nature of its object, and how can this be done if there is no resistance?"[28] Beauty, he goes on to say, is the "form of form," or the "form of perfection."

In one respect, then, form represents the perfection of a thing, which means its adequation to its concept, and yet form remains *more* than this: it is the expression of the thing's not being reducible to the mere concept. This "more" is what will turn out to be the thing's self-manifestation or revelation. We ought to notice, here, that form in the aesthetic sense is not simply different from form in a logical sense—which would return us to the Kantian implications we just mentioned—but it *includes* the logical sense within itself even while it surpasses that particular sense. This makes the logical form, as it were, *implicit within* the aesthetic form: the phrase "form of form" ought to be understood as a subjective genitive. The "both/and" character of form, as Schiller presents it, offers an important insight for the field of aesthetics proper. It allows us both to affirm the experience of recognizing beauty prior to understanding a thing, and at the same time allows us to say that our appreciation of the beauty of a thing can in fact *deepen* with our progressive understanding of it, something that a Kantian view would not permit. This is no small gain for aesthetics.

What does Schiller mean by the curious verb he uses here, "overcome" (*überwinden*)? He strikes a similar note in the letter of February 23, writing that we experience a thing as beautiful when we see mass

---

27. Cf., Kant, CJ, §16, Ak 229–31 (Pluhar: 76–79), in which Kant distinguishes between "free" beauty (*pulchritudo vaga*) and "adherent" beauty (*pulchritudo adhaerens*), calling the judgments concerning the form *pure* judgments of taste.

28. 25 Jan, 1793, 147 (SW.8.632).

An Aesthetics of Freedom

"completely dominated by form."[29] He is speaking in this case of a physical thing in art (artifact) or nature (organism), but it is not difficult to see how his explanation would apply analogously through all the levels of being, from abstract mathematical objects to human deeds.[30] As in the previous case, he makes here a distinction between two essentially different but inseparable senses of form: the *general* form—i.e., that which makes it a "thing" and gives it mass—and the specific form, which is what makes it be the thing it is, what establishes it according to its "particular" nature.[31] The nature of an animal, he says, includes both its being subject to natural laws (mass) and the principle that determines its proper essence (for example, horse). There is an analogy, here, between the distinction Schiller is making and the scholastic distinction between quantitative form designating "signate matter" and the quiditative form that establishes the nature of a thing;[32] and perhaps a more distant analogy to Aristotle's distinction in living things between first and second actuality. In any event, none of these represent numerically distinct forms, which are as it were "aggregated" into the one being, but rather distinct aspects within form itself. Judged aesthetically, the beauty of an animal depends on the extent to which the former, the mass, is subordinate to the latter, the inner nature, which differs in different types of animals and within a species. The formed matter (in scholastic terms, the "signate matter") of a horse makes it a physical body, subject to the laws of nature. A horse is heavy, which means that gravity pulls it to the earth. But a beautiful horse is one that shows that this pull does not strain it, which means that the necessity imposed on it does not burden it as a foreign power, as something that disrupts, as it were, its attempt to be what it is, i.e., to realize and express its "horseness." Quite to the contrary, a beautiful horse takes the necessity imposed on it precisely as a means of self-expression, as an opportunity to show itself for what it is. In doing so, the external imposition is transformed; it appears as a function of the inner principle of the horse's own being. This transformation, of course, admits of degrees; a thing will be more or less

---

29. 23 Feb, 1793, 164 (SW.8.653).

30. And, indeed, Schiller shows this analogy by illustrating his discussion in terms of both human deeds (18 Feb, 1793; 157–58; *SW*.8.644–46) and geometrical figures (23 Feb, 1793, 172–73 [SW.8.664]).

31. Because of the "analogical" character of form, the claim that matter must be dominated by form does *not* necessarily entail a collapse back into Kantian formalism, as Taminiaux suggests: *La nostalgie de la Grèce*, 113.

32. See Thomas Aquinas, *De ente et essentia*, chapter 2.

successful in "internalizing" the foreign necessity, but the ideal of beauty is the "complete domination" of mass.

There are two related things to notice about this domination. In the first place, we see that this transformation is the overcoming of form *from within* rather than the substitution of a new form for the old one. Being a horse does not make it any less a physical thing in the world, but makes its thingness beautiful, that is, makes whatever is outwardly "there" expressive of an internal meaning.[33] It is precisely for this reason that the overcoming allows the difference to be one of analogy rather than one of equivocity. As abstract as this point may seem, we will come to see that it is crucial for the whole of Schiller's aesthetics. Second, the domination of matter that Schiller describes here—again, because of the principle coming from the inside—does not mean the "suppression" of the matter: indeed, there is an undeniable sense in which a beautiful horse is more *physically present*, more imposing in its concrete reality, than a clumsy horse that has never achieved mastery of its movements.[34] The point here is not elimination but integration: a beautiful horse "has it together," which means that the multiplicity of the diverse aspects of its being does not stand outside of its unity. To the contrary, these aspects are expressive of that very interior principle. In this, Schiller is recovering the fundamental feature of Neo-Platonic aesthetics, the very feature that makes that tradition of aesthetics *ontological*, namely, the identity of beauty and unity.[35] But Schiller improves upon this tradition in a decisive respect: whereas the Neo-Platonic tradition insists relentlessly on the ultimate reduction of multiplicity to unity,[36] Schiller

---

33. Schiller speaks at the end of Letter XXIII in the AEM of outward form making manifest inner life: AEM, 169 (SW.8.384). This is an expression of the same idea articulated here in the *Kalliasbriefe*.

34. This affirmation requires a qualification that Schiller himself never gives. The examples Schiller uses encourage what could be a called a "triumphalistic" aesthetics, even though his principles allow for an even more radically "dramatic" aesthetics than he himself offers, namely, the free submission of a figure to absolute necessity in tragedy. Strangely, Schiller doesn't exploit what seems to be the full potential of his own principles in his theory of tragedy. See Schiller's essay "On the Art of Tragedy," and Beiser's illuminating account of his theory and its historical development: *Schiller*, 238–62.

35. See *Ennead* I.6.2: "We hold that all the loveliness of this world comes by communion in Ideal-Form. . . . But where the Ideal-Form has entered, it has grasped and coordinated what from a diversity of parts was to become a unity: it has rallied confusion into co-operation: it has made the sum one harmonious coherence: for the Idea is a unity and what it moulds must come to unity as far as multiplicity may" (McKenna translation). On the presence of Neo-Platonic themes in Schiller, see Koch, *Schillers philosophische Schriften und Plotin*, and Pugh, *The Dialectic of Love*.

36. A more thorough demonstration of this point is necessary than we can give in

insists on the dramatic phenomenon of an asymmetrical reciprocity. Thus, while the Neo-Platonic tradition would say only that beauty increases the more diversity reveals an inner unity, Schiller can affirm this and at the same time claim something that makes no Neo-Platonic sense: beauty also increases the more unity reveals itself to be diversified. This is yet another gain for aesthetics.

This interpretation of form's "dominating" mass, or indeed aesthetic form's "overcoming" logical form, opens up in turn the meaning of two of the best known phrases from the *Kalliasbriefe*, namely, that moral beauty exists when "duty becomes . . . nature"[37] and, as we will see in the next section, the specific definition of beauty as "freedom in appearance." To do something "naturally"—or, as Schiller puts it, "with the ease of someone acting out of mere instinct"—means to do it without the addition of deliberately willed effort. Such acts would include not only the desires that spring from the necessities of one's bodily nature, but also the events that make up one's affective life. When one hears one's child cry, one responds to it immediately and without thinking: care for one's children is a perfectly natural reality. But not all instinctive responses are beautiful. They acquire aesthetic form only if the action represents a duty, which means only if it is something that would have been commanded by reason, with all of the absoluteness and universality that such commandments imply. In other words, with respect to human action, form becomes aesthetic only if it contains *within* itself the rational form that corresponds to moral duty, according to the analogy we presented above. An action is morally beautiful, then, *if* on the one hand it is the fulfillment of a duty that is "imposed," so to speak, as an absolute necessity, and, on the other hand, it occurs *as if* it springs directly from the inner being of the agent as a wholly spontaneous act. That is to say, it comes simultaneously *from without* and *from within*.

To illustrate his point to Körner, Schiller tells a version of the "Good Samaritan" story from the Gospels, which is meant to set in relief the distinctions between merely instinctive action, merely pragmatic action, the mere carrying out of one's duty, the mere triumph over self-interest (without feeling), and finally a genuinely noble deed. We could call it the story of the "Beautiful Samaritan." The point, in any event, is that the last mentioned deed is the most fully human because it *contains* within itself all the partial aspects of the others. It is not, in this respect, simply another

---

the present context. See Schindler, "What's the Difference?," 583–618.

37. 19 Feb, 1793, 159 (SW.8.647).

example to be juxtaposed to all the others. The wholeness of beautiful action is, of course, the theme of Schiller's first major philosophical essay, *On Grace and Dignity*, which we cannot discuss here, though it is worthwhile making two observations in relation to our particular question. First, because of this comprehensiveness, Schiller is able to affirm all of the unconditionality of Kant's deontological ethics, even though he places this at the same time within a larger context that transforms it. We will come back to this point at the end of the chapter. Second, we have to be careful to avoid reading the "as if" Schiller presents here in a *merely* phenomenal sense. When we speak of someone doing something *as if* it were second nature, we are attributing a real quality, not just a "mere appearance," to the action, even though we don't mean the person was born playing tennis, or would have shown his ability to do so without lessons. He has learned to play, and so it is something introduced to him from the outside, but at the same time it has entered so deeply into him that it springs "naturally" from his being. Similarly, for Schiller, a beautiful moral action is one in which duty has been so thoroughly internalized that it *really does* spring from one's inner being. Schiller in fact says that "duty *has become* its nature." If he elsewhere speaks in a more conditional sense, it indicates only that the duty was not there, as it were, from the beginning. It is precisely this point, according to Otfried Höffe, that distinguishes Schiller's ethics from those of Kant, who would make the strain of moral effort paradigmatic of virtue.[38] Once again, it is a point on which Schiller stands closer to Aristotle than to Kant. The important thing in this context, in any event, is that we have here the "overcoming" of moral form, once again, by aesthetic form, which means we have the appropriation of an external imposition to an internal principle.

IV. Manifest Freedom in Nature

How, in light of this, are we to understand the definition of beauty as "freedom in appearance"? From a Kantian perspective, the definition is oxymoronic: freedom is something noumenal in the strictest sense; the phenomenal realm is from first to last subject to a contingency and

---

38. Höffe, "Gerne dien ich den Freunden," 17.

necessity that excludes freedom.[39] While Schiller agrees with this in principle,[40] the central aim of the *Kalliasbriefe* is to overcome this separation by locating a real analogy to freedom *in* the realm of nature. To see the analogy, we must first ask what Schiller means by freedom here, and then how he understands nature. Schiller's definition of freedom is easy to state, but requires some analysis to interpret it properly. He takes over with great enthusiasm Kant's definition, namely, that freedom is self-determination, or *autonomy* as opposed to *heteronomy*: "It is certain that *no* mortal has spoken a greater word than this Kantian word, which also encapsulates his whole philosophy: determine yourself from within yourself."[41] Later, he affirms that "It is the same thing to be free and to be determined from within yourself."[42] Despite affirming the same definition of freedom, Schiller's difference from Kant comes to light the moment we ask after the "*auton*," as it were, of the *auto*nomy. For Kant, reason alone is capable of the spontaneity of self-determination. For Schiller, by contrast, the fullest meaning of "self"—as he makes especially clear in the AEM—is the body-soul composite, the unity of reason and nature. It seems to be the case that Schiller was unaware of how different his view was from Kant's, in the end, which is why he always insisted that the spirit of Kant's philosophy embraced this larger view even if the letter denied it.[43] For his own part, Schiller never saw Kant's affirmation as posing any difficulty to integration within his own understanding.

One of the most immediate implications of this broader view of the "self" in self-determination is that it is precisely what opens up the possibility of analogy to freedom in nature, which in turn implies a significantly different conception of nature more generally. Schiller indicates

---

39. See Kant's solution to the third antinomy of reason: CPR A532–58 B560–86 (Kemp Smith: 464–79). Cf., the critical elucidation of the analytic of pure practical reason in CPrP, 92–110; CJ, §61, Ak 359–61 (Pluhar: 235–37).

40. See 8 Feb, 1793, 151 (SW.8.637) and 19 Feb, 1793, 159 (SW.8.647).

41. 18 Feb, 1793, 151 (SW.8.637).

42. 23 Feb, 1793, 161 (SW.8.649).

43. See AEM XIII, 87fn (SW.8.344fn); cf., *Naive and Sentimental Poetry*, 180fn (SW.8.434fn). Of course, Kant *also* insisted that human reason is finite, which means embodied within particular conditions: this is why he rejects intellectual intuition for human beings, affirming it only for God. Nevertheless, when he explains the meaning of autonomy, he is clear that the "conditionedness" of finitude must be left out of account; and that self-determination is therefore *reason's* determination of itself, or, if you would prefer, the body-soul composite's determination of itself *according to the demands of reason alone*. On this, see the discussion between Anne Margaret Baxley and Frederick Beiser: *Inquiry* 51:1 (2008): 1–15; 63–78.

the analogy thus: "When a rational being acts, it must act on the basis of *pure reason* if it is to show self-determination. If a mere natural being acts, it must act from *pure nature* if it is to show self-determination; for the self of the rational being is reason, while the self of the natural being is nature."[44] We need to keep in mind that, for Schiller, the whole human being is neither "pure reason" nor "pure nature" but a complex whole derived from the asymmetrical reciprocity of both. If we thus see a natural being acting on the basis of its nature, we will ascribe to it "*similarity to freedom* [*Freiheitsähnlichkeit*] or just *freedom*."[45] A being is free because it is constituted by an active, determining principle, an *archē*, which is what enables it to be a "self" in the sense Schiller uses the term here; it is what gives the being an "interior" reality, which is, of course, the precondition for its being able to determine itself *from within* itself. But natural beings, for Schiller, likewise bear such an interiority, they likewise have a self. In fact, Schiller goes so far as to ascribe something like *personhood* to things in nature.[46] Personhood, as Schiller explains in the AEM, is the irreducibly unique identity of a thing; that which sets it apart from all other things or that by which it transcends whatever might happen to be at any given moment the conditions in which it exists.[47] It is often observed, quite casually, that Schiller emphasizes the "apparentness" of freedom in nature because he never thinks for a minute that nature in *reality* is anything other than subject from first to last to the laws that govern all things physical.[48] While there are passages throughout the series that do indeed give the impression that Schiller follows Kant without much qualification on this point, there are not only very strong passages that point in the other direction, but this is also undeniably the "drift" of the aesthetic theory as a whole.[49]

44. 8 Feb, 1793, 151 (SW.8.635).

45. Ibid.

46. 23 Feb, 1793, 163 (SW.8.652): "Es ist gleichsam die Person des Dings." Robert Spaemann has along similar lines argued on behalf of such an "anthropomorphism" in our approach to the natural world: see his essay, "Wirklichkeit als Anthropomorphismus," 13–34.

47. AEM XI, 73–77 (SW.8.337–39). See our discussion of this matter below. Thomas Buchheim has recently argued that the "life expressions" analogous to human freedom in nature depend on the possibility of positing a transcendentally-identical "subject" (which he insists is "horizontally" rather than "vertically" transcendent, in order to avoid a Cartesian sort of dualism) as that to which the expressions are ascribed: see Buchheim, *Unser Verlangen nach Freiheit*, 41–42.

48. See, for example, J. M. Bernstein, "Introduction," xx–xxii; cf., Beiser, *Schiller*, 26–27.

49. Taminiaux makes a similar judgment: although Schiller does fall into a Kantian privileging of subjectivity at times, Taminiaux says, on the whole he gives priority to

An Aesthetics of Freedom

Indeed, the most explicit definition of "nature" that Schiller gives is far closer to that of Aristotle than that of Kant:[50] "What would nature be in this sense? The inner principle of the existence of a thing, which can be at the same time seen as the ground of its form: *the inner necessity of form.*"[51] To have a nature, from this perspective, is to have an active, determining principle—an *archē*—that gathers up the multiplicity of a thing and establishes it as what it is in distinction from all that it is not, a principle that is not simply *one* of the many features of a thing, but that by which it, as a relatively independently existing thing, possesses whatever features it does in fact have. It is what makes it a unique self: "When I say: *the nature of a thing; the thing follows its nature, it determines itself through its nature,* I am contrasting nature with all that is different from the object, what is regarded as merely coincidental and can be abstracted without negating its essence."[52] This use of the term "nature" has a surprising implication: not only does it make nature no longer simply the "opposite" of freedom, as it is for so many late medieval, enlightenment, and modern thinkers, the analogy allows Schiller in fact to use the word "nature" *in the place of freedom* in certain contexts: "I prefer the term *nature* to that of *freedom* because it connotes both the realm of the senses, to which beauty is limited, and the concept of *freedom* as well as its intimation in its sphere in the sense-world."[53]

What Schiller is affirming here regarding nature is subtly but quite significantly different from what Kant means by speaking of "teleological" judgments regarding nature. Kant distinguishes teleological from mechanistic causality. Nature is taken to be mechanistic when we judge it as operating blindly according to chance and necessity; by contrast, we judge a being in nature as teleological when we see it as "*An organized product of nature . . . in which everything is a purpose and reciprocally also a means.*

---

nature: *La nostalgie de la Grèce*, 125.

50. According to Lesley Sharpe in her survey of the secondary literature on Schiller's philosophical thought, Carl Engel long ago fruitfully compared Schiller to Aristotle—though primarily in terms of the Stoff-Form and Person-Condition distinction rather than the view of nature as an internal principle of change: *Schiller als Denker* (1908), and she concludes that this is "an area of inquiry which has still to be fully explored" (*Two Centuries*, 34).

51. 23 Feb, 1793, 166 (SW.8.656). Cf., Aristotle, *Physics*, book II.1 and book III, in which Aristotle identifies form with the inner principle of a thing's activities, and indeed with its final purpose. This, as we shall see, is just what constitutes a thing as a "*lebende Gestalt*" in Schiller's thought.

52. 23 Feb, 1793, 162–63 (SW.8.652).

53. Ibid., 162–63 (SW.8.651).

The Perfection of Freedom

In such a product, nothing is gratuitous, purposeless, or to be attributed to a blind natural mechanism."[54] Interestingly, this view introduces a tension into the claim that Kant makes about the relationship between art and nature in aesthetics. For Kant, the judgment of beauty is that of purposiveness *without* a purpose, that is, the experience of a thing as meaningful without our being able to articulate any particular meaning, without our being able to subsume it under a determinate concept. This is what separates beauty from notions of perfection, which assume such a logical concept, as we discussed above. But to see nature as teleological is to see it as full of purpose, or better, as being *governed* by purpose, which means to view it as serving some concept, whether it be external or internal.[55] Oddly, then, to view a natural being as an organized whole would mean to cease to see it as beautiful, because we would be reducing it to a logical concept. This is why Kant explains that he must divide the third *Critique* into two separate parts:

> This is the basis for dividing the critique of judgment into that of *aesthetic* and that of *teleological* judgment. By the first I mean the power to judge formal purposiveness (sometimes also called subjective purposiveness) by the feeling of pleasure or displeasure; by the second I mean the power to judge the real (objective) purposiveness of nature by understanding and reason.[56]

Counter to our intuition in this matter, and indeed our experience of it, according to Kant's principles the organization of nature represents a hindrance to its beauty, so that we would have to overlook that organization in order to perceive its beauty. But for Schiller, to speak of the *nature* of a thing is to make reference to its internal organizing principle, that

---

54. Kant, CJ, §66, Ak 255 (Pluhar, 376).

55. Kant makes an important distinction between a thing that serves an extrinsic purpose (*bonum utile*) and a thing that serves an intrinsic purpose (*bonum honestum*). See CJ §15, Ak 226–29 (Pluhar, 73–75). This distinction would seem to hold some significance for his discussion of teleological judgments of nature, but Kant does not put it to use in that context.

56. Kant, CJ, Introduction VIII, Ak 193 (Pluhar, 33). This division seems to be in tension with Kant's later claim, which Schiller found extremely fruitful, that we find art beautiful when it looks like nature *and vice versa* (see §45, Ak 306–7; Pluhar, 173–74). There are two points to make here: first, *nature* in this context means what is non-intentional, i.e., without purpose, which for Kant means that it is non-organized. So he is appealing in nature *precisely* to its non-teleological aspect when making this comparison to art. Second, Schiller is right to say that his own theory, which affirms an *objective* criterion for beauty, is alone capable of explaining what Kant here affirms without support from his own suppositions.

An Aesthetics of Freedom

which is responsible for making it the whole that it is. But it is this very same principle that makes the natural thing (analogously) free, which is to say that it is the very same thing that causes its beauty.[57] He can claim this, and still insist that beauty and perfection are distinct, because organization, far from reducing all the aspects of the organized thing in one respect to a means, i.e., far from making every aspect "purposive," is precisely what lifts a thing, as it were, outside of the continuous chain of cause and effect and therefore outside of conceptual articulation. This is why Schiller, like Goethe, objects to a "teleological" approach to nature.[58] To have an internal principle, that is, to have a "self" that forms the basis of all that one is, is to be, in oneself, an "endpoint" of explanation, or, in other words, not to require reference to something outside of oneself in order to be intelligible. If to explain something is to show what purpose it serves, then a truly natural thing, for Schiller, is ultimately inexplicable, or perhaps better: *is itself* its own explanation; "A form is beautiful if it explains itself ... if it *demands no explanation*, or if it *explains itself without a concept.*"[59] While to see nature as non-mechanistic is, for Kant, to affirm that there

---

57. This is the point that Goethe admired in Schiller's *Kalliasbriefe*, and which provokes his own reflections and elaborations, which he sent to Schiller bearing the title, "The Extent to Which the Idea 'Beauty is Perfection in Combination with Freedom' May Be Applied to Living Organisms," around August 1794.

58. See AEM XIII, 89fn (SW.8.346fn); the complaint that "modern philosophy" was inclining observers to *anticipate* nature through the imposition of simple causal schemata was a regular one in Goethe. It is often claimed that Goethe taught Schiller the significance of nature; we can see, however, that Goethe only liberated elements already there for Schiller: a non-mechanistic view of nature was already present in Schiller here in the *Kalliasbriefe* and thus before his decisive encounter with Goethe (Safranski is correct to observe that Schiller already had a robust notion of nature before meeting Goethe: see Safranski, *Schiller*, 371–72). It should be noted that the term "teleology" is an ambiguous one; typically, it is contrasted to mechanism (as it is in Kant). In fact, however, teleology can be conceived mechanistically if one thinks of nature as serving an extrinsic purpose, which would make nature a mere instrument. See Robert Spaemann, *Natürliche Ziele*. Also see, for example, Iris Murdoch who seeks to reject teleology precisely *in order* to affirm the inherent goodness of nature (*Sovereignty of Good*, 79). The most decisive question to be raised in determining the presence of teleology in nature would seem to be, not the controversy about *design*, but in the first place the question of the existence of an *internal principle* of order in nature. We will discuss this and related themes at length in the third chapter on Schelling.

59. 18 Feb, 1793, 155 (SW.8.642). Cf., Goethe, *Selections from Maxims and Reflections*, 307: "The ultimate goal would be: to grasp that everything in the realm of fact is already theory. The blue of the sky shows us the basic law of chromatics. Let us not seek for something behind the phenomena—they themselves are the theory." The difference between Schiller and Goethe here is that Goethe carries over Schiller's *aesthetic* observation into the realm of science proper.

is nothing gratuitous or without purpose in nature, for Schiller, a non-mechanistic view of nature is that in which all is *ultimately* gratuitous, to see that nature "is free and purposeless [*absichtlos*] and comes from itself."[60] What distinguishes the two seems in the end to be that Schiller affirms an *internal determining principle* as the decisive feature of nature here, whereas Kant identifies nature only with what appears, i.e., with the phenomenal realm. In other words, the key to understanding Schiller's aesthetics in the *Kalliasbriefe* is to read him not, in the first place, as a Kantian but as an Aristotelian, and thus to see that what he is offering is a *metaphysical* interpretation of nature.[61] For Schiller, the world can exhibit freedom *because freedom is in some basic sense natural*. This is just what Hegel appreciated in him.

It is, moreover, specifically the "internal" character of nature that accounts for the curious, and difficult to discern, distinction that Schiller draws between "autonomy" and "heautonomy." Etymologically speaking, the words are not essentially different: they both simply mean "self-determination," though the second word sets into greater relief the reflexive character of this determination insofar as *heautos* is simply the reflexive form of the pronoun, and "autonomy" is, in any event, normally understood in a reflexive sense, which would make the additional emphasis rather redundant. Schiller himself uses the terms but does not explicitly articulate their difference. The English translator of the *Kalliasbriefe* interprets the distinction on the basis of Kant's own use of the word in the third Critique,[62] stating: "heautonomy refers to a necessary self-determination of the power of judgment in its relation to nature which is nonetheless merely subjective since it is not legislative for nature."[63] This interpretation is not uncommon,[64] presumably because of the tendency to read Schiller along Kantian lines. But it is hard to explain how to justify this interpretation given Schiller's claim in the very next paragraph that "nature and

---

60. 23 Feb, 1793, 170 (SW.8.660).

61. Here we see the importance of Cassirer's observation regarding the significance of Leibniz as the conceptual background for Schiller's thinking about nature: see Cassirer, *Freiheit und Form*, 296–97. If it is true that Schiller moves away from Kant and toward a *metaphysical* view of freedom, as Bertha Mugdan observed many decades ago (1911) (see Sharpe, *Two Centuries*, 33), it is because he also moved toward a metaphysical view of nature.

62. See the first introduction to the CJ, Ak 225 (Pluhar: 414).

63. Bernstein, *Classic and Romantic German Aesthetics*, 166, fn4.

64. See, for example, Röhr, "Freedom and Autonomy in Schiller," 119–34, here: 120, and fn7.

heautonomy are objective characteristics of the objects which I have been describing, for they remain, even if they have been abstracted from by the thinking subject"[65] unless one has simply taken for granted a priori that Schiller is operating within a Kantian notion of nature. If we consider Schiller's use of the term, we get a different picture. According to Schiller, "The perfect can have autonomy insofar as its form is purely determined by its concept; but heautonomy is possible only in beauty, since only its form is determined by its inner essence."[66] Both terms imply a kind of self-determination, but while autonomy represents the determination *by a concept*, heautonomy is determination *by one's inner essence*.[67] Another way to articulate the difference would be that autonomy represents the determination of the self generally, while heautonomy is self-determination *from within oneself*. We can illuminate this by referring once again to the "beautiful Samaritan" story: action driven by a pure sense of duty is autonomous, in the sense that there is nothing outside of duty, no interest, end, or inclination, that would adulterate its purity. But a *beautiful* act is one that does indeed fulfill duty, but does so as springing spontaneously from one's inner being. Such an act is *more radically* free, more radically self-determining, both because it implies the conformity of the whole of oneself to the determination rather than simply the rational aspect of one's being and also because it demands in some respect no reference outside of the agent for its explanation; it comes simply from within (which does not mean that it ceases to be his duty or that it thus does not come also, if merely implicitly, from without).

We might also distinguish the autonomy of an instrument, in which there exists nothing that does not express the concept, and the heautonomy of a work of art, in which even service of a concept springs, as it were, spontaneously from the work's inner being:

> The musical instrument a skilled craftsman makes may be purely technical but still may not lay claim to beauty. It is purely technical if everything is form, if it is everywhere the concept and not matter, or if it is a lack on the part of his art which determines the form. One might also say that this instrument has autonomy; one could say this as soon as one places the *auton* into thought, which is completely and purely law-giving and which has dominated matter. But if one places the instrument's

---

65. 23 Feb, 1793, 167 (SW.8.657).

66. 23 Feb, 1793, 169 (SW.8.659).

67. Beiser makes a similar observation: see *Schiller*, 65, fn. 50. He insightfully describes heautonomy as the "intensification" of autonomy.

auton into what is its nature and that through which it exists, the judgement shifts. Its technique is recognized as something foreign, independent of its *existence*, coincidental, and is thus regarded as outside violence.[68]

Unless we affirmed an internal principle, a kind of "personhood" in nature, there would be no basis for the distinction in the natural world—and we would be forced to find some obscure definition for heautonomy that fails to illuminate because it fails to show what is in fact different between the two terms. Notice, even autonomy represents the "domination of matter by form," but it is not yet beautiful because of the form of this domination. In the end, beauty is identical with heautonomy insofar as they both represent the "overcoming" of logic or morality by form, which means the gathering up of a whole by virtue of an internal principle. We also see the connection between heautonomy and *nature*, as Schiller uses the term in this context: they both indicate being by virtue of oneself, or as Aristotle puts it with respect to substance (*ousia*) and Plato with respect to form (*eidos*), it exists "*kath' auton*"—that is, *kata*, "by virtue of," "according to," "in reference to," *heauton*, "itself." Once again, the brightest light for illuminating Schiller's theory comes from the classical metaphysical tradition.

This interpretation of heautonomy reveals the genuinely metaphysical character of Schiller's notion of freedom. This is, as we have said above, just what enables him to elaborate an analogy between human freedom, which is of course freedom in the most proper sense, and the "self-being" of things in the realm of nature and art. If freedom concerned simply a deliberate act of will, there would be no basis for comparison. But, for Schiller, the reason the human will is free in the *proper* sense is that it is the most perfect expression of determination from within, which is another way of saying it is the paradigmatic expression of being a self. Indeed, it is only because it gives expression to this general principle of being a self, a "person," in a complete way that it represents freedom. In this respect, there is something about human freedom that reveals a truth about being in general, which is why Schiller's investigations into the meaning of beauty open up insights both into human morality and into the nature, so to speak, of nature, as we will see in our studies of Schelling and Hegel. Freedom, in this context, means in the first place *being in possession of oneself*, which is another way of saying, having a principle of unity capable of gathering up the various aspects of what a thing is into an integral

---

68. 23 Feb, 1793, 165–66 (SW.8.655).

An Aesthetics of Freedom

whole—which is of course simply what it means in classical metaphysics *to be*. Schiller recovers this tradition by way of aesthetics. It is only by virtue of this metaphysical reading of freedom that we can understand how freedom can be the objective ground of beauty: it is the revelation of a thing's *inner* being; inner because the entire content of what is expressed comes to expression as emerging from the principle that makes the thing be what it is. The understanding is not referred outside of the thing to grasp it, because the light of intelligibility radiates from the thing's own center. It is also for this reason that Schiller affirms that *taste*, i.e., the organ so to speak of beauty, "regards all things as ends in themselves" (*als Selbstzwecke*).[69] The "heautonomous" quality of things, perceived as beautiful, makes them in a certain respect absolute, a kind of closed circle in which the principle joins with the purpose, so that the thing ceases to be simply a link in some other chain.[70] To be free is to be absolute in this sense, to be a thing that rests in itself. We can see, moreover, both how freedom would in this interpretation stand for a *state*, a way of being, before it described any particular act, and also how it can indeed describe discrete acts to the extent that they either actualize this possessing of oneself or give expression to it.

Let us take one of Schiller's examples in order to see the significance of the metaphysical character of this interpretation of freedom and also to lead us to our final point with respect to the *Kalliasbriefe* before moving onto the AEM. Schiller draws for his friend Körner two different lines, one, a line that cuts back and forth at a precise distance from a central axis, and another that curves gently back and forth, implying the existence of a central axis as a sort of rule, but not making this axis explicit, as in the other line. See image 1.

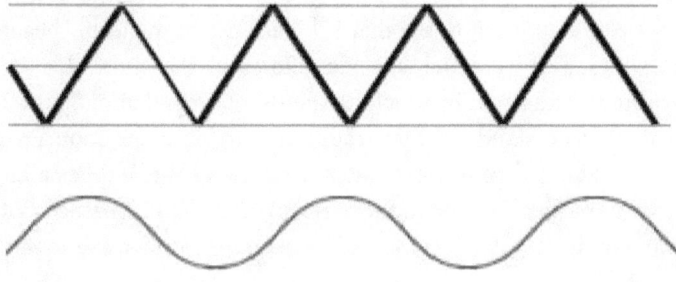

---

69. 23 Feb, 1793, 170 (SW.8.661).

70. Again, we hear an echo here of Aristotle's identification of agent, formal, and final causality in living organisms.

Schiller offers this drawing as a kind of "proof" of his theory: he claims that there is an objective quality in the second line that makes it more beautiful than the first. What is that quality? It is the fact that the "jagged" line appears to have its form determined from outside of itself: the reason the line changes directions at regular intervals is that it reaches a point established, so to speak, a priori. The crucial thing to see, for Schiller, is that it changed direction *ex abrupto*;[71] this is significant because it sets into relief precisely the *extrinsic* character of the determination. From within, the line "wishes" simply to go straight; the change of direction runs simply *counter* to its internal direction, and forces therefore what we would recognize as a rather "mechanical" change. With the curved line, by contrast, the change occurs so to speak "organically," or as Schiller puts it, it occurs almost "unnoticed." The line itself inwardly anticipates the change, so much so that one cannot say exactly when it takes place: "a movement seems free . . . if one cannot name the particular point at which it changes its direction."[72] The movement was always-already prepared for, which is another way of saying it is simply the unfolding of what already lies *within* the line itself. When, further along the line, we see it moving in a completely different direction from the one in which the line started, we therefore recognize that this new direction is in some sense a fulfillment of what went before; it is not an interruption, the intrusion of some foreign element. Of course, there is a perfect unity in both cases. But the first is a "merely" autonomous unity, the unity of a concept, while only the second is heautonomous unity. They are both formed; but only the second expresses the "formality" of form, it is more *perfectly* formed because it is more comprehensively organized according to an inner principle. It is therefore what the scholastics would have described as "*formosus*"; that is, as "beautiful."

It is also important to see that Schiller's use of the term "heautonomy" provides, as it were, the "specific difference" that marks his uniqueness within the tradition in which he stands, namely, that of Spinoza. But it reveals that he stands in that tradition with only one foot: Freedom springs, for Schiller, from one's inner nature, and this implies a kind of necessity, to be sure. Such natural necessity is the basic character of Spinozist freedom.[73] At the same time, however, for Schiller, the root of this

---

71. 23 Feb, 1793, 173 (SW.8.604).
72. Ibid.
73. Baruch Spinoza, *Ethics*, part 1, no. 7, 31: "A thing is said to be free (*liber*) which exists solely from the necessity of its own nature."

An Aesthetics of Freedom

impulse lies in the unique *self* of the being. Spinoza would have no basis for the distinction between heautonomy and autonomy: freedom for him is simply *action* in accordance with nature in the sense of the "whatness" that defines a thing, or its "substance." The distinction Hegel will make between "substance" and "subject" is of no concern to Spinoza. But this distinction makes all the difference in the world for Schiller's conception: heautonomy is, we might say, the subjectivity of being, i.e., the internal principle of being that Schiller refers to as its "person" or its "selfhood," which "overcomes" the substance or whatness of a being. This overcoming is what makes freedom truly spontaneous, even though it remains for Schiller a "fruit" of nature. The distinction between heautonomy and autonomy, then, becomes the "place" where the arbitrariness of choice lies in human beings.[74] It is not difficult to see how the act of free will represents an analogous fulfillment of this self-determination rather than the introduction of something *simply* novel. Interpreting choice from within the self-determination that defines nature in general, Schiller is able to affirm simultaneously a continuity and discontinuity between freedom and nature in human beings, as we will see in our discussion of the AEM. We may note here, as well, the connection between Schiller's use of the term "heautonomy" and the features of the dramatic style we discussed in the last chapter, namely, the "personification" of principles, the attribution of a kind of "self-hood" to things. Again, it is a deep notion of freedom that entails Schiller's sense of the world as essentially dramatic.

V. Heautonomy and Heteronomy

For all of the light that a metaphysical interpretation sheds on the *Kalliasbriefe*, it presents an important problem. The notion of freedom that emerges here is *radically* self-centered: being self-centered is in fact the

74. In this regard, Beiser significantly misunderstands Schiller: he believes the notion of heautonomy is simply *contrary* to that of freedom as choice (since Schiller explains it as an action according to the inner necessity of form), and so it ends up in his mind creating confusion in Schiller's theory of freedom, which Beiser says wants to affirm the reality of *liberum arbitrium* but ends up, he claims at one point, falling into Spinozist determinism (see Beiser, *Schiller*, 213–37, esp. 37). In another venue, however, he presents Schiller, along with Kant and Humboldt, as clearly *rejecting* this kind of determinism: see his "Response to My Critics," 63–78, esp. 66, in which he writes that Schiller espouses an idea of freedom "utterly opposed to the Leibnizian (i.e., deterministic in the Spinozist sense) conception." The fact of the matter is that elements of *both* can be found in Schiller, not because he is confused, but because he does not see free choice and determination as *exclusive* of one another, as Beiser does.

very definition of freedom, insofar as we understand self-centeredness to be another way of expressing the determination of oneself wholly from within oneself. But this prompts the question, how does Schiller avoid a kind of ultimate individualism with this view of freedom? Even more directly, we can ask: On what basis, given this view of freedom, is Schiller able to insist on the importance of respecting the freedom of others, or even more, what allows him to say that true freedom is, in a certain sense, *constituted* by the mutual respect for the freedom of others?[75] In more specifically metaphysical terms, we are asking a question that will return even more forcefully when we explore Hegel's notion of freedom, namely, what place the *other* has in self-determination, whether there is a role for heteronomy in heautonomy.

Schiller does not confront this question in any thorough and explicit sense himself, and what he says seems to leave in place a fundamental ambiguity in spite of the fact that it is quite suggestive in itself. We will face a similar ambiguity once again later in Hegel. In the first place, in classic Schillerian fashion, he affirms a basic tension here, and yet, without seeking simply to diffuse the tension, insists that an adequate response does full justice to both irreducible distinct poles: "The first law of gentility is: *have consideration for the freedom of others*. The second: *show your freedom*. The concrete fulfillment of both is an infinitely difficult problem but gentility requires it relentlessly, and it alone makes the cosmopolitan man."[76] The example he offers is the English dance in which complex and free movements of individuals are coordinated into a radiant whole. The tension occurs because being free means, as we have seen, being in a certain sense absolute, an end in oneself. Showing one's freedom, then, means giving expression to the fact that, at least in some respect, everything that surrounds one, and indeed everything that exists, does so relative to oneself, as a means to oneself as an end. How can this phenomenon be integrated with *anything*, much less with other claims to the same absoluteness? The best response to this problem that Schiller offers would seem to lie once again in his notion of form, which is connected to his notion of beauty.

The relevant aspect of these notions shows itself in Schiller's occasional mention in these letters of the proper relationship of parts to a whole. Consider these three passages: "[w]e call [a whole] beautiful if we do not need to be helped by the idea to see the form, if the form is free and purposeless and comes from itself, and all the parts seem to limit

75. See 23 Feb, 1793, 171–72 (SW.8.662).
76. Ibid., 174 (SW.8.665).

themselves from within themselves";[77] "[i]t is necessary for every great composition that the particular restrict itself to let the whole reach its effect. If this restriction by the particular is at once the effect of its freedom, that is, if it posits the whole itself, the composition is beautiful. Beauty is power limited through itself; restriction of power";[78] "[b]ut what becomes of the harmony of the whole if each only looks out for itself? Freedom comes about because each restricts its inner freedom such as to allow every other to express *its* freedom."[79] Notice the forcefulness of this last point: self-restriction is affirmed as a *condition* of freedom, as one of the *constitutive causes* of freedom, and not simply, say, an important or even necessary *use* that one ought to make of one's freedom, which is understood as boundless in itself.

The notion of form, interpreted in relation to the principle of heautonomy, serves to illuminate the sense of these passages and to respond to the "problem of the other" in two respects. In the first place, it explains why *limit* would be a constitutive element of freedom, and not simply an extrinsic regulation of it. There is no form without limit, insofar as form represents determination. But this is not—contrary to what Spinoza wrote—"*omnis determinatio negatio est*," "every determination is a negation,"[80] because form is "other-excluding," i.e., that it *negates* what lies outside of itself in its expression of its own reality; instead, it is because form implies an internal principle of unity.[81] In this respect, determination is *positive* before it is negative. A multiplicity without limitation would be formless in the sense that the various parts would bear no relation to one another, which is another way of saying they would *have* no unity: it would not be clear where one thing ended and another began; things would flow "into" one another so completely we would not even be able to speak of a multiplicity, since that implies a "what" and therefore a determinate unity. Now, there are, of course, two different ways in which such unity can obtain: it can be imposed from the outside, in which case there is no internal connection between the form and what is formed, or it can emerge from within. In this latter case, we have a thing that *limits itself of itself*, which means that it expresses organic order. It is beautiful.

77. Ibid., 170 (SW.8.660).
78. Ibid., 171 (SW.8.662).
79. Ibid., 171–72 (SW.8.662).

80. See Spinoza's letter to Jarigh Jelles, 2 June, 1674. Cf., Hegel's use of the expression in his *Logic*, first book, first section, second chapter.

81. Which thus makes it an "individual" in the classic sense, i.e., of being "undivided" within itself: see Thomas Aquinas, *De veritate*, 1.1.

The Perfection of Freedom

Here we come to the second way in which Schiller's notion of form responds to the "problem of the other." The question that emerges from the first consideration is whether it is possible to possess form in the way described and still resist integration into a larger whole. We can imagine, for example, the beautiful horse that Schiller presented in the earlier letter remaining stubbornly "free" and wild, at the expense of everything around it. This is, indeed, the decisive question. Schiller's answer would seem to be yes and no. In reference to itself, a thing can have a form that "completely dominates its mass," and can in this respect be free. But we can see that such a freedom will remain a relative freedom, and thus a *restricted* freedom, precisely to the extent that it *resists* participation in a greater whole. To be integrated into a whole means that a thing "posits the whole itself," as he puts it, which means that the principle that gives form to the whole gets appropriated to the principle that governs the part in itself. In other words, the form of the part acquires an internal relationship to the form of the whole, which means, if form is precisely an inner principle of unity, that the form of the *part expands beyond itself*. Integration into a whole is an inner expansion of its own being—inner, once again, because the order is not imposed on it from the outside. We thus come upon two remarkable paradoxes: first, the freedom of a part becomes less precisely to the extent that it refuses to limit itself, both with respect to itself, in which case it would surrender the unity that makes it be what it is, and with respect to what is greater than itself, in which case it would define its own being against the being of the whole, and so lose the possibility of including that whole implicitly in itself. *Self-restraint*, as an expression of participation in a larger whole, *is self-transcendence*; it is the inner growth of form. Second, it turns out that heautonomy, though it is the intensification of "self-centeredness," is, ironically, more capable of being integrated into a larger whole in principle because it does not allow itself to be finally defined by the logical concept that excludes it from all that it is not. Schiller's example of noble behavior, which we will discuss at the end, makes this point clearly.

We are now in a position to articulate the central dimension of Schiller's notion of freedom, which will provide the key to our interpretation of the AEM: in a word, *to be free means to have form*. One of the great benefits of this view of freedom is that it is, from the first, positive and inclusive rather than oppositional. The notion thus does not define itself immediately negatively *against* nature (as a purely rational transcendence of the senses would) or lead us to affirm the self *against* the other (as a merely "autonomous" view of self-determination would), but embraces

An Aesthetics of Freedom

both nature and the other members of the whole as part of its meaning. It can do so because of both the depth and comprehensiveness of the unifying principle. Freedom and order, far from representing competing principles as they do in the popular imagination and indeed in many of the main currents of the history of philosophy, turn out to be in a certain respect *identical*, once we interpret form aesthetically and metaphysically rather than merely logically, and we interpret order organically rather than merely mechanistically. To be without order is to lack any internal principle of being, which means that one does not possess oneself, and indeed that there is no self there either to do the possessing or to be possessed. To have a strictly mechanical order—as represented, for example, by the jagged line that Schiller drew in his *Kalliasbriefe*—is indeed to have *some* measure of freedom and therefore *some* measure of beauty precisely because there is form present, which is why Schiller can use the term "autonomy" to describe such a thing. But *true* freedom comes only with organic order, which is when form reaches, as it were, all the way down to the inside of a thing's being. But this is, of course, simply another way of describing one of Schiller's formulations of the concept of beauty, namely, the complete domination of matter by form.

This view of freedom allows us, moreover, to avoid what would be an easy mistake to make in reading the *Kalliasbriefe*. When Schiller describes a "free" form in contrast to a mechanical instrument, we might think that the form is free precisely to the extent that it possesses *less* order than the mechanism. Miller, for example, distinguishes between moral freedom, which he says is allied with law, and aesthetic freedom, which he describes specifically as "freedom from law."[82] The curved line, from this perspective, would seem to some to be *less* restricted by limits than the jagged one. But it is not so much a question of the "amount" of order as it is *depth*: the order in the jagged line is literally "superficial," because it is merely extrinsic. The free form is ordered *from within*, not from without. Note how the curved line represents a much more complete domination of matter by form: whereas the jagged line only runs up against form, we might say, *in extremis*, the curved line is governed at every moment by the order it has, so to speak, internalized, in the sense that it always already has anticipated each turn in its movements. This is why we can say the curved line demonstrates an intensification of order; it reveals its total domination by form precisely in being in some basic respect unpredictable. This is why we also have to understand that beauty is the transformation and

---

82. Miller, *Schiller and the Ideal of Freedom*, 92.

elevation of rational form, the overcoming of it from within, rather than a destruction of it and substitution for it. It is important to see that "form" in reference to the jagged line and to the curved line is not simply equivocal; there are indeed two distinctively different uses of the term in this context, but they retain an analogy: *both* are principles of organization, it is just that one organizes from the outside and the other organizes from within.

When Schiller says that "beauty is power limited through itself," then, because beauty is the manifestation of freedom, it means that true freedom is power limited through itself, that is, power actualized in true form. The absolutizing of freedom, thus understood, in no way implies the chaotic despotism of ego-atoms, but the flourishing of the *whole*, which is necessarily coincident with the flourishing of the members that constitute that whole;[83] it implies, in short, a community of ends: "In this aesthetic world," Schiller affirms, "even the gown that I wear on my body demands respect for its freedom from me, much like a humble servant who demands that I never let on that he is *serving* me."[84] It is just this "aesthetic world" that Schiller envisions as the goal of education in the AEM, to which we now turn.

VI. Freedom and Human Nature

The AEM is often—and, justly, if we accord weight to Schiller's own assessment[85]—viewed as Schiller's masterpiece, summing up into a unified whole Schiller's philosophical achievement.[86] It is not surprising that this

---

83. In a speech Schiller gave for the birthday of the Countess Franziska von Hohenheim at the Karlsschule in 1780, Schiller distinguished between the "outer" effect of virtue, which makes the entire *"Geisterwelt"* more perfect and happy, and the "inner" effect of virtue, which makes the self more perfect and happy: see SW.8.34.

84. 23 Feb, 1793, 170 (SW.8.661).

85. In correspondence with his publisher Cotta, January 9, 1795, Schiller claims that the *Letters* are "the best thing that I have ever done and indeed the best that I will ever be able to produce," believing they, more than anything else he had written, would bring him "immortality."

86. Of course, though common, this judgment is by no means undisputed. There are some, e.g., who stress that the AEM are incomplete, insofar as Schiller mentions two "kinds" of beauty (in fact, he actually says that the *one* beauty surprisingly fulfills two opposed functions: see AEM X, 63 [SW.8.332]), namely, "melting" and "energizing" beauty, and in fact gives a detailed account in the AEM only of the former. See, e.g., Pugh: "The *Ästhetische Briefe* as published in the *Horen* should thus be seen, not as a definitive text departing from the earlier conception because of further reflection, but rather a provisional and fragmentary text that falls short of the basic conception expressed by Schiller both before and afterwards," (*Dialectic of Love*, 307). Typically, it

An Aesthetics of Freedom

work has received the most attention of Schiller's writings on aesthetics. Rather than give a detailed account of this exceedingly rich and fruitfully provocative treatise or offer a commentary on the whole, we will focus on the significant role Schiller gives to form in these letters in the light of our discussion above, specifically with a view to how that notion, so conceived, opens up a way to respond to problems often raised regarding the consistency of Schiller's philosophy. We will first discuss the tensions in human existence and culture, and show how the freedom of play for Schiller resolves these tensions in all their complexity. This will allow us, afterwards, to discuss the charges of contradiction and sum up his remarkable insights into the meaning of freedom.

We have seen the role of form in the manifestation of freedom in objects in the world, and discovered that freedom is coincident with the domination of mass by form, that to be free essentially means to possess form. When we move into the properly human sphere, which was not central in the *Kalliasbriefe* but is arguably central in Schiller's aesthetics more generally,[87] the situation becomes much more complex in a couple respects. In the first place, there is a more immediate connection between nature and heautonomy in the natural world, so that this "freedom" of nature is simply *given* whereas what is given to human beings must *also* be achieved: the connection between nature and freedom, as we observed above, is mediated by choice and therefore far from automatic, which is precisely why *"Erziehung,"* the deliberate formation of freedom, is necessary:

---

is then said that Schiller's essay "On the Sublime," published only in the 1801 collection of his works that Schiller himself edited, but written at some (disputed) time earlier, is the missing part of the treatise, which Schiller kept separate because it was "incompatible" with the *Letters*: see, e.g., Sharpe, *Friedrich Schiller*, 167–68; 352fn40. Cf., Kaiser's rejection of this claim, *Vergötterung und Tod*, 48–49 fn16. Those who make this claim are often among the critics who say that, in any event, it is wrong-headed to try to identify a culminating philosophical work, since *restlessness* is the defining mark of Schiller's thinking, and his writings are best conceived as provisional solutions to ever-changing, and ultimately unresolved, problems (see for example, Sharpe, *Two Centuries*, xii–xiii, 5, 17). The problem here is the assumption that tension and harmony are incompatible, an assumption it was our intention in the previous chapter to subject to criticism. Our own claim is that the *opposition* between reason and the senses in no way compromises their dramatic unity, and so it does not matter *when* "On the Sublime" was written: it is not a recantation of Schiller's sense of harmony, which he emphasizes in the AEM.

87. In the *Kalliasbriefe*, Schiller observes that humanity is the "highest beauty" (25 Jan, 1793, 146 [SW.8.632]) and in *Anmut und Würde*, he observes that the Greeks included "alle Schönheit und Vollkommenheit" in "die *Menscheit* allein": Grace, 126 (SW.8.172).

The Perfection of Freedom

> Nature deals no better with Man than with the rest of her works: she acts for him as long as he is as yet incapable of acting for himself as a free intelligence. But what makes him Man is precisely this: that he does not stop short at what Nature herself made of him, but has the power of retracing by means of Reason the steps she took on his behalf, of transforming the work of blind compulsion into a work of free choice, and of elevating physical necessity into moral necessity.[88]

The second, and related, complicating factor is that the constitutive principles of human nature are no longer simply those of form and matter, but now are the form-drive (*Formtrieb*) and the material-drive (*Stofftrieb*[89]), which actively work *against* one another as much as converge harmoniously. The question of unity, and therefore of freedom, is thus much more directly dramatic in this case. Nevertheless, as we shall see, the difference between human freedom and the heautonomy of natural beings and works of art remains, for all that, stretched out within a genuine unity.

Schiller's conviction about the radical duality of human nature goes back to his earliest writings,[90] and is arguably one of the central preoccupations of his thinking, the development of which can be traced as an ongoing attempt to find a satisfactory reconciliation of this native conflict—without, for all that, simply eliminating the conflict.[91] The problem

---

88. AEM III, 11 (SW.8.309–10).

89. Schiller will occasionally also use the term "*Sachtrieb.*"

90. His two theses, the "Philosophie der Physiologie," which was rejected by the faculty, and the "Versuch über den Zusammenhang der tierischen Natur mit seiner geistigen," both placed the dual character at the center. Though it is true that he sought to reconcile this duality in a *certain* respect, he was *equally* careful to preserve the difference. On the one hand, he lays particular emphasis on his rejection of the denigration of the body for the sake of the soul, which he considers a more common temptation than the opposite in the philosophical tradition, and he nevertheless insists on the soul's transcendence of the body: he begins with a discussion of the "physical connection" and the "philosophical connection" between the two, and ends the thesis with a section called "Trennung des Zusammenhangs" (see SW.8.41–76). On this theme in Schiller's early writings, see Riedel, *Die Anthropologie des jungen Schiller*, 72.

91. Under the influence of the "systema influxus physici," which he learned in the Karlsschule, Schiller's first writings sought a *Mittelkraft* to mediate between the disparate elements of the human being, but the materialist bent of this resolution seems to have driven him close to a crisis that religious belief, in the fideist form he inherited, could not forestall (see his early text, *Philosophische Briefe*, for a dramatization of this problem). One of the reasons Kant made such an impression on him was the solid rational justification for his native idealism (see Beiser, *Schiller*, 42–45). Schiller correspondingly read Kant in light of his own need, which made for interesting misinterpretations (see Schaper, "Schiller's Kant," 99–115). This general trajectory would seem

An Aesthetics of Freedom

that the AEM seeks to address can be put in cultural or political terms, on the one hand, or in more philosophical terms, on the other. As is well-known, the immediate historical background of the AEM is what Schiller perceived to be the failure of the French Revolution, which aimed to restore human dignity but quickly degenerated into violence. As he explains in Letter V, Schiller believed that an anthropological fragmentation lay behind this political disaster; specifically, the lack of order in man's animal nature (what he refers to as "savagery") inevitably calls down on itself in reaction the imposition of order in a violent fashion, that is, as coming wholly from outside of man's natural being and thus without any organic correspondence to it (what he calls "barbarism").

In the next letter, Schiller considers this fragmentation from a wider historical perspective, comparing contemporary culture to the ancient Greeks. In the ancient world, he says, each human being contained the whole within himself; each person was a relatively independent totality. In the modern world, by contrast, precisely because of the progress of science and technology and the resultant increase in the specialization of human activities and the corresponding division of labor, each person represents only a part, and we find the whole only in adding them up: "Everlastingly chained to a single little fragment of the Whole, man himself develops into nothing but a fragment; everlastingly in his ear the monotonous sound of the wheel that he turns, he never develops the harmony of his being, and instead of putting the stamp of humanity upon his own nature, he becomes nothing more than the imprint of his occupation or of his specialized knowledge."[92] Modern culture, and the modern human being, he goes on to say, is becoming increasingly *mechanized*, which means, as we saw in the last chapter, that the parts do not participate as relative wholes in the life of the whole, and indeed in turn give that whole life, but fall instead outside of one another into purely extrinsic relations. The larger problems that Schiller seeks to address can be formulated, in fact, in terms of "disorganization";[93] that is, the breakdown of the part-whole relationship, whether that be in the individual person or in the culture at large.

---

to be behind Goethe's judgment that Schiller was interested in physical freedom in his youth and later in spiritual or ideal freedom: this would mean reading "freedom" here as "integration," which is the interpretation we have been proposing.

92. AEM VI, 35 (SW.8.320). Note that the expression "putting the stamp of humanity upon his own nature" articulates precisely what Schiller means by "heautonomy."

93. The term is *"Zerrüttung"* (VI, 35 [SW.8.319]), which can also be translated as "breakdown," "destruction," "disintegration," or "shattering."

The possibility of this disorganization occurs because of the genuine diversity of the elements that constitute human life. The human being for Schiller represents a kind of intersection of relatively opposed currents, or indeed even an intersection of two intersections. On the one hand, as he explains early on, the human being is, so to speak, a concrete universal: "Every individual human being, one may say, carries within him, potentially and prescriptively, an ideal man, the archetype of a human being, and it is his life's task to be, through all his changing manifestations, in harmony with the unchanging unity of this ideal."[94] Thus, he represents more than what he is, namely, humanity as a whole, and this representation is a constitutive dimension of his real existence. On the other hand, the human being is also the simultaneity of a transcendent identity and an immanent, and ever-changing, reality: "When abstraction rises to the highest level it can possibly attain . . . it distinguishes in man something that endures and something that constantly changes. That which endures it calls his Person, that which changes, his Condition [*Zustand*]."[95] The terms "Condition" and "Person" replace the more traditional terms he had used in his youthful writings—animal and spiritual natures, matter and spirit, body and soul. Presumably, Schiller adopted this new terminology, which he appears to have borrowed from Fichte, because it describes not two separate *parts* of a human being—which would then have to be mediated by some third "part," i.e., a "*Mittelkraft*"—but two irreducibly different perspectives on the same complex whole. Schiller brings to light the "aspectual" difference-in-unity and unity-in-difference in the way he describes the necessity of both dimensions: "Only inasmuch as he changes does he *exist*; only inasmuch as he remains unchangeable does *he* exist."[96]

But, as we have regularly observed, Schiller does not rest content with a "static" view of reality, which would incline us to think of the two aspects as two fixed elements within the person that thus remain forever separate from one another. Because a whole anthropology exists as a *task* to be accomplished, the different "states" in man express themselves in two different drives. The *Stofftrieb*, or "material drive," stems from the changeable aspect of man, his "reality." The goal of this drive is to "set man within the limits of time, and to turn him into matter."[97] It seeks variety and

---

94. AEM IV, 17 (SW.8.313).
95. AEM XI, 73 (SW.8.337).
96. Ibid., 75 (SW.8.338).
97. AEM XII, 79 (SW.8.340).

An Aesthetics of Freedom

movement; it wants to feel, to be *in* the world.[98] The *Formtrieb*, by contrast, which has its roots in man's "Person," strives to attain what lasts, to give the variety of man's experiences unity, to preserve identity, to discover the formal or ideal dimension of things. One of the things that makes Schiller's thought so fruitful, and at the same time so easy to misinterpret, is his relentless insistence on the necessity of *both* dimensions for a "complete anthropology."[99] They are typically presented as competitors, and even pleas for a holistic sense of the human being often mean by that some essentially materialistic reduction that would read any claim for a timeless and transcendent aspect of the human being an inevitable return to traditional dualisms.[100] On the other side, traditional anthropologies that affirm the *whole* human being—like the Thomist view, for example—typically insist on the body's being *necessary* to the soul but without being able to show what *genuinely positive* contribution the material aspect of existence promises to make.[101] Whatever significance Schiller may have in the end in philosophy, it will certainly have something to do with the complex unity, the dramatic anthropology, that demanded his spiritual energies for so many years. It is difficult to find any thinker before Schiller who insisted so uncompromisingly on the positive meaning of both dimensions.

The first point that Schiller makes after describing the two dimensions is that they are, at least in one respect, incompatible: "At first sight nothing could seem more diametrically opposed than the tendencies of these two drives, the one pressing for change, the other for changelessness. And yet it is these two drives which, between them, exhaust our concept of humanity, and make a third *fundamental drive* which might possibly reconcile the two a completely unthinkable concept."[102] Of course, he goes on straightaway to produce precisely what is "completely unthinkable," namely, a mediating "third." It may seem to be sloppiness or inconsistency, but we should notice how clear an example this is of the dramatic style:

98. See AEM XI, 77 (SW.8.339).

99. AEM IV, 19 (SW.8.313).

100. See, for example, the line of argument presented in Varela et al., *Embodied Mind*. We will see at the end of this chapter that the same assumption lies behind David Pugh's interpretation of Schiller.

101. Aquinas does indeed argue that the unity of body and soul is not in the first place for the sake of the body, but in fact for the sake of the soul (see ST I, 76.2 ad 6), which implies that the body *does* "add something" to the soul. But there are grounds for arguing that, rather than being something genuinely positive, the body is simply necessary to the soul because of the finitude of the human soul: it is something more like a "necessary evil" than a real good.

102. AEM XIII, 85 (SW.8.343).

he states that the difference between the two cannot be overcome, and then he proceeds to overcome it. And the very nature of the problem is the reconciliation of what remains, in some sense, forever opposed. He is thus carrying out what he is describing: form and content converge in a dramatic whole. But even granting the appropriateness of this manner of expression, we have to look more closely at the nature of the opposition he posits. He explains in the body of Letter XIII that the opposition is merely apparent since the two drives have, in fact, two different objects, which keep them distinct from one another in principle. In this case, if they come into conflict it is because they *overstep* their natural boundaries; the conflict is not an essential one: "The sensuous drive does indeed demand change; but it does not demand the extension of this to the Person and its domain, does not demand a change of principles. The formal drive insists on unity and persistence—but it does not require the Condition to be stabilized as well as the Person, does not require identity of sensation."[103] We might say that one of the signs of the "disorganization" that Schiller laments is thus the result of a confusion: we make flexible what ought to be rigid and make rigid what ought to be flexible. The tension between these is not a sterile conflict, but an expression of fertile complexity. We recall here once again the beautiful style, discussed in the last chapter, which consists of a necessary inner concept expressed in a fluid variety of external appearances.

Schiller's footnote clarifies the importance of avoiding making the conflict *natural*: "Once you posit a primary, and therefore necessary, antagonism of the two drives, there is, of course, no other means of maintaining unity in man than by unconditionally *subordinating* the sensuous drive to the rational. From this, however, only uniformity can result, never harmony, and man goes on for ever being divided."[104] It seems to be the case that the two are so deeply intertwined that the conflict is *de facto* inevitable even though it does not belong to nature as such. The reason it does not is that the complexity of human nature is itself natural. In other words, it is not the case that division represents a problem and unity its resolution, but rather that a certain kind of unity can itself be problematic just as tension can have positive value. On this score, the footnote makes a decisive point: if we make *antagonism* natural, Schiller claims that we are forced to try to overcome it by eliminating nature; that is, by eliminating difference through the subordination of the sensuous drive in a

---

103. Ibid.
104. Ibid., 85fn (SW.8.343fn).

one-sided way to the rational drive. This approach has two results: first, it enforces a monotony, or "uniformity," insofar as it makes unity and difference *simple* opposites, and at the same time it always fails to overcome the antagonism because the hostility remains for all that natural. We get both a false unity and a false difference. Schiller's proposal, by contrast, is to reject a reduction *in either direction*.[105] It therefore remains the case that the sensual must be subordinated to the rational because the rational has an absoluteness about it that can never emerge from the mutability of the sensual. At the same time, however, precisely because of its absoluteness, the rational cannot produce the multiplicity of the sensual. This is the failing of the Platonic tradition. It is also what is lacking in the *letter* of Kantian philosophy, as he says further in the footnote to this letter, if not in its spirit.[106] There is a sense then in which matter necessarily represents a "more" with respect to form, and this "more" is something positive and good, something that needs to be preserved: "Both principles are . . . at once subordinated to each other and co-ordinated with each other, that is to say, they stand in reciprocal relation [*Wechselwirkung*] to one another: without form no matter, and without matter no form."[107] It is not simply the case that, to avoid confusion, each needs to be kept in its own separate sphere. Instead, the two aspects are mutually dependent on one another, and indeed this mutual dependence is so profound that *both* will suffer if either is encroached upon; which means that, if one drive is absolutized in itself, that very drive will undermine itself. The drives thus have an internal relationship to one another in their distinction, so that the tension created by the *Wechselwirkung* between the two is essential for the "highest expression" of either one individually.[108] Thus, Schiller affirms succinctly in the thirteenth letter, "From the moment that man is merely a content of time, he ceases to exist, and *has* in consequence no content either. . . . From the moment man *is* only form, he ceases to *have* a form; the annulling of

---

105. Schiller offers a wonderfully dramatic presentation of the simultaneous unity and difference of unity and difference in a brief dialogue he wrote in his youth, "Der Jüngling und der Greis," in which the youth argues that "Rest is not the destiny of our nature, a secret voice constantly calls to us and whispers of unknown dark scenes" (SW. 8.81–82) while the old man insists that the goal of even this desire is for ultimate reconciliation. Characteristically, the dialogue ends without a final victory; human nature includes the reality of both, however incompatible they may seem.

106. AEM XIII, 87fn (SW.8.344fn).

107. AEM XIII, 85fn (SW.8.343–44fn).

108. AEM XIV, 95 (SW.8.348).

his Condition, consequently, involves that of his Person too."[109] *Having* a form, as opposed to simply *being* form, implies a subject that is distinct from that form: i.e., the complex whole constituted by the *Wechselwirkung* of form and matter. The interesting implication of this point, which he makes at the close of this letter without any elaboration, is that man's *independence* turns out to be *dependent* on there being an independent reality outside of him. We will return to this point at the end of the chapter.

This insistence on the reciprocity between form and matter would seem to take Schiller clearly outside of the position he elaborated in the *Kalliasbriefe*, which affirmed not a reciprocity but a total domination of matter by form. Closer inspection reveals, however, that he is not abandoning that position, even if he is enriching it within the human sphere. In the first place, what he refers to in the AEM as a one-sided subordination of matter to form does not correspond to the domination of matter by form in the *Kalliasbriefe* that he identified with true freedom. Instead, it expresses what he called autonomy there in distinction from free heautonomy, namely, a thing's perfect service of its concept. In other words, the term "form" in the AEM is the logical form *rather than* the aesthetic form, which is different from, though of course analogous to, the latter.[110] And we must see *both* the difference and the unity if we are to understand Schiller's general position in the end. Logical form is form understood in abstraction from a thing in its concreteness and thus in relative opposition to the matter from which it is abstracted. This is why it corresponds to the "timeless" ideal that transcends the limiting and ever-changing conditions of a person's state. But rather than simply repeating the term "Form" to distinguish the thing taken "non-abstractly," that is, as a concrete whole, and thus speaking again of the "form of form" as he did in the *Kalliasbriefe*, Schiller introduces a new notion that more clearly preserves the irreducible polarity that nevertheless lay implicit in the earlier notion, namely, between a thing's matter and its form.[111] This new notion is that of the *lebende Gestalt*, living form, which takes the place now of the manifestation

---

109. AEM XIII, 91 (SW.8.346).

110. This is why Schiller is also able to make an assertion in the AEM that directly echoes the text from the *Kalliasbriefe*, namely, that the consummate artist is one who "*can make his form consume [vertilgen] his material*," AEM XXII, 157 (SW.8.378).

111. As we pointed out earlier, the domination of mass by form did not mean the "suppression" of matter, but its liberation, insofar as the form that dominates here is an analogous "third" that includes what it integrates rather than one side of a simple binary opposition that competes with the other. We have here, to say it again, a liberating difference *within* form, understood analogously.

of freedom as the definition of beauty.[112] While there can be no doubt that this notion is due to the constant contact Schiller had had with the mind of Goethe during the time of redacting those letters, this should not cause us to overlook the way the term deepens his earlier insight rather than overturns it.[113]

We see the connection when we ask what it is that Schiller means by "life" in this context. He is quick to point out that the term is not intended in a mere biological sense: a block of marble can have life in the way he intends it here, while a human being can, in fact, be lifeless, even though he continues to breathe and move about on the earth. The best way to interpret the term "life" in this context is in reference to his use of "freedom" in the *Kalliasbriefe*: it indicates the "taking hold" of one's being by virtue of the inner principle that represents one's selfhood and thus animating that being with a vibrant unity. As we recall, this reading of freedom is what opens up the possibility of an analogy for things that do not possess will, but do possess a real unity that illuminates their being; a unity that is truly outwardly visible. Here too life would be the *spontaneity* of a thing's inner being, which is why it provides satisfaction to the *Stofftrieb* that demands variety and surprise. Taken separately from a thing's form, this dimension would reveal itself as "randomness," as change without any continuity other than succession in time. But in union with form, it designates a particular quality of the composite being. Calling this spontaneity *life*, Schiller stresses the positive significance of the phenomenon as well as the wholeness of its subject. The term "life" adds moreover a dimension of temporality and movement that is perhaps not so obvious in the concept of the appearance of freedom. On the other hand, if freedom, from the *Kalliasbriefe*'s definition of beauty, corresponds to life, "appearance" is connected then with *Gestalt*, which means the *outward form* of a thing, but also adds both a note of independence and irreducible uniqueness and also a sense of integration. A *Gestalt*, in this respect, is not a mere "show," but a way of talking about a complete reality as it presents itself. Thus, the new definition of beauty in the *Aesthetic Letters* follows the earlier one while enriching it with a more concrete point of reference. The two terms "life" and *"Gestalt"* are not two halves of a whole, but both express the whole from an irreducibly different perspective.

---

112. AEM XV, 101 (SW.8.351).
113. See our account in fn 58 above.

VII. Living Gestalt and Human Wholeness

The question, once again, is how—and indeed *whether*—Schiller is able to unify what not only *seems* opposed, but according to him is in one respect *truly* opposed, namely, the timeless determinateness of form and the spontaneous movement of life, conditions he insists "are *diametrically opposed* and can never become One."[114] Schiller raises this question in all of its sharpness in the eighteenth letter, calling it "the point on which the whole question of beauty must eventually turn." He continues: "And if we succeed in solving this problem satisfactorily, we shall at the same time have found the thread which will guide us through the whole labyrinth of aesthetics."[115] How can beauty bridge the literally "infinite" gap between "sensation and thought"? Schiller proposes a response here, and adds an important elaboration three letters later. As we mentioned above, his interest is not merely unity, but *genuine* unity that would coincide with the preservation of genuine difference: he wants unity without confusion and distinction without separation.[116] To understand his account here we need to draw on our discussion from the last chapter, which revealed the essentially dramatic character of an authentic whole. If we wish to grasp a whole, we must grasp the interdependence of the parts, which means we cannot understand each without already having understood the other. This is why we cannot proceed simply from one item to the next, but must see the disclosure of the whole, which is simultaneous with the self-explication of each of the parts. Dramatic disclosure turns out to be the key to a proper understanding of beauty, and the various confusions on this score may be attributed to the lack of a properly dramatic method in interpreting the phenomenon. Without this method, one cannot help but begin *simply* with feeling, which then cannot ever make room for reason in its absoluteness, or begin *simply* with reason, which then blocks access to feeling: one either has an indistinct whole or a fragmented series of parts:

---

114. AEM XVIII, 123 (SW.8.362).

115. Ibid.

116. See AEM IV: "Removed alike from uniformity and confusion, there abides the triumph of form": 23 (SW.8.315). In AEM XXIV, he refers to the importance of both in a complete picture: "It is, after all, peculiar to man that he unites in his nature the highest and the lowest; and if his *dignity* depends on his distinguishing strictly between the one and the other, his *happiness* depends on the elimination of this distinction. Culture, which is meant to reconcile his dignity with his happiness, will therefore have to see to it that those two principles are maintained in their utmost purity even while they are being most intimately fused" (translation modified), 173 (SW.8.386).

> Those among the philosophers who, in reflecting on this matter, entrust themselves blindly to the guidance of their *feeling*, can arrive at no *concept* of beauty, because in the totality of their sensuous impression of it they can distinguish no separate elements. Those others, who take intellect as their exclusive guide, can never arrive at any concept of *beauty*, because in the totality which constitutes it they can discern nothing else but the parts, so that spirit and matter, even when most perfectly fused, remain for them eternally distinct. . . . Both, therefore, are bound to miss the truth: the former because they would make the limitations of discursive understanding vie with the infinity of nature; the latter because they would limit the infinity of nature according to the laws of discursive understanding.[117]

We see in the structure of Schiller's sentences an expression of the point he seeks to make. He creates a tension by pulling taught the two extreme possibilities from a central complex whole ("concept of beauty" and then the intersection of "laws/limits of discursive understanding" and the "infinity of nature"), which brings to light, and to life, the "truth" at this center. The "truth" that the extreme approaches miss in their exclusivity is the dramatic revelation of the living *Gestalt*. One has to begin with both aspects of the complex unity at the same time, which means, as we saw in the last chapter, that one needs to be engaged *as a whole* in one's philosophizing.

The key to the response to the problem Schiller poses is just this wholeness, this totality or comprehensiveness. There are two essential aspects of this wholeness that are important in the present context. In the first place, it preserves the reciprocal dependence of the parts, rather than simply affirming the necessity of each in succession. When Schiller describes the reality of beauty, he constantly stresses the paradox of reciprocal relation:

> We must expect from beauty at once a releasing and a tensing effect: a *releasing* effect in order to keep both the sense-drive and the form-drive within proper bounds; a *tensing* effect, in order to keep both at full strength. Ideally speaking, however, these two effects must be reducible to a single effect. Beauty is to release by tensing both natures uniformly, and to tense by releasing both natures uniformly. This already follows from the concept of a reciprocal action, by virtue of which both factors necessarily

---

117. AEM XVIII, 125 (SW.8.363). In fact, these sentences are simply representative of a longer series that repeats a similar pattern in several other respects.

condition each other and are at the same time conditioned by each other, and the purest product of which is beauty.[118]

That ideal avoids being the contradiction some make it out to be if we affirm it *dramatically*.[119] In the second place, and most significantly, it is only in the affirmation of a complex totality *all at once* that we can perfectly unify opposing principles so that they are in a certain respect identically one, and at the same time preserve their abiding difference. If the opposing principles were not already one, they would compete with one another, so that we would have to balance the determinateness of form out against the indeterminacy of freedom. The tension in a violin string is achieved only by pulling it in two directions at once; pulling one side *after* the other would obviously be an exercise in Sisyphean vanity. But this simultaneity, Schiller explains, transforms what we mean by each: freedom proves to be "not just lawlessness but rather harmony of laws, not arbitrariness but supreme inner necessity," and the "definiteness" of form "does not reside in the *exclusion of certain realities*, but in *the absolute inclusion of all realities*; that it is, therefore not limitation but infinity."[120] It is a transformation of each because each, as "always already" related to the other in the complex whole, partakes inwardly of the other and so expresses something of its opposite in its own being.[121]

Schiller specifies the crucial point regarding infinity as inclusion in Letter XXI. Here, anticipating something we will see again in Hegel, he calls indeterminacy "an *empty infinity*," in contrast to "aesthetic freedom of determination," which "must be regarded as an *infinity filled with content*."[122] The "infinity" that we normally oppose to the limit that determination necessarily entails is here made *dependent* on determination. Indeed, Schiller speaks of a "*Wechselwirkung*" also in the relationship between finitude and infinity.[123] What is it that makes aesthetic determination infinite? The key

118. AEM XVI, 111 (SW.8.357).

119. As Gerhard Kaiser observes, Schiller always presents ideals in the shape of a *polarity*: *Vergöttung und Tod*, 20.

120. AEM XVIII, 125 (SW.8.363).

121. On this point, see AEM XVI, 111 (SW.8.357), in which Schiller says that this sort of paradox "already follows from the concept of reciprocal action [*Wechselwirkung*], by virtue of which both factors necessarily condition each other and are conditioned by each other, and the purest product of which is beauty."

122. AEM XXI, 145 (SW.8.373).

123. In addition to the description in AEM XVIII, see AEM XIX, 131 (SW.8.366): "We do then, admittedly, only reach the whole through the part, the limitless only through limitation; but it is no less true that we only reach the part through the whole,

seems to be that aesthetic form contains the determinacy within itself; it is, we might say, the possession of determinacy, rather than being the determination of something extrinsic. In this respect, infinity of form *coincides perfectly* with the way Schiller defines freedom here, namely, as "supreme inner necessity." It is an expression of the same heautonomy that Schiller had made the hallmark of beauty in the *Kalliasbriefe*. Determination encroaches on freedom only insofar as it comes from the outside. Inner determination is not only compatible with freedom, but is an *indispensable condition* thereof. Formlessness, completely random spontaneity, is not in itself freedom, which secondarily can be more or less bound by laws. Instead, it expresses a *lack* of freedom, since it will invariably turn out to be contingent on some external source of determination.[124] Freedom is thus infinite determination, rather than non-determination; it is infinite because it *includes* possibility within its super-abundant reality. The infinity of form therefore arises from the reciprocal dependence of the irreducibly different constitutive parts of the whole. Schiller expresses a similar idea in his poem, "Der philosophische Egoist," in which he criticizes the desire for isolation and independence and affirms that the infinite lies in *reciprocal exchange* itself.[125] True infinity is the internal richness of aesthetic form; the living *Gestalt* is the manifestation of freedom.

Notice how this view of freedom coincides with an actuality that is inclusive of possibility, rather than being identified with "mere" potentiality alone. The infinite determinability that Schiller describes is not just the state of "not-yet-being-determined," but is always already wholly inclusive of determination. The former would be threatened by any particular actuality: if I make a decision, I am imposing a limit on myself; it may be a limit I deem good or at least necessary, but it is one that I pay for through

and limitation only through the limitless."

124. David Pugh thus betrays a fundamental misunderstanding of Schiller when he claims that Schiller did not consider freedom an unqualified good, and takes as evidence for this the fact that Schiller "subordinates" it to the order of laws: see his essay, "Schiller as Citizen of His Time," 50. Pugh is projecting a conventional notion of freedom onto Schiller, which sees law as a limitation of freedom. In fact, it is essential to the meaning of freedom, as Schiller understands it, so that an *absolutizing* of freedom implies by the same stroke insertion and integration into a larger, law-governed order.

125. This poem was published in the sixth issue of *Die Horen*, 1795, just a few months after the AEM. After a description of the beauty of interdependence in the mother-child relationship, the poem closes with the lines: "Selbstgenügsam willst du dem schönen Ring dich entziehen, / Der Geschöpf an Geschöpf reyht in vertraulichem Bund, / Willst, du Armer, stehen allein und allein durch dich selber, / Wenn durch der Kräfte Tausch selbst das Unendliche steht?" Notice that the ring that binds creature to creature—i.e., the "closed circle" or *Gestalt*—is described as beautiful.

the surrender of a certain amount of my freedom. *To the extent* that I have thus limited myself, *within* those limits, I am no longer free. Here we have the notion of freedom espoused generally by the Anglo-liberal tradition. Schiller's connection of freedom with form entails a radically different assessment. If I have made no choices, and in that respect am "unlimited," I am in Schiller's eyes only potentially free, or free in a limited respect. I would express a kind of infinity, to be sure, but it would be what Schiller calls an "empty infinity," life without shape. By making decisions, insofar as those decisions are *defining* of who I am and thus serve to give my life shape, then far from putting boundaries to my freedom, those limitations *liberate* my freedom. My freedom increases, it deepens and grows rich with content, the more comprehensive the form that gives my life its radiantly intelligible shape. Choice is clearly crucial in this case, but everything depends on the *quality* of the choice; the mere fact of choice determines very little. This is something we will see, too, affirmed forcefully by both Schelling and Hegel. If my choice is reactive, aimless, thoughtless, and so forth, it will express only a superficial freedom, and erode even that insofar as it undermines form. Schiller describes the man whose life has not yet acquired form as one who, though unrestricted in his choice in some respect, has no freedom: "What is man before beauty cajoles from him a delight in things for their own sake, or the serenity of form tempers the savagery of life? A monotonous round of ends, a constant vacillation of judgements; self-seeking, and yet without a Self; lawless, yet without Freedom; a slave, yet to no Rule." [126] By contrast, truly dramatic choice, which gathers up the moments of a life, past and future, and includes a wide range of relationships with persons and things in the world, will be a free choice in Schiller's sense, and will give rise to a truly *human* freedom. The real mark of freedom, for Schiller, is completeness, and such completeness depends on having the form that integrates the parts of the human whole:[127] Freedom "arises only when man is a *complete* being, when *both*

---

126. AEM XXIV, 171 (SW.8.384–85). It is worth citing the continuation of this passage: "At this stage the world is for him merely Fate, not yet Object; nothing exists for him except what furthers his own existence; that which neither gives to him, nor takes from him, is not there for him at all. Each phenomenon stands before him, isolated and cut off from all other things, even as he himself is isolated and unrelated in the great chain of being. All that exists, exists for him only at the behest of the moment; every change seems to him an entirely new creation, since with the lack of necessity *within him* there is none *outside of him* either, to connect the changing forms into a universe and, though individual phenomena pass away, to hold fast upon the stage of the world the unvarying law which informs them."

127. See Wessell, "The Aesthetics of Living Form," 193.

his fundamental drives are fully developed; it will, therefore, be lacking as long as he is incomplete, as long as one of the two drives is excluded, and it should be capable of being restored by anything which gives him back his completeness."[128] One of the most appealing features of this notion of freedom is that it does not leave anything out: the demands of the good are part of freedom, so is rational reflection and careful analysis, so are the desires that spring from our natural being, so is the imagination rooted in the heart, and so forth.

Before moving on, it is good to pause for a moment to compare the *Kalliasbriefe* and the AEM on the notion of freedom. In both cases, Schiller links freedom to aesthetic form. In the latter case, that form acquires a more explicitly dramatic character for being interpreted specifically in terms of human existence, which introduces a much more "volatile" phenomenon, as it were, since the elements to be integrated are more clearly dynamic and since the "art" of choice, culture, and education—themselves works of freedom—must recapitulate and supplement what is given already in nature. For this very reason, however, the aesthetic potential is greater: in human beings, there is the capacity for more freedom, more form, and thus more beauty.[129] The *difference* between the elements is greater (indeed, it is now "infinite"), but there is greater possibility for unity. Thus, the "Goethean" notion of the living *Gestalt* turns out to be much more richly concrete than the apparently more "Kantian" notion of beauty as "form of a form," which could be interpreted still fairly "formalistically."[130] What the *Kalliasbriefe* add to the AEM is the association of freedom with a metaphysical interpretation of nature, which gives the elaboration of freedom in the AEM an ontological depth we would otherwise miss, and so would be inclined to pit freedom against nature and likewise (and therefore) to pit freedom against determination. On the other hand, the AEM give the earlier view an important dynamic dimension. They further illuminate the concept of "Person," which proved to be so important, but because of the *analogical* sense of freedom, they allow this insight without blurring the difference between human freedom and the "freedom" that Schiller attributes to nature.[131] In this respect, the two

---

128. AEM XX, 139 (SW.8.370).

129. In AEM II, 7 (SW.8.308), Schiller speaks of the construction of a true political freedom as the "most perfect of all works of art" (translation modified).

130. See Taminiaux's observation in this regard: *La nostalgie de la Grèce*, 113.

131. On this score, we discover a helpful qualification to the observation made by S. S. Kerry, that Schiller simply transfers freedom into natural objects without regard for philosophy (Kerry, *Schindler's Writings on Aesthetics*, 57).

pieces stand in a relationship of *Wechselwirkung*, which ultimately brings to light the *totality* of the meaning of freedom.

VIII. The Seriousness of Play

The notion of completeness leads us to another of the basic notions in the AEM, namely, that of play. According to Schiller's well-known phrase, "With beauty man shall *only play*, and it is *with beauty only* that he shall play"; and this is because "man only plays when he is in the fullest sense of the word a human being, and *he is only fully a human being when he plays*."[132] Because of the link between beauty and freedom, to say that beauty entails play means that play itself is an essential expression of freedom, as Schiller understands it. For Schiller, the "play drive," the "*Spieltrieb*," is a third that represents the unity of the *Formtrieb* and the *Stofftrieb*; it reconciles reason with the senses by removing the "physical compulsion" that the senses entail, and it reconciles the senses with reason by removing the "moral compulsion" that the laws of reason entail. It therefore introduces "form into matter and reality into form."[133] As we recall, it was just this reciprocity that Hegel admired in Schiller, and is no doubt why he considered the AEM a masterpiece, as he wrote to Schelling when they appeared.[134] The object of the play drive, according to von Wiese, is the living form that we have been discussing.[135] The question for us is: what exactly is the connection between *Gestalt* and play?

There are three aspects of significance here. In the first place, play involves a "closed circle," which is a fundamental feature of the *Gestalt*. It is a closed circle because it is determined according to rules it sets itself, which is another way of saying it is ordered from within, it is spontaneously self-limiting, or it is in a certain respect "heautonomous." The rules of a game are both contingent *and* necessary in the sense that they are not "forced" upon the play by virtue of some external need or interest,[136] but they are

---

132. AEM XV, 107 (SW.8.355). Cf., the classic texts on the human significance of play: Huizinga, *Homo ludens*, Rahner, *Der spielende Mensch*, and the incomparably profound ontological interpretation of play by Ferdinand Ulrich, in a section entitled "Dasein als Spiel," in *Der Mensch als Anfang*, 122–40.

133. AEM XIV, 99 (SW.8.351).

134. See his letter to Schelling, April 16, 1795.

135. See von Wiese, *Friedrich Schiller*, 491.

136. See AEM XV, 103–5 (SW.8.353), in which he observes that linguistic usage "is wont to designate as 'play' everything which is neither subjectively nor objectively contingent, and yet imposes no kind of constraint either from within or from without."

An Aesthetics of Freedom

no less binding for all of that: games often have rules that govern every move, and in this respect they are much more precise and demanding than, say, civil laws. In this sense, a game, like a *Gestalt* or like a free form, explains itself, presenting its own intelligibility without having to make reference to something outside of itself. Second, play represents a kind of transcendence of reality *within* reality; the play drive is "directed toward annulling time *within time*, reconciling becoming with absolute being and change with identity."[137] As we have seen, this reconciliation of the ideal and the real also lies at the heart of aesthetic form. Third, play in the most complete sense engages the whole human being precisely *as a whole*. As Otfried Höffe perceptively describes it, play is the devotion of body and soul to a *"zweckfreie Sache,"*[138] which means the engagement of a whole in what is itself a whole, and not simply an instrument of some further end. Because a living *Gestalt* is just as much a sensual reality as it is an intelligible ideal,[139] and indeed because the two dimensions are so profoundly and thus paradoxically related that the intelligibility is made visible to the senses and the sensual form itself illuminates the understanding,[140] engagement in play demands the complete "gift of self" that we discussed in the last chapter. It is no wonder that one *forgets* oneself in real play, and that time both speeds by and seems to freeze forever: we are no longer in our own hands when we play (although we feel completely at home with ourselves and "non-alienated"[141]), but this self-transcendence is altogether different from the not-being-present-to-oneself of distraction, which makes play impossible. Play is a response to the superabundance of absolute determination,[142] of beauty, and at the same time as a life-giving reciprocity it is the *creation* of that infinity. We return here to the theme of the last chapter: the proper disposition toward the dramatic style is *play*.

---

137. AEM XIV, 97 (SW.8.350).

138. Höffe, "Gerne dien ich den Freunden," 14.

139. And so the game both "makes man whole and unfolds both sides of his nature at once," AEM XV, 105 (SW.8.354).

140. See AEM XV, 101 (SW.8.351).

141. See AEM XII, 80–81fn (SW.8.341fn).

142. Interestingly, studies of nature have shown that animals cease to play in times when food is scarce, and not simply because there is no time for it: see "Taking Play Seriously," by Robin Marantz Henig, in *New York Times Magazine*, 17 February, 2008, page 3. Schiller had intuited the same truth: "An animal may be said to *be at work*, when the stimulus to activity is some lack; it may be said to *be at play*, when the stimulus is sheer plenitude of vitality, when superabundance of life is its own incentive to action," AEM XVII, 207 (SW.8.401).

The Perfection of Freedom

The connection between play and form allows us to avoid the easy mistake of interpreting play as a subjective disposition, rather than seeing it above all as an objective reality that has its being in the world, however much it transcends the "worldliness" of that world. If we were to ask for an example of play in the sense Schiller means the term, the clearest is just that, namely, a *play*, i.e., a dramatic action performed on the stage.[143] It is doubtless no accident that the word "play" is in fact used for drama in some languages. A drama presents a meaning, an intelligibility, but it does so, as it were, empirically rather than "merely" conceptually: one watches a play.[144] Moreover, the play displays this meaning through time, but is itself "timeless" (in the sense that *Maria Stuart* has remained in a certain respect identically the same for over two hundred years, and in spite of the fact that it is significantly different in every single performance). A play, too, is a perfect representation of a closed circle that is still part of reality: it unfolds on a determinate stage, but this stage lies before a real audience (who both contribute in a basic way to the meaning of the play as it is performed, and at the same time *receive* that meaning: "The play-drive, therefore, will endeavor so to receive as if it had itself brought forth, and so to bring forth as the intuitive sense aspires to receive"[145]). And indeed the theater lies within a real city.[146] Finally, drama, like play in general, as Schiller claimed repeatedly, engages us, and in fact engages the whole of us all at once. Nevertheless, it should be clear that the living *Gestalt* that Schiller describes is not *exhausted* by theater, but theater represents simply a concentrated form that finds analogous examples through every sphere

---

143. Schiller claims that "arts which affect the passions, such as tragedy," are impure to the extent that they *aim* to produce this effect (AEM XXII, 157 [SW.8.379]), but this leaves open the possibility of a drama that would "respect the freedom of the spirit even amid the most violent storms of passion."

144. With a nod, perhaps, to Lessing, Schiller suggests that a perfect art would be one in which the movement of music would tend to form and the structure of sculpture incline toward movement (AEM XXII, 155 [SW.8.377]). Arguably, this is what is unique about drama.

145. AEM XIV, 97 (SW.8.349).

146. Consider Schiller's raising of the question of the contribution of the stage to education in his early essay ("Was kann eine gute stehende Schaubühne eignetlich wirken?," SW.8.84–97), coupled with his insistence that drama, like all art, needs to be independent of any practical or moral end: "No less self-contradictory is the notion of a fine art which teaches (dialectic) or improves (moral)," AEM XX, 157 (SW.8.379); cf., AEM XVI, 201–3 (SW.8.399–400). While his views on the matter certainly evolved in the decade between these two, the two affirmations do not represent a 180 degree turnabout, but are aspects of a single, complex vision of the matter. *As* an end in itself, drama teaches.

An Aesthetics of Freedom

of existence, and even in, for example, the writing of philosophy, as we discussed in the last chapter.

We can see now why Schiller claims that play is indispensable for humanity: this is not hyperbole, but a simple statement of fact, since play is defined by its appeal to the complexity of human nature *in* its complete complexity. In this respect, play represents a response to the fragmentation he eloquently described in letters V and VI. We are reaching here what we take to be the heart of Schiller's contribution to the meaning of freedom. Schiller's complaint about modern civilization is that it has increasingly taken the form of a "mechanism," and that human beings have grown fragmented as a result. These are both symptoms of a kind of *disorganization* that beauty is meant to address, which is why beauty, and the play it provokes, is capable of liberating: it promises a restoration of order. Let us consider both aspects of the problem we mentioned at the outset of our investigation of the AEM, beginning with the cultural dimension. Schiller had diagnosed his contemporary culture as tending toward the (dis-)order of a *machine* because of its separation of the constitutive "parts" of culture, which therefore no longer participate in one another and so "condition" each other: state and church, he observes, are divided from one another, law and customs, enjoyment and labor, means and ends, and effort and reward.[147] Because of this isolation, each aspect becomes lifeless in itself, and for that very reason an instrument of something other than itself. It is not a surprise, then, that this fragmentation coincides with a division of individuals from the community, of the so-called "private" sphere from the public, and a division of labor, in which each activity has *literally a part* to play, but never genuinely shares in the whole.[148] In this culture, everything comes to represent nothing more than an "instrumental good," and comes to possess only "exchange" value. A genuinely human culture, by contrast, would thus cultivate things that are *ends* in themselves. This involves giving things aesthetic form by rendering them "heautonomous"—that is, allowing them to be ends in themselves even in their service of ends outside of themselves. For example, one treats a chair not merely as an instrument for sitting, but as a thing of beauty that accomplishes this end with grace, and one builds chairs deserving of such treatment. It also involves giving human interactions a form that lifts them beyond the fulfillment of whatever material transaction that occasions them. But this means "ritualizing"

---

147. AEM VI, 35 (SW.8.320).

148. We will see this observation argued at length in Hegel's critique of civil society in the *Philosophy of Right*, which we will discuss in chapter 6.

these actions, i.e., idealizing them, following a certain manner and set of rules that they possess just as games do. In other words, it means infusing them with the spirit of play by lending them beauty. Schiller speaks in this context of the importance of *"Höflichkeit,"* which may be translated as "politeness," or even more literally as "courtesy."[149] In this way, the things and activities that make up a culture become so many *"lebende Gestalten."* The physical necessity of eating becomes the beautiful form of sharing a meal; the material need of sex and procreation becomes the elaborate cultural forms of courtship and marriage. These forms are a sort of social theater, in which real needs are given an ideal character and meaning is allowed, as it were, to be freely displayed, rather than directly and literally "injected" from one abstract mind into another. This leaves both the giver and the receiver free in the complete sense as we saw in the "free style" discussed in the last chapter. The meaning that is thus displayed, moreover, is of a more-than-merely-conceptual sort that engages both body and soul.[150]

The centrality of play as cultural form cultivates human freedom, understood here as human wholeness, in terms of both of the anthropological polarities Schiller described in the early part of his series of letters: namely, that between the individual and the universal and that between man's timeless and temporal nature. On the one hand, according to Schiller's vision, the human being *represents* in a certain respect more than he *is*. We saw the importance at the end of our discussion of the *Kalliasbriefe* of the parts "positing the whole themselves," which entails an expansion of form. Only if we interpret freedom and nature in metaphysical terms as reciprocally dependent will this self-limitation avoid becoming alienating, because this perspective entails precisely an internal share in the ideal, an inner expansion of form. There is an interesting critique implicit here of the theory that would think of free political order as that generated by the mechanical tallying of votes, each of which represents only itself. Schiller offers the possibility of a fundamentally different interpretation of political participation, a possibility that Hegel will realize in great depth, as we will see in chapter 6.

On the other hand, the notion of play provides a way to transcend the limitation of matter in a decidedly non-dualistic fashion: whereas the mere immediate satisfaction of natural desires is by its very nature time-bound,

---

149. See, e.g., AEM XVI, 199 (SW.8.399fn).

150. On the significance of such forms for a human culture, see the classic study by Douglas, *Natural Symbols*. On the meaning of "form" in the classical model of education, which was replaced in the later Middle Ages by a more abstract model, see Jaeger, *The Envy of Angels*.

An Aesthetics of Freedom

as we have all experienced with frustration, giving form to the consumption of goods—that is, "ritualizing" them or transforming them into a kind of play—infuses them with a more-than-temporal significance. They share immediately in the meaning of all the other "instances" of the ritualized act, and they thus share immediately in the significance of transcendence, of form, itself:

> Not just content with what satisfies nature, and meets his instinctual needs, he demands something over and above this: to begin with, admittedly, only a superfluity of *material things*, in order to conceal from appetite the fact that it has limits, and ensure enjoyment beyond the satisfaction of immediate needs; soon, however, a superfluity *in material things*, an aesthetic surplus, in order to satisfy the formal impulse too, and extend enjoyment beyond the satisfaction of every need. By merely gathering supplies around him for future use, and enjoying them in anticipation, he does, it is true, transcend the present moment—but without transcending time altogether. He enjoys *more*, but he does not enjoy *differently*. But when he also lets form enter into his enjoyment, and begins to notice the outward appearance of the things [*die Formen der Gegenstände*] which satisfy his desire, then he has not merely enhanced his enjoyment in scope and degree, but also ennobled it in kind.[151]

In this sense, rather than satisfying his sensual nature in some activities and his intellectual nature in others—which would have man simply *alternate* between being an animal and being a mind, but never allow him to be a human being—form thus understood satisfies all of him at once. In other words, while such an alternation would leave the human being a "machine" with all his parts remaining external to one another, the overcoming of fragmentation requires both the "realizing of form," as Schiller puts it, and the physical enjoyment of transcendent meaning—and these are not two things, but a single reality: the *lebende Gestalt*. A ritualized practice, one that has received a form, thus "represents" more than it "is," just as does a complete human being. It is therefore indispensable to freedom. Schiller simply mentions these insights without developing a complete cultural or political theory; for a further exploration of ideas along these lines, we will have to wait for the study of Hegel.

To make play, or beauty, fundamental to a culture, however, is not to reduce human life in general to a mere game, to deprive it of its seriousness. Schiller was acutely aware of this possible misunderstanding, which

---

151. AEM XXVII, 205–7 (SW.8.401).

is in part why he wrote so insistently about the dangers of allowing beauty to encroach on truth or goodness.[152] It is crucial that beauty and the play that necessarily follows it be kept in their proper place, and not be allowed to transgress the limits that belong to them by nature. Of course, their proper place happens to be directly at the center. In a genuine human culture, there is a need for work, for the fulfillment of moral obligations, for self-sacrifice and service, and these may not be trivialized. When Schiller insists on the centrality of play, he means simply that these activities, if they are to be genuinely human, need to be rooted in cultural form, which is another way of saying that the activities never be wholly instrumentalized as mere means to external goals. Instead, they must always remain *at bottom* ends in themselves, intrinsic goods, even in their accomplishment of further purposes. Plato spoke of the need for the highest human affairs to be carried out in a spirit of serious play and playful seriousness;[153] Schiller's philosophy of freedom offers a notion that explains this simultaneity, namely, that of moral or rational form contained within aesthetic form. Without an integrating center, by contrast, the parts of a culture will become narrow and rigid, that is, resistant to integration, because they remain "formless." Once again, we see why indeterminacy represents a *lack* of freedom. In this case, the parts will be inclined to expand beyond their proper boundaries, and to turn up missing when sought in their proper place. Schiller explains, for example, that in a mechanistic culture, "[w]e disown Nature in her rightful sphere only to submit to her tyranny in the moral, and while resisting the impact she makes on our senses are content to take over her principles."[154] To be free, in a word, is to make what is central indeed central, which is not necessarily to make it first or last, primary or ultimate. Or to put it in Schiller's terms, to be free is to give one's life shape and one's shape life: it is to possess living form.

IX. A Criticism and the Question of Contradiction

At this point, it is necessary to reckon with two objections that have been made to Schiller's aesthetics: first, Gadamer's criticism of Schiller's notion of *"Schein,"* "appearance," which for Schiller is the ruling principle of the realm of play, and, second, a more general claim that Schiller contradicts

---

152. This was the theme of the two essays published directly after the AEM, "Über die notwendigen Grenzen des Schönen," and "Über die Gefahr ästhetischer Sitten."

153. Plato, *Letter VI*, 323d.

154. AEM V, 27 (SW.8.316).

An Aesthetics of Freedom

himself by elevating the aesthetic state into an ideal in itself and instrumentalizing the aesthetic disposition for the sake of non-aesthetic ends.

According to Gadamer, far from overcoming Kant's subjectivizing of spirit, Schiller radicalized it by transforming what was a mere methodological presupposition—namely, the "unreality" of art—into a substantial claim.[155] Schiller effectively abstracted art from human culture, Gadamer claims, sealing it up within its own sphere (*art pour l'art*) by identifying it with the realm of *appearance*, and thus setting this realm explicitly in opposition to that of reality.[156] This would seem to subordinate the sphere of true human activity—in politics and ethics—to a world of "make-believe," an impression that would seem to be reinforced by the importance Schiller gives to play. There are two points to make in response to Gadamer's charge. On the one hand, Schiller's insistence on a clear distinction between art and reality, appearance and being, is driven precisely by the desire to avoid "reifying" appearance, as it were, into a "thing-in-itself" in its own right and as juxtaposed to reality, which would lead us to substitute one for the other. This would simultaneously glorify art beyond its due and trivialize it, because art would cease to be an *appearance*, that is, a display or revelation of something *other* than itself, namely, of reality. Emphasizing the *"Schein"*-character of art, and so of play, in its proper distinction from being has the effect, according to Schiller, of intensifying in turn the reality of the real: "For [man] cannot keep semblance clear of actuality without at the same time setting actuality free from semblance."[157] In this respect, Schiller does *not* oppose art to reality, as Gadamer claims, because only another reality could be so opposed. Gadamer's misunderstanding of this point is behind his obviously mistaken judgment that Schiller directs education to the production of the "culture of an 'aesthetic state'" *rather than* to the acquisition of moral and political freedom.[158] Schiller avoids this dualism, again, by insisting on the very distinction that prompts Gadamer's complaint.

155. Gadamer, *Truth and Method*, 82.

156. Ibid., 82–85. Cf., the similar claim by Taminiaux, *La nostalgie de la Grèce*, 114. John Ruskin had registered a complaint along the same lines: see *Modern Painters*, part 3, section 1, chapter 15, §9, page 178.

157. AEM XVI, 197 (SW.8.397).

158. Gadamer, *Truth and Method*, 83. Gerhard Kaiser defends Schiller against the charge of "aestheticism" by arguing that Schiller affirms a dialectic between the real and ideal in which each is distinct from, but dependent on, the other. In this case, Kaiser says, the more decisively one engages in life, the more decisively one swings up into the ideal, and vice versa. See *Vergötterung und Tod*, 25–28.

The Perfection of Freedom

On the other hand, while Schiller does emphasize the clear distinction of art from reality, he does not in this context go on in his customary fashion to reveal at the same time their "intimate union." In this particular respect, Gadamer's observation is correct. But it is correct only to the extent that Schiller fails to work out the implications of his own principles in this sphere. In Letter XVI, which is where he addresses the issue most at length, he focuses almost exclusively on the difference. Arguably, according to Schiller's own insight into the nature of order, such an exclusivity threatens to undermine just what it intends to protect: specifically in this case, it would be impossible to avoid hypostasizing appearance if one repeatedly insisted only that it is different from, and thus set over against, reality. It would be more in accordance with Schiller's general "dramatic style" to affirm a new kind of unity that the separation of appearance from reality would allow, and thus make it a "mediating third" in a paradoxical polarity rather than one side of a dualism. Indeed, as we have seen, it is the essence of beauty to "bridge the gap," as it were, between "mere" appearance and "mere" reality by being the free self-disclosure of reality. As Schiller describes art's role in this particular letter, he tends much more toward Kant's subjectivizing formalism—as we see in his insistence here that art draw no support whatever from the real—than his explicit intentions in both this series and the *Kalliasbriefe* would seem to promise. Schiller's basic aim is *not* toward a radical subjectivizing of art, but toward a paradoxical *Wechselwirkung* between the subject and object, as we saw typified in the "dramatic style."[159] The *Wechselwirkung* expresses itself precisely in the reciprocity between necessity and contingency that we have identified with play, as opposed to the "mere seriousness" that would attach to the didactic or the scientific style, on the one hand, or the experiences of the agreeable or the good and true, on the other. If we associate the agreeable with appearance, as "separate" from being, and goodness (and truth) with being considered in itself, as "separate" from appearance, beauty represents the "full *Schein*," the "superabundant determinacy" that combines both. And "play" rests on this simultaneity: "The agreeable, the good, the perfect, with these man is *merely* in earnest; but with beauty he plays."[160]

---

159. In this sense, he does indeed aim to overcome just what Taminiaux identified as the fundamental tension in classical German philosophy, namely, that between the subject and nature: see Taminiaux, *La Nostalgie de la Grèce*, 119. As we will see in the next chapter, this is also the aim of Schelling's *Naturphilosophie*.

160. AEM XV, 105–7 (SW.8.354).

An Aesthetics of Freedom

It is curious that Gadamer, for whom aesthetic play has such significance, would not have made more of Schiller.[161]

Once we grasp what may be called a "dramatic" sense of the part-whole relationship in Schiller's thought, we are in a position to give a fruitful response to the problem of apparent contradiction in the AEM. Schiller seems to make the "aesthetic" condition—the sphere indicated by the word "play"—the supreme state of human existence, while in other places he fairly clearly states that this state is a means to moral action or some other human activity, which is where the human being expresses the best of his nature.[162] Another way to put this charge is that Schiller seems, on the one hand, to identify freedom with human integration, while on the other, he makes reason and the will's sovereign indifference to the demands of the sense world the highest expression of freedom. This apparent inconsistency bears an evident connection to another one that likewise receives a good deal of attention, though it concerns primarily the earlier essay *On Grace and Dignity*, namely, Schiller's claim that the ideal person possesses *both* grace (harmony between soul and body) and dignity (opposition between the two, in which reason triumphs).[163] Finally, we have the complaint that Schiller attempts in various ways to join beauty and the sublime together in his aesthetics, when in fact they are logically incompatible.[164] This problem—for it is a single problem, though it finds

---

161. Gadamer claims as part of his own project in *Truth and Method* to liberate the notion of play from the merely subjective significance it has in Schiller (*Truth and Method*, 557). But we have seen that Schiller does *not* in fact have a subjectivistic conception of play. Gadamer seems to misread Schiller because of Schiller's identification of play with freedom, and Gadamer's assumption that freedom is something purely subjective (see ibid., 101, where he describes Schiller as presenting "the freedom of a subjectivity engaged in play"). But this overlooks the transformation of freedom into something that lies beyond the merely subjective sphere, the study of which has been the point of our chapters on Schiller.

162. See, for example, Reginald Snell's observation: "I do not think it is possible to defend Schiller against this charge of an absolutely central inconsistency. . . . He is presenting, at the same time, a Three Levels theory of aesthetic development, and a Synthesis theory—and he is mixing them up. . . . In one, Beauty is merely a means of enlightenment, of transitory value; in the other, an end in itself, a work of the reason, of absolute value" (Snell, "Introduction," 15).

163. See Hamburger, "Schillers Fragment," 393.

164. Lesley Sharpe observes that Schiller's attempt to synthesize the two is so interesting precisely because it is "impossible," given their contradictory nature: *Two Centuries*, 29. In her review of studies on Schiller, Sharpe criticizes those who emphasize the reconciliation—which Schiller repeatedly claims—for overlooking this contradiction.

different expressions in a variety of spheres—is arguably the principal issue in critical studies of Schiller.

It would, of course, be impossible to address this literature at any length in the present context, but we can at least take a representative, David Pugh. As we mentioned in the last chapter, his book, *The Dialectic of Love*, is one of the most important works on Schiller's philosophy written in English. The book is a major contribution in that it argues for Schiller as a metaphysical rather than a critical philosopher, and thus recovers a position that had been lost in recent decades. As Pugh shows, making reference to Humboldt's observation in the mid-nineteenth century, many of Schiller's insights that are generally considered due to his reading of Kant were present in his work before 1791. What Schiller in fact *praises* in Kant is the fact that he vindicated through the provision of rational justification what the human race had always believed[165]—which, of course, means that Schiller is not celebrating Kant's "Copernican turn" in epistemology: "such famous and quintessentially Kantian doctrines as the thing-in-itself or the a priori status of time and space do not interest him in the slightest."[166] The reason Kant made such an impression on Schiller was his elevation of the ideal, which Schiller interpreted—here is one of the main theses of Pugh's book—in a distinctively Platonic fashion rather than within the guidelines, as it were, of the new transcendentalism in philosophy. One of the implications of this Platonic interpretation (and here we have another principal aspect of Pugh's thesis) is that Schiller thus inherited a contradiction that has always lain in the Platonic metaphysics that has governed Western thought, namely, that caused by the strict incompatibility of two basic Platonic themes: the theme of *chorismos*, i.e., the *separation* of the ideal realm from the real (the "transcendence" theme in Plato), and the theme of *methexis*, i.e., the *participation* of the real in the ideal (the "immanence" theme in Plato). Pugh's claim, in a word, is that Schiller wishes to affirm *both* unity (immanence) *and* difference (transcendence), and that, even

---

165. See Schiller's letter to Goethe, 28 October, 1794, in which he says that he has no fear that the foundation of Kant's philosophy will last forever, whatever may be the fate of the *form* of Kant's philosophy, because this foundation represents what the human race has implicitly believed from the beginning.

166. Pugh, *Dialectic of Love*, 22. Saying that Schiller took no interest in such questions is no doubt an overstatement: though Schiller does not discuss the issues in technical language, he was keenly aware of the "existential" implications of the most abstract philosophical positions. In any event, he clearly does not have a typical Kantian position on the matters Pugh mentions: consider the richly suggestive claim Schiller makes, for instance, on the "reciprocity" of a priority and a posteriority in our grasp of space and time: AEM XIX, 131 (SW.8.365–66).

though these are exclusive of one another, Schiller "absurdly" attempts to bring them together because he is the unwitting heir of Platonic metaphysics.[167] Thus, he says, we often find in Schiller a strong emphasis on harmony between reason and the senses, but this emphasis always turns out to be undermined in the end by a unilateral supremacy of reason.

We have discussed the simultaneity of unity and difference in Schiller at length in these two chapters, and have affirmed that simultaneity as the hallmark of his thought. One of the most obvious features of Schiller's thinking on this matter that belies Pugh's interpretation is that the "opposition" between the two is not in the least hidden to Schiller; it is not a tension that catches Schiller unawares, the function of an old metaphysics that thwarts Schiller's intentions to resolve conflict, but lies explicitly on the surface as the point Schiller *intends* to make. The primary problem with Pugh's thesis, however, is not in the *first* place his interpretation of Schiller, but his interpretation of Plato. Or in other words, he does not offer any philosophical argument why the transcendence and immanence of the ideal are incompatible, but simply takes it as self-evident in Plato and then attributes it to Schiller—though it is *precisely this question that Schiller means to beg*, to say nothing of Plato's own objections to this interpretation. Pugh is thus criticizing Schiller in terms of an unexamined assumption about the nature of reality that Schiller himself rejects for strong philosophical reasons, reasons he himself elaborates at length. Schiller *states* just what Pugh presents as the problem, and he states it as something to which he has found a solution. Extraordinarily, Pugh repeatedly restates the problem and never philosophically weighs Schiller's proposal for a solution. This neglect leads Pugh to force Schiller's philosophy in directions in which it does not naturally go, and thus to marginalize what lies in the center. To take just one example, he claims that Schiller's tendency to look for an analogy to freedom in nature is inconsistent with his thinking, and constantly gets re-absorbed into his general line, namely, what amounts to a rational despotism over nature.[168] But this analogy, as we have seen, is not a foreign element that never gets integrated in Schiller's thinking.[169]

---

167. Pugh, *Dialectic of Love*, 64.

168. Ibid., 166. Cf., Kerry, 57; 70; 98. Wilcox also claims that Schiller differs from Kant precisely in viewing nature in *noumenal* terms, i.e., seeing it as free: see *Die Dialektik der menschlichen Vollendung*, 43–44. Jeffrey Barnouw observes that Schiller detects a "glimmer of freedom" in animals, which Kant's theory would exclude: "Freiheit zu geben durch Freiheit," 159. Cf., also, Hoffheimer, "The Influence of Schiller's Theory of Nature," 231–44.

169. Though this is, of course, merely anecdotal evidence, it is worth noting that

The Perfection of Freedom

Instead, it is a central point that integrates the rest. Pugh's line of interpretation would make Schiller simply incoherent. Pugh seems himself to be the unwitting heir of the Enlightenment tradition of incompatibility between reason and nature, so that he can accept unity only when he sees difference wiped out. Thus, because genuine difference, and the asymmetry it implies, remains in Schiller, he has to assume contradiction. But for Plato as well as for Schiller transcendence and immanence, far from being incompatible, are *mutually dependent* on one another even in (indeed *precisely by virtue of*) their asymmetry, as a significant amount of scholarly work on Plato has shown.[170] Schiller, too, is attempting to demonstrate that what *seems* to be incompatible in the end turns out to have a surprising unity, without losing its tension. It is no doubt the regular failure to see what is admittedly a subtle and profound point that led Schiller to feel his basic philosophical insight was so rarely understood.[171] In our estimation, in short, Pugh is right that Schiller is best interpreted in the light of the classical tradition rather than immediately in terms of Kant, but his own judgments regarding that tradition are overly simplistic and rest on conventional assumptions that warrant the scrutiny Schiller himself offers.

Let us consider in brief the aspects of Schiller's position that respond to the charge of contradiction. There are three aspects that open up immediately. In the first place, as we have seen, Schiller has an *analogical* notion of form, in which there lies both similarity and difference. Thus, form represents, on the one hand, a principle of *reason*, the object of the *Formtrieb*, which governs both the practical and the theoretical realm. In other words, it is the referent both for understanding and for moral action. On the other hand, form is the concrete *Gestalt*, the object of the

---

Schiller had an abiding interest in nature. He was a member of the naturalist society while in Jena and regularly attended their lectures (for a brief account of his participation, see Kratzsch, *Friedrich Schiller und die Naturforschende Gesellschaft zu Jena*. This society was founded in the 1790s, largely thanks to Goethe's efforts: ibid., 5). Indeed, his famous encounter with Goethe began after one such meeting, after which, through casual comments, Schiller and Goethe realized they both agreed in their criticism of the fragmentary approach to nature that the lecturer represented. On this, see Goethe's account, "Fortunate Encounter," 18–21.

170. For a discussion of this issue and the scholarship surrounding it, see Schindler, *Plato's Critique of Impure Reason*, especially the book's coda, which is devoted specifically to this theme. Pugh's account of the history of ancient philosophy on this point is simplistic in the extreme: see Pugh, *Dialectic of Love*, 87–92, for example.

171. Indeed, after Schiller's AEM appeared, Wilhelm von Humboldt wrote (15 August, 1795) to Schiller to tell him that they were greeted in Berlin by silence: a well-known philosopher explained to him that they were hard to understand, and contained more unclarity than even Kant.

An Aesthetics of Freedom

Spieltrieb, which governs the realm of contemplation, play, and beauty, and thus represents the integrating principle of humanity. This aspect of form, we have been arguing, is the principle of heautonomy in a thing, its *internal* self-determination, which includes within itself autonomy, without eliminating what distinguishes that autonomy. It is therefore true that the "complete" notion of form relativizes form in its abstract sense, but it does so without compromising its absoluteness within its own order. We saw in the last chapter that taste, properly understood, has room, as it were, to accommodate the full demands of logical rigor. Similarly, here, the living *Gestalt* has room for the whole of moral rigor in its integrity. This is precisely why Schiller was able to affirm Kant's *Unbedingtheit*, "unconditionality," in questions of duty and at the same time criticize any position in morality that eliminated the significance of nature. To the incomprehension of many, he called himself a Kantian to the end, and yet he offered one of the most memorable critiques of a merely "deontological" ethics. Schiller does not seek to say less than Kant, but rather affirms Kant . . . and goes further.[172] The most significant explicit statement Schiller makes in this regard in the AEM, in which we see both the affirmation and the transformation, can be found in an important footnote to Letter XXIII:

> The moral philosopher does, it is true, teach us that man can never do *more* than his duty; and he is perfectly right if he merely has in mind the relation between actions and the moral law. But in the case of actions which are merely end-serving, *to exceed the end, and pass beyond it* into the supra-sensible (which in the present context can mean nothing more than carrying out the physical in an aesthetic manner), is in fact *to exceed duty*, since duty can only prescribe that the *will* be sacred, but not that *nature itself* shall have taken on sacral character. There is thus no possibility of a moral transcendence of duty; but there is such a thing as an aesthetic transcendence; and such conduct we call noble.[173]

---

172. In this respect, Muehleck-Müller's interpretation is correct: Kant is speaking of ethics, while Schiller's context is the larger one of anthropology (see her *Schönheit als Freiheit*, 177–78). The question of course is to what extent the difference in context affects the meaning of the particular claims. Cf., Höffe's contrast between Schiller and Kant on this point: "Gerne dien ich den Freunden," 17, and Baxley's different attempt to do the same: "The Beautiful Soul and the Autocratic Agent," 493–514.

173. AEM XXIII, 167fn (SW.8.383fn).

The Perfection of Freedom

One question that would remain open for further exploration is the extent to which there is a moral demand to be noble. In any event, we ought to note how much of what Schiller wishes to argue in general turns on the status of nature. We will investigate this further in our study of Schelling in the next chapter.

Regarding the other way of expressing this apparent contradiction, namely, the tension between freedom as integration vs. freedom as moral transcendence, it is important to keep in mind the analogy constantly at work in Schiller's terminology. Thus, as we indicated at the outset, commentators have observed that form can mean the concrete whole, and it can also mean one aspect of what is integrated in that whole. Similarly, freedom can mean the integration of reason and the senses, or it can indicate one element of that integration, namely, reason. Indeed, it is even possible to say that integration or "harmony" itself can stand for the whole, or it can represent one aspect of that which is to be harmonized.[174] This complexity, it bears repeating, is not simply a sign of confusion, but is an expression of the "dramatic" reality that Schiller was attempting to articulate. It is one of the things that makes him unique in philosophy, and for that reason one of the main causes of the regular misunderstandings in the interpretation of his thought.

Second, as we have emphasized repeatedly, the living form Schiller is presenting here is a complex whole that cannot be reduced in the end to any particular external purpose. Even if it may *also* turn out to serve some end outside of itself, in a proper whole this "duty" springs as it were from the subject's nature, which means that the external duty is appropriated to the internal principle. One of the implications of genuine wholeness, as we have seen, is a rejection of unilateral hierarchy without a rejection of asymmetry. Schiller often speaks of *reciprocal* subordination.[175] This follows necessarily from an organic whole, as we saw in the last chapter. In such a whole, each part is itself a relative whole, which means that each part is in a certain sense an end in itself, to which everything else is subordinate. To take an example that Schiller cites in the essay we discussed last chapter, St. Peter's, we have pillars supporting what he calls the "artful firmament." There is a way in which the pillars serve the ceiling, indeed, since they keep it aloft; at the same time, however, the ceiling serves to cover the pillars, which are things of beauty in their own right, giving

---

174. For a more elaborate presentation of this pattern in his thought, see WW, 348–50.

175. See AEM XIII, 85fn (SW.8.344fn).

them not only protection from the elements but locating them in aesthetic space. To argue for a simple priority of one part of the whole over the other, or to insist that these two affirmations of relative priority are somehow inconsistent would be obviously absurd. At the same time, it is clear that the ceiling remains "over" the pillars, and the relative priority of the pillars does not imply that they change their position of subordination to the ceiling, so that one would have to see the ceiling as a support for the pillars in order to affirm a reciprocal subordination. Genuine reciprocity requires that each be specifically what it is in relation to the other. The only way there could be a reduction to a single order would be if the ensemble served some particular and exclusive function outside of itself, e.g., to support a lookout tower. But if St. Peter's clearly does not serve some such external function, it is even more clear that the human being, in Schiller's view, is never simply an instrument.

The play drive, moreover, represents the whole of the human being in a way that neither of the others can, even though, properly integrated, each of them shares in the totality. It remains true that, for Schiller, the whole possesses a dependence on the parts, just as the parts do the whole, but the whole remains the integrating power. Within that integration, moreover, there is a reciprocity of functions but no simple symmetry. It seems to be just such a symmetry that Pugh is seeking as evidence of Schiller's having successfully overcome the traditional "Platonic dualism." But Schiller would regard simple symmetry as confusion, as another example of "disorganization." A proper integration means that the parts retain their uniqueness, which means further that they maintain the particular function that belongs properly to them in fostering the wholeness of the whole. Thus, more specifically, Schiller insists that, in perfect freedom, nature and the reality of the senses are treated as ends in themselves. What matter *is*, as good in itself, is the *real-ization* of form, a realization that form cannot accomplish on its own. But this uniqueness is, of course, relative to form, and relative indeed to the reciprocal *uniqueness* of form, which lies in its own unconditionality. To deny this unconditionality for the sake of "symmetry" would undermine not only form, but matter as well, and vice versa. Schiller is quite clear on this point.

Finally, along similar lines, if it is true that the wholeness of the whole *requires* and liberates the individuality of the parts in their own right, then it follows that the cultivation of the whole does not substitute for the cultivation of each of the parts, even while it remains a precondition for the proper cultivation of those parts. In a footnote to the twentieth letter,

Schiller specifies what he means by "aesthetic education," in relation to the education for "health," "understanding," and "morality."[176] These three correspond to the complexity of the unity of the human being, who is not only physical, but spiritual, i.e., capable of moral and intellectual acts. Aesthetic education corresponds to the *unity* of that complexity. To be educated in beauty, to be formed in play, evidently does not satisfy the demands of the other dimensions, though it is the principle for their proper relation to the whole. Far from substituting for them, then, aesthetic education, to the extent that it succeeds, makes them more truly what they are in themselves: it makes physical education more genuinely physical, reason more reasonable, and morality more moral. Here is the wonderful paradox: the more morality is relativized to the humanity, the more it becomes what it is, namely, the unconditional response to the demands of goodness, which means it becomes more truly absolute the more it is genuinely relative. To put the matter more concretely: Schiller explains the aesthetic state as the engagement of all the human powers at once, which is what makes a person, so to speak, "ready for anything."[177] But *because* he is ready for anything, he is ready for specifically *moral* action—or physical, or intellectual. Aesthetic determination, we recall, is infinite because it *includes* all possibility. There is, obviously, no incompatibility between being ready for anything and being ready to do one's duty. Because one is inclined to transcend oneself in play, one can act "independently" of one's inclinations—because that is what one wants to do, that is one's *delight*. A full human being is able to act selflessly on another's behalf when demanded, and in that act his wholeness becomes the means to the end pursued. But it serves as such a means only because it is itself an end. To put it another way, the perfect integration of reason and the senses is dependent on reason's perfect transcendence of the senses, and the senses' being a kind of *telos* for reason. This is why Schiller is able to affirm the simultaneity of grace and dignity as his ideal of human freedom,[178] not as an afterthought or a slip in thinking, but as the carefully chosen final sentence of his main philosophical work. He describes the community of genuinely free human beings as one in which "men make their way, with undismayed simplicity and tranquil innocence, through even the most involved and complex situations, free alike of the compulsion to infringe the freedom of others in

---

176. AEM XX, 141–43fn (SW.8.372fn).
177. See AEM XXII, 151 (SW.8.73).
178. Grace, 163 (SW.8.216).

order to assert their own, as of the necessity to shed their Dignity in order to manifest Grace."[179]

The philosophical insight at the core of these various paradoxes is the notion we identified in chapter 1 as the governing principle in Schiller's philosophical style, and the key to interpreting the content of that work: the completeness of a concept is what allows it to enter so perfectly into the external expression that the expression takes on a life of its own. In more general terms related to the question of contradiction we have been discussing, the *transcendence* of form over matter is precisely what enables it to be wholly immanent in the matter. There is thus, in other words, a single cause for both the harmony between soul and body (grace) and the heroic triumph of the soul over the body (dignity) in tragedy, for example. They are both expressions of the very same freedom, and both are essential elements of a *lebende Gestalt*.

X. Nobility or Bourgeois Aestheticism?

The paradoxes that arise from Schiller's dramatic anthropology are summed up in the figure Schiller presents as the emblem of freedom, namely, the "noble soul," and it is fitting for us to conclude with a description of this figure. According to Schiller,

> In general we call noble any nature which possesses the gift of transforming, purely by its manner of handling it, even the most trifling occupation, or the most petty of objects, into something infinite. We call that form noble which impresses the stamp of autonomy upon anything which by its nature merely *serves some purpose* (is a mere means). A noble nature is not content to be itself free; it must also set free everything around it, even the lifeless. Beauty, however, is the only way that freedom has of making itself manifest in appearance.[180]

To be noble is to have the "expansive form" that we saw in the *Kalliasbriefe*: one can possess such a form only if one acknowledges it in others, which means that one's freedom is quite really *dependent* on the freedom

---

179. AEM XXVII, 218 (SW.8.408). In the original publication of the letters in *Die Horen*, the passage cited was contained in a footnote to the final sentence. But when Schiller published the text as a whole in his collected works in 1801, he eliminated the footnote, and placed the content in the main body of the text as the final paragraph. Subsequent editions have done the same.

180. AEM XXIII, 167fn (SW.8.382–83fn).

of others. Schiller depicts it here as the bestowal of a gift, and he remarks elsewhere that we cannot be a harmonious whole ourselves "if we lack the power of receiving into ourselves, faithfully and truly, natures unlike ours, of feeling our way into the situation of others, of making other people's feeling our own."[181] We might say that this freedom is just as much a gift received: it arises when one "transforms" whatever one comes into contact with into a thing of beauty, i.e., a heautonomous whole, and thus a kind of *end* that one serves. One becomes noble only by ennobling those around one. The aesthetic form in which one's own freedom is crystallized, in other words, is not a private possession but an embracing objective order in which one participates with others. The play that beauty provokes tends of itself to cooperation; understood as aesthetic, freedom proves to be inherently social in principle.

But play can degenerate into a mere game; nobility can become nothing more than a show of gentile manners; the cultivation of aesthetic form can turn into superficial aestheticism. Although Schiller's notion of the *lebende Gestalt* provides a breakthrough beyond subjectivism, as we have been arguing over the course of this chapter, this development can be sustained only if the freedom that is thereby won can be shown to have genuine *roots* in the objective order. Otherwise, the form that gives freedom substance can collapse into empty appearance. There are two things necessary to prevent this collapse: On the one hand, what is needed is a philosophy of nature, which shows how the physical world, down to its most elemental parts, is ordered to freedom, and a corresponding reinterpretation of the highest realm of spirit as having a natural principle. On the other hand, there is a need for a philosophy of political order, which reveals that subjectivity is always-already *inter*-subjectivity, and that freedom can therefore never belong to the bourgeois individual in isolation, but necessarily has a social character. Gestures in these directions are present in Schiller's thought, but the systematic development of these philosophies is just what Schelling and Hegel seek to provide, as we will see over the course the rest of the book.

---

181. AEM XIII, 89–91fn (SW.8.347–48fn).

3

The Dark Roots of Life: Organic Form as a Symbol of Freedom in Schelling's *Naturphilosophie*

I. The Philosophy of the Future

IT IS OFTEN CLAIMED, particularly in English-language studies, that Schelling was the quintessential philosopher ahead of his time.[1] Though he was given public honor in the evening of his life by being appointed to a prestigious chair at the University of Berlin that had been held by his onetime roommate at the Tübingen Seminary, his brief collaborator in what might be considered the first journal of German Idealism,[2] and eventually the most significant "foil" for the development of his late philosophical ideas, namely, Hegel, Schelling's ideas cannot be said to have established themselves at his death in the middle of the nineteenth century.[3] On the

---

1. See Bowie, *Schelling and Modern European Philosophy*, 178–91; Wirth, *The Conspiracy of Life*, 1–4; Grant, *Philosophies of Nature*.

2. Schelling and Hegel founded the *Kritische Journal der Philosophie* in 1802 while they were together briefly in Jena.

3. Arguably, Schelling was given the post not in the first place because of the intrinsic value of his ideas but because the Prussian king, Friedrich Wilhelm IV, thought he might be able to stem the growing tide of Hegel's influence. Karl Freiherr Bunsen wrote to Schelling on August 1, 1840, that the king wanted to bring him to Berlin on account of what the king himself called the "dragon seed of Hegelian pantheism," which, among other things, threatened to erode the sense of discipline in the people. In other words,

The Perfection of Freedom

one hand, in spite of Schelling's apparently having the "last word," Hegel has generally been thought of as the major representative of this period in the history of philosophy, Schelling being essentially one of the steps from Kant to Hegel. On the other hand, even those who were inclined to "go beyond" Hegel at the time were not inclined to "follow behind" Schelling in doing so, even if they initially expected to receive inspiration from Schelling for their own philosophical projects. In what is no doubt one of the great events in the history of philosophy, Schelling gave his "Eintritsrede" in Berlin on November 15, 1841, nearly ten years to the day after Hegel's death, and presented his thought to an immense audience that included Jakob Burkhardt, Frederick Engels, Søren Kierkegaard, and Michail Bakhunin, among others, as opening up a new direction for philosophy, one capable for the first time of embracing history, personal freedom, and the positivity of existence.[4] Though filled with excitement at first, the lectures proved to be a disappointment for most, and the numbers of the once overflowing lecture hall dwindled significantly as the weeks went by.[5] Kierkegaard left attending because, as he wrote in a letter, Schelling cut a ridiculous figure presenting such claims when he was already clearly a thing of the past.[6]

So it is ironic that he is now seen as having anticipated the thought of twentieth-century figures like Heidegger, Tillich, Lacan, and Deleuze.[7]

---

he seems to have been given the post for political more than philosophical reasons. On the other hand, it was nevertheless the case that Schelling's importance was recognized at the time, even in France; a French philosopher wrote a book introducing Schelling to his compatriots as the summation of the *whole* of German philosophy and its most important living thinker: Matter, *Schelling et la philosophie de la nature*, 1.

4. For a good, brief account of both the atmosphere and content of these lectures, see Gräb, "Anerkannte Kontingenz," 141–54.

5. See Kirchhoff, *Friedrich Wilhelm Joseph von Schelling*, 55–56.

6. Kierkegaard wrote to his brother Peter Christian of his decision to leave off listening to Schelling's lectures in February of 1842: "I am too old to attend lectures, just as Schelling is too old to give them. His whole doctrine of potencies betrays the highest degree of impotence." Cited in the "Historical Introduction" of *The Concept of Irony*, xxiii.

7. On Tillich's reprisal of certain ideas found in Schelling, see Brown, *The Later Philosophy of Schelling*, 9. Žižek suggests Schelling anticipates Lacan (see *The Indivisible Remainder*, 75), and Grant that his *Naturphilosophie* anticipates Deleuze: *Philosophies of Nature*, 199–206. Bowie presents Schelling as anticipating some of the fundamental insights of Heidegger, among others: see his translator's preface to HMP, ix. Moreover, he notes that ideas in Schelling reappear later, not only in Freud, Heidegger, Derrida, and Lacan, but also in "big bang" theories in science and contemporary thinking in ecology: see *Schelling and Modern European Philosophy*, 6.

Indeed, the irony lies deeper than initially apparent insofar as his present actuality (*Schelling Now!*[8]) is due largely to his being celebrated as a philosopher quite literally *of the future*: one of his major contributions is his revolutionary interpretation of eternity, not as "timeless" but as "time-full," and so not simply opposed to the novel "coming to be" that time entails. Schelling's deep intuition was that freedom must have an "open," an "as-yet-undecided" character, and if we are to understand the world on the basis of freedom, this quality must belong to reality itself in some respect. Thus, being itself must stand before us as something unexpected, as a surprise, as *"unvordenklich,"* not as something already concluded, but as a constant *beginning.*[9] Indeed, being must be unpreconceivable not simply in relation to us, but *in itself*. This leads him to the surprising inference that, in contrast to the God of the philosophers, who has always already come to a definitive end[10]—God as "eternal"—the *true* God is a Personal one, and a Person is essentially (and not just in relation to us) *"unvordenklich,"* so that we would have to affirm that God himself has in some respect an undecided future.[11] A philosophy of freedom is, for Schelling, of its essence a philosophy of the future, even more decisively than Nietzsche's would be.

It would be difficult to exaggerate the depth and breadth of the implications of such a line of thinking, which on its face presents a straightforward contradiction. There is a tendency, in fact, to celebrate precisely the contradiction, to claim Schelling as important for contemporary thought primarily for having acknowledged the reality of the unconscious and irrational, and thus for liberating thought from its totalizing drive.[12] While such an impulse is certainly to be found in Schelling, especially in the lectures he gave after the appearance of his last major published work, *On the*

8. Wirth, *Schelling Now*.

9. See Lawrence, *Schellings Philosophie des ewigen Anfangs*, 1.

10. HMP, 132 (W.5.193–94).

11. See PO, 174–79. We will discuss Schelling's view of God at length in the next chapter. According to Baumgartner and Korten (*Schelling*, 11), the most decisive development in Schelling's thought is his introduction of the notion of a *personal* God. Even as early as the *System of Transcendental Idealism*, Schelling presents God as the playwright of history, but a history in which human beings—who are not separate from God—freely invent their own roles: see STI, 210 (KA.I.9-1.301).

12. For example, see Jason Wirth's observation that "the system of freedom is a contradiction and that, rather than being an argument against the system, is the secret to its vitality," in the translator's introduction to *The Ages of the World*, xxi. See also Žižek's essay, "The Abyss of Freedom," in *The Abyss of Freedom/Ages of the World*, 3–104.

The Perfection of Freedom

Essence of Human Freedom (which we shall explore in the next chapter), the decontextualized elevation of this element distorts his philosophy. If we interpret Schelling simply as tearing down order for the sake of freedom then we will simply repeat the dualism that he sought continuously to overcome. Against the habit, which indeed began with Hegel, of seeing Schelling as a philosophical Proteus who "carried out his education in public,"[13] Heidegger claimed that Schelling was rather dominated by a single idea from the beginning to the end of his thinking.[14] To put it in the most basic terms, Schelling—just like Schiller before him, and often along similar lines—endeavored from the beginning to *reconcile* the ideal and the real, the basic rift that had grown in modern thought between the subject and the object. Even as late as 1833–1834, when Schelling was in the thick of developing the (unfinished) masterpiece of his late philosophy, the *Ages of the World*, he aspired to the creation of a *system* of freedom as complete as Spinoza's.[15] In other words, at the heart of Schelling's efforts lies the same desideratum that we studied in Schiller, namely, the *coincidentia oppositorum* as the ultimate reference point for the thinking of any other philosophical problems. Heidegger is also correct to say that the meaning of freedom, which Schelling famously referred to as the Alpha and Omega of philosophy,[16] is bound in its essence to this coincidence.[17] According to Schelling's phrase, which bears unmistakable Schillerean tones, the goal of his philosophy is to bring it about that "Nature shall be visible spirit, and spirit invisible nature."[18] If we lose nature, we lose spirit.[19]

---

13. See Hegel's Hist of Phil (JA.19.647).

14. Heidegger, *Schelling*, 7–8. Walter E. Ehrhardt makes a similar argument: "Nur ein Schelling," 111–22.

15. HMP, 66 (W.5.105–6). See Lawrence, *Schellings Philosophie*, 12. Lawrence gives the date as 1827, which is what Schelling's son had assumed when compiling the collected works, but it has become evident that the lectures on the history of modern philosophy presented in the collected works belongs to a later period, either 1833–34 or 1836–37.

16. Schelling's letter to Hegel, 4 February, 1795. See also Ideas, 167 (KA.I.5.69). Schelling claimed in his *Freiheitsschrift* that making freedom the founding principle of all philosophy was the greatest revolution in the history of thought: Freedom, 232 (W.4.243). On this, see Marx, *Geschichte, System, Freiheit*, 102.

17. Heidegger, *Schelling*, 73.

18. Ideas, 202 (KA.I.5.107).

19. See HMP, 173 (W.5.247), and *Clara*, 3 (W.4E.105–6). Grant justly observes that, for Schelling, we cannot have a metaphysics if we neglect physics: Grant, *Philosophies of Nature*, viii.

The Dark Roots of Life

There are few thinkers in the modern period who saw the importance of a philosophy of nature more than Schelling. To claim that freedom is the first and last in philosophy demands that we rethink the meaning of nature *on the basis* of freedom and with a view to the ultimate meaning of freedom.[20] This we discovered in our study of Schiller: if freedom does not have its roots already in the natural world in some respect, it will collapse into an empty subjectivism. Schelling, in fact, refers to Schiller's notion of the manifestation of freedom in nature as the starting point in one of his major works in *Naturphilosophie*.[21] Schelling claimed that the transcendental philosophy he was developing would be the first to grasp the proper meaning of freedom, and this coincided with an observation that modern philosophy had not yet known the existence of a genuine philosophy of nature.[22] The first period of his philosophical studies was given to filling just this gap, and though he set aside explicit engagement with the findings of experimental science in his middle and later periods,[23] he referred to his earlier philosophy, which he insisted was not replaced but rather complemented by his later,[24] generally as the "philosophy of nature" simply.[25] He

---

20. We thus hear a clear echo of Schelling in the passage from the "Oldest Programme for a System of German Idealism": "The first idea, of course, is the representation *of myself as* an absolutely free being. With this free, self-conscious being a whole *world* comes into existence—out of nothing—the only true and conceivable *creation from nothing.*—Here I will descend to the realm of physics; the question is this: How must a world be constituted for a moral being? I would like to give wings once again to our physics, which is otherwise sluggish and progresses laboriously via experiments," in *Classical and Romantic Aesthetics*, ed. Bernstein, 185. On this echo, see Wieland, "Die Anfänge der Philosophie Schellings," 412.

21. WS, 67 (KA.I.4.67, 25. Anmerkung 275).

22. See Freedom, 236 (W.4.248).

23. Although he did not continue to elaborate his *Naturphilosophie* in his writings, it does not mean that the issue of nature ceased to be important for him: see Grant's argument and evidence: Grant, *Philosophies of Nature*, 4–5. He did, however, present a lecture on March 28, 1832, on "The Discovery of Electromagnetic Induction by Faraday," commenting on the significance of that event, which is considered a remarkable exception (along with a few others, such as Oersted's work in electromagnetism: see Friedmann, "Kant-*Naturphilosophie*-Electromagnetism," 60) to the claim that Schelling's *Naturphilosophie* had no relevance for experimental science. Faraday confessed explicitly that his investigations were guided by Schelling's philosophy.

24. See Zaborowski, "Geschichte," 48–52.

25. In HMP, 120 (W.5.177), he explains why he preferred this name, in spite of the fact that it designates what is only a part of his philosophy, to the name that had become more popular, namely, the "Identity System." It is also interesting to note that one of the first presentations of Schelling's thought more generally in French summarized the whole of it under the name "philosophie de la nature": see the book by Jacques Matter referenced in fn 3.

is the first to try to bridge the gap between the practice of science and the insights of philosophy in the wake of the maturity, if not the birth, of what is called modern science proper.[26] In spite of his efforts and those of a few others, the split that had just begun in the middle of the nineteenth century[27] has arguably grown considerably since Schelling's time, so that his complaint about the lack of—and so need for—a philosophy of nature has become even more urgent.[28] In this respect, Schelling may turn out to be a philosopher of the future *especially because* he is a philosopher of nature. Our own engagement with Schelling is prompted by the conviction that the problems to which Schelling attempted to respond are still with us, and that an adequate philosophy of freedom *still requires* a reflection on the nature of nature.

Because of the complexity of the path Schelling's thought took in this area, it is good, here at the outset and in anticipation of our discussion, to sketch out the argument we will be making. We aim to show, in this chapter, why Schelling rightly insisted that a mechanistic conception of nature, for all of the power it might promise to human technological projects, entails in the end a radical impoverishment of freedom. The problem here is not simply that the apparent determinism of mechanistic physics excludes the indeterminacy of free choice, so that saving freedom requires finding a way—as Leibniz and Kant attempted to do,[29] for example—to reconcile physical necessity with the spontaneity of the human spirit. Such a reconciliation, indeed, takes for granted that freedom in its essence is self-determined choice, and so betrays the very impoverishment that the thinkers we are exploring in this book sought to remedy. The deeper problem is the loss of substance in the notion of freedom, due ultimately to a

---

26. See Wieland, "Die Anfänge der Philosophie Schellings," 436, who claims he represents last great attempt to appropriate science in a philosophically systematic way. Cf. also Bach, *Biologie und Philosophie*, 247fn382.

27. See Sandkühler, "Ein Werk im Werden," 13.

28. The fact that Hans Jonas is able to make the same observation in 1974 suggests that the problem of an adequate philosophy of nature is still with us: see his "Introduction" to *Philosophical Essays*, xii–xiii. The best work being done in the philosophy of science in the contemporary academy is not evidence to the contrary: it tends to be a specialized branch of epistemology, and not a study of the meaning of nature itself (i.e., it is, in fact, a philosophy of *science* rather than a philosophy of *nature*).

29. Leibniz makes a distinction between logical and causal necessity and insists that freedom is only incompatible with the former: see his brief essay, "On Freedom," in Leibniz, *Philosophical Essays*, 94–98. Kant allows freedom only to the *noumenal* self, and admits that the phenomenal self is, from the first to last, subject to mechanical laws: see his "Critical Elucidation of the Analytic of Pure Practical Reason" in the CPrR, 92–110.

division between subject and object, or the ideal and real. As Schelling repeatedly insisted, healing this division requires rethinking the cosmos in such a way that organic form, which is an integration of subjectivity and objectivity, comes to represent not an epiphenomenon of physics or a mere product of (wholly subjective) reflective judgment, as Kant claimed, but the very paradigm of nature and so the epitome of the real. In this case, the organism as an integration of the real and ideal will reveal, as it were, the genuine *nature* of spirit. The organism will therefore prove to be the symbol of freedom.

The trajectory of the present chapter runs as follows: we will first indicate the lacunae in modern thought that Schelling developed his *Naturphilosophie* to fill. A failure to see the ultimate integration of subject and object entails both a deficient view of nature and a deficient view of spirit. We will, accordingly, explore the resultant deficiencies he detected in each, first in more immediate terms and then more globally. On the side of the real, we will see how mechanism undermines both nature and our experience of it, and then makes a coherent conception of organism impossible. More generally, it implies what Schelling calls the "death of the cosmos," in which no genuine intimacy, no true inter-action, between things is possible. On the side of the ideal, we will see that mechanism implies an essentially solipsistic conception of subjectivity and a positivistic sense of human agency. More broadly, as Schelling shows in the lectures on academic studies in his middle period, it entails a general fragmentation of reason that follows the fragmentation of its object. Against this backdrop, we will then present the general features of Schelling's *Naturphilosophie*, showing why it culminates in the organism, as the expression in nature of the Absolute, understood as the ultimate integration of the ideal and real. After this presentation, we will consider its implications for Schelling's view of freedom in his middle period, and then conclude with a look at a fundamental ambiguity that threatens to undermine his achievement, and leads to the development of the late philosophy that we will study in chapter 4.

II. The Origins of Schelling's *Naturphilosophie*

Schelling elaborated his *Naturphilosophie* in a series of relatively short works that followed one another rapidly, especially in his early years.[30]

30. For a relatively complete bibliography of Schelling's writings, see Schneeberger, *Eine Bibliographie*.

His groundbreaking work was the *Ideas for a Philosophy of Nature*, which appeared in 1797, when Schelling was twenty-two years old and working as a tutor in Leipzig.[31] His next was *On the World Soul: A Hypothesis of Higher Physics as an Attempt to Explain the Universal Organism* (1798). During this time, he began lecturing on *Naturphilosophie* at Jena, and was in regular contact there with Fichte, Schiller, Goethe, and others. The very next year, he wrote his *First Sketch of a System of Naturphilosophie*, and then published separately a substantial introduction to that work. In 1800, he began to produce a journal called the *Zeitschrift für spekulative Physik*, in which appeared what some consider his most complete *naturphilosophische* work, the "Universal Deduction of the Dynamic Process." In this same year, he completed his *System of Transcendental Idealism*, in which he began more explicitly to connect his *Naturphilosophie* with philosophy generally. This effort characterized the majority of his *naturphilosophische* works after this time. Most significant of these is the *Exposition of My System of Philosophy* (1801) and his *Further Expositions of My System of Philosophy* (1802), as well as his philosophical dialogue, *Bruno: On the Divine and Natural Principle of Things* (1802) and the essay he wrote for his journal, *On the Relation of Natural Philosophy to Philosophy in General* (1802). Finally, he wrote another version of the *System of Philosophy in General and of the Philosophy of Nature in Particular* (1804), which remained unpublished, his *Aphorisms on the Philosophy of Nature* as well as an introduction to this work (1806), and his *Exposition of the True Relationship of the Philosophy of Nature to the Improved Version of Fichte's Teaching* (1806). He also published lectures that drew on and developed aspects of his philosophy of nature: the *Lectures on the Method of Academic Studies* (1803) and *On the Relationship of the Plastic Arts to Nature* (1807).[32]

What prompted such prodigious productivity in such a brief period of time? Schelling's *Naturphilosophie* arose as a response to two distinct lacks that Schelling perceived in the intellectual currents of his time, at the core of which lay a single problem. We will first sketch in broad strokes the

---

31. Schelling revised this work for re-publication in 1803. As Schelling accompanied his "tutee" to the university lectures from 1796 to 1798, he immersed himself in the study of math, science, and medicine, acquainting himself with a great deal of the contemporary work being done in those fields. There is some debate about the degree to which he achieved any genuine mastery in them.

32. This list does not include his smaller texts and miscellanea, nor does it include the discussion of the philosophy of nature in the context of his later philosophy, such as in the lectures *On the History of Modern Philosophy*.

The Dark Roots of Life

deficiencies and the single problem that gave rise to them, and then offer a more thorough exploration of Schelling's interpretation. On the one hand, Schelling believed that the natural sciences were encumbered by a significant deficiency. The positivistic empiricism that was becoming dominant in Schelling's day as the ideal method in science—even if it can remain, at least in some respect, entirely consistent both with its own internal principles and with the data derived from experiments—does not do justice to the proper demands of science, in Schelling's view, because it leaves unintelligible its own foundations. Moreover, if it is taken to be the authoritative method in science, it ends by allowing the various sciences to retain the name only insofar as they become mechanistic, and excludes any aspect of reality that resists such a reduction. The most immediate victim of this reduction, of course, is nothing less than life and everything it implies. On the other hand, Schelling also felt the need for a kind of corrective to the "subjective idealism" developing within the new transcendental philosophy of Kant, Reinhold, and Fichte. Philosophy concerns truth, truth is attained, properly speaking, in knowledge, and knowledge is, so to speak, the encounter between the intellect and being, or to put it in the language of the time, between the subject and the object or the ideal and the real. A philosophy that attempts to account for this encounter *wholly* as a result of the unfolding of the subject's faculties, or even joins the two in a merely extrinsic way as an accidental event, will invariably falsify the truth of that encounter. Subjectivity so conceived ends up surrendering its substance and its principle of unity. Schelling decided that a genuine philosophy will therefore have to supplement subjective idealism with a new objective idealism, or indeed idealism with a new realism, at the core of which is a philosophical illumination of nature down to its most basic mechanical laws. An elaboration of these two deficient bodies of thought—positivistic empiricism and subjective idealism—will illuminate essential features in Schelling's *Naturphilosophie*. As we will see, the *Naturphilosophie* emerges precisely at the point at which these two lacks intersect.

According to Schelling, the single problem at the source of this twofold deficiency goes back most decisively to the sixteenth century. As he sees it, the philosophy of Descartes is ultimately what eliminated the possibility of a philosophy of nature.[33] By making the distinction between the *res cogitans* and *res extensa* the basis of his thinking about nature, Descartes begins with the subjectivity of the subject and the objectivity of the object as defined in the first place *in* themselves and to that extent *over*

---

33. See AS (W.3.341–42).

against the other, which lies, so to speak, wholly outside. This, in a nutshell, is the core problem: namely, a separation between the ideal and the real that leaves them opposed to one another in principle. As far as nature goes, then, the opposition gives us a series of "things," the entire "inner" content of which is nothing more than the filling up of space. Extension, so conceived, is not intelligible in itself, insofar as the light of intelligibility implies, as it were, "translucence," which means that a thing can be understood in some respect only by being related to something else as its ground: if we cannot ask about the "cause" of a thing, we cannot understand it. Instead of understanding matter in itself, we grasp it according to the way material things interact, in the only terms mere extension allows: quantities. Our investigation of the meaning of the world thus turns into predictive calculation of the movements of the bits of matter. As far as spirit goes, it ends up filling the empty spaces in a mechanistic world and so comes to reflect back the same void. In the next two main sections, we will explore the two aspects of this problem in greater depth in order better to appreciate the significance of Schelling's *Naturphilosophie*.

III. The Impoverishment of Nature

A. Empiricism and the Destruction of Science

There are three immediate implications of this reduction of the meaning of matter: the loss of science, of the content of experience, and of the possibility of natural life. Let us look at each of these in turn. The first implication is that the study of nature ceases in fact to be a science in the strict sense. In his *Ideas*, Schelling presents a sharp critique of one of the most successful contemporary representatives at that time of this approach to nature, namely, the Swiss physicist George-Louis Le Sage (1724–1803). He explains that Le Sage purports to explain everything in the cosmos on the basis of three axioms: the assumption of indivisible atoms, movement, and space.[34] But although the system Le Sage presents is internally very mathematically precise, Schelling writes, it leaves its axioms themselves "wholly groundless"[35] because it never asks after the *possibility* of matter or the original source of movement.[36] Ironically, this makes physics wholly "speculative," not in Schelling's or Hegel's sense, but in the sense that it trac-

---

34. Ideas (KA.I.5.197–202).
35. Ideas (KA.I.5.200).
36. Ideas (KA.I.5.204).

es out what *would* necessarily be the case given an unverified hypothesis rather than what in fact *is* the case.[37] In the end, no experiment can verify the science that prides itself on experimental verifiability. Not only can this science therefore not claim in an ultimate sense to be experimental, it also cannot claim to be a *science*. Since, in Schelling's understanding, a science in the proper sense must grasp its own principles, which means it must always interpret its subject matter in relation to the absolute, physics as the study of matter in motion is necessarily secondary to and dependent on genuine science. As Schelling explains in a later work, mechanistic physics can only trace movement back to previous movements, and cannot think the original movement out of essential rest.[38] But if *all* change in matter has an external cause as Kant affirmed, then there cannot ultimately be any change in nature.[39] In this case, mechanistic physics undermines itself on its own terms and so calls for a more fundamental science, one that is able to grasp *self*-movement.

Another implication of this approach to physics is the inability to account for what constitutes the foundation of our experience of things, namely, their qualities. The reduction of matter in mechanistic physics excludes the possibility of sense experience of things in two respects: In the first place, having reduced the physical world to bits of matter in motion, it assumes that an outside object impinges on me as a force *acting on* what is not force, and indeed has no relation to force, namely, the ideality of consciousness. But a physical force can affect only a counterforce, which is a basic supposition of mechanics. Thus, one cannot give a physicalistic account of sensation.[40] Second, sensation implies the real existence of qualities, which implies in turn that matter has some content of its own. This would be possible, Schelling claims, only if matter possessed an "inward" being. But matter conceived merely as *res extensa* does not: it is by definition pure externality, and the search for an inner cause in things by opening matter up is simply a further exposure of more and more surfaces, but

---

37. Ideas (KA.I.5.205).

38. EEE (KA.I.8.32–33). One might raise the interesting question here whether this criticism is outdated given the vast amount of scientific study of the origin of the universe in the twentieth century, not to mention the non-deterministic (and indeed non-local) model of causality in quantum mechanics. It is important to realize, in raising this question, that contemporary science would rise above Schelling's criticism at the most essential point only insofar as it recovered a sense of interiority and subjectivity within being.

39. See Lawrence, *Schellings Philosophie*, 79.

40. Ideas, 175–76 (KA.I.5.79).

nowhere the "place" wherein a quality could reside. As Schelling puts it in his *Universal Deduction*, what is improperly taken to be dead nature, i.e., purely physical reality, in reality lacks only the final potentializing act whereby its qualities can be changed into experiences, its matters into intentions.[41] But given the Cartesian separation of body and soul, we can find no place for qualities, for the content of sense experience: qualities in this case have nothing in common with the nature of consciousness, and also nothing in common with the nature of nature. If qualities are to be at all possible, there would have to be some point of unity between subject and object in principle. In the *Ideas*, Schelling writes: "How did the impression get to *this* region of your soul where you feel entirely free and independent of impressions? You can insert as many intermediate members as you like between the affection of your nerves, your brain, etc., and the representation of an external thing. Yet you deceive only yourselves; for according to your own representations the transition from body to soul cannot be continuous, but must be made in a leap, which you purport to wish to avoid."[42] The nature of this unity between body and soul, as we shall see, will be one of the primary objects of *Naturphilosophie*.

Furthermore, the Cartesian division between subject and object eliminates what are the most basic realities of nature, namely, organisms. If the essence of the material world is inert particles that are moved by external forces, then we never have an integrated whole in which parts are internal to one another because of their sharing in a unifying principle, but only aggregates.[43] In Schelling's words, it is insufficient to view a living body "as an accidental aggregate of organized corpuscles, or a hydraulic machine, or a chemical laboratory."[44] If there is in fact organization, there must be an integrating principle that is not simply one of the processes being integrated. Schelling complained about the enthusiasm of the age for interpreting all organic manifestations as mere chemical processes (and indeed chemical processes as mere physicalistic events).[45] But he argues that chemical processes that occur in a living thing *presuppose* the life rather than explain it,[46] which is demonstrated by the fact that they cease

---

41. UD (KA.I.8.365).

42. Ideas, 178 (KA.I.5.81–82). We have here a succinct criticism of Schiller's early attempts to articulate a holistic anthropology by identifying a *Mittelkraft* between body and soul.

43. Ibid., 196 (KA.I.5.100–101)

44. Ibid., 197 (KA.I.5.101)

45. AS (W.3.357)

46. WS (KA.I.6.189)

when the organism is dead. It is better, then, to think of chemical processes as "imperfect organic processes," since they are derivative.[47] Outside of this derivation, chemistry would in fact lose its claim as a science, since the objects of chemistry do not appear to behave mechanistically in the manner of the objects of physics, which is, for example, why Kant did not allow it to have that status.[48] In short, if we draw an absolute distinction between subject and object, consciousness and matter, we become unable to grasp the integrated wholeness of things as intelligible, and in turn lose the foundation for the sciences. Indeed, insofar as the substantial reality of nature depends on the existence of integrated wholes that cannot be reduced to mere aggregates, we lose nature itself. According to Schelling, this can be avoided only if science *begins* with its roots in what is ultimate, which is the unity of subject and object. It is precisely this that *Naturphilosophie* takes as its founding principle.

If we do take the mechanism of physics as both the paradigm of rationality and for that reason the most basic description of the natural world, we may be led to posit, Schelling says, a kind of "vital force" to account for the organism that appears to transcend the bounds of mechanism:[49] after all, since it is impossible to imagine activity and life coming from "within" parts that are themselves inert and lifeless, it would be natural to supplement this conception of matter through the addition of some new energy, as it were. Because Schelling is sometimes taken to be a vitalist,[50] it is crucial to see why he so vehemently rejects this approach. In the first place, vitalism is not a critique of mechanism but essentially a concession to it. It takes life to be a significant factor only insofar as it intrudes as yet another physical force. In other words, it leaves in place the fundamental problem, namely, that of merely extrinsic relationships, and simply introduces another force that acts on things from the outside, albeit in a more mysterious fashion. Schelling explains that forces can be understood only in relation to other forces, and that the principle that integrates those relations cannot be itself a force—indeed, it cannot be physical at all, since

---

47. Ideas, 197 (KA.I.5.101).

48. Bach, *Biologie und Philosophie*, 241–46. Kant believed that chemistry is more a "systematic art" than a science: see the preface to his *Metaphysichen Anfangsgründe der Naturwissenschaft*. For a general discussion of Kant and chemistry, see Carrier, "Kants Theorie der Materie," 170–210.

49. Ideas, 197 (KA.I.5.102).

50. See Esposito, *Schelling's Idealism*, 11, and Richards, *The Romantic Conception of Life*, 293, in which Richards calls Schelling's position "a kind of synthesis of materialism and vitalism."

force is the highest activity in the physical realm, but must in some sense transcend this realm altogether.[51] The more serious problem, however, is that it undercuts Schelling's essential aim in developing a *Naturphilosophie*. The point of this philosophy is ultimately to overcome the simple separation between the world of spirit and the world of matter. As Grant has so clearly seen, the basis for a problematic two-world metaphysics is a two-worlds physics; that is, the positing of a chasm between the organic and the inorganic.[52] If one leaves the inorganic as, so to speak, sealed in itself and then tries to avoid materialism simply by "adding" further dimensions to one's account of nature, one in fact reinforces the very problem one seeks to resolve. The way to overcome materialism is not to emphasize something in addition to matter, but *to understand matter itself differently*. Physics is crucial for Schelling's philosophy of freedom precisely because it represents the hard case: if freedom is the beginning and end of philosophy, it will have something to do with reality in its most rudimentary forms, its matter and motion.

In the end, if we accept experimental physics understood in the mechanistic sense as the basic science of nature, we paradoxically no longer have science, nature, or even experiment (understood at least as having some connection to the sensible experience of things). Science thus conceived undermines itself and in this respect demands *of itself* what Schelling will call the philosophy of nature. To sum up the point being made here, it is helpful to consider Schelling's claim that empiricism (as scientific positivism) is necessarily bound to dogmatism (the loss of science in the strict sense) and mechanism (the loss of nature). In the *Ideas*, Schelling names "dogmatism" the position that "presupposes that all things are originally *present* outside ourselves (not *becoming* and *arising out of* ourselves)."[53] In other words, it takes the physical presence of things in their self-enclosed, individual existence as an absolute starting point for any further reflection, rather than seeing in things a reality that provokes inquiry of itself. But this means, of course, that the only sphere open to the mind regarding the things of nature is the sphere of their mechanical interaction: the understanding can do nothing other than record the pat-

---

51. See Ideas, 197 (KA.I.5.102). Schelling interestingly hesitates to call the principle "spiritual" for two reasons: it is not clear how spirit can act "on" matter, and so we are left with a new dualism, and also we would need in any event to find an additional principle of unity.

52. Grant, *Philosophies of Nature*, 15. See also Heuser-Kessler, "Schellings Organismusbegriff," 29–31.

53. Ideas, 190 (KA.I.5.93).

terns of the movements of these opaque bodies; that is, it will follow an essentially empirical method. Furthermore, if the ultimacy of bodies—i.e., irreducible bits of matter—is thus taken for granted, then the only possible interaction between things will be *extrinsic*: their relations to one another will be accidental to their own reality, which means that they can affect one another only "from the outside," in terms of the mechanism precisely of *force*. To insist on the appearance of things as the foundation of the study of nature, a foundation that is taken for granted rather than penetrated into by thought, is to absolutize mechanism as a view of the natural world: "As soon as [the dogmatist] raises himself above particular appearances his whole philosophy is finished; the limits of mechanism are also the limits of his system."[54]

One might object that an account of things as "becoming or arising out of ourselves" is not the only alternative to dogmatism. Indeed, without further qualification, which Schelling will provide as his thinking matures, this claim seems no different in principle from Fichte's idealism. Schelling will eventually make this difference explicit. In any event, his intention in the *Ideas* is not to develop his own idealism but simply to insist that there has to be ultimately an *intrinsic* connection between subject and object in order for us to have knowledge of things in themselves, which is, in turn, the only alternative to taking them as opaque and independent things existing merely outside of us and therefore outside of one another—as simply "particular appearances." Schelling claims that physics, thus understood, limits itself to the surface of reality, the purely external.[55] To the extent that we fail to penetrate to this unity between subject and object, we can only see things as externally related, and thus only as interacting mechanistically. In a word, if one allows only the surface of things in the world to have significance for the intelligence, then nature can behave *only* mechanistically as far as one is able to see, insofar as surfaces can interact only, quite literally, superficially. In this respect, Schelling's criticism would extend not only to banal empiricism of, say, scientific positivism, but even to the "critical empiricism," which is the counterpart to a Kantian transcendental idealism. The only possibility of avoiding mechanism is to allow a "speculative" access to the internal reality of nature.[56] Here,

---

54. Ideas, 190 (KA.I.5.93).

55. EEE (KA.I.8.32–33).

56. Joseph Lawrence claims that Schelling's *Naturphilosophie* implies that nature, and above all the organism, remains *essentially* inaccessible to philosophy, but he seems to take for granted an essentially Kantian view of reason (*Schellings Philosophie*, 57). For Schelling, the constructive activity that belongs to reason is in fact a participation

once again, we see what Schelling would claim to be an indispensable demand for the "speculative" physics he develops as an essential part of his *Naturphilosophie*. The only alternative to seeing things superficially, for Schelling, is to view them "arising out of ourselves." To understand how this insistence does not commit him to a kind of subjective idealism, we must consider his critique of this approach to philosophy, why the lack in this current of transcendental philosophy prompted, with the lack in the newly emerging experimental science, the development of his *Naturphilosophie*. Before turning to this in the next main section, we will reflect on the broader implications of the subject-object dualism for nature.

B. Mechanism and the Death of the Cosmos

Positivism in science entails what Schelling identified as the fundamental problem of the age, and thus the main reason for the *Naturphilosophie*. He named this problem "mechanism," but also referred to it as the death of matter, which means the death of nature *tout court*. His diagnosis comes to take the form, in his middle period, of a radical critique of the Western tradition, which in many surprising respects anticipates that of both Nietzsche and Heidegger.[57] A particularly suggestive statement of this

---

within nature's own productivity, so that reason always thinks from *within* nature. In this respect, it is never left outside. See UD (KA.I.8.297–98, 365) and Schelling's claim that the question of the nature of construction is the most important in philosophy: *Über die Construktion in der Philosophie* (W.3.545). This notion of construction lies at the basis of what Edward Beach has described as the "empathetic" method that represents Schelling's most characteristic mode of thought: "The Later Schelling's Concept of Dialectical Method," 35–54.

57. Like Schelling, Nietzsche and Heidegger acknowledge a health and depth in the most ancient Greek thinkers, and identify Plato as, in some respect, the beginning of the "error" (as Nietzsche puts it) that essentially defines Western civilization. Though we cannot explore this fascinating connection here, it is important to see that Schelling differs from these others, on this score, in at least three respects: first, he does not blame Plato himself but rather a vulgarization of Plato that has its paradigm in Descartes' dualism (cf., Schelling's mention of Plato in contrast to Descartes in his WA (1815), 50 [W.4.646]); second, far from taking Christianity to represent the highpoint of the error ("Platonism for the people"), Schelling takes Christianity to be the fullness of truth, even if he affirms a kind of gnostic version of it in some respects; third, while Nietzsche and Heidegger seem to imply that the original insights of the ancient thinkers were lost until their own philosophies, Schelling affirms that the "one, true philosophy"—which is arguably, in its essence, the philosophy of Plotinus—has survived over time, even if championed by only a marginal few or even a persecuted One. It is not an accident that Schelling names his dialogue *Bruno*, after the Renaissance Neo-Platonist Giordanno Bruno who was burned at the stake for his divinizing the cosmos.

problem comes toward the end of the *Bruno*, which is no doubt Schelling's most perfectly achieved work, if not his most significant. This dialogue, clearly inspired above all by the Platonic dialogue, the *Timaeus*, which Schelling had commented on as a student,[58] presents a comprehensive metaphysical cosmology emerging through a conversation between various speakers, each of which represents a partial perspective that finds its fulfillment in its being reconciled with the others in the whole.[59] He had argued over the course of the dialogue that there could in the end be only one philosophy—a point to which we will return—and so what may seem to be various philosophies are in fact various perspectives on that one philosophy, which are properly understood then only in light of that basic unity. Alexander, the last character to present his perspective, represents materialism. According to him, the truth about matter was lost in some sense already with Plato.[60] The so-called pre-Socratic thinkers understood that matter was part of a whole, and so ultimately inseparable from form.[61] In this unity with form, matter is, not a mere substrate, but a philosophical *principle*. The basic confusion arose when philosophers began to associate matter with body, which defines itself over-against the soul. It is easy, then, to move from there to the identification of matter with what Schelling calls "raw inorganic stuff." Once this move is made, we have rendered impossible the primordial insight that body and soul, and within the body, the inorganic and the organic, were distinctions within the original *unity* of matter.[62] Now, they are oppositions, only one fragmented piece of which is taken to be matter.

What are the consequences of this fragmentation? Schelling claims that it is "the death of all science," and it is this, as we shall see, because it represents the death of reason: mechanism means that reason no longer has itself the order of an organism, but gets reduced to a power, specifically, the sheer power to introduce (mechanical) change. Schelling details

---

58. Schelling, *"Timaeus"* (1794). On this commentary, see Viganó, "Schelling liest Platons '*Timaeus*,'" 227–35, and Franz, *Schellings Tübinger Platon-Studien*.

59. See Michael Vater's detailed presentation of the dialogue and its main argument in the substantial introduction he wrote to his translation: *Bruno*, 3–107, esp., 17–69.

60. As we pointed out in footnote 57 above, Schelling qualifies this judgment of Plato. The character Alexander in the dialogue also praises Plato for his understanding of Eros as "the child of Wealth and Poverty," which he says expresses the "relation that obtains between matter and the original forms": *Bruno*, 206 (W.3.207).

61. *Bruno*, 207–8 (W.3.209).

62. Ibid., 206 (W.3.206–7).

the fragmentation implied by what would now be known as "mechanism" thus:

> Once matter was killed and its bare image replaced the [living] reality, the notion almost automatically evolved that forms are all impressed on matter from without. And since forms were thought to be purely external, and since there was thought to be nothing eternal over and beyond them, the forms had to be posited as unchangeable. In this way, the inner unity and affinity of all things was annihilated, and the world fragmented into an endless aggregate of fixed differences, until the general conception finally prevailed that the living totality of the universe is like a receptacle or chamber, in which things are placed in such a way that they do not participate in one another, nor live in community with each other, nor interact with each other.[63]

If matter does not possess an *original unity* with form, which implies both that matter always-already has an internal relation to form (i.e., that its own meaning *includes* its participation in form, and conversely that form itself always-already shares in matter so that this relation is likewise constitutive of its own most original meaning), then the two can, of course, be brought together only extrinsically. This means that forms, on the one hand, turn out to be eternally fixed "identities," which, as always-already set, and thus self-enclosed, necessarily possess what we could call an "atomistic" existence. Matter, on the other hand, turns out to be nothing more than an opaque object, which, lacking any internal relation to form, cannot "mean" anything in itself, cannot invite the mind's communion, but can present something for the mind only in its external activity. The upshot is twofold: life is henceforward excluded, at one stroke, from the universe as far as the human mind is concerned because life depends on and in fact in some sense *is* nothing more than the integration of form and matter. Similarly, there can be no more genuine community in the cosmos because community depends on a priori unity in the particular sense that communion means intimacy, intimacy means *internal relation*, and internal relation requires that things related not already be complete, self-enclosed, "fixed" identities prior to their encounter. They must, in other words, each be capable of *including* the other in themselves as part of their *own* meaning. Things—whatever sort they may be, from atoms to human beings—make contact with one another only in terms of their surfaces. Schelling's claim is a startling one, then: the domination of the empirical

---

63. Ibid., 209 (W.3.211).

method in physics, when followed out to its furthest implications, means the end of all intimacy. This loss of intimacy entails the impoverishment of spirit to which we shall turn in a moment.

Schelling goes on in this passage from the *Bruno* to explain that this reductive materialism entails the domination of "death": "Since men agreed that, in the beginning, matter was dead, it was decided that death was the principle governing all things, and that life was just a derivative phenomenon."[64] Though he does not explain this implication, it is not difficult to fill in the gaps. "Matter" is indeed the most obvious feature of things in the world, and in the positivistic method physical things allow themselves to be described exclusively in terms of their most obvious features, precisely because what we could call "internal" meanings by definition do not obtrude phenomenally. As Plato saw a long time ago, it is possible to give in one respect a complete account of Socrates' being in jail by describing the nature of his bones, muscles, and ligaments and their respective positions.[65] Schelling similarly allows that one could explain the origin of a Homeric poem through a description of the shapes of the letters and an account of how they are connected and printed on the page.[66] In this case, however, if matter is identified with mechanistic externality and then in turn associated with rational explanation, life will necessarily become a function of what is taken to be real, in this case, raw "stuff"; it will then become derivative, a kind of "epiphenomenon" of "dead" matter. In this respect, there is no such thing as a *separation* between the organic and the inorganic, because the very positing of the separation "kills" the organic, and the inorganic gets juxtaposed only to what no longer exists. In contemporary thought, it is common to criticize the "excesses" of mechanism by showing how, for example, mental phenomena cannot in the end be reduced to mere brain-states, or, apparently more fundamentally, organisms betray features of "intelligent design" insofar as they exhibit a complexity that could not have arisen, as it were, piecemeal. Those who make these claims tend to concede, however, that in most cases a "scientific" account of things is adequate within its limited sphere. For Schelling, however, this approach to the problem of mechanism, far from solving it, *reinforces* the most fundamentally problematic features of the matter. As we stressed at the outset, a genuine philosophy of nature has to begin with

---

64. Ibid. For a similar judgment, see Jonas, "Life, Death, and the Body in the Theory of Being," 9–12.

65. Plato, *Phaedo*, 98c–d.

66. AS (W.3.343).

what is most basic, and this means it must show how the reality of life and freedom is analogously present in the rudiments of the physical world, in matter and motion. If these are simply neglected in themselves as opaque to the intelligence, the real roots of life and freedom will be severed.[67]

As surprising as it may seem to us, for Schelling the very symbol of the death of the cosmos and undermining of all human intimacy is Newton's *Optics*.[68] Whereas light had traditionally represented the most basic presence of life, or "ideality" in the physical sphere,[69] it becomes in

---

67. Again, Hans Jonas has made the same observation, which is worth quoting at length: "One expects to encounter the term [freedom] in the area of mind and will, and not before: but if mind is prefigured in the organic from the beginning, then freedom is. And indeed our contention is that even metabolism, the basic level of all organic existence, exhibits it: that it is itself the first form of freedom. These must sound strange words to most readers, and I do not expect it otherwise. For what could be further from freedom, further from will and choice which are required for it by any normal understanding of the word, than the blind automatism of the chemistry carried out in the depths of our bodies? Yet it will be the burden of one part of our discourse to show that it is in the dark stirrings of primeval organic substance that a principle of freedom shines forth for the first time within the vast necessity of the physical universe—a principle foreign to suns, planets, and atoms. Obviously, all consciously 'mental' connotations must at first be kept away from the concept when used for so comprehensive a principle: 'Freedom' must denote an objectively discernable mode of being, i.e., a manner of executing existence, distinctive of the organic *per se* and thus shared by all members but by no nonmembers of the class: an ontologically descriptive term which can apply to mere physical evidence at first. Yet, even as such it must not be unrelated to the meaning it has in the human sphere whence it is borrowed, else its extended use would be frivolous. For all their physical objectivity, the traits described by it on the primitive level constitute the ontological foundation, and already an adumbration, of those more elevated phenomena that more directly invite and more manifestly qualify for the noble name; and these still remain bound to the humble beginnings as to the condition of their possibility. Thus the first appearance of the principle in its bare, elementary object-form signifies the break-through of being to the indefinite range of possibilities which hence stretches to the farthest reaches of subjective life, and as a whole stands under the sign of 'freedom,'" ("On the Subjects of a Philosophy of Life," 3). The resonance with Schelling's *Naturphilosophie* could not be clearer. Nevertheless, two qualifications must be made here: on the one hand, while Jonas insists on a strict separation between the organic and inorganic, Schelling, as we will see, interprets the organic itself as the unfolding of the inorganic. On the other hand, Jonas's description suggests he conceives of freedom yet in "possibilistic" terms.

68. To see this, one must connect his judgment of Newton's optics in the *Lectures on the Method of Academic Studies*—"Newton's optics is the greatest proof of the possibility that an entire building may be constructed out of false inferences, a building that is grounded in all of its parts on experience and experiment" (W.3.352)—and his pointing to the mechanistic conception of light as spelling the death of the cosmos in the *Bruno* (209 [W.3.211]).

69. Plotinus, for instance, explains that fire is the highest element because it is a material expression of the ideal: see *Ennead* I.6.3. Schelling characterizes light,

Newton's experiments a wholly mechanical reality, the mere production of forces acting on dead bits of matter. As is well known, Goethe was horrified by Newton's theory on this point above all, and the passion with which certain philosophers engaged the controversy would be perhaps difficult to understand without this background.[70] As Schelling's analysis reveals, there is much more at stake in the nature of light than simply the nature of light: in the balance is the nature of nature itself, and in turn, of course, the nature of freedom.

The point, in short, that Schelling is trying to make in the *Bruno*, and indeed in his *Naturphilosophie* more generally, is that "materialism," understood as Alexander presents it in the dialogue, is an essential aspect of a comprehensive philosophy. In this sense of the term, moreover, materialism means an interpretation of matter in relation to what is ultimate—in other words, a specifically *philosophical*, or as he would say, "speculative," account of matter. If matter is separated out as belonging to the domain of experimental science, while more "meaningful" questions are given to philosophy, as it were, in compensation, it is not simply that matter will no longer be understood in its inner depth, but in fact the philosophical questions will turn out to be less "meaningful" than one had initially assumed. Once again, the problems in our view of nature will bear bad fruit in our view of freedom. Let us now turn to investigate more closely the subjective implications of the split between the real and the ideal.

IV. The Impoverishment of Spirit

A. The Problem of Subjective Idealism

Given Schelling's insistence on overcoming the inner deficiency of experimental science by accounting for nature "from within" our consciousness,

---

similarly, as subjectivity itself as it exists in nature, and thus as an analogy in the extended world for *Geist*: HMP, 119 (W.5.175). For a reflection on the meaning of light and its implications for philosophy in the oldest Greek text, namely, Homer's *Iliad*, see Schindler, "Homer's Truth," 161–82.

70. Note, for example, the sharpness of Hegel's critique of Newton in the *Encyclopedia* philosophy of nature (E [1817], §221 [GW.13.134–35]), which betrays a passion that exceeds anything else in that text. Schelling's own appreciation of Goethe's theory is more complex. Though, on the one hand, he shared Goethe's horror regarding Newton's optics, he criticizes a view, presumably Goethe's, that would take light to be merely "simple" in itself, and to become differentiated only through the introduction of something external (shadow). For Schelling, everything basic must be already relational in itself: see EE (KA.I.7.95).

we might think that Schelling would develop an idealism that deduced the natural world from the exigencies of his own subjectivity. But Schelling was convinced from the beginning of the inadequacy of this approach.[71] His conviction about this inadequacy arose not simply from within his own reflection on the subject matter, but in dialogue with other thinkers, and so requires a more historical elaboration. Schelling shared with Fichte the conviction regarding the need to get beyond Kant's doctrine of the "thing-in-itself." As Schelling explains it in his later lectures, Kant's theory ends up with a plurality of supersensible "things," without ever explaining how they relate. In essence, we have what we might call the foundation of subjectivity (*Ding-an-sich* as the immortal soul, as the essence of freedom) and the foundation of objectivity (*Ding-an-sich* as the independent reality of the world) as separate "objects," but no account of their reciprocal relation (*Ding-an-sich* as God).[72] One of the early Fichte's most original and distinctive concerns was to "win back" the systematic unity of knowledge by deriving the whole from a single principle, which for Fichte was the spontaneous activity of the individual self positing a not-self, and then relating the two.[73] It might seem that Schelling initially followed Fichte in this endeavor, but from the beginning his emphasis lay more on an "absolute" starting point than on the individual "I," which led him, unlike Fichte, to draw in a creative way primarily from Spinoza and Leibniz.[74] Nevertheless, he was entirely at one with Fichte in his belief that freedom is the highest, that one can never account for freedom as a product of something other than it, and that the absoluteness of freedom depended on the ability to successfully derive the whole from a single principle: for if freedom is simply a *part* of the whole, it will turn out to be derivative, and derivative freedom is simply a contradiction.[75]

71. Zaborowski, "Geschichte," 43.
72. HMP, 102 (W.5.154).
73. See Henrich, "Fichte's Original Insight," 15–53.
74. Schelling appears to follow Fichte especially in his early essay, "Vom Ich als Princip der Philosophie und über das Unbedingte im menschlichen Wissen," in which he argues, for example, that "the I contains all being, all reality" (KA.I.2.111). But in fact even here Schelling is trying to expand the I, as it were, into a kind of absolute synthesis. As Jean-Marie Vaysse observes, "Schelling contra Hegel," 364, in the *Philosophical Letters*, at any rate, Schelling begins not with the I's self-positing, but with an original positing of the I and not-I.
75. Schelling is very clear about this point in his early writings (see "Vom Ich," KA.I.2.90, in which he explains that the "I" can never be an object, and so is absolute). He qualifies this position substantially, however, by the time of the *Freiheitsschrift*, in which he affirms that the notion of a "derivative absolute" is the central concept of all

As Aristotle may have predicted, however, the subtle divergence at the beginning led to a great difference in the end, and so Schelling eventually broke with Fichte. The point of contention centered on the question of the need for a *Naturphilosophie* as relatively independent of a philosophy of consciousness.[76] The fact that the break, which was no doubt inevitable, was so long in coming shows that Schelling understood his *Naturphilosophie* as *demanded* by the starting point he shared with Fichte, and so he held onto the belief that Fichte would come to adopt his endeavor himself as soon as they succeeded in overcoming superficial misunderstandings. This hope led to the dialogue *Bruno*, discussed above. Here, Schelling attempted to demonstrate that Fichte's perspective, represented by Lucian, and his own, represented by the character Bruno, were only seemingly opposed, but in fact were ultimately reconciled with each other in the whole. When Fichte rejected even this attempt at reconciliation, Schelling finally published a forceful and explicit criticism of the direction he saw Fichte taking, significantly calling the piece, not a rejection of Fichte, but an *improvement* of Fichte's ideas: "Exposition of the True Relationship of the Philosophy of Nature to the Improved Version of Fichte's Doctrine," published in 1806. Again, Schelling always saw his *Naturphilosophie* as an unfolding of the inner logic of, not an external supplement to, the transcendental standpoint.

The heart of the matter in fact turns on the very point of his difference with Fichte, and elaborating it shows the inadequacy of transcendentalism that Schelling saw his own philosophy as filling. As Schelling explains the philosophy in this essay, Fichte seeks to overcome Kant's dualism by recovering a dynamic notion of subjectivity. Thus, the subject, at its deepest level, is not the empty stillness of the thing-in-itself—what Hegel will eventually describe as abstract subjectivity—but is rather a kind of *event or activity*. He can affirm it as such because it "becomes" what it *is*, and it does so by positing an other outside of itself, namely, being, the object, or nature, and then overcoming this opposition. Its unity consists

---

philosophy (Freedom, 228 [W.4.239] [B, 20]).

76. Hegel's "Habilitation," so to speak, on the "Difference between the Fichtean and Schellingian Systems," which Hegel wrote in Jena while working with Schelling on the *Kritische Journal*, speaks in the preface about the "need for a philosophy that will recompense nature for the mishandling it suffered in Kant's and Fichte's systems" (DS, 83 [GW.4.8]). For Fichte, from the highest standpoint, "nature has the character of absolute objectivity, that is, of death" (DS, 140 [GW.4.51]). In 1833, in a review of the history of modern philosophy, Schelling claims as one of his main achievements to have rescued nature "from death" by revealing it to be autonomous and self-positing: HMP, 130–31 (W.5.191).

in the activity of self-positing, an event that includes within itself both the self and its other. This conception of the self would seem, then, in principle capable of having a world, that is, a whole in which subject and object are united even in their opposition to one another. But in Schelling's eyes, this is a deceptive appearance, and the problem he identifies in it, as subtle as it may at first seem, has radical implications both for Fichte's philosophy and (as we will see at greater length in the chapter that follows) also for what is called Schelling's "late" philosophy. According to Schelling, Fichte rightly understands that opposition of some form is indispensable for a dynamic sense of the subject, which is, in turn, crucial for a "productive," that is, a "non-inert" principle of reality. The problem is that Fichte sees this opposition as something *achieved* rather than as something simply *given* from the first. But if it is not in some sense given from the first, then it is in fact second, which means that it is not the ultimate principle of reality. This point may seem quite subtle in the context of Fichte's view of the subject as "self-positing," insofar as he seems to want to say that this complex event is itself, in some sense, first, so that the achieved is, as it were, always already accomplished. However this may be, our purpose here is not primarily to interpret Fichte, but to understand Schelling in light of his evaluation of Fichte. As Schelling insightfully points out, the fact that Fichte, in effect, places all "life" on the side of the self-affirming subject and, as a consequence, makes the objectivity of being in essence nothing more than a lifeless foil for the subject, reveals that the principle of reality is itself in its most original essence something lifeless, regardless of what is made of it secondarily (or, in fact, *precisely because* something has to be made of it secondarily). As he puts it, for Fichte, being in itself is first "simple"—that is, without relation and therefore inert—and *for that very reason* has to come *out* of itself in order to be alive.[77]

Identifying this problem in Fichte points up one of the most basic originating aims of Schelling's *Naturphilosophie*: in order to affirm *life*, and thus *freedom*, as absolute, the principle of reality cannot itself be merely simple, but must always already be in some sense oppositional within itself. If being is already a complex life, then the other that faces the self will never be an inert object but will necessarily reflect back to the subject the very life that it possesses in itself, albeit according to a different order (namely, as "objectified"). Being other is therefore already part of being self, and so the other that the self encounters in the realm of the object will reveal something familiar even in its strangeness. The proper disposition to

77. Anti-Fichte (W.3.663)

nature, Schelling concludes, is not the smugness of the master, but *piety*.[78] The world, in its very worldliness, bears traces of the divine, the origin of all things—including all subjectivity. If the difference between Fichte and Schelling appears subtle in some places, it becomes quite evident on this point. Fichte's "teleological" view of nature, which sees it from first to last as an instrument of some purpose outside of it, far from overcoming the lifeless nature of mechanism, seals it forever shut.[79] Nature there evinces value only insofar as it can demonstrate its utility, and whether that be for God's or man's use, the outcome is the same: it is wholly reducible to the subject. While Fichte stubbornly resisted Schelling's promptings in this direction because he thought that the life given to nature would be so far taken from the subject, and that we would therefore be forced back to the Kantian dualism it is the very point of the transcendental turn to overcome, Schelling reveals that the very opposite is the case for subjectivity. To hold onto its life is to lose it.

Schelling's later assessment of Fichte's thought in the lectures on the history of modern philosophy delivered in Munich in the early to mid thirties is more easily grasped once we have understood this fundamental point. The most obvious complaint against the "pure" transcendentalism of Fichte is that it would seem to collapse into the most banal sort of subjectivism: if the entire world is derived, not simply from the "absolute I," but in fact from my very self, it would seem to make the world the product of my whim and nothing more. Fichte countered that charge by showing that the self would lose its subjectivity, its freedom, if it were not en-countered by a non-self that imposed a necessity which provoked that freedom. For Fichte, because that non-self is thereby *produced* by the self, it remains within the transcendental subject and therefore remains entirely a factor of the subject's ideas, his deliberate will. But, for Schelling, to affirm this is precisely to compromise the *necessity* that the self needs; we can "feel" the imposition only if it is outside of our explicit vision and deliberate "willful" activity. It must therefore arise from a nature that *exceeds* the will:

> The absolute idealist cannot avoid thinking of the I as *dependent* in relation to its ideas (*Vorstellungen*) if [sic] the external world—even if it is not dependent on a thing in itself, as Kant called it, or on a cause outside itself, it is at least dependent on

---

78. Anti-Fichte (W.3.703).

79. Anti-Fichte (W.3.704). Schelling, to be sure, does not reject teleology altogether, but only an instrumentalist understanding of it, as becomes clear, for example, in his discussion of nature in the *System of Transcendental Idealism*.

> an inner necessity, and if Fichte attributes a production of those ideas to the I, then this must at least be a production which is blind and not grounded in the *will* but rather in the *nature* of the I. Fichte showed himself unconcerned about all this, he related to necessity as a whole more like someone who indignantly negated it than someone who explained it. Left now to take up philosophy where Fichte had left it, I had to see above all how that undeniable and inevitable necessity, which Fichte, so to speak, only tried to scare off with words, could be united with Fichtean concepts, thus with the assertion of the absolute substance of the I.[80]

This move, again apparently subtle, has profound implications, which we can illuminate by comparison with Schelling's critique of empiricism: we can no longer think of the subject as "ready-made" entering a world of objects in itself anymore than we can think of objects simply as ready-made. As we saw above, to do so is to make all relations extrinsic, which means *secondary*, which means in turn to eliminate from the universe—from *both* the subject *and* the object—the life that depends on internal relation. What we need to do, by contrast, is realize that the subject "emerges" out of the object, just as the object "emerges" out of the subject, or better yet, to see that they both emerge into their own unique identity out of an original identity that always-already and non-reductively includes both. This is why Schelling insists in his historical account of Fichte's thought that he was lacking a "history of consciousness," an account of the genesis of subjectivity[81]—which would, of course, be for Fichte, as he never tired of complaining, a total misunderstanding of the nature of freedom.

We may mention here, moreover, one of the more distant implications of the separation of the subject from the object for our understanding of the nature of subjectivity. If the subject is indeed understood in separation from objectivity, then freedom will be understood in separation from nature. According to Schelling, this separation will incline us to see human activity itself in the superficial terms of empiricism. We might interpret the origins of the new science to emerge in the nineteenth century, namely, sociology, as having its roots in the phenomenon Schelling describes here. His focus is the novel approach to history that was becoming standard at the time. If nature is conceived wholly outside of freedom, then freedom in turn lies wholly outside of nature. If, moreover, nature is viewed mechanistically, which means as subject from first to last to the

---

80. HMP, 108–9 (W.5.162–63).
81. HMP, 109–10 (W.5.164–65).

external determination of laws, then freedom will turn out to be its simple opposite; that is, it will turn out to be utterly "lawless," as Schelling shows in the *Bruno*.[82] But to be lawless means to be without any determination. For Schelling, it follows that, once we conceive of freedom in isolation from nature, freedom will no longer be a revelation of any internal order, that is, it will not be intelligible in itself. Instead, since freedom thereby becomes, as it were, totally "open-ended," it can be significant for the intelligence only in terms of its surface. Just as mechanistic physics does not allow the mind to penetrate into natural things but only record the external shape of their behavior, so too does the novel approach to history refrain from trying to understand the inner nature of historical figures, but simply observes their outward deeds.[83] This view of freedom thus leads one to look only at the products of freedom as so many facts, with only an accidental or in any event superficial connection to one another: "The freedom that one seeks or thinks one sees in empirical action is just as little true freedom, and is just as deceptive, as is the truth one thinks one has in empirical knowledge."[84] The study of history, then, becomes the purely empirical one of gathering and rearranging facts, and thus one justifies one's scholarship, not by penetrating more deeply into the meaning of things—which is an approach that would encourage a community of thinkers—but by uncovering "new" facts or indeed spinning a "novel" interpretation of the old ones:

> In the same way as nature had been turned into mere externality, into a game without any inner life, without a real life-interest, people liked no less to make history appear as the most contingent game of lawless arbitrariness, of a meaningless and pointless hustle and bustle; indeed the scholar who most emphasized the senselessness, indeed the absurdity of history, was regarded as the most intelligent, and the bigger the event, the more sublime the historical phenomenon was, the smaller, the more contingent and base were the causes that he could come up with to explain it.[85]

---

82. Bruno, 202 (W.3.202).

83. With great insight, Henry B. Veatch presents the character that historical explanation acquires when the modern logic of relation (beginning with Hume) comes to replace classical, substance-based logic and therefore when scientific knowing replaces humanistic knowing in *Two Logics*, 222–41.

84. AS (W.3.244).

85. HMP, 131 (W.5.191–92).

This is precisely the sort of study of history that Schiller had famously attacked a few years earlier in his inaugural lecture at the University of Jena, lamenting the loss of its philosophical dimension and its degenerating into what he called a *"Brotwissenschaft."*[86] For Schelling, if we wish to avoid an intrinsically senseless notion of freedom, we have to include a philosophical penetration of nature within transcendental philosophy, which entails a view of freedom that reflects the order of nature, just as nature reflects the shape of freedom.

B. Mechanism and the Fragmentation of Reason

What people generally think of as the *birth* of science, at least in its proper modern form, Schelling refers to as its *death*. Indeed, he calls it the death, not only of physics or the natural sciences, but of *all* science—i.e., the death of intelligence simply. Before we begin to elaborate the principles of Schelling's response to the problem of mechanism, it is important to follow out his claim, to see why the split between subject and object leads to the unraveling, so to speak, of the human spirit generally. In a celebrated series of lectures that Schelling gave in Jena the same year he published the *Bruno*, called "On the Method of Academic Studies," Schelling argues that the vitality of any particular discipline, or in his language, "science," depends on an integrated connection to all the others in relation to a center. He elaborates that center as the primordial unity of the ideal and real, which is, of course, the founding principle of *Naturphilosophie* itself, and indeed of Schelling's philosophy simply. The sciences, as we shall shortly see, receive a creative impulse from this center because it is so to speak the "soul" of the sciences, which establishes the particular identity of that science and in so doing gives that science its own life. By contrast, if a science is detached from this animating center, its intelligibility will no longer be due to the illumination it receives from this internal life-giving principle, but will shift, so to speak, to the surfaces, as we have seen with regard to the study of matter and of history. If the one reality that the various sciences study, as Aristotle says, under different aspects atrophies

---

86. Schiller distinguished between *"Brotgelehrter"* and *"philosophische Köpfe"* in the approach to history in his famous inaugural address, which he delivered as he took up his position as a professor of History at Jena in 1789. Significantly, he had used the term *"Brotwissenschaft"* in his dissertation from the Karlsschule to describe a purely technical approach to medicine that assumes a mechanistic understanding of the human being: see his *Versuch über den Zusammenhang der tierischen Natur des Menschen mit seiner geistigen* (SW.8.40).

from neglect, those sciences will begin to bear evidence of this in their increased isolation from one another and their loss of ultimate significance. What is "objective" in the various sciences will be the superficiality of inert "facts," and the "subjectivity" will be added only, as it were, from the outside in the form of the manipulation of those facts.

Schelling's focus, in the first few lectures, is the effect on the student of this detachment from a center: the more the student desires a sense of the whole, the more he will have the impression at the university "of a chaos, in which he cannot yet make out anything particular, or of a vast ocean, into which he finds himself transposed without a compass or a guiding star."[87] In a fragmented university, students will necessarily become passive because no living engagement—no community or intimacy—with purely external things is possible, and one's activity in their regard can consist essentially of nothing more than the "recording" of what is already complete in itself. Such information can then in turn justify itself only in relation to its capacity to produce some outcome. In other words, one of the implications of the loss of a center—and so a division between subject and object—is the instrumentalization of knowledge and the relentless subordination of theory to praxis.[88] We recall here Schiller's insight into the meaning of a free "*Darstellung*" and the reader's free engagement with it, which we called a *dramatic* style; the absence of a dramatic encounter between the author and reader makes learning the lifeless repetition of empty content. By contrast to this mere passive reproduction, Schelling lays down the ultimate rule of what we could call genuine academic freedom: "All the rules one could proscribe for the student can be summed up in a single one: study only in order to be able to create yourself."[89] Schelling articulates this rule after having distinguished the historical (material) aspect of study from the philosophical (formal) aspect, and says, like Schiller, that one has truly appropriated the material only when one can give it living form: "Genuine reception is complete, not when one reproduces the given material in its given, particular form, which must be learned, but only when one reproduces it in one's own form that comes to be from oneself."[90] What he means by this is that the proper intellectual grasp of a thing is an appropriation of it from the inside, which presupposes that the matter indeed *has* an inside. And because the "inside" of things is the

87. AS (W.3.233).
88. AS (W.3.233–44).
89. AS (W.3.263).
90. AS (W.3.263).

absolute principle, which unites subject and object in a productive activity, the proper understanding of reality will perfectly coincide with a creative radiation of it further, since understanding is in fact an inward appropriation of its originating principle. Schelling insists that the separation of theory and praxis, contemplation and action, rests on a basic misunderstanding of nature. At the heart of the world, these are one, and the ultimate point of the academy is intellectual intimacy with reality, that is, to come to know, appropriate, and give creative expression to, its living heart.

It must be noted here in passing, however, that there is an ambiguity present in Schelling's formulation about the centrality of creativity in knowing, insofar as it creates some tension with the receptivity that would necessarily follow from the absolute priority of the absolute over the particular realization. How different, in the end, is Schelling's rule, "Study only to create!," from the constant refrain that he so sharply criticizes: "Act! Act!"?[91] We will address this ambiguity, which we will see repeated at every turn in Schelling's *Naturphilosophie*, in chapter 4, but for now it is important to see the point of his affirmation. The life of the sciences, and thus the life of the university in general, depends on the reality of a unifying center, the relation to which is what specifies the science called philosophy.

It is crucial to see that what is at stake in the question of the nature of nature is very much the "life" of the university, on which depends more generally the life of the mind—for, as we recall, "life," whether of art or of nature, means for Schelling (as for Schiller) that both the whole and each of the parts has a life of its own as well: "The relation of individual parts in the closed and organic whole of philosophy is like that of the various figures in a perfectly constructed poetic work, where each, in being a member of the whole, is at the same time, as a perfect reflection of that whole, absolute and independent in itself."[92] Because of the nature of the philosophy that holds the center, so to speak, each particular science becomes *more independent* the more it is approached philosophically, because to approach it philosophically means to interpret it as an expression of what is ultimate, which means in turn to appropriate it from its own principle: "By means of this primal knowledge, all other knowing lies in the absolute and becomes itself absolute."[93] At the same time, as the sciences become independent they nevertheless always reveal an inner interdependence on

---

91. AS (W.3.240).
92. 1802 System (W.3.527).
93. AS (W.3.238).

one another—which is natural, insofar as what gives them their independence is the very same thing that unites them, namely, the absolute that represents the end of philosophy. Schelling does not elaborate examples of this interdependence in much detail anywhere in his work, but one can find a few suggestive instances. In this series of lectures, after elaborating the philosophical principle of the center, he presents the implications for the study of theology, history and law, the natural sciences and medicine, and art.[94] He observes that the study of physics and psychology should not be separated from one another, since their simple separation implies a dualistic division between body and soul.[95] While this may seem to some an anticipation of, say, cognitive science and even more of "neurophilosophy," it is significantly different insofar as what Schelling proposes entails a transformation of the physics to which psychology is united. An obvious counterexample to the more common contemporary version of this body-soul holism would be Schelling's exposition in the *System of Transcendental Idealism*, in which he develops the nature of the world, from the ground up, as it were, in perfect tandem with the nature of the powers of the soul.[96] Further, Schelling claims that a proper *Naturphilosophie* will bear an intrinsic relation even to poetry, and thus calls for poets and scientists to work together.[97] Perhaps the most concrete example we have of a "Schellingian" transformation of a particular discipline, in this case the interpretation of literature, is his essay on Dante, appropriately titled, "On Dante in Relation to Philosophy."[98]

94. Art was a topic of particular interest to Schelling because of its capacity to integrate: see his lecture series *Philosophy of Art*, his important lecture *On the Relationship of the Plastic Arts to Nature*, and his discussion of art in the *System of Transcendental Idealism*, in which art is presented as the organ of philosophy: on this, see Velkley, "Realizing Nature," 149–68. The *Philosophy of Art* lectures are especially interesting in this context, for, as is often observed, much of the *content* of his view of art was cribbed from Schlegel; but in fact Schelling's appropriation of this material from his distinctive philosophical perspective transforms it and gives it a creative impulse rather than making it simply a historical study of a variety of forms. Schelling himself was convinced that his was the *first* philosophy of art in history (see Phil of Art, 11–12 [W.3.381]), in the particular sense of a philosophy of *poēsis*, the productive activity of the artist, rather than, he claims, the empirical psychology in English and French thinkers.

95. AS (W.3.292–93).

96. See his three epochs of the history of consciousness, from original sensation to productive intuition, then to reflection, and finally to the absolute act of will: STI, 51–154 (KA.I.9-1.92–229).

97. See his "Anhang zu den vorstehenden Aufsatz," KA.I.8.249–50.

98. W.3.572–83.

The Perfection of Freedom

Schelling's grand proposal for a new idea of the university marks a significant moment, indeed, in the historical development of the self-understanding of the university insofar as it aims to recover the *unity* of knowledge, which characterized the first universities in the middle ages, but to do so for the first time after the fragmentation of specialization and according to an explicit philosophical principle. But for this very reason, one might object that it tyrannizes the variety of the sciences with the "unquestionable" absoluteness of philosophy, and thus threatens their integrity. It is important, then, to see that, at least in principle, philosophy is a sine qua non for the preservation of that integrity, and indeed for the unity of reason in general. *If* we do not view each of the sciences as an expression of the absolute in a particular respect, and so according to its own particular inner "laws," in Schelling's words, we evacuate those sciences of their *soul*, because we separate them from an internal principle.[99] "Every bit of knowledge," he says, "and every particular discipline is embraced within this whole as an organic part; and thus any knowledge that is not somehow, whether in an immediate or mediated way and regardless of the number of intervening links, connected to the primal knowledge, is without significance."[100] What we are left with, as we have just seen, is merely a variety of outward appearances, a series of disconnected facts that receive a connection externally through an imposition of order. But this means that, precisely in their isolation, all of the sciences fall to the tyranny of a single methodology, namely, a kind of empiricism. They can, in turn, avoid a banal objectivity only by becoming the object of novel interpretations, which are *necessarily arbitrary* manipulations precisely insofar as this novelty gets imposed on the "facts" from the outside. It turns out, then, that the various sciences can be "saved," as it were, from the tyranny of philosophy only through either the inevitable monotony of subordination to another philosophy, namely, that of empiricism, or by becoming subject to the whim of individuals. An interesting implication for contemporary discussions is that, if academic freedom has some connection to the preservation of the proper integrity and relative autonomy of the sciences, then academic freedom requires the affirmation of the absoluteness of philosophy: their freedom depends on its authority.

In the end, then, just as mechanistic physics undermines the possibility of a genuine *uni*-verse—that is, an ordered whole rather than an

---

99. In the seventh lecture, he relates philosophy to the "positive sciences" as soul to body, or better, as "inner organism" to "outer organism," AS (W.3.298–307).

100. AS (W.3.239).

accidental aggregate of merely extrinsically related things—so too does it undermine the possibility of a *uni*-versity. If the positivistic method of science, so conceived, is made the paradigm of rationality, reason surrenders the unifying center that by its nature eludes such a method. As a result, the human spirit comes to reflect the obtrusive passivity of inert matter, and it loses the life it had stolen from nature. To revive nature, and so the human spirit, requires revisioning the objective world as centered on the organism, which in turn implies opening science itself to the *absolute*, the unity of the real and ideal, in the manner appropriate to it. Rather than modeling philosophy on science, Schelling insisted that science must model itself after philosophy.

V. *Naturphilosophie* and the Place of the Organism

Having elaborated some of the issues and problems that prompted Schelling to develop his *Naturphilosophie*, we are now in a position to present basic principles of that philosophy itself. It is difficult to elaborate this philosophy in any systematic fashion because, as regularly observed,[101] the various works of *Naturphilosophie* exhibit subtle but significant differences from one another, and it is not always evident how they fit together. It often seems as if he is, with each new work, starting all over again from a different point, in a way that seems to render what went before obsolete.[102] Rather than give a step-by-step account of each work as it appeared, we will seek to distill some of the basic general themes in their development. Our intention will be given to the more directly philosophical aspects of the work—the understanding of the organism and its relation to the rest of nature, for example, or the founding metaphysical principles—rather than the more "scientific" details of his work, since it is the former aspects that are above all of enduring value.[103] It is not accidental that his very

---

101. Xavier Tilliette's book is the classic expression of this observation: *Une philosophie en devenir*, though he, too, insists that there is a fundamental unity to Schelling's thought. Bonsiepen describes a swift shifting of starting points from 1797–1801: Bonsiepen, *Die Begründung*,147–48; cf. Jantzen, "Die Philosophie der Natur," 82–83.

102. Schelling himself claims that he never changed his *Naturphilosophie*: see My System, 344 (KA.I.10.109–20). When he presented its founding principles at this relatively late point (1801), he explained that he had had these in mind from the beginning. It does seem to be the case that the essentials are never incompatible with one another even if he does revisit the same issue from different perspectives, which sheds a new light on what is otherwise a similar insight.

103. We recognize that making this distinction already creates a certain tension with Schelling's philosophy, in the sense that Schelling himself would not approve of

substantial introductions to his more scientific works—the *Ideas* and the *First Sketch*—tend to receive the most scholarly attention.

Bonsiepen puts the heart of the matter quite nicely: "Ultimately, the birth of Schelling's *Naturphilosophie* is the spirit's search for forms of self-organization in nature that correspond to its own organization."[104] Schelling's *Naturphilosophie* is an attempt to think nature through from the beginning in terms of an absolute characterized by the unity of the subject and object, and thus to acknowledge in each a reflection of the other: "Nowhere, not in any sphere, is there anything merely subjective or merely objective, but only a unity of the two."[105] As we have already observed, his interest is above all in the organic aspect of nature, because, we might say, if nature has no life, it is so to speak impotent in relation to subjectivity.[106] One of Schelling's most profound insights is that this impotence would not mean the triumph of the subject but in fact the undermining of subjectivity. The world of nature will always willy nilly express something about the world of spirit, and if it is simply dead, it reveals that formless void to be the form of spirit—and thus the form of freedom as well. In this sense, Schelling's desire to recover the life of the world of nature is an essential expression of the fact that freedom is, for him, philosophy's Alpha and Omega.

In terms of his relation to the history of philosophy, Schelling was, in the first place, inspired by Plato's endeavor in the *Timaeus*, a dialogue he had commented on in his youth, to give an account of the material world in relation to the highest principles of philosophy.[107] More proximately, Schelling was provoked by Kant's *Critique of Judgment*, in which Kant addresses the nature of the organism in distinction from the mechanics of mere matter, but Schelling criticizes Kant's surrender of chemistry as a

---

separating the specifics of the nature of magnetism, electricity, and so forth from the more general metaphysical principles. But one can agree that metaphysical principles will necessarily have "empirical" implications, even if one takes the particulars of the expression of those implications to be time-bound and thus able to be revised both in light of new data and the same basic principles.

104. Bonsiepen, *Die Begründung*, 210. Hegel will follow Schelling on this point. In the 1830 *Encyclopedia*, he claims that the goal of the philosophy of nature is to find the counterpart of spirit in nature, which means liberating the spirit latent in nature (§246Z [JA.9.38–49]).

105. HMP, 119 (W.5.176).

106. Joseph Lawrence has argued that, for Schelling, freedom *needs* the abiding independence of nature: *Schellings Philosophie*, 45.

107. On the historical sources, see Jantzen, "Philosophie der Natur," 82; Baum, "Die Anfänge der Schellingian Naturphilosophie," 95.

proper science,[108] and takes this as a result of his failure to integrate the organism in fact: the organism becomes a mere exception to the otherwise universally regnant mechanical laws, and so represents at best a regulative idea rather than a description of what nature really *is*. If this is the case, then even the organic dimension of nature, as far as the subject is concerned at any rate, is itself only a function of the subject.

The main figures in Schelling's attempt to remedy this fundamental problem are Leibniz and, above all, Spinoza.[109] For Schelling, Spinoza's achievement was his insight that the first principles of all things must be the perfect unity of subject and object (or in his language of subject and substance), which is, of course, the key for the *Naturphilosophie*.[110] What Spinoza failed to see is that this relation must be a *living* one, which implies a kind of *exchange* between subject and object, in which the two remain irreducible even in their perfect unity.[111] Because he misses this, which is to be sure quite difficult to conceive, Schelling felt that he ends up absorbing the subject into substance, so to speak, so that his system betrays the quality that, interestingly, Goethe came most to admire, namely, the perfect contemplative stillness of sheer "objectivity." It is, however, just this point—the absorption of all individuality into the divine substance— that called down upon the "Spinozists" the charges of pantheism.[112] Leibniz represents, at least superficially,[113] the opposite of Spinoza in two respects. First, rather than dissolving the Many into the One, he infinitely multiplied the absolute identity of spirit and substance into the spiritual "monads," each of which contained implicitly the whole of the cosmos within itself. Second, rather than identifying spirit with *substance*, like Spinoza, he identified substance with *spirit*. For Schelling, what is missing in both philosophies, at least as they are commonly understood, is the life that is generated when both identities are affirmed as absolute even in

108. See Jantzen, "Philosophie der Natur," 90.

109. Bonsiepen, *Die Begründung*, 147.

110. See Ideas, 173 (KA.I.5.76).

111. SS, 214 (W.4.335). Schelling goes on to say that, because there is no internal opposition in Spinoza's absolute substance, Spinoza ends up with a mechanistic sense of nature.

112. For an outstanding account of the pantheism controversy, see Beiser, *The Fate of Reason*. Schelling for his part always affirmed the importance of Spinoza in spite of the great pantheism controversy, seeing his own philosophy more as a refinement of it than a rebellion from it, and like Hegel *rejected* the notion that it entails pantheism. See his most detailed account in Freedom, 222–31 (W.5.232–42; B, 12–23).

113. Schelling believes that Leibniz is generally misunderstood and so presents a reading that challenges typical interpretations: see HMP, 75–84 (W.5.118–29).

their opposition, which will ultimately require a higher originating principle that is neither identity nor difference, but "indifference." We will save a full discussion of this important term for the next chapter.[114]

The living concern in Schelling's study of nature is therefore the following: if we can find a *single atom* in the entire cosmos that behaves merely mechanistically,[115] that is, one that is in itself merely "object," without a trace of "subjectivity," then we will, on the one hand, lose a genuine unity to the cosmos (because there would be something then that lies outside of this unity, which would force us to posit an ultimate dualism of principles) and, on the other hand, we would have a dimension of reality that resists integration, which would make a physical organism a contradiction in terms.[116] Schelling's rejection of mechanism leads him to deny that an absolute distinction between the organic and inorganic can be sustained. Or perhaps better, if mechanism reduces the organic to the inorganic, *Naturphilosophie* will have to interpret the inorganic on the basis of life (but without simply reducing physics, as it were, to biology[117]). This means that even the most insignificant physical thing in the world will turn out to exhibit, *in some analogous sense*, the features of an organism.

In his first major *naturphilosophische* work, the *Ideas*, Schelling draws his account of the nature of an organism largely from Kant's Third Critique,[118] though he transforms what he takes over into the new context. There are three interrelated features that we can discern in his brief presentation of the organism here.[119] First, in an organism, there must be a reciprocal interdependence of whole and parts, or more specifically, the

---

114. For a brief account of the meaning of the term, see Vater's introduction to the *Bruno*, 101fn27.

115. See Intro to Aph #69 (W.4.69).

116. See Heuser-Kessler, "Organismusbegriff," 30–32.

117. Küppers, in *Natur als Organismus*, 88, complains that, in the end, Schelling's organicism leaves no room for the inorganic. But in fact, and in spite of a tendency toward acosmism that we will discuss next chapter, Schelling remained committed to affirming a place for the mechanistic features of reality. It is simply that he would not permit these features to *define* the physical as such. Dale Snow's observation that Schelling "decided to eliminate mechanism and efficient causality from his philosophy of nature" ("The Evolution of Schelling's Concept of Freedom," 332) represents a common misunderstanding. For Schelling, mechanism represents, so to speak, the "outward body" of nature (see EEE [KA.I.8.40]), and, of course, the whole point of Schelling's *Naturphilosophie* is to preserve the reality of the body in relation to the spirit.

118. Cf., Kant, CJ §§64–65, Ak 369–76 (Pluhar, 248–55).

119. See Ideas, 190–91 (KA.I.5.93–95).

parts that constitute a whole must be reciprocally intertwined with one another, in the sense that each part is both cause and effect of the other parts. What this means, of course, is that one cannot have a whole without having parts that are so related, and at the same time the parts cannot be such as they are without participating in this "priorly" existing web of interrelations that the whole is. Second, an organism must be both cause and effect of itself, or, as Schelling more explicitly puts it, it is the nature of an organism to be "self-caused."[120] This point becomes, in a sense, the hallmark of Schelling's *Naturphilosophie* and has received a good deal of contemporary attention, in part because it seems to be the most directly relevant proposal in relation to developments within the field of biology and indeed contemporary debates within that field.[121] Schelling's insight is in fact in many respects a recovery of Aristotle's theory regarding organisms,[122] and it leads Schelling to a theological position that is ultimately very similar to Aristotle's: *if* organisms are self-caused, then it implies that they cannot have any extrinsic cause.[123] For Aristotle, this

---

120. As Heuser-Kessler observes, Schelling radicalizes Kant's point here: "Organismusbegriff," 19. While Kant interprets this to mean that organisms are caused by other organisms of the same species, Schelling argues that each organism, *qua* organism, must be in a basic way a cause of itself.

121. The strongest champion of Schelling's significance in contemporary biology is Heuser-Kessler, above all in her book *Die Produktivität der Natur*. She has been sharply criticized, however, by Bernd-Olaf Küppers who disputes his significance because Schelling affirms the transcendence of ideas as the basis of his biology, which Küppers says has no place in contemporary science: see *Natur als Organismus*, 116–17. On this debate, see Bonseipen, *Die Begründung*, 287fn784.

122. On Schelling's similarity to Aristotle in the realm of nature, see Lawrence, *Schellings Philosophie*, 93–117. It ought to be noted, however, that Schelling rejects the notion that his theory is a kind of *hylomorphism* (SS, 215 [W.4.336]) because this, in his view, implies a still too passive notion of matter.

123. Schelling's inference here is of decisive significance because, as we will see, it will eventually create insuperable problems for him in his later, more explicitly theological reflections. It is important to see that Schelling does not entertain the possibility of a *genuinely transcendent causality* that would not be opposed but in fact in a basic sense would *necessitate* a view of nature as in some respect self-caused—a possibility that we find, for example, in Aquinas's metaphysics of creation (see Ferdinand Ulrich's argument that being acquires the character of "not-being-caused" through its participation in the pure generosity of God's creative act: *Homo Abyssus*, 127–31). It is remarkable, indeed, how insignificant medieval philosophy was in the accounts of the history of philosophy in the nineteenth century: see, for example, the scant treatment in Hegel. Schelling, too, makes virtually no reference to this period, in spite of his own theological leanings, though his formulations and the frequent use of Latin terms and phrases in his positive philosophy betray a study of medieval thought (see, e.g., Laughland, *Schelling versus Hegel*, 131–34). On the relationship between a genuinely

entails a positing of the "eternality" of species, each of which is in some respect identical to the eternity of God's perfect actuality; it also entails the claim that there cannot be an absolute coming to be of the species.[124] The centrality of the organism leads Schelling, likewise, at least before the developments in his later thought, to reject an ultimate distinction between God and the universe, and so to reject the possibility of a divine creation. In his early thought, prior to the "revolution" in his thinking that begins with his *Freedom Essay* in 1809, Schelling tends to affirm God and the world as a single "organism."[125] We will investigate in the next chapter Schelling's reconsideration of this point.

The third feature is not mentioned explicitly by Kant, for what are perhaps good reasons in relation to his interpretation of reflective judgments, but Schelling draws it out as an implication of the other two points; namely, in an organism, form and matter cannot be separated. He himself refers to it as the *essence* of organization.[126] This feature is directly connected to the second, insofar as it, too, reveals the impossibility of an external cause "making" nature according to the model of an artifact; that is, by the imposition of form on separately existing matter. It is less obvious, but equally important, to see how this third feature connects with the first here mentioned. One aspect of this third feature is no real revelation: matter that is altogether without form simply does not exist. The "bite" of this feature is the other aspect, namely, that organic form is always already united to matter. In an artifact, material elements—which already possess their own individual forms—are gathered together under a new form that is imposed on them from the outside.[127] But this means that the form of

---

transcendent causality (a metaphysics of creation) and the immanent intelligibility of science, see the important work being done by Michael Hanby.

124. See Lear, *Aristotle*, 293–309.

125. See Matter, *Schelling*, 21; My System, 359 (KA.I.10.130); 1804 System, 153, 167 (W.2E.87, 107): "God is not the cause of the universe, but the universe itself"; PandR, 621 (W.4.95).

126. WS, 188 (KA.I.6.188). A year later Schelling refers to the reciprocity of cause and effect as the essence of organic nature (EE [KA.I.7.202]), but as we are arguing, these two points imply one another. There is no contradiction here.

127. Except, one might argue, in the case of a genuine work of art: as has often been suggested, a great artist does not simply *impose* a form, but gives it to an object while at the same time "eliciting" it in a certain sense from the material itself. Michelangelo has been described as "releasing" his statues from the block of marble, in which they already in some sense lay. In this respect, the act of artistic creation is a kind of co-act, a reciprocal (though asymmetrical) exchange between the artist and the object. This is why we can draw an analogy between a natural organism and a work of art. It is not a surprise that Schelling, for whom the reciprocity between the subject and object was

the whole does not "enter into" the individual forms of the various parts. Instead, it is, as it were, layered on top of the form they already have. Their meaning does not, therefore, involve in itself the meaning of the whole. And because that is the case, the parts can relate only externally to one another: they are not mediated "into" one another by the form of the whole. It is precisely this extrinsic relation that makes parts in an artifact replaceable in principle with other parts. In an organism, by contrast, the forms of the individual parts are always-already interwoven with one another by virtue of the indwelling of the form of the whole. In this respect, the form and matter grow together (*con-crescere*) as a concrete whole. Not only, then, is matter inseparable from form, but organic form is always-already *real*-ized, which means that it, too, is inseparable from matter in an asymmetrical way. If the first feature accounts for the organism being *organized*, and the second for its being *self*-organized, this third accounts for its being an *ontological whole*.

Kant's failure to see the significance of this third feature of the organism (and arguably the second, at least as Schelling interprets it) is related to the great diverging of the paths between the two thinkers. The inseparability of form and matter in the organism presents a basic challenge to the proposal of organicity being a merely "regulative," as opposed to a "constitutive," idea, and indeed challenges the very distinction between noumena and phenomena itself. The inseparability leads Schelling immediately to conclude that, if there are organisms at all, the features of organic being must necessarily belong to nature in a *real*, i.e., metaphysical, sense.[128] Insofar as the reflective judgment at the root of a regulative idea implies that the intelligible form does not have its ultimate basis in the thing itself, but rather in the judging subject, it is contradictory to speak of a reflective judgment of organic teleology, for it amounts to saying that one is imposing on a thing a logical form, the content of which is that the form does not come as it were from the outside, but arises from within the thing itself.

---

fundamental, would have given art such a central place in his (middle) philosophy. See the analogy between the products of art and nature: STI, 219 (KA.I.9-1.312–13); art, indeed, is made here the *organon* of philosophy (STI, 231 [KA.I.9-1.328]), a position it does not hold for long for Schelling: already in the *Bruno* of 1802, Schelling relativizes the position of art (see Vater's "Introduction" in Bruno, 1/1–/38).

128. Those who seek to read Schelling's *Naturphilosophie* within the strictures Kant establishes are therefore mistaken: see Wieland, "Die Anfänge der Philosophie Schellings," 411; Mutschler, *Spekulative und empirische Physik*, 27. Manfred Baum speaks of Schelling's "vigorous Kantianizing of Plato's philosophy" ("Die Anfänge der Schellingian Naturphilosophie," 111) which is inadequate; if anything, the reverse would be a more apt description.

The Perfection of Freedom

One does not avoid the contradiction by explaining one is not *denying* the reality of organic being, but merely suspending judgment about it and articulating only something regarding one's understanding—in other words, by appealing to the distinction between phenomena and noumena.[129] To say that such a suspension is *possible* at all is in fact already to reject organic being in principle, insofar as that being rests on the *inseparability* of form and matter. The self-limitation of reason turns out, in this regard, to be, not a gesture of modesty at all, but quite (literally) self-imposing.

The reason Kant gives for making teleological judgments reflective is revealing. As he explains, the kind of causality we attribute to organic being "has nothing analogous to any causality known to us"[130]—i.e., the linear sequence of cause and effect characteristic of mechanism—and it must therefore be acknowledged that if the organization of nature bears a distant analogy to our own rational purposiveness, we cannot meditate on the organic aspect of the world "for the sake of gaining knowledge either of nature or of that original basis of nature."[131] Underlying this judgment is the assumption that nature is intelligible just insofar as it is mechanical. Once again, we see a certain kind of physics assumed as the paradigm of rationality. According to Kant, natural science would not be possible, physical being would not be intelligible, if we rejected the second law of mechanics (the law of inertia), which affirms that "all change in matter has an external cause."[132] For Kant to concede the inseparability of form and matter in organisms, which Schelling draws out as a necessary implication of Kant's own definition of the organism, would require him to rethink not only his natural science, but fundamental tenets of his philosophy more generally, including the operation and derivation of the basic category of causality in the understanding and, indeed, the distinction between phenomena and noumena. In this respect, the "sticking point" between Kant and *Naturphilosophie* is much more than simply the question of whether

---

129. To press the point by arguing that while it may be a contradiction *in reality* (i.e., from an ontological perspective) it is not a contradiction for me simply to *think* organic being, is equally inadequate. One is, in this case, no longer merely suspending judgment regarding the noumenal realm; one is in fact positing an essential and complete lack of correspondence between the two realms. Schelling expressed criticisms of the critical standpoint, which would claim a separation between knowledge and what is real, from the very beginning of his philosophical reflection, and in his middle period offered a substantial argument why "knowledge of the absolute and the absolute itself" must be one and the same: see Further Expositions (W.1E.413–24).

130. Kant, CJ, Ak 375 (Pluhar 254).

131. Ibid. (Pluhar 255).

132. Kant, *Metaphysische Anfangsgründe der Naturwissenschaft*, 120–21.

the concept of an organism were regulative or constitutive,[133] or, at least, there is much more at stake in that question than simply modes of judgment. Precisely because Schelling wishes to affirm the reality of organisms he does indeed rethink both the status and the nature of physics; moreover, he also criticizes a critical approach and even begins to move beyond a transcendental approach to philosophy.[134] It is the reality of the organism that undermines a dualistic understanding of the relationship between the ideal and the real. We thus have already in Schelling's first writings the seeds of his break with Fichte.[135]

The question for Schelling, then, is: what does it imply about the world—and, ultimately, about the nature of being and reason, identity and difference—if we begin by affirming the real existence of organisms? Schelling's second major work in *Naturphilosophie*, the *World Soul*, develops this question directly. Beginning with a reference to Schiller's affirmation of the manifestation of freedom in nature, Schelling argues that if we are to view nature *as a whole*, then the direct opposition between mechanism and organism must fall away.[136] Because one of these would have to be the positive and the other the negative if they are to exist in unity, Schelling argues that organism has to be ultimate and, therefore, the basis for both the existence and the intelligibility of mechanism. His reasoning here is compelling: organism has to have this role because of the circular and self-contained nature of organic causality. As an endless succession of causes and effects, mechanism can neither exist nor be understood as absolute.[137] This means that it can have only a *derivative* reality. Thus, Schelling affirms that matter is not an inert "stuff" that forms the building blocks of what we would recognize as a living thing, but precisely conversely, *matter is the product of life*. Mechanical activity is not a primordial activity,

---

133. See Beiser, "Kant and *Naturphilosophie*," 20. Because of its implications for the whole of his thought, Beiser is right to say that the "most exasperating concept" for a Neo-Kantian is the *organic* notion of nature (7).

134. Schelling's criticism of criticism comes early: see his Phil Letters, 173 (KA.I.3.76). According to Bonsiepen (*Die Begründung*, 148), while Schelling's starting point in the *Ideas* was still "quasi" transcendental, he quickly moved in a different direction, which we clearly see already with his next work, the *World Soul*.

135. Claude Piché claims that Schelling and Fichte were in agreement at the outset, insofar as both affirmed an organic view of the world and so rejected mechanism ("Fichte," 214–15). The question, however, is whether they understood these in the same way, or, indeed, whether an organic view of the world is possible if this view derives *simply* from the "I," as Fichte would have it.

136. WS (KA.I.6.68).

137. WS (KA.I.6.69).

but rather represents some kind of a limitation on what is primordial and most essential, namely, life itself. It follows that inorganic matter is not "dead in itself" but is rather what he calls "extinguished life."[138] Schelling concludes to what he explicitly identifies as a resurrection of the ancient (Neo-Platonic) notion of the world-soul, a principle that is far different from what is often called a vital force, insofar as such a force, as we saw above, is conceived merely as the opposite of natural laws, which means it simply adds another force to what is otherwise purely mechanical.[139] Instead, it "transcends" the cosmos so as to be able to gather it up from within the cosmos into a single whole, a whole that must be taken to be a kind of ultimate organism.[140]

While this does appear, indeed, to recall the ancient idea, we have to see that Schelling introduces an interesting difference, which seems subtle but has radical implications that will not cease to rattle the foundations of Schelling's *Naturphilosophie* and constantly threaten to bring about its collapse. According to the Neo-Platonic idea of the world soul, matter and the externality (mechanism) it implies at the limit is very much the "negative" that corresponds to the "positive" of life (and, in turn, of intelligence, and ultimately of unity); but this means that it is ultimately reducible back to its positive principle. In this respect, to put the matter somewhat over-simply, for Neo-Platonism, there *can be no* essential opposition between the two principles, but only an *appearance* of tension that is due, not to any positive cause, but in the end to ignorance alone. To deny this is to deny the unity of the cosmos, which is indeed simply to deny the One. Schelling risks this denial, though, as we will elaborate more fully in the next chapter, he intends to retain the unity. He insists from the beginning that the negative principle *cannot* simply be reduced back to the positive: this, as we saw in a different context above, can be said to be the founding principle of *Naturphilosophie*. *If* it were so reducible, according to Schelling, it would be simply passive—that is, inert or dead. We would thus return to the death of nature implied by mechanism that provoked Schelling's *Naturphilosophie* in the first place, since we would have "raw inorganic stuff" as a starting point for science. He therefore makes it what he calls an *actively negative* principle,[141] which the positive principle itself requires, he claims, in order to be positive. Thus, there is no unilateral rela-

---

138. WS (KA.I.6.189–90).
139. WS (KA.I.6.215).
140. WS (KA.I.6.257).
141. WS (KA.I.6.192).

tion, but rather always a reciprocal dependence of principles in Schelling's thought. There emerges, here, a pattern that determines essentially all of Schelling's thinking: the negative principle is *active* because it is not simply the opposite of the positive, but shares in its positivity. Nevertheless, it remains, for all that, negative insofar as it is not reducible to its unity with the positive.[142] For its part, the positive has *its* positivity only by virtue of the negative being itself actively opposed.

What we have here is a complex inter-relation between parts that are independent *only in* their mutual dependence. The result is a kind of explosive unity, which is more *event* than thing: it is activity itself. As Schelling elaborates it in the *First Sketch*, the first cause in nature cannot presuppose duplicity, but must produce it, and then it must produce identity in turn out of duplicity. He finds the basic natural expression of this complex causality in the phenomenon of magnetism, in which what is the same repulses itself (duplicity) and what is different attracts itself (unity), and determines, then, that magnetism is the universal cause of all activity in the cosmos.[143] In his later introduction to that work, Schelling formulates this principle by playing on an ambiguity in German grammar: "Opposites must eternally flee one another [or themselves], in order eternally to seek one another [or themselves], and eternally seek one another [or themselves], in order never to find one another [or themselves]; only in *this* contradiction lies the ground of all the activity of nature."[144] Because it is the *whole* of this interaction that describes the primordial cause of nature, and not, for example, just the unity which would require us to look elsewhere for multiplicity and vice versa, all of the things in nature that would seem to be opposed are intrinsically related. This cause, again, is what Schelling calls here the world soul, and it is at the source of *both* the organic and the inorganic dimensions of nature. As Schelling puts it, the organic and inorganic coexist interdependently as a single product because of their common origin.[145]

Nature therefore acquires two basic and related features in Schelling's *Naturphilosophie* as a result of the centrality of organism, namely,

---

142. Or at least not absolutely. Schelling does not reject the reducibility to unity, but he constantly seeks to couple that with the affirmation of abiding difference. The "decisive condition," according to Dieter Sturma, "for every form of non-reductive theory" of reality is to affirm the emergence of what cannot be reduced back to its ground: see the reference by Dale Snow, "Evolution," 325.

143. EE (KA.I.7.255–57).

144. EEE (KA.I.8.74, fn L).

145. WS (KA.I.6.132).

dynamism and *productivity*, which we shall consider in turn. In the place of the *mechanism* of modern physics, Schelling's organic view of the cosmos leads him to put *dynamism*.[146] In the *First Sketch*, he calls his *Naturphilosophie* a "dynamic atomism," which is opposed to the atomism that lies at the basis of mechanism.[147] A mechanistic approach to physics seeks out the most basic physical elements of things, which are then taken as the starting point for scientific explanation. But these elements are "mere" unities, and therefore essentially inert. To start with them will inevitably be to end with them, and thus never to have life at all. Kant offered a different approach to the natural world in his *Metaphysische Anfangsgründe* by introducing the idea that there were two forces, the attractive and the repulsive, that constituted the various things that we see. But Schelling felt that Kant did not go far enough, insofar as he nevertheless takes the actual physical *things* of the world for granted as a starting point—thus failing to get beyond the position Schelling criticized, as we saw, in the *Ideas*—and interprets the forces relative to these things.[148] Schelling, by contrast, made the forces *themselves* primordial and deduced things *from the forces*. Thus, what exists ultimately, for Schelling, is not solid things, but *actions*. Matter is not essentially static but rather an especially low degree of action, and the fixed figures we see in the world occur only through the inter-action of basic impulses.[149]

Schelling began to work out the specifically metaphysical foundations for his *Naturphilosophie* in the introduction to his *First Sketch* (1799), as a preparation for the broader integration of his *Naturphilosophie* with transcendental idealism in his general system. In this introduction, Schelling transposed Spinoza's philosophy into more directly dynamic terms. Thus, he refers to the *natura naturans* as *productivity*, and identifies this living force with nature simply. *Natura naturata*, then, is the *product* that nature generates. The generation of relatively fixed products gives rise to what he calls the *world*, in distinction from nature itself, and includes the variety of corporeal things that mechanism mistakenly takes to be nature simply.[150] What nature is in reality, for Schelling, is an (infinite) internal energy, so to speak, which he later will also call *essence* [*Wesen*]. It is this that the *Naturphilosophie* studies as its formal object, and it can be called specula-

---

146. EE (KA.I.7.271).
147. EE (KA.I.7.86).
148. See Lawrence, *Schellings Philosophie*, 78.
149. EE (KA.I.7.91).
150. EEE (KA.I.8.40).

The Dark Roots of Life

tive physics because it must look beyond the surface to find nature in its truth. The surface, then, is, so to speak, the (finite) body of nature, and it is this body that forms the object of the positivistic empiricism that we generally identify with science simply. We recall the criticism Schelling made in the *Bruno*: the identification of matter (i.e., nature) with body entailed the death of the cosmos. Instead, interpreted in its original sense, matter included within itself the distinction between body and soul; it is not the inert stuff to which order is added, but it is self-organizing in its most primordial roots.[151] A true science of nature, Schelling says, must not investigate the products of nature, but rather the productive activity that properly defines nature.[152] Significantly, he says here that nature must therefore be lifted up out of mechanism and enlivened with freedom.

A difficulty arises here that Heuser-Kessler has called the "Kernproblem" in Schelling's *Naturphilosophie*.[153] If nature is essentially an active energy, what accounts for there being a world (i.e., any stable thing) at all? According to Schelling, because nature is its own cause, the finitude of its products cannot be due to something outside of the natural world. In this respect, nature is not only activity, but it is essentially a self-limiting activity.[154] To explain this limitation, Schelling posits a third force in nature in addition to the attractive and repulsive forces Kant had identified, namely, *gravity*, which he says Kant mistakenly assimilated to attraction.[155] The only way for the active forces of nature to come to rest in a static figure is for them to be directly opposed to one another, and they can be so opposed only in one and the same subject. The reality of this subject, according to Schelling, requires a synthetic activity over and above the two opposed forces.[156] It is interesting to note that Schelling associates gravity in his later philosophy with the ground of (egoistic) individuality, which is in tension with selfless universality.[157] In any event, the fact that this unity is precisely what allows the expansive and contractive forces to remain infinite within themselves in their opposition means that the coming to rest does not entail, for Schelling, the silencing of nature's activity. Quite the contrary, it means that there is always something "provisional" about

151. UD (KA.I.8.298).
152. EE (KA.I.7.79).
153. Heuser-Kessler, "Organismusbegriff," 104 and *Produktivität der Natur*, 102–4.
154. Lawrence, *Schellings Philosophie*, 72.
155. STI, 85 (KA.I.9-1.140).
156. STI, 81–82 (KA.I.9-1.134–36).
157. Freedom, 240 (W.4.250).

the static-character of nature's products; each product is, as it were, nature's progressive attempt at bringing its essential infinity to expression in the finite. In fact, Schelling refers to the things that compose the world as "*Scheinprodukte*," because they are not themselves adequate to nature's infinity, even though they each reflect that infinity in some respect in themselves.[158] Nature cannot produce an infinite product, but nor can it content itself with the finite, and so has to be both finite and infinite at once: and this, Schelling says, is an endless development.[159]

Schelling traces out this development in exquisite detail in several *Naturphilosophie* works, which we cannot elaborate here in all its parts. To sketch it in broad strokes, nature, as Schelling understands it, builds itself up from the simpler to the more complex: first, there is the most basic composite unity of opposed forces, the straight line (i.e., movement in two directly opposed directions "captured" in a single figure), which Schelling associates with the polarity of magnetism. Then, the line itself becomes the site of a polarity in the next dimension, and so extends into a plane; Schelling identifies this figure with the phenomenon of electricity. Finally there is the same pattern at a higher level, by which breadth expands into depth. It is at this level, Schelling says, that we first reach physical reality. While the science Kant had connected with the physical world in its simplest form is physics, Schelling links this basic figure of reality, interestingly, with chemistry, insofar as it presents the genuine interpenetration, or as he sometimes puts it, intussusception,[160] of forces rather than their mere external opposition. Here again, we see the different judgment Schelling makes by virtue of his privileging of the organism in nature.[161] Schelling's "construction" of nature, moreover, differs from the philosophical one Plato presented in the *Timaeus*, by which Schelling's is clearly inspired, both in the fact that Plato begins with the simple point while Schelling begins with the line, so that the simplest feature is already for him essentially polar, and also that Schelling does not simply describe

---

158. EE (KA.I.7.81).

159. EEE (KA.I.8.46). Heuser-Kessler claims that Schelling's view anticipates Darwin's notion of evolution: *Die Produktivität der Natur*, 27–28, though Küppers insists the two notions are radically different: *Natur als Organismus*, 116–17. A profound difference between the two, of course, is that Darwin accepts without qualification a mechanistic view of the basic operations of nature, whereas Schelling criticized just this understanding.

160. EE (KA.I.7.247).

161. For a succinct account of this "construction" of nature we have sketched, see UD (KA.I.8.301–36).

geometrical entities in abstraction but links them from the first with real, dynamic processes. Both of these differences set into relief the essentially "living" character of Schelling's conception of nature. At each stage of nature's development, there is a relative stability simultaneous with a drive to progress to a higher level.[162]

But, as Schelling makes especially clear in his later "retrospective" account of the *Naturphilosophie*,[163] even fully-formed matter, dynamically conceived, does not constitute the whole of the natural world, but points beyond itself to the explicitly organic. As Schelling describes it in these late lectures, matter, in turn, has its reality in a polar relationship with *light*, which fills space like matter, but is not itself material.[164] According to Schelling, "Light is, therefore, itself not matter, but in the Ideal it is precisely that which matter is in the Real; for it fills space in *its* way, i.e., in an ideal way, precisely as matter fills space in all its dimensions; light is, therefore, the *concept* of matter, not just inwardly or merely subjectively, but it is the itself objectively posited concept of matter."[165] At first, light is *opposed* to matter as subject to object, but it is, as objectively posited, meant to belong to nature, and so must be brought into unity with matter. As Schelling understands it, light (as ideality or subjectivity) does indeed join together with the objectivity of matter in the organism, which thus represents the integration of subjectivity and objectivity, in relation to which matter (extension) and light (consciousness) now become attributes.[166] Viewed in relation to the organism, and as thus ordered to it, matter reveals itself to be the essentially dynamic and self-developing reality that we described above. For Schelling, the geometric order exhibited by the inorganic is a reflection, at a lower level, of the living order possessed by the organism, though this becomes apparent only when geometry itself is understood in terms of the productivity of nature.[167]

In the transition from the inorganic to the organic, the essential "locus" of nature, so to speak, passes from matter to form. As Schelling points out, organisms in the natural world do not seek to preserve their own *material* substrate in the first place, but instead their *form*, which transcends their material particularity as universal species.[168] Schelling then explains

162. UD (KA.I.8.340).
163. HMP, 114–33.
164. See UD (KA.I.8.337).
165. HMP, 119.
166. HMP, 121.
167. EE (KA.I.7.202).
168. HMP, 122.

that the hierarchy of organisms in the natural world can be interpreted thus as revealing the gradual in-forming of matter, so that, for example, the external shell at a lower level becomes an internal skeleton at a higher, and so forth. Without entering into the details, which he had elaborated elsewhere in his system at greater length, Schelling points in the Munich lectures to the progression from plants to animals to human beings. At this highest level, we have another transition to a more directly *ideal* objectivity of self-consciousness. But this means that, just as life is simply a higher transposition of what we see exhibited as geometrical order at the inorganic level, consciousness is itself the higher transposition of life. This is why the natural world is intelligible in the first place, and why man can achieve genuine insight into the *objectivity* of nature precisely through an introspective turn.[169] The point in all of this, in other words, is to show that the organic is, in fact, an unfolding of the highest principles of inorganic nature,[170] and the realm of spirit is itself built upon the world of nature in a manner that is genuinely fitting.[171] Though there is indeed a leap from one level to the next, there remains, nevertheless, a continuity between them: we are never pure spirits, Schelling says, even at the highest levels of spiritual life.[172] For the very same reason, we may regard nature, not as wholly unrelated to spirit, but, so to speak, as "solidified intelligence."[173] While Kant affirms nature to be essentially inertial and so moved exclusively from the outside, which means that the spontaneity of freedom is exactly *unnatural*, Schelling can say that human freedom in fact reflects in a more explicit and concentrated form what belongs already in some respect to nature.

VI. Natural Freedom

If nature is "solidified intelligence"—or as he put it in his first *naturphilosophische* text, the *Ideas*, "spirit made visible"—it implies that freedom, which belongs to spirit and intelligence, does not face nature as something utterly foreign to itself, but in fact has a home in the objective realm of nature. Objective being is not, in other words, the opposite of freedom, but is "freedom suspended" (*aufgehobene Freiheit*), or the "expression of an

---

169. See Buchheim, "Das 'objektive Denken,'" 327.
170. UD (KA.I.8.298).
171. Clara, 4–5 (W.4E.107–8)
172. UD (KA.I.8.365).
173. UD (KA.I.8.366).

impeded freedom."¹⁷⁴ If Newton's science leaves man outside of the world as an alien spectator,¹⁷⁵ Schelling's *Naturphilosophie* allows man to see himself reflected in nature, and nature reflected in himself. As we saw in our study of Schiller, such a view of nature is indispensable if we are to affirm freedom as something other than an empty and wholly subjective power of self-determination. According to the *Naturphilosophie* such as we have presented it here, the organism, as the highest level of the natural world, is, so to speak, a "borderline phenomenon," which exhibits the integration of subjectivity and objectivity, the ideal and the real, and *for precisely this reason* reveals to us the form of freedom. It is thus that nature makes visible the essence of spirit. There is, we recall, nothing in nature that is mere mechanism, and so there is nothing in nature that is not *in some respect* revelatory of organic order. Just as nature expresses the meaning of spirit even in its opposition to spirit, so too does the inorganic express the inner meaning of organism even in its opposition to it, and thus there is nothing in nature that does not reveal in some way, however distantly mediated, the spirit. Schelling concludes, then, in a justly oft-quoted passage that nature, from first to last,

> is a poem lying pent in a mysterious and wonderful script. Yet the riddle could reveal itself, were we to recognize in it the odyssey of the spirit, which, marvelously deluded, seeks itself, and in seeking flies from itself; for through the world of sense there glimmers, as if through words the meaning, as if through dissolving mists the land of fantasy, of which we are in search.¹⁷⁶

Schelling believes that spirit is essentially organic, and claims that reason is the most perfect organism.¹⁷⁷ Further, he affirms that "every plant is a symbol of intelligence."¹⁷⁸ Although spiritual activity cannot be

---

174. STI, 33, 35 (KA.I.9-1.67, 70).

175. As E. A. Burtt describes it, the implications of Newton's science are that man becomes "a puny, irrelevant spectator (so far as a being wholly imprisoned in a dark room can be called such) of the vast mathematical system whose regular motions according to mechanical principles constituted the world of nature. . . . The world that people had thought themselves living in—a world rich with colour and sound, redolent with fragrance, filled with gladness, love and beauty, speaking everywhere of purposive harmony and creative ideals—was crowded now into minute corners in the brains of scattered organic beings. The really important world outside was a world hard, cold, colourless, silent, and dead," *Metaphysical Foundations*, 236–37.

176. STI, 232 (KA.I.9-1.328).

177. AS (W.3.340).

178. STI, 122 (KA.I.9-1.188).

The Perfection of Freedom

detected at the lowest levels, Schelling argues, if it were not present there in some degree it could not exist at the higher levels.[179] Only *because* the seed of freedom, so to speak, is in nature is man capable of acting freely precisely *in* the world—and not simply "transcendentally," as Kant necessarily affirms.[180] As Heidegger succinctly put it, the heart of Schelling's philosophy is to uncover both a free sense of nature and therefore a natural sense of freedom.

But if the organism reveals freedom to itself by being its objective manifestation, what precisely does it teach us about freedom? In the first place, it reveals that the human spirit is not just a "power" to know and to will, each of these being interpreted simply as empty instruments capable of being filled indifferently with any possible content. We recall that this problem represented the heart of Schelling's complaint against the modern university. Because there is no center in this university, there is no organization, which means no internal integration of the various "parts" of knowledge. Thus, the bits of knowledge lie "inertly" adjacent to one another. The absence of a *Naturphilosophie*, which means the failure both to view nature *philosophically* and thereby perceive the organism as its paradigm, renders nature, and by implication the *real* in general, the world as it is grasped by the human spirit, a *form-less* chaos. The human spirit then becomes, for that very reason, a formless chaos itself. If the world is bereft of life, the mind too becomes a purely passive instrument. In contrast to this formlessness, the organism, as we have seen, is an organized form; that is, it is a "closed system," a reciprocity of cause and effect, form and matter, which gives it a living and creative integrity. If Schelling says that the intelligence is an organism, he means that it is not a mere power indifferent to content, but that it flourishes only as an organized whole wherein content and form coincide. We will see this particular point—which Schelling indicates but does not elaborate very far—developed at length in Hegel. But nonetheless, for Schelling too, the inseparability of form and content in spirit is another way of expressing the reciprocal dependence of subjectivity and objectivity, the ideal and the real. The flourishing that this overcoming of fragmentation and death expresses is part of the proper meaning of freedom.

But Schelling also develops the implications of this integration directly for the will and human action. In the *System of Transcendental Idealism*—the first major work that Schelling wrote after developing his

---

179. Intro to Aph #72 (W.4.90).
180. STI, 213–14 (KA.I.9-1.305–6). See Lawrence, *Schellings Philosophie*, 53.

Naturphilosophie, and which was meant to complement it as its ideal counterpart—Schelling discusses the meaning of freedom in relation to the question, in what sense is it possible to be free as an empirical, and so limited, self? We note that this question is an echo of the problem in the *Naturphilosophie* of explaining the existence of finite natural products given the infinite productivity of nature. The gist of his argument is to show why freedom is not opposed to the necessity of limitation, but, in fact, has its complete form only integrated with it. The background of his discussion, of course, is Schelling's fundamental insight that there is no such thing as *pure* objectivity or *pure* subjectivity; instead, just as the objectivity in nature always-already bears an essential relationship to subjectivity, the subjectivity of human being always-already bears an essential relationship to objectivity. We will present Schelling's view of freedom here in simple strokes, first by investigating the "absolute act" of self-consciousness, and then by looking at the actual exercise of freedom in human praxis.

Contrary to Fichte, who sought ultimately to reduce reality to the ideal, Schelling asserts that the real and the ideal "mutually presuppose each other."[181] At the basis of the self, which is the principle of transcendental idealism, is the "absolute act" of self-consciousness. While one might assume that this act belongs simply to the realm of the ideal, Schelling explains that it is, in fact, from the first a *synthesis* of the ideal and real. The reason for this is that self-consciousness is the intuition of the self, not qua subject, but, because consciousness is always *of* an *object*, it is the self qua object. Or better, in self-consciousness, the subject-object intuits the object-subject. Schelling describes this intuition as the limitation of the otherwise infinite "activities" of ideality and reality. We are reminded, here, of nature's self-limitation of the expansive and attractive forces, each of which is infinite in itself. Here, too, the limitation is, so to speak, an explosive event, insofar as it brings about a "conflict of absolutely opposed activities."[182] If we think of the infinite objectivity of reality as "selfhood" (which is how Schelling later describes it) and the infinite subjectivity of ideality as consciousness, only the necessarily limited union of the two gives us *self-consciousness*. It is only here, in this synthesis, that the free act of self-consciousness is achieved, which thus arises in connection with the necessity that objectivity implies. To illuminate his point, Schelling refers to the notion that God's action is simultaneously absolute necessity and absolute freedom: "Such an act is the original act of self-consciousness;

---

181. STI, 40–41 (KA.I.9-1.77).
182. STI, 49 (KA.I.9-1.90).

The Perfection of Freedom

absolutely free, since it is determined by nothing outside the self; absolutely necessary, since it proceeds from the inner necessity of the nature of the self."[183]

There are two implications of this conception of self-consciousness. First, because it consists of an "infinite conflict," Schelling explains that it implies an infinity of actions, which presents the "content of an infinite task."[184] Just as the living energy of nature in his conception led to a progression of ever greater products in the pursuit of adequation to the productivity itself, so too does self-consciousness, thus conceived, entail a progression of ever more ample actions. This gives rise to what Schelling refers to as the various "epochs in the history of self-consciousness," which we might say constitute the life of the mind. Second, because self-consciousness is conceived *from the first* as an integration of subjectivity and objectivity, the increasingly complex relations to the extra-subjective world never pose a threat to the meaning of the self. Thus, the various moments of imposition by external realities, encounters with other intelligences, the inner promptings of one's nature, the eventual restrictions of the civil and moral law, and so forth, prove to be *part* of the meaning of freedom rather than intrusions upon it.

This last point brings us to the second discussion of freedom in the STI we wished to consider, namely, the universal level of action, or the level of history. Here, we find what is certainly one of Schelling's most unique contributions to the notion of freedom. He observes that, for all of its vicissitudes, history exhibits an unmistakable order, which we see, for example, in the tendency toward progress and the existence of a moral order.[185] How are we to reconcile this prevailing order with a view of free individuals? Given the notion of the self he had developed in the previous sections of the STI, and indeed, given the insights gained in his *Naturphilosophie*, Schelling affirms that there is a necessity *within freedom itself*.[186] The novelty of his view becomes evident in his explanation of this point: In each of our actions, he says, a co-active principle is operative that lies beyond our deliberate consciousness. In other words, we always do more than we intend to do. What he means by this is not simply that our actions have further consequences beyond those we explicitly intend, for this would imply a wholly *extrinsic* relationship between subjectivity

---

183. STI, 47 (KA.I.9-1.87–88).
184. STI, 50 (KA.I.9-1.90–91).
185. STI, 202 (KA.I.9-1.291).
186. STI, 204 (KA.I.9-1.293).

The Dark Roots of Life

and objectivity. Rather, he means that there is an objective dimension that *co-acts* "inside of" our action (which is possible, of course, only given an organic conception of objectivity):

> To say that necessity is again to be present in freedom, amounts, therefore, to saying that through freedom itself, and in that I believe myself to act freely, something I do not intend is to come about unconsciously, i.e., without my consent; or, to put it otherwise, the conscious, or that freely determining activity which we deduced earlier on, is to be confronted with an unconscious, whereby out of the most uninhibited expression of freedom there arises unawares something wholly involuntary, and perhaps even contrary to the agent's will, which he himself could never have realized through his willing.[187]

Schelling illustrates the point he is making by appealing to the notion of tragedy, in which actors gradually come to see that a "hidden necessity" was working itself out, beyond their limited views and so beyond what they consciously and deliberately sought, but nevertheless precisely *through* their free actions. He also says that we have just this in mind when we speak of fate or providence, however vague these concepts might appear in ordinary conversation. Moreover, Schelling points to our sense of participating in the general progress of our race, which has an inevitability about it even though it depends on freedom. He later brings up the production of works of art as presenting precisely the same phenomenon, and, indeed, in a paradigmatic way.[188] Drawing on Kant's notion of genius,[189] whereby *nature* acts through the artist, Schelling observes that the infinite satisfaction the artist experiences is conceivable only if we acknowledge the interdependence of subjectivity and objectivity he has been developing throughout the system.[190] The artist is aware of an unconscious impulse in his activity, so that he is unable to make wholly explicit what he seeks to accomplish in a work. But far from experiencing this as an intrusion on his subjectivity or a compromise of his freedom, the artist riding the crest of a wave of creative inspiration feels *perfectly free*.

The insight into the nature of freedom Schelling has here becomes most apparent if we contrast it with the notion of freedom he critiqued in his *Naturphilosophie*, namely, freedom as *wholly arbitrary*; that is, as

---

187. STI, 204 (KA.I.9-1.293).
188. STI 219 (KA.I.9-1.312–13).
189. See STI 222 (KA.I.9-1.316).
190. STI, 223 (KA.I.9-1.317).

arising from nothing more than the subjective intentions of the agent. This freedom is empty, as we saw; it does not reveal anything; it has no inner meaning for the intelligence, and so can be understood only from the outside—i.e., superficially—as productive of (mere) historical facts. "Natural" freedom, if we may use the term here, precisely because of its internal unity with objectivity, is, by contrast, full. It has substance, a weight of its own, and a significance in relation to the larger whole of the encompassing order of the world. Schelling describes this significance in a memorable image: we are actors in a play, but the playwright is not a separate subject imposing direction upon us. Rather, the author depends on the characters, who co-write their parts through their actions in history.[191] This is not to say that they are self-creators, therefore, in a banal, existential sense. Instead, they bring into being a meaning beyond what they intend, a meaning that, in its objectivity, transcends them—i.e., is truly and substantially meaningful—but that at the same time passes in and through them. Their deeds are both theirs and greater than themselves. It is this that gives freedom, in Schelling's understanding, an objective substance. This is natural freedom, of which the organism, as the integration of subjectivity and objectivity in the world, is the symbol.

VII. Freedom or Form?

To conclude this chapter, and prepare for the next, we must reflect explicitly on the question of the relationship between freedom and form entailed in the foregoing. As we will see, there is a profound ambiguity in Schelling's conception that works directly against the very integration between subject and object at which he aims.[192] The ambiguity can be put fairly simply: Schelling appears to remain undecided whether the life that he affirms in nature has its most direct expression in the *organic form* that lies at the summit of the natural order, or in the *infinite activity* at the source of nature's various products. In other words, what ultimately represents, for Schelling, the alternative to mechanism in physics? Is it simply *dynamism* or, in fact, *organism*? There was, we recall, an ambiguity in Schiller's conception of the *living Gestalt*, but that ambiguity, we determined, was

---

191. STI, 210 (KA.I.9-1.301).

192. This is not, of course, the only ambiguity in Schelling's thought. Zaborowski, for example, presents another in the relation between being and consciousness, which he says is essential to Schelling's philosophy: "Geschichte," 42. We might say that the ambiguity we are presenting reflects a general pattern.

The Dark Roots of Life

deliberate and necessary. Indeed, we saw that it was the key to understanding Schiller's philosophy of freedom. The ambiguity in Schelling, by contrast, is a problematic one. Elaborating the difference between Schiller and Schelling helps us see why this is so. In Schiller, we came to see that the transcendence of the concept over its external appearance—its inner completion and so independence from the expression—is precisely what allowed the concept to be perfectly immanent to the appearance, which is what, in turn, allowed the expression itself to be independent. This is what Schiller meant by the noble freedom that is identical to beauty, and what he explained, at the human level, as the ability to devote oneself wholly to one's particular task. To transpose this into Schelling's terms, we could say that the subject is most perfectly independent and complete in its pouring itself unreservedly into the object. Schelling himself, however, lacks this particular notion of paradox. Revealingly, he criticizes Spinoza for allowing the subject to pass wholly over into the object, which Schelling claims extinguishes life by eliminating the subjectivity.[193] Schelling seems to imply that, to remain living, the subject must hold itself back from its relation to the object. In spite of his insistence on the interrelation between the subject and object, there remains a kind of hostility between them: *if* the subject pours itself wholly into objectivity, it loses its proper reality. In other words, *either* subject *or* object; *either* life as infinite activity *or* life as organism;[194] in short, *either* freedom *or* form.

Let us look, then, at both sides of this ambiguity. On the one hand, Schelling emphasizes the *perfection* of order in finite forms. This emphasis tends to come primarily in Schelling's middle period (1800–1807), at the

---

193. HMP, 114 (W.5.169): "But the difference between *this* [i.e., in Schelling's philosophy] becoming object from what must also be thought as preceding Spinoza's substance is that the latter loses itself completely, thus wholly without reservation, when it goes over into the object, and thus is only encountered as *such* (as object); but the subject is not blind, but rather *infinite* self-positing, i.e., it does not stop being a subject in becoming object; infinite self-positing, then—not in the merely *negative* sense that it is only not finite or could not become finite at all, but rather in the positive sense, *that* it can make itself finite (make itself into something), but emerges victorious from that finitude, again as subject." Note, Schelling explains that the subject must in some sense conquer its objectivity in order to become subject (again). Schiller would say, by contrast, that the subject becomes more perfectly subject the more completely it enters into the object.

194. The most striking instance of this either-or is no doubt the passage in EE in which he goes so far as to *deny* the living character in animals, making them, he admits explicitly, into Cartesian machines. He does so, he explains, only to be able to affirm the life of nature in general: EE (KA.I.7.207). See Lawrence, *Schellings Philosophie*, 88.

same time that art, significantly, acquires a central role in his thinking.[195] It is, indeed, the moment in Schelling when he is closest to Schiller. In an inspired lecture given in 1807, "On the Relation of the Plastic Arts to Nature," Schelling considers the deleterious effects on art of the mechanistic view of nature. Such a view would incline one to seek creative energy precisely by destroying or otherwise transcending form, which is indeed the direction in which much of Romantic aesthetics began to move. But Schelling challenges this move by challenging the view of nature on which it is founded. While it is the case, he says, that nature presents us at first with so many fixed structures, by going *beyond* form we do not leave form behind but rather return to it; we regain it now as a living *expression* of the infinitely productive essence of nature.[196] The key to this reversal is the interdependence of form (structure) and essence (life):

> Once everything positive and essential had been mentally eliminated from form, it was bound to appear restrictive and, so to speak, hostile to essence, and the same theory which had conjured up the false and feeble ideal inevitably operated in the direction of the formless in art at the same time. In any case, if form were necessarily restrictive to essence it would exist independently of it. But if it exists with and through essence, how could the latter feel restricted by that which it creates itself? Violence might certainly be done to essence by form which was imposed upon it, but never by that which flows out of itself. It is bound rather to rest satisfied in the latter and feel its existence to be autonomous and self-enclosed. Definiteness of form in nature is never a negation but always an affirmation. Generally, of course, you think of a body's shape as a restriction which it undergoes; if, however, you were to turn your attention to creative energy, it would strike you as the bounds which this latter sets itself and within which it appears as a truly meaningful force. For the ability to set one's own bounds is everywhere regarded as an excellence, indeed as one of the highest.[197]

Schelling achieves in this passage perhaps the highest integration of form and freedom in his work. In another text, namely, the *Aphorisms*, which he wrote about the same time, Schelling expresses a similar insight,

---

195. See Bowie, *Schelling and Modern European Philosophy*, 45–54. One occasionally finds references to the perfection of finitude in his late philosophy of revelation as well: see, e.g., W.6.417–18. It is interesting to note that he specifically refers (in a "Schillerian" vein) to the *aesthetic* quality of the form in this case.

196. Plastic, 329 (W.3E.399).

197. Ibid., 334 (W.3E.403).

which echoes something we saw in Schiller: "The true infinity is not formlessness, but rather it is that which limits itself from within itself, that which is closed within itself and so complete."[198] If organization is the "closed system," the reciprocity of cause and effect, and organization is at the same time the inner content, as it were, of the ideal, then *limit* proves to be—contrary to the reigning assumptions of modern thought[199]—a *perfection*. The reality of subjectivity, which comes to expression in the organism, is not pure spontaneity, it is not what we could call the endlessly "expansive" power of self-affirmation, but is the far more complex event of the reciprocal interaction of expansion and contraction, the synthesis of self-affirmation and self-limitation that Schelling early on identified with organization.[200] For this very reason, the "closedness" of form is not negative; it represents, to the contrary, a completion, a fulfillment (*Vollendung*), the achievement *sought* by spirit.[201] In short, spirit recognizes itself in nature precisely in organic order. Organization is absolute because it is the simultaneity of freedom and form. What is most lacking in modern thought is just this integration, and this lack is directly connected to its lack of a philosophy of nature. To deny the reality of the organism is thus *both* to deny integration, and also to deny the reality of nature. There is a connection between an utterly mechanistic conception of physics that dissolves nature into its parts and a conception of freedom as the sheer spontaneous capacity for choice and action. For Schelling, *only* an organism can be free.

Thus, spirit does not represent the Absolute alone, but, as we will see at greater length in the next chapter, the Absolute is more than mere spirit: God includes, as it were, within himself the opposition between spirit and the world. In the present context, we see that the organism is not a mere physical thing, a mere form, but is the integration of form and essence, i.e., of external structure and inner activity. It is for this reason that Schelling can make bold to say that the organism represents the "birth of God" in the world;[202] it does not simply represent the absolute in an extrinsic sense, but is itself the revelation of the very interpenetration, the difference in unity and unity in difference, that the Absolute represents: "The absolute convergence [*Ineinsbildung*] of both unities [i.e., A=B and B=A] in the real

---

198. Intro to Aph, #17 (W.4.77).
199. See AW (1815), 7 (W.4.588).
200. WS (KA.I.6.77).
201. AW (1815), 93–94 (W.4.700–701).
202. Anti-Fichte (W.3.653).

in such a way that, in this reality, matter is wholly form and form is wholly matter, is the organism, the highest expression of nature as it exists in God, and the highest expression of God as he exists in nature, in the finite."[203] Schelling affirms that the organism is a totality in the strict sense because in it alone the absolute exists *immediately*.[204] In his later lectures, Schelling explains that, in the organism, life depends on the *form* of the substance, or again that form itself becomes the essential. In this sense, life, which is identical to organic form, is the unity of the ideal and the real.[205] In the *Aphorisms*, Schelling likewise says that absolute identity is not only God, but the essence of all things.[206] This allows us to claim, not only that the cosmos is divine, but so is each part of the cosmos, insofar as we see it in relation to itself, i.e., as a relative absolute or organism.[207] God is, indeed, so fully present in the world that, interpreted properly, we see him in *every atom*.[208] According to Schelling, we cannot eliminate the tiniest thing in the world without eliminating God himself.[209] Clearly, Schelling is going to have to confront the issue of pantheism, and reckon with the implications of that question for his general ideas about nature, as we will investigate in the next chapter.

We see again why the organism lies at the center of *Naturphilosophie* and why *Naturphilosophie* is fundamental to all philosophy, including the philosophy of freedom. According to *Naturphilosophie*, the heart of nature is not *res extensa* externally set in motion, but productivity; though we need to qualify that as form-making productivity rather than sheer blind force. If this is true, then the organism presents the highest point *of reality*, which reveals the nature of objectivity, of being, more generally. Being, as Schelling claimed (contra Fichte), is not merely object but is always already the self-relation in the opposition between a self-and-other.[210] Being is thus always an activity, a kind of self-affirmation, a multiplicity gathered into unity and unity differentiated into multiplicity, and therefore something that calls to itself both vital interest *and* thought, insofar as

---

203. Further Expositions (W.1E.474). It is important to see that Schelling qualifies this elsewhere, claiming that the organism is *not* the highest, but rather *reason* is: see Phil of Art, 27 (W.3.398).

204. My System, 101 (KA.I.10.204).

205. HMP, 122–23 (W.4.180).

206. Intro to Aph., #73 (W.4.90–91).

207. Intro to Aph., #18 (W.4.77).

208. Intro to Aph., ##192, 194 (W.4.113).

209. Intro to Aph., #224 (W.4.123).

210. Anti-Fichte (W.3.647–48).

The Dark Roots of Life

thought can have only the absolute as its object and the absolute is this interpenetration. In the end, Schelling's interpretation of the organism turns empiricism on its head: what we *see* in things, that is, what is most *real* in them and directly accessible to perception, is not inert stuff but the activity itself of self-affirmation; we do not see time, but only eternity: the *speculative* approach thus turns out to be most immediate, the most truly based on experience,[211] and empiricism a relative abstraction from it, which in the end eliminates nature if made absolute. Schelling calls empiricism "physoclastic" precisely because it is "ikonoclastic," that is, because it does not see in nature the activity of the absolute, which means it does not see the "seeing" that nature itself is.[212] The self-seeing, or self-affirmation, of being in the organism, in a word, is the revelation of the absolute and thus the revelation of freedom.

On the other hand, by virtue of the ambiguity in his conception of life, there is a tendency in Schelling to dissolve form precisely in the name of freedom. To say that being is "freedom suspended," can mean, not that objective being is the physical manifestation of freedom that reveals to the subject its inner content, which is how we have interpreted it above in the section on "natural freedom," but also simply that, in being, freedom is cancelled, so that the subject ceases to be free precisely to the extent that it extends, so to speak, into the objective world. In his earliest writings, in which Schelling was closest to the transcendentalism that passes through Fichte, Schelling had written that the "essence of the I is freedom,"[213] and the I must be understood in purely subjective terms: "No objective freedom belongs to the I because it is not an object at all." It follows, he says, that objective freedom is a contradiction. He thus comes to *identify* freedom with the exclusion of "all that is not-I absolutely."[214]

Although, as we have seen, Schelling moves beyond this subjectivistic conception of freedom through the development of his *Naturphilosophie*, the ambiguity we have set into relief suggests that his aim was never satisfactorily attained. Even though Schelling insisted on the simultaneity of the infinite and the finite in nature, the infinite seemed in the end always to overwhelm any finite form. In the next chapter, we will explore this problem in greater depth, and follow out Schelling's new attempt to

---

211. Anti-Fichte (W.3.694–95).

212. Anti-Fichte (W.3.694). Schelling calls the true physicist the "liberator" of *"das Sehende"* in nature.

213. "On the 'I,'" 84 (KA.I.2.103).

214. Ibid., 85 (KA.I.2.103).

The Perfection of Freedom

resolve it through a radically new philosophical conception of God. If bringing God into nature threatens to eclipse the particular integrity of the world precisely *in* its objectivity, the logical response, as we will see, is to bring nature into God.

4

From Organism to Incarnation: The Fall and Redemption of Finite Form in Schelling's Late Philosophy

I. Ontological Freedom

A SUCCINCT WAY TO articulate the single goal that Schelling pursued over the course of his philosophical reflection from the beginning[1] is to say that he sought to develop a *properly ontological notion* of freedom;[2] that is, a substantial notion of freedom, which owes its substance to the fact that in the exercise of freedom something more comes to expression than simply the deliberate subjectivity of an acting agent. It is interesting to note that, as Schelling's thinking matured, he began to attempt to present his philosophy in the form of a work of art: not only do we have the philosophical dialogue *Bruno*, but Schelling also composed what one might call a philosophical novella, *Clara*, and moreover set to work on the great philosophical epic "poem" that he meant to be his *Meisterwerk*, namely, the *Ages of the World*. We see in these an expression in the *manner* of his thinking of the recognition that genuine freedom—which is what philosophical reflection is—must take an organic form. For Schelling, freedom acquires endlessly rich tones the moment we recognize that it resonates

---

1. His first major philosophical publication, *The Philosophical Letters* (1795), aimed to develop an affirmation of the coincidence of freedom and necessity in the absolute (see, for example, KA.I.3.101), an insight Schelling says in the *Freedom Essay* is the goal of *all* philosophy in general: Freedom, 221 (W.4.230).
2. John Laughland provides this formulation in *Schelling versus Hegel*, 63-64.

beyond the strictly human sphere all the way into the deepest crevices, as it were, of the world: "Only he who has tasted freedom," Schelling writes in 1809, "can sense the desire to make everything its analogue, to spread it throughout the whole universe."[3] Human freedom gives expression to the world because the world itself is already, in some latent sense, free: "the essence of the moral world is the same (in the final instance) as the essence of nature."[4] In the previous chapter, we saw what Schelling meant by interpreting *nature* on the basis of freedom. But if both man and nature are, in analogous ways, free, it can only mean that freedom has its roots in being itself. Speaking of the integration of both the real and ideal in a comprehensive system, Schelling writes that "[i]n the final and highest instance, there is no being other than will. Will is original being [*Wollen ist Urseyn*], and to it alone all predicates of being apply: groundlessness, eternality, independence of time, self-affirmation."[5]

The passage just cited comes from Schelling's 1809 essay entitled *Philosophical Investigations into the Essence of Human Freedom and Related Matters*. There are some who take this text to be the culmination of Schelling's philosophy, and, indeed, of German philosophy simply.[6] But even if one is not inclined to grant it this significance, it is nevertheless generally acknowledged to mark the transition from Schelling's early, more rationalist, philosophy to his later philosophy, which is defined in a basic way by freedom.[7] Far from representing a complete break from his earlier thought, however, as frequently suggested, the *Freedom Essay* and the new philosophical approach that springs from it in fact deepen a concern that lay at the heart of his *Naturphilosophie*, namely, to defend the "vitality" of the real in the face of consciousness, and so its irreducibility to the ideal, without surrendering genuine unity. But in deepening this insight, his late thought intensifies the problems that arose from this early philosophy as Schelling developed it. At the same time, the new solution to these problems that the greater emphasis on freedom provides does not come from thin air, but draws on principles Schelling had already estab-

---

3. Freedom, 232 (W.4.243).

4. Ibid., 224 (W.4.234).

5. Ibid., 231 (W.4.242).

6. Heidegger famously took the essay to be "Schelling's greatest achievement, and ... at the same time one of the deepest works of German and therefore of Western philosophy," Heidegger, *Schelling*, 2. In his later re-assessment of the essay, Heidegger called it "the summit of German metaphysics," Heidegger, *Die Metaphysik des deutschen Idealismus*, 1.

7. B, ix.

lished in his *Naturphilosophie*. There is, in other words, a significant continuity between the early and late periods of Schelling's thought in spite of the very real discontinuity between them. As a way into the thematic that will occupy the present chapter, let us sketch out two of the problems that began to emerge from our discussion at the end of chapter 3, showing how both the insight and the difficulties quicken with the new emphasis on freedom, and then suggesting in a nutshell the direction Schelling's response to these problems comes to take.

The first problem concerns the relation between the finite and the infinite, which Schelling calls the "most important issue in philosophy."[8] After a long struggle with this problem,[9] which emerged explicitly already in his first published work,[10] Schelling declared in 1804 that the "origin of matter belongs to the highest mysteries of philosophy."[11] Why should this origin be so obscure? As Dieter Sturma has observed, the "decisive condition for every form of non-reductive theory" is an emergence that "can neither be traced back to its ground nor explained entirely from its ground."[12] It is indeed difficult to see how there could, in the end, be anything at all ultimately *different* from the absolute principle of all things, because to call it an absolute principle is to affirm that there is no other source for things, and if a thing owes absolutely every aspect of its being to this single principle—if, in other words, the thing is *wholly* derived from that principle—then it would seem to follow that it can be wholly reduced back to its source. In this sense, the origin of matter—of something genuinely

---

8. Intro to Aph (W.4.123).

9. One gets the impression that Schelling constantly second-guessed the affirmations he presented each time as the only solution possible: in the beginning of his thinking, he criticized Spinoza for being unable to account for the transition from the infinite to the finite (see the seventh letter of the Phil Letters [KA.I.3.82–85], and then he insisted in 1801 that such an account cannot be given, because finitude itself does not properly exist (My System, 353 [KA.I.10.120–21]). The following year, he explained in what is by far the longest and most complex passage in the *Bruno* that it is not only possible, but *necessary* for the finite to "depart" from the infinite (Bruno, 158ff. [W.3.152ff.]), even as he maintained in another text that things are different from the absolute, not in reality, but only for reflection (Further Expositions, 285–86 [W.1E.441–42]). As we will suggest, though this appears to be a confusion, there is a consistent logic running through it.

10. Here, Schelling articulates the essential problem of philosophy thus: "How is it at all possible for me to proceed from the absolute to something posited over against it?" (KA.I.3.60).

11. PandR, 633 (W.3.37).

12. Sturma, "Präreflexive Freiheit," 157–58. Cited in Snow, "The Evolution of Schelling's Concept of Freedom," 325.

other than the absolute—is indeed a supreme mystery. But the affirmation of the reality of finite freedom deepens this problem, for whatever else it is freedom would seem to be *itself* a kind of source or origin. Being an origin, however, would make it, in some respect, unconditional (i.e., not wholly conditioned by something other than it) and so absolute. The problem, in this case, is no longer explaining simply how there can be something *other* than the absolute, but now how there can be something *absolutely other* than it. In other words, it becomes the problem of accounting for what Schelling calls a "derivative absolute," which seems *prima facie* to be an oxymoron.[13] Because it is the paradigm of the problem of the relation of the finite and the infinite, explaining the possibility of derivative absoluteness resolves once and for all the problem of the origin of matter, and indeed of the origin of any world at all.

The second problem follows immediately from the first once we consider it in concrete terms. If we can affirm the distinct reality of finite freedom in the face of God's absolute freedom, can we also allow the *disordered use* of that freedom? This problem, too, intensifies once we give freedom an ontological weight, for either we deny finite freedom the possibility of going astray, which would seem to compromise its free character, or we *introduce disorder into being itself*: "If the enquiry into the reality of freedom thus becomes an enquiry into the ontological status of evil, then the metaphysics of freedom also becomes a metaphysics of evil."[14] Deeper than the origin of matter is the origin of that reality that is not only independent of its origin and so absolute in itself, but is even capable of turning *against* its own origin. Schelling believed that the idealistic bent of philosophy had inclined modern thinkers to neglect this great problem:

> The abhorrence of everything real, the belief that every contact with the real contaminates the spiritual, must naturally make one blind to the origin of evil as well. Idealism, if it does not receive a living realism as its basis, becomes just as empty and abstract a system as the Leibnitzian, the Spinozian, or any other dogmatic system. All new European philosophy since it began with Descartes has this common defect, that nature does not exist for it and that it lacks a living ground.[15]

---

13. Freedom 228 (W.4.239).

14. Laughland, *Schelling vs. Hegel*, 70.

15. Freedom, 236 (W.4.248). It is interesting to recall in this connection that Schelling wrote his Latin magister dissertation at Tübingen on the question of the origin of evil: see his *De malorum origine* (1792) (KA.I.1.59–181).

As we saw in the last chapter, Schelling himself, in the STI, affirmed rather glibly that independent individuals, through their autonomous actions, nevertheless accomplish universal goals and serve the general progress of history. But is there not also ample evidence of the *thwarting* of that progress, of the *upsetting* of order in history? As Schelling explains in the first few pages of the *Freedom Essay*, to understand the meaning of freedom, it is not enough simply to explore the concept simply "formally," in abstraction from other philosophical questions. Instead, while the question of the essence of freedom retains its relative autonomy and integrity as a problem in its own right, a comprehensive understanding requires an investigation of its place relative to a "whole world view"—which, for Schelling, means its place within a broader system. The relationship between freedom and system is indeed the relationship between freedom and reason, freedom and order, in short, between freedom and form. But if anything resists systematization, it would seem to be freedom, and if this resistance is not immediately apparent in freedom understood in the Spinozist sense as "*amor intellectualis*," which seems to make freedom the perfect expression of order, it is glaringly obvious in evil. Whatever else it may be, evil is *dis*-order. According to Schelling, unless we wish to deny that evil is due to freedom,[16] we will have to face the problem of showing how even the disorder of evil and the irrationality of sin "fits" into the system. If it does not, then there is, in the end, no possibility of freedom and form, as he conceives them.

Schelling forestalls this despair by pointing in the introductory section of his *Freedom Essay* immediately to God: God is omniscient, and reason is essentially systematic; it follows that the twists and turns of history, no matter how dark and perverse they may become, ultimately belong to a divine system.[17] The key will be to see how to affirm this *without compromising* the spontaneity of freedom or indeed the dis-order of evil, which is another way of saying the *evil* of evil. The question in its simplest form becomes: How do we "integrate" disorder and order? Schelling claims that the reduction of either one to the other *ultimately ends in the dissolution of*

---

16. We will suggest, in the conclusion, that we ultimately *must* deny that evil is due to freedom, strictly speaking, if we want to affirm the reality of freedom. This, however, is a possibility that Schelling considers only in a problematic form.

17. Schelling repeats the observation in SS, 197 (W.4.313). On this, see Marx, *The Philosophy of Schelling*, 8. Marx's classic book is centered on precisely this problem, which is clearly a central one that preoccupied Schelling over the course of his philosophical developments.

both.¹⁸ We cannot let go of this paradox. As we will see, the resolution of this ultimate problem of the integration of freedom and form, according to Schelling, requires witnessing in the end the way that God deals with evil in history.

If Schelling's early thinking occupied itself above all with nature, his late philosophy was "God-obsessed." Nevertheless, we are suggesting that there remains a continuity in his thinking in spite of the shift of focus. We argued in the previous chapter that Schelling strove to overcome the impoverishment of the conventional notion of freedom by revealing its "dark" roots in nature. Freedom thus acquires a reality, a depth, precisely because it possesses an objective principle, a dimension that lies beyond deliberate subjective consciousness—and so in this respect is "dark"—and yet at the same time is not foreign to subjectivity. We intend to show in the present chapter that, in his late philosophy, Schelling endeavors to resolve the problems we described above precisely along these same lines, but now in more absolute terms. Schelling argues for the need to understand God himself, not as pure (and so "poor") subjectivity—i.e., as the perfect transparency of self-thinking thought, for example—but as a living *person*, that is, as free. But *real* freedom, for Schelling, requires the tension of a "dark ground," of something that resists simple order. Once this view of freedom is accepted, the "derivative absoluteness" of finite freedom and its eventual opposition to God ceases to be a problem, and instead becomes an essential medium for the actualization of God's perfection. If freedom is what intensifies the problem of the relation of the finite to the infinite, properly understood it also turns out to open up the solution to this problem. The key is a substantial—that is, a *natural* or *real* and *living*—concept of freedom.

We will follow out the development of Schelling's integration of freedom and order in the present chapter, first by exploring in more detail the relationship between the finite and the infinite in Schelling's early thought, sharpening the problem that arose therein in order to set into relief the answer he provided in the *Freedom Essay*. The point here is to uncover the notion of the absolute that lay behind the ambiguity that we discussed at the end of the last chapter so that we may see the significance of Schelling's attempts to rethink the nature of the absolute in his late philosophy. Next, we will see how the response he offers in the *Freedom Essay* brings philosophy into an essentially historical register.¹⁹ The question about the nature

18. Freedom, 221 (W.4.230).
19. Zaborowski, "Geschichte," 44–45.

of the absolute thus becomes a reflection on the personal God who reveals himself in history, and most definitively in Christianity. We will thus consider how Schelling's philosophical interpretations of the doctrines of the Trinity and the Incarnation that he presents in his famous Berlin lectures of WS 1841/42 stand as his final response to the question of the possibility of integrating freedom and form. In the end, as a result of Schelling's insight into the absolute priority of existence over thought, the integration is not something human beings can accomplish, but must be achieved by God, and if man is subsequently able to comprehend the integration in thought it is only because God has accomplished the integration in reality. As we will see, for Schelling, God's entry into history is the condition of the possibility of finite freedom, and we might add, the condition of possibility of nature, and indeed of there being any world at all. The chapter will conclude with a general assessment of Schelling's philosophy of freedom.

II. The Fate of the Real in the Early Systems

It is a strange irony that the very system—namely, the *Naturphilosophie*—that was developed precisely in order to "rescue nature from the dead" and maintain its relative autonomy, its life, in and with the human spirit, should bear an inexorable tendency to deny the existence of the physical world, and indeed of reality altogether. But in fact the primary means by which Schelling attempts this rescue itself tends to lead to this end. As we saw at length in the last chapter, Schelling sought to overcome the empiricism-dogmatism-mechanism complex by getting behind things, as it were, in their emergence rather than facing them as "ready-made" objects, and entering through reason into their originating source, which is at the same time the science of subjectivity itself, so as to accompany nature, so to speak, in its birth. Schelling avoids subjective idealism in his early thought, significantly, *not* by allowing the object to surprise the subject as a reality that the subject cannot rationally anticipate ahead of time (as *das Unvordenkliche*), but rather by insisting that the essence of nature is *also* a priori. In this respect, it may be a more faithful description of his approach to speak, not of "construction," but of a "generative dialectic."[20] This pro-

20. Beach has helpfully termed Schelling's method "Erzeugungsdialektik" in contrast to Hegel's better known "Aufhebungsdialektik," 38. See E. Beach, "The Later Schelling's Conception of Dialectical Method," 84–85. Thomas Buchheim offers a sophisticated explanation of the meaning of *"zeugen"* in Schelling: it does mean positing the other outside of oneself, but not as if the self were the author of its being; rather, the other is the cause of the identity of the self: *Eins von Allem*, 57. Interestingly, the word *"zeugen"*

ductive a priori is decidedly not an affair of the concept alone, as it will be for Hegel, since, for Schelling, the concept is opposed as a universal to the particular.[21] Instead, it is "*urbildlich*,"[22] which carries the sense of being an originating principle, a kind of *archē* (*ur*), as well as the concreteness and particularity of the image (*Bild*). The subjective correlate of the originating principle, thus understood, is intellectual intuition, which Schelling says is a unity of the universal and particular, the infinite and the finite.[23] The question, however, is the extent to which the origin can itself already be concrete, or, to put it another way, the extent to which the particular as such can be *a priori*. We will see in our studies of Hegel that follow how Hegel presents a distinctive solution to this problem, but here we need to follow out Schelling's own, very different, attempt. If we think through its implications, we realize that the entire question of the integration of freedom and form rests on the solution to this very problem, and the whole of Schelling's late philosophy can be interpreted as an extended effort to respond to all of the difficulties contained therein.

The fundamental pathos of Schelling's *Naturphilosophie* is the "piety" that Schelling wrote of in his 1806 text on Fichte: one does not see nature properly if one looks simply at the surfaces of things. To see truly, one must look, so to speak, *through* things in order to catch a glimpse of the activity that produced them, or better, the activity that is even now producing them.[24] As Schelling put it in his lectures on the plastic arts, at the moment in which his affirmation of the finite was at its peak, in order

---

means both "to beget," and "to bear witness to." In other words, Schelling aims at a radical reciprocity between subject and object, reflected in the very method of thought.

21. Here is a difference from Hegel: Schelling, in his exchange with Hegel after the latter had sent him a copy of the *Phenomenology*, notes his surprise at the role Hegel accords the concept, as *itself* concrete, and seems to express a certain betrayal in this: "I admit that as yet I do not comprehend the sense in which you oppose 'concept' to intuition. By concept you can mean nothing other than what you and I have called 'Idea', whose nature it precisely is to have one aspect whereby it is concept and another whereby it is intuition": Schelling to Hegel, 3 Nov, 1807 (*Briefe* 3, 431, cited in Vater, "Introduction," *Bruno*, 96). Hegel does indeed echo the distinction Schelling refers to here insofar as he presents the Idea as the unity of the concept and existence, but he nevertheless does not seem content to allow the concept as such to remain simply in opposition to intuition and therefore abstract.

22. See Further Expositions, 243 (W.1E.399).

23. Bruno 142 (W.3.138). On the concept of intellectual intuition in Schelling's middle period, see Vater, "Intellectual Intuition," 213–34. Vater points out that Schelling will occasionally substitute the term "reason" for "intellectual intuition" for this unity of the universal and particular (ibid., 216), which thus anticipates Hegel.

24. See Anti-Fichte (W.3.694, 703).

From Organism to Incarnation

to contemplate forms as positive even in their limited determinateness, we need to look past them to the infinite creativity at their source. But if we do so through the destruction of the finite, in a Romantic celebration of creativity, we in fact undermine that very creativity, which would thus be frustrated in its most proper end, namely, to give birth to forms. The genuine eye for nature returns to the finite from the infinite; it sees the finite as an *expression* of the infinite rather than a limitation of it, and so its very finitude (*End-lichkeit*) becomes, not a place where the infinite *ends*, as it were, but where it finds fulfillment or perfection (*Voll-end-ung*). In this sense, we might say that the infinite "extends" itself in the finite; it becomes paradoxically "more" by virtue of the finite. When we look at a person, we do not simply stare *at* his physical features as so many sense data, from which we infer the subjectivity of the person through an inference based on an analogy to our own inhabiting of a body.²⁵ Rather, we look *through* the features, *at* the person. The person's personality comes "immediately" to expression *in* the physical features. Schelling insists on a similar point with respect to nature: the life of nature is what we most directly see *in* the particular things in the world.²⁶ We do not see simply natural phenomena, but we see Nature herself, i.e., Nature as subject, *in* the objectivity of the finite forms. But as we suggested at the end of the last chapter, an ambiguity remains: Everything hangs on the precise meaning we accord to the little word "in." Is it meant extrinsically (i.e., instrumentally) or intrinsically, is it meant in the manner of an agent "in" a vehicle, or in the manner of an organic form immanent in matter?

For all of his intentions to the contrary, we noted that Schelling betrays a tendency in his early thinking to relate the ideal and real extrinsically, as outrageous as the claim may seem given the ferociousness of the attack he urges on those who do this very thing. This tendency appears in Schelling's ambivalence toward *difference*.²⁷ In his more directly

---

25. This is essentially how Husserl describes the perception of the Other [*Fremderfahrung*], although he qualifies this inference as a "prelogical" one: see *Cartesianische Meditationen* V, §§48–54, *Gesammelten Schriften*, vol. 8, 107–23.

26. Anti-Fichte (W.3.655).

27. In "Schellings logisches Prinzip," Jürgensen describes three "stages" in the development of Schelling's thought on difference and identity: first, difference without identity, second similarity (identity viewed from the perspective of difference), and third, identity without difference (see esp., 143). Although he offers helpful insights into Schelling's evolution on this subject, the schema is far too simplistic. There is a sense, indeed, as we will argue, that Schelling begins with pure identity without difference, and gradually elevates it until we have difference without identity. It is better to say that the relationship between identity and difference is a fundamental theme in

"*naturphilosophisch*" writings, Schelling identifies his approach as that of a "dynamic atomism,"[28] which he explains later as the expression in the empirical realm of a speculative approach to philosophy.[29] As we discussed last chapter, this dynamism has difficulty accounting for fixed forms in nature, which must thus appear as "thwarting" the dynamism, or "stopping it up"—Schelling uses the term *Hemmung* in this context. Thus, we find Schelling saying that individual things ought to be seen as "failed attempts" at absolute organization, and that the independent structured figure, the *Gestalt*, represents non-freedom, insofar as it is a place wherein the life and freedom of dynamism, which is nature in its truth, comes to an end.[30] In fact, Schelling goes so far as to concede a Cartesian notion of animals as *machines*, though he claims he deprives them of life only in order to be able to affirm the life of Nature in general.[31] Notice, it is possible to make such a claim only if one thinks of the life of the individual organism and the life of Nature as fundamentally in competition with one another, which would be the case only if they were extrinsically related as opposites, in which the elevation of one entailed the diminution of the other.

In Schelling's early *Naturphilosophie*, then, what counts in nature is what is active, what is in motion or productive. A thing is dead, and to that extent insignificant, insofar as it comes to rest. To rescue nature from death, in this case, means to see that what appears to be at rest is in reality and in truth in motion. To be sure, "motion," here, is not meant simply univocally in the crass sense of local motion. As Schelling's thought progresses, the "horizontal" activity of the dynamic action gets "verticalized," so to speak, so that the activity is interpreted, not in the first place as physical movement understood exclusively as a result of the interplay of force, of efficient causality, but rather more metaphysically as generative productivity. Schelling comes to adopt a kind of Platonism, or better Neo-Platonism, with strong notes of Spinoza and Leibniz, but with the new twist given by the *Naturphilosophie*. In the more mature, systematic expressions of his philosophy of nature, he thus speaks of the divine Ideas, which are the true life of things, on the one hand, and are identical with

---

his thought, in which the two are connected in different and developing ways from the beginning.

28. EE (KA.I.7.86); EEE (KA.I.8.49).
29. Cf., UD (KA.I.8.364).
30. EE (KA.I.7.81, 101–2).
31. EE (KA.I.7.207).

From Organism to Incarnation

the Absolute itself, on the other.³² Because God is essentially creative, the Ideas, which are in some respect *identical* to God, are themselves creative.³³ They represent the *soul* of things, or as Schelling will also call them, their *essence*, while things in their physical externality, their structured shape, are the *body* or the *form*.³⁴ As we saw in the last chapter, Schelling does not allow this physical aspect, in fact, to be called nature, but instead distinguishes it as mere "world"³⁵—a notion, it bears remarking, that carries the religious overtones of "fallenness," which will become significant below. In short, for Schelling, the reality of nature often appears to get subsumed wholly under the concept of creativity, and what does not fit under this concept becomes at best insignificant.

As Mutschler has seen, this tendency to eclipse the positivity of the finite in its finitude reaches a high point in Schelling's Identity System.³⁶ In Schelling's initial exposition of that system in 1801, in which he claims to be articulating the first principles of his *Naturphilosophie* for the first time,³⁷ he begins by establishing what he claims is both the ultimate law of reason and thus of being, namely: $A=A$. He takes this to imply that there cannot be any difference as such in the Absolute.³⁸ Because of the lack of difference, the Absolute is by definition infinite. But if the Absolute is in fact the law of being, and the finite is by definition not infinite, it follows that the finite, qua finite, does not properly exist.³⁹ The problem of accounting for the emergence of the finite from the infinite, in this case, simply dissolves. *There is no finite outside of the infinite*; to emerge from or depart from the infinite is to depart from being.

Regarding the issue of difference, we find two immediate implications: in the first place, the only possible difference ultimately is *quantitative*.⁴⁰ No-*thing* can be "added" to the infinite from the outside, which means that things can differ from one another only formally, that is, in the mode in which they present what is ultimate, and without real difference.

---

32. See AS (W.3.340–41). Cf., 1804 System, 171 (W.2E.117).
33. AS (W.3.340–41).
34. AS (W.3.340); Intro to Aph, #73 (W.4.90–91); PandR, 616 (W.4.20).
35. EEE (KA.I.8.40).
36. Mutschler, *Spekulative und empirische Physik*, 14, 44.
37. My System, 348 (KA.I.10.114–15).
38. He makes this especially explicit in his Further Expositions, 285–86 (W.1E.441–42).
39. My System, 353 (KA.I.10.120–21).
40. Ibid., 355 (KA.I.10.125).

Here is the metaphysical roots for the notion of "potencies" that, as we shall see, comes to dominate Schelling's late philosophy: Schelling adopts it in order to be able to differentiate moments of the absolute (A^1, A^2, A^3, etc.), which nevertheless preserve a strict identity (A).[41] In the second place, even this difference exists only for reflection, or as he puts it in another place, in *appearance*.[42] In other words, for the finite apprehension of reflection or understanding, things appear, as interacting with one another externally, which means that, phenomenally, they are reciprocally conditioned by one another, subject to causality and therefore to time.[43] But for the non-finite mode of reason, or to put it another way, with respect to things in themselves, things are no longer individualized, and so distinct from one another, but are rather absolute: "Each individual in relation to itself is a totality."[44] In short, there is only *one* absolute essence or reality, and the differences among things reflect different determinations of that essence in appearance, but no change in the essence itself.[45] Quantitative difference is not real, but "exists" only as *"non ens"* [*nicht Wesen*].[46] The relative non-being is itself the appearance that is distinguished from the Idea.[47]

Though it may seem from this brief account that Schelling's philosophy represents a straightforward "acosmism," it is crucial to see that this inference can never simply be made without qualification at any point in his thinking, and that an ambiguity is present from the very beginning and remains unresolved, as we will see, even to the very end and in spite of the deep transformation it undergoes with the emergence of his positive philosophy. Schelling himself never clearly admitted any inconsistency or incompatibility between his early and late thinking.[48] From what we

41. See David, *Le vocabulaire de Schelling*, 48–49. David quotes V. Jankélévitch here who describes the potencies significantly as "successive concessions that Identity is obliged to make to otherness."

42. My System (KA.I.10.117; 127; 129). Cf., 1804 System (W.2E.117)

43. 1804 System (W.2E.125). Cf., My System (KA.I.10.117).

44. My System (KA.I.10.134).

45. Phil of Art, 14 (W.3.385–86).

46. 1804 System, 17 (W.2E.134). Cf., PandR, 61/1–/30 (W.4.23), where Schelling says this is only the possibility of a difference, and not a real difference, and also Intro to Aph #176 Anmerkung (W.4.124).

47. 1804 System, 175 (W.2E.117).

48. To be more precise, Schelling admits, for example, in his late lectures on "System of the Ages of the World" (1827/28) that the *Naturphilosophie* is *deficient* from the perspective of the positive philosophy, but becomes *mistaken* only when it claims to be adequate to the whole (see *System der Weltalter*, edited by Peetz, 55). He also confesses

have seen, it is not a surprise that Schelling would continue to have deep sympathies with Spinoza, for whom there is ultimately only one substance, since Schelling, too, wants to resist the idea that things can ever truly relate to one another in a merely extrinsic—i.e., mechanistic—way, and so wishes to affirm an ultimate unity to things.[49] At the same time, however, he is critical of Spinoza from the beginning. As we mentioned at the outset, already in the *Philosophical Letters*, he complains that, because Spinoza cannot account for the transition from the infinite to the finite, he simply denies the existence of the finite.[50] It cannot be the case that Schelling forgets this criticism and falls into the same problem;[51] it must be that he at least understands himself to be doing something very different. The key to this difference, once again, lies in his criticism of the lack of a "living relationship" between subject and object in Spinoza. The problem with Spinoza, to his mind, was not the one usually mentioned, namely, pantheism, but rather *mechanism*, which is logically connected with Spinoza's reduction of subject ultimately to substance.[52] Ironically, as we indicated, one avoids "degrading" the object to an inert mechanism precisely by resisting the absorption of the subject into the object, or in other words, by resisting the absolutizing of objectivity. If subjectivity has its "own" reality beyond the object, then the object has the possibility of sharing in something other than itself, i.e., of participating in subjectivity.

Here we see the critical importance of the organism in Schelling's thought: it represents, we suggested, the key to Schelling's resistance to acosmism. Whereas Spinoza simply identified things with God's thought

---

in fact that the assumptions of his age inclined him to make this mistake: ibid., 93.

49. See My System, §12 with its 2 additions: "*Everything that exists is absolute identity itself.* For it is infinite, and as absolute identity it can never be eliminated, . . . and therefore everything that exists must be the absolute identity itself." Add. 1: "Everything that is is, in itself, one . . ." Add. 2: "The absolute Identity is the sole [reality] that exists in itself, or simply, which means that everything is only insofar as, in itself, it is the absolute identity itself, and insofar as it is not the absolute identity, it does not exist at all in itself" (KA.I.10.120).

50. Phil Letters, 177 (KA.I.3.82–85).

51. Interpreting every stage of Schelling's development in its relationship to Spinozism, Alan White finally judges that Schelling is unable to avoid collapsing into a nihilistic mysticism in the end: see *An Introduction*, esp. 1–6; 187–91. Insofar as he takes Schelling to advocate that one "abandon the metaphysical quest for rationality altogether" (ibid., 189), White seems to see only one aspect of what is essentially ambiguous in Schelling, a more complete view of which would require a fuller treatment of the late philosophy than White offers.

52. Freedom, 230 (W.4.241); SS, 210 (W.4.335); cf., HMP, 114 (W.5.169); Ideas, 186–87 (KA.I.5.90).

of them, and identified that thought in turn with God himself, Schelling allowed things a life of their own. For him, the Ideas that express the essence of things are themselves *organisms*.[53] He insists that ideas *are not* simply universals, which would allow them to be reduced back simply to God's substance, but rather they combine the universal and the particular in a living unity.[54] It is just this that distinguishes them from concepts, which are by their nature opposed to particulars.[55] The unity of the universal and the particular is exactly how Schelling defines the organism.[56] If the divine ideas were interpreted in a wholly rationalistic manner and thus simply excluded particularity, then we would have to say that the absolutizing of the idea would necessarily imply straightforwardly the elimination of the reality of nature and the particularity of physical, limited things that make up the natural world. And although Schelling often formulates his ideas in a way that suggests just this elimination, his position is in fact quite subtle. It is not that particulars in themselves are not real; rather, Schelling eventually clarifies that they lose their reality only insofar as they *depart* from the Absolute. Schelling expresses this departure in theological language in *Philosophy and Religion*, in which he refers to it as a *fall*, but the notion is in line with his thinking in the *Naturphilosophie* and the Identity Philosophy, even if it adds a new emphasis on freedom, which we will discuss in a moment.[57] Though things surrender their substance to the extent that they fall from the Absolute, it does not mean that they avoid this only to be absorbed by the Absolute on the other side. Instead, *in the Absolute, they exist in their particularity*, or perhaps more adequately put, in the unity of particularity and universality. As Schelling puts it in his *Aphorisms*, the "All" does not repress individual things, but is coincident with the freedom of their particular life.[58] The particular, he goes on to say, can be interpreted either as a limit in relation to the whole, in which case it

---

53. AS (W.3.34/1–/31). In fact, Schelling drew this conception of the ideas directly from Plato: see his 1794 commentary on the notion of the *zōon noēton* in the *Timaeus*: Schelling, "*Timaeus*" (1794), 29ff.

54. Intro to Aph, #99 (W.3.96).

55. Bruno, 142–43 (W.3.138–39).

56. Phil of Art, 15 (W.3.387).

57. He explains in PandR that forms are *ideally* identical to essence (616 [W.4.20]) and can only exist *positively* through a fall (624 [W.4.28]). But as we will see shortly he makes the freedom of a thing its "*in-sich-selbst-seyn*," which it *has* in God (625–26 [W.4.29]). This is quite similar to his claim in his 1801 System that things exist *in themselves*, which is identical with their being in God, and forfeit their own being only outside of God.

58. Intro to Aph, #91 (W.4.95).

is negative, or as a totality in itself (as we saw in the last chapter), in which case its perfection exists in the same degree as its particularity.[59]

It is interesting that Schelling mentions love in a significant way for the first time in his writings in the context of the mutual existence of the finite and the infinite, describing love as consisting in a unity that desires multiplicity in freedom.[60] This insight will become important later on. Perhaps we could say that, at this stage in Schelling's thinking, finitude becomes disorder, it "falls," insofar as it *opposes itself* to the Absolute, but the Absolute is not *in itself* opposed to the finite. In this case, a paradox arises: if a thing asserts its particularity, it loses it, but if it surrenders its particularity to the Absolute, it finds itself affirmed even in that particularity.[61] Things, then, are *free* to the extent that they possess that freedom inside God, who is the perfect coincidence of freedom and necessity, and they lose their freedom precisely to the extent that they lose divine necessity.[62] They become more perfectly themselves as unique individuals the more wholly they live in God.

We are just about at the peak of Schelling's insight, the place at which a radical turn occurs, but in order to reach this peak we need to go one step further in our analysis. For all of the sophisticated articulation and formulation that Schelling gives of the relationship between the finite and the infinite, he never succeeds in resolving the basic ambiguity. It becomes sharpest in the last substantial piece he wrote before his investigation into human freedom, the "Improved Version of Fichte's Doctrine," in which there also appears for the first time the insight that will bear fruit in the *Freedom Essay* regarding the necessity of otherness.[63] As we discussed in the preceding chapter, Schelling criticizes Fichte's attempt to affirm the ultimacy of life, for, according to Schelling, the logic of Fichte's argument betrays his intention in making it. Being, he explains, has to come out of itself in order to be alive.[64] But this means that being *in itself* is simply

---

59. Ibid., #103 (W.4.96–97).

60. Ibid., #163 (W.4.108): "This is the mystery of eternal love, that that which could be absolutely does not consider it a deprivation to exist for itself, but is only in and with others. If each thing were not a whole, but only a part of the whole, then there would be no love: but there is love because each is a whole and at the same time is not and cannot be without the other."

61. PandR, 649 (W.4.53).

62. PandR, 625–26 (W.4.29–30).

63. See Anti-Fichte, 54 (W.3.648); Buchheim, "Persönlichkeit," 17.

64. Anti-Fichte, 69 (W.3.663).

dead.⁶⁵ The irony is that the very same criticism can be made of Schelling himself. Against any philosophy that would allow the possibility of there being even the slightest instance of a reality in the universe that was simply inert, which would necessarily entail a thoroughgoing metaphysical dualism, Schelling insists in this text that there is no "thing" in the universe that is an object and nothing more, no "thing" that is simply "being." Instead, at its deepest root, being and knowing are, as Parmenides long ago put it, "the same," which means that everything that exists is not just known (object), but also a knower (subject), not just posited, but also positing, indeed, self-positing. Being, he says, *is* self-affirmation.⁶⁶ The self-undermining character of Schelling's argument here is subtle, but once we grasp it we discover it running through the whole of his early work. By insisting that being is meaningful—and for Schelling something has meaning only insofar as it is productive or creative—*precisely because* what appears to be merely posited is in reality self-positing, he deprives objectivity of all significance *qua objective*. The object has its truth, in other words, not as object *but only insofar as it is in fact subject*. To say that the object always already *is* subject, and so never has to be "subjectivized" in order to be brought to life, does not resolve the problem but only deepens it. The irony, to put it another way, is that Schelling's attempt to save nature from mechanism by affirming its essential dynamism—*"Natur als Subjekt"*⁶⁷—in the end collapses back into mechanism, because it lifts nature from "mere objectivity" only by lifting it from its natural being altogether, at least insofar as we associate nature with the things we encounter in the world.⁶⁸ In our language, we could say that Schelling overcomes a dualism between freedom and form by constantly dissolving form into freedom and at the very same time constantly protesting this dissolution.

To prepare for our exploration of the turn in Schelling's thinking, it is necessary to see the notion of God that lies behind this restless ambiguity. From the very beginning, Schelling realized the need to avoid *above all else* a "reductive" notion of the Absolute—either as pure subject or as

---

65. Anti-Fichte, 80 (W.3.674).

66. Anti-Fichte, 52–53 (646–47).

67. For a succinct account of Schelling's philosophy of nature in this regard, see Krings, "Natur als Subjekt," 111–28.

68. Though positively disposed to Schelling's approach, Bonsiepen likewise criticizes Schelling for thinking of nature in abstraction from its products: Bonsiepen, *Die Begründung einer Naturphilosophie*, 281. Hans Urs von Balthasar claims that, for all of his protesting to the contrary, Schelling ends up ultimately with a notion of matter very much like that of Descartes: *Glory of the Lord*, vol. 5, 564.

pure object, which would in either case ultimately undermine freedom. At the same time, he was equally committed to a non-dualistic view of the universe, since dualism cannot ultimately be rationally sustained. But how does one affirm an absolute simplicity without being simplistic? Though Schelling constantly altered his formulations, in sometimes slight, sometimes significant ways, which we do not have the space to explore,[69] the primary notion to emerge from his early work as it matured is that of *Indifference*. Indifference is meant to allow an ultimacy of *both* identity *and* difference without simply leaving their relationship unresolved as a duality of principles that cannot be reduced further.[70] It does this by remaining distinct from both identity and difference, and thus being able, as neither the one nor the other, to unite the two without removing the differences between them. In this sense, both reality and ideality become equal expressions of the Absolute, and indeed *perfect* expressions of it, insofar as the transcendence of indifference from the two allows it to be *wholly* present in each, rather than its being divided up, so to speak, between them as two of its parts. But if each is in truth equally the perfect expression of the Absolute, then each is simply absolute. Because of the paradox that lies within this notion so conceived, Schelling is able to make various claims that might, at first glance, appear to be inconsistent. Thus, he asserts in the first exposition of his system, as we have seen, that *reason*, as the "indifference" of subject and object, is absolute, and governed by the law of identity, A=A.[71] He reaffirms in his "Further Expositions" that there is no actual difference in the Absolute.[72] In between these two texts, however, he had written in the *Bruno* that the first principle is not *mere* identity, but, borrowing a line that Hegel had used to distinguish his system from that of Fichte, Schelling referred to it as the "identity of identity and opposition."[73] A few years later in *Philosophy and Religion*, Schelling

69. See Sandkaulen-Bock, *Ausgang vom Unbedingten*.

70. In one of the earliest articulations of the meaning of indifference, Schelling defines it as "identity out of duality" (UD [KA.I.8.305]).

71. My System, 349–50 (KA.I.10.116–18). Cf. Anti-Fichte (W.3.646), where he claims that opposition is as primordial to reason as identity. Though this was implied in his conception at least from the moment he articulated it as the "identity of identity and opposition" in 1802, and arguably more deeply latent from the very outset of his philosophizing when he presented the absolute as the identity of the I and the not-I, he seems only gradually to have confronted the implications. It seems to be that his philosophy begins to "crack open" with the anti-Fichte treatise.

72. Further Expositions, 28/1–/36 (W.1E.441–42).

73. Bruno, 136 (W.3.132). Hegel had written in his *Differenzschrift*, "the Absolute itself is the identity of identity and non-identity; being opposed and being one are both

specifies further that the Absolute differentiates itself in self-knowledge, but not as subject and object. Rather, it remains *absolute* in *both sides* of the "knowledge" relationship, but in one it is absolute simplicity, while in the other it is absolute difference.[74] The question however is whether the paradoxical simultaneity of the unity and non-unity of identity and difference in Indifference amounts to an *integration* of the two, a mutual interpenetration, or whether they are simply affirmed both together even in their exclusivity.[75]

It is right here that the ambiguity we have been discussing lies. On the one hand, if the absolute Indifference itself genuinely mediates between the two it unites in difference, then it would communicate an intrinsic relationship whereby each principle would share in some sense in what belongs properly to the other. We saw this sort of mutuality come to expression on occasion in Schelling's insights into the nature of the organism in the last chapter. On the other hand, however, for reasons we will discuss at the end of this chapter, Schelling's methodology inclines him more basically to affirm a kind of dialectical alternation, a mirrored-image, rather than mutual interpenetration, so that identity always turns out to be the flip-side of difference on the very same coin—which makes it both extrinsic to difference and inseparably joined to it. At least in these earlier writings in which Schelling has not yet faced the implications of difference remaining in some sense absolute, identity turns out to be the *real* side of the coin, the more fundamental and authentic truth of being. It is in 1809 that he begins to give more substance to difference, as we shall now see.

III. The Positivity of Finite Freedom

Schelling's last published major work,[76] *The Freedom Essay*, represents the convergence of deep intuitions scattered through his early writings that,

---

together in it" (DS, 156).

74. PandR, 619 (W.4.22–23).

75. For example, in the *Bruno* Schelling discusses precisely this question and opts for the absolute opposition without any mediation and thus without any internal "mingling" of the two (136–40) (W.3.132–35).

76. Smaller works appeared after 1809, including Schelling's significant critique of Jacobi in 1812, but in spite of scuttled plans at two times in his later years, Schelling never published any part of his "System of the Ages of the World" or the positive philosophy. There are many speculations about why Schelling suddenly stopped publishing after the constant flood of writings in his early period. The most common theories are either that Hegel's implicit criticism of Schelling in his 1807 *Phenomenology* made

From Organism to Incarnation

when brought together in this text, amount to a new step forward, in the sense that they reconfigure his thought into a new whole. There is more continuity between this text and the ones preceding it than many scholars admit, but an undeniably new note enters here, a note that is new not only in relation to Schelling's thinking but indeed in some sense to the history of philosophy. Schelling attempts, here, to offer a solution to the problem of evil, which he believes has not yet received a satisfactory resolution. In doing so, he presents a novel definition of freedom, which has great consequences for his late philosophy: according to Schelling, *freedom is the capacity for good and evil*.[77] As we will see, he is motivated by the desire to take the reality of sin and evil—and by implication the accidental and irrational in nature and in history—seriously for what he claims to be the first time, while simultaneously remaining faithful to the perennial affirmation of God's perfection and the ontological depth of goodness. It is significant that he titles this a study specifically of *human* freedom: while Idealism (at least his own version of it) is able to show the *universality* of freedom, as the intelligible, in-itself reality of all things, it is not of itself capable in its generality of accounting for the specificity of *human* freedom, the drama of choices in history that seem to elude all attempts at explanation.[78] There is evidence, here, of a shift from a more Spinozist conception of freedom (as identical to the necessity of nature), to which he had previously adhered, to one in which the notion of spontaneity or unpredictability dominates.[79] What is necessary in order to account for history, Schelling continues, is a new realism, which is itself possible only on the basis of the philosophy of nature that modern thought had lacked until his own efforts.[80] Schelling is implying that idealism without realism will tend toward an abstract generality that will eclipse the *particularity* that represents the neuralgic point of freedom, even as realism must be interpreted as *genuinely* and *concretely*

Schelling hesitant to expose his thoughts in writing; that the death of his beloved wife Caroline in 1809 shook his life to its foundations and thus spoiled his taste for public activity; or that the discovery of the essentially "unsystematizability" of freedom made his thinking unruly and frustrated his attempts to bring it to complete and satisfactory expression.

77. As Heidegger observes, and as we will discuss below, this conception overturns the traditional interpretation of freedom as a capacity for good (*Schelling*, 117), which turns Schelling's fundamental inquiry into being essentially a "metaphysics of evil" (ibid., 125).

78. Freedom, 232 (W.4.243).

79. See Marx, *The Philosophy of Schelling*, 71-72. Cf., White, *End of Philosophy*, 418-19.

80. Freedom 235-36 (W.4.248).

real, which means non-mechanistically and therefore (contra Spinoza) in a living relation with the ideal. On the basis of our earlier discussion, we can say that Schelling is aware of the tendency toward acosmism that any systematic philosophy would betray, even his own, and is drawing on the resources of his own early attempts in the *Naturphilosophie* to "rescue nature," and thus rescue the real, the physical, and so forth, in order to muster a new impulse to clarify the ambiguity.

Schelling begins the substance of his essay on freedom by defending a certain kind of pantheism from its unthinking critics. What pantheism expresses is simply the radical dependence of all things on God. But to affirm this, he explains, is not to identify God with any particular being or even with the sum total of all beings; nor is it to eliminate the reality of particular things in their relationship to God. According to Schelling, the root of this confusion is a misunderstanding of the law of identity: "S is P." This proposition does not assert that S and P are one and the same in every respect, such that each would be reducible to the other. Instead, it simply expresses the inherence of P in S (e.g., "The object is blue" means simply that the quality of blue inheres in the object, and not that the object and this quality are interchangeable). P, however, still retains its particularity in this inherence, and in fact in some sense receives the reality that belongs to it only in the relationship (blue does not exist as such, but only *in* blue things). By analogy, then, to say that God is the world, in this sense, would mean nothing more than that the world has its own being as world *only in* its inherence in God. Thus understood, the proposition expresses precisely the relationship between the finite and the absolute that Schelling appears to have held more or less from the beginning. The law of identity, if we interpret it in this way, does not exhaustively determine the intelligible content of the terms, but only shows their relationship, and so it still requires us to ask after the particularity of what inheres. There is therefore no opposition in principle, he claims, between dependence and the absoluteness of self-being, or indeed of free autonomy.[81] Switching his example, Schelling points out that a child may owe his being entirely to his parents, but that does not make him any less a free human being. To the contrary, properly understood, his dependence liberates his freedom, insofar as his dependence in this case is precisely what gives him his humanity and therefore everything that essentially belongs to it, including liberty. Indeed, as Schelling affirms, citing Leibniz, there is no incoherence in the concept of a derivative absolute; even the notion of a God being be-

---

81. Ibid., 227 (W.4.238).

gotten is not in principle logically contradictory.[82] Far from limiting God's absoluteness, the capacity to be the origin of beings who are themselves free in a radical sense only proves God's sovereignty: God reveals *himself*, his sovereignty, in fact, only in *free* beings:

> God is not a God of the dead, but of the living. It is incomprehensible how the most perfect being could delight in a machine, even the most perfect one possible. However one might think of the manner of consecution of beings from God, it can never be mechanical, never a mere effecting of positing, where what is effected is nothing for itself. Nor can it any more be emanation, in which case what flows out remains the same as that from which it flowed, and thus is nothing of its own, nothing autonomous. The consecution of things from God is a self-revelation of God. God can reveal himself only in what is like him, in free beings that act by themselves, for whose being there is no ground except God, but who are as God is.[83]

We see in this argument a deepening of the insight we saw above, namely, that the *idea* of things, which is their identity with God, is not only their general concept but includes as well their particularity in a *living* unity. As we saw above, the question this assertion raised is how this particularity can be "contained" always already in the absolute priority of God. This treatise marks the beginning of Schelling's focused endeavor to answer the question. The first decisive step consists in two claims being made in these opening pages. The first is the radical generativity implied in the divine knowing that gives rise to the Ideas:

> Even if all the world's beings were only thoughts in the divine mind, for this very reason they would have to be living. Thus thoughts are certainly engendered by the soul; but the engendered thought is an independent power, continuing to act by itself, indeed growing to such an extent in the human soul that it vanquishes its own mother and subjugates her. Yet divine imagination, which is the cause of the specification of the world's beings, is not like human imagination, which imparts mere ideal actuality to its creatures. The divinity's representations can be only autonomous beings; for what limits our representations other than our seeing the limited? God looks at the

---

82. Ibid., 227 (W.4.238). See B, 101.
83. Ibid., 228 (W.4.238–39).

things-in-themselves. But only the eternal is in itself, resting in itself; it alone is will and freedom.[84]

The second is that this autonomy, or "*Selbständigkeit*," is in no wise in competition with God's reality but represents something "good" for God; it is an absolute *positivity*, and not merely a *relative* one, which would be then eliminated in the Absolute. As he states it here *in nuce*, "man is not outside God, but in God, and . . . his activity itself belongs to the life of God."[85] Exactly how it belongs to the life of God is what we will have to unfold as we proceed. For Schelling, the immanence of the world in God, which he approvingly calls "pantheism" here, is the very condition for the autonomy of the world, because, given that the world is *essentially* finite and so not its own source, if it were dependent on what was *extrinsic* to its being, and at the same time what was absolute, its own being would have no ultimate justification, and so would necessarily be annulled.[86]

In order for this claim to be sustained, as we were saying, it is necessary to show that the autonomy of the world is something "good" for God. It is precisely here that Schelling's thinking takes its most radical turn, and hails the arrival of his late philosophy. As we argued above in relation to the *Naturphilosophie*, the preservation of the reality of the finite requires an integration of freedom and form, subjectivity and objectivity, the ideal and real, and the infinite and finite, in God himself. But according to Schelling, the traditional purely "abstract" and ideal notion of God as "*actus purissimus*" makes this impossible.[87] In its place, we need to develop a notion of the *living* God. What does this mean? Schelling had come by this point to insist that life is impossible without opposition; that pure simplicity without qualification is simply inert.[88] A living concept of God thus has to include the radical reality of difference, though it remains the case that this cannot compromise in the least God's unity and perfection.

In order to fulfill the conditions of this concept, Schelling draws on a distinction that he had already developed in his *Naturphilosophie*, and which he claims to have been the first to see: the distinction between the

---

84. Ibid. (W.4.239).
85. Ibid., 222 (W.4.231).
86. See ibid., 228–29 (W.4.239).
87. Ibid., 235 (W.4.248).
88. See Anti-Fichte (W.3.646), WA (1811), 124, and SS, 208 (W.4.327): "Ohne Gegensatz kein Leben." On this point in general, see Bensussan, "La vie comme contradiction," 132–42.

ground of a thing and its *existence*.⁸⁹ Because this distinction does not in principle indicate a difference between separate things, but a radical difference within unity, he applies it to God. We can distinguish ground and existence, or as he also puts it, nature and existence, in God without compromising his simplicity: "This ground of existence which God has with himself is not God viewed absolutely, i.e., insofar as he exists; for it is only the ground of his existence, it is *nature*—in God, a being which, though inseparable from him, still is distinguished from him."⁹⁰ It is important to see that "nature" in this context is not meant in the scholastic sense as intelligible essence, but rather in the very "earthy" *naturphilosophisch* sense as real origin, as the source of a thing to which it owes its being, and thus which lies beyond it, as the dark ground out of which the plant springs. In relation to God, as Schelling uses the term here, "nature" or "ground" is the positively enabling condition, as Thomas Buchheim helpfully describes it,⁹¹ the condition that gets taken up and actualized in the reality that makes it be. Buchheim illustrates this in terms of the food and water that "enable" an organism, substances that are taken up into the existence of the organism itself and so transformed. In this illustration, however, the distinction between ground and existence is that between separate and independent things. At a higher level, we might think of the physical features of a face that enable its expression, but which are distinct from the expression itself, which is the light-filled reality into which the enabling ground gets taken up. Schelling insists that, although God is perfectly *one*, even in him there is a difference—which to be sure has always already been bridged—between God's actual existence, which Schelling identifies with God *himself*, and his enabling ground, his nature. We have to be clear that, while in all other finite beings, the ground lies outside of existence, at least logically if not physically, there is nothing outside of God's unity, not even his own enabling ground. There is neither temporal nor logical priority of ground to existence in God, but they are rather reciprocally dependent in a paradoxical way: "God has within himself an inner ground of his existence which to this extent precedes him in his existence; yet God is just as much prior to the ground insofar as the ground, also as such,

---

89. Freedom, 236–37 (W.4.249). Buchheim points out that there were "foreshadowings" of this distinction, which is made explicitly in the 1801 System, as Schelling himself points out in his footnote, not only in Schelling's earlier writings, but also in thinkers that had significant influence on Schelling, namely, Baader, Jacobi, Leibniz, and Böhme: see B, 114–15.

90. Freedom, 237 (W.4.250).

91. B, 113–14.

could not be if God did not exist *actu*."⁹² The paradoxical notion of a *precondition* that is in some sense *second* is crucial, and will arise again later.

Speaking somewhat metaphorically, Schelling goes on to identify ground with darkness, gravity, contraction, longing, and "self-ness," while existence is associated with light, generosity, love, understanding, and universality. These associations reveal to us what is for Schelling the *essence* of personality, a concept he claims has never yet received sufficient philosophical illumination: to be a person is not something simply *given* in nature, but is rather a kind of *achievement*, a triumph over nature, an existential transformation of nature.⁹³ Personality takes on substance, clarity, and depth; it acquires strong roots, precisely as a result of this "overcoming" of nature. A person with a weak nature, with no sense of self, will also have a weak personality. The force of personality increases in proportion to the resistance of the nature, the force of "ownhood," that it must overcome in expressive generosity. We might compare Schelling's distinction to Freud's distinction between the *id* and the *ego*, which it clearly anticipates insofar as Schelling elsewhere associates the nature in God with "object" and existence with "subject." Nature would then be, as it were, the internal "energy" essential for a full personality, which would at the same time represent a destructive force to the extent that it was not given form in the personality. In the last chapter, we saw that Schelling sought to substantialize freedom by giving it natural roots; this insight comes to flower in the distinction, indeed, the *tension*, between nature and person, which is for Schelling precisely what gives freedom a potency or a vital reality.⁹⁴

This line of reflection has two implications relevant for our own discussion: in the first place, it gives philosophical sense to the religious notion of God as a *person*. For Schelling, to posit an internal distinction in God is the same as saying that God is *alive*; it brings into the notion of God, not the reality of becoming, since becoming in the strict sense requires temporality and external causality, but at least the analogous foundation

---

92. Freedom, 237–38 (W.4.250). See Brown, *The Later Philosophy of Schelling*, 127. While Brown denies that their relationship is one of temporal sequence, he affirms it is nevertheless a logical sequence. However, it is more adequate to Schelling's conception to say that, because they are reciprocally dependent in their meaning, the principles are also *logically* prior to one another.

93. On this, see Buchheim, "Persönlichkeit," 22–27.

94. It is for the very same reason that he will argue that the *revealed* religion of Christianity requires the natural religion of mythology precisely in order to be a *free* religion in a substantial sense. See lecture 10 of the PM, 159–73 (W.6.230–54).

in God for what we would recognize as becoming in the creaturely realm. Schelling believed that the positive philosophy that he developed in the last part of his life was the first to do justice to God *in his truth*, i.e., as the living, personal, and free Lord of being and Creator of the world. Secondly, it provides what has been needed all along in Schelling's philosophy from the beginning, namely, a principle for human autonomy, and thus the positivity of the real, "which is in God but is at the same time *not God himself*"[95]—or to use language he employs elsewhere, it is God but not yet *as* God. With this distinction, we have a way of avoiding, on the one hand, an ultimate metaphysical dualism that would locate human freedom in something outside of God, and thus in something that is evil by definition, and, on the other hand, making human freedom dependent in a reductive manner on God, which would both make freedom an illusion and would make God responsible ultimately for the evil due to human freedom. The "cause" of human being is from this perspective essentially complex. As we saw above, the divine Idea of things had to be both universal *and* particular, which meant that these must be integrated in the Absolute; here we see that integration expressed in the duality within unity of God's nature and existence. Because of the complexity of the cause, human being reflects the same duality: he has nature, which is his self-will or his particularity, and he has his existence, which is the identification of this self-will with the extension of his being beyond himself to others. This existence is his *personhood*, his self-communication. The difference between God and man is that in God this unity is indivisible; in man it can be divided.

We are now in a position to understand how and why evil plays a crucial role in what Schelling calls the *real* notion of freedom. Let us first consider what Schelling means by evil. Because Schelling wishes to articulate an ontological notion of freedom, he seeks to develop a properly ontological (as opposed to merely moral) understanding of evil, and he does so through an analogy to disease.[96] As we have just explained, the human being is constituted by a dark and a light principle: the dark principle is the formless longing of self-hood, to be one's own and thus to withdraw from all relation.[97] This is, so to speak, the *ground* of personality. But this

---

95. Freedom, 238 (W.4.251).

96. Interestingly, disease is crucial for Schelling as a "proof" of life: it reveals the autonomy of order, which alone is capable of the real disorder that disease implies. There are some who believe that Schelling's tragic experience of disease in the death of Auguste, Caroline's daughter, and his inability to "master" it as a thinker, is in part responsible for his insights here.

97. In reference to God, Schelling calls this principle in the WA (1815) an eternal No!: 11 (W.4.595).

formless longing must be given form, it must be raised up to the light of existence in personality, and it is so raised through the achievement of relation with others along with the deepening of understanding.[98] It is crucial to see, in this context, that the principle that Schelling refers to as dark *is not itself evil*. Rather, it is the autonomous being of the self, which Schelling identifies as due to God (God's nature in particular, or the ground in God that is not yet *as* God) and essential to the perfection of human finitude. A truly human life would be one in which the particular will subordinates itself to the universal will, in which case man unites himself in his particularity with God, and with all things in God. Evil, as the failure of such a life, as a kind of *disease*,[99] is thus defined as the dis-order of this relationship; that is, the subordination of the universal will to man's particularity. In the beginning of the treatise, Schelling had observed that disease is the proof of freedom. What he means by this is that disease is possible only if a thing possessed a dependent autonomy; that is, its *own* being, which it has by virtue of a relation to a whole greater than itself.[100] Only thus is it capable of subordinating that relation to the whole, which is an essential part of its own being, to its particularity. And this, for Schelling, is the essence of disease. In the light of this analogy, we may say that man is an autonomous individual whether he subordinates himself to the whole or not, but in the first case, when he *does* subordinate himself, his individuality lies in God as suffused with the light of personality. In the second case, by contrast, his individuality defines itself over against God, and thus against all other things: the positive principle of self-hood in this case becomes a principle of separation. Thus, while it is true that the dark principle is not *in itself* evil, it nevertheless represents the *positive principle* of evil—though it does so without making evil itself something positive.

Here, then, is the reason Schelling redefines freedom as the capacity for good and for evil: goodness and evil stem from the same positive principle. A person has a natural body whether or not he is good or evil; in both cases, it is a condition of being a self. It becomes *evil* only when the soul serves the body, rather than the reverse. Schelling believes this

---

98. In this respect, Wirth's making longing more fundamental than understanding in Schelling's philosophy requires significant qualification (see his *Conspiracy of Life*, 5–6). The absolute most fully is the unity of longing and understanding.

99. Interestingly, disease is crucial for Schelling as a "proof" of life: it reveals the autonomy of order, which alone is capable of the real disorder that disease implies. There are some who believe that Schelling's tragic experience of disease in the death of Auguste, Caroline's daughter, and his inability to "master" it as a thinker, is in part responsible for Schelling's insights here.

100. Freedom, 228 (W.4.238).

interpretation is the only way to avoid the shortcomings in traditional views on the subject. He rejects the notion of evil as simply a privation, due to something like a *deficient* cause (in distinction from the *efficient* cause of goodness, which is ultimately God himself), as well as the view that would make evil the result of imperfection, because neither of these views would be able to explain why only human beings can sin, while the far less perfect animals cannot. At the same time, it can avoid, like the traditional views it rejects, making evil something essential. It does so, however, while achieving something it claims the traditional views cannot, namely, the affirmation of evil as something quite real—not "nothing" and not simply a lesser good.[101] Schelling insists that evil is not a privation of unity, because differentiation, and the finitude it implies, is in itself something *good*. It can only be a privation of *true* unity, which is coincident with true difference, which is another way of saying that evil represents *a false unity* precisely and insofar as it represents a false difference.[102]

In short, finitude is something quite dramatic for Schelling. It is good in itself, but it bears the weight of a task, namely, the transformation of selfhood in love. Schelling describes the pathos of finitude, here, in colorful terms as the "*Angst des Lebens*," the fear of life, which Buchheim explains is meant in both the subjective and the objective sense of the genitive:[103] it is the fear that a living thing possesses on account of its fragility and capacity for failure, and at the same time a fear of life itself, of unity with God, because of the mortification of the self in its separateness that this life implies.[104]

IV. The Actuality of Evil and Love in History

There are two questions that this novel interpretation of freedom has to face in order to be complete: in the first place, how can the conception of freedom as the capacity for good and evil, which implies that freedom in itself is indifferent to either, avoid degenerating into the purely indeterminate conception, the purely "positivistic" or "empirical" conception,

---

101. See Augustine, *City of God*, XII.7, and *Enchiridion*, 11; Dionysius the Areopagite, *Divine Names*, IV.18; and Aquinas, ST, 1-2.25.2. For a comparison between Schelling and Augustine on the notion of evil, see Oesterreich, "'Der umgekehrte Gott," 483-95.

102. Freedom, 247–48 (W.4.262–63).

103. B, 145.

104. Freedom, 256 (W.4.273).

that Schelling had consistently criticized up to this point? Indeed, in the *Stuttgart Seminars* he gave in the year after publishing the *Freedom Essay*, Schelling explicitly identifies human freedom with the point of *indifference* between nature and God.[105] How is this any different, one might legitimately wonder, from a pure, indeterminate capacity to choose? Second, since this view radicalizes the particularity that has to be integrated with universality in the first principle to the point of becoming explicitly historical, then how must we think of God such that history is no longer *foreign* to him, excluded from his eternal reality, without surrendering that eternity that defines his divinity? This second question becomes, of course, all the more imposing once we acknowledge, as we must, that the history we are speaking about is one in which evil has been actualized, an evil that can no longer be explained away as an illusion or simply a lesser good whose existence is somehow necessary. How, in short, can we reconcile God and sheer contingency, which has determined itself *against* God? We will see, in the next section on the philosophy of revelation, that, for Schelling, this is a reconciliation that man cannot in fact achieve, but only God can—or, more precisely, that man can achieve only in dependence on God's achievement. Already in the *Freedom Essay*, however, we have the principle of a response, which parallels in a sense the response to the first problem: on the one hand, Schelling raises up the contingency of human freedom into eternity, and, on the other hand, he "lowers" divine freedom into history.

After explaining the *real* notion of freedom, namely, as the capacity for good and evil, Schelling begins his treatment of the *formal* concept of freedom with a criticism of the conventional association of freedom with the "undetermined capability for willing one of two contradictory opposites without any determining grounds except that this is wanted, purely and simply."[106] He thus provides us with an answer to our first question. We recall that Schelling sought, in this treatise, not simply to develop a notion of freedom in itself, but in fact to integrate it with a larger worldview. This notion of freedom as indeterminate capacity for choice is supremely resistant to integration; it is essentially opaque and unrelational, regardless of how important one wishes to make the relationships into which this freedom gets secondarily inserted. Schelling's criticism of the notion, here, ought to prevent us from interpreting the notion Schelling just presented simply along these lines, as the mere indifferent capacity

---

105. SS (W.4.350).
106. Freedom, 256 (W.4.274).

to choose either good or evil. The argument Schelling presents against freedom as indeterminate choice is incontrovertible: if there is nothing that *sufficiently* motivates the choice one makes between alternatives, then freedom becomes something wholly arbitrary, nothing more than the Epicurean "swerve."[107] The seemingly opposite view that affirms the necessary predetermination of all actions is also inadequate insofar as the location of necessity in empirical causality, he says, does away altogether with the will. It is interesting to note that Schelling concedes, nevertheless, that this determination would be preferable to voluntarism, insofar as determinism can be integrated "with reason as with the necessary unity of the whole," for it shows the depth of Schelling's desire not to sacrifice order in the end to freedom.[108] However this may be, he claims that determinism and voluntarism are in the end simply two sides of the same coin. They both miss what is *essential* to a genuine conception of freedom, namely, "an inner necessity welling up from the essence of the agent himself."[109] Once again, we hear an echo of what we have called Schelling's "natural" sense of freedom.

We discussed at length in our treatment of Schiller the importance of the notion of inner necessity for the integration of freedom and form, and we saw how Schiller's view, with the absolutizing of self-being in the

---

107. Freedom, 257 (B, 54–55).

108. There is no room in the present context to discuss this issue to the extent that it requires, but this observation gives at least some weight to the oft-disputed thesis of Schulz's classic book on Schelling's late philosophy, namely, that Schelling intends ultimately, not to champion the "extra-rational" for its own sake, but rather to *recover* reason *after* its collapse. (Bowie's observation is important: "Schelling, however, insists that 'conceptless being' is posited in order to 'again make it the content of reason.' This is, therefore, not a celebration of the irrational ground of the illusions of reason of the kind that has recently again become all too familiar but rather a correction of a particular conception of reason in which reason becomes narcissistic and only sees the world as a reflection of itself," "Translator's Introduction," HMP, 34. Cf., Fuhrmans, "Vorrede," *Grundlegung*, 8, and Buchheim, *Eins von Allem*, 5–6.) The question is simply whether the scales begin to tip as Schelling develops his positive philosophy ever further. Schelling does indeed deny that the positive philosophy can ever be systematized "in the same way" as negative philosophy (see GPP, 182–83 [W.6E.133]). Nevertheless, he insists that it remains a *system*, even if in an unusual sense (GPP, 183 [W.6E.133]). In one of his latest texts, from the philosophy of religion (see W.6E.419), Schelling says that reason *must* have an end, though he goes on to say that end is astonishment before the incomprehensibility of God. Zaborowski is right to argue that there is an ambiguity "built into" Schelling's philosophy on this point ("Geschichte," 46–47). In this respect, the debate over whether Schelling is a rationalist or an irrationalist can go on indefinitely.

109. Freedom, 257 (W.4.275).

notion of heautonomy, differs from the natural necessity one finds in Spinoza's concept of freedom. Schelling's own view lies much closer to Schiller's than to Spinoza's, though he elaborates the theological dimension of the conception, which remained implicit in Schiller, and gives this dimension a radical interpretation. His interpretation was in fact prepared for in his *Naturphilosophie*. For Schelling, the notion of internal or natural necessity is incompatible with freedom only if we think of nature as "dead," i.e., as pure object. As we have observed several times, this is the heart of his complaint against Spinoza. There is no tension if we recognize that nature is essentially *activity*, which has its paradigm in subjectivity. If nature is productivity, then human nature, which is, so to speak, the highest instance of nature, is self-productivity. As Schelling puts the point in the *Freedom Essay*, "man's essence is essentially *his own deed*," and thus, "necessity and freedom are interrelated as one being which appears as the one or the other only when viewed from different aspects: in itself it is freedom, formally it is necessity."[110] Notice, this is a version of Schiller's distinction between autonomy and heautonomy: on the one hand, we have (logical or moral) form dominating matter; on the other, the whole being taking possession of itself. In any event, from the perspective of Schelling's distinction, freedom is never empty, because it has always already been fully determined, and at the same time this determination is never the imposition of a foreign necessity because it has always already sprung from the inner being of the agent and has no other principle of origin.

In order to avoid the obvious contradiction into which this conception would seem destined to fall—doesn't the self as determining subject have to exist prior to itself as determined object, and if so wouldn't this self have to be *either* as yet undetermined *or* "objectively" *pre*-determined, which would land us back in precisely the same dilemma the proposal was meant to save us from?—Schelling reflects on the nature of the relationship between eternity and time. The question of "priority" implies temporality, and indeed if self-determination were an event that took place in time it would in fact be self-contradictory.[111] But Schelling insists that it is *not* a (merely) temporal event; rather, it is an eternal one. It has to be eternal,

---

110. Ibid., 259 (W.4.277).

111. Dale Snow makes the important observation that self-determination cannot occur in time because everything in time is interdependent ("Evolution," 327). This same observation could apply as well to the notion of organic form, as self-organization, which we discussed last chapter. On the other hand, of course, self-determination cannot be "merely" eternal, in the sense of timelessness, without returning us to the dualism the notion seeks to avoid: see Beach, *Potencies*, 64–65.

From Organism to Incarnation

in fact, precisely because self-determination cannot occur according to the cause-effect schema that is indeed bound to time. The paradox that Schelling posited in the ground-existence reciprocity thus appears once again at the level of human being. We recall here, moreover, the "nonthingness," i.e., the *unconditionality* or absoluteness, of the organism that we discussed in the last chapter; such a conception is a precursor to the notion of freedom Schelling is elaborating in this treatise. If self-determination is not (merely) temporal, Schelling continues, then there is a sense in which it "extends" beyond time, which means beyond creation itself, so that we would have to say that a person is who he is in some respect *from eternity,* "*before*" the foundation of the world.[112]

God's act of creating the human being is not an *extrinsic* activity in the sense of something imposed on an object from the outside. Instead, creation is a *co-act*; it is something in which the human being shares from the beginning, not as a mere object, but as both subject and object at once. We thus recover a notion that Schelling mentioned as early as 1800, but did not elaborate to any significant degree, namely, that history is a drama, of which God is the author even while each of us invents, in some sense, his own role.[113] Whenever we act in time we are thus bringing to light the inner content of an eternal action, namely, our created self-determination. Our freedom is therefore coincident with an inner necessity, and for that very reason is a *revelation* of meaning, of our internal essence, rather than being a mere empirical fact, which cannot be understood but only recorded. Schelling affirms what he refers to as the ancient teaching about predestination, which he praises for allowing our comprehension of history as an *order* rather than an arbitrary and endless series, though he ridicules the extrinsicist view of this order as imposed on history simply by divine decree: "We, too, assert predestination, but in a completely different sense, namely, the following: as man acts now, so he has acted from eternity and even in the beginning of creation."[114]

A qualification is required here in order to avoid what would be an easy mistake to make in interpreting Schelling's view, and perhaps he

---

112. Freedom, 259–60 (W.4.277–78).

113. STI, 210 (KA.I.9-1.301).

114. Freedom, 261 (W.4.279–80). It bears remarking that Plato posits a similar origin for man's character in *Republic* X, 617d–21b. The *daimon* that Heraclitus had said determines one's character, Plato says the soul chooses for itself. It makes this choice in Hades, and so in some sense "outside of temporal life." As Plato sees it, one chooses one's eternal character paradoxically based on the choices one makes in one's temporal life.

is not altogether clear about it himself. "*Pre*-destination" cannot mean simply *prior*, insofar as this would make it a temporal event. One might imagine that Schelling is saying that the choices made in one's life are simply the unfolding of a previous, fundamental choice one made "before" the beginning of the world in some sort of "pre"-existence. But this view would not only return us to the contradiction described above, it would also make the reality of history an illusion: everything would already have been decided; we would have no future, and indeed no real present, but only an absolutely oppressive past. In this case, however, there would be no freedom. The problem here would be analogous to the one regarding methodology in Schelling's *Naturphilosophie*: though he intended to integrate the real and ideal, he insisted on the *strictly* a priori method of construction, which would necessarily eliminate the *reality* of the real and tend to reduce it to mere ideality. Here, interpreting eternal self-determination as an event that has already taken place *before* time would eliminate the reality of history and undermine the goal of integrating the particular into the universal. Indeed, the solution to the former problem depends in an essential way on the solution to this latter. Rather than referring to eternity as something that comes "before" time, Schelling claims it is an act that "moves through time (untouched by it)," a life that is "prior to this life—except that it is not thought of as preceding in time, since the intelligible is outside of time altogether." Instead of making this determination simply *a priori*, Schelling says that "in the prior the subsequent, too, is already coacting."[115] This qualification also keeps us from oversimplifying the matter by interpreting freedom as simply a kind of self-creation: we are who we make ourselves to be.[116] Schelling is trying to integrate the active choice with receptive determination rather than simply reducing the latter to the former.

Now, there is a slight inconsistency in these formulations regarding a crucial matter. If time does not in some sense "touch" eternity, if the universal is not in *some respect* dependent on the particular, what sense would it make to assert that the subsequent is "already coacting" with the prior? The second formulation would seem to be the more consistent one, and the more adequate to the problem Schelling is attempting to resolve. If self-determination is eternal, it need not be opposed to time at all. But if it is not opposed to time, it can include time without compromise of its

---

115. Freedom, 260 (W.4.279).

116. Bernard Freydberg likewise qualifies the choice that defines one as non-temporal, but he does not see how this eternal choice would have to be itself reciprocally dependent on action in time: see *Schelling's Dialogical Freedom Essay*, 72–73.

From Organism to Incarnation

eternal character. What this means is that we can affirm *both* the novelty of historical choice, *and* the eternity of self-determination, by explaining that one's choices are not, in one respect, anticipated by eternity, but, *once made*, have always, from eternity, been what they are—this particular choice at this particular time. In this case, not only would the "deed" of one's eternal self-determination determine each of one's choices in time, but the reverse would also be, in some sense, true: who one eternally *is* depends on one's life in time; one's eternal character is co-determined by the sort of person one has chosen to be over the course of one's temporal history, even while it remains true "at the same time" that those very choices are informed by the eternal identity they help create. This would imply, among other things, that one's future choices *bear on* one's present choices, without either simply anticipating the other. However paradoxical this view may seem, there is no other way to integrate the particular and the universal in a manner that would do justice to both, there is no other way to interpret the "subsequent" as *coacting* in the prior. There has to be a real, albeit asymmetrical, reciprocity between the infinite and the finite, the eternal and the temporal, in order to have an adequate conception of either.[117] We will return to this issue and assess Schelling's position more fully at the end of this chapter.

The moment we affirm a reciprocity between the infinite and the finite, God and man, the moment, that is, that we make man's historical self-determination an eternal truth, the problem of evil acquires itself a literally infinite weight. The free choice of evil, in this case, cannot simply be something added to the Absolute from the outside. Instead, evil must somehow have something to do with the meaning of God himself. How are we to understand this? The core of Schelling's response to the problem of evil lies in the distinction he had described between nature and existence in both man and God. As we saw above, the "divisibility" of these two principles in man is the *positive ground* of the possibility of evil. But it is also the principle of genuine, real goodness: goodness would be abstract and superficial if it did not have a *self* in it, that is, a kind of resistance to universality that thus gives the universality, once achieved, a kind of force, character, or, best, "personality." Personality is the unity of ground and existence. Moreover, self-revelation is essential to being a person.[118] One cannot be a person without an other to whom one can reveal oneself,

---

117. We recall that Schiller made the same observation in his AEM. See Letter XIX, 129–37 (SW.8.365–70).
118. Buchheim, "Persönlichkeit," 20.

since the overcoming of nature requires an *other for whom*, and as it were "toward whom," the nature (as contraction into self) is overcome. In this respect, a personal conception of God requires an "other," both within God and at the same time not God. But while these aspects are divisible in man, they are wholly and absolutely one in God. While this is precisely a function of God's perfection, in one respect, in another respect it presents a sort of lack. As Schelling explains, for the unity of the two principles to be living and "actual," some kind of division and conflict is required for it to overcome, and this is something that cannot belong to God by definition. In this way, God is dependent on man *at least in order* to reveal himself as Person, or indeed, as Schelling puts it later, as *love*:

> For if God as spirit is the indivisible unity of both principles, and this same unity is actual only in man's spirit, then if it were just as indissoluble in him as in God, there would be no difference between man and God. Man would be absorbed in God, and there would be no revelation and no movement of love. For every being can be revealed only in its opposite: love only in hate, unity only in conflict. Were there no division of principles, unity could not demonstrate its omnipotence; were there no discord, love could not become actual. Man is placed on the pinnacle where he has the source of self-movement towards good and evil equally within him; the bond of principles within him is not a necessary but a free one. He stands at the junction; whatever he chooses, that will be his deed. But he cannot remain in indecision, because God must necessarily reveal himself and because in creation nothing whatsoever can remain ambiguous.[119]

In other words, God cannot reveal himself as love except as having overcome his inner will to remain in himself, i.e., his ground, but this ground cannot be overcome except as resistant, and it can be resistant only by "awakening" self-will in man, which, though itself good, is the principle of the evil that in turn provokes God's total self-revelation as almighty love.[120]

With this complex formulation, Schelling wishes to assert that God can make evil possible without being responsible for it, and indeed that, far from evil threatening the reality of God's love, it is only *because* of the reality of love that evil exists at all. As Schelling explains, evil is not a "conditio sine qua non" for love, but only in a certain respect for the

---

119. Freedom, 250 (W.4.265–66).

120. As Freydberg has put it, God needs to undergo an evil of which he is not the cause in order to be a *living* God: *Dialogical Freedom Essay*, 63.

ground, insofar as it represents self-willing, which is the possibility of evil. But God cannot eliminate the will of this ground without eliminating his own existence. Thus, the reality of love entails the possibility—always already eternally realized and witnessed as such by God—of evil. In this sense alone, Schelling claims, one can say that God wills evil: it is *de facto*, but not *de jure*, included in his willing the eternal victory of love.[121] Evil, we might say, gives God an indispensable opportunity to reveal the depths of his being that would otherwise have remained eternally submerged.[122] In this respect, and in a way that we will have to spell out further in our discussion of the philosophy of revelation, God can include within himself the whole of human history, which is in some respect a disordered history, without compromising either his eternal sovereignty as God or the contingency, the vicissitudes, and even the darkness, of human history. God remains supreme, not by eliminating what is other or oppressing it, but allowing it to *be* in freedom and always already outflanking it, so to speak, in love.

What are the implications of all this for the question of God's freedom? According to Schelling, as the perfect unity of two principles of being, God also represents the perfect unity of necessity and freedom, not as two parts of a whole, but as an identity: necessity in God *is* freedom, and freedom is necessity. Although he will explain the matter differently in the philosophy of revelation lectures, as we will soon see, in the *Freedom Essay* he affirms that there is, first of all, no *choice* in God, understood as deliberation between alternatives.[123] On the other hand, there is no mechanical necessity, since there is nothing outside of God to compel him. Instead, God is the perfect coincidence of apparently opposed elements, each of which takes on the character of the other by virtue of the unity. Thus, the will of the ground is the necessity that enters into all of God's acts, but it is not "blind mechanical necessity," essentially un-conscious and thus opposed to God's conscious reality; it is rather always already in union with that consciousness as a kind of natural longing. On the other hand, God's conscious will is not "sheer" will in abstraction from nature, but carries with it the weight of his substance. God's freedom, then, is a deep longing that is always willed, and a moral inclination that always becomes a metaphysical necessity. Each is, in a way, the condition and cause of the other, in a kind of reciprocal causality that cannot be separated out

121. Freedom, 272–73 (W.4.293–94).
122. Marx, *The Philosophy of Schelling*, 79.
123. Freedom, 269 (W.4.289).

into a sequence of distinct moments. In the view of a God whose nature perfectly inclines to what he wills as Person, Schelling presents us with a kind of perfect model of the simultaneity of necessity and spontaneity in the eternal self-determination that constitutes the essence of human freedom, with the difference that human freedom bears the anxiety of life that springs from its finitude and temptation to indecision or sinful self-assertion.

Before concluding his treatise, and after apparently resolving the various possible objections that could be raised, Schelling takes a final step in his argument, which, though one might say it feels tacked on somewhat gratuitously,[124] Schelling claims is the "highest point of the entire investigation."[125] Here, he returns to the question of the unity in difference in God, and adds a significant new dimension to what had preceded in the treatise, which both recollects a basic point in his earlier identity philosophy, and anticipates some of the formulations of his later philosophy, as we will see in a moment. He introduces this dimension in response to a question that he says he has left unanswered up to this point: in what sense can these two principles, ground and existence, be one in reality? "For either there is no common midpoint for these two—then we must declare ourselves for absolute dualism; or there is such a midpoint—and then in the final analysis the two coincide again."[126] As we recall from the last chapter, unity in difference simply by itself is unstable without a mediating third; here, he points out that it will collapse either into an ultimate monism or an ultimate dualism. There must therefore, he goes on to say, be a "being" that is absolutely prior to the distinction into ground and existence. Schelling gives this being a new name, "unground" (*Ungrund*), but describes its essence using a very familiar word in his system, as absolute *indifference*. As Thomas Buchheim observes, the term "unground," which Schelling no doubt borrowed from the mystical theosopher Jacob Boehme, whom he had been reading a great deal in this period, is meant simply to designate God as he is in himself, i.e., precisely not *qua* enabling ground for his self-revealing personality in relation to *us*.[127] This nonground, Schelling specifies, is *not* the unity of opposites, which he says would imply either the confused identification of what is different or the

---

124. This is a common reaction to this part of the treatise; one finds it, for example, even in Heidegger: *Schelling*, 191–92.

125. Freedom, 276 (W.4.298).

126. Ibid. (W.4.298).

127. B, 161–62n336.

preservation of the principles implicitly within *as* opposites: we would thus fall back to the very problem to which the unground is meant as a response. Instead, as we saw earlier, indifference implies the *total transcendence* of the opposites, precisely so that it can perfectly and completely indwell them: it is not simultaneously both, but rather impartially either. According to Buchheim, this indifference is what allows God to be wholly involved in each of the "levels" of revelation: from indifference to God's self-generation to the differentiation of principles to creation to judgment to love. For Schelling, this "super primordial" first principle, if you will, is essential ultimately for *love*. As he had affirmed in his 1806 Aphorisms, the mystery of love consists in a relation that is both necessary and free, "it combines what could be by itself and yet is not and cannot be without the other."[128] If there were no primordial indifference, the two "constitutive" principles of God's being, the light and the darkness, the universality and self-being, would either be extrinsic to one another without any internal need for the other, or they would require the other for their own being, which would imply too much necessity. But, as he says, there can be no love when there is mere indifference or mere need. The complete inner life of God thus proves to be complex (though without ever losing the simplicity of either indifference or love): the initial distinction between ground and existent is initially allowed to remain until the fulfillment of history, in which the dark principle dissolves into the light of spirit, which in turn is subordinated to nothing other than that which is highest *simpliciter*, the love that is now "all in all." How Schelling further specifies the inner life of God through a more differentiated confrontation with history is a theme he did not stop working on from the time of his *Freedom Essay* (1809) until his call to Berlin in 1841. It is here that he articulated his final understanding of the matter, among other things, through a philosophical appropriation of the central doctrines of Christianity.

V. Creation as Theogony

It is, of course, not possible to give a full account of Schelling's late philosophy, one of the basic parts of which he presented in Berlin, most famously in WS 1841/42, under the general name of "Philosophy of Revelation."[129]

---

128. Intro to Aph, #163 (W.4.108).

129. The "Philosophy of Revelation" had come to represent the final moment of Schelling's positive philosophy, which some believe itself is the completion of the *Ages of the World* project he had worked on for decades, beginning just after the *Stuttgart*

The Perfection of Freedom

The lectures represent one of the most original attempts in history to give a thorough and sophisticated systematic philosophical argumentation for the "positive" data of Christian revelation (Hegel's philosophy being another one). It is important to note that, for Schelling, the moment philosophy becomes historical it cannot avoid an engagement with the claims of Christianity, which is at the very least an undeniable fact of history, without betraying its own essence.[130] Although this engagement involves

---

Seminars, in 1811. In its final form, the positive philosophy had three "stages," a first part in which Schelling expounded a philosophy of God and creation, in light of a general historical account of the emergence of the positive philosophy: the "Grounding of Positive Philosophy"; then, a series of lectures on the "Philosophy of Mythology"; and finally the "Philosophy of Revelation." These main parts were prefaced by a history of modern philosophy since Descartes, which explained the relationship this new positive philosophy had to the thinkers that preceded it. This "cycle" was essentially complete in 1832, after which year Schelling would present the parts over again without significant changes in the lectures he delivered in Munich. When he was called to Berlin for the 1841/42 WS, he announced his system, no longer as the "System of the Ages of the World," which was the title they had in Munich, but simply as the "Philosophy of Revelation." In his first semester at Berlin, Schelling thus presented the whole cycle in a concentrated form, beginning with a shorter history of modern philosophy, providing an overview of myth, and ending with a shorter version of the philosophy of revelation. Although he lectured again on the philosophy of myth, as well as new lectures on the "Principles of Philosophy," and even, somewhat surprisingly, on his old *Naturphilosophie*, before retiring from lecturing in 1846, the "Philosophy of Revelation" can be said to represent the final form of Schelling's oft-changing philosophy. On all of this, see Fuhrmans, *Grundlegung*, 26–46.

In spite of some gestures in this direction, Schelling never published any of these late lectures, though he left instructions for his son regarding the inclusion of his manuscripts in his collected works. The rationalist theologian H. E. G. Paulus, who had attended his original lectures in Berlin, took it upon himself to publish his own transcription of Schelling's lectures. Schelling took up a law suit against Paulus, but lost. This transcription has been edited as the "Paulus-Nachschrift" by Manfred Frank, (3rd edition [Frankfurt am Main: Suhrkamp, 1995]). This text forms the basis of our presentation. It has the disadvantage of not being from Schelling's own hand, but it has the decided advantage, for our purposes, of offering the "system" in a compact form, whereas the texts in the collected works often retrace the same ground at great length. Indeed, as Frank points out, these texts themselves have the disadvantage of being presented as "finished versions" of texts that never stopped evolving (PO, 42). Moreover, it is impossible, as Xavier Tilliette has concluded after many years of study, to find a paradigm in the collected works that would explain how what he calls the "*disjecta membra*" fit together (see "Une philosophie en deux," 68). On the general reliability of the Paulus-Nachschrift, see PO, 46–52. According to Frank, this text contains Schelling's own words, even if a comparison with other notes taken from the lectures suggests that not every word was recorded here. We will occasionally refer to the texts in the collected works when clarification is necessary.

130. See GPP, 190 (W.6E.144–445). Jean-Marie Vaysse explains that, once reason recognizes its inability to ground itself (as Schelling realizes "contra Hegel"), it will

From Organism to Incarnation

faith, Schelling claims that it does not thereby cease to be philosophical.[131] In the years following the *Freedom Essay*, Schelling made a discovery that he eventually took to be his most important contribution to philosophy, namely, that the fact of reality is irreducibly different from its definable "whatness" (i.e., existence is different from essence), so that reason, which works with essences, depends on what lies outside of itself to come to realize its own end, which is to come to know reality in its truth.[132] When we realize that philosophy *always* depends in some respect on a kind of "*unvordenkliche*" *prius*, something it cannot account for on the basis of reason alone—this is indeed what it means to say, as Plato did, that philosophy begins with wonder[133]—the absolute *prius* of faith, however unanticipated it necessarily will be, does not introduce something foreign to thought, which would thereby make it an "*Unphilosophie*," even if it does involve a reconception of philosophy. Thus the most complete philosophy, for Schelling, *includes* faith within it as an extra-conceptual ground for thinking, and thereby becomes positive philosophy.[134] We will in the present context only be attending to the themes directly connected with our discussion so far, specifically Schelling's development of the primordiality of difference and unity in the Absolute, the role of human history in the coming to be of divine personality, and the implications all of this has for the meaning of freedom.

We will focus on three essential moments in Schelling's exposition, each of which is not a mere logical distinction but a dramatic event, or as Schelling himself calls it, a "process." First, the distinction of God in himself whereby pure act becomes a three-fold possibility; second, the positing of the world "outside" of God whereby God's possibilities become the three potencies; and third, the incarnation of God in history as the redemption of finite freedom, whereby the potencies become personalities. In other words, we will explain Schelling's view of God in himself, in

---

necessarily have to engage with the historical data of pagan and Christian revelation ("Schelling Contra Hegel," 376–77).

131. See GPP, 183 (W.6E.133–34), in which Schelling explains that positive philosophy is not religious because revelation does not possess any authority for reason in this philosophy other than its factuality.

132. Schelling points to his polemical essay on Jacobi (1812) as the place wherein he first gave a public intimation of his new positive philosophy (GPP, 149 [W.6E.86]).

133. See WA (1827), 183, PO, 161, and Rev (W.6.404–5).

134. Although Schelling was influenced by Jacobi (and the theosophists) in the development of his positive philosophy, his clearest difference from him lies in his claim that faith perfects philosophy in transforming it, rather than simply bringing philosophy to an end, as Jacobi thought. See WA (1827), 58–74.

his creation of the world, and in his personal entry into the history of that world.

A. God in Himself (God as *Spirit*)

According to Schelling, purely rational philosophy—which he calls "negative" philosophy, the philosophy of the academy as opposed to life[135]—aims at showing the logical necessity of things that lie, so to speak, within the boundaries of concepts. Consistently developed, it leads up to God, but not *as* God. Instead, it is only God in theory, as the foundation for the intelligibility of all things, and so as the *primum cogitabile*. At the summit of this philosophical task is the ontological argument, which affirms the necessary existence of God. But one of the most recurrent themes of Schelling's late thought is that this argument does not, in fact, attain existence; it remains within conceptual necessity, and so its conclusion is best formulated: *if* God exists, he exists necessarily.[136] What distinguishes positive philosophy, then, is that it begins with the sheer *fact* of existence, which is something that can never be deduced from a concept. Existence is simply there, and it is always-already there, before one can reflect on it and as presupposed by that reflection. Schelling calls this philosophy positive, because it starts with a reality posited outside of reason, a positing that therefore makes reason "ecstatic."[137] Its task is then to show how this "*unvordenkliches Sein*," "unforethinkable being," or what he calls the "blindly existing" reality, is in fact divine.

To understand why we cannot simply identify this sheer existence with God gets us to what most specifically characterizes Schelling's late philosophy. Revealingly, Schelling accuses Spinoza of making the mistake of this identification.[138] This is connected to the fact that a genuine understanding of freedom is missing from Spinoza's system. Sheer existence, according to Schelling, lacks all potential: it is not act from potency,

---

135. GPP, 198 (W.6E.156).

136. Schelling expounds this especially in his presentation of Descartes' philosophy: HMP, 42–61 (W.5.74–99). Cf., GPP, 199–201 (W.6E.156–60); PO, 156. A similar point had been made by Aquinas in his treatment of the argument, and also by Kant. For Aquinas, the argument works only if one accepts the real existence of that than which nothing greater can be thought (ST 1.2.1ad1). For Kant, existence is not a real predicate, and so is not included in any concept of a thing, even the most perfect: see CPR A592–602 B620–30.

137. GPP, 203 (W.6E.162–63). Cf., Schulz, *Die Vollendung*, 49–52.

138. Ibid., 199 (W.6E.156–57).

Schelling says, but act prior to all potency, which is precisely what makes it prior to all thought. Potential belongs to an essence, a definable "what," and so it is by definition conceivable. But this unforethinkable being, prior to all potency, thus has no *ability* to be anything other than it actually is, which is another way of saying it lacks all freedom. Drawing on the same distinction he had made in the *Freedom Essay*, Schelling explains that, in order to be *free*, and indeed in order simply to be divine, God must distinguish himself from it, as nature; he must be able to be other than it.[139] Here, Schelling introduces the groundwork for his famous doctrine of the "divine potencies," which are a sort of hybrid between logical principles and real living powers.[140] We understand them best as developments from Schelling's early articulations of the simplicity in complexity of the highest principle: his early notion of the I and not-I in the Absolute, subject (A=B) and object (B=A) in their union in his identity systems, and ground, existence, unground, and love in the *Freedom Essay*; developments that incorporate Schelling's constant desire to affirm reality as living, or as he put it in the *Freedom Essay*, being ultimately as *will*, without sacrificing rational order. As we observed earlier, in the most general sense, potencies, viewed "mathematically," represent in a paradigmatic way the difference Schelling allows truly to coexist with unity: namely, quantitative difference, the sameness of content (A) multiplied to different degrees (A^1, A^2, A^3, etc.).[141] But the term also has a "dynamic" sense, which expresses the very things Schelling tends to associate with freedom, namely, possibility, power, force, and drive. This accounts for the increasing significance the notion acquires in his late thought. In the present context, Schelling begins by elaborating these as three fundamental "possibilities," which then become "potencies" and finally "personalities" as they increase in strength, which corresponds to their increasing relation to the reality of the world. Conceived on the basis of pure actuality, they are significantly different from the pure possibility articulated in the negative philosophy, since they exhibit the real vitality and substance that comes with a hard won achievement.[142]

139. Schelling affirms the traditional notion of God as pure actuality, but with a paradoxical twist: the *purely actual* God is only *potentially* God, insofar as pure act describes only God's *nature*, and not his personal existence, which, as we will see, is understood by contrast in terms of potency: see PO, 156.

140. See Beach, *Potencies*, 108.

141. See his earlier explanation of the potencies in Phil of Art, 14 (W.3.385-86).

142. Clearly responding to what Marx (Marx, *Philosophy of Schelling*, 81) takes to be a criticism Hegel made of Schelling—namely, the passage in the *Phenomenology*:

The Perfection of Freedom

The distinction of the initial possibilities from the blind actuality of unforethinkable being constitutes what we might call God's inner life. Blind existing is not outside of God, but nor is it simply identical with God. It is God but not *as* God. According to Schelling, God is truly God only as spirit, which will eventually come to mean only as free personality. But the passage from blind being to free personality passes through a series of (fairly complex) steps. The first is to see God in himself, which means as spirit, the primary feature of which is *power*. Blind being is not God because God can be *as* God only through his *will*: God's being is a self-willed being. But blind being by definition is not willed; it is always already "there" as the absolute *prius*. For this to be divine requires it to be *affirmed*. But this self-affirmation is a complex event, which Schelling distinguishes into three moments. What is lacking in blind being, what makes it not God himself, is *possibility*. For God to be *as* God is to distinguish himself from blind being, which is, in other words, to posit himself precisely as potentially *other* than it. This is the *decisive* moment in Schelling's interpretation of God in the philosophy of revelation. He calls this moment "*das Seinkönnende*," "the ability-to-be," or making its content more explicit, the "ability-to-be-other"(= B).[143] It is just here, Schelling says, that God's *divinity* begins, because it is only in this possibility, in this power (*Stärke*), that we can speak of this reality as God. This ability-to-be is therefore what Schelling calls the "*principium divinitatis*."[144] Again echoing a point we saw in the *Freedom Essay*, Schelling says that "man, too, has to liberate himself from his being [*von seinem Sein sich losreißen*], in order to begin a free existence [*ein freies Sein*]."[145] God, as B, is not

---

"Thus the life of God and divine cognition may well be spoken of as a disporting of Love with itself; but this idea sinks into mere edification, and even insipidity, if it lacks the seriousness, the suffering, the patience, and the labour of the negative" (Phen, 10 [GW.9.18])—Schelling refers to the inner life of God as *wisdom*, which is achieved by God's principle passing through "all the delights and tribulations" of the process of coming to consciousness: PO, 185–86.

143. PO, 169. This possibility is designated as "B" precisely because it is *other*, and therefore in a certain sense *secondary*. In his early thought, Schelling identified "B" with objectivity or the real. It represented the *first* moment of his *Naturphilosophie*, but specifically as A=B, or as Subject-Object, i.e., objectivity that results from the activity of subjectivity. Although he never specifies it as such in these lectures, one may assume that the "A" that precedes the "B" in the philosophy of revelation is unforethinkable being. Schelling does not make this explicit, presumably because unforethinkable being is strictly undefinable and lacking any content whatsoever.

144. PO, 169.

145. Ibid., 170.

identical with being, but is the *Lord of being*.[146] It is just this notion of God that overcomes pantheism once and for all, because pantheism just is the identification of God with being.[147]

With this distinction of God from sheer existence, however, not all is said. Unforethinkable being is not eliminated in the distinction from it of the ability-to-be, but the concepts get reversed in a way that creates a tension. Unforethinkable being, which in itself is pure act, becomes in relation to the ability-to-be mere potential, while the latter, as potential, in fact defines the divinity of God, and so is a sort of actuality. But pure act, Schelling goes on to say, cannot bear to be mere potential, and so becomes *effective* (*es wirkt*), i.e., it re-actualizes itself, now no longer as blind being but, mediated by the negation of otherness (B), as determinate, or as "developed essence" (*entwickelte Wesen*). In contrast to the ability-to-be, this is a "having-to-be," a "*Seinmüssende.*" The tension between these two, according to Schelling, is what keeps God from being something merely static, and instead revealing himself to contain within himself "life and process."[148]

But the complete notion of God is not this tension between competing "possibilities"; it also includes the transcendence of this tension, without which God would be in a sense subordinate to these moments rather than the *Lord* of possibility. God's inner freedom, for Schelling, lies in his ability to be or not to be, to act or not to act. This is the third possibility, which unites the first two and in so doing produces for the first time, so to speak, the reality of *spirit*: "It is therefore the ability-to-be-having-to-be, the necessary essence that does not lose itself, or in other words, *spirit.*"[149] We find an echo, here, of two patterns that characterized Schelling's *Naturphilosophie*: first, the generation of life from two opposed

---

146. As Schelling says in his WA (1827) lectures and inspired by Newton's explanation of the name "Dominus," God is nothing merely "in himself"; God is a *relational* notion, he is himself only as Lord of being: "God is the Lord of being. Here, God is taken in relation to being, and this notion runs counter to the new conception [*Vorstellung*] of God as *absolute*. But the *first error* lies in determining God according to what he is simply and absolutely. *God as such is nothing at all in himself; he is nothing but pure and total relation.* He *is* only Lord of Being. He exists only to be a Lord of being. God is the only free nature not occupied with himself, who has absolutely nothing to do with himself. Every substance is occupied with itself; but he is sui securus; and so he occupies himself with others and stands in a relationship to all substances" (WA [1827], 105). See Baumgarten and Korten, *Schelling*, 163.

147. PO, 170.

148. Ibid., 173.

149. Ibid., 173.

principles brought into a potent unity by virtue of a third; and, second, an identification of the preservation of selfhood with the resistance to absorption in relation. In other words, just as, in the *Naturphilosophie*, the subject does not pass over altogether into the objectivity, so too, here, the "ability-to-be" withholds itself from necessary essence. This is what allows God's necessity, paradoxically, to be a *free* one, which Schelling describes as the "ought-to-be" (*das Seinsollende*).[150]

The three-fold articulation of possibility in God's "inner life" is strictly comprehensive, Schelling says. Every future possibility is contained *in nuce* herein. In fact, Schelling describes the divine ideas at the basis of things as so many configurations of these possibilities.[151] The question now is, how do these possibilities become actual?

B. The Positing of the World *Praeter Deum* (God as *Person*)

One of the points Schelling most emphasizes in his philosophical account of creation is that the independent being of the world does not follow from God with logical necessity. God does not *need* the world in order to come to know himself, as, for example, Hegel thought.[152] We would be forced to affirm some such thing only if we remained within the limits of negative philosophy. In the positive philosophy, by contrast, we begin with actual existence, from which God is distinct, which means that, since there *is* something rather than nothing, and since this fact is not deduced from any concept, what was possibility must have been actualized in a manner independent of logical necessity. Schelling infers from this that God is not bound to the world; it makes no difference to God in himself whether there is a world or not. God is in this sense free to create or not to create. At the same time, however, Schelling insists that we may not therefore assume that *there is no reason* for the world. God is not arbitrary. There

---

150. Although Schelling repeats this formulation of the tripartite structure of spirit in his own manuscript (see, e.g., W.5.57–59), in other places he describes the three moments somewhat differently: the first is the "ability-to-be," which is pure subject, the second is "the purely existing thing [*das rein Seyende*]," or pure objectivity, and the third is the "subject that posits itself or exists as such" (*das als solches gesetzte oder seyende Subjekt*). This last, which is the complete notion of spirit, according to Schelling, does not cease to be potential (i.e., free subjectivity) even *in* its objectivity. See W.6.305–12. Christian Danz has interpreted this to mean that spirit, for Schelling, is "determined indeterminacy," "Die Philosophie der Offenbarung," 178.

151. PO, 184–85.

152. Ibid., 183.

must, therefore, be a necessity based not on logical derivation but rather on the nature of spirit, such as Schelling describes it. Spirit, we saw above, is free necessity. The cause that corresponds to the free necessity of spirit, according to Schelling, is the need to be known, which he thus posits as the reason for the existence of the world.[153] In other words, there must be a necessity to create, without which the world would be simply unintelligible, but that necessity must not be imposed by something lower than God; instead, it must spring from his highest nature, his divinity itself. Schelling explains this by saying that God cannot be God except as Lord of creation, but his lordship is defined as the ability to create or not. "Before" creation, in other words, God is, so to speak, pure possibility; this possibility becomes effective *potency* only in the actual production of a world that is other than God.

In order to understand what it means for God to create, it is helpful to recall the insight Schelling articulated in the *Freedom Essay* regarding the possibility of being *in* God but at the same time *other than* God. The same insight reappears here in a more differentiated fashion. God cannot be *actually* God except in relation to being that is *actually* different from him; prior to this is only the real ability-to-be other. Contrary to the sterility of self-thinking thought, the God of negative philosophy, Schelling cites Goethe: "*Ich denke nur, wenn ich produziere*"; true spiritual blessedness occurs only when one is outside of oneself, full of concern for an other.[154] God, too, ought to be so understood: his blessedness lies in his (non-compulsory) self-transcendence in a world. At the same time, however, because this possibility of otherness lies *in* God, creation is not something "added," so to speak, to God. Instead, it occurs, we might say, in the space God clears within himself through the "suspension" of his existence as *actus purus*: "God *does not empty himself into the world*, but rather withdraws into his divinity; . . . insofar as he *suspends the act, he enters into himself*. At the same time however God *suspends the act of his necessary existence in order to posit a being different from himself in the place of that first existence*."[155] As a result, creation is to be understood as *other than* God (*praeter deum*) but as nevertheless still *in* God.

---

153. Ibid., 189. Laughland (*Schelling versus Hegel*, 133) affirms God's non-compulsion to create in order to be able to claim Schelling's orthodoxy in this matter, but he does not take into account the necessity that Schelling nevertheless attributes to creation.

154. "I am truly thinking only when I produce." Ibid., 17/1–/37.

155. Ibid., 177. Italics are Schelling's.

The Perfection of Freedom

In relation to the real otherness of the world, Schelling reinterprets the three "possibilities" that constitute the inner life of God now as effective *potencies*. The ability-to-be other (B) is now boundless will, which Schelling calls the *causa materia*, or that out of which the world comes to be. This recalls the *Ursein* that Schelling had identified with will in the *Freedom Essay*. He explains here that the emptiness of the primal will out of which all things come is the only intelligible meaning of the traditional *ex nihilo*.[156] With the existence of the world, the "having-to-be" of God's inner life becomes the second potency (A^2), which Schelling explains as that which "overcomes" boundless will by setting determinate limits on it. He calls this potency the *causa efficiens*, or that *per quam* the world comes to be. The third potency (A^3) regulates this process so that it happens gradually in stages, building up the relative levels of being in nature. We recall here nature's progressive self-construction in Schelling's *Naturphilosophie*. This third potency is the "*causa in quam* or *secundum quam omnia sunt*."[157] As regulating the process, A^3 posits what "ought-to-be." Because, he says, this confirms the overcoming of B by A^2, it seems to render B— i.e., the will precisely as boundless—that which "ought-not-to-be," that is, to reveal it as evil.[158] However, once again echoing the *Freedom Essay*, he clarifies that B is only the *positive principle* of evil; it is not itself evil. It can become so only through human freedom, as we shall see in a moment. The "stage" is nevertheless set here because what were simply possibilities have now been externalized, set in motion, and therefore separated into a living tension with one another through the act of creation. The separation of the potencies will turn out to be a precondition for their being actually dis-ordered in evil.

We said that, for Schelling, creation is not necessary to God. But, given Schelling's understanding of creation and its relation to God's inner life, we ought not simply to infer that creation is therefore a free act in the sense of an act that follows from a God understood as free in himself.[159] Instead, as Emil Brito has helpfully put it, God, for Schelling, is only *potentially* free prior to creation, but *requires* creation in order to be free in a *real* sense.[160] Indeed, we will see in a moment that more is needed for real

---

156. Ibid., 179.

157. Ibid., 182.

158. Ibid., 182–83.

159. See Laughland, *Schelling versus Hegel*, 133, and Marx, *The Philosophy of Schelling*, 84–85.

160. Brito, "La création chez Hegel et Schelling," 265.

freedom than the simple fact of a world distinct from God. For Schelling, just as God is *spirit* only in the unity of two opposed *possibilities* (ability-to-be and having-to-be), so too is he *personal* only in the unity of the potencies, which are the actual causes of creation. To be free personality, God must be Lord of being that is actually different from himself. Creation is therefore a free act in the sense that, in this act, God is free.

Schelling calls the notion of God as Creator the properly *monotheistic* conception of God, and calls monotheism the *dogma kat'exochēn*, because it is the essence of *revelation*, that act by which God freely makes himself known *as a person* (as distinct from merely manifesting his being in nature).[161] Monotheism has generally been interpreted in terms of mere theism, Schelling observes, which always collapses in the end into either pantheism or atheism, insofar as, failing to distinguish God from being, it posits God as *one* over against the world's multiplicity and so either absorbs the world into God or God into the world.[162] Interpreted, by contrast, within positive philosophy, monotheism reveals itself to be a notion of God, not simply as one (versus many), but as a *totality*, a one-all. God transcends the world only as Lord of the potencies, as a unity that includes multiplicity within itself. It is for this reason, he says, that the Christian doctrine of the Trinity brings monotheism to completion.[163]

C. Divine Personalities in the Face of the World *Extra Deum* (God as *Trinity*)

We must now see how the potencies that constitute the personality of the *one* God (monotheism) become personalities in themselves in relation to human freedom. The creation of something different from God, we said, is the opening in God of the *possibility* of the *nicht-Seinsollende*; the actuality of creation is the handing over of this possibility into the hands of human freedom. According to Schelling, because God created in order to be known, the summit of creation is man, in whom the whole of creation lies enclosed. It is through human freedom that the closed circle, however, is broken open, and the being that is different from God (as *praeter deum*) becomes foreign to God (as *extra deum*). The difference between these two is analogous to the distinction we discussed last chapter between *nature* (inner living principle) and *world* (external mechanical existence)—the

161. PO, 189.
162. Ibid., 190.
163. Ibid., 194.

latter term, we noted, evoking the religious notion of fallenness. Schelling affirms the human being quite literally as the creator of the world outside of God.[164] He is perhaps the first in history to see the evil due to human freedom as having implications for the most basic meaning of worldly being, and to think through those implications in a systematic way.[165] In any event, he claims to be the first to be able to explain how *created freedom* is possible in the face of (absolute) divine causality, and he does so by showing that it shares in a decisive way *in* that causality.

Schelling describes human freedom as being like a baby rocking back and forth in a crib.[166] His elaboration is reminiscent of the treatment in the *Freedom Essay*: man is created, as it were, in the difference *between* the boundless will of God (as nature, =B) and the determination of form (A^2), a difference preserved by the unity of the third potency, the Spirit (A^3): "it is free from the first cause through the second, and by having B as its basis, it is free with respect to [*gegen*] A^2."[167] In a word, it is precisely in relation to the Spirit that man is free. This is what accounts for man's nature being "super-material," and thus being identical with freedom. This freedom is called, as it were, to realize itself in the subordination of blind being, boundless will, to the perfect order of universality coincident with self-limitation.

In fact, however, Schelling says that man's rejection of this call was inevitable. The *real-ization* of freedom transforms freedom as given to itself into freedom as self-posited, which means it falls from God as its ground. This is an inevitable event precisely because of Schelling's conception of freedom (as we will elaborate in our concluding section): it cannot be actualized without the introduction of difference, and difference is the rupture of unity.[168] We will see in a moment the different difference in Christ's actualization of freedom. What occurs as a result is that man "sides," as it were, with the first potency (the boundless will), rather than taking his place with the second, and so, instead of receiving the being that is given, as in the proper order of the potencies, he makes himself "like one of us," as the God of Genesis says; he takes over the productive power of God. Thus, instead of internalizing what was "breathed out," or rather, being in his freedom the internalizing itself, and so serving the perfect unity

---

164. Ibid., 199. See Schulz, *Die Vollendung des deutschen Idealismus*, 232n2.
165. See Horst Fuhrmans, *Grundlegung*, 15.
166. PO, 200.
167. Ibid., 200.
168. See Danz, "Die Philosophie der Offenbarung," 276–77.

From Organism to Incarnation

of the whole, man *externalizes* it, giving us the fallen world as we know it. Sin, for Schelling, is the first actualization of finite freedom, and it is thus what creates the extra-divine world.

This moment of externalization is the beginning of history. Its implications for the meaning of God, as Schelling understands it, are radical. The potencies, which enjoyed an absolute unity in God "before" creation now become relatively independent, or indeed opposed to one another insofar as their own meaning is now interpreted *against* one another in the dis-integration occasioned by evil, rather than from within the context of unity. The theogony becomes, as it were, a the-agony. Here we have what is no doubt one of Schelling's most original ideas. The mythological gods of the pagan world, he explains, are *not* mere allegories or symbols, but are the revelation of a particular truth about God, namely, that his unity is not inert oneness but totality, except that this truth has been severed, as it were, from the whole truth of God through the fall.[169] The mythological gods are therefore the divine potencies externalized and separated, so that they are now in dramatic tension with each other. Given this interpretation, there is thus a place for the "mythological process" that is essential in the revelation of Christianity itself.[170] Following a pattern known to ancient Gnosticism and medieval Joachinism, but adding a significant "twist" to these,[171] Schelling thus divides the whole of history into three "ages" or "periods": the first is the age of the Father, which is, so to speak, super-historical (as pure potentiality). The second is the age of the Son,

---

169. Beach's book, the *Potencies of God (s)*, is an excellent explanation of this point. See especially the introduction to this book, 1–14, and chapter 2, 25–45.

170. See PM, 171–72 (W.6.249). Cf., PO, 208–50. Schelling thus interprets mythology as a *natural religion*, not in the classical sense of a religion accessible to natural reason, but rather in the organismic sense of nature he developed in the *Naturphilosophie*, and so as real event. It is in relation to this alone that Christianity can be revealed as free, and why that revelation is not simply a teaching but an equally real *person*: Jesus Christ.

171. Marcion (ca. 110–60) divided the New Testament from the Old by opposing the teachings of Jesus to what he considered the essentially pagan demiurge that the Jews worshiped. Schelling wrote his Latin theology thesis at the Tübingen Stift on Marcion: see KA.I.2.211–96. Joachim of Floris (1145–1202) divided history into the past, the age of the Father (law and obedience), the present, the age of the Son (reading and thought), and the future, which will be the age of the Spirit (contemplative prayer). This final stage will bring history to a close as it eliminates the institutional aspect of Christianity and represents the universalizing of love. Schelling differs from Joachim in making the Father supra-temporal, making the age of the Son twofold, and making the final age one of speculative philosophy. Nevertheless, the similarities between Schelling and Joachim are striking: for example, Schelling also identifies the coming of the third age with the elimination of the institution of the church: see PO, 324.

which has two essentially different moments: the first is that in which man is wholly delivered to the power of "B" and so the natural, boundless will, i.e., the pagan world, and then there is the age in which the Son subjects himself to this power in order to effect a reconciliation, the Christian age. The third age, the age of the Spirit, is yet to come: *das Sein-sollende*. The whole of history stands under the second Person, in his two-fold aspect, as wrath and as love. As in the *Freedom Essay*, God permits evil in order to be love. In the philosophy of revelation, Schelling claims that the Father wills the creation of the world, in spite of its inevitable production of the disorder of externality, because he sees, from eternity, the Son's reconciliation of the whole through his death and resurrection.[172]

We thus see the justice of Christian Danz's claim that, for Schelling, Christology is the ultimate condition of the possibility of finite freedom.[173] "The Father," says Schelling, "creates the concrete multiplicity of being in order to hand it over to the Son as an independent [*selbständiger*] Personality (*panta moi paredothē para tou patros mou*, Mt 11:27). Without seeing his Son beforehand, without a positing, before the world, which included the Son (*prothesis*), without positing the Son as an independent Personality beforehand, there would be no freedom, there would be no world as we understand the term."[174] God desires difference because difference is what allows God to know and be known—in other words, to be a Person—but this means that he desires it only for the sake of his greater unity, or better: totality. Difference simply in itself would be a break-down of unity, but difference within the context in which the Son places it—difference as redeemed—represents the total victory of unity. There is, here, a reciprocal dependence between unity and difference, but it is clearly asymmetrical: it would be true to say, in fact, as Schelling does, that the Person of Christ "existed" before the creation of the world, precisely as its condition of possibility.[175] We recall here the "non-linear" notion of time that Schelling introduced in the *Freedom Essay*.[176] For Schelling, this is another way of saying that the first potency is in fact actualized as *Father* only in the actualized Personality of the Son, which means in fact only at the completion of history, even though this is in some sense a condition for

---

172. PO, 205.
173. See Danz, "Christologie als endliche Freiheit," 265–86.
174. PO, 206.
175. See ibid., 271–77.
176. On Schelling's notion of time, see Adolphi, "Warum ist überhaupt Zeit," 355–95.

the possibility of creation.[177] To deny this would ultimately lead to a subordinationism, which would entail the breakdown of the unity of God and so the loss of monotheism *tout court*. We can therefore see why Schelling would refer to the incarnation as "the most important and most essential of our investigation."[178] It is arguably Schelling's ultimate response to the problem of the integration of freedom and form, the very *event* in which that integration is achieved.

We might best understand Schelling's philosophy of the incarnation by looking at it from the side of his earlier thought, for indeed it presents, not a *deus ex machina* in a fideistic and superficial sense, but in fact a kind of inner fulfillment of his earliest insights, for all of its genuine *Unvordenklichkeit*. As articulated most clearly, perhaps, in *STI*, Schelling sought an integration of the ideal and the real that was genuinely *both* ideal and real, which would among other things mean an integration both within consciousness and outside of consciousness, in a real being. He sought this integration, there, in a double polarity: on the one hand, on the side of the subjective, as a providential historical deed, and on the other hand, on the objective side in the polarity between the organism (as unconscious integration of consciousness and the unconscious) and the work of art (as the conscious integration of the conscious and unconscious). In the Person of Christ, who is, as Schelling insists, fully God and fully man, we have the convergence of all three at once. He is the paradigm of providential history insofar as he arrives at the fullness of time, and indeed because he is the condition of possibility of history, he may be said to contain all of time without compromise of its spontaneity and unpredictability. At the very same time, the Person of Christ is wholly *objective* in Schelling's sense: he is, of course, a *conscious* integration of the ideal and real, but it is equally important to realize that this integration lies at the same time, as it were, *in his very organism*. Schelling insists that we will have altogether misunderstood Christianity if we think of Christ as bringing a (merely subjective) *message* of salvation rather than understanding him to *be* salvation in his Person, which is at once both a *being* and a (historical) life.[179] The incarnation, moreover, is the final response to the question we began this chapter with: how can the finite exist in all of its relative absoluteness without eclipsing, however slightly, the Absolute itself, which would be simply a contradiction? The incarnation is, as it were, both the condition

---

177. See Danz, "Die Philosophie der Offenbarung," 181.
178. PO, 285–86.
179. Ibid., 260.

The Perfection of Freedom

of possibility of the *departure* of the finite from the infinite *and* the "outflanking" of that possibility, showing that the Absolute is so Absolute that it has room for the total negation of its Absoluteness, which is implied in the disorder of evil.

In order to see how Christ plays this role in Schelling's thought, we need to understand Schelling's soteriology, which he develops above all in his speculative exegesis of the well-known christological hymn of Philippians 2:5–11. As we saw above, disorder was introduced both into the world and, in a certain sense, into the inner life of God through the actualization of finite freedom as sin. The most radical consequence of this disorder is the division of the divine potencies from one another, which make them "*außergöttliche*" divinities, "gods" separated from one another (mythology). It is, in fact, precisely this division that, according to Schelling, made the incarnation possible, which is indeed God's entry into what is "outside" of himself. It would not be possible for God to introduce the necessary division himself, since this would run contrary to his nature.[180] The movement into human nature, then, is not at all a departure from the divine nature. Thus, Schelling qualifies the traditional notion: "*It is therefore not correct to speak of God's becoming man*, even though there is indeed an incarnate God [*Menschgewordene Gott*]. *The extra-divinity of the divine made itself man, or became man.*"[181] God remains God; it is just that he renounces his separation *qua* separate.[182] Instead, he embodies it, so to speak, in human being, in the finite freedom that is defined by its capacity for good and evil. Because this is willed by the divine Person *qua* divine, it remains "over" the human being (*das menschliche Sein*), which thus can be said to belong wholly to the personality that contains it within itself.[183] There is therefore *one* divine Person, coincident with *one*

---

180. This is the significance of Schelling's claim that "we have seen the *Son in a state* in which he is posited without his assistance [*ohne sein Zutun*] and purely as a consequence of man, *as an extradivine potency while at the same time in 'the form of God.'* This potency *emptied itself, not of its divinity, but of its extradivine being as a divinity*, whereby the incarnation emerges as the highest act of the divinity that has remained in him" (PO, 287).

181. PO, 289.

182. In this respect, the claim that Schelling's Christology is wholly a kenotic Christology is in fact incorrect: see Baumgarten and Korten, *Friedrich Wilhelm Joseph Schelling*, 182. As Brito has seen, Schelling falls more into a "Sabellianism" insofar as he makes the personalizing of God in the Son and Spirit a *purely economic process*, on the other side of which is the absolutely unchanging God: "La création chez Hegel et Schelling," 268–72.

183. As Buchheim observes, the freedom of spirit *from* nature exemplified in

human being. But indeed at a deeper level, even this formulation is not yet adequate. It is not enough to identify the divine Person with the finite freedom as still undetermined; rather, it is only possible with a freedom always-already wholly resolved, namely, to renounce its *difference* from God, the very difference that the actualization of sin produced. The *real* expression of this renunciation is the death of Jesus undertaken wholly in obedience to the Father, which amounts therefore to the elimination of the "extra-divine" reality of the finite (i.e., as *extra* deum but not as *praeter* deum) and so the restoration of unity.

We saw above that the fall was inevitable insofar as the actualization of finite freedom necessarily introduces difference. In this respect, the late philosophy of revelation remains continuous with the metaphysics of evil articulated in the *Freedom Essay*.[184] The fall would be inescapable except for the fact that a new act of finite freedom, executed by and with divine freedom, can introduce a difference into this difference, as it were, can negate the negation, and therefore *posit itself* (which is the essence of finite freedom), not as independent, but rather wholly *as given*. It is thus a single act that is both infinite and finite, divine and human. The age of wrath, whereby man appropriated to himself the (Father's) divine power and for that reason became wholly subject to it, is thereby turned into the age of love, wherein the finite *receives* its otherness as a gift in the Son, and so without threatening the unity of God's being. It is thus that God becomes all in all. The *final* act in the drama therefore occurs *not* in the death of Christ, but in his resurrection in the Person of the Spirit, which reveals that the finitude that the Son assumed in the incarnation is not ultimately eliminated, but rather justified for all eternity.[185] Christ is neither absorbed

---

personality allows the spirit, in its purest form, to *exchange* its nature ("Persönlichkeit," 26). It is this concept of person that lies behind Schelling's Christology.

184. Although it is true that Schelling shows evidence of having studied in depth while in Munich not only scholastic theology and Aristotle, but also the church fathers, it is not the case that his theological positions become increasingly orthodox from the early to the mid nineteenth century as Laughland asserts (see *Schelling versus Hegel*, 1–2; 119–21; 133). Cf., the contrary judgment of Brito, "Schelling et la Bonté de la Création," 499–516. In fact, his basic positions remain remarkably similar on this point in spite of an enormous increase in sophistication.

185. With the preservation of the finitude assumed in the incarnation, there is also preserved in some respect the relative difference of the mythological age, rather than the elimination of it, along with Christianity itself, in the final age of the spirit. As Siegbert Peetz observes, this is a significant way in which Schelling differs from Hegel, for whom each stage simply surpasses (and so leaves behind) the previous one (see Peetz, "Die Philosophie der Mythologie," 157). The resurrection is therefore also the foundation for the difference between Schelling's "Erzeugungsdialektik," which constantly

into God nor absorbed into humanity, he is "outside of God through his eternal humanity and is outside humanity through his divinity."[186]

Let us put the pieces together from the start into a single picture as a way of concluding this exposition. The possibility of the real, and thus the possibility of its genuine integration with the ideal, requires a ground in God himself, which means it must ultimately have a divine justification. To be personal, which is, as Schelling repeatedly stresses, the most godly conception of God, God has to *reveal himself* and not simply *be*. But neither the absolute indifference of the nonground, nor the merely implicit original difference between ground and existence, as Schelling articulates it in the *Freedom Essay*, is a sufficient basis for the self-revelation constitutive of Personhood. For this, an independent otherness is necessary, which God cannot generate on his own, but can only co-generate in allowing finite freedom to posit itself over against God and then to triumph over that opposition through the miracle of love, which reveals itself to be even more "*unvordenklich*" than the pure act of being, the absolute *prius*, we spoke of at the outset.[187] Divine love is, in this sense, the ultimate reason for creation. Because it is only through this love that God becomes Person, or as we see now, the Trinitarian Life of Persons, in which, as a perfectly personal exchange of being, the uniqueness of the Personalities is utterly coincident with the unity of the whole, the Father is the personal Father, and not merely the "*Seinkönnende*" of the first potency, only in the actuality of the incarnate Son, and vice versa, and this reciprocity is itself the actualized Person of the Spirit—who now is revealed as the Spirit of love. But God can create freely only as Trinity.[188] Thus, if it is the case that God

---

produces a "more" that cannot be reduced back, and Hegel's "Aufhebungsdialektik," which simply logically unfolds what is always already implied in the beginning: see Beach, "Dialectical Method," 37–41.

186. PO, 308.

187. Werner Marx affirms the necessity of opposition for the life of God, and thus the need within God for human freedom—not just as autonomy but indeed as the *possibility* of evil—but he does not fill out the full paradox that the possibility of evil itself depends on God *as living* (see *Schelling*, 130–31). Both sides are essential for a full understanding of what Schelling is communicating here. It is also crucial to understand Schelling's criticism of the alienation in the transition from logic to nature in Hegel's system as a free act in the sense of being wholly blind (see HMP, 155 [W.5.223–24]). Marx interprets Schelling as arguing for just this in his own concept of God (see Marx, *Schelling*, 120). In fact, Schelling seeks to affirm it as *both* spontaneous *and* necessary, not as one over against the other.

188. As Sven Jürgensen observes, the notion of God as *love* is what allows Schelling to pass from the identification of individuality with guilt (in PandR) to a view of the individual soul as a created image of God: "Schellings logisches Prinzip," 141–42.

From Organism to Incarnation

depends, for his full actualization as Person, on the actualization of the world *against* God, it is even more the case that the "breathing forth" of the world, as a Trinitarian act, depends on the full Personalization of God, so that in the end Schelling can indeed say that the process of creation is identical with the process of God's own "coming-to-be" as Person, the transformation of the potencies into Personalities. Creation and theogony are therefore one and the same: "If . . . divinity exists as perfect and absolute only in the three Personalities, then with respect to things the process is creation, while with respect to God, it is a process of theogony."[189] This is another way of putting something Schelling had in fact already proposed in the 1810 *Stuttgart Seminars*, namely, that God in a certain sense creates himself.[190] As Schulz insightfully observed, God posits *himself* in a sense *praeter deum* and even outstrips in this positing the *extra deum* introduced by sinful finite freedom, so that "the distance between the Creator and the creature is a distance *within God himself.*"[191] This is why Schelling can continue to speak in the end—even after his "overcoming" of Spinozism and his total affirmation of the doctrine of "monotheism" and all that it implies regarding God's freedom with respect to the world, and the world's freedom with respect to God—of a genuinely *Christian* pantheism:[192] God's being can embrace, without absorbing, human freedom, and with it the whole of the created world unto the very materiality of nature, precisely because God's being is essentially ecstatic, which is another way of saying, simply, that God is love: *Deus caritas est.*

What, then, does all this imply for the meaning of freedom? Although he calls his positive philosophy the "truly free philosophy,"[193] it nevertheless recapitulates on a new basis, we have argued, the same aspiration as his early, negative, *Naturphilosophie*, namely, to develop a *substantial* notion of freedom beyond mere subjective self-determination. Schelling does so, first, by revealing freedom's roots in nature, and, then, by showing that these roots lie even more profoundly in divine being itself. Schelling thus manages to offer a genuinely *ontological* notion of freedom, and indeed to an extraordinary degree: the exercise of freedom is not simply activity carried out on the objectively given stage of the world; instead, human

---

189. PO, 197.

190. SS, 206 (W.4.324).

191. Schulz, *Die Vollendung des deutschen Idealismus*, 234.

192. See PO, 266. Here he claims that *"Christian pantheism is . . . the most perfect monotheism."*

193. GPP, 182 (W.6E.132).

freedom participates in a mysterious way already in God's own creating, both of the human being himself and of the world simply. Human freedom, therefore, reverberates into the very structures of the cosmos. This is undoubtedly one of the most radical views of freedom in the intellectual history of the West. But whether it actually succeeds in integrating freedom and form and resolving the ambiguity we presented at the end of the last chapter is a question we must now address in a general conclusion.

VI. Love, Nature, and Freedom: A Final Assessment

Having sketched out some of the developments in Schelling's late philosophy in broad strokes, it is good, now, to consider the success of these developments in relation to the issues that emerged from Schelling's *Naturphilosophie* as we discussed in the previous chapter, and indeed in relation to our overarching problem of the relationship between freedom and form. As we have mentioned before, there is no one in the modern era who has argued more compellingly than Schelling on behalf of the need for an adequate philosophy of nature in order properly to understand freedom. At the center of the philosophy of nature lies the distinctiveness of the organism, which discloses both the fullest meaning of nature and at the same time presents a *symbol of freedom*, revealing it to be in some sense identical to form, understood as *self-organization*; that is, as the creative reciprocity of parts and whole, cause and effect. Schelling ultimately seeks a ground for the internal differentiation of the relatively absolute organism in the radical personality of God. Our question here is whether the notion of freedom that Schelling articulates in his late philosophy, as the capacity for good and evil, or indeed as sinful and redeemed self-positing, fulfills Schelling's goal of integrating freedom and order. It seems that, for all of the insights Schelling's reflections offer into nature and the philosophical meaning of God, his final views undermine in a radical way his original goal, or indeed they arguably absolutize, rather than resolve, the problematic ambiguity that was present in his thinking from the start. Rather than rehearse all the stages and developments of Schelling from the beginning, we will simply summarize four points of critique.

1) The most essential issue, which may be said to include all the others, is that Schelling's reflection, whether in the early period or in the later, proceeds from simplicity to complexity; it is, so to speak, a constructive movement generated wholly from below. But this means that what is primordial in his system, what is most basic, is always a kind of absolute

poverty or emptiness. We see this in the *Naturphilosophie* in the fact that his criticism of mechanism was not directed principally to the reductionism it implies but to its *lifelessness* above all, which is why he opposes, not its atomism, but merely the internally static character of its atomism, and offers as an alternative simply another version of reductionism: *dynamic* atomism, in which things are produced through the relation of essentially simple actions. But if actions are *essentially* simple, they can interact only extrinsically; they will lack a radical receptivity, which would take the other *in*, and exhibit instead a kind of forceful spontaneity. Schelling never objected simply to Kant's sense of freedom as autonomy, nor to Fichte's notion of a purely spontaneous subjectivity, but merely insisted on universalizing it; a universalization that reached its peak in his 1809 claim that *being is essentially will*, on which more in a moment. But the pure spontaneity of being cannot finally be integrated with a notion of organic form, which, as we have seen, is constituted essentially by internal relations and therefore requires a receptivity that is as fundamental as spontaneity. Schelling's dynamic atomism will always thwart his desire for an organism, for one cannot "assemble" a whole, one cannot achieve a genuinely complex organization through the combination of essentially simple parts, no matter how dynamic those parts may be, merely by adding yet another external force to hold them together. The constant tendency to *lose* precisely the organism Schelling sought to affirm is only superficially an inconsistency; in truth, it is the basic logic of his philosophy asserting itself.

In spite of appearances, this same logic persists even in the *Freedom Essay* and his late thought. While Schelling insists here on an inwardly differentiated Absolute, he betrays this insistence in two ways. The first, which we will elaborate below, is that he conceives that difference dialectically. The second is that, while he develops an equiprimordial unity and difference in God through most of the treatise, he ends by saying that *prior* to the unity in difference of ground and existence in God is the "unground," which must be understood as the absolutely simple indifference that can be fully present within each precisely because it wholly transcends both, or as Schelling puts it, it is a completely separate being.[194] The new step taken in the *Freedom Essay* in fact returns to the absolute indifference founding the unity in difference of subject and object in the identity philosophy. Although Schelling eventually comes to affirm God, not as a

---

194. Hans Urs von Balthasar links Schelling's view of indifference with the "univocal" concept of being in the late middle ages, out of which one can construct indifferently either God or the world: *Glory*, V, 564–65.

simple One, but as a totality that is beyond and so inclusive of both unity and difference—which would seem to be an essentially *rich* notion of God, infinitely distant from the "night in which all cows are black" sort of absolute Hegel apparently attributed to him—he nevertheless understands totality as constructed, so to speak, from essentially simple principles. Each of these principles is defined *first* in itself and so in opposition to what is then posited over and above it, which makes each therefore *empty*. Thus, unforethinkable being is altogether without potency and so without any intelligible content in itself. The ability-to-be other, likewise, is in itself pure possibility and so likewise without content. Rich content, and indeed life and eventually freedom itself, is generated only in the oppositional relation of what is internally void. The willing, the life, the potency, that Schelling wishes to affirm of being always, in the end, stand out against a dark background of empty silence: one might say that Schelling himself never clears his own thought of the harsh charges he brings against Fichte's philosophy in 1806. To rescue nature would ultimately require an affirmation of the positivity of the object *precisely in its objectivity*. Schelling closes off this possibility in as radical a way as can be imagined by identifying being with will. While this seems to be a different formulation of the integration of freedom and form (subjectivity and objectivity), it is in fact the opposite. It enlivens being only by making it, at bottom, subjective, i.e., will, and at the same time makes the will (as now in a sense, by virtue of the identification, merely objective) an imperfection that has to be overcome through transformation into free personality.

2) If absolute simplicity, or poverty, turns out at the decisive moment always already to have been prior, regardless of where it arises in the system, and if difference does not, *qua* difference, always already belong to the absolute *prius*, it can only be ex-trinsic to what comes before.[195] This makes difference by definition superficial, which is another way of saying it can only ever be purely formal, "formal" understood here precisely as that which has been abstracted from all content and therefore as being a mere "external" modification of it ("external" is meant here, first, in a logical sense, but eventually and necessarily also in a spatial sense). It is not a surprise, then, that Schelling insists in his early and middle periods that *all difference is ultimately only quantitative*.[196] While Schelling speaks less often of purely quantitative difference in his later philosophy, he nevertheless gives expression to what is effectively the same notion in his

---

195. See Hegel, GL, 612–18 (GW.12.43–48).

196. See, e.g., My System, 355 (KA.I.10.125); 1804 System, 170 (W.2E.111).

"*Potenzenlehre*." The Potencies, as we mentioned above, are an attempt to integrate—in a living way—the simultaneity of identity and difference insofar as they represent an essentially quantitative increase, a potentializing *by degrees*, of what is identically the same with respect to content. Hegel is correct to complain that such a conception is, so to speak, irremediably abstract.[197] Insofar as the modalities of being are determined thus in abstraction, their concrete meaning can come only afterwards, secondarily, and so cannot bear inwardly on the form.[198]

However abstract this formulation of the problem may appear, its implication is quite concrete: it represents the complete separation of form and content, and by implication of form and matter. But, as we argued in the previous chapter, the inseparability of form and matter is the sine qua non of the organism, and for the same reason the essence of an integrated notion of both reason and freedom. Without a notion of organic form at the center of nature, we are left with a series of related problems in our intellectual relation to society and the world: the sciences will collapse into an increasingly self-absolutizing of positivism (scientism and historicism); philosophy will dissolve into an abstract formalism coupled with an equally abstract empiricism, to the extent that it remains rational, or else it will simply surrender to the irrational (Anglo-American analytic philosophy or contemporary Continental philosophy); and freedom will either lose all potency in relation to nature, which has now become either wholly mechanized or wholly historicized as the merely actual, or it will divide itself from a nature so conceived and will define itself as the pure potency of indeterminate choice (biological and sociological determinism or liberalism). Schelling's basic assumption and fundamental methodology make inevitable in his thinking the very thing he sought most persistently to overcome. In the early years of the nineteenth century, Schelling insisted that there could be in the end *only one* philosophy, and that this philosophy represents the ultimate safeguard of the unity of the university and so the life of the mind.[199] It is a tragic irony that Schelling insists toward the end of his life that there are two philosophies that remain irreducibly different from one another,[200] and thus only ever externally related, however

---

197. Hegel, GL, 841–42 (GW.12.251–52). Cf., Hegel's critique of Schelling in Hist Phil, III, 525–26) (V.9.182).

198. Hegel, GL, 233; 324–25 (GW.11.144–45; 187–88).

199. See *On the Essence of Philosophical Critique in General* (1802), 408 (W.3.512); Bruno, 205 (W.3.205–6); AS, (W.3.236).

200. See for example his claim in 1827 that "Two poles must now arise inside of philosophy, and, with them, a system of dualism" (WA [1827], 64).

The Perfection of Freedom

else their connection is determined: one, the negative, which remains perfectly abstract in itself, and the second, the positive philosophy, which reveals its tendency toward a reduction to the pure actuality of history in its ultimate identification with theology, its appropriation of revelation. That which is meant to preserve the unity of the whole in the end itself splits irreparably in two.[201]

3) Moreover, if a kind of poverty is affirmed as the beginning of all beginnings, the relationship between unity and difference will always remain simply dialectical, that is to say, that which is related will always be in some sense oppositional even in their identity. Another way to put this is to say that the things differentiated from one another will always be in some radical sense *outside* of one another, so that their relationship will always be first negative before it is positive. This lack of integration appears in the fact that unity regularly presents itself in Schelling as struggling with difference, and vice versa, so that each in itself represents a denial of the other, a denial that has to be productively "channeled" in some way (e.g., as *personality*). Thus, on the one hand, Schelling constantly speaks of differentiation using the implicitly oppositional verb *"überwinden,"* to overcome. The first potency, in Schelling's ultimate articulation of God,

---

201. This is not to say that Schelling meant to present the two as fragmented, but the fact that he insists the positive philosophy is *added to* the negative after the latter's completion without changing in any respect the content of negative philosophy (GPP, 146 [W.6E.81]) suggests that they essentially remain extrinsic to one another. Unfortunately, Schelling's explanation of their relation remains at best suggestive (see, e.g., PO, 150–53; GPP, 141–54 [W.6E.74–93]), and requires further work of interpretation. Tilliette, who had originally argued for their integration, ended up modifying that judgment and deciding, in the end, that it is not clear how they may be brought into unity (see "Une philosophie en deux," 55–69). There have been some interesting explanations of their difference and connection: Buchheim has compared the relationship of the two philosophies to the difference between taking food merely as the means to satisfy hunger and the more fully human sense of eating a meal (*Eins von Allem*, 7) (see also his "Zur Unterscheidung," 125–45). Beach has explained the contribution of positive philosophy as increasing a sense of religious awe in thinking and as showing *how* God created the world so as to make it more meaningful: see *Potencies*, 159. The question is the extent to which negative philosophy is assumed to account, within itself, for the purely rational *content* of reality, which would make the relationship to positive philosophy merely external in just the way we have been elaborating (see HMP, 133 [W.5.194–95], where Schelling explains that negative philosophy must "leave a space free *outside itself* for the philosophy which relates to *existence*, i.e., for the positive philosophy"; first italics added). Our claim, which would have to be worked out in greater detail in another context, is that this will be inevitable to the extent that an attempt to articulate the unity in difference of the two philosophies does not involve a radical revision of the basic principles of Schelling's thought from the beginning to the end, one that would take account of the various criticisms we are developing here.

is depicted as having *overcome* sheer actuality, and so achieving its potency, its power, precisely in freeing itself *from* being, in asserting itself as the ability to be *other* or *different from* what is, as it were, purely given.[202] This is an essentially negative notion of freedom, as we will elaborate in the last point. Along the same lines, Schelling defines personhood as in some fundamental sense *contra naturam*, it represents a *victory over* what is given, which is more truly itself the more powerful the opponent it has overcome. In Schelling's earlier thought, we find differentiation requiring a kind of *"Hemmung"* of force, which by its nature *has* to be introduced from the outside. But this reveals, of course, that relationality is secondary and so derivative. Aware of the inadequacy of this implication, Schelling tries repeatedly to articulate a sense of freedom as self-limitation, which is coincident with the positivity of finite form, but even his strongest affirmation of this point in his lectures on the plastic arts remains ambiguous, so that he ends up affirming that the most perfect form in fact dissolves into the energy of essence.[203] The need for inward self-limitation comes to be projected onto God in Schelling's reflections on the meaning of creation, but, revealingly, even here the possibility of self-limitation depends on opposition from the outside: the creation of the world, which Schelling interprets as God's making room *within* himself for the other, requires the actualization of human freedom as sin, so that God's determinateness as Personhood is inseparably bound up with the resistance of human freedom. Love, as we will see in a moment, tends to have for him the negative meaning of restoration rather than the primordially positive meaning of *"unvordenkliche" gift*. We will come back to this in a moment.

The ultimacy of negativity in Schelling's dialectic becomes perhaps most clear in three claims Schelling makes: first, in the *Freedom Essay*, Schelling associates the difference of man from God—which is implied in freedom as a possibility even independently of its negative realization—with *sadness*, with a melancholy running through the being of all things, rather than most fundamentally with the positivity of *joy*. Man's individuality

> is only loaned to him, is independent of him, thus his personality and selfhood can never rise to perfect act. This is the sadness clinging to all finite life, and if in God, too, there is a condition which is at least relatively independent, then within him there is a well of sadness, which, however, never comes to actuality, but serves only for the eternal joy of overcoming. Hence the veil of

202. See PO, 162–63.
203. The fullness of form, he says, does away with form: Plastic, 336–37 (W.3E.405).

> despondency spread over all of nature, the deep, indestructible melancholy of all life. Joy must have sorrow, sorrow must be transfigured into joy.[204]

In other words, joy is not *primordial*, coincident with the positive gift of otherness, but *exists only as otherness overcome*. To be an individual is a state suffused with regret, even if that regret is always, in the end, vanquished. Second, in spite of his increasingly radical affirmation of difference, Schelling never has room in his thought for externality *as such*, as belonging essentially to finitude, and so *good* precisely *in* its finitude, for the physical world *precisely qua* physical, i.e., as extension into space and time:

> The theory of the cosmos [*Weltsystem*], of the spreading out of spatially extended bodies into the absurd boundlessness of infinity rests on presuppositions that, more closely considered, do not hold up to any criticism. If space is on one point of the cosmos the necessary form of existence, it does not follow that distances that appear to *us* as spatial are not expressions *of merely ideal differences*. If it is man who has posited the spatial world, we ought not to infer from this that this effect stretches out beyond what he is able to grasp. Heaven is precisely that from which man has separated himself in his present existence.[205]

Spatial distance, in other words, is evil: it is an expression of the fall, and exists in its truest essence only as purely ideal difference. Finally, if Schelling's interpretation of the resurrection would seem to be an ultimate justification of the difference between God and the world, the infinite and the finite, it is nevertheless *not* an integration, but in the end only the paradoxical simultaneity of what is essentially mutually exclusive: "*Christ is outside of God through his eternal humanity and is outside of man through his divinity.*"[206] What we have here is not an ultimate integration, but rather an absolute "extra-gration."

4) Finally, one may ask whether all of the preceding kept Schelling's interpretation of the essence of human freedom bound in some respect to the subjectivism from which he constantly strove to liberate it, first in his *Naturphilosophie* and then in his positive philosophy. When Schelling comes in the *Freedom Essay* to identify freedom with ability or power *rather than* a kind of actuality or perfection, he makes the integration

204. Freedom, 270–71 (W.4.291).
205. PO, 311–12.
206. Ibid., 308.

with order, not something simply that has to be achieved, but something in fact *impossible in principle*, or at the very least possible only through a radical "subversion" of the meaning of order. Schelling is himself, of course, critical of the interpretation of freedom as indeterminate choice or as indifference before alternatives with an equal capacity for either, because this leads to irrationalism, a wholly arbitrary notion of freedom. But rather than integrating possibility *within* actuality, Schelling instead tries to make each so equally primordial that they converge into an identity: choice is not subordinated to, and therefore in-formed, by actuality, but is instead *substituted* for form insofar as the determination that "precedes" any choice ultimately turns out to be an eternally "prior" choosing. The entire content of human nature is, from this perspective, a *human deed*. This is another version of the tendency to dissolve the objectivity of form into the subjective dynamism of life we discussed at the end of our study of Schelling's *Naturphilosophie*. Schelling presents an imitation of the transcendence of order through the eternalizing of the temporal, which means that choice is integrated, not into form or order, which is genuinely *other* than it, but only into *itself* as always-already choosing and having chosen. This does not solve the problem of indeterminacy, but simply buries it forever in the inscrutable darkness of eternity. Freedom then becomes irrational in a radical sense, perhaps as radical as any other philosophy in the Western tradition.

This fate of freedom becomes evident in the negativity that becomes essential to it, which appears in two ways. In the first place, God's freedom is interpreted in its most basic sense as a freedom *from* his being, as we mentioned above. According to Schelling, the "*Seinkönnende*" of the first potency is the pure possibility of empty indifference: divinity is free, he says, to consent or not to consent to his being.[207] This possibility is a novelty, he goes on to explain, since it does not *precede* the absolute *prius* of the unforethinkable being, but *arrives*, so to speak, afterward as something wholly unexpected. "When" it arrives, however, it does so as something that has always-already been the case from eternity. In this sense, God is an eternal surprise to himself, since his being is eternal, endless, possibility. But one might say that this surprise is itself nevertheless essentially monotonous, since it consists of a possibility that is total indifference, the as yet undetermined power either to consent or to reject. There is a fundamental negativity in indifference, which *is* what it is *precisely* in *not* being anything else. We may contrast this with the integration of freedom and

---

207. Ibid., 163.

form proposed by Schiller, in which the *realization* of freedom in particular and actual choices becomes an increase and deepening of the reality of freedom, rather than a negation of freedom that then has to assert itself, over against what has been actualized, with a new claim to be able to be other. It was precisely this view in Schiller that Hegel hailed as the "break through" philosophy needed to get beyond Kant's subjectivism. In this respect at least, Schelling's late philosophy represents the proverbial "two steps back" rather than a genuine philosophy of the future.

Because in his most developed philosophy, Schelling conceives of freedom as negative in its essence, its possibility lies in its being the opposite of actuality, which means it is "suspended" as indifference, while its actuality therefore cannot consist of anything but being the opposite of what is already actual. In this respect, the actuality of freedom can only be *in its most original expression* a rejection of God, the real-izing of evil.[208] And it is, then, just this realization that in turn allows God's freedom to be love: capable only of being free in general by means of negation, God is given the opportunity, as it were, by human sin to be negative in a positive way, so to speak: he is able to be free by negating the actuality of evil, and in this sense to be good. One might object that God gives the *possibility* of evil in giving freedom, but, however likely it may have been that this freedom would be abused, it was not necessitated in the original gift. But in fact for Schelling prior to the actualization of freedom in sin, there is in God only a *possible* ground for difference, not a *real* one, as Schelling puts it in the *Freedom Essay*. A unity that is actualized without difference, which for Schelling *cannot* mean anything but opposition in the first instance, would be a false unity: "For if God as spirit is the indivisible unity of both principles, and this same unity is actual only in man's spirit, then if it were just as indissoluble in him as in God, there would be no difference between man and God. Man would be absorbed in God, and there would be no revelation and no movement of love."[209] In other words, man cannot be *different* from God, which means cannot be *really* (and not just *potentially*) free, except in some relation to sin, either as the reality of evil or as having been redeemed by love; he cannot be free in the innocence of the first creation, which ultimately means that creation is *never really*

---

208. It is rare that this implication of the identification of freedom with indeterminate choice is thought through to this extent, but we see it occasionally. See, e.g., the striking claim by Kohler, "Selbstbezug," 78: "The human will in its created character is free only to the extent that it says 'no,' and thus becomes the origin of evil, and is in no way free if it remains related to God and the good."

209. Freedom, 250 (W.4.265).

innocent. This is another way of saying that freedom is never *positively* given to man, as becomes most evident in Schelling's philosophy of revelation; if he has it at all, it is only because he has in some sense stolen it. God *gives* man freedom in the end only by allowing him ultimately to keep what he initially stole.

It is true that Schelling makes the final redemption the first intention in God's being, so that the victory of goodness has a priority over evil insofar as the good is anticipated from eternity. Nevertheless, the definition of freedom as the capacity for good and evil in the end makes goodness dependent on evil, which is another way of saying it excludes *in principle* the genuine integration of freedom and form. As we have seen in the unfolding of Schelling's philosophy of revelation, Schelling's final attempt at this integration is a sort of extrinsic imposition of order on what which is of its very essence indifferent to it: a purely *forensic* justification, if you will. Insofar as this order can only be extrinsic, can only be a stamp on what looks to all appearances still to be disorder.[210] There is no warrant to speak of integration here, for this implies an order that is internal to freedom as in-forming it, and form as the perfect real-ization of freedom, an expression that allows it to be even more what it is. In other words, integration requires a freedom that is not at all indifferent to the good, a freedom for which the good is not simply one of two equally possible options. Schelling argues that *the only way* to explain why man, the most perfect of God's creatures, is the only one capable of sin, is to define freedom as the capacity for good *and* evil, which would make the choice of evil just as much an expression of freedom as the choice of good (and indeed to remain consistent with the logic of this position if not with some of the actual claims Schelling makes in its real-ization, the choice of evil is in fact a *truer* expression of freedom). But he overlooks a long tradition in Western thought begun most explicitly by Augustine, though present *in nuce* already in Plato and Aristotle: it is possible to say that only a free being can commit sin without that sin being the expression of freedom, just as one can say it is possible to trip and fall, and indeed stumble into and over other things and people, *only because and insofar as one walks*, without making that fall the *expression* of one's ability to walk.[211] In this case,

---

210. "The *same thing* that becomes evil by the creature's will (when it tears itself free in order to be for itself), is in itself the good as long as it remains swallowed up in the good and in the ground," Freedom, 271 (W.4.292). Italics added.

211. As Etienne Gilson puts it in his explication of Augustine, "Man is free, and by his own choice he does evil, but not by that which makes his choice free," *Introduction à l'étude de Saint Augustin*, 318. This formulation allows us to affirm what Schelling

freedom would be linked with actuality, with form, which is inclusive of ever new possibility, and so would *never* be simply indifferent to goodness or order, but would rather instead rise and fall with it. It may seem a subtle distinction, but to deny this is, in the end, to fall back into the oppositional one-sidedness of mechanism and a subjectivistic transcendentalism that Schelling sought finally to overcome.

The very failure, however, brings to light an essential aspect of the problem of the relation between freedom and form, and so opens up a possibility that emerges from time to time in Schelling's reflections. If the dis-integration is due to the primordiality of poverty, the ultimacy of dialectic, the absolutizing of productivity, and the primacy of the negative over the positive—all of which might be summed up in Schelling's making indifference the prior condition for the possibility of love—then integration would require reversing that primacy, so that one would make the fullness of love, not something *achieved* in the first place, but given from the very beginning. It would require starting in some sense with the whole as given; at the highest level, this would mean *beginning* not with the monolithic *actus purus* of unforethinkable being, but with the trintiarian life of God as a life of Persons, who are always already fully disclosed to one another. In this sense, as Richard of St. Victor, for example, saw, it is possible to affirm the equiprimordiality of unity and difference in God as a precondition of the gratuity of creation, and not as a goal for which creation is an indispensable means.[212] This would make, in other words, the *possibility* of creation already included in the perfectly rich actuality of God's life, which would allow the difference implied in the existence of freedom to be received from the first as a gift rather than as a theft.[213] The possibility implied in indifference would be seen in this case as the fruit of love, as always contained *within* it, rather than as its precondition. Schelling's insight into the meaning of love is essential: it makes both unity and difference equally real, and so fills each with life. Thus understood, God himself, as internally self-revelatory in the Trinitarian perichoresis, would be understood as being always already the realization, not just the

---

does, namely, that only a higher creature is capable of evil, without forcing us to reconceive freedom in negative terms either as indifference or as rejection of order.

212. Richard of St. Victor, *De trinitate*, book 3.

213. See Ulrich, *Der Gegenwart der Freiheit*. See also Bieler, *Freiheit als Gabe*. According to Bieler, "Freedom is either gift or it is independence (Selbständigkeit), which owes itself only to itself. There is hardly any clearer way to put the alternative notions of freedom" (ibid., 24).

potential form, of love, which is to say that God is himself the integration of freedom and form.

Hegel was critical of what he took to be the "poverty," the abstractness, of Schelling's notion of the absolute. As a result, as we will see, one of the most fundamental features of his philosophy is an affirmation of the positivity of the objective *precisely in its objectivity*, which is something we have repeatedly claimed is essential for a proper integration. Whether Hegel succeeds where Schelling fails is a question that will occupy us in the final two chapters of this book. Schelling, with his notion of love, has in any event provided us with the standard by which to measure Hegel's own philosophical project.

5

Freedom as the Concrete Form of Reason in Hegel's *Philosophy of Right*

I. Introduction: Hegel's Uniqueness

According to Hegel, no idea is more misunderstood and underappreciated than that of freedom.[1] While this claim is no doubt true enough in itself, we understand immediately why Hegel in particular would make this judgment once we come to see what he himself meant by the term. In relation to the general conception of freedom in the Western intellectual tradition, Hegel's sense of freedom is certainly peculiar.[2] The most succinct definition of freedom that he offers is *bei-sich-selbst-sein in einem Anderen*, "being at home with oneself in an other."[3] We will have to flesh out the meaning of this notion through a discussion of the philosophy of spirit that informs and is in turn developed by Hegel's political philosophy. By way of introduction, however, to set the uniqueness of his view into relief, it is worthwhile specifying briefly some of the ways his notion of freedom most evidently differs from what we might call the "normal" understanding of freedom one has in the contemporary West. In anticipation of more thorough discussion of each of these points below, we

---

1. E (1830), §482A (GW.20.476).

2. Cf., Lewis, *Freedom and Tradition*, 1. Pelczynski claims it is the richest and most comprehensive concept of freedom in history: "Freedom in Hegel," 150.

3. E (1830), §24Z2 (JA.8.87); §23A (GW.20.66); Intro to PH, 20 (JA.11.44). Cf., Neuhouser, *Actualizing Freedom*, 19–20.

will mention simply three.

In the first place, while freedom is typically identified with possibility,[4] Hegel insists on thinking freedom most fundamentally as *actuality*. In other words, it is not in the first place, for him, the power to choose, the ability to realize or determine oneself, or to accomplish what one wills, even if the full notion of freedom includes all of these in some manner.[5] Instead, for Hegel, freedom is the actual realization or accomplishment *itself*. Freedom, for him, is not primarily a characteristic of action, but rather a particular way of being (which includes, but does not reduce to, a way of acting). This understanding leads us to the second peculiar feature of Hegel's notion: thinking of freedom not as a power to act, but most fundamentally as the basis and result of action would seem to "reify" freedom. And, indeed, what is perhaps most difficult to grasp in Hegel's notion is the emphasis he lays on its *objective* dimension.[6] Freedom in its most perfect form possesses a reality *in itself* and in some respect transcendent of any individual agent, which gives freedom a substance-like character. Finally, this individual-transcending character is reinforced by the third feature that distinguishes Hegel's conception, namely, its fundamental reference to the *other*. According to Levinas, the Western notion of freedom is essentially egological, meaning that freedom, interpreted as autonomy, defines itself in terms of the self and precisely to the exclusion of the other.[7] While Hegel does, indeed, affirm autonomy, as well as other apparently "egological" notions such as self-determination, he nevertheless at least

---

4. After a fairly comprehensive survey of philosophies of freedom in the history of the West, Mortimer Adler boils them down to variations on three formulations, and concludes that "[t]he word 'able' is found in [all three]. This is the most obvious point they have in common. It suggests that freedom, in any conception of it, involves an *ability*, or *power* of some sort," *The Idea of Freedom*, 608.

5. In his classic essay, "Hegel on Freedom," Richard Schacht sums up Hegel's notion of freedom as "rational, self-conscious self-determination." While this formulation captures a part of what Hegel means, it does not do justice to the whole. In fact, as we will show, it overlooks what is in fact most distinctive about Hegel's notion of freedom, and instead conforms that notion to the more conventional views that Hegel intends to critique.

6. Neuhouser, *Actualizing Freedom*, 115–16.

7. Levinas, "Philosophie et l'idée de l'Infini," 165–78, esp. 167. According to Mortimer Adler, the tension between self and other is a constant feature of conceptions of freedom in the West. Only God, he says, is completely independent in the sense of having no other. The assumption, here, is that having no other would define freedom in the absolute sense. Hegel's view at least apparently suggests otherwise, which makes his conception, once again, unique.

The Perfection of Freedom

appears to be unique in the Western tradition in making reference to the other explicit in the very definition he offers of freedom.

As we will point out along the way, each of these aspects will, of course, require further elaboration in order to show their relation to one another, and, moreover, argument and justification to make a case for them as important features of any conception of freedom. This latter requirement is particularly pressing in the present age. Taken together, these aspects point to a view in which freedom does not have its "locus" in the first place in the individual agent, but rather in a whole that non-reductively includes such agents within itself.[8] Because of its supra-individual character, it is appropriate to call this a distinctively *social* conception, and because this character, as we will come to see, requires some sense in which freedom has a substantial reality of its own, we may also call it *metaphysical*.[9] It is precisely this dimension that reveals its connection with form. While the first characteristic has great contemporary appeal, the second is almost universally regarded in the English-language scholarship as problematic. We will have to show, then, why the metaphysical character is indispensable to Hegel's conception, so that to dismiss it is not only to render impotent the thrust of the social character of freedom, but to undermine the basic integrity of Hegel's philosophy of freedom more generally. After distinguishing between a "weak" and a "strong" interpretation of the social character of Hegel's conception and admitting that the latter is closest to Hegel's own view, Friedrich Neuhouser rejects it without argument, saying simply that it is "unattractive" and that it has nothing to do with anything that we would recognize as freedom.[10] It may be the case that the failure to recognize what Hegel means stems from an inadequacy in *our own* conception, so that we in fact genuinely have something to learn from an engagement with Hegel. One of the goals in these two chapters on Hegel is to show why this "strong" sense of social freedom in Hegel is a good and indeed necessary conception, and also how it surpasses other, more easily recognizable, concepts of freedom only by fulfilling them even on their own terms. The strong sense of social freedom will almost necessarily be filtered out as long as we interpret him in light of the conventional notion of freedom; it stands out as central, by contrast, when seen in the light of Schiller's view of freedom as living form.

8. See Plamenatz, "History as the Realization of Freedom," 32–35. See also Riedel's chapter on objective spirit in *Between Tradition and Revolution*, 3–30.

9. Paul Franco observes that Hegel's notion of freedom is essentially metaphysical (and not merely moral): *Hegel's Philosophy of Freedom*, 186.

10. Neuhouser, *Actualizing Freedom*, 38–45.

Freedom as the Concrete Form of Reason

We will attempt to accomplish our goal by elaborating Hegel's notion of freedom essentially as overcoming and supplementing the inadequacies of the general view—which we argued that Schelling tends to share in spite of himself—that thinks of freedom in its most ideal instance as a power or ability of some sort possessed by individuals. Accordingly, the first of these two chapters on Hegel will seek to show why freedom ought not to be thought of primarily as a *power*, and the second why freedom is not possessed first by individuals *qua* individuals. We will then come to see why freedom, for Hegel, is, on the one hand, an actual, objective, substantial reality, and, on the other hand, why it is fundamentally social. To accomplish this first task, we will examine the guiding principles of Hegel's *Philosophy of Right* as he lays them out in the preface and introduction to that book. More specifically, we will reflect on the relationship between reason and actuality, and what this implies about Hegel's notion of spirit in relation to the philosophical tradition he inherits and also to certain ideas of his time. Then, in the same chapter, in light of this notion of spirit, we will examine Hegel's critique of the view of will as a *faculty* with the attendant understanding of freedom as indeterminacy or choice, and present in contrast to this view Hegel's own notion of will in terms of concrete freedom.

In the second of these chapters, we will follow through Hegel's critique of what we could call a classical liberal conception of political order in light of this concrete notion of freedom.[11] This will require a discussion of the meaning of *Sittlichkeit*, ethical substance, in relation to the "social" notion of spirit Hegel develops elsewhere, especially in the *Phenomenology*. The guiding concern in this second chapter will be the question, How significant is the reference to the "other" in Hegel's definition of freedom? This concern will confront us with the oft-discussed problem of the "totalizing" tendency in Hegel's thought. Does his notion of *Sittlichkeit* swallow up individual, subjective freedom? To what extent is his a romantic, organic notion of the state that has no place for what are generally recognized as the values of modern liberalism? While most recent discussions "save" Hegel from totalitarianism by interpreting him in an "anti-metaphysical" way, we will argue that such a strategy fails because it inevitably presupposes the very conception of will, spirit, and freedom that Hegel criticizes.

---

11. This is not to say, as we shall see, that Hegel simply *rejects* liberalism; rather, he considers it impotent on its own to give rise to and sustain genuine political order: see K. -H. Ilting, "The Structure of Hegel's *Philosophy of Right*," 90–110. Domenico Losurdo identifies Hegel's position, somewhat paradoxically, as "liberal anticontracturalism": see *Freedom of the Moderns*, 53–70.

Instead, we will argue that, rather than retreating from actuality back into a possibilistic conception of freedom, it is necessary to deepen the notion of actuality along the very lines Hegel himself establishes, but in a way that carries us beyond Hegel: in order to arrive at the actuality of absolute spirit in and for itself, which both unifies and preserves the distinctness of subjective and objective spirit, and so is necessary to avoid collapsing everything either into one or the other. If a "totalizing" interpretation of Hegel reduces absolute spirit to objective spirit and so eliminates subjective spirit, the "anti-metaphysical" interpretation instrumentalizes objective spirit as a function of subjective spirit, and so turns into yet another version of the contractarian view of the political order with which we are all-too-familiar.

II. Preliminary Considerations

Our investigation of the basic meaning of freedom, as Hegel understands it, will focus on the *Philosophy of Right*; in this chapter, we will discuss above all the preface and the introduction to that work, and in the next chapter the third part of the work devoted to *Sittlichkeit*. It is already significant that this is the work in which Hegel most fully elaborates his conception of freedom—rather than, say, in his anthropology or psychology or even in his treatment of absolute spirit.[12] While the notion of freedom makes an appearance regularly throughout his writings, and sometimes in unexpected places[13]—it is, after all, arguably *the* central notion of his philosophy[14]—Hegel offers the fullest presentation, appropriately, at the

---

12. Will Dudley has recently argued that freedom, for Hegel, consists most basically in self-determination, which is in the end characteristic only of spiritual beings capable of internalizing the external world to which they are subject: *Hegel, Nietzsche, and Philosophy*, 24. While he is right that this entails a critique of freedom merely as "will," and also of liberalism, it still ties freedom too strictly to an individual agent. What is missing, here, as we shall see, is the *actuality* of spirit, which for Hegel links freedom directly with objective spirit.

13. Towards the end of his *Encyclopedia Logic*, for example, Hegel attributes freedom to the concept as its most proper feature: E (1830), §160 (GW.20.177). For an illuminating interpretation of Hegel's notion of freedom in the *Logic*, see Wallace, *Reality, Freedom, and God*. Wallace is right to insist that Hegel's political philosophy has to be understood on the basis of his logic and metaphysics, which tends to be neglected in English-language studies: xxvi–xxvii, fn. 5.

14. Bruno Liebruck claims that "human freedom is the only theme of Hegelian philosophy" ("Recht, Moralität und Sittlichkeit," 12). In the *PR*, Hegel says that "it is the absolute end of reason that freedom should be actual," §258Z (JA.7.333–34), and of course he makes this actualization of freedom the end of history itself: see Intro to

Freedom as the Concrete Form of Reason

place where the notion reaches its inwardly targeted destination. The book Hegel published in 1820,[15] called *The Elements of the Philosophy of Right*, or as we may translate it, *The Fundamentals of a Philosophy of Political Order*,[16] and meant primarily as a textbook for students attending his lectures at that moment in Berlin, is an elaboration of the middle section of the third part of the *Encyclopedia*, in which Hegel presents, as it were, the skeleton of his system as a whole. While the word "system" often has a pejorative ring to it in contemporary Continental discussions, for Hegel the word indicates, in the first place, simply an acknowledgment that things cannot be understood outside of their context, so that each item depends on its relations to other items for its own meaning, and so it is ultimately in principle necessary to have some sense of the whole in order to understand any one of the parts.[17] The context of the *Philosophy of Right* thus has philosophical significance.[18]

The middle section of the third part of the *Encyclopedia* treats spirit specifically in its *objective* realization. It follows upon the elaboration of subjective spirit—i.e., Hegel's anthropology, phenomenology, and psychology—in which he articulates the nature and structure of the acting and theorizing human agent, and it precedes the absolute spirit, which unites the subjective and objective aspects of spirit in the successive forms of art, religion, and philosophy. The "location" of freedom in the system is significant because it reveals the importance Hegel gives to objective realization in his understanding of the term. As we already mentioned above, freedom is not primarily a property that belongs to the individual subject,

---

PH, 22 (JA.11.46–47).

15. There is some controversy over the precise publication date, since the publisher put the date 1821 on the book, though it seems, according to a mention in one of Hegel's letters, to have in fact been published in September or October of 1820. See HK, 576–77; cf., Peperzak, *Philosophy and Politics*, 1.

16. The term *"Recht,"* like its corresponding Latin term *ius*, has no single equivalent in English: it means not only right, but also law, or even, more generally, the principle of political order (*ius* is the root of the English word "justice"). We will be flexible in the way we render the term in the text, following the standard English translation for the title, but giving preference in our account to the most ample translation, "political order," for this seems to do most justice to the richness of Hegel's use of the term: it signifies the actualized political sphere, but specifically with reference to its *archē*, its ordering principle, which is reason understood concretely as freedom (as we shall see).

17. The notion of system is often associated with the method pioneered in the modern period by Reinhold and Fichte (and in a certain sense Schelling), which sought to deduce the whole of thought from a single proposition. But Hegel was sharply critical of this approach, and made, not a proposition, but a concrete, complex *whole*, his absolute: see E (1817), §8 (GW.13.19); cf., DS, 103–5 (GW.4.23–24).

18. See Peperzak, *Modern Freedom*, 43–45.

but has its truth in the political order, wherein subjectivity acquires substance (and vice versa) in its interaction with the world and the reality of other subjects. Hegel's notion of freedom, then, not unlike Schiller's, concerns a whole that is greater than the sum of its parts, and in which the parts find their fitting place. It is objective in the specific sense that the political order represents what Hegel calls the *idea* of freedom, which is the unity of the concept with its actual existence, or in other words, where the reality that exists in the world is adequate to the concept of that reality.[19] At the same time, what is often overlooked is that the objectivity of spirit is not yet its fully realized truth, but is itself superseded by spirit in its absolute form. The question will inevitably arise—and will be addressed directly in the following chapter—whether freedom has an absolute form distinct from its realization in the state, and, if so, what implication this form has for the political realization.

The reason we begin our study with the preface and introduction of the PR is that it is here that Hegel presents, as it were, the fundamentals of the fundamentals. In the preface, Hegel makes explicit his view of the relationship between philosophy and politics, which guides his investigation of the nature of realized freedom, and contrasts this view with some of the more common alternatives available in his contemporary context. Although it is written in a popular style, it helps to show in general terms the broader context in which Hegel approaches the particular problems that occupy him in the body of the work. In the introduction, Hegel presents in more systematic fashion an overview of the subject-matter of the work, namely, the idea of right. Significantly, this introduction is occupied almost entirely with a clarification of Hegel's understanding of the *will*. This approach to the political order, in which Hegel follows in his own way a path opened by Rousseau above all, is significant because it shows, on the one hand, that the sphere of objective spirit, for Hegel, is a realm of practical philosophy, but even more because it suggests, on the other hand, a conviction that the general view of the will—and therefore of the meaning of practical philosophy, of the political order, and of freedom—is deficient and in need of re-thinking. Over the course of this chapter, we will interpret the preface as sketching out a particular notion of reason and of actuality in view of their essential unity, and then interpret Hegel's notion of will as a further exposition of this unity. Needless to say, though we will focus on these two texts, we will draw on other writings: for Hegel,

---

19. PR, §1, §1A (GW.14-1.23), and §1Z (JA.7.38–39).

more than for most other thinkers, concepts suffer distortion when isolated from their role in the system.[20]

There is scarcely any phrase in Hegel's work that has generated more intellectual shudders than the line in the preface to his *Elements of the Philosophy of Right*—which is set off in the text like a proverb—"What is rational is actual; and what is actual is rational."[21] It has often been taken to represent a surrendering of the more reformationist impulses of his earlier writings on political matters, and a capitulation to the new circumstances in which he found himself as he was revising his *Philosophy of Right* for publication and composing the preface. The 1819 "Karlsbad Decrees," issued after the political fomenting of a student fraternity led to the murder of a well-known conservative writer, among other things, provided for the removal of any university professors whose influence threatened to undermine support for existing political institutions. As evidence that Hegel approved of the academic repression here installed, one might point, above all, to the harsh criticism he expresses in the preface of his former Jena colleague and rival Jacob Friedrich Fries (1773–1843), who had been dismissed from his post under the decrees. But not only is such an interpretation of the phrase blind to Hegel's criticisms, on the other hand, of known conservatives and the various efforts he made to promote others associated with the student fraternities,[22] it is also, at the very least, short-sighted. In any event, it is un-philosophical. Hegel made clear in a footnote to his opening discussion in the 1827 *Encyclopedia* that, by the "actual," he did not simply mean that which happened to exist, but rather the "genuine" or "authentic", which could indeed be quite different from existing institutions.[23] To make this point here, moreover, he simply drew attention to the discussion of "actuality" in his *Greater Logic*, written in 1812, many years before the political events that led to the Karlsbad Decrees. More significantly, however, even if one were to accuse Hegel of taking refuge in fine "academic" distinctions in order to maintain the approval of the censors, one still has to reckon with the fact that this statement does not express in the first place simply a political opinion, but rather articulates what may be the central guiding notion of *all* of Hegel's philosophy from the very beginning, namely, a conception of the absolute that is not

20. See Theunissen, *Hegels Lehre*, viii.

21. See the various reactions to the phrase cited in the appendix to HK, along with echoes of this phrase in other parts of the Hegelian corpus: 399–404, endnote 27.

22. See Avineri's note, *Hegel's Theory*, 130–31.

23. Steinberger enters important qualifications of the judgment that Hegel is an "accommodationist," in *Logic and Politics*, 3–43, esp. 40–43.

opposed to the relative, and thus which serves to reconcile the ideal and real, the infinite and the finite, in a non-reductive manner.[24] What is at stake in this phrase, in other words, is precisely what is most distinctive about Hegel's philosophy. Whatever political implications the phrase may have had at the moment of publication, it also has a distinct philosophical significance, which must be attended to first and most fundamentally.[25] Those who criticize Hegel for making this statement invariably neglect to reflect on what the implications of denying it would have for the coherence of Hegel's thought more generally.[26]

The purpose of the preface Hegel wrote to the *PR* just before submitting it for publication is to justify to a broader and more popular audience a *philosophical*, or as he puts it here, a *"wissenschaftliche"* treatment of a political theme, namely, the issue of *"das Recht," jus*, the order that grounds political life. Of course, to "justify" in Hegel's sense means simply to explain why it is in fact the only justifiable method in the end. What is necessary is to understand the *truth* regarding the order of politics, and truth does not consist simply in a collection of correct statements about that order, but always represents for Hegel a systematic whole.[27] A statement is not ultimately true except as integrated with other statements on which it depends and which it in turn supports. In this respect, the order of the exposition bears in an intrinsic way on the content of what is set forth, or as Hegel puts it here, "in science, the content is essentially inseparable from the *form*," the latter term being misconceived if it is thought to be nothing more than a "purely external quality indifferent to the matter [*Sache*] itself."[28] Hegel concludes that the truth of the political order must be

---

24. This is our interpretation of the actualization of the absolute as the "identity of identity and non-identity," which Hegel first formulates in the DS (156 [GW.4.64]). We will qualify this interpretation over the course of these two chapters. In that early writing, Hegel adds that philosophy has never been "about anything else than positing the finite in the infinite," 178 (GW.4.80).

25. Robert Pippin has compellingly argued that philosophical reflection, for Hegel, does not belong within the sphere of praxis, and so it is misunderstood if it is accused of being conservative or liberal, quietist or revolutionary: "The Rose and the Owl," 7–16. According to Eric Weil, "Hegel, like Plato and Aristotle, did not take a position on the issues of the day," because, as a philosopher, his interest was politics in general: *Hegel and the State*, 9.

26. For example, he claims in the 1830 *Encyclopedia* (§6A [GW.20.44–46]) that this is the principle of all religion, by which he means all theory and praxis that takes the actuality of the absolute as its founding principle.

27. Phen, preface, 11 (GW.9.19).

28. PR, 10 (GW.14-1.6).

thought through philosophically, which means unfolded according to the internal necessities of the matter itself, rather than approached through the extrinsic methods of empiricism, as Schelling also saw.[29] Such an affirmation makes sense, however, only if the matter does indeed possess internal necessities, which is to say only if it can indeed be made transparent to reason. But it can be thus illuminated only if it is already radiant in itself; in other words, it can be comprehended only if it is itself inherently *rational*. Hegel thus decries those who would admit that the realm of nature is rational—i.e., that, insofar as the physical world obeys the *laws* of nature, it gives expression to the order of reason—but would imagine the realm of spirit to be "at the mercy of contingency and arbitrariness, to be *god-forsaken*, so that, according to this atheism of the ethical world, *truth* lies *outside* it, and at the same time, since reason is nevertheless *also* supposed to be present in it, truth is nothing but a problem."[30] In other words, Hegel insists that a contradiction lies in supposing that the realm of spirit, i.e., *Geist* or mind, is not itself rational, a contradiction he expresses in the provocative phrase "atheism of the ethical world."

One might see Hegel's "argument" here as an example of his often-lamented tendency facilely to dismiss a serious objection on the thin basis of a linguistic ambiguity. It is easy to see that an action produced by a mind may nevertheless be irrational or at least inexplicable in terms of internal logical necessities: no one would deny that human behavior is much less predictable than the "behavior" of merely physical entities. In the light of this, one could object more basically that Hegel is begging the question right from the start: he justifies a philosophical interpretation of political order merely by asserting that political order is philosophical. The problem, however, is that such an objection is itself facile, and begs the very question it believes it is raising. If it is true that this reality is philosophical, it will in fact be evident only philosophically; in other words, it will not be possible to justify this *before* investigating the matter itself, i.e., in a non-philosophical manner. To assert that one can is to assume—from the outset, and without providing a justification—that, contrary to what Hegel says, form and content are indeed merely extrinsically related to one another and so are indeed separable in principle. To put it more essentially, it is to take for granted that truth is *not* the whole, but is ultimately a kind of correctness that can be determined as it were from the outside. To take this position is not to evaluate Hegel's thought

29. See our discussion of this in chapter 3: 136–38.
30. PR, 14 (GW.14-1.8).

from a vigorous philosophical standpoint, or submit his work to serious scholarly criticism, but is rather to dismiss it mindlessly from the start. What Hegel "assumes" at the outset, as he explains in a variety of places, he can show to be true only at the end. An extrinsic critique of Hegel, at least in this respect, is not possible.[31] As he says somewhat glibly at the end of the preface, "the author will regard any criticism [of what he presents in the PR] expressed in a form other than that of scientific discussion of the matter [*Sache*] itself merely as a subjective postscript and random assertion, and will treat it with indifference."[32]

The various notions and perspectives that Hegel criticizes in this preface can in fact be reduced to a single problem: they all represent some version of the separation of reason and reality, which is a problem that occupied Hegel's political reflections from the very beginning.[33] Hegel's point in the preface, then, will be to deny this separation, which means to affirm that reality always-already has an intrinsic relationship to reason, and that reason always-already has an intrinsic relationship to reality. Given that the unity of reason and reality is arguably one of the most traditional philosophical assumptions in the intellectual history of the West,[34] it may seem surprising that Hegel's affirmation should have generated such controversy. But what is unique in this case is that the affirmation occurs in the preface to an account of politics. It is essential for us to explore the meaning of this claim in this new context, for, as we will see, it is indispensable for an adequate understanding of what Hegel means by freedom. In the following two sections, we will consider what is at issue, and what is at stake, in the two sides of this affirmation respectively.

III. Rational Politics

According to Hegel, it is not simply that philosophy and politics *ought* not to be separated; they are *in fact and in principle* inseparable. But it is the higher that always, willy-nilly, determines the lower. In this respect,

---

31. This reveals the inadequacy, for example, in Voegelin's criticism of Hegel: see his *Science, Politics, and Gnosticism*, 43–44. For a paradigmatic counter example, see Hegel's "refutation" of Spinoza's system, GL, 580–82 (GW.12.14–15).

32. PR, 23 (GW.14-1.17).

33. See Charles Taylor, *Hegel*, 3; cf., Avineri, *Hegel's Theory*, ix–x.

34. Articulated first explicitly by Parmenides (DK2.7–8 and 3), it has been a working assumption, in different ways, of Plato and Aristotle, all of the varieties of Neo-Platonism (see, e.g., Perl, *Theophany*, 5–6), almost all of the major medieval philosophers, whether Christian, Jewish, or Muslim, and many figures in modern philosophy.

Freedom as the Concrete Form of Reason

it is of course true that the observations Hegel makes in the preface are, as it were, "politically charged," but rather than interpret the philosophical judgments on the basis of (prior) political convictions—which would in fact make those convictions ultimately arbitrary, would by implication erect rational castles on the sands of contingency, and so would amount to the implicit denial of the very possibility of philosophy in this realm—one ought to read the political positions as a function of philosophical judgments, however implicit. This is not to say that philosophical judgments "cause" political positions in an efficient sense, or that explicit philosophical judgments always precede political ones, but simply that one's political positions will always be a function of what one takes to be the nature of order, so that, for example, even the setting aside of philosophical ideas for the sake of more immediate practical concerns reflects a judgment regarding the relationship between the theoretical and the practical orders: this is a theoretical judgment, however implicit it may be, which precedes the practical judgment.

The embeddedness of politics in philosophy becomes apparent in the present context in the following manner: in outline, Hegel shows that the rejection of an essential internal connection between reason and reality, among other things, prevents the objective matter itself from being an internal standard for reason. Absent such a standard, thought will tend to collapse into subjective opinion. Hegel describes this collapse in terms of the romantic phenomenon of assuming truth to be what immediately "wells up in one's heart," an essentially unmediated experience that renders philosophy an immediate, and therefore trivial, possession. But, Hegel says, this superficiality in the sphere of truth "leads automatically" to superficiality in ethics, whereby one adopts principles that "identify what is right with *subjective ends and opinions*, with *subjective feeling and particular [partikulär] conviction*, and they lead to the destruction of inner ethics and the upright conscience, of love and right among private persons, as well as the destruction of public order and the laws of the state."[35] Without an intrinsic connection to the real, thought has no essential obligation to political order—*das Recht*—an obligation that would imply integration and thus the differentiation of hierarchy. What results is dis-integration, the separating out of one thought next to an other, which logically accords each such thought "absolute" value (insofar as none can be measured by

---

35. PR, 18 (GW.14-1.12), italics are Hegel's. Cf., Hegel's criticism of Fichte for subjectivizing reason and the implications of this reduction for politics: DS, 119–54 (GW.4.34–62).

something other than itself) and thus renders each completely equal to all the rest: "For by declaring the cognition of truth to be a futile endeavour, this self-styled philosophizing has reduced all thoughts and topics *to the same level*, just as the depotism [sic] of the Roman emperors *removed all distinctions* between patricians and slaves, virtue and vice, honour and dishonour, and knowledge [*Kenntnis*] and ignorance."[36]

The connection Hegel sees between philosophical and political disintegrations sheds light on the judgment he makes of Fries in this context: he quotes a passage from a notorious speech given to the student fraternities at the Wartburg Festival in Eisenach in 1817,[37] in which Fries advocates the founding of political order "from below," assuming, of course, that the people were instilled with "a common spirit."[38] Hegel's disdain for Fries is tangible. Not only does he fail to engage directly with any particular point Fries makes in this speech or in Fries' political thought more generally, but he even neglects to quote any complete passage from Fries, instead breaking off the quotation after a few phrases with an obviously contemptuous "and so on." He then accuses Fries—again without argument—of reducing the well-formed (*gebildeten*) structure of the political order to a "mush of 'heart, friendship, and enthusiasm.'"[39] Given this summary dismissal, it is easy to see why Hegel is often assumed to be motivated here, if not altogether by political considerations, at least by personal enmity.[40] But to assess this properly we have to reckon with the nature of the claim Fries is making and the form in which he makes it. To champion the founding of political order merely "from below" amounts, as we have suggested, to a philosophical claim about the nature of order more generally. It affirms that a whole is reducible to the sum of its parts, so that, to have a whole— in this case, political order—one need only assemble the parts together, or more accurately, to urge or to allow them to come together "from below."

There is a fascinating self-contradiction in this very notion, which is worthwhile pausing to consider. One exhorts a people to come together "from below"—What role does this exhortation play, what sort of causal power does it have or at least aspire to? Is it also simply "from below"? It cannot be. It is inevitably at some point and in some manner the presentation of an ideal, of a goal, *to which* the people as a whole are called, and

36. PR, 19 (GW.14-1.13).
37. See HK, 398, endnote 18.
38. PR, 15 (GW.14-1.9).
39. Ibid., 16 (GW.14-1.10).
40. See Allen Wood's comments in ibid., 382–83fn6.

thus it represents the presentation of a unity that is prior to, and meant precisely by virtue of that priority to be effective of, the coming together of the people. In this sense it is in its form the affirmation of a whole greater than the sum of its parts, which is what it denies in its express content. True political order wholly from below would be indistinguishable from disorder, since it would reduce to whatever individuals *qua* individuals are already doing naturally. One cannot appeal to the not uncommon incidence of spontaneous organization "from below" as a counter example unless one is willing to admit the affirmation of a unity greater than the sum of its parts—and thus to admit a principle that is no longer merely "from below"—as a criterion for distinguishing this from the disorganization out of which it presumably emerges. Again, the affirmation of *wholly* "from below" causality requires the affirmation of whatever happens already to be the case as an equal instance of order. The call to order from below is therefore disingenuous, and is, however unwittingly and unwillingly, a form of manipulation by its very logic. From a Hegelian perspective, it is not a surprise that "populist" politics is so often accompanied by demagoguery.[41]

Fries makes reference in his appeal to the motivation of a "common spirit." The ambiguity of the notion is important because it bears on a basic point in the interpretation of Hegel's philosophy. Is this spirit "common" in the sense that there is one spirit, which is in some respect a subject in itself, in which all the members of that common spirit share, or is it instead simply more or less the "same" spirit that repeats itself individually, as it were, in each separate consciousness? This difference, which Hegel does not set into explicit relief in this particular context, lies at the heart of his regular criticism of Rousseau.[42] Because of the great importance of this figure in Hegel's political thought, it is important to address the issue at the outset, for Hegel's critique of Fries illuminates aspects of the criticism of Rousseau that can easily otherwise go unnoticed.[43] One might think

---

41. Shakespeare illustrates this phenomenon, for example, in the *Corialanus*, in which the politicians working to give a voice to the people are quite plausibly the ones seeking power in fact for themselves.

42. See, e.g., PR §258A (GW.14-1.201–4).

43. Even as sympathetic a reading of Hegel's political philosophy as Avineri's betrays a failure to see Hegel's difference from Rousseau, and ends up in the conventional position of suggesting Hegel simply misunderstood Rousseau: see Avineri, *Hegel's Theory*, 184. One of the most intelligent recent accounts of Hegel's political philosophy, Friedrich Neuhouser's *Actualizing Freedom*, presents a useful case in point. Neuhouser interprets Hegel as essentially developing Rousseau's vision of social freedom with an aim similar to that of the present book, namely, to discover an alternative to the

that Fries's reference to a "common spirit" ought to have softened Hegel's critique since an affirmation of a "common spirit" could arguably be said to be a primary purpose of his own political theory. And yet he strides over this mention in Fries without any second thoughts, and proceeds to describe Fries's sense of political order as an "Epicurean universe," i.e., as made up of atoms in the void. The reason for this description, in spite of Fries's mention of a "common spirit," is that, as we just indicated, it is possible—at least apparently—to interpret this common spirit in a way that remains atomistic. The question is whether this spirit has any reality *in itself* (what this reality consists of will be an important question, of course, later on) or if it is *nothing but* the coincidence of what each individual happens to think. If it is the latter, it is common only in an accidental sense; that is, as a sort of epiphenomenon, the reality of which is the collection of individuals *qua* individuals (in classical philosophy an accident has its being, not in itself, but only in the substance in which it inheres). In this case, the "substance" is not one, but the multiplicity of individuals. But this means that, strictly speaking, we do not have *an* accident, but many accidents. We cannot in truth speak of a common spirit in this case, but rather of a multiplicity of spirits that are in some accidental respect, not "the same"—for that would again imply a kind of unity that transcends the various individuals—but relatively similar. The implications of this point are striking: it would not, in this case, be possible, strictly speaking, to say that various individuals are aspiring to *the same* goal, because if we deny

---

impoverished view of freedom in contemporary thought. Given the importance that Neuhouser gives to Hegel's indebtedness to Rousseau, which is undeniable, it is surprising that Neuhouser does not attempt to account for Hegel's frequent and stringent criticisms of Rousseau—which suggests in fact that, whatever Hegel owes to Rousseau, there remains nevertheless a fundamental difference between the two thinkers (for an account of Hegel's critique of Rousseau, see, e.g., J.-F. Suter, "Burke, Hegel, and the French Revolution," 52–72, esp. 52–57). The essence of Hegel's criticism is that Rousseau lacks any philosophical foundation for the distinction he wishes to draw between the *volonté générale* and the *volonté de tous*, and so will necessarily tend to collapse the former into the latter. The significance of this insight is fundamental to Hegel's thought; it lies behind his criticism, for example, of the "impotence of the ought" and abstract formalism in morality. But it is impossible to do justice to this insight if one insists, as Neuhouser does, on a strict "anti-metaphysical" reading of Hegel, which denies any sense to speaking of spirit "in itself." It is not a surprise, then, that Neuhouser ends up in the very place Fries does in this preface, namely, attempting to *enrich* the sense of the political order, not ultimately through substance, but through *sentiment*. What Neuhouser aims at, then, is a "feeling" of unity, not a real unity: see, e.g., *Actualizing Freedom*, 226–27. Neuhouser in fact reduces *objective* freedom, in the end, to the collective sum of subjective freedoms, since it exhausts itself in its promotion of the individuals that constitute society.

a unity greater than the sum of its parts the realization of that goal can be understood only as relative to each individual taken individually. Thus, we would simply have, not a unifying goal, but a collection of individual goals that happen to be, in an accidental way, relatively similar. This does not mean that there can be no interrelation between individuals, or cooperation in bringing about the collection of goals, but only that the activity that constitutes the cooperation will be structured in each case relative to the individual end pursued. There is no other real basis for action, for the formation of institutions, for the ordering of the community, other than that which alone is real: individuals taken individually. Hegel's criticism of Fries thus echoes, for example, Plato's criticism of Lysias's reduction of eros to *égoisme à deux* in the *Phaedrus*, and the response is also the same: we can avoid this only if there is a reality that transcends individuals, such that it cannot be simply reduced to them.[44]

Hegel's criticism makes it clear why "heart, friendship, and enthusiasm" have the prominence that they do for Fries. Sentiment is the sole suitable vehicle for the common spirit as Fries understands it, for it allows the universal to appear, but to do so only in a reductively subjective manner. In other words, in sentiment, we have a universal content in a particular form.[45] Individuals *feel* united, but this unity is just that, namely, a feeling, which means that it lies only within the hearts of the individuals who therefore remain in their being nothing more than an accidentally connected collection of individuals. The surest sign, according to Hegel, that this unity remains a purely subjective one is that it inevitably regards any substantial reality of that unity—for example, authority, duty, or law— as "a *dead, cold letter*, and a *shackle*,"[46] or in other words as a threat to the feeling in which "warm" unity resides *precisely because* this substantial reality represents an objective "check" to particularity. Sentiment is best

---

44. The very first point that Socrates makes in his "recantation" of Lysias' argument is that eros has in fact a divine (i.e., a supra-worldly) origin: the best things we possess, he says, "come from madness, *when it is a gift from the god*" (*Phaedrus*, 244a, emphasis added). Socrates then goes on to interpret the *subject* of love as the immortal (i.e., non-temporal) soul and the *object* of love as the transcendent form of beauty. The point is that a good that is truly common, and so irreducible to particular interests, must lie in some respect "beyond" the mundane.

45. In this respect, Mark Tunick's observation that Hegel's critique of Fries concerns the *form* of politics: "rationalism vs. confused sentiment," as he puts it (*Hegel's Political Philosophy*, 68), is correct, but he is wrong to think this therefore does *not* concern content. For Hegel one cannot separate these. Behind this misunderstanding is the non-Hegelian assumption that reason is essentially an individual faculty, which is incidentally also how Tunick characterizes will and therefore freedom: *Hegel's Political Philosophy*, 38.

46. PR, 17 (GW.14-1.11).

described, therefore, as the *appearance* of unity, which explains its appeal, but also its potential danger: a powerful appearance can convince itself to do without the reality. It also explains, at least in principle, the manner of Hegel's treatment of Fries. If the order that Fries seeks to inspire is essentially a sentimental unity coupled with a rational individualism, the method is essentially emotional appeal rather than argumentation, and one can offer a *counter*-argument only to an argument.[47] "Heart, friendship, and enthusiasm," in abstraction from a rational understanding of their substance, is "mush" in the sense that it lacks distinct form. This comment need not be interpreted as a rejection of sentiment, of course: it represents the appearance of unity, and the appearance is part of the whole reality, but the "warmth" of feeling ought to arise from the reality of the unity, it ought to be the appearance *of* the reality.[48] Real unity requires universality not only in (unmediated) content but *also* in form. What lies beyond the capacity of sentiment represents the essence of reason. Atheism in ethical life, as Hegel put it earlier, or, to make reference to a favorite text Hegel cites from Goethe in this context, a "diabolical politics," occurs when we resort to

> the simple household remedy of attributing to *feeling* what reason and its understanding have laboured to produce over several thousand years, all the trouble involved in rational insight and cognition, guided by the thinking concept, can of course be avoided. Goethe's Mephistopheles—a good authority—says much the same thing in lines which I have quoted elsewhere: "Do but despise reason and science, / The highest of all human gifts— / Then you have surrendered to the devil / And must surely perish."[49]

It now becomes clearer why Hegel insists on the rationality of the political order, and why this insistence is not simply an arbitrary assertion. As we see with the consideration of Fries, even those that would reject the possibility of an objective grasp of truth, and would thus seek to found political order on sentiment *rather* than reason, nevertheless *intend* a reality that lies beyond the limits they artificially set: an appeal to some kind of transcendent unity lies implicit, willy nilly, in *any* conception of political

---

47. Along similar lines, Hegel had also dismissed the superficiality of Fries's *System of Logic* when writing his own, explaining that the conception was so shallow it spared him the trouble of engaging with it: see GL, 52, fn.1 (GW.11.23fn).

48. Hegel, for example, refers to the *warmth* of the actual world's unity, which is due to reason: PR, 22–23 (GW.14-1.16).

49. Ibid., 16 (GW.14-1.10).

order. In a word, one is always an "idealist" in one's political theorizing; the question only concerns the rational quality of one's ideals. In this respect, the insistence on the rationality of the political order does not present itself as simply an alternative approach to political theory—which one may or may not choose to adopt; a choice that can have no criterion and so is necessarily arbitrary—but rather as the fulfillment of what its competing claim itself seeks unknowingly and thus often in vain.

It is nevertheless not enough to insist on the rationality of politics, for Hegel, unless one also has an adequate conception of the nature of reason. We thus turn to the complementary side of Hegel's consideration of the relation between philosophy and politics.

IV. Political Reason

An insistence on the importance of reason in politics is hardly new in philosophy, whether ancient (Plato) or modern (Hobbes). What makes Hegel's contribution distinctive is his political development of the integration of the temporal into the eternal order, which also represents a fundamental aim in Schelling's thought, as we saw in the previous chapter: for Hegel, it is not simply that politics must be rational, but also that reason must be political—the word "political" here meaning realized in the concrete order of actual community. After having criticized the romanticism which founds unity on feeling rather than reason, the dialectical movement of his thinking leads him in the preface to criticize the opposite problem, what we could call a "rationalistic" approach to politics. This approach is typically associated with Plato, but in fact, though Hegel accepts this association, he does so only by reversing the assumptions on which this association is typically based, which makes this moment in the preface much more complex than it initially seems. To help clarify, we will first elucidate his criticism of rationalism, and then turn to his criticism, specifically, of Plato.

The problem of rationalism, for Hegel, is relatively straightforward: it represents one of the "misunderstandings" of the relationship between philosophy and politics, which views the task of philosophy as "the setting up of a world beyond—which exists God knows where—or rather, of which we can very well say that we know where it exists, namely, in the errors of a one-sided and empty ratiocination."[50] Hegel's critique is not very

---

50. Ibid., 20 (GW.14-1.13–14).

different from the one Nietzsche will make several decades later,[51] namely, while universality is, so to speak, the medium of reason, universals do not exist as such in reality (as Hegel points out in a favorite anecdote of the man ordered by his doctor to eat fruit, but who despairs because he can find only apples, cherries, etc.[52]). The *unreal*, since it is placed in a "world beyond," is by the very same token divinized. But, after the pause of a "*Gedankenstrich*," Hegel shows that, because it exists nowhere real, it can exist only in individual minds. Hegel had described this empty reasoning as spinning itself on and on in its own web, thus developing Francis Bacon's image of the spider as symbol of the rationalist that draws only from what is inside itself; Hegel's rationalist for that very reason likewise entangles himself within himself. We return to a problem similar to that of sentiment, which we just elaborated above. The difference is that sentiment presents an "apparently" accomplished unity—or we could say unity merely as unmediated content—whereas rationalism presents this unity as an "empty ideal," that is, as a *form* that lacks content and therefore stands as what Hegel elsewhere calls an "impotent ought." It represents something that is supposed to be brought into existence, which means that as of yet it does not exist. The problem with such a view, which Hegel explains repeatedly in a variety of contexts,[53] is that its impotence is essential. One cannot give rational form to what is not already rational in itself except as a superficial overlay, which as such preserves a merely extrinsic relation between form and content and so undermines the very rationality that "ought" to be imposed. The "ought" can have genuinely effective power only if it is a derivation of the "is." In classical language, actuality is always ultimately logically, if not chronologically, prior to possibility. In this sense, reason can have a task, paradoxically, only if it is in some respect already accomplished.[54] Philosophy is therefore best understood as always

---

51. See his passage on "'Reason' in Philosophy" in *Twilight of the Idols*, 479–84, in which he complains that philosophers "think that they show *respect* for a subject when they de-historicize it, *sub specie aeterni*—when they turn it into a mummy. All that philosophers have handled for thousands of years have been concept-mummies; nothing real escaped their grasp alive. When these honorable idolators of concepts worship something, they kill it and stuff it; they threaten the life of everything they worship" (ibid., 479).

52. E (1817), §8A (GW.13.19); E (1830), §13A (GW.20.55).

53. E.g., E (1830), §6A (GW.20.45–46); cf., DS, 132 (GW.4.45).

54. This is ultimately the basis for Hegel's claim, in E (1830), §212Z (JA.8.423), that the world must be taken as always-already redeemed, i.e., as already historically *accomplished* at some level. While the claim strikes one as shocking, it in fact follows from Hegel's transposition of the classical absolute priority of actuality into a historical key, as we will discuss below.

catching up with itself: its task is to comprehend what is actual and present in thought (the ambiguity is intentional).[55]

Hegel's discussion of Plato here helps to fill out what it would mean for reason to *include* content. The *Republic* is generally taken as the "proverbial example" of a one-sided reason, but Hegel qualifies this judgment in a significant way. The problem is *not*, he insists, that Plato separates the rational and real as rationalism does; in fact, he explains that the *Republic* "is essentially the embodiment of nothing other than the nature of Greek ethics [*Sittlichkeit*]"—the latter term signifying for Hegel what is sometimes translated as "ethical *substance*," and meant as a contrast to the *morality* that, in abstraction, tends toward an empty formalism. Plato's ideal *is* the real, and is thus not an empty concept but a *substance*.[56] Nevertheless, Hegel goes on to say that it remains for all that one-sided. For Hegel, Plato stands at the cusp of what he calls a "world revolution." A new movement of the spirit was occurring, which introduced a tension that enters into Plato's philosophy precisely because of his genius. On the one hand, Plato perceives this movement—and *has* to perceive it—as destructive of Greek *Sittlichkeit*, but, on the other hand, Hegel says that he himself makes use of this longing *against* itself. How are we to understand this ambiguity?

The new impulse is what he calls here "free infinite personality." In the preface to the PR Hegel leaves unnamed the historical moment he identifies with the emergence of this principle, but he makes it explicit when this point comes up again in the body of the work. Here, he points to the "principle of the *self-sufficient and inherently infinite personality* of the individual [*das Einzelnen*], the principle of subjective freedom, which arose in an inward form in the *Christian* religion and in an external form (which was therefore linked with abstract universality) in the *Roman* world."[57] The external form of personality in the Roman world is the right to possess private property, which is abstract insofar as it does not fully realize the subjectivity of the person but only the person in its (abstract) personhood, i.e., the particularity of its being-for-itself realized in the particularity of the mere being-in-itself of property. While property represents a "fallen" concept of subjectivity in one respect, since it objectifies that subjectivity, Christianity represents a complete expression of subjectivity

---

55. PR, 21 (GW.14-1.15).

56. This is not to say that Hegel thinks Plato is merely *describing* the existing Greek society, as M. J. Inwood believes (see "Hegel, Plato and Greek *Sittlichkeit*," 40–54). Rather, it is a rational *core*, which as such remains a prescriptive norm for what exists in the more mundane sense, as we will elaborate in the next section.

57. PR §185A (GW.14-1.161–62).

The Perfection of Freedom

for Hegel insofar as it posits as *infinite* what remains necessarily finite in the Roman world. Interestingly, one of the marks of Christianity and the "discovery" of subjectivity that Hegel notes in the *Encyclopedia Logic* is its doctrine that God "wills that all be saved"[58]—in other words, the Christian doctrine affirms a universality that is specifically inclusive of every (subjective) individual, and thus accords "infinite value" to subjectivity in its very particularity. This affirmation sets into relief what Hegel sees as lacking in Plato's unity of the ideal and real. As Hegel explains it in the remark to §185, Plato excluded everything associated with "self-sufficient particularity" from his notion of the perfect state: private property, family, free choice, and so forth. To penetrate to the philosophical roots of these "political policies," as it were, we might say that, while Plato does indeed identify the ideal and the real, he does so in a one-sided fashion. The real—i.e., the particular—in this case reduces without remainder to the ideal, which means that the real as such does not contribute anything to the ideal.

But Hegel does not insist only that the "rational is the actual," he *also* insists that "the actual is the rational." In other words, the unity between the two that he has in mind is a complex dual movement that never collapses back into a "monochromatic" identity (of the "night in which all cows are black" sort[59]). The implication of this lack in Plato is a notion of universality that is *exclusive* of particularity. It is this sort of universality that Hegel associates with *Verstand* precisely in contrast to the inclusive universality of *Vernunft*. A genuine interpretation of the rational and actual requires a non-reductive unity between universality and particularity. If Plato "makes use" of the longing that is coming to be at this moment in history, but uses it against itself, this seems to mean that he *anticipates* the integration of reason and actuality through a substantial notion of the ideal, but that this integration is inadequate because it is unilateral, and so the very substantiality of the ideal becomes the force that oppresses individuality. The upshot of all of this is that, though Plato's thought is not rationalistic in the usual sense (that is, in the sense that measures the

---

58. E (1830), §147Z (JA.8.334).

59. Phen, 9 (GW.9.17). Hegel radicalized the traditional proverb, apparently first recorded by John Haywood in 1546 ("When all candles bee out, all cats be gray") and quoted also by Cervantes (see *Don Quixote*, pt.2, ch.33), which Hegel may have picked up from Friedrich Schlegel's citation. For Hegel, it means the dissolution of all difference, and he is somewhat controversially taken to have Schelling's notion of absolute indifference in mind. See Terry Pinkard's reference in *Hegel: A Biography*, 704fn90; cf., Bonsiepen's note to the *Phenomonologie des Geistes*, 562.

real by abstract universals), it nevertheless ends up, like rationalism and the "politics of *Verstand*," representing an "external" form that is imposed "from on high," to use Hegel's words here.[60]

At this point we may pause to take stock of where we are. The preface, for all of the superficiality and externality of its style that Hegel himself confesses at the end, betrays a dialectical structure. It begins with an insistence on the unity between form and content, proceeds to criticize the founding of politics on the formless content of sentiment (romanticism) and then criticizes the founding of politics on the contentless form of abstract reason, in order to return at the end to the unity of form and content, now with a concrete meaning.[61] The first proceeds *from below*, which means from the perspective of the multiplicity of particular individuals, and because of its one-sidedness cannot achieve unity in anything but appearance. The second proceeds wholly *from above*, on the basis of an abstract unity, which is thus sheer self-relation without content. The absence of content renders this an instrumentalist conception of reason that acts *on* the multiplicity of content, but is never *in* it. For all of their opposition, the two problems turn out to represent flip sides of the same coin, namely, a failure to integrate reason and reality, philosophy and politics.

To integrate this truly requires a concrete sense of reason, which holds together in an intrinsic but non-reductive unity both form and content. We have seen a similar insistence on the integration of form and content in Schiller's notion of beauty, and in Schelling's notion of the organism. In both cases, this integration represented some part of the essence of freedom. It will do so, as we shall see, also for Hegel. What is unique about Hegel, here, is that he interprets this integration specifically in the social sphere. In Schiller, the integration required an interpretation of nature beyond Kant's critical strictures, and this became even more explicit in Schelling's interpretation of the organism: one cannot simply "impute" a telos to what exists as a form-matter unity by definition. What Schelling sees in relation to the organism, Hegel affirms now with respect to the political order.

The problem with both romanticism and rationalism is that they both presume that the unity can be formed, as it were, from distinct parts (romanticism from the collection of individuals, and rationalism from the imposition of form on matter), rather than acknowledging a concrete

---

60. PR, 20 (GW.14-1.14).

61. Ibid., 22 (GW.14-1.16): "This is also what constitutes the more concrete sense of what was described above in more abstract terms as the *unity of form and content*."

unity that is already *given* in the actual order of things. But to say that there is a unity of form and content in the political order means, first of all, that reason is not a mere instrument for thinking, indifferent to its infinitely many possible objects, but, second, it has its own content, which is to say that it has a particular kind (yet to be discussed) of being *in itself*, and thus in some respect transcendent of any particular "rational" individuals. Third, if it has being in itself, and is not a mere instrument for some end other than itself in the merely extrinsic sense of "other," then reason exists not only in itself but also *for itself*; it is not that we have reason in our minds and then we *apply* it to the political order, but rather the political order represents the place, as it were, that reason first comes to be. Without concrete actuality, we do not yet have rationality: the actual is the rational and the rational is the actual. If this is the case, it is impossible to interpret Hegel in a strictly "anti-metaphysical" sense—i.e., as representing a form of criticism that refrains from speculation about any sort of reality outside of human experience—without undermining what is most distinctive about his political philosophy.[62]

62. Peperzak provides an excellent critique of the "anti-metaphysical" interpretation of Hegel, which he is right to say represents the dominant trend in English-language scholarship: *Modern Freedom*, 5–19. Cf., Frederick Beiser, "Introduction: Hegel and the Problem of Metaphysics," 1–24. For a prominent example of this school of interpretation that Peperzak does not mention, we might consider Neuhouser's approach, which is quite representative and which helps set the position we are taking into clear relief: Neuhouser isolates Hegel's political thought from his logic and metaphysics on the basis of a distinction he draws between theoretical freedom and *practical* freedom, which concerns the will (*Actualizing Freedom*, 20–21; 134). This leads him to qualify, in an ultimately dismissive way, precisely what he had identified earlier as Hegel's essential formulation of freedom as "being at home with oneself in another" because he claims this is more theoretical than practical (ibid., 105), which means, it appears, that he does not take this claim to apply to Hegel's political philosophy. But Hegel could not be any clearer in his rejection of the separation of the will from reason; indeed, he characterizes the will as a particular kind of thought. Neuhouser simply avoids this basic objection to his approach, presumably because the "anti-metaphysical" drift in contemporary English-language scholarship that Peperzak identifies lends his approach prima facie plausibility.

The most compelling defense of an "anti-metaphysical" interpretation of Hegel is no doubt that offered by Findlay (*Hegel: A Re-Examination*, 351–59), since Findlay bases it on Hegel's own principle of an ultimately immanentist "metaphysics." Nevertheless, we have to see that Hegel makes in this no concession to Kant's *critical* philosophy, since it is precisely the absolute and eternal that Hegel makes immanent to historical consciousness. He is indeed "immanentist," then, but only by radically transforming the meaning of the term, in a manner that the more Kantian interpreters of Hegel fail to acknowledge.

Stephen Houlgate has recently offered a specifically *ontological* reading of Hegel's *Logic*, as an alternative to the dominant categorial interpretation represented by Robert

Freedom as the Concrete Form of Reason

It is helpful to consider how significantly Hegel diverges in his insistence on the rationality of politics from the way that insistence would be conventionally interpreted. For Hegel, it does not simply mean (subjectively) that one ought to carry out politics in a *rational way*, i.e., to make political decisions guided by reason rather than by something else, such as emotion or desire, for this conception leaves in place an extrinsicism between form and content, in which reason is viewed as an individual faculty that ought to be applied, in this case, to political matters. It is also not sufficient to say that politics ought to possess an (objectively) rational form, in the sense that the institutions ought to function and relate to one another according to some conceptual plan. This, too, formalizes reason. What Hegel has in mind is something far more concrete. People often talk about Hegel's "organic" conception of the state,[63] a description that does indeed reveal something important—namely, that the political order has a kind of "life of its own"—but we have to keep in mind that Hegel, like Schelling, interprets the organism according to the model of reason. We will address this issue more directly in the following chapter; the main point in Hegel's conception we wish to highlight here is that reason is *more* than just individuals acting rationally, even though it necessarily includes such individual action, and this is precisely why reason will always take on a social dimension. It is also why Hegel sees freedom as the concrete actualization of reason. To understand this, we will have to unfold in more depth what Hegel means specifically by actuality in the preface, and then, with a study of the will in the introduction, to see the relation this bears to freedom.

V. On the Meaning of Actuality

One's first inclination in interpreting what Hegel means by actuality in this context is to view it as external particularity. Hegel says here that the "rational ... becomes actual by entering into external existence."[64] If actuality were simply identified with external existence then there would be some grounds for the charge that Hegel resigned himself in the end to the conservatism of a historically positivistic sort, for the unity of reason and actuality in this case would identify reason with the particular in-

---

Pippin: see *The Opening of Hegel's Logic*, esp. 115–43, and 436–41.

63. See, e.g., Suter, "Burke, Hegel, and the French Revolution," 59–62.

64. PR, 20–21 (GW.14-1.14). It is closer to the original German to say that the "rational, in its actuality, at the same time enters into external existence."

stitutional form existing at his particular historical moment, and would thus, in effect, absolutize the one relative instance. But this is clearly not what Hegel has in mind: not only is he sharply critical elsewhere in PR of just such a conservatism,[65] but even here he immediately describes the particular existence into which reason enters as a sort of husk that *surrounds* the truly rational core. While "consciousness" initially finds a dwelling place in these myriad external forms, he goes on to say, when consciousness becomes speculative it penetrates through the husk to the core. Somewhat surprisingly, Hegel insists that philosophy ought never to occupy itself with particulars *as such*, and he cites examples from Plato and Fichte that show philosophy straying from its specific task, thereby making itself foolish. One might think, in this context, of William Traugott Krug's famous objection to the new speculative system represented by Schelling and Hegel that, for all of its intelligence, it does not allow them to deduce the existence of "this pen." Hegel responded that the very demand that one do so betrays the failure to grasp what philosophy is.[66] We thus pass from an absolutizing of the particular to a complete trivialization, for it now seems as if Hegel is saying that, although reason externalizes itself in existence, what in fact exists is *not* reason, but a mere outward display that philosophy ought to ignore. Is this not a contradiction, or at least a confusion?

As we mentioned above, the controversy and misunderstanding of what Hegel meant by asserting the actuality of the rational led Hegel to add a note to his 1827 edition of the *Encyclopedia* in an attempt to clarify.[67] The gist of his clarification is to point out that not all existences are actual; instead, only a certain *kind* of existence is qualified to receive that designation: we do not call just anyone who attempts to be productive in a certain way a "real" (*wirklich*) poet or statesman.[68] Note that there is a connection between the mistaking of all contingent things as actual and thinking of reason essentially as subjective representation: both assume the separation between reason and reality we discussed above. For Hegel, actuality is not mere *existence*, but is the *unity* of existence and essence.[69] Hegel also calls

---

65. The essence of Hegel's scathing criticism of the romantic reactionary Karl Ludwig von Haller, for instance (see PR, §258Afn. [GW.14-1.204–7fn]), is that he absolutizes the historically contingent and so undermines reason altogether.

66. See Hegel's early essay, "How the Ordinary Human Understanding Takes Philosophy (as Displayed in the Works of Mr. Krug)," in *Miscellaneous Writings of G. W. F. Hegel*, 226–44 (GW.4.174–87).

67. See E (1827), §6 (GW.19.32–33). Cf., Peperzak, *Philosophy and Politics*, 92–103.

68. E (1830), §142Z (JA.8.321).

69. Ibid., §142 (GW.20.164).

it the unity of the "outer and the inner world of consciousness,"[70] what is outer and what is inner become identical. He goes on to say that the actual, in its external actuality, remains something essential, even as the essence has its essentiality only in the actuality. The sorts of existence that do *not* qualify as actual are purely contingent insofar as they remain bound up in possibility: the very quality of their existence expresses the fact that they could just as well *not* exist. He claims that, in contrast to this, the "actual" is not subject to "passing over," or we could say, "passing away."[71] Mere appearance, the externality that is *not* unity with inward essence, is thus "transient and insignificant."[72] In the actual, the unity of essence and existence is *posited*, so that what is there (*Dasein*) is the manifestation of the essence.

How are we to understand all of this concretely? Let us take the example Hegel himself mentions: the poet. A bad poet, we might say, has no "staying power," and such is the case if the poet does not say something *essential*. But if he does say something essential, this does not mean that he gives expression to a universal content that can, indeed ought to, be abstracted from the necessarily particular form in which it is expressed. A philosophical exposition of the meaning of *King Lear*, if it could be achieved, would not give us more direct access to Shakespeare, and would never simply substitute for the play. Instead, the meaningful, particular words themselves are essential. In his lectures on the *Philosophy of Art*, Hegel rejects any interpretation—for example, a didactic one—that would instrumentalize the work of art itself in relation to a purpose external to it.[73] Art is the sensuous manifestation of truth, and so possesses the absoluteness that all truth does.[74] If, in the system, philosophy supersedes art, it is only because it attends to this manifestation specifically *qua* truth (rather than *qua* external manifestation). To return to the PR preface, it is the externalized and thus existing essence, the actuality, that forms the true object of philosophical interest, even if it is not *in* the externality

---

70. Ibid., §6 (GW.20.44).

71. In this sense, Engels's attempt to reinterpret Hegel's proposition diverges sharply from Hegel's own meaning. Engels concludes: "The proposition regarding the rationality of everything actual dissolves, in accordance with all of the rules of the Hegelian method of thinking into another: Everything that is deserves to perish," cited in HK, 404.

72. E (1830), §6. (GW.20.44)

73. Introductory lecture, Phil of Art, 80–87 (JA.12.82–89).

74. This is the main thesis of William Desmond's important work, *Art and the Absolute*.

qua external. It may be helpful to see that there are at least two "layers" of form-content relationship here: *experience* is the consciousness of the actual as appearance, i.e., in its sensuous externality. Philosophy has the same content as experience, but gives that content a rational form. This does not mean, however, that philosophy focuses on the rational essence while experience is occupied with external existence, but rather that the *content* of both is the content-form, inner-outer, essence-existence unity of actuality, albeit in a different *form* in each case. We are thus able to understand Hegel's dismissal here of the "infinite wealth" of forms, appearances, and shapes that "surrounds" the essential core in a non-dualistic way: if the concept penetrates to this core to find the inner pulse, it does not grasp it in abstraction from its actuality, but "detect[s] its continued beat *even within* the external shapes."[75]

The section from the *Encyclopedia Logic* helps to illuminate this further. Here, Hegel associates actuality with the Greek notion of *energeia*, which always subsists within a polarity with *dunamis*, potentiality. These are not simple opposites, but bear a reciprocal, and yet asymmetrical relation to one another. Actuality depends on potentiality to be actual, but potentiality is ordered to act. This gives rise to a dynamic and organic sense of actuality, which *comes to be*. Hegel describes it as "inwardness that is totally to the fore," i.e., as the complete externalization of what lay within.[76] The completeness of this movement ("*schlechthin heraus*") is essential: Hegel implies that nothing may be left merely inward, since the discrepancy this implies would compromise the identity of the inward essence and outward existence (we will explain this in the next section). An actualized potency is the manifestation of reality itself, and not a mere "part" of reality. We may think of the growth and blossoming of a flower, which unfolds itself, makes what it was merely implicitly into its explicit reality. This growth is not a merely additive process, which would be a conception that reduces the organism to a mechanism, but presupposes that the flower has its complete being in some sense already within it. Actuality can only be conceived in relation to potentiality, but the reverse is true as well: insofar as the actual being is the unfolding of a potential, and not the mere addition of something new, it is already contained in the potentiality, which means that potentiality is a kind of inward actuality.

75. PR, 21, emphasis added (GW.14-1.14).

76. E (1830), §142Z (JA.8.322). In the preface to the Phen, Hegel defines the "actual" as "that which posits itself and is alive within itself—existence within its own Notion. It is the process which begets and traverses its own moments, and this whole movement constitutes what is positive [in it] and its truth," 27 (GW.9.34).

Freedom as the Concrete Form of Reason

That is why this coming forth from itself is meaningful: it is the outward manifestation of something essential. In a word, actuality is manifestation or self-revelation. It is helpful to compare Hegel on this point to the sense of actuality Schelling embraces above all in his positive philosophy. Although, as we will see in a moment, Hegel's view of actuality owes a certain debt to other currents in Schelling's thinking, their difference on this point is quite stark. For the late Schelling, actuality in its most ultimate sense bears no relation at all to potentiality, which is why the positive philosophy necessarily begins, as we saw, with the sheer *thereness* of being, devoid of all concepts.[77] Similarly, for him potentiality is *separate* from actuality, which is what allows the negative philosophy to be a complete system in itself. In a nutshell, act and potency are inwardly independent, even if extrinsically connected, for Schelling, while for Hegel they are intrinsically intertwined, which is what makes actuality for him an essentially "organic" notion.[78]

We discussed the problems of Schelling's tendency toward extrinsicism in relation to his conception of freedom in the last chapter, but we ought to see that the *point* of separating actuality and potentiality so completely from one another is precisely to preserve the possibility of genuine novelty. Hegel rejects the extrinsicism for the sake of an organic notion of actuality, so the question arises whether he surrenders the ground for novelty. If, for Hegel, actuality is merely the bringing to the fore of what "already exists" potentially, it would seem to be the case that it cannot in fact introduce anything that is new. But, to connect this question with the concerns of the PR preface, if philosophy disregards outward manifestation in its externality, then does this mean that Hegel is taking back with one hand what he had given with the other? Doesn't this render this insistence on the actuality of reason empty? In more precise terms: if nothing *new* is added in manifestation, we can say that only the form changes (from inward to outward) while the content remains the same.

---

77. One may wish to insist on a distinction between the epistemological and the ontological, and say that actuality itself always bears a relation to potency, but that our understanding of it begins with actuality as separate and subsequently proceeds to concepts. But there can be in fact no such clear separation between the epistemological and the ontological. If actuality *in reality* bears an intrinsic relation to potentiality, then we cannot separate it from this in our understanding without falsifying it. As Plato insisted long ago, we can only properly be said to know *what is*.

78. See, for example, Schelling's PM, 123 (W.6.177–78), in which Schelling contrasts actuality with essence because actuality represents for him empirical reality, "thereness," merely real being, whereas for Hegel actuality is always the real-ization of essence.

But philosophy takes the actuality as its content, though in the form of reason rather than in that of experience. This would seem to mean, then, that philosophy removes the only thing that actuality "added," namely, external form. The only way to avoid this problematic conclusion is to affirm that the change of form *does indeed*, in at least some respect, change content. This affirmation is plausible simply because of Hegel's regular affirmation of the ultimate inseparability of form and content: if one could change without the other, they could be related only in an extrinsic fashion. But we must consider what this might mean more concretely. In order to flesh out Hegel's notion, let us first situate him with respect to some of the philosophical sources for his notion. We will compare Hegel to his sources in order to see both what he adopts from them, and also how he differs, which will give us a more concrete notion of what actuality means for him. This will allow us in the section that follows to raise the question more directly what it is that actuality "adds" in Hegel's thought.

VI. Philosophical Sources

Hegel's view of the nature of actuality, and the relationship it has to reason and freedom, is a configuration of insights from both classical and contemporary sources. His synthesis of these insights represents a whole greater than the sum of its parts, and so his appropriation of these sources transforms each of them. As appropriate, therefore, we will point out how his understanding differs so as to give concrete shape to the uniqueness of his own view.

There are three main sources for Hegel's view of actuality in contemporary thought. The first is Schiller, whom Hegel credits, as we saw in chapter 2, with "the important service of having broken through the Kantian subjectivity and abstractness of thought, and of having ventured the attempt to pass beyond it by comprehending unity and reconciliation in thought as the true and realizing this truth in artistic production."[79] This breakthrough lies at the heart of Hegel's own project, which carries out just such a reconciliation, and rather than realizing it in artistic production, points instead to its actualization in the real order of politics. This integration of reason and history occurs, not in the mode of an application to the world of subjective rational principles, as we have said, but actually *in* the world as an objective form, which bears a direct analogy to Schiller's reconciliation of spirit and body in the *lebende Gestalt*. For Hegel, too, the

---

79. *Lectures on Aesthetics* (JA.12.96).

Freedom as the Concrete Form of Reason

form is essentially living, it is actuality as an organic unity, which means, as it does both in Schiller and in Schelling, a reciprocal dependence of parts.[80] This form, moreover, is the *expression* of the interior: as we saw in chapter 1, Schiller interprets this as the gift of the self, the pouring of the whole of one's self into one's activity; Hegel similarly speaks of a self-surrender, which is the "flip side," as it were, of a self-unfolding. By interpreting this movement of ex-pression as actuality, Hegel turns what was an existential mode in Schiller into a general metaphysical principle.

The second most basic source is the current in German Idealism represented by Schelling's interpretation of absolute subjectivity. As we have seen in our discussion of the early Schelling, subjectivity, insofar as the notion implies consciousness at all, requires an object, but insofar as it is *absolute* subjectivity, the object cannot simply be *other* than the subject (though it must *also* be that); rather, it must be, in some fundamental respect, the objectification of the subject to itself. Behind this notion is, of course, Fichte's original insight into the ego's need to generate a non-ego out of itself in order to be a subject, an insight to which Fichte himself came as a way of closing Kant's apparently unbridgeable dualism between the phenomenal and the noumenal realms. Schelling's novelty with respect to Fichte, which Hegel both identified and approved of in his *Differenzschrift*, was to make this internal dialectical energy, as it were, not merely a principle of subjectivity but of being in general, including that form of being one would normally assume to be most lacking in subjectivity, namely, the matter of physics. Schelling thus sees that there is nothing simply inert in reality, even at its most elemental level, but rather that all things contain, at their core, a dynamic interplay between self and other, which Hegel will call the "contradiction" that lies at the heart of all things and makes them live.[81] As we have pointed out, Schelling seeks to affirm both identity and difference as equiprimordial, but, in Hegel's view, he ultimately leaves these too extrinsic to one another. Nevertheless, his own notion of the dialectic depends on Schelling's overcoming of both Kant and Fichte along the path opened by Schiller, even if he attempts to solve the problem that arises in Schelling by thinking through the relation between self and other at the root of being in more intrinsic and organic terms. In any event, behind Hegel's notion of actuality is this dialectical energy.

A third source for Hegel's notion of actuality lies in Goethe's morphology. The high regard Hegel had for Goethe is well-known. Not only

---

80. See Phen 2 (GW.9.10).
81. GL 439–43 (GW.11.286–90).

did he admire Goethe's achievements in poetry and drama, but Hegel had particular esteem for Goethe's scientific work, which, like Schelling, he saw as presupposing a much sounder understanding of the nature of reality than the mechanism represented by Newton: without a doubt, the most impassioned language Hegel uses in the entire *Encyclopedia* occurs in the denunciation of Newton's optics and the fundamental option, as it were, for Goethe on this point.[82] Goethe's interpretation of nature was *essential* for Hegel, so much so that Gustav Mueller was able to call the two "metaphysical twins differing only in the media of thought and poetry, in which they express the same worldview."[83] Indeed, toward the end of his life, Hegel wrote to Goethe that "when I look back over the course of my intellectual development, I see you everywhere woven into it, and may call myself one of your sons: what is inward in me has been nourished by you [in its growth] toward resilient strength in the face of abstraction, and has oriented its course by your forms as by beacons."[84] Note that what Goethe helps Hegel overcome is abstraction, and he does it precisely through the actuality of form.

The reason for Goethe's importance for Hegel appears early. Hegel often referred to lines from a lesser poet, which he took to represent a position he was fundamentally critical of: "Ins Innre der Natur dringt kein erschaffner Geist. / Zu glücklich, wenn sie noch die aüssre Schale weist."[85] Hegel presented his criticism by citing Goethe's poetic response to this verse, the last couplet of which runs: "Natur hat weder Kern noch Schale, / Alles ist sie mit einem Male."[86] Goethe rejected a dualism between the hidden "inner" reality of nature and the "external" forms, and instead affirmed an inseparable unity between the two. This affirmation lay at the basis of his scientific methodology, which gave priority to what one may call natural observation with the senses over experimentation, the use of instruments intended to reveal what does not naturally disclose itself, and

---

82. See E (1817), §221A (GW.13.134–35). There may be several reasons for the language: in part because he assumed Goethe, a man he so greatly admired, would read the text; also no doubt because Newton was clearly winning the battle for popular favor. However that may be, it remains the case that Hegel, like Schelling, thought that the meaning of the universe was at stake in Newton's interpretation.

83. Mueller, *Hegel*, 13–14.

84. April 24, 1825, cited in *Hegel: The Letters*, 708.

85. "No created spirit can penetrate the inner world of nature. / We are already fortunate enough that she should present her external shell."

86. "Nature has no 'core' or 'shell,' / She is rather the whole all at once." See DS, 193–94fn60 (GW.4.92; E (1830), §140A (GW.20.163)).

Freedom as the Concrete Form of Reason

a "protection" of physics from a reduction to mathematics.[87] For Goethe, theory (i.e., the ideal) does not lie invisibly behind the (real) external manifestation, but is *in* it—for those with eyes to see.[88] This, we recall, was the essence of the dispute Goethe had with Schiller. Schiller affirmed the *unity*, but as a matter of the aesthetic achievement of spirit, not as a natural given.[89] This natural unity entailed, for Goethe, a kind of "ethics" of scientific observation, in which the subject was personally involved with the object, respectfully receiving what the object gave of itself. One of the main definitions Hegel offers of actuality, as we have seen, is unity between the *inner* and the *outer*. If we connect it with earlier comments, we may see how this unity, for Hegel, reflects a kind of achievement, with an increasing degree of external dependence as the being becomes more complex. Manifestation is a perfection,[90] the real-ization of what would otherwise lie inert—dead—within. A lower-level being, a stone for example, presents an identity of outer and inner in an immediate sort of way (though Hegel insists that there is no being in the universe, however lowly, that does not transcend itself in some degree[91]); a plant must grow out from a seed, a process that can be thwarted by both internal and external failures; *Geist* requires much more sophisticated resources to become properly perfected in this manner. The necessary conditions for this actualization will be a question that will occupy us as we proceed.

There are also classical sources for Hegel's notion of the significance of actuality. When Hegel mentions the inner-outer dualism in the contemporary philosophy of nature in the *Encyclopedia*, he observes that the theological expression of this dualism is the non-Christian notion of a jealous God, and says that both Plato and Aristotle already overcame this problem.[92] Let us consider the three counter-positions he refers to here, which, as we will see, form a sort of Hegelian triad when viewed together.

Hegel does not elaborate how Plato and Aristotle overcome this dualism in this particular context, but we can infer it from what he says about

---

87. "A strict separation must be maintained between physics and mathematics," Goethe, *The Collected works*, vol. 12, 310.

88. Ibid., 307.

89. See our discussion of this in chapter 2 (65).

90. In E (1830), §140Z (JA.8.316), Hegel refers to the non-manifestness of inward potential as a "deficit" and "imperfection." Note that the point is made clear in the German word: *Unvollkommenheit*, which expresses, more literally, that it has not reached the fullness of its potential.

91. GL, 134–35 (GW.21.121–22).

92. E (1830), §140Z (JA.8.315).

them in other places. In his history of philosophy, Hegel notes that Plato's notion of God is "much higher than most of our moderns," insofar as Plato recognizes God's *manifestness* in nature, which he explains through the claim that God is not jealous.[93] It is only a jealous God that would keep himself hidden: for Hegel, a strong "negative theology" presupposes an imperfect God.[94] It is the perfect goodness of God, by contrast, that allows a unity between the "inner" and the "outer," which lies at the basis, as we have seen, of the unity between reason and actuality. It is thus that Hegel can ascribe to Plato the point that he himself makes in the PR: in Plato's philosophy, Hegel says, "the eternal world, as God holy in himself, is reality, not a world above us or beyond, but the present world looked at in its truth, and not as it meets the senses of those who hear, see, etc."[95] This transparency of the present to its eternal meaning, which Hegel later describes in Plato as a "unity of indivisible substance and other-being," for all of its concreteness, nevertheless remains a concreteness essentially in thought, one that does not yet embrace the whole "reality of nature and of consciousness."[96] In order to progress toward this more comprehensive perspective, it is necessary to think of the concrete explicitly as *energeia*. We thus pass to Aristotle.

Rather than simply speaking of *ideas* as highest, Aristotle describes the absolute as the *concrete*: it is not just substantial thought as an absolute content, but is rather thought thinking itself, the activity of thinking in perfect identity with the object of thought, a content that grasps itself in a manner that is perfectly adequate to itself, and therefore represents the perfect coincidence of form and content. It is thus that Hegel is able to praise Aristotle as having discovered the principle of individuality or subjectivity.[97] The significance of living subjectivity is what led Aristotle, on the one hand, to recognize the truth of nature, but, on the other hand, inclined him to lose sight of the unity of the whole, and thus to "immanentize" the absolute as one concrete individual among many in the cosmos.[98] Nevertheless, the importance of Aristotle's notion of actuality for Hegel cannot be overstated. He presents it as the proper understanding of the

---

93. Timaeus, 29e; cf., Hist of Phil, II, 72–73 (JA.18.249).

94. See Hegel's "Foreword to Hinrichs' *Religion in its Inner Relation to Science*," in *Miscellaneous Writings*, 351–52 (GW.15.141).

95. His of Phil, II, 96 (JA.18.275).

96. Ibid., 380 (JA.19.10).

97. Ibid., 139–40 (V.8.68). See Ferrarin, *Hegel and Aristotle*, 105–8.

98. Ibid., II, 229 (JA.18.421).

ultimate reality: contrary to—presumably Schelling's—"dead" notion of the identity of indifference, this "is a unity which is activity, movement, repulsion, and thus, in being different, is at the same time identical with itself."[99] That Hegel makes Aristotle's principle fully his own is revealed nowhere so clearly as in the fact that the famous text from the *Metaphysics* (xii.7) is the last page of his *Encyclopedia*, and strikingly it appears there without a number, as if to say that the insight that Aristotle articulates is not simply the *final stage* of the development of spirit, even though it is the most succinct expression of what Hegel means by the Idea, or Absolute Knowledge. If it were merely the last point, as it were, it would betray symbolically the very insight it expresses, insofar as it would reduce to a particular content. Rather, as Hegel explains in the preface to his *Phenomenology*, truth is not just the result; nor is it just the process leading up to it, but "the true is the whole,"[100] it is both process and result at once, as a perfect unity that nevertheless accommodates the abiding difference between the two. The Aristotelian text that stands as the crowning of Hegel's philosophical system is therefore not present only at the end, so to speak, but is "at work," in *act*, already from the beginning and throughout, so that the "process" leading up to it does not fall outside of it as something extrinsic to the pure actuality of spirit.

And this reflection brings to light another essential feature of Hegel's understanding of actuality with respect to Aristotle. Hegel, as we saw, highlights the energy, movement, or *activity* contained in Aristotle's notion of actuality. Now, Aristotle distinguishes two different kinds of activity, *motion* on the one hand, and actuality more properly speaking on the other (*kinēsis* and *energeia*).[101] In motion, the end of the activity is external to the activity itself, which means that the activity comes to a stop when the end is reached. In the more basic sense of act, by contrast, the end is internal to the activity, which means that the activity is an end in itself, even though this being an end in itself is not exclusive of being an end as other. Hegel makes a similar observation in comparing efficient causality to final causality: in the former, cause and effect lie outside of one another so that the effect leaves the cause behind, as it were, while the cause is preserved within the effect in final causality,[102] which is thus the causality more fitting

---

99. Ibid., 149 (JA.18.332). In fact, making a clear allusion to Schelling, Hegel observes here in passing that "Philosophy is not an identity-system; that is unphilosophical."

100. Phen, 11 (GW.9.19).

101. Aristotle, *Meta.*, ix.6.

102. E (1830), §204A (GW.20.209–11).

for spirit. According to Aristotle, the prime mover causes all things in the sense of finality, as being desired.[103] And we can see that it does so *precisely by* being the actuality that all acts imitate. Genuinely spiritual activities are always of this second sort. Aristotle gives the supreme example of knowing, which indeed has a specific object in a given case, but at the same time is its own end. A knower, as Hegel himself often observes, is always at home in himself, even when knowing the most extreme things.[104] This notion of actuality is the reason Aristotle makes the act of contemplation, in a certain respect, at least the highest act, but at the same time accords it only to God, for whom the other—the object of knowing—coincides completely with the self, the knower. Human beings, as mortal, exist in a certain tension, desiring the perfect actuality of contemplation, but able to realize themselves only in the finite order of political society. And here we see a decisive difference that marks Hegel's novelty with respect to Aristotle: while, for Aristotle, the god lives in total independence by virtue of his perfection, for Hegel spirit finds its ultimate actualization only *in* the political order:[105] only here does it find the freedom of "being with itself in the other." As Alfredo Ferrarin has shown, Hegel appropriates what he interprets as Aristotle's notion of being as "containing" within itself the movement and activity of becoming.[106] What Hegel adds to Aristotle is his "historicizing" of actuality, so that the pure act of Aristotle's *nous* is no longer simply a time-transcending nature, but ultimately gets filled with the concrete content of the world.[107]

This points to the significance of Christianity for Hegel.[108] If Plato made logic concrete, and Aristotle included nature, it is the revelation of the meaning of spirit that opens up the philosophical significance of histo-

---

103. Aristotle, *Meta.*, xii.7. Cf., Hist of Phil, II, 146 (JA.18.328-29).

104. See, e.g., his observation in Hist of Phil, introduction, 230-31 (JA.17.51-52).

105. Whether it ultimately *reduces* to that actualization is a basic question for our next chapter.

106. Ferrarin, *Hegel and Aristotle*, 26.

107. Ibid., 368-69. Part of what accounts for Hegel's difference from Aristotle, according to Ferrarin, is the intervening Christian notion of the *Menschwerdung Gottes*.

108. It appears to have been Franz von Baader, and especially Jacob Boehme, who opened to Hegel the specifically philosophical content of Christianity: see the preface to the 1827 Encyclopedia, 75. Cf., O'Regan, *Gnostic Apocalypse*. Whether Hegel ends up in fact *reducing* Christianity to its philosophical content in the end is a crucial question. According to William Desmond, Hegel so "immanentizes" revelation as to render God a "counterfeit double," reason's own idea that continues to masquerade as the God of religious belief: see *Hegel's God*, 49-78. We will return to this issue at the end of the next chapter.

Freedom as the Concrete Form of Reason

ry. In general terms, spirit for Hegel can be defined as the concrete coincidence of substance and subjectivity, self-consciousness that embraces the most objective being or substance of the self. Hegel points to the Christian religion as having introduced most decisively this notion of spirit, insofar as it conceives of God in the essentially "spiritual" terms of self-revelation, which we will explain in just a moment. It is not the case, however, that Christianity *invented* this view, or that it is a theological notion that belongs in a special, and so exclusive, sense to Christianity. Instead, Hegel affirms that the notion of God as spirit is the *properly* philosophical concept of God,[109] and that such a concept was already implicitly posited by Plato and Aristotle, since they—as opposed to the Jews, for example—did not affirm God as jealous, and so were able to grasp his *rational*, i.e., self-revelational character. In this respect, Christianity merely serves to make *explicit* what spirit always has been, namely, that which makes itself explicit. This introduction has a performative character, it achieves or actualizes what it says, namely, its content, which makes it not simply a new idea *about* spirit, but the self-manifestation *of* spirit.

There are three things in particular that we can point out in Hegel's understanding of Christianity specifically in relation to the question of actuality. In the first place, as we have already indicated, what distinguishes Christianity is that it is *revealed* religion. While God has always been manifest implicitly in nature, Hegel believes, he now reveals himself explicitly as he is in himself. Hegel says that the general concept of spirit is not just self-manifestation but indeed the very act of making itself manifest:

> Spirit, if it is thought immediately, simply, and at rest, is no spirit; for spirit's essential [character] is *to be altogether active*. More exactly, it is the activity of *self-manifesting*. Spirit that does not manifest or reveal itself is something dead. "Manifesting" signifies "becoming for an other." As "becoming for an other" it enters into antithesis, into distinction in general, and thus it is a *finitizing* of spirit. Something that is *for an other* is, in this abstract determination, precisely something finite. It has an other over against itself, it has its terminus in this other, its boundary. Thus spirit that manifests itself, determines itself, enters into existence, gives itself finitude, is the second moment. But the third is its manifesting of itself according to its concept, taking its former, initial manifestation back into itself, sublating it, coming to its own self, becoming and being *explicitly* the way it is implicitly. This is the rhythm or the pure eternal life of

---

109. LPR, 164 (V.3.73).

spirit itself. If there were not this movement, then it would be something dead. Spirit is the having of itself as object. Therein consists its manifestation, in its being the relationship of objectivity, its being something finite. The third moment is that it is *object to itself*, is reconciled with itself in the object, has arrived at freedom, for freedom is being present to itself.[110]

The culmination of this self-objectification of spirit is the "unity of its absoluteness and particularity," in the Christian notion of the incarnation of God in Christ. The historical unfolding of salvation in the revealed religion is not accidental for Hegel: the most *perfect* objectification occurs in the finitude that is *opposed* to the infinite, i.e., in evil, and so a God could not be spirit without becoming incarnate specifically in the mode of entry into the furthest extremities of evil, and therefore entering into hell, God's perfect opposite, so to speak.[111] There is thus an essential connection between the fact of revelation, and the particular content it has in Christianity (the incarnation, crucifixion, and descent into hell), and this coincidence is essential to the conception of God as *spirit* and of spirit as actuality.

The second aspect of Christianity of importance in the present context is the doctrine of the Trinity.[112] The moment of the incarnation is, for Hegel, only the *implicit* unity of the absolute and particular; this unity must itself be made explicit, and it becomes so, to speak in the language of *Vorstellung*, in the resurrection of Christ, which is the return of pure objectivity to the subject, or the spirit's grasping itself for the first time *as itself* in what is other than itself. The gospel says that in Christ God is revealed in *spirit* and in *truth*, and these, of course, necessarily coincide for Hegel: it is only in the Holy Spirit—the Person whose proper name is in fact a description of the *essence* of God, and thus the "moment" in which God becomes perfectly God—that God is *true*, i.e., is the whole and so

---

110. Ibid., 176–77 (V.3.85). Note the presentation of freedom, here, not as some *ability*, but precisely as something achieved, as a perfection.

111. In the E (1817), §40A (GW.13.38), Hegel identifies freedom with negativity, which becomes positive at its furthest extreme: this is, as it were, a transposition of the theological dogma (interpreted, one ought to add, in a particularly Lutheran mode) into a logical key. On this, see Léonard, "La reprise hégélienne du dogme christologique," 160–71.

112. On Hegel's philosophical appropriation of the Christian doctrine of the Trinity, see Pannenberg, "Der Geist und sein Anderes," 151–59. Pannenberg shows that Hegel compromises the otherness of the other, in contrast to orthodox Christian thinking about the Trinity, by subordinating the Father and the Son to the Spirit, which reverses the traditional understanding of the relation among the divine Persons.

Freedom as the Concrete Form of Reason

complete. Hegel affirms that if the Deist God of the Enlightenment is the understanding's God, which views God as separate from the world and so leaves in place an opposition between the infinite and the finite, the Trinity is *reason's* God.[113] It is when spirit exists explicitly *for itself* as spirit that self-manifestation reaches its end, which is the coincidence of subject and object, when the appearance becomes *perfectly adequate* to its being. Again, we see that this is the very meaning of actuality for Hegel, the unity of the inner and the outer.

But it is important to note a deep ambiguity that lies herein, which we will return to at the end of the next chapter. Hegel suggests that, at this ultimate stage in religion, "there is no longer anything secret in God,"[114] or, in other words, there is nothing internal that has not become externalized, no potential that is not actualized. For Hegel, to deny this, it would seem, would be to reject the definition of spirit as the act of self-manifestation, for it would content spirit with an incomplete manifestation and so identify its essence with what Hegel would call an inert abstraction. It would be "dead." The irony, then, is that the revelation of God as Trinity, which is the most specifically theological concept of God, is the moment God ceases to be "theological," and instead becomes wholly transparent to reason—and thus in need of a specifically philosophical form that is no longer theological.[115] This ambiguity is why we cannot finally decide whether Hegel affirms the reality of the Trinity, the life of God in himself, or rather interprets it as a symbol, the reality of which consists in the community of the political order.[116] In other words, he speaks for example of the Holy Spirit, the third moment in which the universal becomes concrete, not as a divine Person, but as the community of believers. The question that this prompts will bear in a surprising way on Hegel's philosophy of freedom, and will furnish a central theme for us in the next chapter.

The third aspect of Christianity significant here is its relation to freedom. According to Hegel, it is Christianity that introduced freedom

---

113. E (1830), §182Z (JA.8.385-86). Cf., LPR, 124-25, fn31 (V.3.40-42fn.).

114. LPR, 184, fn 85 (V.3.92fn.), see also 332 (V.3.234): "Authentic religion corresponds to its content, in it we have the ultimate summit where the content raises itself up to itself, where spirit appears as it is in and for itself, and the *content* accords with the *concept* of spirit. In this authentic mode, God is manifest to himself or quite generally has become manifest, for there is no longer anything hidden in him."

115. Here we see an example of what Ferdinand Ulrich has disclosed to be the "pseudo-theologumena" that have been appropriated into philosophy in what defines modern thought: see *Homo Abyssus*, 1-6, 273-77.

116. Desmond, *Hegel's God*, 167-86.

thematically into Western civilization, it is Christianity that revealed that *all*—not just one or many—human beings are free.[117] Central to Christian revelation is God's will to universal salvation. There is a connection between this doctrine, for Hegel, and the notion of spirit as actualization in history. As we pointed out earlier, universal salvation implies an ultimate affirmation of all individuals precisely *qua* individuals, which means that the subjectivity of the individual cannot be subsumed by the universality, as Hegel claims it is, for example, in Plato. On the other hand, it is not enough to absolutize individuals in opposition to the whole. There must, instead, be a reconciliation between the objective substance of the whole and the subjective particularity of the individuals, which is precisely what Hegel means by "salvation." But this can occur only if the relation is not an extrinsic one, which means that the universal would require of itself the differentiation into individuals. As we will address further in the following chapter, in Hegel's view, Christianity reveals that spirit is, so to speak, inwardly ample enough to allow in principle infinite space, as it were, for the individuals to pursue their particularity, and still reconcile them in the end, which is something we saw in Schelling as well. For Hegel, the objectivity of this wholeness, however, is not provided by spirit in its *religious* incarnation, but requires the state. While for Schelling the state is an essentially fallen institution that is meant ultimately to dissolve, and the final integration is achieved (merely) eschatologically,[118] for Hegel the church is ultimately subordinated to the state, which achieves the integration (merely) in the immanent order. On the other hand, this makes the state in a certain respect the "outside" of religion.[119] The upshot, in any event, is that the freedom that represents the essence of spirit entails both an inward differentiation and an external manifestation, both of which are meant by the word "actualization."

It has been said that Hegel's thought consists of a retrieval of classical philosophy within the modern philosophical tradition,[120] and we can see how his thinking on actuality is an example of this. But one may equally characterize his thought as a rethinking of ancient ideas on the basis of

---

117. Intro to PH, 21 (JA.11.45–46).

118. SS 227 (W.4.353–54).

119. Obviously, certain qualifications would have to be entered here, insofar as religion has its place, not in *subjective* spirit but in *absolute* spirit. Also, it is the case that Hegel begins to affirm later the significance of some of the *positive*—and thus objective—dimensions of Christianity, which he had rejected in his early theological writings. We will discuss this at greater length in the next chapter.

120. See Wood, "Hegel's Ethics," 211.

modern insights. Perhaps the best way to describe Hegel is as an example of the ideal presented by Schiller in his essay *On Naive and Sentimental Poetry*: a third option, a recovery of the ancient unity through the modern differentiation, which integrates both in transformative ways. On the other hand, Hegel affirms the central modern notion of freedom with all of the enthusiasm of Schiller and Schelling, but at the same time he interprets it as, so to speak, an organic development of the classical metaphysical theme of actuality, in a way that includes nature. What results, then, is an ontological notion of freedom that is more dynamic than at least the conventional interpretation of classical ontology and at the same time does not, in its dynamism, oppose itself to the apparent fixity of nature, as so much of modern thought on freedom does. We will return to the significance of this point at the end of the chapter.

VII. The Importance of Being Finite

While we have fleshed out the notion of actuality in Hegel by giving a brief account of his appropriation of his sources on this point, it remains to be seen what significance actuality has for Hegel simply in itself. Although as fundamental the theme runs throughout Hegel's thought, he makes explicit remarks on this question in the introduction to his lectures on the history of philosophy, specifically in relation to the notion of development and the concrete.[121] The reason Hegel offers for the importance of actuality depends on his particular terminology, and the new context into which he brings the notion. He begins by observing that a goal of philosophy is to explain what was previously taken as known, in this case the notion of development. Development is a transition, and thus a passing from one state to another. First, we have the state of potency, which Hegel names in both Latin (*potentia*) and Greek (*dynamis*) and to which he also gives his own designation, namely, "being-in-itself." The subsequent state is actuality (*actus, energeia*), which he calls "being-for-itself." We note that what Hegel's terminology clarifies here is that the transition is not a change of being, but rather of the mode in which the same being relates to itself. To simplify, we could say that the content remains the same while the form changes (though we have to keep in mind that form and content are never simply independent of each other for Hegel). Now, Hegel refers here to this transition from potency to actuality as *development* (*Entwicklung*), a notion he indicates finds further treatment in the *Logic*. In the *Encyclope-*

---

121. Hist of Phil, I, 19–28 (JA.17.48–56).

dia Logic, Hegel distinguishes the transition he calls *development* (which corresponds to the concept) from the lower-level transitions he had called "passing over" (*Übergehen*) (being) and "shining" (*Scheinen*) (essence).[122] What distinguishes it from these lower forms is the unity, the wholeness of the being, that remains throughout the change—as opposed to a replacement of one quality by another, or a mere appearing differently. It is for this reason that Hegel calls it the transition that occurs to a *free* being, that is, the sort of being we could describe in at least a relatively complete way as the abiding *subject* of the transition. This is why the new state cannot be strictly novel, but simply a new mode of self-relation of the same subject, as we just said. The very word "development," even more clearly in the German "*Ent-wicklung*," designates an unfolding, which means that what *results* was already contained in the beginning *in nuce*.

Hegel uses two sorts of examples in this section of the introduction to the lectures on the History of Philosophy to elucidate the notion of development, the organic one of a plant growing from a seed, and the more spiritual one of a human being coming to know himself as free. Now, it is not an accident that Hegel should use an organic image, since this way of understanding actuality was so fundamental to Aristotle, the philosopher who first introduced the notion. It is in organic being that what might be called *teleological* potency makes its appearance, that is, not mere passive possibility to which something can occur, but being that already is as im-plicit (en-folded) what it is to become, so that its transition to the state in which that potentiality is brought to realization is something that *it does*.[123] In the latter case, the transition is done *to it*, but this means that the novelty is not an unfolding, a de-velopment or a making ex-plicit, but is rather the addition of something extrinsic *per definitionem*. We see why development, and by implication actuality in general, presupposes freedom in the sense of subjectivity. This is why the very first characteristic Hegel attributes to the concept is in fact freedom.[124] It is also clear why actuality would appear so evidently to be a perfection for Aristotle, insofar

---

122. E (1830), §161 (GW.20.177).

123. As Thomas Buchheim has observed, all of the expressions we use for "*Lebensaüserungen*" [expressions of life] presuppose grammatically an organism in the place of the subject, and that this grammatical fact rests on an ontological truth about the nature of an organism: see *Unser Verlangen nach Freiheit*, 37–62; here, 39. Hegel has the same thing in mind here. While we normally do not think of a tree as an acting subject, as it were, it remains the case that we say a *tree* grows (and not that growth is something that happens to the tree).

124. E (1830), §160 (GW.20.177).

Freedom as the Concrete Form of Reason

as it cannot be understood except in relation to potency, and therefore teleologically. An organic being is an *entelecheia*, which means it possesses its end "already" in itself. Only such a being can be "actualized." All living things, and in some analogous sense all things in general,[125] seek the actualization of their being: and this is what is meant by perfection, *Vollkommenheit*, coming to the fullness of one's being.

But the more basic example Hegel uses for actualization provides an even more comprehensive explanation. A child, he says, is implicitly rational, but does not become rational *in fact* until he *knows* that he is rational. This end lies beyond the organic development, insofar as a fully biologically mature human being does not yet necessarily grasp himself as rational. Here, a spiritual act is required for the actualization of nature, so that, even if it is not an event that simply happens naturally, it is still a natural event in the sense that it is still an unfolding of an inner potential. But it is even clearer in this case why the possibility of development is given only to a free being. The human being who comes to know himself as such represents a paradigm of what all natural beings seek by nature.[126]

---

125. For Aristotle, nature, which has its paradigm in the organism, is not simply one type of being among others, but is what illuminates the meaning of all being in the world, and so represents the reference point for understanding whatever exists. Even artificial being, the apparent opposite of the natural, imitates nature (see Spaemann, "Was heißt: 'Die Kunst ahmet die Natur nach'?," 247–64). The scholastic "extension" of this organic conception of being—which we find for example in Aquinas's statement that existence represents a perfection for all being whatever (see *De Veritate*, 21.2), is thus by no means a violence to the Aristotelian concept. Or, for that matter, to the Hegelian as we now see.

126. While it is true that Hegel often "opposes" nature and spirit (and therefore freedom), it is wrong to assume that they are in the end simply opposed to one another, as Manfred Riedel does ("Nature and Freedom," 136–50). Riedel concludes that Hegel draws analogies between nature and freedom (ibid., 142), but nevertheless insists that "The idea of freedom—and Kant's *Critique of Pure Reason* makes this abundantly clear for the whole modern era—can no longer find in nature the analogy of natural ends, and therefore turns in upon itself. This is also of decisive importance for Hegel's *Philosophy of Right*" (ibid., 142). In essence, Riedel is saying that the best interpretation of Hegel involves reading him according to the very presuppositions he himself criticizes—indeed, a criticism that lies at the heart of his philosophy. As we saw above, Hegel is explicit about following Goethe's sense of nature *as opposed to* the Newtonian sense adopted by Kant, for whom freedom remains extrinsic to nature. Thus, Riedel reads Hegel's description of the world of concretely free spirit as "a second nature," not in the Aristotelian sense (and, we should add, Schillerian sense), but rather explicitly in the Hobbesian sense of a product of human work that precisely *substitutes* for the "first" nature (ibid., 137). Riedel's interpretation involves ascribing an essentially non-teleological view of nature to Hegel, which, though fairly common (see, e.g., Franco, *Hegel's Philosophy of Freedom*, 184), simply cannot hold

The Perfection of Freedom

Hegel illuminates this point with a further observation, which is again not an example chosen at random but rather one that represents the end in which both philosophy and history—reason and actuality—meet: while it is true that human beings in themselves are free, that truth has not yet been fully actualized insofar as the phenomenon of slavery exists, Hegel observes, even at this late stage of history. Here we see the significance of Hegel's terminology: it is not enough to speak of making explicit what was initially only present *in virtute*, but this explication must be explicitly recognized for what it is, namely, the objectifying of the subject itself. It is just this recognition that allows the subject to take hold of itself, which is what it means to be for-itself. We now see why Hegel is able to present actuality, *energeia*, and *für-sich-sein* as ultimately synonymous. If the implicit points "outward" to its real externalization, the externalization points back to the being-in-itself of which it is the fulfillment, and in this sense the actualized being exists for itself. We saw above that actualization requires the unity of the being that so comes to completion; we see now that this unity remains implicit in natural being but becomes actually actual, we might say, only in this return movement wherein the subject *identifies* itself with its objectification. But only *spirit*, according to Hegel, is capable of such an identification. As Hegel says here, in nature the flower and the seed, for all their subjective unity, stand over against one another as two separate units; as he says elsewhere, the blossom "refutes" the seed.[127] In spirit, by contrast, the end is resolved back into the beginning. While the unity of the growing plant exists only "for us" (and, of course, "in itself"), reason's self-actualization exists "for itself." As we see in the example Hegel gives, and as we will discuss at length in the following chapter, this achievement of spirit spontaneously opens beyond the individual to the social sphere. It also becomes clear why Hegel describes freedom as the *telos* of historical development.[128] Freedom is not the end simply because it is a great good,

---

up to a reading of Hegel's philosophy of nature, the goal of which, he states, is to find the counterpart of spirit in nature, and to liberate the spirit in nature: E (1830), §246Z (GW.9.48). He is not critical of analogy but only what he calls its "irresponsible use" in the modern *Naturphilosophie* (§190Z [JA.8.394–96]). Stephen Houlgate offers a more integrated interpretation of nature as specifically a "rational whole" that "necessarily leads to consciousness" in *Freedom, Truth, and History*, 179.

127. Phen, 2 (GW.9.10).

128. Intro to PH, 22 (JA.11.46–47). Plamenetz points out that it has become increasingly clear, since Hegel, that history is not moving inexorably toward greater freedom, "History as the Realization of Freedom," 45–51. To assess this judgment would require a distinction between an empirical claim and a philosophical claim, which bears a clear resemblance to the question of the meaning of the rationality of actuality

Freedom as the Concrete Form of Reason

like wisdom or goodness, and so forth, but it represents the very *meaning* of development. All development, of whatever sort, is in this respect an image of freedom, which, like all images, in fact seeks the reality itself.

But what specifically is gained in this achievement? Hegel has several responses to this question, only two of which he makes explicitly in this context. In the first place, Hegel says that reason that is merely implicit is, for all intents and purposes, non-existent. A child possesses reason in an implicit sense but cannot actualize that possession: "it is just the same as if he had no reason; reason does not yet exist in him since he cannot yet do anything rational, and has no rational consciousness."[129] Unless it is actual, it is not *effective*, and in this sense not real, i.e., *wirklich*, capable of doing the "work" it is made to do. Actuality marks the difference between reality and unreality. Furthermore, while Hegel explains that actualization does not add any new content, he nevertheless affirms that the difference between the implicit and explicit, as he has been describing it, "is quite enormous." In fact, "this form of being for self makes all the difference."[130] In this context, he says that this difference accounts for all of the great variety present in the world through history. While it has always been the one reality of spirit that has been the subject of history from the beginning, that one reality has actualized itself in an essentially infinite variety of ways. Every culture, in this sense, is an expression of the one spirit, but in a *particular* way, which is therefore in some sense wholly unique. We thus have, in the notion of the actuality of spirit, a coincidence of perfect unity with, in principle, infinite difference, which explains how we can recognize ourselves in, and so come to understand, a culture that at least initially surprises us in its foreignness.

This second response points to a more general insight in Hegel. The movement outward entailed in actualization, which is an explication of being, represents in Hegel's thought a moment of determinacy. As an externalization, it is, as it were, a departure from the implicit, and in that sense a negation. It must be negative insofar as something strictly "positive" would represent an addition to what previously existed, which would mean that the determination is no longer an actualization of potency but simply a change into something different. Its being essentially negative is why one could describe this moment in the dialectic, as Hegel does on occasion, as an alienation, an entry into otherness (the *aliud*), which is the

---

we discussed above.

129. Hist of Phil, I, 21 (JA.17.49).
130. Ibid., 21 (JA.17.50).

not-self. It is also why Hegel speaks of this movement as an essential contradiction: contradiction because it is a negation of what preceded, but essential insofar as this negation was already implicitly contained within the being itself.[131] Now, Hegel takes as his own the Spinozist principle *omnis determinatio est negatio*; for him, this negation is positive in the sense that it articulates, it "spells out," we might say, what was implicit, and so posits it as full of content. Without content, it remains abstract—a term Hegel uses to describe a moment of the whole considered in isolation from that whole—and so empty, unreal, and strictly speaking untrue. Actualization represents a differentiation, which is what distinguishes Hegel's sense of the absolute from Schelling's unmediated intellectual intuition: it is what makes the absolute transparent, what gives it to reason.

Precisely because it is a "specification," as it were, of the implicit, actualization requires the acceptance of finitude. To take objective form is necessarily to take *this* form, rather than *that*. Determination is negative, then, also in the sense that it negates the indeterminate, abstract, infinity of pure possibility. This is thus also the moment that Hegel associates with *particularity*. We see in this context the significance of the Christian notion of subjectivity. For the Neo-Platonic tradition, the particular can have only a negative status as a negation of universality, which is why multiplicity has to represent a fall from unity, regardless of how much importance is put on the productivity of the One.[132] For Hegel, particularity is, even in its negation, an achievement insofar as it provides content; though it is recognized as such only in the recovery of unity, when the negation is negated, as Hegel puts it. Multiplicity and differentiation are thus not a fall from unity for Hegel but a progress toward unity, properly conceived. We thus have, not an abstract universal, opposed to the particular, but the *individual*, which is a concrete universal. Thus, what actualization provides in this sense is, in its defining and making real, the giving of concrete form to spirit. And if freedom is in fact the paradigm of actualization, then it follows that the concrete form that spirit acquires is its freedom. Let us now consider this connection between freedom and concrete form specifically in terms of the understanding of will that Hegel presents in the PR. We will see that the unity of rationality and actuality that Hegel argued

---

131. We could borrow Houlgate's felicitous phrase here: "one is explicitly *included* in the other as *excluded* from it." Houlgate is describing the paired categories of the logic of essence. See "Why Hegel's Concept Is Not the Essence of Things," 19–29, here: 21.

132. For a more thorough argument in support of this judgment, see my "What's the Difference?," 593–601.

for in the preface is not an extrinsic addendum to the PR, but is in fact a way of articulating the *idea* of freedom he develops therein.

VIII. The Will as Concrete Freedom

A question that we have faced repeatedly in this book, because it lies at the basis of the relationship between freedom and form, gets posed here in a new formulation: in what sense can the implicit infinite *identify itself* with a finite realization? To address this question, we return to the *Philosophy of Right*, in which Hegel presents most fully his understanding of the *will*. It is precisely the will that gives spirit its actual reality for Hegel,[133] which represents one of the most succinct differences between Hegel and Aristotle on the meaning of actuality. Our discussion of this notion in Hegel puts us in a position to understand this section of Hegel's philosophy in terms of its significance for the general style it presents.

If we interpret what Hegel says about the will against the backdrop of the preface, as we have presented it in the light of some of the basic principles in his thought, we come to see that Hegel's understanding of the will differs significantly, as we would expect, from the normal connotation of the term. Since an understanding of will is crucial for an understanding of freedom, which represents, of course, the principle and end of politics for Hegel, it shows a fundamental misunderstanding to abstract the philosophy of right from Hegel's logic and metaphysics—as, for example, Frederick Neuhouser explicitly does, on the supposition that, as a philosophy of the will, a *practical* philosophy, its intelligibility is independent of these more theoretical dimensions of his thought.[134] Such an assumption betrays precisely the "classical liberal" notion of the will that Hegel makes a central target of criticism, and will inevitably lead to dilemmas regarding the relation between subjective and objective freedom that Hegel's thought leaves behind.[135] For Hegel, the will bears an intrinsic relationship to reason, and both the subjective and the objective stages are reciprocally dependent realizations of spirit. It is true that the philosophy of right represents, for Hegel, the sphere of *objective* spirit, and thus practical philosophy, which mediates between the nature of the agent (elaborated

---

133. See Intro to PH: "For actuality, there must be a *second* element added—and that is activity or actualization. The principle of this is the will," 25 (JA.11.50).

134. Neuhouser, *Actualized Freedom*, 287fn10.

135. Which is not to say Hegel does not face the dilemma from a different direction, which we will address in the next chapter.

The Perfection of Freedom

in the three moments of subjective spirit: anthropology, phenomenology, and psychology) and the absolute spirit that represents Hegel's theoretical philosophy. But it is also the case that the practical philosophy cannot be separated from these others, since the will is the real-ization of reason. It is not an autonomous order juxtaposed to the order of reason, but rather each level (subjective, objective, absolute) represents the whole of actualized spirit in a particular respect. Indeed, although the system culminates in the theoretical philosophy, it is interesting to note that Hegel identifies the end of history, not with *science*, but with *freedom*. Although he presents Aristotle's *noēsis noēseōs* as the crown of the system, he reinterprets it as we saw in historical terms: it is *both* thought thinking itself and, to borrow a phrase from the PR, the "free will which wills the free will."[136] We will have to pursue the question of the relation between subjective, objective, and absolute spirit in more depth in the next chapter, but it is important to note, in the present context, that the will has its meaning in the substance of spirit, which is itself the coincidence of the rational and real. Only thus will we be able to avoid an otherwise inevitable tendency to drift into a conception of freedom as a subjective faculty.

Hegel's most elaborate treatment of the will—which appears in a variety of places in his work[137]—appears in the Introduction to the *Philosophy of Right*, and indeed comprises almost the whole of that introduction. Since freedom is the very substance of politics, and is essentially tied to the will, we cannot understand the political order, *das Recht*, as we have said, without first unfolding the proper meaning of the will. After explaining in the opening sections of PR (§§ 1–4) that freedom represents the idea, the concrete realization of the concept in existence, of right, Hegel first differentiates the basic *form* of the will into its three distinct moments (§§ 5–9), and, second, elaborates the *content* of freedom in its three moments as immediacy (in itself) (§§ 10–13), free choice (for itself) (§§ 14–20), and actual freedom (in and for itself) (§§ 21–28). He then concludes with further brief remarks on the concept of right and how to approach it (§§ 29–32).[138] For Hegel, the realization of a thing reveals most fully and clearly what that thing is; in the present context, this means that we look to

---

136. PR, §27 (GW.14-1.45).

137. E.g., the Intro to PH, cited above (JA.11.50); E (1830), §233–34 (GW.20.227–28). Perhaps most significantly, we find a discussion at the end of the philosophy of subjective spirit, which precisely marks the transition into objective spirit (E [1830] §§469–82 [GW.20.466–77]).

138. See Peperzak, *Modern Freedom*, 191–93, for a fairly detailed chart of the structure of the introduction.

Freedom as the Concrete Form of Reason

the third moment in each case to discover the definition of the will and of freedom. As Peperzak suggests, it is best to interpret Hegel by reading him backwards.[139] The three moments represent what we could call, given our discussion above, a *development*, insofar as they represent a movement from potency, through determination, to act. The importance of Hegel's distinctive approach cannot be overstated, since it lies at the heart of his difference from conventional views, and also precisely from that aspect of Schelling's thought which we saw created insurmountable problems. According to this view, the will, and freedom, are defined in their first moment *as potentiality or possibility*, and then the movement toward the determinacy is viewed simply as an application of what is already complete in itself. To see why this understanding is problematic, let us consider each (the *form* of the will and the *content* of freedom) in turn.

The three moments of the form of will are the typical "Hegelian" moments: first is an implicit, indeterminate infinity, the second is explicit determination, and the third is the unity of the two. He refers to the first as the *self* by itself, as it were, the second is specific *determination*, and thus the third is when the self identifies itself in some respect with the particular determination it has willed: *self-determination*. The essence of the will, for Hegel, is self-determination. This may seem to be a simple restatement of the usual notion of will, but in fact, interpreted as *result*, it is a precise reversal of the usual notion. Hegel's reinterpretation is, in this respect, exactly analogous to Schiller's reinterpretation of freedom as heautonomy, which we discussed in chapter 2. To say that will is self-determination normally means that it is the *power* or *ability* to determine oneself, whether one goes on to specify this determination in terms of one's natural inclinations, one's deliberate choice, or the universality of the moral law. There is scarcely a figure in modern philosophy, indeed in contemporary philosophy, that does not think of self-determination in this way. But for Hegel self-determination is not a power; it is an actuality. It is the *particular form* one has given to oneself through the exercise of the will. Note the conception of actuality is not a lifeless *fact*, mere "*Dasein*"; it is not, in other words, the second moment taken abstractly, but is rather the concrete determination *as* an expression of the will, and so is actuality as including the exercise of the will. To use Hegel's customary terminology, the truth of the whole is not just result but also principle and process. Thus the will is not, in the first place, *that which acts*, but is in truth the

---

139. Ibid., 194.

actualized whole. We capture something of what Hegel means here when we point to a particular resolution and say: "This is my will."

Now, in his own remarks on this reflection, and in the additions from his lectures, Hegel explains the problems that necessarily follow if we identify the will with only one of its moments.[140] Isolating the first moment, he says, is implied in thinking of the will as a mere *faculty*, and thus as a potency. But what defines potential *as* potential is its indeterminacy. If this is what constitutes the will in fact, the will will be understood as opposed to determination, since any particular determination will represent a limitation of its infinity. This flight from limitation is what Hegel identifies as *negative* freedom, which he says is freedom such as the *understanding* (*Verstand*) sees it—insofar as understanding isolates moments in abstraction from the whole. He goes on to say that this negative view of the will can take two different concrete shapes in the political order, an Eastern one and a Western one, as it happens. The first he refers to as "Hindu fanaticism," which he identifies as the pure passivity of contemplation, in which one retreats into the "void" of absolute possibility and detaches from all differentiation as unreal. The other is that the negativity of the will externalizes itself actively in the political order, which has two sides. On the one hand, there is the idealization of equality,[141] and, on the other hand, there is the tendency to destroy any particular institution that takes fixed shape. He points in his lecture to the recent French Revolution as an example of this latter.[142] While it is typically thought that the Terror represents a betrayal of the Revolution, in fact Hegel reveals that there is a profound logic uniting the two: they both represent two possible modes of intolerance toward difference, and for that very reason the destruction of actualized form, either implicitly (the leveling of difference in equality), or explicitly (in the form of violence). What is crucial to see is that all of this follows from a conception of will *as a faculty*.[143] Spirit necessarily strives

---

140. PR, §5 (GW.14-1.32), §5A (GW.14-1.32–33), §5Z (JA.7.55–56).

141. In his *Logic*, Hegel describes equality or likeness (*Gleichheit*) as the most abstract relation of identity and difference, since it allows no more difference than the externalization that distinguishes one thing from its identical other: See GL, 419–20 (GW.11.268).

142. PR, §5Z (JA.7.55–56).

143. Charles Taylor interprets Hegel as criticizing the French Revolution for its *absolutizing* of freedom (Taylor, *Hegel and Modern Society*, 100–111), and eventually argues for what he calls "situated freedom," which is freedom relativized, so to speak, through its contextualization. This interpretation, however, concedes too much to the notion of will Hegel intends to criticize; will, properly understood as actuality, is self-limited. In this case, absolutizing is not a problem. The problem arises only when one

toward actualization. If the will is a mere faculty, and thus pure potency, it will actualize itself either by (paradoxically) never actualizing itself, in the withdrawal of pure passivity, or it will take some real form of negativity. It would be interesting in this context to consider the proceduralism of modern liberalism as another actualizing of the pure possibility of empty form, which is unfortunately beyond our scope here.

Hegel's statement of the problem of absolutizing the second moment, in PR §6A, is much less colorful. It is essentially the identification of the will with a particular determination, as the opposite of indeterminacy, and therefore one that remains still negative. He associates this, somewhat cryptically, with Kant and Fichte. The essential problem, he says, is that it gives rise to a purely finite conception of the self, the problem of which becomes clear only in relation to the third moment, which is what alone provides a genuinely positive notion of the will, and first gives us *freedom*, according to Hegel. He describes this third moment—and thus the realization of the formal concept of the will—as an idealization of the particular determination through the self's identity with it. This determination thus becomes ideal, Hegel says, because the will embraces it as something *it* has willed, and thus raises it to the self's own universality. In other words, the will's abstraction from any particular content in the first moment is the establishment of the as-yet merely ideal *self-hood* of the self, its transcendence from all other things; it overcomes its abstract ideality by making a real choice, which requires it to sacrifice its infinity; and it then recovers that infinity, now as concrete individuality, by claiming that choice, so to speak, as the expression of itself.

The example Hegel offers is illuminating:[144] the freedom of the will in its complete form is found in the phenomenon of love or friendship: here, I am attached to *this particular* person, but this "limitation" is not felt as a restriction or imposition since the individual finds fulfillment in the recognition of the other here as other. To speak of fulfillment is to say that spirit remains "with itself" even in this other, which is, of course, Hegel's definition of freedom. This view of the will relates it positively to the particularity of determination precisely because the will is not defined by its potentiality, which would make any particular actualization external to it, either as something wholly accidental to it or an intrusion on its self-containedness. In other words, Hegel can make the concrete realization

---

absolutizes a *particular* conception. Taylor's failure to see this is no doubt tied to his reading of freedom in Hegel as self-realization, which remains ultimately, in the terms we have been using, a possibilistic notion.

144. PR §7Z (JA.7.59–60).

essential to the meaning of will because he conceives of spirit in terms of actuality such as we have been describing it over the course of this chapter. It is only at this point, Hegel explains, that we can speak in the strict sense of the freedom of the will, since it is only in this moment of completion that the will becomes substantial, and the substance of the will, for Hegel, *is* freedom.

The only thing that remains to be noted here is that, when we say that *the will is* universal and that *the will* determines itself, we speak as if the will were already assumed to be a *subject* or *substratum*. But the will is not complete and universal until it is determined, and until this determination is superseded and idealized; it does not become will for Hegel in the strict sense until it is this self-mediating activity and this return into itself.[145] This gives freedom in Hegel's thought, from the outset, a character that was lacking in Schelling's notion, which is the most basic reason an ultimate integration eluded him. As we saw, for Schelling, freedom is conceived negatively, which makes determination a termination of freedom that then has to recover itself in indifference. Nearly unique in the history of philosophy, Hegel claims that "freedom lies neither in indeterminacy nor in determinacy, but is both at once."[146]

But how is such a union of opposites possible? How is the implicitly infinite self able to identify itself with a necessarily finite and limited determination? At the end of the *formal* consideration of will, Hegel remarks that the I identifies with the determination *precisely by representing it as a mere possibility*, or, in other words, by seeing it as simply one of the many things it *could have* willed—which is what is meant by the ideal or the universal—and thus, we could say, transforms its givenness or positivity into a function of the will itself. It would be tempting to interpret this move as the achievement of integration, as, for example, one scholar does, who makes this pattern the key to reconciling freedom and tradition; another scholar, in a similar vein, presents freedom in Hegel as a suspended tension between detachment and commitment: I embrace something but always only against the background of the ability to let it go at any moment.[147] Such positions are essentially tempting insofar as they would

---

145. Ibid., §7A (GW.14-1.34-35).

146. Ibid., §7Z (JA.7.60). The closest anticipation of this judgment is no doubt Schiller's characterization of aesthetic freedom, which is infinitely "determinable," not because it is *in*determinate, but because it is perfectly determinate: see AEM, XXI.145 (SW.8.373).

147. Tunick, *Hegel's Political Philosophy*, 50–51: "I can abstract if I want, this is a possibility that I know; but I choose not to, for I am satisfied with this content." Thomas

represent the assimilation of Hegel into the liberal tradition most familiar to the English-speaking world: we reconcile ourselves to what is imposed on us by taking a critical distance and then embracing it, not as "given," but now as our choice. We might consider in this context, for example, Rousseau's observation with respect to familial relationships.[148] While this is not entirely opposed to Hegel, who likewise seeks at least in *some* sense to overcome givenness as given,[149] it is inadequate insofar as it ends up conceding the very negative concept of freedom it initially criticized, since this character is bound to an identification of freedom with possibility. I can embrace something finite and particular in this case as not a restriction only by thinking of its limitation as merely one of my limitless number of possibilities.[150]

The inadequacy of this view becomes apparent when we place this reflection back into its context, and realize that we have not, at this point, come to the realization of will *per se*, but only in a formal sense. After elaborating the formal concept of will as actualizing self-determination, Hegel directly turns his attention to the *content* of that particular determination,[151] and raises an objection to any perspective that would consider the will in itself as indifferent to any possible content, calling this the "understanding's" concept of will, which is abstractly finite:

> Finitude, according to this determination, consists in the fact that what something is *in itself* or in accordance with its concept is different in its existence [*Existenz*] or appearance from what it is *for itself*.... The understanding stops at mere *being-in-itself*

Lewis makes a similar observation with respect to habit: *Freedom and Tradition*, 57.

148. Rousseau, *Du Contrat social*, bk. 1, ch. 2, 236. We will discuss this text from Rousseau in comparison to Hegel in the next chapter.

149. This is behind his claim, for instance, that freedom is meant to unify itself with nature, but *as* freedom and not *as* nature: "Preparatory Lectures on Philosophy of Law" (1824–25), in *Miscellaneous Writings*, 314 (*Vorlesungen über Rechtsphilosophie*, vol. 4, 80).

150. See PR, §14 (GW.14-1.38). Terry Pinkard (*Hegel*, 473) takes this to be the essence of Hegel's understanding of freedom, and thus makes Hegel's spirit into Goethe's mephistophelian *"vernichtender Geist."* If Pinkard were correct, Hegel would absolutize the Romantic spirit of irony as the perfection of spirit, which he very obviously does not: he absolutizes the positive actuality of spirit. Pinkard's interpretation of freedom thus represents a paradigm of distorting Hegel by isolating a point out of the context of the systematic whole. One wonders what sort of interpretation Pinkard would give, for example, of Hegel's claim that philosophy is freedom only as *system* (E [1817], §7 [GW.13.19]).

151. Tunick likewise observes the importance of the content of choice for determining the question of freedom: *Hegel's Political Philosophy*, 60.

> and therefore calls freedom in accordance with this being-in-itself a *faculty* [*Vermögen*], since it is indeed in this case a mere *potentiality* [*Möglichkeit*]. But the understanding regards this determination as absolute and perennial, and takes the relationship [*Beziehung*] of freedom to what it wills, or in general to its reality, merely as its *application* to a given material, an application which does not belong to the essence of freedom itself. In this way, the understanding has to do with the abstract alone, not with the Idea and truth of freedom.[152]

It is finite because it separates form and content, making the "for itself" determination wholly extrinsic to the will, which is complete "in itself" as a faculty that merely *applies itself*.

Now, to get beyond this abstract sense of will, it is necessary to advance to a consideration of the will's content, which, because of the integration, will turn out to be increasingly adequate descriptions of what the will itself is. Hegel (unsurprisingly) distinguishes this content into three particular kinds. In a nutshell, the first is determination in the form of immediacy, which Hegel describes as the drives, desires, and inclinations given by nature. The second is contingent choice, now considered as the actual content of the will. The third is the content as liberated from contingency to *concrete* infinity—the free will in and for itself—through the education, or *form-ation* (*Bildung*), of the will.[153] To see why only the third moment brings the will and its freedom to fruition is to grasp what is most characteristic about Hegel's notion of freedom, and indeed about his philosophy of spirit in general.[154]

The first is inadequate because the natural drives *as such* do not involve the will, which is revealed in the fact that we share them with the will-less animals. A person who acts merely on instinct is one who does not, in truth, act, but merely follows his nature. While his nature is in fact his, and this determination remains thus a form of self-determination, it is so nevertheless only in a wholly passive sense. Such a person has no character; he drifts aimlessly. To say he is passive means that his will remains "in itself," since its content is nothing more than the immediacy of the natural

---

152. PR, §10A (GW.14-1.35–36).

153. See Peperzak, *Modern Freedom*, 192, who presents these moments in a helpful schematic outline, and interprets *education* as the transition from the second to the third moment of concrete freedom.

154. David Kolb provides a very lucid explanation, drawing ultimately on Hegel's *Logic*, for why the self-determination of the will essentially requires the full mediation of membership in a social whole: *Critique of Pure Modernity*, 98–102.

Freedom as the Concrete Form of Reason

drives. It is *resolution*, Hegel says, that moves one beyond this immediacy. In explaining what he means by this, Hegel points to the rich ambiguity of the German language, which can state this act in either of the apparently opposed expressions, *etwas beschließen*, literally, "to close something," and *sich entschließen*, "to open oneself up."[155] There is a truth in this paradox: the will takes concrete shape, and so "closes" its open determinacy, only by opening up and going outside of itself to something particular. Hegel alludes in contrast here to what he described as a "beautiful soul" in the *Phenomenology*, which is a soul that remains in the ideal realm of pure possibility, not wishing to soil its purity by anything actual.[156]

But resolution in itself also remains inadequate until it reaches its proper form. Interpreted simply as resolution without any reference to *what* is resolved, we have at this point an identification of freedom with choice, *Willkür*. This, Hegel says, is "the commonest idea we have of freedom," and sees it both in Wolff and in Kant. The latter, in particular, may seem surprising insofar as Kant insists that a will is free only insofar as it wills the moral law, but this becomes clear when we understand more precisely Hegel's criticism of this view. The point is not, in the first place, that this view makes freedom random and unpredictable, which would indeed make his criticism of Kant miss its target.[157] The problem, rather, is formalism: it is not yet the *truth* of freedom, which requires that freedom be the fully determined *content* of the will. One sign of this formalism

---

155. See PR, §12A (GW.14-1.137). One can compare Hegel fruitfully here to Heidegger's quite similar notion of *Erschlossenheit*, "resolution." One difference, however, is that it remains formalistic in Heidegger, for, as Heidegger describes the phenomenon, it does not matter what one decides, as long as one is resolute. While, for Hegel, the point is the concrete realization of the will, for Heidegger, though he does not oppose this resoluteness to actuality, actuality is not the primary point: "In resoluteness the issue for Dasein is its ownmost potentiality-for-Being" (*Being and Time*, 346). Indeed, the *end* for Hegel is *actuality*; for Heidegger, "Higher than actuality stands *possibility*" (ibid., 63). Heidegger is arguably closer to the conventional notion in his conception, at least as he articulates it in *Being and Time*.

156. Phen, 400 (GW.9.354–55). It becomes quite clear how Hegel's use of the term differs from Schiller's. For Schiller, it represents precisely the *integration* of the ideal and the real; Hegel will occasionally use the term in a positive sense, particularly when talking about the Greek culture, but will otherwise use it ironically. His use of the term thus reflects what we have indicated is his basic position with respect to Schiller: Hegel takes Schiller's integration to be *decisive*, but sees it as tending toward a bourgeois aestheticism if not developed further in terms of the social order.

157. Allen Wood believes Hegel misunderstands Kant because he thinks Hegel is criticizing Kant's view of the will for its *arbitrariness*: see Wood's commentary in PR, 399. But Hegel was fully aware of the distinction Wood indicates. His criticism rather concerns the abstraction of the notion of choice.

is that a thinker will make the primary question regarding the meaning, nature, and possibility of freedom the question of the relationship between free will and determinism.[158] For Hegel, this problem is insoluble in the terms in which it is typically posed, but at the same time not worth solving, insofar as the real philosophical problem lies in the terms themselves. This view thinks of freedom as (formal) self-activity, and then raises questions about various possible *contents* of this self-activity. But this makes the content external to the will, which means that it will always tend to represent a determination that is foreign to freedom. As Hegel sees it, because there is no integration between form and content in this conception, whether we speak of free will or determinism in any particular case simply does not matter; they represent two different perspectives that are so external to one another that they simply do not intersect. In this case, it becomes possible to affirm the very same thing as wholly mechanically determined and completely free, as both Kant and Locke do in different ways, for example.[159] Here we do not have an integration—freedom as determinate and indeterminate at once—but an "extra-gration," as we saw in Schelling's late philosophy: the opposites lie side by side, parallel lines that do not intersect even when extended into infinity.

This last image points to the distinctiveness of Hegel, who precisely distinguishes between "bad infinity" and "good infinity" as between a straight line and a circle.[160] The key difference between the two is that the first is *opposed* to finitude, while the latter *requires* it. The will becomes in-

158. As Kant does, for instance: see his "Critical Elucidation of the Analytic of Pure Practical Reason," in CPrR, 92–110. The relationship between free will and determinism occupies nearly the whole of the massive discussion of freedom in contemporary analytic philosophy.

159. For Kant, the difference involves simply shifting from an empirical to a transcendental perspective on one and the same act (*Practical Reason*, 101). Locke initially contented himself with a notion of freedom as the power to carry out one's preference in reality, without concern about the source of those preferences. He thus considered the question of the freedom of the will to be a useless one: see his *Essay Concerning Human Understanding*, bk 2, ch. 21, pars. 14; 21–22. After publishing this book, he was brought to consider the matter further, adding in a second edition the claim that the ability to *suspend* one's desires is the essence of freedom (bk 2, ch. 21, par 48). It is to be noted that this change—which did not lead him to modify what was already written but simply to add this further observation—does not in fact get beyond the question of determinism, for it leaves in place the question concerning the source of the desire to suspend one's desire, and so on.

160. PR, §22Z (JA.7.74) Cf., also Hegel's observation that Plato is critical of the boundlessness of unnecessary physical desires in the *Republic* precisely because they represent a "bad infinity," significantly because they "do not form a closed circle" (PR, §185Z [JA.7.266]).

finite in an actual, concrete way only when it exists *for* itself, which means when it finds its inner being made objective, brought to the light of day, which, as externality, can occur only in a finite form. The image is helpful: it is only when the line closes itself in a particular, definite shape, that it becomes actually infinite. It is endless, in this case, because it has itself all at once. By contrast, if we think of infinity in an indeterminate sense as endless extension, in its very opposition to finitude it never reaches infinity, since, as Aristotle proved long ago, infinity can never be actual.[161] The irony, then, is that if we oppose infinity to the finite, we render the infinite actually finite, and thus always incomplete, whereas if we integrate the two, the infinite becomes actual precisely *in* the finite. We can return, at this point, to Hegel's observation in the preface regarding the philosophical vision of the spirit *in* the concrete forms of actuality. In relation to the present issue, this means that, in fact, the will is not indifferent to its content, but rather requires a unity between form and content, which means the content, the particularity of whatever is "arbitrarily" chosen, has to be adequate to the form. The only way for this to occur is for the object of the will to be freedom itself, so that form and content become one. It is just this identity of form and content that Hegel means by real infinity:

> The will which has being in and for itself is *truly infinite*, because its object [*Gegenstand*] is itself, and therefore not something which it sees as *other* or as a *limitation*; on the contrary, it has merely returned into itself in its object. Furthermore, it is not just a possibility, predisposition, or *capacity* (*potentia*), but the *infinite in actuality* (*infinitum actu*), because the concept's existence [*Dasein*] or objective [*gegenständliche*] externality is inwardness itself.[162]

But, of course, it is crucial to interpret the free embrace of freedom in the proper sense, which means in light of the spirit's drive to become actual. "The free will which wills the free will" does not mean the choosing of the power to choose, as we almost cannot help but assume. This would represent an utterly contentless abstraction. Instead, if freedom is not a power but is actuality, this phrase means the spirit's total embrace of its full, comprehensive realization. This embrace is by definition full of content. The free will willing the free will is thus the human spirit's wholly being its whole self, its pouring itself unreservedly into being what it is.

---

161. Aristotle, *Physics* iii.5–8.
162. PR, §22 (GW.14-1.42).

We cannot help but hear an echo of Schiller here. He, too, interpreted the most fundamental sense of freedom as human wholeness, which includes within it the ability to engage itself *as a whole* in all of its particular acts. Interestingly, Schiller identifies this with the aesthetic state, beautiful form, which he describes, like Hegel, as a filled infinity, and which he distinguishes both from the abstract, empty infinity of indeterminacy, and from mere finite determination. What makes beautiful form infinite is the fact that it actually includes all possibilities: it is, as Hegel would much later say, a closed circle, which as such is both determinate and indeterminate at the same time.[163] Now, Schiller identifies the achievement of beautiful form as the *center*, if not simply the *end*, of education; it is this because it represents the ideal of humanity.[164] As we have mentioned, one might worry that Schiller's notion of freedom threatens, unless more is said, to settle unsatisfactorily into a bourgeois aestheticism. The cultivation of beautiful form, if absolutized, could lead to an individualistic effete obsession with gentile manners. Whether Schiller has the resources in the logic of his own position to avoid this problem remains an open question; in any event, Hegel offers the requisite qualification. On the one hand, he affirms the indispensable role of education in decidedly Schillerian terms: through its form-ation [*Bildung*] of individual particularity, it ennobles the individual by universalizing him.[165] On the other hand, however, this moment does not yet represent the ideal of freedom. It is ultimately, for Hegel, the *state* wherein freedom finds its paradigmatic realization,[166] whereas *Bildung* is that whereby individual subjectivity becomes a part of the substantiality of freedom.

It is at this moment, we could say, that the Schillerian aesthetic form opens up most directly into social form: for Hegel, as we will explain more fully in the following chapter, the individual can be *wholly* whole ultimately only within the supra-individual wholeness of a community. Schiller had described the aesthetic form of the human being as that wherein "duty becomes nature,"[167] that is, wherein reason takes on flesh; it manifests it-

---

163. AEM, XXI.145 (SW.8.373).

164. Ibid., XXIV.171–81 (SW.8.384–90).

165. PR, §20 (GW.14-1.41); cf., §187A (GW.14-1.162–64), where Hegel identifies education as that by means of which the "*form of universality* comes into existence," which is precisely what allows the spirit to be "*at home* and *with itself* in this *externality* as such," i.e., to be free in the Hegelian sense.

166. As Hegel puts it already in the Phen, "Human nature only really exists in an achieved community of ends": 43 (GW.9.47–48).

167. Kallias, 19 Feb, 1793 (159) (SW.8.647).

self in the externality of the body. Making clear allusion to Schiller, Hegel describes *Sittlichkeit*, ethical substance, as that wherein "self-conscious freedom becomes nature."[168] The incarnation of reason, in this case, takes on a more directly "corporate" dimension. What is common to them both, nevertheless, is an integration of form and content that can occur only as a real *Gestalt*, a historical phenomenon of spirit. While Hegel is well-known to have criticized Kant's formalism of reason, insisting that reason cannot be understood without the particularity of concrete content, it is less often perceived that he makes the same criticism with respect to *freedom*. This criticism, however, stands out in clear relief when we read Hegel in light of Schiller.

IX. Conclusion

We may now sum up the foregoing with a review of Hegel's initial definition, which we will then develop in the next chapter by returning to Hegel's first description of the meaning of freedom in section 4 of the introduction to the *Philosophy of Right* and the light of its subsequent unfolding in the introduction and our discussion of the preface that precedes it.

While we generally think of freedom as a quality that may or may not—depending on circumstances—belong to the will, which is conceived as a distinct faculty within the human spirit, Hegel takes a more concrete view insofar as he interprets freedom, not as a quality of the will but its very essence, and, second, he sees will, not as a separate faculty but as integrated with reason in the one reality of spirit. As he puts it, will and thought are *one and the same*, though viewed from two different perspectives.

Here we can draw together a number of threads. If will is freedom in its essence, then freedom represents the fulfillment of reason. And if reason and actuality are ultimately identical, we may likewise identify freedom and actuality. Hegel, as we have explained, defines freedom as "being at home with oneself in the other": the *being at home* is this reality viewed as reason; the being at home *in the other* is the reality viewed as will, insofar as it is this movement *into* determinate reality, beyond abstract ideality, and therefore the movement of actualization, which is reason's own goal. The one word "freedom" captures all of this at once. This whole complex configuration represents the perfection of spirit, for Hegel, because there is no higher perfection possible. We understand then

---

168. E (1817), §430 (GW.13.232–33).

The Perfection of Freedom

in what sense Hegel can identify freedom as both the end of history, and as the end of philosophy.

Let us return, in the conclusion, to our opening comments on Hegel's notion of freedom, and consider them in the light of this fuller unfolding, and with a view to its positive achievement. We suggested, at the outset, that although Hegel's notion of freedom may appear to be wholly discontinuous with prior conceptions, his view intends to provide what is lacking to other views, and so complete them even on their own terms, while carrying them forward to a more comprehensive truth. To see how this is the case, let us consider three common notions associated with freedom: choice, self-determination, and autonomy. We discussed Hegel's explicit rejection of the first as inadequate because its content is arbitrary. Here we ask, in what sense does Hegel's concrete notion of freedom fulfill the view of freedom as choice? In the first place, we can say that Hegel necessarily *includes* choice in his view since there is no way for the will to "open" its mere abstract in-itselfness and enter into external existence *for* itself except by means of choice. Affirming this allows us to see what choice itself seeks. Hegel is showing us that the reason we desire the power to choose is that we wish to extend ourselves, as it were, into the world, to realize ourselves.[169] The objection that we find sufficient satisfaction in simply having the *power* to choose, irrespective of any particular choice—which would imply that, contrary to Hegel's protests, the will has its perfection in potentiality—reveals a superficiality in the fact that the power one desires already has an ordering, i.e., an actuality: ultimately indeterminate power is impotent in its emptiness. We desire not just any power, but specifically the power *to choose*, and once we admit this dependence of potency on actuality in principle, we are immediately picked up and carried along in the Hegelian dialectic, for we must then face the question of the desirability of that to which the power is directed, namely, choice. Facing this question, we thus find that the desirability derives from the actuality of the end that choice seeks in any particular case. An investigation of the various possible ends in turn raises the question of the adequacy of the actuality to its potency, and we are then talking about the actuality of spirit once again in concrete terms. Hegel's rejection of choice as the definition of freedom is nevertheless a completion of this particular view in a more comprehensive

---

169. In the introduction to the Lectures on Aesthetics, Hegel points to the "child's first impulse," the little boy's throwing pebbles into a lake and watching the ripples it makes, as an expression of this: what prompts this play, he says, is the spirit's need to see itself objectified in the world (JA.12.58).

one, which means it is an *internal* criticism rather than an *external* one:[170] it brings this view to the form that this view itself seeks but cannot attain because of its self-imposed limitation. On this score, Hegel's approach to choice is remarkably similar to that of Plotinus, who likewise "systematically" reduces potency to act in his meditation on freedom, to the point of identifying freedom and being.[171] Hegel may be said to be recovering a classical view, then, by insisting that choice is never simply indifferent to content, and yet he does so in an obviously modern context: while in the classical view, the content was provided, as it were, by the *good*, in Hegel it is defined more directly as self-determination.[172] We will consider the significance of this difference in the general conclusion to this book.

This brings us to the second notion, self-determination. In a manner similar to what we have just seen regarding choice, one typically locates the *freedom* of self-determination in the *power* that the self possesses: I am free because I am *able* to determine myself in a way that I direct. Now, the focus on potency prompts the same criticism we just made above, but we can also consider a more subtle and profound problem. Determination is actuality. If what makes the self free, however, is possibility, then "self"-determination becomes a straightforward contradiction. The self, to the extent that it is *defined* as possibility, is opposed to determination. In this respect, it is clear how Hegel fulfills this notion. Connecting freedom to actuality is necessary in order to save the notion of self-determination from incoherence. But let us dwell for a moment on the implications. A possibilistic view of freedom locks the subject, as it were, forever outside the actual order of the world. We mentioned this problem in our discussion of Schiller, and saw that it lay at the foundations of Schelling's *Naturphilosophie*. If we define subject and object *outside* of one another, we can never overcome a dualism between the ideal and the real. Schelling sought to overcome this by positing a dialectic between subject and object

---

170. Maletz, "Hegel on Right," 33–50, likewise sees Hegel as offering a view of freedom that *accommodates* choice (*Willkür*) rather than eliminating it (ibid., 40–41). However, Maletz says he does so by *justifying* the more comprehensive order *to* subjective will, when in fact it is an elevation of this will to the larger order. Peperzak, by contrast, is right that the lower moments need to be read in light of the later resolutions, rather than the reverse.

171. Plotinus, *Ennead* VI.8.

172. In the initial section of the final part of morality, marking the transition from subjectivity to the objectivity of *Sittlichkeit*, Hegel identifies goodness with the *realization of freedom* (PR, §129 [GW.14-1.114]). In other words, *because* it is the realization of freedom, it is, for him, good. The classical view, of course, would be that it realizes freedom because it is good.

in an ever more originary way until it comes to constitute the very being of God. But no matter how original, for Schelling, as we saw, identity and difference, we argued, always remained ultimately external to one another, which is most clearly revealed in the fact that he retains in the end a "possibilistic" notion of freedom (as the capacity for good and evil). For Hegel, the reconciliation is, as it were, more fundamental than the opposition, so that subjectivity has its reality *in* objectification; it comes to itself in its other. It is not, in other words, defined *first* in itself, and *then* set in relation to objectivity. It is this always-already presupposed reconciliation that is expressed in the claim that the rational *is* the actual and the actual, rational, and it is what makes possible a concrete notion of self-determination.

This concrete notion has two further benefits. If spirit is not essentially actual, not only does the subject remain in opposition to objectivity, but it will always therefore be opposed to itself in the concrete order. Interpreted as mere power, the self that the self possesses in self-determination necessarily shrinks to a non-existent point.[173] It can never possess itself as real, but only as "ideal," since any realization slips just so far into the actuality that is opposed to the self. This self must therefore retreat into abstraction, as Hegel has described it in a variety of contexts. Indeed, not only would we have to say that the self does not possess itself in its being, but only in its subjective power, but even this power cannot be actually possessed, but only potentially sought—an "ought." We might think of the potential neuroses produced here by defining the individual in terms of an essential abstraction that necessarily and eternally elude its grasp, which imposes on the self a need to be what it cannot possibly be. Philip Rieff has made very interesting observations, in this regard, on the ideal of individuality in contemporary culture.[174] Ironically, the self as *potentiality* becomes endless *activity* that has no essential rest. If we view spirit essentially as actuality, by contrast, subjectivity has room in itself for objectivity, indeed in principle in its most objective form. In other words, in this case self-determination becomes comprehensive: the self may come to possess itself unto the very somatic cells. In the *Encyclopedia*, Hegel talks about having knowledge even in the *limbs* of our body.[175]

And this leads to the second benefit: this reconciliation allows an overcoming of the division between freedom and nature that haunts the

---

173. On this, see Murdoch, *The Sovereignty of Good*, 18.
174. Rieff, *The Triumph of the Therapeutic*.
175. E (1830), §66 (GW.20.107-8).

modern mind, and it does so without collapsing the difference.[176] There is, as we have seen, a connection between a possibilistic view of freedom and a one-sidedly subjective view. To see spirit as actuality, by contrast, not only changes our notion of spirit, but also of actuality. It thus gives freedom ontological depth. All of being, for Hegel, from top to bottom has the form of self-determination, analogously realized at every level. Freedom in the sense of spirit, then, brings to explicit perfection what implicitly represents the structure of reality as such. In this respect, freedom is never foreign to nature, and conversely, nature always expresses intimations of freedom, more clearly the more complex it appears. Hans Jonas has called our attention to the importance of this point, though his appeal has found little echo.[177] Schelling before him sounded out the problem here far more profoundly and extensively, especially in his early writings, than did Hegel. But, because of governing presuppositions about the nature of freedom, we have argued that he was never able to resolve it in a satisfactory way. It is interesting to consider the fruitfulness this view would have in resolving the problem of the interaction between body and soul, how an act of the soul is able to move the body: here, the body is an integral "part" of the meaning of soul, and is always already contained within it, while the soul has its actuality in the body. This makes its activity not that of an agent acting on an external object, but rather the body is always already the actuality of the soul in this case; it is an intrinsic dimension of the spirit's freedom. Only from such a perspective could we say that the body is in some basic sense *me*, and not merely an "external" object that "I" possess as property. Ultimately, it is only in Hegel's view of self-determination that we are able to conceive ourselves as dwelling *in* our body, or in fact *being* our body: this affirmation requires an integration of freedom and form.

Finally, autonomy. We find this in Rousseau: the free self is one that gives a law to itself. The good sought in this conception is the kind of self-possession we have been discussing, which is coincident with the integrity of one's being. But if we achieve this good primarily in terms of power, rather than actuality, it comes at the cost of opposition between the self and the other. Hegel very clearly and very emphatically affirms autonomy

---

176. See Franco, 154, on Hegel's difference from Kant on this score.

177. Alfred North Whitehead is a notable exception: see his *Science and the Modern World*. On the influence of Hegel, and even more significantly of Schelling (through Coleridge), on Whitehead, see Braeckman "Whitehead and German Idealism," 265–86.

in his notion of freedom,[178] and so we can confidently say he does not reject this view. But if autonomy is understood in *opposition* to otherness, it will concretely always be threatened in society. We see this threat in Rousseau, who regarded society as alienation, as primarily a problem that had to be resolved on the basis of the assumption of natural autonomy. For Hegel, by contrast, once we see spirit as actualization, and see that actualization implies at least a kind of otherness from the very beginning, the spirit cannot in fact have its autonomy, it cannot be *"bei sich," except in the other*. This view allows, in principle, the self to be at home in the midst of the social order. Indeed, it *requires* it. At this point, however, we have seen this only as the concrete realization of the individual's will. The social dimension of freedom, and the success of Hegel's affirmation of otherness, is the topic of our next chapter.

---

178. See, for example, PR, §135A (GW.14-1.118). Interestingly, in the introductory lecture on the Phil of Hist, Hegel defines freedom as *"bei-sich-selbst-sein,"* without reference to the other: 20 (JA.11.44).

6

"The 'I' That Is 'We' and the 'We' That Is 'I'": On the Sociality of Freedom in Hegel and its Excesses

I. The Controversy Surrounding Hegel's Conception of the State

NEXT TO HEGEL'S IDENTIFYING rationality and actuality in the preface of the PR, which we discussed last chapter, few statements by Hegel have generated more controversy than the claim that occurs in the *Zusatz* to one of the opening sections on the state in the PR:

> The state in and for itself is the ethical whole, the actualization of freedom, and it is the absolute end of reason that freedom should be actual. The state is the spirit which is present in the world and which *consciously* realizes itself therein, whereas in nature, it actualizes itself only as the other of itself, as dormant spirit. Only when it is present in consciousness, knowing itself as an existent object, is it the state. Any discussion of freedom must begin not with individuality or the individual self-consciousness, but only with the essence of self-consciousness; for whether human beings know it or not, this essence realizes itself as a self-sufficient power of which single individuals are only moments. The state consists in the march of God in the world, and its basis is the power of reason actualizing itself as will.[1]

---

1. PR, §258Z (JA.7.333–36).

The Perfection of Freedom

No comment is needed to explain why this passage should cause concern. Some seek to lessen the concern by pointing out that the most threatening phrase, "The state consists in the march of God in the world," occurs only in transcribed lecture notes and has no precise equivalent in any of Hegel's published works, or by observing that the German is ambiguous: Wood's translation, which we cite here, is a somewhat free rendering; as Kaufman and Avineri have both argued, a more literal translation would be "It is the way of God in the world, that there should be the state,"[2] which certainly has a different implication. But, while this translation is no doubt the more accurate one,[3] it scarcely eliminates the problem. It is true that Hegel would affirm—as it was the burden of our last chapter to show—that it corresponds essentially to the nature of God (or, in more directly philosophical language, of *Geist* in its most complete sense, in its truth) to exist in the world, but it is also true that the *fact* of spirit's existence for Hegel cannot be detached from essence, without dissolving what he means by actuality. In other words, it is not simply that the fact of the state's existence reflects the will of God; Hegel also claims that the *essence* of the state is a realization of the essence of absolute spirit.

Kaufman and Avineri's efforts to soften the point are thwarted by the very next sentence in the *Zusatz*: "In considering the Idea of the state, we must not have only particular states or particular institutions in mind; instead, we should consider the Idea, this actual God [*diesen wirklichen Gott*], in its own right."[4] Thus, after the observation about the state being "the way of God in the world," Hegel immediately draws our attention, not to any external existence, but to the *Idea*, which represents the realized essence, and he calls the Idea the "actual God." If this phrase does not recur specifically in this form in his published writings, it does have close parallels in other lecture notes,[5] and it nevertheless gives expression to the essential movement of his thought, as we have begun to see in the last chapter and will elaborate in the present one. The issue here is thus not merely one of grammar. An engagement with Hegel's political thought will have to confront the question why Hegel attributes a divine

---

2. Walter Kaufmann, "Introduction," 4. See Avineri, *Hegel's Theory*, 176–77.

3. We say "no doubt" because one would expect in this case that Hegel would have put the phrase in the subjunctive mood. The use of the indicative leaves open the possibility of interpreting the "es" as a place holder for the relative cause, which would make Wood's translation at the very least justifiable.

4. PR §258Z (JA.7.336).

5. For example, just a few pages later (§272Z [JA.7.370]), Hegel notoriously refers to the state as an "earthly divinity" that should be venerated as such.

character to the state and whether the totalitarian implications of this attribution can be avoided without jettisoning the concrete conception of freedom, the contribution of which surely counts as one of Hegel's greatest achievements.

The long passage we cited above introduces all of the major themes we will address in the present chapter. In the first place, it sets into relief the fact that *Geist*, for Hegel, is essentially a "supra-individual" reality, even if, at the same time, it is as it were constituted only by individuals in relation. Accordingly, we will discuss below the "communal" aspect of Hegel's conception of spirit. Extending the point that we ended with in the last chapter, namely, that spirit requires an other in order to become actual, we will show here that spirit's other must ultimately be spirit as well, so that the truth of spirit consists in the relation between irreducible spiritual individuals. The main text we will draw on in this context is Hegel's explication of the meaning of spirit in the *Encyclopedia*, though we will also refer to key texts from the *Phenomenology* and from the *Logic*.

Second, Hegel describes the state as the "ethical whole," and it is precisely as such that it represents the actualization of freedom. There are indeed grounds for interpreting the state as the ultimate whole that Hegel identifies with the true.[6] As we have seen, freedom, for Hegel, is not a mere possible quality of the faculty of will, but is the very essence of the will, which in turn is essentially the actualization of spirit. This is why Hegel often calls freedom the substance of spirit. But precisely because spirit is supra-individual, it has its substance not in consciousness nor even in what we would call intersubjectivity, but rather in the political order understood primarily in the objective sense that includes the positivity of politics—institutions and the like. Here, we will discuss the meaning of what is arguably the central term in Hegel's political theory, namely, *Sittlichkeit*, in the light of the communal sense of spirit we have just developed. Then, we will explore the basic articulations of *Sittlichkeit* as fulfilling that meaning. *Sittlichkeit* will turn out to represent freedom as social form, a complex unity that seeks to do full justice to the irreducible autonomy of each of its members, and thus stands in a certain respect as the culmination of the integration of freedom and form that we have been pursuing over the course of this book.

Thirdly, and finally, Hegel calls the "ethical whole" of the state, which as such represents the actualization of freedom, the *absolute end of reason*. In other words, he seems to say, here, that there is no higher fulfillment for

---

6. Phen, 11 (GW.9.19).

reason than the state. Indeed, he often claims that freedom is the ultimate goal of spirit, it has no purpose other than "*sich zu sich zu befreien*,"[7] and also that the essential *home* of that liberation lies within the rich bonds of *Sittlichkeit*. It is thus not a departure from his general view to refer to the state as the "*Gang Gottes in der Welt.*" But this raises a fundamental question, the exploration of which will bring our study of Hegel to a close: What exactly is the relationship between the objective spirit, realized most perfectly in the *Sittlichkeit* of the state, and *absolute spirit*, which ought to transcend objective spirit and thereby give full range to subjective spirit and the specific freedom that belongs to it? As we will show, this basic question takes the most concrete form in the question of the relationship between church and state. This question will turn out to be a central one as well for the integration of freedom and form, which represents the broader goal of this book.

It is helpful already at the outset to sketch the shape of the argument we will advance in this chapter with respect to general currents in the scholarship on Hegel. In the first place, we will attempt to show that there is something desirable, indeed, indispensable, in Hegel's notion that the state represents, in some respect, the very substance of spirit. Among other things, it is only such a conception that allows us not only to think of freedom in something other than purely formalistic and thus "possibilistic" terms, but by the very same token to understand spirit as truly social in its structure and not just as a power individuals have, which enables them in a secondary sense to establish relations with others. In other words, a substantial conception of spirit is indispensable in any attempt to think of freedom as *social form*. To affirm this will require us to embrace what Neuhouser has described, and dismissed, as a "strongly holistic" reading of objective spirit in Hegel.[8] We will insist that to dismiss this is in fact to reject Hegel's political theory *in toto*,[9] even if one resists strong holism for the very good reason that it appears to threaten any substantial autonomy for the individual as such. Our argument will be that, in order to avoid this

---

7. E (1830), §442A (GW.20.437).

8. Neuhouser, *Actualized Freedom*, 38–39. Neuhouser does not give a reason for rejecting this interpretation, but simply asserts that it is "unattractive" and has nothing to do with what we recognize as freedom (ibid., 45). But of course that is what we should expect if Hegel claims that the concept is generally misunderstood.

9. This does not mean that one could not continue to affirm one idea or another found in Hegel's thought, but only that one will have rejected the ultimate form, and so the foundation, of his political theory. In this case, even the aspects of his philosophy that one affirms will take on a different, non-Hegelian meaning.

threat, it is ultimately self-defeating to give a weak reading of objective, and by extension, absolute spirit, since it will turn out to be only a strong sense of absolute spirit, in the end, that allows due place for *both* subjective and objective spirit in their unity *and* their difference. While making this argument simply follows the inner logic of basic Hegelian concepts, we will see that it leads to a place significantly different from Hegel's own, or at the very least that it helps to resolve a basic ambiguity in Hegel's thought regarding the ultimate significance of difference or otherness in a way that recasts some of his most fundamental notions—for example, his notion of freedom—and requires in turn a revision of the position he takes on the relationship between religion, philosophy, and politics.

II. Communal Spirit

One of the questions that quite palpably tortured Schelling from the beginning of his philosophical reflection to the very end was the ever ancient and ever new question of the One and the Many: how does the finite emerge from the infinite, or how does difference emerge from absolute unity? As we saw, Schelling attempted, in his early writings, to respond to the question at one point by affirming the absolute as a kind of "identity of identity and non-identity" (a phrase he seems to have borrowed from Hegel's formulation of his position in the *Differenzschrift*[10]), by describing it somewhat later as an *in*-difference, which transcends both unity and difference, and ultimately by seeking an answer to this question in the realm of revealed religion.[11] In contrast to Schelling's restlessness over the question, Hegel appears to have settled it fairly early, with great tranquility, and once he settled it he never looked back. Hegel asserts that simple infinity, or the absolute concept, at the purest level of ideality contains an internal division that nevertheless does not compromise its perfect unity: each of the divided "parts" of the concept is so purely opposed to the other it is a sort of mirror reflection that is identically the same, and each other contains its opposite in itself thus *without difference*. He then goes on to say—perhaps with Schelling in mind?—the following: "Accordingly, we do not need to ask the question, still less to think that fretting over such a

10. DS, 156 (GW.4.64). Hegel repeats this definition of the absolute, considered in its most abstract form in the GL, 74 (GW.11.37).

11. We recall that, although this placed it beyond the reach of philosophy as traditionally understood, Schelling insisted that this insight does not become a matter of strictly theological faith, but remains philosophical, although to be sure this requires a whole new "kind" of philosophy, i.e., the positive philosophy.

question is philosophy, or even that it is a question that philosophy cannot answer, the question, viz., '*How*, from this pure [unified] essence, how does difference or otherness *issue forth* from it?'"[12] In the *Logic*, he observes along the same lines that beginning with an absolutely immediate unity dooms one to an empty notion of infinity from which one will never be able to escape no matter how much difference is subsequently added.[13] We discussed precisely this problem as the central one in Schelling at the end of chapter 4. This criticism represents a fundamental position that Hegel adopts, which illuminates a primary feature of his thinking: if unity is always-already mediated by difference—even so perfectly as to become thereby "self-identical" to itself without any difference—this means that difference will never, in principle, represent a threat to unity, and vice versa. Quite to the contrary, division, or "self-sundering," always turns out to be, in the end, what we might call a self-transcendent rediscovery of the self. The importance of this point in all Hegel's thinking cannot be overstated. This dialectical relation between self and other reveals why the movement of the *Phenomenology of Spirit*, for example, is an *essentially* two-fold one: ex-tension and in-tension are in this book one and the same—in contrast, say, to Schelling's *System of Transcendental Idealism*, which unfolded the complexity of consciousness as one part of philosophy, but awaited the complementary development of the world in itself in the *Naturphilosophie* and later in his historical positive philosophy. Instead, for Hegel, the starting point is the most abstract immediacy, and one moves toward the concreteness of the self and the concreteness of the world at the same time. The immediacy of the "here and now," with which the *Phenemonology* begins, allows for neither self nor other; the more complex and comprehensive the object becomes, the more profound and receptive becomes the corresponding subjectivity, so that the broadening of the sphere of consciousness to the outer bounds of history and beyond is simultaneously for Hegel a deeper penetration into the depths of the self.

This is, incidentally, why there will always be a certain plausibility to the anti-metaphysical reading of Hegel, which insists that he never transgresses the boundary of the immanent experience of consciousness, and so may be said to *expand* Kant in a manner similar to Fichte, to stretch the

---

12. Phen, 100 (GW.9.100).

13. GL, 841–42 (GW.12.251–52). Again, Hegel appears to have Schelling—or at the very least his disciples—in mind.

limits he set, but never in fact to overturn critical philosophy.[14] But this interpretation is only half-true. Hegel does indeed rigorously avoid talking about reality in a non-immanent way—as we just said, the *otherness* in Hegel will never turn out to be *foreign* to the self—but at the same time the immanence for him is not in the end to individual consciousness, or understanding, or even reason itself insofar as this is understood as a faculty of the individual subject. Instead, it is, in the end, immanent precisely to what transcends all of these: it is immanent to spirit. In the *Phenomenology*, self-consciousness shows itself to be limited insofar as it possesses itself, as it were, in opposition to the world, even though it still requires otherness to be itself (*Anerkennung*; lordship and bondage).[15] Reason is higher than self-consciousness insofar as the relation to the other becomes something positive.[16] But while this relation, perfected in reason's discovering itself in its other, is true *in* itself, it becomes true also *for* itself only in spirit. In a sense, spirit represents a consciousness of what transcends any particular consciousness, which is why—assuming that substance is the objective correlate to consciousness—Hegel calls spirit the simultaneity of subjectivity and substantiality.[17] As substance, it is, as it were, large enough to "contain" individual self-consciousnesses in itself, and yet it is not a mere object to these self-consciousnesses as an other, but is rather in turn fully comprehended by each; it is, in other words, they themselves. Spirit, to put it another way, is for Hegel inseparable from community: his definition of spirit is "absolute substance which is the unity of the different independent self-consciousnesses which, in their opposition, enjoy perfect freedom and independence: 'I' that is 'We' and 'We' that is 'I.'"[18]

The significance of this description of spirit cannot be overstated; it is worth dwelling on for a moment. Let us first note that it represents a different "model" of the part-whole relationship from any that we have seen in this book thus far. Schiller had placed a notion of a beautiful whole, the *lebende Gestalt*, at the center of his thought, wherein the whole, which transcends the parts, is alive to the extent that each of the parts is alive, and, indeed, one can say that the whole, in turn, serves the parts by bringing them to life. Schelling had affirmed, in his early thought, an organic whole in which form and content converge, and, as Kant had already affirmed,

---

14. On this point, see Beiser, "Hegel and the Problem of Metaphysics," 1–24.
15. Phen, 111 (GW.9.109).
16. Ibid., 139 (GW.9.132).
17. Ibid., 14 (GW.9.22).
18. Ibid., 110 (GW.9.108).

The Perfection of Freedom

each part is both cause and effect. Hegel's notion of spirit as a community or a *social* whole affirms all of this, but takes it a step further, since he goes beyond the organic to the spiritual, which he calls the *truth* of nature, its *absolute prius*.[19] For Hegel, an organism does not yet represent a perfect integration to the extent that it is as yet *both* insufficiently simple *and*—perhaps what is less obvious—insufficiently diverse. The reason the organism is insufficiently simple is that it is an essentially material being (which is not to say it is merely material, in which case it would have no unity at all). Hegel defines matter in a way similar to the classical philosophical tradition more generally, in terms of externality, as that which has its center outside itself.[20] For this reason, a material being is necessarily composed of parts, which, precisely because none has its center in itself, are all relatively separable from one another. Spirit, by contrast, is defined precisely as that which has its center in itself. It follows, incidentally—again, as the classical traditional affirmed but the modern tradition has tended to forget[21]—that to the extent that material beings have unity at all, they have it in *spirit*, which is why Hegel is able to observe in the *Logic* that all beings, even stones, in some sense transcend themselves.[22]

Now, it is crucial at this point to avoid a misunderstanding that Hegel's way of contrasting spirit and matter could easily occasion. If matter transcends itself precisely because its center is outside itself, it might seem that spirit therefore precisely does not transcend itself. It is easy to think this in fact because, once again, it is half-true—and, indeed, as we shall see at the end of this chapter, also because certain key moves Hegel will make eventually remove any obstacles to prevent a collapse into this partial verity. The thrust of his thinking, in any event, is to affirm a rather complex paradox: self-transcendence, far from being lacking to spirit, is its *very essence*, to such an extent that to be itself it must go beyond itself, or, conversely, the only way to remain within itself is to be always-already outside of itself with its other.[23] Its transcendence of itself is always in this

---

19. E (1830), §381 (GW.20.381).
20. Intro to Phil of Hist, 20 (JA.11.44).
21. See Spaemann, *Natürliche Ziele*.

22. See GL, 134 (GW.21.121). Here, Hegel articulates the self-transcendence of material things in terms of the concept rather than spirit—a stone has its being in its concept, which is always more than any particular stone (as he puts it, the concept includes both the self and the other), but concept and spirit, of course, ultimately converge for Hegel—or perhaps we could say that the concept is spirit expressed at the level of pure ideality, i.e., of logic.

23. In the Phen, Hegel describes consciousness more generally in just these terms:

respect a sort of "catching up" with itself. In other words, the center that lies within spirit is not a center that belongs simply to itself (as opposed to the other), but is, in the most perfect instance, a *shared* center, which to that extent belongs equally to every other self precisely to the extent that the other self is spirit.

This is why it is not enough, for Hegel, simply to define spirit as the "We" that is "I," but he also affirms that it is the "I" that is "We." These are complementary affirmations, to be sure, but they move in literally opposed directions, and we fail to grasp the essence of spirit if we do not see that it includes within itself both opposed movements at once. There is a sense, then, in which spirit—as we will unfold more concretely in our interpretation of *Sittlichkeit*—is most completely the spirit of a community, which is in a certain respect absolutely independent of its individual members, so much so that Hegel is able to describe the community as a substance, which means as having its being in itself, in relation to which individual members are mere accidents.[24] Any strictly "anti-metaphysical" reading of Hegel will always seek to downplay this independent, substantial being of the community, and, as we shall see further on, will have difficulty avoiding finding themselves on the wrong side of Hegel's criticism of Rousseau.[25] Instead, it will highlight the "opposite" side of Hegel's thought, which is, to say it yet again, equally true, namely, that the "We" is always also an "I" (which means that Hegel's description of the individuals as "accidents" of the community needs to be complemented by the claim that the individual-community relationship is not, for Hegel, a simple part-whole relationship). Rather, each "I" is *also* the whole; each *is* the We, which is because the center that belongs to the community at the highest level lies, for Hegel, perfectly within the individual self as spirit. It is this coincidence of centers that makes spirit, in contrast to matter, absolutely simple.

One of the basic preconditions for this coincidence of centers is what Hegel calls the particular quality that defines spirit (*die Bestimmtheit des Geistes*), namely, *manifestation*.[26] It is, as he goes on to say, the very *being* of spirit and not merely one of its activities. This qualification is crucial because it is what allows us to avoid the sort of dualism that would keep

---

"Consciousness . . . is something that goes beyond its limits, and since these limits are its own, it is something that goes beyond itself," 51 (GW.9.57).

24. PR, §156Z (JA.7.236).

25. Specifically, that Rousseau did not in the end have a basis to sustain a distinction between the general will and the will of all. See footnote 43 from chapter five.

26. E (1830), §383 (GW.20.382). Cf., Lewis, *Freedom and Tradition*, 36.

the centers from coinciding. If manifestation were not the being of spirit, then spirit would not in fact manifest itself in truth but only some aspect of itself (even if that aspect were something like the appearance of itself as a whole, which, for all its completeness, would still not be the self itself, the "real thing"). In this case, manifestation has to be, as it were, the giving away of spirit, its "self-gift": We hear an echo in this of Schiller's notion of total self-gift being a precondition of freedom, which we discussed in chapter 1. Only thus do we have the perfect convergence of form and content, which Hegel stresses in the *Zusatz* to this section: as opposed to the conventional understanding, which thinks of manifestation as a mere act, which can therefore, as an in principle "empty" form, be filled up indifferently with any content, "[i]n spirit . . . form and content are identical with each other. . . . The true content contains, therefore, form within itself, and the true form is its own content. But we have to know spirit as this true content and as this true form."[27]

But this coincidence requires more than that manifestation be the being of spirit, it is also necessary to have an adequate "medium" for manifestation. Thus, spirit, to give itself *as* itself, has to be received by nothing less than spirit. This is another way of saying that the essence of manifestation is *self*-manifestation, understanding "self" here to be both direct and indirect object. To prevent ourselves from envisioning absolute manifestation of self to self as a pure monologue, a sort of absolute autism, we have to recall that spirit is just as much a "We" as it is an "I."[28] To speak of the self-manifestation of spirit is not to minimize the other, because, as we affirmed above and will explicate further in just a moment, the other belongs just as much to the "self" of spirit as does the individual self. It is just that this other does not lie *outside* of spirit, which is to say that self-manifestation does not represent a compromise of unity, but is rather—and this is no doubt the heart of Hegel's notion of spirit—precisely what allows it to be absolutely simple.

27. E (1830), §383Z (JA.10.34). For the sake of consistency, the translation has been modified, here as elsewhere in our citation of the spirit section of the *Encyclopedia*, by exchanging "spirit" for "mind" whenever it appears in the English.

28. Jean-François Courtine suggests that one of the things that distinguishes Schelling's view of the manifestation that defines spirit from Hegel's is that, for Schelling, the manifestation is a genuine revelation to an *other*, while for Hegel it is simply what Courtine calls "auto-manifestation," which ultimately has no room for otherness and the various things connected with it (finitude, exteriority, and positivity). See "Temporalité et Révélation," 9–30. While we will make a similar criticism in the end, it must be said that the matter is essentially ambiguous for Hegel insofar as the "self" of the self-manifestation always necessarily includes a relation to the other.

This point, then, picks up the argument from the previous chapter, namely, that spirit is essentially actuality. There we saw that spirit has to externalize itself in relation to an other in order to be what it is: this, we observed, raised the question of an actual determinacy that would be adequate to the potential of what determines itself. Here we see that the only thing that allows this adequation is spirit itself, which means that the realization of spirit that represents the essence of its freedom must necessarily take a social form, a relation between and among spiritual beings. Only such form allows for a perfect unity between the "inside" and the "outside," which is how Hegel defines actuality, or, in other words, allows the concept, or ideal possibility, to coincide perfectly with the "external" realization, or actuality, of the concept so that possibility and actuality become identical: "The spirit is not some one mode or meaning which finds utterance or externality only in a form distinct from itself: it does not manifest or reveal *something*, but its very mode and meaning is this revelation. And thus in its mere possibility spirit is at the same moment an infinite, 'absolute,' *actuality*."[29] To connect this point again with the previous chapter, it is only in spirit's social form that the real is the rational and the rational is the real, which is what gives that ancient philosophical insight a distinctive "modern" twist.

We observed earlier that social form, for Hegel, supersedes organic form both because the latter has less unity *and* because it has less diversity. From what we have been saying, it may seem that the unity of spirit allows only the most minimal diversity, or even that whatever diversity it possesses is illusory or at the very least a mere moment that is overcome and thus left behind. Spirit, after all, finds precisely *itself* in the other—whereas the material parts of an organism always remain external to some degree to one another and therefore their otherness abides. But, in fact, in Hegel's view spirit also contains a more complete degree of otherness within itself than does material being. If it were the case that the merest fact of otherness sufficed to have the reality of spirit—or the more minimal the otherness the better—then mere subjective spirit would represent already in itself the perfection of spirit, and indeed the notion of spirit would collapse back into individual self-consciousness. For Hegel points out that the "I," which is the simplest determination of spirit, already contains within itself a difference in what we might call the "vertical" direction of the universal-particular relation and the "horizontal" direction of the relation of self-consciousness:

29. E (1830), §383 (GW.20.382).

> If we consider spirit more closely, we find that its primary and simplest determination is the "I." The "I" is something perfectly simple, universal. When we say "I," we mean, to be sure, an individual; but since everyone is "I," when we say "I," we only say something quite universal. The universality of the "I" enables it to abstract from everything, even from its life. But spirit is not merely this abstractly simple being equivalent to light, which was how it was considered when the simplicity of the soul in contrast to the composite nature of the body was under discussion; on the contrary, spirit in spite of its simplicity is distinguished within itself; for the "I" sets itself over against itself, makes itself its own object, and returns from this difference, which is, of course, only abstract, not yet concrete, into unity with itself. This being-with-itself of the "I" in its difference from itself is the "I"'s infinitude or ideality.[30]

The unity Hegel is describing here is *merely* ideal, because it is not yet actualized, and it is not yet actualized because it has not yet achieved perfect difference. Thus, Hegel immediately goes on to say that "this ideality is first authenticated in the relation of the 'I' to the infinitely manifold material confronting it."[31] The "I" requires not merely an ideal difference, but a real one, and in order to find this it must, so to speak, go out into the world. But it turns out, of course, that the things in the world, for all their reality, nevertheless also fail to present sufficient resistance to the "I," and so fail to real-ize it, because the relationship is essentially unilateral. We might think here of Adam naming the animals, but not yet receiving a name himself, the personal identity of being a man, without a co-equal spirit to turn to him, i.e., the woman. Material things, we said above, do not have their centers in themselves but ultimately only in spirit, which in this case is the "I" that faces it: "This material, in being seized by the 'I,' is at the same time poisoned and transfigured by the latter's universality; it loses its isolated, independent existence and receives a spiritual one."[32] In this particular account of spirit in relation to its other, which occurs in the opening pages of the *Philosophy of Spirit*, Hegel argues that the "I," as *religious* consciousness, seeks beyond things to their infinite ideality in the divine spirit. But this move leaps over, as it were, the essential moment of objective spirit that Hegel would usually mention at this point, which is the indispensable means from subjective spirit (the "I") to concrete infi-

---

30. Ibid., §381Z (JA.10.24–25).
31. Ibid., §381Z (JA.10.25).
32. Ibid., §381Z (JA.10.25).

nite spirit. We must therefore fill this gap by considering Hegel's account of this moment elsewhere.

In the *Phenomenology*, the transition to religious consciousness occurs with the event of confession and reconciliation.[33] The independence of self-consciousness had emerged through the antagonism of lordship and bondage, and then that self, initially no more than the abstraction of being recognized as other, was enriched by being variously both further particularized and further universalized through the diverse relations of reason and culture, until it became a substantially concrete individual. At the end of what will eventually be called in Hegel's system the realm of "objective spirit," and at the threshold of the absolute spirit in religion and then philosophy,[34] the two selves that were at war with each other stand, as it were, before one another once again, their abstract difference having become concretely perfect:

> Each of these two self-certain Spirits has no other purpose than its own pure self, and no other reality and existence than just this pure self. But yet they are different; and the difference is absolute because it is set in this element of the pure Notion. It is also absolute, not only for us, but for the Notions themselves which stand in this antithesis. For these Notions, though *specific* in relation to one another, are at the same time in themselves universal, so that they fill out the whole range of the self, and this self has no other content than this its own determinateness, which neither goes beyond the self nor is more restricted than it; for one of them, the absolute universal, is equally the pure knowledge of itself, as the other is the absolute discreteness of individuality, and both are only this pure self-knowledge. Both determinatenesses are thus pure conscious Notions, whose determinateness is itself immediately a knowing, or whose *relationship* and antithesis is the "I." Consequently, they are these sheer opposites *for one another*; it is the completely *inner* being which thus confronts its own self and enters into outer existence.[35]

To say that the antithesis of mere self-consciousness is abstract means that the difference in the two lies simply juxtaposed to whatever

33. Phen, 408 (GW.9.424–25).

34. We will briefly discuss the ordering of the "parts" of spirit in the Phen and the *Encyclopedia* in the last section of this chapter. At this stage in his thinking, Hegel included art within his longer treatment of religion, and so the absolute spirit has as it were only two faces in the Phen, religion and philosophy.

35. Ibid., 408–9 (GW.9.361–62).

(abstractly) unifies them, so that what is different is merely different, and what is the same is therefore merely the same. The reason Hegel can call the difference genuinely *absolute* at this stage is precisely because of the more fundamental integration of these dimensions, so that now the very universality of the individual spirit as concrete has been turned *against* itself in the other. According to Hegel, this is difference made most real, and he gives it the name "evil."[36]

We are generally accustomed to thinking of sub-human things as presenting *more* difference to man than would different individuals within the same species, but this is only because we take for granted an abstract sense of difference that would decrease in proportion as unity increased.[37] Hegel could point out, however, not only that sub-human things are incapable of the extreme opposition of evil, but also that sub-human things betray the impotence of their difference, so to speak, in the fact that they can be appropriated by a human being: I can consume a material thing and I can own an animal. These sorts of beings are thus, in Hegel's eyes, not different *in truth*. But another human being cannot be appropriated in principle. The historical fact of slavery is no objection to this claim, because to possess a slave is precisely not to possess a human being *qua* human being, but rather to reduce a human being to an animal, which is the very reason the practice cannot be justified. One cannot *take* a human being, but only *receive* an "other" of this sort, which presupposes that the other has *given* himself freely. Only thus does self-manifestation occur—since spirit can show itself as spirit only to spirit and in a spiritual manner, which Hegel here describes as reciprocal confession and reconciliation.[38] This act rests on a concrete sense of unity and difference, which is why the reconciliation does not actually eliminate the difference, but only intensifies it within a more perfect union. While evil represents difference in its most "real" moment, reconciliation sublates this moment in a more comprehensive whole and thereby fulfills it. We no longer have two spirits, two absolutes, that relate to each other only from the outside, and so

---

36. Ibid. (GW.9.361). Cf., also PR §139 (GW.14-1.121) and E (1830), §382Z (JA.10.31–32).

37. We might consider Derrida's affirmation that animals are "more other" to me than other human beings: *The Gift of Death*, 69. This claim reveals that Derrida has what Hegel would call an "abstract" notion of otherness that simply opposes it to likeness. This leads Derrida to insist on the sort of absolute silence with respect to God that Hegel targets centrally in his philosophy of religion.

38. As Franco observes, self-consciousness can find satisfaction only in another self-consciousness: Franco, *Hegel's Philosophy of Freedom*, 89.

"The 'I' That Is 'We' and the 'We' That Is 'I'"

negatively, but, without compromising their independent being, they now relate *intrinsically*, which means that they have (also) become in some real sense numerically one. It is here that spirit emerges in its truth, as the "I" that is "We" and the "We" that is "I": "The reconciling *Yea*, in which the two 'I's let go their antithetical *existence*, is the *existence* of the 'I' which has expanded into a duality, and therein remains identical with itself, and, in its complete externalization and opposite, possesses the certainty of itself: it is God manifested in the midst of those who know themselves in the form of pure knowledge."[39]

It is significant that Hegel calls this moment the appearance of God in our midst, which indicates the true transition into religious consciousness. We noted above that objective spirit, which we have just described in terms of a communion of two subjective spirits, so to speak, is an essential mediator of absolute spirit. If we can put the reason for this in a nutshell— which we will open up further at the end of the chapter, and make some essential qualifications of what is being said here—a direct leap from subjective spirit into religion will inevitably leave infinite spirit as an impoverished abstraction: God will appear, in his infinity, as the mere opposite of finite consciousness, and so, in this dialectical opposition, will either collapse back into subjectivity or will remain wholly beyond as an opaque, and therefore meaningless, other.[40] The reason this fruitless dialectic is inevitable is that finite spirit cannot undergo difference in a concrete and perfect sense, and therefore in union with unity, except in the reciprocity of communion with another finite spirit. Only in this reciprocity are unity and difference simultaneous and reciprocally dependent on one another. When Hegel calls this the manifestation of God in our midst, though he is using what he would call the language of *Vorstellung*, he means it quite literally: the "I" that is "We" and the "We" that is "I" *is* in fact what Hegel means by the infinite, by absolute spirit.

In order to understand how this is so, we have to recall our discussion of the infinite in the last chapter. Hegel understands infinity in a decidedly concrete sense, which means it is not abstract indeterminacy but rather includes the rich determination of the finite. Indeed, the infinite not only includes the finite, but is at least in a certain respect identical with it. Such an affirmation requires a significantly different sense of the two terms from their usual connotation, and this is, of course, just what Hegel

---

39. Phen, 409 (GW.9.362).

40. Hegel describes this dialectic quite vividly in his "Foreword to Hinrichs' *Religion in its Inner Relation to Science*," in *Miscellaneous Writings*, 337–53 (GW.15.126–43).

insists on. As he explains in his discussion of the relationship between finite and infinite spirit in the philosophy of spirit: "The genuine definition of finitude here . . . must be that the finite is a reality that is not adequate to its concept."[41] On the one hand, this means that a finite thing's concept—Hegel takes the concept of the sun to illustrate—includes more within it than what the thing itself is: the concept of the sun includes a reference to the solar system, etc., which represents a number of things *in addition to* the sun. This is what makes the sun finite. On the other hand, as Hegel emphasizes in other contexts, it means that there is a discrepancy in the finite thing between form and content, which is another way of saying that the ideal (indeterminate) possibility of a thing does not perfectly "match up" with its determinate actualization. The only reality in which this discrepancy wholly disappears is spirit, which means that only spirit is truly infinite in Hegel's sense. But this is spirit only as wholly self-manifest, and so as related to its perfect opposite as to itself. For this reason, Hegel says it is, strictly speaking, meaningless to affirm the existence of finite spirits, since spirit *qua* spirit is infinite.[42] However, lest one think that Hegel is here dissolving the particularity of individuals into some mystical One, we have to keep in mind his criticism of the "bad" infinity that is opposed to the finite. Contrary to this view, Hegel insists that infinity properly understood non-reductively *includes* the finite within itself. But in this concrete sense, finitude itself acquires a new, more perfect, meaning. Indeed, in a way similar to the paradoxical interdependence of unity and difference we just saw, not only is remaining finite, as it were, essential to achieving the infinite, but for Hegel infinity actually *intensifies* rather than dissolves the finite.[43]

In order to see how the finite becomes more truly finite in its identity with the infinite, we must recall what was said above about social form. Hegel explains that natural objects have a kind of imperfect finitude, since "their limitation does not exist for the objects themselves, but only for us who compare them with one another."[44] There is a certain sense, for example, in which a stone has no absolute definition, and therefore no true ultimate finitude or limit that distinguishes it from other things: it is, as it were, all the same to a rock whether it is broken up into two, crushed into

41. E (1830), §386Z (JA.10.44).

42. "Spirit is also by its nature impersonal or suprapersonal. It is not *my* exclusive spirit or *your* exclusive spirit, but something which by its nature transcends the distinction of persons," Findlay, *Hegel*, 39.

43. Ibid., 40–41.

44. E (1830), §386Z (JA.10.44).

sand, dissolved into trace minerals and digested by an organism, or shaped into a statue and placed atop a cathedral. To be truly, perfectly finite is to be finite for oneself, i.e., to know that one is finite and thus to possess one's limits in all the sharpness that defines one. But, as Hegel loves to point out, to know one's limitation is already to have transcended it—which emphatically does not mean left it behind, since we cannot speak of knowledge about something unreal. Socratic ignorance is a genuine transcendence, in contrast to the sophistic presumption that one knows everything precisely because one does not know what one does not know. According to Hegel, the paradigm of the perfection of finitude that transcends itself is the interpersonal relation that actualizes spirit in its truth: "we make ourselves finite by receiving an Other into our consciousness: but in the very fact of knowing this Other we have transcended this limitation."[45] Thus, "spirit is, therefore, *as well* infinite *as* finite, and *neither* merely the one *nor* merely the other." The simultaneity of finitude and infinity is why spirit is adequate to its concept, an adequation wherein the finite determination coincides with the indeterminate, ideal "infinite" concept. Spirit is not merely more infinite than matter, it is also more finite, more definite, more "boundable," or capable of limitation. As we will see, this is why it can be free.

The concrete limitations of *Sittlichkeit* in which spirit finds its fulfillment will be the theme for our next major section, after which we will face the question that arises quite emphatically given the point we have just made, namely, if the absolute spirit exists *in* social form, why does Hegel's system not come to an end with objective spirit? But it is fitting at this point to conclude the present section by tying in what we developed here with the account of freedom offered in the last chapter. In section 382 of the *Encyclopedia*'s philosophy of spirit, Hegel affirms that "the essential, but formally essential, feature of spirit is freedom: i.e., it is the notion's absolute negativity or self-identity," and adds in the *Zusatz*: "the substance of spirit is freedom, i.e., the absence of dependence on an other, the relating of self to self."[46] This statement of the meaning of freedom strikes a different chord from what we have been arguing, since it appears to define freedom in opposition to otherness. There are some who take this negativity to be the essence of Hegel's view of the matter,[47] but to do so either overlooks or fails to grasp the significance of the fact that he qualifies this as merely a formal definition. If we took this formal definition to be the

---

45. Ibid. (JA.10.44).
46. Ibid. (JA.10.31).
47. See, e.g., Pinkard, *Hegel*, 473.

final one, we would collapse the essence of spirit into the abstraction of mere self-consciousness. In this case, there would be no need, for example, to transcend the antagonism of lordship and bondage, and indeed no means of doing so. We ought to notice, moreover, that the description of freedom that Hegel offers in this context bears a striking resemblance to the essentially limited form of consciousness found in the self-withdrawal of stoicism, and then the skeptical negation of this withdrawal, which he had described in the *Phenomenology*.[48] It is not that this formal definition is false, but only that it has to be interpreted concretely. Thus, Hegel goes on to insist, in the *Zusatz*, that "freedom of mind or spirit is not merely an absence of dependence on an Other won outside of the Other, but won in it; it attains actuality not by fleeing from the Other but by overcoming it."[49]

Here is a decisive movement beyond the negativity of stoic self-possession. The positive relation to the other is thus essential to the actualization of spirit and so to the reality of its freedom. The formal definition of freedom as self-identity finds its fulfillment in the concrete definition of freedom as "being at home in the other." It is significant that the section of the *Encyclopedia* that immediately follows this formal statement of freedom is the description of manifestation as the determinateness of spirit, which is also when its "mere possibility" is actualized. Reading it along the lines we have been suggesting, this means that the formal definition of freedom is not first true in itself, and then simply filled with content depending on whatever particular sort of manifestation it carries out. Instead, it is true *only concretely*; that is, spirit is in fact self-identical, it achieves its ultimate definition, only in relation to another spirit, and so only as mediated to itself by an other. It is often the case that Hegel articulates the concrete definition of freedom without reference to the other, simply as "*bei-sich-sein*," being "at home."[50] Moreover, he emphasizes at

---

48. "This thinking consciousness as determined in the form of abstract freedom is thus only the incomplete negation of otherness. *Withdrawn* from existence only into itself, it has not there achieved its consummation as absolute negation of that existence.... *Scepticism* is the realization of that of which Stoicism was only the Notion, and is the actual experience of what the freedom of thought is. This is *in itself* the negative and must exhibit itself as such," Phen, 122–23 (GW.9.118–19). The unity of these is the unhappy consciousness, which Hegel describes as the internalizing of the lord and bondsman conflict (126 [GW.9.121]). All of this lies at the level of mere self-consciousness: we have not yet entered the realm of spirit proper, and thus of freedom in its authentic sense.

49. E (1830), §382Z (JA.10.31).

50. See, e.g., E (1830), §23 (GW.20.66); cf., E (1817), §5A (GW.13.18), §32A (GW.13.32), §301 (GW.13.179).

decisive moments that, ultimately, *there is no other for spirit*.[51] While it is true that such affirmations are one-sided—a crucial point that we will return to at the end—we need to recognize that such affirmations are not in principle "monological" or "egological," as it were. To say it again, spirit is not spirit without being a "We," and so if this excludes an other in an extrinsic sense, it is only because it includes perfect otherness already within itself.[52] Being "*bei sich*" is essentially a social event.

This interpretation of spirit brings home the argument made at the end of the last chapter. There we argued that it is inadequate to think of will as a faculty of spirit because will is not in the *first* place a faculty, but instead an actualized reality (which integrates it concretely with reason in a single whole). But we have now taken a further step, which allows us to see an even more fundamental inadequacy, namely, that this way of interpreting the matter assumes an essentially individualistic sense of spirit, which we now see is contrary to the nature of spirit. In the preface to the 1827 edition of the *Encyclopedia*, Hegel makes an observation which reveals the basic aim of his philosophy of spirit perhaps better than any other: presenting the significance of Jacob Boehme, whom he says has rightly been called the "Teutonic Philosopher."[53] Hegel says that at the foundation of Boehme's thought lies the thesis "that the spirit of man and all things else are created in the image of God—and of course, of God as the Trinity."[54] Hegel is praising Boehme, in other words, for the insight, both that the nature of spirit illuminates the meaning of all other things, and that one cannot understand spirit *except* in trinitarian terms—which is true, moreover, not only for divine spirit, but for spirit *as such*, and this means for spirit also in its most ordinary, human sense. This rethinking of the meaning of spirit in trinitarian terms is the heart of Hegel's political

---

51. E (1830), §377Z: "An out-and-out Other simply does not exist for spirit" (JA.10.10).

52. Whether this is an ultimately adequate sense of the other is a point to which we will return in the final section of this chapter.

53. E (1827), 15 (GW.19.16). Hegel's approbation of this appellation seems to indicate that he takes Boehme to have introduced precisely what is the most decisive German contribution to philosophy. Schelling similarly observes, "One cannot help but say that J. Boehme is a miraculous appearance in the history of humankind, and particularly in the history of the German spirit. If one could ever forget what treasure lies in the natural depths of the heart and spirit of the German nation, then one would only need to remember this man," Schelling, GPP, 176 (W.6E.123). Here is a rare point on which the late Hegel and the late Schelling are in agreement.

54. E (1827), 15 (GW.19.16).

philosophy, and so is indispensable for understanding the same.[55] While he often uses the Christian notion of the Trinity to illustrate the meaning of spirit, Hegel believes that the significance of this revelation requires the work of transposition into philosophical thought. Indeed, because this insight is the key to our grasp of all other things, coming to understand and achieve the essence of spirit as Trinity is not only philosophy's highest task, but it is the ultimate purpose of every single occurrence in the cosmos. Hegel could not be more emphatic: this notion "is the supreme definition of the Absolute. To find this definition and to grasp its meaning and burden was, we may say, the ultimate purpose of all education and all philosophy: it was the point to which turned the impulse of all religion and science: and it is this impulse that must explain the history of the world."[56]

Interestingly, for Hegel, this view of spirit as communal would remain extrinsic to thought until philosophy recognized "the concept and freedom . . . as its object and soul." Freedom and the social form of spirit are so closely bound up with one another for Hegel that we cannot understand freedom without the trinitarian articulation of spirit, and we cannot appropriate spirit in thought unless we recognize freedom as the soul of philosophy: once again, we find a perfect convergence of form and content. To know that freedom is the goal of knowledge is to become free, and we know this indeed only as living within a common spirit.

One of the implications of this interpretation of freedom and spirit as social form is that we have to think of freedom in the first place, once again not as an attribute of an individual agent, but most fundamentally as a property belonging to the community as a kind of subject in its own right, and only thus as also belonging to the individual members in their individuality. To spell out this admittedly quite peculiar point more concretely requires an investigation of the principle features of *Sittlichkeit*, the fulfillment of objective spirit.

III. *Sittlichkeit* as Social Form

It is not possible to enter into the details of Hegel's treatment of *Sittlichkeit* (a term we shall generally leave untranslated[57]), which is an exceedingly

---

55. See Houlgate, *Freedom, Truth, and History*, 189–99.
56. E (1830), §384A (GW.20.382–83).
57. *Sittlichkeit* would be most literally translated by "ethicality," which is awkward in English, and which would in any event convey the meaning of Hegel's term only if we heard echo in it the Greek notion of *ethos* (habit or custom) as well as its related

rich text, the heart of Hegel's PR, and so of objective spirit. Our treatment here will not, therefore, be a commentary on that text in each of its details, but instead we will focus on the basic "structure" of *Sittlichkeit*, and the specific forms it takes in its three moments, that of the family, of civil society, and of the state. All of this will be done specifically in relation to the notion of spirit we sketched out above and with a view to an understanding of the meaning of freedom.

The section on *Sittlichkeit* is part three of PR, following upon a treatment of (abstract) right and of morality, and it thus represents the fulfillment of objective spirit, i.e., it presents most adequately what objective spirit *is*. All three parts display some aspect of the actuality of freedom, which is the "function" of objective spirit, but the first two do so in a relatively abstract manner: to speak somewhat loosely, "right," which centers on property, is objective but only of the person[58] and not yet of spirit, while "morality" is the recovery of spirit, but in a withdrawal into subjectivity and so no longer in a fully objective sense; *Sittlichkeit* brings these two forms to unity. Alluding no doubt to Aristotle's criticism of Plato's political theory, Hegel describes *Sittlichkeit* at the outset as the "living good," rather than an empty and abstract ideal,[59] and defines it as "the concept of freedom which has become the existing [*vorhandenen*] world and the nature of self-consciousness." If Aristotle thinks of virtuous freedom as the communication of rationality to the natural body, so that one does what is excellent spontaneously, we might say that Hegel expands Aristotle's "*aretē*" to the social sphere: *Sittlichkeit* is the real-ization of rationality not only in the individual nature, but in the structures that make up the social order, so that the social whole becomes a second nature, as it were.[60] If Schiller, moreover, thinks of freedom as "duty become nature," Hegel

---

word *ethnos* (a people bound together by custom). *Sittlichkeit* includes all the customs and traditions of a people, but it is not simply identical to these, as some assume (cf., for example, Inwood, *A Hegel Dictionary*, 91–93). Instead, for Hegel, customs are the *phenomena* of *Sittlichkeit*, not (simply) its *being*. His use of the term is thus not primarily moral, as the English "ethicality" might suggest, but first of all decidedly *metaphysical*. This becomes clearest, perhaps, in the fact that Hegel often uses the phrase "*die sittliche Substanz*" when speaking of *Sittlichkeit*, indicating a reality which possesses, as we shall see, a being in and for itself. It is this metaphysical dimension that leads Hegel to distinguish it systematically from "morality": see, for example, PR, §33A (GW.14-1.49).

58. Specifically of the "legal" person, which Hegel defines rather narrowly: PR, §35 (GW.14-1.51).

59. PR, §142 (GW.14-1.157), cf., §156Z (JA.7.236).

60. E (1817), §430 (GW.13.232–33).

thinks of freedom as "morality become *Sittlichkeit*," or as reason acquiring a social body that has become so fundamental to all one does or says as to be nature, i.e., the unconscious principle of all else. In other words, *Sittlichkeit* represents freedom that has become literally *real*, in the sense that we described in the previous chapter; it has become a sort of "thing" in the world, a substantial entity,[61] and, as such, it forms the ground of the self-consciousness of its individual members. At the same time, *Sittlichkeit* is reciprocally dependent on the individuals, which represents its actuality as its differentiation and particular determination. The relationship between *Sittlichkeit* as a substantial whole and the members that constitute it is a complex one, and characterizing this relationship is the main theme of Hegel's preliminary remarks on the meaning of *Sittlichkeit*. Our claim is that this complex reality can be adequately understood only against the backdrop of Hegel's concept of spirit, as the perfection of both unity and difference, and in light of the notion of freedom as actuality elaborated in the last chapter—else one will inevitably end up opposing the dimensions of togetherness and independence and subordinating them to one another in an improper way.

Towards the end of Hegel's preliminary comments, he observes, in a *Zusatz*, that one can think of the ethical in only one of two possible perspectives, either "from above," i.e., from the perspective of substantiality, or "from below," as the coming together of individuals.[62] But Hegel simply rejects this latter possibility: if we start with individuals, who have their own reality in themselves *first* as individuals, we will never end up with anything other than an aggregate, and never a *whole*, which is what *Sittlichkeit* is. We saw this point at the beginning of the previous chapter. What Hegel adds in this context to what we saw there is the claim that

---

61. It is worth pointing out that Hegel means "substance" in this context in a strict sense. For Aristotle, substance—*ousia*—is defined as what exists *kath' hauton*, that is, what is capable of standing independently on its own (Aristotle, *Metaph.*, vii.1.1028a10–30). We would thus normally think of substance in terms of natural beings, in which case we would attribute the notion of "substance" to something like a community in only a loose, metaphorical sense, since it does not appear to have its *own* being, but instead only to be made up of individual beings. But while Hegel understands spirit as essentially "organic," as we have seen, spirit nevertheless represents, in turn, the *truth* of nature (E [1830], §381 [GW.20.381]). This means that substance for Hegel is most directly the true designation of spirit, and natural beings are substances only in a relative sense. Spirit, moreover, has its truth in social form. It follows that the paradigm of substance, for Hegel, is a "We" that takes shape in actuality, and that all other substances are relative imitations of this one. For example, as we shall see, marriage is a paradigm of substance in the Hegelian sense.

62. PR, §156Z (JA.7.236).

such an aggregate "excludes spirit," and it does so because "spirit is not something individual but the unity of the individual and the universal."[63] Spirit exists only in community. Hegel goes so far here as to describe spirit as the actual substance, and consequently to refer to the members of *Sittlichkeit* as "its accidents."[64] But we also saw in the previous chapter that Hegel likewise rejects a simple top-down approach, which would assume that the whole has its existence prior to the individuals, since this would imply an abstract notion of universality. While Hegel does not explicitly reject this "top-down" approach in the present context, as he does the "bottom-up" approach, he nevertheless provides the proper qualifications all through these opening paragraphs in his insistence that *Sittlichkeit* cannot be viewed abstractly. Again, *Sittlichkeit* is a *living good*. What saves it from abstraction is precisely the individual self-consciousness of its members.

Let us consider this closely. The opening sentence of part 3 reads, "Ethical life is the *Idea of freedom* as the living good which has its knowledge and volition in self-consciousness, and its actuality through self-conscious action,"[65] and he later qualifies *Sittlichkeit* as a substance, the substance of spirit, which is what has *actuality*, while the individuals are accidents. There is a paradox here, but it is essential: while it is spirit (as the whole) that has actuality, it has that actuality *in* the individual members. In this respect, there is a *certain sense* in which there is no spirit except what exists in self-conscious individuals—which is why there is a certain truth to the liberal interpretation of Hegel's political theory and its corresponding "anti-metaphysical" affect—but it is *also* the case that it is precisely a "supra-individual" spirit that therein exists. It follows that spirit does not exist "until" self-conscious individuals come together, but that what thus comes into existence is prior to those individuals in an ontological sense, and it is prior to them by definition precisely because it is a whole, a community, that integrates the individual and the universal, and not a conglomeration of externally related individuals.[66] If Hegel calls individuals the "accidents" of spirit, we must nevertheless recall that, according to Aristotle, from whom this language comes, accidents are the

---

63. Ibid. (JA.7.236).
64. Ibid. (JA.7.236).
65. Ibid., §142 (GW.14-1.137).
66. K. Westphal is right to emphasize a reciprocal dependence between the whole and parts in Hegel's view of the state, but wrong to conclude that "The issue of the ontological priority of individuals or society is bogus," in "The Basic Context and Structure," 236–37. Reciprocal dependence is not the same (and in fact is arguably incompatible with) symmetrical equality.

expression of substance, which serves to actualize it, so that if all accidents were removed no actual "thing" would remain. Even more, and uniquely in the case of spirit, the expression—i.e., the manifestation of spirit—is indeed the very self of spirit; spirit as we saw is always self-manifestation. To call individuals the accidents of spirit, then, is to say that each individual is spirit and indeed *wholly*, but at the same time is the whole only in relation to other individuals (and indeed only in relations of a particular sort, as we shall see in a moment). In other words, each individual is the whole—but only by being a mere "part" of the whole, which is simply a different way of saying that the "I" is "We" and the "We" is "I."[67] Thus, *Sittlichkeit* is simply spirit *tout court*, viewed from an objective perspective. This is what Hegel means by calling *Sittlichkeit* concrete substance *"as infinite form*,"[68] which achieves concreteness through the subjectivity of its members. It is form as thus determinately differentiated, but, as we saw above, this form is infinite as the transcendence of limitation *in* limitation.

Now, to say that the spirit that the individuals actualize is not (merely) their own spirit but rather the spirit of the whole, indeed, "spirit itself," is *not* to say that the individuals do not *also* actualize their own spirit, but only that actualizing spirit is, so to speak, the precondition of being spirit themselves. Objective spirit is not the elimination of subjective spirit, but represents rather the home in which subjective spirit comes to its freedom. For this reason, Hegel affirms that individuals possess their rights and their freedom specifically as *belonging to* the ethical whole.[69] This paradoxical relationship of spirit to its actualization concretely gives rise to a number of the recognizable features of life in a political community, but which take on a new significance when viewed against the backdrop of this notion of spirit.

Let us look briefly at his understanding of law and the relationship between social obligations and rights, on the one hand, and freedom, on the other. Thus, for example, Hegel presents laws and institutions as things that *"have being in and for themselves."*[70] The strangeness of this affirmation should not be passed over. Having being "for itself" is something for Hegel that typically belongs to subjectivity. In this case, what could it possibly mean to say that laws and institutions have their own "subjectivity"? We

---

67. As Hegel puts it in the Phen, "I regard them as myself and myself as them," 213 (GW.9.195).
68. PR, §144 (GW.14-1.137).
69. Ibid., §153 (GW.14-1.142).
70. Ibid., §144 (GW.14-1.137).

would normally want to say that only human beings have self-conscious being for themselves, and institutions are artifices, at best meant to protect that self-conscious being. They exist only because they are *made* by people, and *for* people, and they can just as easily be *unmade* by them, or, in other words, their reality is wholly a function of the individuals they are designed to serve. But this view would return us to the atomism that Hegel invariably criticizes. For him, while it is true that only human beings are self-conscious, that very self-consciousness, when it is real, is the actualization of something greater than and therefore non-reducible to the individuals in their individuality. Note, Hegel says that *Sittlichkeit* "has *its* knowledge and volition in self-consciousness, and *its* actuality through self-conscious action."[71] There is, in other words, a very real sense in which *a community* knows, wills, and acts. The "being in and for itself" of laws and institutions is a concrete expression of the subjectivity that belongs to the community in distinction from its individual members. It is what therefore gives them what Hegel calls—in contrast to what he says is the natural law tradition as commonly understood—"an absolute authority and power, infinitely more firmly based than the being of nature."[72]

At the same time, this power does not stand over and against the individual as a foreign entity, as it inevitably would if spirit did not have a metaphysical reality of its own.[73] Instead, Hegel affirms that the ethical substance, with its laws and powers, is the internal essence of the subject "in which it has its *self-awareness* [*Selbstgefühl*] and lives as in its element which is not distinct from itself—a relationship which is immediate and closer to identity than even [a relationship of] faith or trust."[74] The reason the substantiality of *Sittlichkeit* is not alienating to the members of the community is that they are *its* actuality.[75] It has its reality, in other words, not over-against them, but only *in* them. Hegel's notion of *Sittlichkeit* in this respect bears a strong resemblance to what Rousseau calls the general will, because both of them represent authority, that is, a wholeness that lies beyond individuals and therefore functions in some sense as their measure, but in an essentially non-alienating manner, insofar as that measure is not extrinsic to the individuals. But the difference between these two

---

71. Ibid., §142 (GW.14-1.137). Emphasis added.
72. Ibid., §146 (GW.14-1.138).
73. See Houlgate, *Freedom, Truth, and History*, 84.
74. PR, §147 (GW.14-1.138).
75. In Phen, Hegel observes that spirit is the *actuality* of the ethical substance: 263 (GW.9.238).

notions is profound, and it is subtle because it is profound. Rousseau's general will is essentially pragmatic, achieved through the actual willing of all individuals *qua* individuals; this is why his view is necessarily tied to a social contract theory of political order, which subordinates that order to the individuals that constitute it. It is also why Rousseau affirms democracy in the crudest sense, that is, he requires individuals to vote as far as possible in isolation from one another.[76] For Hegel, *Sittlichkeit* is not pragmatic but *ontological*; it represents the *truth* of spirit, and so the most basic reality presupposed in all spiritual acts. And spirit thus understood is constitutively relational. Spirit has a social form. This view—as we will elaborate below—leads Hegel to take positions fundamentally opposed to Rousseau: he rejects social contract theory as expressing a basic confusion regarding the nature of community, and he is sharply critical of democracy in the crude sense that conceives of political order as emerging from the atomistic existence of separate individuals.[77]

Social contract theory in its classical articulation is founded on an affirmation of natural rights, i.e., rights that belong to an individual by nature and so independent of the social order. Because of their priority, they set the terms, as it were, for that order. Natural rights give the individual a claim on society and establish a certain sphere of freedom with respect to it. Hegel's concept of *Sittlichkeit* entails a radical reordering of these relationships.[78] It implies an essentially reciprocal relationship between duty and freedom, on the one hand, and duties and rights, on the other. Duty, Hegel says in §149, does not limit freedom but rather, as it were,

---

76. See Rousseau, *Du Contrat social*, book 2, chapter 3, 252, in which Rousseau claims that the General Will will always be good to the extent that the citizens have *no communication* among themselves. As we will see, Hegel believes that the individual is strongest qua individual specifically as bound to others in a family or in a corporation.

77. On Hegel's criticisms of social contract theory, see Alan Patten, "Social Contract Theory," 167–84.

78. The fact that Hegel does not *reject* individual freedom and natural rights is insufficient for K. Westphal's claim that Hegel is ultimately a liberal progressive who, in common with social contract theorists, takes "the analysis of the individual will and its freedom as the starting point for justifying basic political principles and institutions," "Context and Structure," 244. Westphal argues that whatever criticisms Hegel makes of the various iterations of social contract theory stem from their relative ability to promote the individual: this is a functionalizing of the state, however, which surrenders precisely its *Sittlichkeit*, which we have claimed is the heart of Hegel's political philosophy. Hegel does indeed begin his analysis with the individual will, but he certainly does not simply *build* on this. Instead, he progressively reinterprets the meaning of the individual will as he unfolds the essence of the political order.

"The 'I' That Is 'We' and the 'We' That Is 'I'"

liberates it precisely because it gives freedom substance.[79] As he explains, it *does* limit freedom in its purely formal sense (I=I), but, as we saw above, formal freedom does not exist as such; instead, it exists only concretely, which means only as mediated by an other. This was the case, we recall, because transcendence and limitation, or infinity and finitude, are reciprocally dependent. Ultimately, freedom is the substance of *spirit*, not simply a feature of self-consciousness, and spirit includes *both* the self *and* its limitation by its other. This inclusion of the other, rather than opposition to it, is why Hegel refers to this freedom as "affirmative freedom."[80] It is illuminating to consider Hobbes' view of the relationship between law (duty) and right (freedom), which represents a perfect contrast to Hegel on this point. Hobbes statement of his position is worth quoting in full:

> The right of nature, which writers commonly call *jus naturale*, is the liberty each man hath to use his own power, as he will himself, for the preservation of his own nature; that is to say, of his own life; and consequently, of doing anything, which in his own judgment and reason, he shall conceive to be the aptest means thereunto.
>
> By *liberty*, is understood, according to the proper signification of the word, the absence of external impediments: which impediments, may oft take away part of a man's power to do what he would; but cannot hinder him from using the power left him, according as his judgment and reason shall dictate to him.
>
> A *law of nature, lex naturalis*, is a precept or general rule, found out by reason, by which a man is forbidden to do that

---

79. See PR, §149 (GW.14-1.139–40). Z. A. Pelczynski distinguishes between civil liberty and political liberty in Hegel, the latter being rooted in the common good rather than private interest: see "Political Community and Individual Freedom," 76. While the distinction is helpful, it should not obscure the fact that these represent stages of a single freedom for Hegel, so that political freedom would be the sublation of freedom in its civil iteration.

80. It is important to keep in mind that "affirmative" freedom in Hegel is not the same as Berlin's "positive freedom," however similar they may appear *prima facie*. "Affirmative freedom" is not a "freedom *for*" in the sense of a power possessed by an individual that ought to be used in a particular way for the benefit of others, nor is it, by the same token, an order imposed on the individual from above. Instead, it is a description of the nature of freedom, its *being*, as constituted socially, that is, as residing in the individual only as always-already related to the other. Will Dudley has correctly pointed out that, for example, Wood's response to Isaiah Berlin (*Hegel's Ethical Thought*, 52, 258), which defends Hegel by subordinating subjective freedom to other, more satisfying goods, simply recapitulates Berlin's objection to Hegel: see *Hegel, Nietzsche and Philosophy*, 269fn25. What is needed is a deepened understanding of the essential *nature* of freedom.

> which is destructive of his life, or taketh away the means of preserving the same; and to omit that by which he thinketh it may be best preserved. For though they that speak of this subject, use to confound *jus* and *lex*, *right* and *law*; yet they ought to be distinguished: because *right* consisteth in liberty to do or to forbear, whereas *law* determineth and bindeth to one of them; so that law, and right differ as much as obligation and liberty; which in one and the same matter are inconsistent.[81]

It is not difficult to see that Hobbes presupposes just that "possibilistic" notion of freedom that Hegel is at pains to critique.

Because Hegel has a concrete notion of freedom, which differs in a fundamental way from that of Hobbes, he is able to make the perhaps startling claim that "*duty* and *right* coincide in this identity of the universal and the particular will, and in the ethical realm, a human being has rights in so far as he has duties, and duties in so far as he has rights."[82] Abstractly, it means one cannot have a right unless an other has the duty to respect it, and so these turn out to be reciprocally dependent. But the more concretely we consider the social order, the more we realize that "right" and "duty" are in fact two ways of viewing one and the same reality; the very relation that binds one to the whole (duty) is a relation that liberates one's individuality (right). In this case, Hegel observes that the more deeply involved one is in the social order, the less one is inclined in fact to concern oneself with rights: "uncultured people insist most strongly on their rights."[83]

Hegel's treatment of rights comes accordingly in the first and most abstract part of the political order, and the notion becomes altogether relativized at the concrete level of *Sittlichkeit*.[84] If, however, one has no rights except as a member of society, as Hegel affirms, one might fear that the social order would no longer possess the measure it had in classical

---

81. Hobbes, *Leviathan*, ch. XIV, 163.
82. PR, §155 (GW.14-1.143).
83. Ibid., §37Z (JA.7.91). What Hegel means by "uncultured" here is "unsocialized," in the sense of being a person who has not internalized membership in the community.
84. Rights are defining of the person, which Hegel defines specifically in abstraction from all relation (see PR, §§35–36 [GW.14-1.51–52]). Considered concretely, a human being is a *member*—i.e., part of a family—before being a person in the legal sense. This is why rights become an issue for a family only when the family breaks down (PR, §159 [GW.14-1.144]), and, moreover, as we just saw, Hegel observes that it is *uncultured* people who tend to insist most strongly on rights, namely, those who do not belong to a whole greater than themselves.

political theory, namely, nature. We will discuss the threat of the totalitarian state in Hegel's thought at the end of the chapter, but we ought to point out that Hegel's identification of rights and duties does not lead to this inference in principle: to say that one possesses a right only as a member of society does *not* necessarily mean that rights are not natural, but may also mean that nature is itself relational and human nature thus essentially social. In this case, we would say that one possesses a right *in* the political order, *by* nature, because one has one's nature only socially.[85] Along a similar line, for Hegel freedom is not (simply) something given in (abstract) nature, something that an individual possesses in himself, which allows him subsequently to enter into social relations and thus fulfill the duty to others that these relations entail. Such a conception would regard duty as a curtailment of freedom, albeit one accepted willingly, perhaps, insofar as one regards the preservation of order as necessary for the enjoyment of freedom. In other words, according to this view, one accepts the limitation of freedom by duty in order to avoid the more radical loss of freedom that social disorder would bring.[86] Hegel, by contrast, believes that freedom

---

85. On Hegel's critique of the classical liberal notion of rights, see Smith, *Hegel's Critique of Liberalism*, 57–97; for an articulation of Hegel's own theory, see ibid., 98–131. Smith argues that, in contrast to the liberal view, the fundamental right at the basis of all others is the inherently social right to recognition (*Anerkennung*). While this is true, its truth is grounded in the more basic metaphysical truth of the inherently trinitarian structure of *Geist*. For the classic debate over Hegel's relationship to liberalism, see the contributions by Sidney Hook, Shlomo Avineri, and Z. A. Pelczynski in *Hegel's Political Philosophy*, ed. Walter Kaufmann.

86. This is essentially Locke's view of the matter: see his *Second Treatise of Government*, chapter VI: "For law, in its true notion, is not so much the limitation as the direction of a free and intelligent agent to his proper interest, and prescribes no farther than is for the general good of those under that law. Could they be happier without it, the law, as a useless thing, would of itself vanish; and that ill deserves the name of confinement which hedges us in only from bogs and precipices. So that however it may be mistaken, and the end of law is not to abolish or restrain, but to preserve and enlarge freedom. For in all the states of created beings, capable of laws, where there is no law there is no freedom. For liberty is to be free from restraint and violence from others, which cannot be where there is no law; and is not, as we are told, 'a liberty for every man to do what he lists.' For who could be free, when every other man's humor might domineer over him? But liberty to dispose and order freely as he lists his person, actions, possessions, and his whole property within the allowance of those laws under which he is, and therein not to be subject to the arbitrary will of another, but freely follow his own." From *The English Philosophers*, edited by E. Burtt, 425. Note that this view of law "enlarges" freedom, not by expanding it from within through the inclusion of others, but rather by extending its boundaries, which it fills in a wholly self-related way. For all of the positive value given to law, Locke's thus remains a formal, "possibilistic" conception of freedom.

grows by virtue of law and duty in a positive way, rather than affirming simply that it is protected by them.

In sum, the reconception of the relationship between freedom and duty, like that between rights and duty, reveals Hegel's distance from the classical liberal tradition, a distance that follows from a substantial, or metaphysical, conception of the political order. The distinctiveness of Hegel's view becomes evident in his articulation of spirit in the three interdependent expressions of social form that represent the basic division of *Sittlichkeit*: family, civil society, and the state. Let us explore each of these in turn. Because our aim is primarily the meaning of the social form of freedom, we will attend in each case essentially to the articulation of the relationship of members to the community, which will require us to pass over many of the details in Hegel's account.

A. The Family

Significantly, the basic "unit" of *Sittlichkeit* is not the individual person, but the family: here is another way that Hegel's political theory differs significantly from that of Rousseau, who affirms at best only an instrumental function for the family, as a means of educating the individual.[87] *Sittlichkeit* is a manifestation *of spirit*, and spirit, as essentially relational, cannot be broken down into atoms, but at most into molecules, as it were. The family represents what Hegel calls the "immediate substantiality" of spirit—it is substance because it is the objectivity of relation, and it is immediate in the sense that it is *Sittlichkeit* in its natural form, that is, in the form of feeling (*Empfindung*). The word "feeling" might seem strange, here, in its association with the objectivity of spirit, since we tend to think of feeling as essentially subjective and individual. The word as Hegel uses it in this particular context seems to indicate the unreflective character of the unity designated by spirit. In fact, Hegel identifies spirit's feeling with *love*, the notion that played such a significant role in Hegel's earliest writings.[88] In the *Zusatz* to the opening section on family in the PR, he

---

87. "The most ancient of all societies, and the only natural one, is the family: but even here the children remain bound to their father only so long as they need him for their own self-preservation. The moment this need ceases, the natural bond dissolves. The children, exempt from the obedience they owe to the father, and the father, exempt from the care he owes to the children, return in perfect equality to independence," Rousseau, *Du contrat social*, bk. 1, ch. 2, 236. See Neuhouser, *Actualizing Freedom*, 89.

88. See the fragment on love Hegel composed, probably around 1797 or 1798, prior to his writing *The Spirit of Christianity: On Christianity*, 302–8.

defines love as the consciousness of my unity with another that results from my having surrendered my independent personhood, an act by which I end up "knowing myself as the unity of myself with another and of the other with me."[89] He remarks, interestingly, that love is simultaneously "the production and the resolution" of a contradiction, namely, that I am not myself, but another, although in being that other I come to be myself. He observes that the understanding cannot resolve this because it has no capacity for paradox. But the reason that belongs to spirit certainly does have such a capacity: indeed, in this contradiction of love we have precisely the essence of spirit, as we developed it above. Because of the profound intimacy of this relation, Hegel goes on to say that the notion of right, though it has its ground in the individuality that arises from this relationship, does not take an actual legal form unless and until the family dissolves. Prior to this, it is precisely the family as a whole that possesses a right "against externality."[90] This point—the family as the basic unit of the concrete social order—is crucial for what follows.

The foundation of the family, of course, is marriage, which represents the paradigm of objective spirit, that is, of social form. Marriage is, so to speak, spirit in its most distilled form. By calling it an essentially "ethical" relationship, using the term in his technical sense, Hegel means to distinguish it from three common misinterpretations of the meaning of marriage. First, he claims that the (modern) natural law tradition, for the most part, misunderstood marriage to the extent that it reduced marriage to a merely natural, i.e., "physical" relationship.[91] This would identify marriage with the "concubinage" Hegel describes later.[92] Second, he criticizes the (modern liberal) interpretation of marriage in contractual terms, and cites Kant as an example. The problem with this interpretation is that it never succeeds in transcending individualism: on the one hand, the form of marriage is the "*Willkür*"—the arbitrary choice—of individuals, and

89. PR, §158Z (JA.7.238).

90. Ibid., §159Z (JA.7.238-39).

91. Hegel here qualifies this as "most systems," showing an acknowledgment that "natural law" has an ambiguous meaning, as he admits and elaborates elsewhere. In his "Prefatory Lectures on the Philosophy of Law," given in Berlin in 1824-25, for example, Hegel distinguishes nature as "natural being," i.e., "the immediate aspect of our being," and nature as the concept. He goes on to explain that the natural law tradition tends to take the naturalistic starting point for its doctrine: see the "Prefatory Lectures" in *Miscellaneous Writings of G. W. F. Hegel*, 310-22 (*Vorlesungen*, Ilting ed., vol. 4, 75-91). For a thorough account of Hegel's critique of the predominant natural law theory of his day, see Riedel, *Between Tradition and Revolution*, 76-104.

92. PR, §163Z (JA.7.242-43).

on the other hand, the end of it is the individuals' reciprocal *use* of one another. In other words, a union that consists in nothing more than a contractualized relation represents the very sort of aggregation that Hegel had said excludes spirit. We will return to this in a moment. Third, he rejects the (romantic) reduction of marriage to "mere" love; that is, to love precisely as a contingent feeling. This is the view that would deny the need for a civil ceremony.[93]

One might wonder how this romantic interpretation differs from Hegel's since he too describes the familial relation essentially in terms of love-as-feeling. The difference is illuminating indeed: the romantic view of love is wholly subjective, which reveals itself in the fact that it regards the objective ceremony as an intrusive imposition, or, at the very least, as irrelevant. If love is wholly subjective, however, it cannot in fact *unify*: it does not, that is, "produce and resolve" the contradiction of individuality, since this is a paradox that can occur only on the basis of an actuality that transcends the individuals in their individuality. Hegel sarcastically compares the view that a ceremony is meaningless to the sort of argument a seducer would make—suggesting that the outcome is similar, namely, the essentially temporary use of the other (no matter how long the time may turn out to be *de facto*). Though Hegel likewise, as we saw, interprets marriage in terms of love and love in terms of feeling, we must recall that he posits it as the feeling *of spirit*, which means that the actual subject of feeling is not either of the individuals *as* individuals, but rather the whole that they actualize. In this sense, it is specifically "objective" feeling, the sort of feeling that essentially transcends the individuals and for that very reason unifies them. This is why Hegel qualifies marriage as "rightfully ethical love," by which he means "substantial." If a romantic reduction of love to subjective feeling makes it essentially temporal in principle, Hegel says that marriage is by its nature permanent, "indissoluble."[94] Similarly, this is why, for Hegel, the "institutionality" of the ceremony, far from interfering with the meaning of marriage as something extrinsic to it, is actually indispensable to it, just as institutions and laws are indispensable to any instance of *Sittlichkeit*: it embodies the supra-individual character

---

93. Ibid., §164Z (JA.7.245).

94. Ibid., §163 (GW.14-1.146). In the *Zusatz*, Hegel explains that its indissolubility is *intrinsic*, which means it cannot be dissolved by anything alien to it. He does allow, however, that it may inwardly collapse, citing Christ's statement that divorce may be permitted "because of the hardness of their hearts" (JA.7.242–43). Nevertheless, "all legislations must make such dissolution as difficult as possible and uphold the right of ethics against caprice." See M. Westphal, "Hegel's Radical Idealism," 79–80.

that enables individuality. As *sittlich*, marital love is a "being in and for itself," a reality that is in a certain respect independent of the spouses; as Hegel puts it, the union itself is a "substantial end,"⁹⁵ which serves in a vivid way to distinguish it from the contractual relation that can have only the participating individuals as its ends (in plural).

Let us penetrate even more deeply this distinction from a contractual relation. Hegel admits that marriage begins with a contract, in the sense that there is no marriage without the free consent of self-conscious individuals, but it begins here, he says, precisely "in order to supersede it [*ihn aufzuheben*]."⁹⁶ In a contract, the other is regarded as a means to myself as an end, though what saves this transaction from being simply unilateral is that the use is reciprocated. In the enactment of marriage, by contrast, though I begin as an individual that is not how I end: the very act that has its roots in my individuality terminates in an end beyond that individuality. In this case, the very choice that I make is that of no longer being able to choose. In other words, in marriage, the spouses consent "to *constitute a single person* and to give up their natural and individual personalities in this union."⁹⁷ There is clearly a radical self-limitation in this renunciation of the power to choose and in ceasing to be a separate individual, but it is crucial to see that, as we would expect from his account of *Sittlichkeit*, Hegel does not call this a limitation of one's freedom. Precisely to the contrary, he claims that it is only in such a self-limitation that freedom is achieved. We see here a concrete example of the meaning of freedom as actuality rather than as possibility, which we discussed at the end of the previous chapter.

This perspective casts a new light on the conventional use of the terms. When we speak of a person "freely consenting" to marriage, we typically mean that one is not being compelled against one's will, that there is nothing preventing one from making this commitment (e.g., a previous marriage), and so one's choice is wholly in one's power. But for Hegel, while all of this is indispensable to the meaning of free consent, it does not yet capture what is essential. Instead, an act of consent is free precisely to the extent that, in it, one hands oneself wholly over to the other in a gift of self that is reciprocated, which means that the other receives the gift *as* the self of the other, which can be done only through the reciprocating offer of one's self in return. To understand this, we must recall the

---

95. PR, §163 (GW.14-1.146).
96. Ibid., §163A (GW.14-1.146).
97. Ibid., §162 (GW.14-1.145).

The Perfection of Freedom

meaning of spirit presented above. Spirit exists as such only in manifestation understood specifically as the externalizing of the whole of "what is inside," or, in other words, the giving of the being-in-itself of spirit, so that it can become also "for itself." But such a manifestation can be made only *to* spirit, which means only to that which wholly hands itself over. In the *Phenomenology*, this act was illustrated as reconciliation, in which two self-consciousnesses reveal themselves to another in order to repair unity. But now we have a more basic instance, insofar as this reciprocal revelation is quite literally a binding pledge of oneself, and, after all, a re-conciliation implies a previous union. If Hegel says that in marriage a natural relation becomes a spiritual one,[98] it is not (only) because one has made an instinctive inclination a choice[99] (i.e., spiritual in the subjective sense of individual agency), but more fundamentally because it is the actualization of social form (i.e., spiritual in the more perfect, because more comprehensive, objective sense).

Thus, marriage is a paradigmatically spiritual reality because it makes real, makes *true*, the transcendence of the individual self.[100] This transcendence occurs, for Hegel, in what we might call both a vertical and a horizontal sense. Vertically, the enactment of marriage results, as we said, in a single person, which lies as it were "above" the two selves in the sense that the marital union becomes an end in itself precisely to the extent that it cannot be reduced to the individual ends of those that constitute it. It is treated legally as *one*. This "one person" is neither the husband nor the

---

98. Ibid., §161 (GW.14-1.145).

99. Thomas Lewis draws an illuminating comparison between the "spiritualizing" of nature in marriage and the spiritualizing of nature in habit in Hegel's treatment of subjective spirit (see *Freedom and Tradition*, 170). However, Lewis places the emphasis in this on the negative sense of spirit's freedom as a freedom *from* the givenness in nature. It is important to keep in mind that the negative sense of freedom, for Hegel, is always situated within a larger, positive sense.

100. Joan Landes describes the role Hegel gives to the family in overcoming atomistic egoism, but she ultimately does not go far enough on this point: for her, Hegel seems to say that "the individual (not mere feeling or sexual love) is the goal of ethical life within the family," "Hegel's Conception of the Family," 26, but in fact the *end* for the individuals is the family itself, which is precisely what makes it an ethical substance. Family is not a mere means of preparing the individual for the liberation of civil society, but is freedom itself. While Landes is right to observe Hegel's normalizing nineteenth-century bourgeois views of the male-female relationship, her suggestion that he contradicts himself by giving only the man the freedom of economic independence in civil society reveals her own normalizing of a contemporary view of freedom. As we will see shortly, Hegel takes economic independence to represent a kind of *threat* to genuine freedom.

wife, nor is it simply the two of them together, which would make each a "half" person. Instead, it is a whole greater than the sum of the parts, and this "greater than" comes to expression in the fact that the family, as Hegel says, becomes the *substance* of which the members are now accidents, which is to say it becomes an ethical reality in Hegel's technical sense.[101] Marriage results in a new person, for Hegel, also in a horizontal sense, insofar as the union between husband and wife results in a child: "The *unity* of marriage, which in substance is merely *inwardness* and *disposition* but in existence [*als existierend*] is divided between the two subjects, *itself* becomes in the children *an existence* [*eine Existenz*] *which has being for itself*, and an *object* [*Gegenstand*] which they [i.e., the parents] love as their love and their substantial existence [*Dasein*]."[102] He adds in the *Zusatz*, "In the child, the mother loves her husband and he his wife; in it, they see their love before them." "Horizontal" transcendence is indispensable, since spirit has to have objective existence in order to be what it is. A childless marriage has this objectivity in the fact that individual property becomes the resources *of the family* and not just of the individuals as such, but the child is the paradigm of the objectivity paradoxically precisely because he or she is not something that belongs to the parents as a possession: "Whereas their unity is present in their [shared] resources only as in an external thing [*Sache*], it is present in their children in a spiritual form in which the parents are loved and which they love"[103]—or in other words, to which they relate not as appropriating but rather in the movement of love that "produces and resolves" the contradiction of individuality. The reason property is not a sufficient objectification of the marriage is that it can be consumed, i.e., it can be reduced back to them in a certain respect as individuals; the child, by contrast, is the truth of the unity of man and woman because he transcends them as spirit, as having being in and for himself just as they do.

Hegel expresses the self-transcending character of marriage symbolically, i.e., in "picture language," by reference to the ancient idea of the Penates, the divinities of the household, and it is significant that he

---

101. Hegel qualifies his judgment by referring to the *Encyclopedia Logic*, in which he describes substance as the "totality of accidents," i.e., clarifies that it is not a "thing" over-against its accidents, but rather is constituted by them: see E (1830), §151 (GW.20.170).

102. PR, §173 (GW.14-1.153). In the Phen, Hegel says that the relationship between man and woman has its *actual* existence, and thus becomes *spirit*, in the child: 273 (GW.9.246).

103. PR, §173Z (JA.7.251–52).

mentions the Penates here twice: first, in connection with the marriage ceremony in which the spouses pledge themselves to one another (vertical transcendence),[104] and second, in relation to the bearing of children, which represents the extension of the family through the generations and in principle without end (horizontal transcendence). In his notes from Hegel's 1824/25 lectures on the PR, Greisheim explains that religion is the foundation [*Grundlage*] of the family for two reasons.[105] First, spirit is a religious notion, and the family—as social form—is essentially a spiritual reality. Second, family life involves the most intimate inner depths of the person. But these two moments are, in a sense, one and the same, insofar as the inner depths of subjectivity have their actualization only in consummated community. The reason we draw attention to Hegel's account of the religious character of the family, its existence as substantial spirit with its own reality, its being in and for itself, is simply to show that the metaphysical sense of spirit that Hegel quite emphatically defends, and as indeed central to his thought, is not the mystical specter floating over history determining events, as the anti-metaphysical interpreters of Hegel seem to imagine, apparently in order facilely to dismiss as absurd. In dismissing the metaphysical dimension, they lose *Sittlichkeit*. The relatively independent reality of spirit, for Hegel, is a fairly ordinary, everyday reality, which is phenomenologically accessible. But it is an ordinary reality we tend to take for granted and so fail to see for what it is. What it is, indeed, implies a rethinking of the meaning of spirit and the shape of human existence in its most basic instances.

In sum, marriage and family represent for Hegel the paradigm of freedom, and it is worthwhile dwelling on why this is so and what its implications are. The PR is a philosophy of the political order, which is the place wherein spirit achieves an objectivity that is adequate to it, and so wherein it has its substantial reality or its truth. But the political order is the sphere of the will[106]—PR is Hegel's practical philosophy—and the essence of the will is freedom. On the other hand, freedom is not a power, but is the actuality of spirit, so that we may call the political order the substance of spirit's freedom. Now, for Hegel, it is only in *Sittlichkeit* that spirit is truly objectified, while right and morality represent merely abstract moments of that objectivity, and marriage and family represent the paradigm of *Sittlichkeit*. It follows that marriage—as social form, as a complex whole

---

104. Ibid., §164A (GW.14-1.148).
105. See HK, 466–67.
106. PR, §4 (GW.14-1.31).

in which spirit exists *as* community—is a perfect model of what freedom means.[107] It is not an accident that, when Hegel first introduces what he calls the "concrete concept of freedom" in the opening sections of the book, he illustrates it with "friendship and love."[108] We observed in the last chapter that, while people recognize Hegel's overcoming a formalistic sense of *reason*, they less often recognize that he likewise overcomes a formalistic sense of *freedom*, and so tend to identify Hegel's notion of freedom with what Hegel explicitly and repeatedly calls merely an abstract moment of freedom. The assumption that freedom means nothing more than possibility apparently lies almost irretrievably deep in our consciousness.

Thinking of freedom in non-formalistic terms has unaccustomed implications, though these are not as foreign to our common experience of things as they initially appear. A substantial and concrete notion of freedom leads us to say that not all acts of the will are equally free, even if they are equally uncoerced. Arbitrarily waving my arms in private may be no less an uncoerced choice I make than opening my heart to someone who had been up to that point a sworn enemy, but the act is infinitely less free precisely because there is virtually no "substance" in the act. Non-coercion is a necessary condition of freedom, since it is a contradiction to say one gives oneself by force, and yet it is insufficient since freedom *is* the realization of self-manifestation. Here we see concretely what it means to affirm choice as an essential moment of a reality greater than choice. We also see that this conception makes "self-determination" an appropriate way to describe freedom even as it fundamentally reverses our usual associations with the term. Waving my arm is not very free because I do not become different thereby in any significant sense: it is an act in my power, but it does not determine me in any remarkable way. Thus, I would call it an act of self-determination in only a very negligible sense. By contrast, there is arguably no act that determines me more completely than the act by which I pledge myself to another in perpetuity. Marriage is a paradigm of freedom because it is thus a paradigm of self-determination.

One of the things most fascinating about this view is that it inverts the typical relationship between freedom and power, understood as having "control over." Waving my arm is not a very free act *precisely because* I have so much control over it. It is thus wholly subordinate to me, and so in performing the act I do not in any significant sense transcend myself, which

---

107. Merold Westphal is thus correct to observe that, for Hegel, the family illuminates the nature of the state by providing a model for it beyond the individualism of civil society: "Hegel's Radical Idealism," 77.

108. PR, §7Z (JA.7.60).

is the very reason I do not thereby determine myself. I can be determined only by an encounter with something that is at the same time beyond me and not alien to me, and therefore most fundamentally by something that, as we saw above, is my *perfect* other, which is to say by an encounter with some*one*. To the extent that the other to whom I am united is other, he remains "beyond my control," and as such the realization of my freedom. In this sense, conceiving and bearing a child is a quintessential act of freedom as Hegel understands it.[109] This reflection shows why freedom, for Hegel, is fundamentally social, and indeed it is freer the more truly social it becomes. Waving my arms can become free in a higher degree if it occurs in the presence of another person, and thereby turns into a *gesture*, i.e., an act of communication or self-manifestation, however rudimentary. And the freedom will increase the more one communicates, that is, the more one "lets go" of oneself and so commits oneself in an irrevocable way, which is another way of saying the more significant—meaning-ful, full of substance—is the self-determination. Hegel's notion of freedom as social form, which has its paradigm in marriage, simply dissolves the problem of "free will and determinism" that dominates so much of the modern and contemporary discussion, not by reconciling freedom as purely inward form with mechanism as purely external content, as Spinoza and Kant do in different ways, for example, but rather by thinking through the meaning of freedom in its moments on the basis of its most complete concrete realization.

B. Civil Society

The child represents the transcendence of the parents in a complete sense: he is implicitly from the beginning and ever more actually an individual person in his own right, and so while being a member of the family he is reared by it to leave the family in a certain respect and enter the world as an independent individual.[110] Thus begins what Hegel calls "civil society," and indeed he appears to be the first to use this term in the distinctively modern sense to designate a sphere of social interaction that is distinct,

---

109. In this, Hegel revives what was, according to Richard Onians, the original etymological association between "freedom" and the "procreative life-element" in Latin and Greek: see Onians, *The Origins of European Thought*, 472–80.

110. Which is at least one reason why Hegel connects the "upbringing of children" and the "dissolution of the family," PR, §177 (GW.14-1.155).

if not separate, from both the family and the state.¹¹¹ Such a thing exists only in the modern world because it requires, first, an extension of society beyond the immediate community of the ancient polis, and, second, the emergence of economic activity genuinely distinct from the more "naturally" differentiated and hierarchical structures of the medieval feudal system.¹¹² In other words, it requires what we would call today a globalized free market. Civil society represents for Hegel the sphere of the individual pursuit of self-interest in which each person is "out for himself," so to speak. The issue for us is what place this sphere could possibly have in Hegel's philosophy of objective spirit, and indeed, more particularly, in the *Sittlichkeit* that Hegel presents as the substance of the social order.

In the first place, it is important to point out that civil society belongs to *Sittlichkeit* in a somewhat paradoxical way. In a certain sense, it is the negative opposite of *Sittlichkeit*, since, as fragmentation into individuality it represents precisely "the loss of ethical life."¹¹³ But this loss turns out to be essential in the following way. Hegel calls civil society the "world of appearance" of *Sittlichkeit*, and in doing so he refers the reader to his treatment of appearance in the *Encyclopedia Logic*.¹¹⁴ There, appearance was regarded as the necessary correlate of essence, which gives it a central role in the *Logic*'s second part. There is no essence that does not appear, and appearance is always the appearance *of* essence. If being, the first part of the *Logic*, is immediacy, the logic of essence is the logic of mediation, or relationality. In the PR, if family is *Sittlichkeit* in an immediate sense, civil society is the sphere of pure mediation, or pure, abstract relationality: Hegel calls it, appropriately, the stage of difference.¹¹⁵ In abstract terms, the differentiation that civil society represents will be just as necessary to ethical life as appearance is to essence in logic. But we have to make this more concrete.¹¹⁶

If we were told that a person were concerned wholly with appearance, we would imagine him as striving in every way possible, whether overtly or discreetly, to "outdo" others, if not in reality by actually *being* better, then at least by *seeming* to be better in the eyes of others. Political

111. See Franco, *Hegel's Philosophy of Freedom*, 249; cf., Riedel, *Between Tradition and Revolution*, 129–56.

112. PR, §182Z (JA.262–63).

113. Ibid., §181 (GW.14-1.159).

114. Ibid. (GW.14-1.159). See E (1830) §131–§141 (GW.20.157–64).

115. PR, §181 (GW.14-1.159).

116. The best brief account of Hegel's view of civil society is Avineri, *Hegel's Theory*, 132–54.

thinkers from Plato to Rousseau recognized the sphere of appearance as one of competition, potential violence, and profound alienation.[117] For Aristotle, those who make honor—*timē*—the highest good prove, in spite of their immoderate concern with themselves, to be wholly dependent on others in a disordered fashion.[118] Hegel seeks to set just this dynamic into relief in his analysis of the internal logic of civil society, which reveals it to represent for him, just as for Plato, the dissolution of order and therefore an expression of irrationality. Hegel sees the absolutizing of appearance in its pure relationality—i.e., its lack of substantiality—as collapsing simultaneously into the abstract self and into pure dependence on the other. Thus, one enters the sphere of civil society essentially as a self-interested individual, which means that one regards all others as mere instruments of one's self. However, one cannot achieve one's own ends except precisely by *means of* others. But it is just this instrumentalization of others, this use of others for one's own ends, that makes one useful to them in what is the exclusive pursuit of their own ends. By using them, and precisely *in* using them, one is being used *by* them.

The self in civil society measures all others by its needs. But Hegel points out that these needs, in another respect, to a significant degree do *not* belong to the self, they do not represent the self in its genuine selfhood. Instead, these needs are largely produced in the self by others through the dynamic of commerce.[119] Absolute independence is the flip side of utter dependence, and one loses oneself in one's selfishness. This is what Hegel means by pure, abstract mediation: particularity and universality collapse into one another without being integrated. The key reason for this collapse is the absence of "substantiality" or "ethicality," i.e., *Sittlichkeit*, in civil society. *Sittlichkeit* implies that individuals are *internally* related to one another precisely because they belong together in the same whole. In this respect, their particularity is always-already mediated by universality, and vice versa. Because of this internal relatedness, their pursuit of their own interests will naturally involve more than just their individual selves, and, by the same token, the promotion of the other will strengthen their own individual reality. If there is no social substance, by contrast, individuals relate only externally to one another. But this means that the reduction of

---

117. We need only think of the figure of Thrasymachus in Plato's *Republic*, or of the implications Rousseau sees, with profound psychological insight, in the distinction between healthy *"amour de soi"* and the destructive *"amour propre,"* which is essentially the former as mediated by appearance.

118. See Aristotle, *Nic. Ethics*, I.3.

119. PR, §191Z (JA.7.273).

others to the self and the reduction of the self to others are "apparently" opposed descriptions of a single relationship.

Civil society gives expression to what Hegel calls "bad infinity"; that is, the sort of infinity that is opposed to finite form. This internal formlessness of civil society, when it is coupled with the contingency of historical accidents and the abstract principles of particularity and universality, will betray an inexorable slide toward fundamental social disorder.[120] If the purely individual satisfaction of needs is made primary, which is another way of saying that mediation as such is absolutized, then work—which represents for Hegel in general the making concrete of subjectivity[121]— ceases to have an intrinsic meaning, and becomes instead simply a means by which human beings, so to speak, consume one another.[122] In other words, in uninhibited civil society, which has no place for intrinsic goods, labor becomes wholly instrumentalized to production, and so made as efficient as possible. According to Hegel, this leads to the boundless accumulation of wealth, on the one hand, and the increased specialization and mechanization of work, on the other, to the point of utter abstraction, "so that the human being is eventually able to step aside and let a *machine* take his place."[123] But if a machine can substitute for him, it is only because he has already himself become more or less a machine. The result is that a significant part of the population becomes bound to work that provides no human fulfillment and requires no culture and education, and so the "rabble" comes into being, and the problem of poverty becomes an inevitable result precisely of the "growth" of the economy. If Hegel remarks that the problem of poverty is an essentially modern problem,[124] it is not because he is ignorant, for example, of the existence of the medieval peasant, but rather because poverty represents for him, not just a lack of abundance, but more fundamentally an abandonment to one's naked individuality and the loss of dignity this abandonment entails. Poverty requires the existence of civil society.

For Hegel, the dissolution of social order that civil society threatens to produce is held in check by two things: first, the administration of justice, and second, the existence of the "police" [*Polizei*] and the "corporation."

120. According to Hegel, civil society liberates the "aptitudes, and all accidents of birth and fortune" of the various individuals that make up a nation: PR, §182Z (JA.7.263).

121. Phen, 117–18 (GW.9.114–15); cf., 213–14 (GW.9.194–95).

122. See PR, §196 (GW.14-1.168).

123. Ibid., §198 (GW.14-1.169).

124. See Hegel's remarks from his lectures of 1819–20, cited in ibid., 453–54.

The Perfection of Freedom

What Hegel means by these two terms, it should be noted, is significantly different from what they typically connote. The "police"—in which Hegel hears the ancient word "*polis*," and which may therefore be more adequately translated as "polity"[125]—represents any official intervention on behalf of the citizens, and so would include, for example, not just the patrolling of streets, but also any governmental regulation of commerce. A "corporation," moreover, is not just a business association, but any sort of community at all that is distinct, on the one hand, from the family and, on the other hand, from the state; it would include, therefore, guilds and even religious organizations.

Now, what Hegel calls the "administration of justice" in civil society is essentially the legal system, the laws and the courts that interpret them, all of which is intended ultimately to protect individual rights, i.e., property. But, while justice protects rights, it does not do justice, so to speak, to human beings in a more concrete and comprehensive sense. According to Hegel, "welfare is something external to right as such," even though it is, at the same time, "an essential determination in the system of needs."[126] The needs that are generated by and drive civil society, therefore, demand more than the administration of justice. The police, thus, ought to be understood as concerned with welfare, i.e., not simply with the *protection* of the rights of individuals, but with their flourishing. It is helpful to note that this activity, which we commonly identify with the state today, is located for Hegel specifically in civil society *as distinct from* the state.[127] Because, Hegel says, civil society tends to erode the family, insofar as it treats the members, not as accidents of a substance, but as independent individuals, it has an obligation to fulfill the family's role when the family fails.[128] Hegel thus refers to civil society as a sort of "universal family," which means it must provide as far as it can: not only regulating commerce to mitigate its destructive effects but also to provide work and even education; indeed, through the promotion of public works of charity, it must seek also to respond to what Hegel calls the "subjective" needs "both with regard to the *particular* circumstances and with regard to *emotion* and *love*."[129]

---

125. This is Nicholas Boyle's suggestion: *Who Are We Now?*, 166. Cf., the discussion of the *Polizei* in Riedel, *Jacob Friedrich Abel*, 152–53.
126. PR, §229Z (JA.7.310).
127. See Boyle, *Who Are We Now?*, 166.
128. PR, §238–39 (GW.14-1.191–92).
129. Ibid., §242 (GW.14-1.193).

Nevertheless, Hegel sees that the government's capacities with respect to welfare are strictly limited. The reason for this is that the problems that are caused by civil society are insoluble simply from within the terms set by civil society. If we penetrate to the logical core, the problem is disintegration, or, more specifically, the separation of the particular and the universal, which can be integrated only in an ethical whole.[130] The police attempt to join these two aspects, but can do so only *extrinsically*: "What the police provides for in the first instance is the actualization and preservation of the universal which is contained within the particularity of civil society, [and it does so] as *an external order and arrangement* for the protection and security of the masses of particular ends and interest which have their subsistence [*Bestehen*] in this universal."[131] The inadequacy of the police, in this regard, gives rise to the *corporation*, in which individuals join with one another, and so the particular takes the universal that is "present in its immanent interests" as the end of its will and activity.[132] In this case, particularity and universality achieve a more *intrinsic* relationship, and so we have a "concrete whole," which allows Hegel to say that, in the corporation, "*the ethical returns* to civil society as an immanent principle."[133] To say that the "ethical" returns means that the corporation represents a genuine whole, a substance, which means that the individuals are once again *members*, and so bear an internal relation to one another. The corporations thus respond directly—indeed, more directly than the welfare offered by the police—to the very problems that are created by civil society: being part of a community, on the one hand, returns a sense of *honor* to the individual, who knows himself to belong to something larger than himself, and it also mitigates in very practical ways the problem of poverty and all that it implies.[134] It does so both because the wealthier members feel bound by the whole of which they are a part, and so fulfill spontaneously their obligations to the less fortunate members, and also because the poor can receive help without humiliation and loss of dignity precisely by virtue of their membership.[135] The key in both of these cases

---

130. We recall that this is just how Schiller characterized the problem posed by modernity in the AEM, VI.31–43, esp. 35 (SW.317–24).

131. PR, §249 (GW.14-1.196).

132. See K. Westphal, "Context and Structure," 259, who points out that the corporations set into relief the "individual contributions to the corporate and social good."

133. Ibid. For a good, concise explanation of the significance of the corporations in Hegel's political philosophy, see Brod, *Hegel's Philosophy of Politics*, 110–14.

134. See Brod, *Hegel's Philosophy of Politics*, 107–10.

135. PR, §253A (GW.14-1.198).

is that the substantiality of corporations restores an internal relatedness to individuals, saving them from the pure atomism, so to speak, that defines civil society generally.

The judgments that Hegel makes regarding civil society set into relief, once again, the significance of the connection between freedom and social form. Hegel affirms, in a remark to §255, that "[t]he sanctity of marriage and the honor attaching to the corporation are the two moments round which the disorganization of civil society revolves." In other words, civil society, as pure relationality or mediation, taken *in itself* and thus in isolation from anything concrete, so that this mediation becomes absolutized, represents sheer "disorganization" or disintegration. What prevents it from becoming such, for Hegel, are the two *essentially concrete* poles of the family and the corporation, which have their unifying ground, as we shall see in a moment, in the state. Both of these are concrete, or as Hegel calls them in this context, "ethical," because both serve to integrate particularity and universality, although they do so in different—in fact, "opposed"—ways: the family gives priority to the objective universal (although it is an essentially "particular" universal, insofar as each family is one among many in the whole) since the individuals are accidents of the immediate substance of spirit, while the corporation gives priority to the subjective particular (although it is a *generalized* particularity insofar as corporations are in principle available to any individual) since the union is founded on the universal precisely insofar as it is immanent within particular self-interest.

Now, it is crucial to see that, when Hegel later speaks of the subjective freedom of civil society, he means primarily freedom *in the concrete* sense that the individual possesses *as* a member of a corporation, which means that, for Hegel, *even subjective freedom properly understood is essentially social, i.e., has its actuality as social form.* Hegel rejects the (Rousseauian) idea that man would be freest if left to the immediate satisfaction of the simple needs given to him by nature, for this immediacy submerges spirit in nature, and, because freedom is essentially spiritual, it thereby submerges freedom.[136] But he also insists that the "liberation from nature" that occurs in being educated into a responsible agent, so that one does not merely blindly follow the impulses of nature, but rather is capable of choosing deliberately and knowingly—i.e., what many would want to call freedom today, freedom in the "liberal" sense, whether on the conservative or liberal end of the spectrum—remains merely *formal* "because the

---

136. Ibid., §187A (GW.14-1.162–64), §194A (GW.14-1.167).

particularity of ends remains the basic content,"¹³⁷ i.e., it is not yet mediated by the universality of society. Not only is freedom in this abstract formal sense perfectly compatible with the concrete *un*freedom of being essentially a cog in the machine of civil society, of being wholly manipulated by the designs of commerce in the deluded pursuit of one's individuality, but in fact it will be the very *cause* of this enslavement to the extent that we take it as the definition of freedom, and thereby absolutize particularity in its abstract sense. If we do, we will tend to minimize the significance of the very ethical realities that bring order to civil society by acting, as it were, as its substantial antipodes, since we will tend to conceive each of them, not in substantial terms, but rather in primarily "contractual" terms as the free association of individuals related to each other in terms of rights and duties, and thereby simply as a function of the civil society to which they ought, rather, to give order.

The result, then, is an essentially irrational dialectic between individual rights and the imposition of order in the form of governmental interventions, neither side of which knowing any bounds because of the disorganization that civil society represents.¹³⁸ Within the logic of civil society, in other words, there is no limit to which the government can "intrude upon" one's personal life, and there is likewise no limit to which I can demand my rights, i.e., claim the service of the government to satisfy my particular needs. In order to grasp what Hegel means by reason and the political order (which we discussed last chapter), as distinct from a more contemporary liberal conception of public reason (as found, for example, in John Rawls), it is illuminating to consider that Rawlsian "public reason" is perfectly compatible with the radical political disintegration we have been discussing here, while Hegel's public reason is basically opposed to it. What is at issue is essentially the difference between a formalistic conception of freedom and a concrete one. Given Hegel's analysis, we can even make the more provocative claim that, to the extent that Rawls takes for granted a formalistic conception of freedom, his theory of justice is not only compatible with social disorder but is a *cause* of it. From a Hegelian perspective, Rawlsian "public reason" is basically irrational.¹³⁹

137. Ibid., §195 (GW.14-1.167).
138. Cf., ibid., §234Z (JA.7.312).

139. Of course, to make this claim one would have to show that Rawls does in fact assume a formalistic conception of freedom, which we cannot do in the present context. It is worth noting that Rawls tends to conceive social order in terms of the administration of justice and welfare—i.e., the police—which for Hegel remains extrinsic, because they have not yet moved beyond the horizon of civil society. Ethical

Because the end of the corporation, even as concrete and to that extent social, remains for all that "limited and finite," it seeks its *truth*, according to Hegel, in an end that is "*universal* in and for itself" and is thus "absolutely actual."[140] We thus pass from civil society to the state.

C. The State

Our discussion of the meaning of spirit, and our elaboration of social form as family and civil society, has put us in a position to grasp the otherwise quite peculiar description that Hegel offers of the state, which we discussed at the beginning of the present chapter. We noted especially Hegel's tendency to divinize the state; while this will indeed require further critical reflection, we ought to recall that Hegel had also called the family an essentially religious institution. He did so, not because it possesses supernatural attributes, but simply because it embodies a kind of absolute (i.e., religious) spirit precisely by being community in a substantial sense: an "I" that is a "We" and a "We" that is an "I." It is interesting to note that Hegel refers once again in his introductory remarks on the state to the Penates, which sets into relief the fact that he conceives of spirit "metaphysically," that is, as having being in and for itself, and so as existing in a way that transcends the individuals that constitute it.[141] Our purpose, here, is

---

wholes such as the family and the corporation, which are the antipodes necessary to make civil society intelligible, do not play a foundational role in Rawls. Stephen Houlgate attempts to show that Rawls and Hegel are much more similar than generally assumed, in part because Rawls agrees that human beings are inherently social, but to say that human beings are always in society is not yet to say that they are social by nature, i.e., in an *essential*, rather than accidental, way. The difference between Hegel and Rawls that Houlgate eventually does affirm in fact stems from a different conception of human nature, or, to use more directly Hegelian language, of *spirit*, and therefore a radically different conception of both reason and freedom. See Houlgate, "Hegel, Rawls, and the Rational State," 249–73. Joyce Beck Hoy notes that, in spite of Rawls' apparently "Hegelian" concern to overcome the abstractness of Kantian autonomy and the aggregation of atomistic self-interest, he nevertheless remains committed in the end to an ideal of the person as an "independent chooser," "Hegel's Critique of Rawls," 418. As we have sought to show in the previous chapter, and in this one, for Hegel such a conception is irrational in form no matter how "rational" the choices made happen to be. For a similar observation, see Kolb, *Critique of Pure Modernity*, 98.

140. PR, §256 (GW.14-1.199). It is interesting to note that many scholars confess an inability to see the necessity of the transition from civil society to the state. The transition would in fact make little sense if one did not accept what we have been calling a specifically "metaphysical" conception of spirit.

141. PR, §257A (GW.14-1.201).

not to comment on Hegel's theory of the state in all of the richness of its details, but rather to consider his theory from the perspective of a notion of freedom as social form, and we will most directly achieve this purpose by working out the precise way in which the state differs from both the family and civil society, so as to be able to be the unity of these two, and so represent *Sittlichkeit* in its most actual form.[142]

Hegel does not explicitly differentiate the state from the family, no doubt because he does not need to: there is no reason one would confuse them.[143] It is nevertheless useful to differentiate them ourselves according to Hegel's principles in order to understand what sort of social form the state is, and we can do so by considering what Hegel believes is lacking in the family as a form of spirit. According to Hegel, the family in itself and on its own does not yet offer the full development of particularity *in its own right*, but only in relation to the universality of the whole, and this is the case because it is the *immediate* substance of spirit. Although Hegel does not explicitly differentiate the state from the family, as we said, he does address what he takes to be lacking in the ancient polis, which had a form analogous to the family in that "universality was indeed already present, but particularity had not yet been released and set at liberty and brought back to universality, i.e., the universal end of the whole."[144] In this respect, there is something clearly to be gained by the elevation of individuality in the rise of civil society. Those who think of Hegel essentially as a romantic who idealizes the Greek polis clearly overlook this point, which we see is not at all a small point in his political theory, even if it is an understandable mistake given that Hegel tended in this direction in his earlier thinking on politics, and also that, while he affirms the indispensable reality of subjectivity, he subordinates it in an important way to the objectivity of *Sittlichkeit*, as we will see momentarily.[145] Nevertheless, the "fragmentation" of civil society, while it undermines the immediate unity of the ancient polis, in the end serves to help constitute a richer sort of unity.[146] In this sense, Hegel's understanding of wholeness in politics is

---

142. Houlgate, *Freedom, Truth, and History*, 120.

143. This is not to imply that Hegel fails to see their difference: see Landes, "Hegel's Conception of the Family," 5.

144. PR, §260Z (JA.7.338). It is interesting to recall in this context that Plato's "noble lie," in the *Republic*, aims essentially to transform the political order into a family (*Rep.*, 414bff.).

145. On Hegel's relationship to the Greeks, see Shklar, "An Elegy for Hellas."

146. For Hegel, the *rich* unity that comprises the state is one that "allows the *opposition* within reason *to develop to its full strength*, and has overcome it so as to preserve

strikingly similar to that of Schiller, who likewise affirmed a "synthesis" that integrated both the wholeness of the ancient order and the individuality of the modern one.[147]

The more dangerous confusion, in Hegel's eyes, because it is the more common one in the modern period, is the reduction of the state to civil society.[148] He thus takes pains to make this distinction explicit: "If the state is confused with civil society and its determination is equated with the security and protection of property and personal freedom, *the interest of individuals [der Einzelnen] as such* becomes the ultimate end for which they are united; it also follows from this that membership of the state is an optional matter."[149] It is important to realize that the judgment Hegel is making here is not a *moral* one—a criticism of a person's subjective intentions—but an *ontological* one, or rather, it is a moral judgment only because it is first and most fundamentally an ontological judgment. *If* individuals have their being wholly in themselves and so relate to others only *qua* individuals, then it is impossible for there to be any end to the relation other than the mere accidental conglomeration of individual ends, which in fact means that the conglomeration itself has no reality in itself but reduces to each individual in particular. This is the case regardless of the quality of the subjective intentions, or what it is that any particular individual happens to will. Given this conception of the nature of the human being, no conception of the state makes sense other than as a "social contract," however this may be understood in its details. The fact that Rousseau embraces such a conception is evidence, for Hegel, that his distinction between the "general will" (a sort of transcendent unity) and the "will of all" (as the mere sum of individuals) is essentially an

---

itself within it and *wholly contain it within itself*," PR, §185A (GW.14-1.161).

147. Schiller, AEM, VI.30–43 (SW.8.317–24). Schiller ends the letter saying that "however much the law of Nature did have that tendency [to sacrifice totality for the sake of cultivating individual powers], we must be at liberty to restore by means of a higher Art this wholeness in our nature which Art has destroyed."

148. Z. A. Pelczynski claims that "the conceptual separation of the state and civil society is one of the most original features of Hegel's political and social philosophy," "The Significance of Hegel's Separation," 1. It is the most original because it rests on what we have called the most "Hegelian" aspect of Hegel's political philosophy, namely, ethical substance or *Sittlichkeit*. It is not an accident that those who take an "antimetaphysical" approach to Hegel, and who therefore have difficulty seeing *Sittlichkeit* precisely as ethical *substance*, would also have difficulty grasping the necessity of the transition from civil society to the state.

149. PR, §258A (GW.14-1.201).

insubstantial one.[150] The essential problem of any social contract theory is that it reduces the state to civil society, which can imagine only contractual relations, and therefore implies the social disorder and threat to freedom we saw in unbridled civil society. One who thinks of the state as a social contract will tend to think of marriage in the same terms and to interpret corporations as associations *of individuals* rather than as *associations* of individuals, which means one will eliminate the substantial antipodes that preserve reason in civil society. For Hegel, the only alternative to a social contract theory of state, if we do not wish to posit it as a fundamentally natural being as the ancients did, is to think of it as *objective* spirit, or *Sittlichkeit*, which arises when we think of spirit, not primarily in terms of individual agency, but as a communal substance, i.e., as social form.

Hegel explains this fairly succinctly:

> Since the state is objective spirit, it is only through being a member of the state that the individual [*Individuum*] himself has objectivity, truth, and ethical life. *Union* as such is itself the true content and end, and the destiny [*Bestimmung*] of individuals [*Individuen*] is to lead a universal life; their further particular satisfaction, activity, and mode of conduct have this substantial and universally valid basis as their point of departure and result.—Considered in the abstract, rationality consists in general in the unity and interpenetration of universality and individuality [*Einzelheit*]. Here, in a concrete sense and in terms of its content, it consists in the unity of objective freedom (i.e., of the universal substantial will) and subjective freedom (as the freedom of individual [*individuellen*] knowledge and of the will in its pursuit of particular ends).[151]

It is precisely *because* the state is the unity of objective freedom and subjective freedom that Hegel can call it "the actuality of concrete freedom."[152] Note, it is the objectivity of the state that allows it to bring unity to the objective and subjective dimension of freedom, which is another way of saying that the objectivity of social form is not simply part of the meaning of freedom, but the whole of it, though its being the whole implies that it does full justice to the "non-objective" aspect of freedom. Clearly, we have two senses of objectivity here, or perhaps better: two levels, one that is relatively opposed to the subjective and one that includes

---

150. Ibid. (GW.14-1.202).
151. Ibid. (GW.14-1.201–2)
152. Ibid., §260 (GW.14-1.208).

this relative opposition within itself. But does the inclusion subordinate the subjective to the objective in an ultimate sense? We will return to this question in a moment.

As an ethical substance, the state resembles the family in which the unity of substance has an absolute priority over the difference of the members (even if its absoluteness does not make it unilateral), though, as we said, it differs in that it, like civil society, gives full play to individuality. It is therefore a more complex relationship than either alone. Both the unity and the difference in the state acquire a particular character by virtue of the complexity that characterizes the state as a whole: as Hegel describes it, the unity is ordered to difference, while difference is ordered to unity, or, more concretely, the end of the state is the flourishing of the individuality of its members, while the end of the individuals is the flourishing of the state. It is just this reciprocal ordering that reveals the intrinsic relation between these two aspects, as opposed to an extrinsic relation, which would make each aspect a threat to the other, and consequently require each to aim at *itself* against the other for the sake of self-preservation. It is just this mutuality that Hegel has in mind when he describes the members of the state as "patriotic," or as "politically disposed" (we might say, "politically minded"), on the one hand, and describes the state *itself* as organic, on the other; though he presents both of these notions in a rather unusual way by virtue of their mutuality. Each of these, for Hegel, represents freedom in a certain respect: "political mindedness" captures the essence of subjective freedom, and the correlative organic conception of the state captures the essence of objective freedom. Let us consider Hegel's understanding of each of these in turn.

What made family spirit an ethical substance is the vow: in this total gift of self, two individuals become a single person, and because the child is the actualization of this unity, he is not a mere addition to the couple, so that we would have now *two* persons, but is rather included *within* that (vertically transcendent) personhood as its (horizontal) expansion. There can be no ethical substance without the unity of the whole having priority over the constitutive elements, and such a priority can "come to be" only in a total, reciprocal, and permanent pledging of self, which is therefore fundamentally different from a mere contract. The completeness of this surrender of self, we observed, is what makes it a paradigm of *Sittlichkeit*, or the actuality of objective freedom. Civil society is ethical, and not simply the chaos of sheer particularity, because of the universality that lies implicit within the particularity of self-interest. Only the commonality of interests, and therefore their individual-transcending character, allows particular corporations or communities to form within the sphere of civil society. These latter "wholes" have the advantage of being founded on the particularity of self-consciousness, and so result from the individual's deliberate choice, but for that very reason are less substantial. As we saw above, the state is the unity of objective and subjective freedom, and this has implications for the character of the citizens' subjective disposition. On the one hand, just as the members of a family take the family as their end, so too do the members of a state take the state as their ultimate end.[153] In the case of the state, however, the members actively pursue this substantial spirit of the state "knowingly and willingly," that is, fully self-consciously. This is possible on Hegel's terms only through a recognition that the universal end of the state is *already* implicit in their particular ends, which means that they understand their own ends would fail if the state should fail, and more positively that the flourishing of the state implies the flourishing of their particularity. This does not imply, though, that their particularity becomes the measure of the state, because that would reduce the state to civil society. Instead—and we need to have Hegel's sense of the infinite in order to grasp this point—what distinguishes the state from civil society is that, while its universality is not juxtaposed to particularity (as an abstract universality) and so *is* in fact included within the particularity in a certain respect, it is so included only by transcending that particularity and including it in turn: it is only because the universal transcends the particular that it lies implicit within it.

Spelled out more concretely in terms of Hegel's view of patriotism, it means that the ethical life of the state is, in the first place, a matter of habit: belonging to this state is, as it were, so much a part of me that, for the most part, I simply am not aware of it. Hegel claims its immediate expression is habit or custom (*Sitte*):[154] in a wholly natural way, I recognize the traditions that constitute the life of the state as a fundamental part of my personal identity. So fundamental, in fact, that I scarcely notice it. If it were a reality simply "above" me, I would be aware of it whenever it was present, as something "other." But its substantiality is truly mine, so that its presence is like the presence of water to a fish: *because* it is so essential, it is altogether invisible. We typically associate patriotism with an intense feeling or enthusiasm, but, while Hegel does not exclude this in principle,

---

153. As Merold Westphal has observed, the patriotism that occurs at the level of the state corresponds to the love and trust at the level of the family: "Hegel's Radical Idealism," 89.

154. PR, §257 (GW.14-1.201).

he relativizes it to the more ordinary reality of habit.[155] Hegel says that the "ethical man is unconscious of himself."[156] Indeed, to insist that enthusiasm is the essence of patriotism would be to trivialize it, to reduce it to something subjective, an "opinion," as Hegel calls it, making one's relation to the whole a matter of certainty rather than truth. Mere certainty constantly needs to reassure itself by making itself explicit to itself over and over again, whereas one relates to truth most generally by taking it for granted. Taking the customs and traditions of a state for granted, as something always-already a part of my being, is the basic expression within the subjective sphere of the state's absolute priority over my individuality, and what distinguishes this relation from the discrete, deliberate acts that make up the moment of civil society. As substance, it cannot be a function of my choice, but has to precede that choice as what is "given" from the outset, but what is then appropriated as my own. While education in its formal sense, as we saw, develops one as a self-conscious individual, its more complete aim is to integrate one into one's community, to reconcile one to the whole of which one is a member: "Education in its early stages always begins with fault-finding [i.e., the development of critical thinking], but when it is complete, it sees the positive element in everything."[157] Similar to the way in which freedom is duty's having become nature in Schiller, for Hegel one is subjectively free when the social order has become "second nature."[158]

To say that membership in the state precedes choice, however, is not to say that choice is irrelevant, but only that the substantiality of the state always conditions whatever choice is made within it. The state is not utterly invisible, wholly implicit within my pursuit of my particular ends, in the sense that the state takes care of its business while I take care of mine. We might think, here, of Adam Smith's notion of the invisible hand, which may indeed have a relative truth in civil society, since the universal is in fact contained in the particular there, but this containment is precisely why the sphere has to be coordinated within a more complete order. The state may indeed have its immediate existence in (relatively unconscious) custom, but it has a "mediate existence in *the self-consciousness of the individual*, in the individual's knowledge and activity."[159] This self-

---

155. See Boyle, *Who Are We Now?*, 167.
156. PR, §144Z (JA.7.227).
157. Ibid., §268Z (JA.7.346).
158. See E (1817), §430 (GW.13.232–33).
159. PR, §257 (GW.14-1.201).

"The 'I' That Is 'We' and the 'We' That Is 'I'"

consciousness takes the form of knowing and willing that my individual end is contained within the universal end of the state, so that I harmonize my interest with the universal interest, rather than the reverse,[160] and moreover that I am willing to "make extraordinary efforts" on behalf of the state,[161] even to the point of, say, sacrificing my life for it in the time of war.[162] What is important to note, here, is that this willingness to sacrifice myself when necessary is, for Hegel, quite significantly different from the Kantian selfless performance of duty, because duty, in Hegel's sense, is simply an explication of the element in which I live day to day, or to put it more directly, it is an expression of the very substance that gives me life as *subjective spirit*: "In the state, as an ethical entity and as the interpenetration of the substantial and the particular, my obligation towards the substantial is at the same time the existence of my particular freedom; that is, duty and right are *united* within the state *in one and the same relation* [*Beziehung*]."[163] My subjective freedom increases the more I appropriate, in my actual knowledge and will, the relation I bear to the substance of the state. By the same token, this appropriation actualizes the substance of the state, since it requires the full development of subjectivity to be fully real itself. The rationality of the state, in other words, cannot come to be *either* merely beyond the individuals *or* merely in the individuals, but only both at once; it is being in itself (in the immediacy of custom) and being for itself (in the mediation of self-consciousness).

This, then, is the subjective freedom of the state. Its objective freedom—and here we find clear echoes of Schelling's early thought—lies in the state's organic character.[164] But, just as Hegel reverses usual conceptions in his presentation of patriotism primarily as an absence of feeling, here too he reverses expectations.[165] We tend to think that an organic conception of the state is one in which unity threatens to tyrannize difference, i.e., that the individuals are submerged in the whole and thus are mere functions of the state. But Hegel in fact emphasizes precisely the

---

160. Ibid., §261A (GW.14-1.208–10). Note, this is decidedly *not* a suppression of particular interests.

161. Ibid., §268A (GW.14-1.212).

162. Ibid., §324 (GW.14-1.265).

163. Ibid., §261A (GW.14-1.208).

164. See Hegel's early criticism of Fichte's "mechanistic" conception of the state, which is specifically tied to Fichte's formalistic conception of freedom: DS, 148–49 (GW.4.58).

165. Cassirer, *Myth of the State*, 265. Cf., Kenneth Westphal, "Context and Structure," 236–37.

inner differentiation of the organism. It is thus that it becomes the natural correlate of, indeed the presupposition for, what he had described as the proper subjective disposition of the members. Hegel explains that in an organism the universal resolves itself into its particulars.[166] To understand this, we must recall our initial reflections on the meaning of *Sittlichkeit*. The state does not have its actuality in itself, but only in the particulars that constitute it, so much so that we can say that in some respect the state is nothing more than the self-actualization of its individual members. Nevertheless, it is in fact the state that thereby becomes actual; *their* life is *its* actuality. Hegel does not mean this as a mere metaphor. The self-actualization of its members *as* members—which, we must keep in mind, means their concrete freedom or their internalization of their dependence on the whole—is the subjectivity of the state. This is what allows Hegel to speak of the state as an agent in its own right, as knowing and willing. It is also what explains the significance of custom, for the universal's resolution into its particulars is what makes it relatively invisible, what makes it the substance in which they have their life and natural existence with others: "The state is actual, and its actuality consists in the fact that the interest of the whole realizes itself through the particular ends. Actuality is always the unity of universality and particularity, the resolution of universality into particularity; the latter then appears to be self-sufficient, although it is sustained and supported only by the whole."[167] Thus, the organic character of the state for Hegel is expressed in the liberation, so to speak, of the particularity of its members. The relative self-sufficiency of the particulars in their difference does not eclipse the importance of unity, but reveals it, insofar as each is fully itself *because* it belongs to the whole. Hegel takes Aristotle's example of a hand, which is not, in fact, a hand unless it is attached to the body, which means its self-actualization depends on its being the expression of an over-arching unity.[168] In one sense, the unity does not exist as such, in the sense that, if you were to remove all the members of the body, you would be left, in fact, with nothing at all, and yet the members have a "vital interest" in its reality. The reality of its unity is the members' existing in a particular way, as having their own existence in their interrelation with all others in the whole.

This last observation leads to a crucial final point regarding the nature of the state as social form. One sometimes reads that Hegel balances

---

166. PR, §270Z (JA.7.362–63).
167. Ibid. (JA.7.362).
168. Ibid. (JA.7.363). See Aristotle, *Politics*, 1.2.1253a.

his organic view of the state with a healthy individualism.[169] While it is true that Hegel integrates the objective form of freedom that one finds most obviously in the ancient polis with the subjective freedom set in relief in the modern conception of the state, it remains the case that Hegel does not equate subjective freedom with individualism in the usual sense of that term. Instead, subjective freedom—as we pointed out above—is *inherently social* for Hegel. In relation to his view of the state, it means that Hegel rejects a democratic understanding of political order—but we might say that he does so precisely in the name of the integrity of the individual and his genuine self-conscious agency.[170] An organic whole liberates its parts specifically as concrete individuals, rather than as separate atoms. We recall the significance of corporations for subjective freedom. "Pure" democracy—i.e., direct plebiscite—would be an affirmation of the individual as an abstraction, a mere unit. To say that everyone ought to participate in the acts of the state as individuals would be to identify the whole with the sum of its parts, which is not an organism. A purely democratic organism, so to speak, is a dead one, already in a state of decomposition.[171] An organism exists by virtue of integration, which means that it is constituted by the essentially asymmetrical relations one necessarily finds in any genuine whole. In a democracy, by contrast, there are only individuals juxtaposed to one another extrinsically. This is why Hegel says democracy is "devoid of rational form"—i.e., it is not a social form, which means that democracy represents an absence of freedom. While democracy would seem to privilege the individual, the appearance is deceptive. Democracy in the crude sense implies a non-substantial view of state, and this means that the whole, the universal, is not implicit, as substance, in the life of its parts, but that instead their only "connection" to the whole is through discrete acts by which they influence what is external to them. My connection with the whole is not already given in my being, in other words, but arises only through my active, explicit, and deliberate participation. But this makes my participation in fact that of a single discrete atom. And as a discrete atom, so to speak, it is effectively *nothing* in comparison to the thousands or millions or billions of other atoms.

---

169. See Neuhouser, *Actualizing Freedom*, 120ff.

170. See Houlgate, *Freedom, Truth, and History*, 122–23. Houlgate makes the point elsewhere ("Hegel, Rawls, and the Rational State," 201) that Hegel rejects democracy, not because he prefers other things (like aristocratic privileges) to freedom, but *precisely in the name of freedom*.

171. I owe this image to my father.

Civil society, in abstraction from any substantial wholes, represents, as we saw, an individualism that tends of its own inner logic to destroy individuality.[172] Pure democracy, understood as a collection of individuals who enter the political sphere only through deliberate acts, thereby collapses the state into civil society, and so likewise threatens to destroy the individual. Prior to Tocqueville's better known observations in this regard, as Avineri has shown, Hegel already perceived that an unmediated democracy, with the atomistic conception of political order that it implies, will eventually lead to the simultaneity of complete disinterest in politics and an overzealous political activism.[173] Ironically, like the importance of habit for real patriotism, the recognition that one does not have to be *directly* involved in the actions of the state can be the affirmation of a far more profound participation in political life. For Hegel, as for Tocqueville, political individuality occurs in and through the mediation of communities larger than the family but smaller than the state: "It is within the sphere of his corporation, community, etc. (see §251) that the individual first attains his actual and living determination, as *universal*."[174]

In the *Phenomenology*, Hegel had described spirit as the unity of substance and subject; in the state, substance becomes total subjectivity insofar as it has its actuality in individuals who have unfolded their own inner being to the furthest extent, and subjectivity becomes pure substantiality insofar as the individuals live, move, and have their being in the ethical whole of the state. Thus, at this point, the social form becomes perfect, the "I" is truly "We" and the "We" is truly "I," which means that freedom reaches its fullest actuality. As a result, the state presents itself as "an absolute and unmoved end in itself."[175]

---

172. Harry Brod observes that "Hegel violates the traditional liberal individualist logic, but he does so in the name of many of the pluralist freedoms liberalism has been concerned with defending," *Hegel's Philosophy of Politics*, 98. According to David Kolb, "Paradoxically, the problem Hegel sees with the free citizen of civil society, who has been liberated from tradition, is that he is not free enough," *Critique of Pure Modernity*, 97.

173. Avineri, *Hegel's Theory*, 49. Cf., K. Westphal, "Context and Structure," 262; Kolb, 110–11; Taylor, *Hegel and Modern Society*, 116–18.

174. PR, §308A (GW.14-1.255).

175. Ibid., §258 (GW.14-1.201).

IV. Freedom and Absolute Spirit

We ended the last section with a somewhat ominous quotation from Hegel. This characterization of the actualization of freedom raises the specter of the totalitarian state, and in doing so compels us to confront a series of dilemmas that cut to the heart, not simply of Hegel's political philosophy, but of his thought more generally, as we shall see. This threat presents itself in a variety of ways: in subordinating morality to *Sittlichkeit*, Hegel undercuts any rights critical reason might have over against the state, so there is no place given in Hegel's system from which to judge the legitimacy of any particular action of the state; in his relating individuals as accidents to ethical substance, the individual, no matter how much it may be the *actualization* of substance, nevertheless has no ultimate grounds for claims *against* that substance and so no real protection from the possible abuse of power; moreover, if it is the case that the state is not founded in some sense on natural rights but is rather itself the source of rights, the state would seem to have no measure beyond itself for its truth; and, because the individual state is truly absolute in itself, there is no higher authority to adjudicate international relations, so states would relate to one another in a manner that is analogous to civil society, which would seem necessarily to reproduce the dangers that we saw arise from the absolutization of civil society, this time on a global scale.[176]

It follows logically from all of this that war turns in fact into the normal state of international relations, and the highest destiny of individuals is to serve their nation's military aims. In this case, there is no ultimate judge over the state other than world history, written so to speak by the victors, which makes it appropriate to end the PR, as Hegel does, with a sketch of the stages of history. As Hegel mentions at the end of the introduction to PR, the state "is freedom in its most concrete shape, which is subordinate only to the supreme absolute truth of the world spirit."[177] This subordination can turn out to be brutal, for, while a state is absolute in itself, any particular state may nevertheless be nothing at all in the larger context. Hegel says, indeed, that the most progressive state at a historical moment is absolute with respect to all other states, so that these "are without rights, and they, like those whose epoch has passed, no longer count in world history."[178] Justice apparently has no transcendent foundation, so

---

176. See Franco, *Hegel's Philosophy of Freedom*, 335.

177. PR, §33Z (JA.7.87).

178. Ibid., §347 (GW.14-1.276). Indeed, this absolute right with respect to all else ultimately falls to the world-historical individual who carries his state forward, even if

that truth would seem to be determined in the end only by the machinations of power.

In the face of this totalitarian specter, there appear to be two possible responses. The most common response is to emphasize what one might call the "liberal" element that is undeniably present in his writings. One says that, according to Hegel's logic, what is "*aufgehoben*" is not for all that eliminated, so the higher synthesis of the state does not have to be interpreted as undermining the critical reason implied in morality.[179] One adds that, even if Hegel does affirm that the individual is meant to serve the state, it is also the case that the state ultimately is meant to promote the individual welfare of its members.[180] This response to the totalitarian specter quite often coincides with a decidedly "anti-metaphysical" interpretation more generally, which is not accidental, since this view affirms that the state *as such* has no substantial reality, because there *is* no "supra-individual" spirit. Indeed, these two positions require one another, because *if* the state has any being in itself at all, then the "liberal" element must necessarily be qualified in such a radical way that it ceases to resemble liberalism, and we are brought back to face the specter of totalitarianism. As we have been arguing here, not only is a liberal interpretation of Hegel forced to deny fundamental principles of his thought, but it is moreover forced to overlook the powerful arguments he repeatedly and consistently makes against this view. The liberal interpretation of Hegel[181] cannot therefore justly claim to be an interpretation of Hegel, but at best a use of some Hegelian ideas for another purpose. More importantly, however, if Hegel's criticisms of atomic individualism carry any weight, then it is a deeply problematic position to take in its own right.

The liberal response, in short, does not solve our dilemma: *either* we conceive of freedom in the abstract and formalistic terms of individualism, and accept all of the consequences, *or* we conceive of freedom as social form, and are forced to reckon with totalitarianism. These alternatives are

---

he is unconscious of this fact (ibid., §348 [GW.14-1.276]).

179. See Lewis, *Freedom and Tradition*, 163–65.

180. Neuhouser, in this vein, reduces Hegel's notion of objective freedom entirely to the promotion of subjective potentialities. As he sees it, objective freedom consists of three things: 1) it forms subjects; 2) it enables them to exercise their freedom; and 3) it allows them to approve of and consent to the laws they obey. See *Actualizing Freedom*, 226–27.

181. To say it once again, "liberal" here does not mean "left-wing," but rather "classical liberal"—many of what we would categorize as "liberal interpretations of Hegel" would generally be considered politically conservative.

mutually exclusive, for spirit is either essentially individual or essentially social. (It is important to note that the second alternative does not exclude individuality in principle, but simply insists that it finds itself concretely only in social form.) To attempt to hold both by affirming the individual as having his essential being in himself *and also* making himself social by relating as an individual to others is an illusion, and does not become more real no matter how many people share it. Hegel was justly contemptuous of the merely additive "and also" in philosophical thinking. This illusion collapses the difference between the state and civil society and reduces what ought to be the communal substance of the state to the mere sentiment of "belonging," which is diabolical, in the end, because it substitutes satisfaction with the mere *feeling* of satisfaction, and recasts reciprocal instrumentalization as cooperation toward the common good.

A much more promising response to the specter of the totalitarian state—because evidently more faithful to Hegel's thought—is to emphasize that the state represents the end, not of spirit simply, but of *objective* spirit, which as such remains subordinate to the expressions of absolute spirit in art, religion, and philosophy. We find variations of this response, for example, in the work of Avineri, Cassirer, and Peperzak.[182] Thus, if subjective spirit ends with the development of the will and cognition,[183] and if objective spirit develops Hegel's practical philosophy, then we can interpret absolute spirit as Hegel's *theoretical* philosophy. And Hegel seems clearly to hold that theory is more comprehensive than praxis.[184] In this case, absolute spirit would present a foundation *higher* than the state from the perspective of which the state can be judged. The state would, then, cease to be an "absolute and immovable end in itself," but would revolve around a more strictly unmoved mover, that is, it would be relativized to something greater than itself. Moreover, the transcendence of objective spirit would in principle allow an affirmation of the subjective sphere, in some respect, at least *beyond* the sphere of objectivity. We say "in principle" because it is an implication that Hegel himself, for reasons we will discuss in a moment, does not accept to the extent that he defines objective spirit as wholly comprehending within itself both objective free-

---

182. Avineri, *Hegel's Theory*, 132; Cassirer, *Myth of the State*, 274; Peperzak, *Modern Freedom*, 45. Cf., Houlgate, *Freedom, Truth, and History*, 125.

183. E (1830), §481 (GW.20.476).

184. The Owl of Minerva, although politically impotent, is capable of surveying the whole in a manner that exceeds the deeds of even the greatest of the world-historical individuals. There is, nevertheless, a persistent ambiguity in Hegel's view of the theory-praxis problem, which we will address shortly.

dom *and* subjective freedom. This definition implies that, however far the subject may develop as an individual, he will never in reality transgress the boundaries of objectivity.

Nevertheless, the principle is presented here, which would allow the subjective and the objective both to be united *and* genuinely distinguished, genuinely *to exceed one another*, without for all that falling apart because in their reciprocal transcendence they would be comprehended by what transcends them both. In this case, the unity is not, as it were, provided by one of the poles in the relation, but rather by that which lies above both poles together, which is precisely what it means to be *absolute* spirit. We will not, in the end, avoid the problem of the totalitarian state by "pulling back" from the state and thereby emptying freedom of the very substance it is Hegel's great achievement to have won for it, but only by "going beyond" the state. This means that we cannot attenuate the metaphysical element in his thought without deleterious consequences, and so we ought instead to embrace it, literally, "absolutely."

As promising as this response would appear to be, however, it sets into relief what can only be called a contradiction in Hegel's philosophy—and, since we are talking about Hegel, we must hasten to add, a contradiction in the "bad" sense, which is not a sign of life, but of inadequate basic assumptions.[185] The terms Hegel sets, in other words, produce the contradiction but do not resolve it. To formulate the contradiction in a succinct manner: while Hegel presents objective spirit as a stage toward absolute spirit, his characterization of spirit entails the definitive subordination of the latter to the former. Let us look at this problem more closely. Though certain passages in the system seem to open up the objective realm to a further explication of spirit,[186] the ways in which he closes off this possible openness are decisive and so undermine whatever significance they may

185. Alfredo Ferrarin has noted the same problem: *Hegel and Aristotle*, 367, though he argues on behalf of right and morality for the relativization of the state rather than the affirmation of religion over politics, as we are proposing.

186. So, for example, at the end of the part on subjective spirit in the *Encyclopedia*, he explains that the notion of freedom he introduced is "intended to develop into an objective phase, into legal, moral, religious, and no less into scientific actuality," E (1830), §482A (GW.20.477). Even this passage, however, is ambiguous. While it suggests that freedom would have an actuality *beyond* the political, in the sense that it would eventually have both a religious and a "scientific," i.e., philosophical, actuality, all of these at the same time seem to lie within the "objective realm." This is expressed not only in the fact that everything in this phrase following "objective realm" appears to represent its explication, but also that legal and moral actuality represent the first two parts of PR, which would identify religious and philosophical actuality simply with *Sittlichkeit*.

appear to have. In the first place, Hegel affirms freedom as the substance of spirit and the final goal that it pursues through all the pathways of history. And Hegel also makes objective spirit the essential reality of freedom.[187] This would seem to make objective spirit the *ne plus ultra* of spirit, so that any movement beyond this sphere would have to be driven by something other than spirit. But, for Hegel, there *is* nothing higher than spirit, which means that any such movement would ultimately turn out to be irrational and unjustified. It is interesting to note that freedom is both the essence of spirit *and* of the will, and that Hegel calls, not knowledge, but freedom, i.e., the specifically *practical* realization of spirit in the objective realm, the ultimate end of the history of spirit.[188] There is in Hegel a clear tendency to absolutize practical philosophy. In this respect, Marx does not flip Hegel's dialectic over and put its feet on the ground,[189] but simply picks up just where Hegel left off.

Perhaps even more decisive is Hegel's particular interpretation of actuality, which leads him relentlessly to purge the real of anything that remains implicit or transcendent, as an empty and therefore meaningless abstraction. In this respect, Hegel's philosophy represents a paradigm of what Stanley Rosen has called "the dream of Enlightenment, or full wakefulness."[190] For Hegel, a concept remains abstract precisely to the extent that it does not expose itself to the light of day, does not achieve finite, real determination, does not unfold itself and so make itself objective. Perfect concreteness in this case means *exhaustive* determination. An actualized concept therefore has nothing left within itself to show; there is nothing more, if we can put it this way, *to give*. It is not an accident that

---

187. Under the assumption that freedom, for Hegel, is self-determination and so the spirit's capacity to internalize what is other, Will Dudley explains that art, religion, and philosophy represent, for Hegel, the fullest achievement of freedom—but does not explain why there is so little textual support for this apparently self-evident interpretation. Dudley misses this tension because he fails to see the essential connection in Hegel between freedom and *actuality*, which is what roots freedom so fundamentally in objectivity. Interestingly, when Dudley explains why philosophy represents the fulfillment of freedom, it ends up being because philosophy "has an indispensable role to play in guiding the realization of freedom in the social and political world," *Hegel, Nietzsche, and Philosophy*, 117.

188. It is most revealing that Hegel concludes his system with Aristotle's *noēsis noēseōs* as the absolute, but only after reinterpreting its perfect *energeia* in the practical terms of history (see Ferrarin, *Hegel and Aristotle*, 368–69).

189. See the 1873 *Afterword* to the second German edition of *Das Kapital*.

190. Rosen, *The Limits of Analysis*, xv. Charles Taylor speaks of Hegel's aspiration toward the "final victory of conceptual clarity," *Hegel and the Modern World*, 166.

Hegel—in sharp contrast to the Christian tradition on this point[191]—takes the fact that God has revealed himself to mean that *there is no longer any mystery*.[192] To use William Desmond's fecund image, Hegel thus exhausts "the reserves of God."[193] It is true that Hegel affirmed, not the replacement of indeterminacy by determination or of possibility by actuality, but rather their perfect simultaneity.[194] But for Hegel this simultaneity can be nothing other than perfect identity, which means that they signify one and the same thing, only from a different perspective, or in other words it is what the scholastics would have called a *distinctio raionalis* rather than a *distinctio realis*. But if there is no real distinction between possibility and actuality, it means that possibility has no real, i.e., ontological, significance in itself that has not already been objectively realized. Indeed, even history presents nothing genuinely new: it is not, strictly speaking, a progressive unfolding of the meaning of spirit, as Hegelians often describe it, but rather the progressive dispelling of an illusion regarding what has already *actually* been accomplished.[195] Hegel notoriously insisted, in the

---

191. Gregory of Nyssa, for example, shows in his *Life of Moses* that there is no opposition between the closure of true knowledge given in revelation and the openness of the greater mystery of God. To the contrary, they imply one another directly, so that one's desire for the ever greater God increases in tandem with one's sure grasp of God, and vice versa. For Gregory, this constant increase never comes to an end; it is the essence of eternal life: "This truly is the vision of God: never to be satisfied in the desire to see him": *Life of Moses*. Because of his conception of actuality, Hegel would be compelled to think of eternal life as endless boredom.

192. See our mention of this point in the previous chapter: LPR, 184 (fn 85) (V.3.92fn), and also 332 (V.3.234).

193. Desmond, *Hegel's God*, 187–208.

194. John F. Hoffmeyer makes a case for the non-subordination of possibility to actuality: "The possible is actual, but not by being subsumed under actuality. Possibility is not merely deficient actuality or would-be actuality that is not yet actualized. Just as there is an actualizing of possibility, there is also a 'possibilizing' of actuality," *The Advent of Freedom*, 68. On the other hand, Hoffmeyer concedes that Hegel's *vocabulary* suggests the opposite; that is, Hegel explicitly describes possibility as a deficiency (ibid., 75). Hoffmeyer is seeking, here, to show that, by virtue of his understanding of eternity, things do not have a fixed meaning that persists through time, but that future contingencies can *recast*, retroactively, the meaning of essences. While Hoffmeyer is correct about this, he does not reckon with the more fundamental exclusion of novelty in Hegel: for him, there is a sense in which history has always-already been accomplished, so that temporal novelty is always ultimately an illusion. The key is the question whether Hegel would acknowledge that *implicit indeterminacy* is a perfection *as such*, and it is quite clear that he does not: see, e.g., E (1830), §140Z (JA.8.316).

195. E (1830), §212Z (JA.8.422). This does not mean that we do not experience genuine contingency or novelty in the living out of history, but only that the novelty *as such* has no ultimate significance.

Phenomenology, that philosophy, as *love* of wisdom, needs to be superseded by philosophy as *Wissenschaft*, since it is irrational, he says, to make something incomplete an ideal.[196] The point, then, is not wisdom as pursued, but wisdom as attained, or in other words, as fully actualized, so that there is in truth nothing left to pursue. And where is wisdom actualized? Only in the state. Let us note that what Hegel seeks to "eliminate from the equation," so to speak, is love, the very thing we noted at the end of chapter 4 as Schelling's deepest insight into the integration of freedom and form. What this implies, then, is that spirit cannot but reach its final end in the objective realm, which culminates in the state.

What does Hegel's notion of actuality, as we have interpreted it, imply for absolute spirit? In the present context, we can respond only briefly to this question, with a view to our general concerns. The final stage of Hegel's philosophy is comprised of three parts, art, religion, and philosophy, which are absolute insofar as they present truth according to various modes, in the form of the sensuous, in the form of imaginative representation, and in the form of knowledge, respectively. For reasons that we cannot develop at any length here, but clearly have some connection with the criticism we are making, the sphere of art seems to be only ambiguously absolute in Hegel's thought.[197] In Hegel's view, the perfect unity and difference that spirit represents above all in its absolute form can exist in matter—which, after all, is for Hegel pure externality as such and so incapable of real unity—in only a wholly implicit, and so abstract, manner. Even if one tries to explain away his famous observation that the age of art has passed,[198] it is worth noting that, not only does he tend to interpret art so much in religious terms that he is able to include it in some contexts for all intents and purposes as part of religion, so that only religion and philosophy stand at the level of absolute spirit in the *Phenomenology*, but in the final paragraph of the PR, which marks the transition to absolute spirit, Hegel does not in fact mention art, but only religion and *Wissen-*

---

196. Phen, 3 (GW.9.11).

197. William Desmond acknowledges the ambiguity, but argues in the end for the abiding absoluteness of art in Hegel even in its *essentially* religious character: see *Art and the Absolute*, esp. chapter 3, 35–56. Desmond argues that the abiding absoluteness of art turns on the fact that the intrinsically "open" wholeness of art is different from the "closed" totality that is erroneously ascribed to Hegel. While we do not deny the importance of this difference, our argument is that it remains difficult to sustain it given Hegel's interpretation of the actuality of spirit. Desmond has become much less willing to defend the notion of an abiding "transcendence" in Hegel in his latest book on the subject: see *Hegel's God*, esp. the preface.

198. See the discussion of the "death of art" in Curtis Carter, "A Re-examination."

The Perfection of Freedom

schaft, i.e., philosophy.[199] In other words, given Hegel's view of actuality as explicitation, art taken in itself (rather than as an expression of religion) necessarily has a "twilight" status.

As for philosophy, Hegel describes it here, in the last sentence of PR, as grasping the truth that remains identical in its unfolding in "the *state*, in *nature*, and in the *ideal world*,"[200] referring of course to the three parts of his system (and, incidentally, allowing "state" to stand for spirit). Our question in this context is the following: in what sense does this grasp of the identity of the three spheres allow philosophy to transcend the state? Hegel offers an answer that differs radically from any that would have been given in the philosophical tradition that preceded him: not only does philosophy *not* transcend the state, but in fact the practice of philosophy as Hegel describes it immerses one all the more completely in the state. Indeed, the point of this final section of the PR is to present the state as overcoming the division—which Rousseau attributes to Christianity, but was indeed present already in Plato and Aristotle—between this world (i.e., the "ordinary realm") and the beyond, precisely by eliminating the "otherworldliness" (i.e., the transcendent character) of truth. The state is *for this reason* the objectivity of spirit, and philosophy as absolute spirit does not in any sense recover a transcendence of truth over the state, but simply grasps for itself the truth that *is* the state, insofar as it sees the state as the culmination of the process of actualization that occurs through the logic and the realm of nature. People have often remarked on the melancholic resignation, the impotence of philosophy's "gray on gray," which allows it to hover over the world with its great watchful eyes after the time of activity has passed, but not to live *in* it by day specifically *qua* philosophy. Thus, while Aristotle recognized the contemplative, or theoretical dimension, of philosophy as introducing a supra-human tension into the "immanent" sphere of politics, for Hegel, philosophy amounts in the end to the perfect unfolding of self-consciousness by which the individual grasps his membership to the state as his absolute and unsurpassable truth, an unfolding in and through which the state finds its own most complete actualization. The point of philosophy, in the end, is ultimately ... patriotism.

The objection that the philosopher's devotion is not to any particular state, but rather to the ideal essence realized in the particular state, may help us to avoid an irrational conservatism such as van Haller's, but it does not resolve the problem in principle, since it still subordinates philosophy

---

199. PR, §360 (GW.14-1.281).
200. Ibid., §310 (GW.14-1.282).

to objective spirit. For Plato, by contrast, even the ideal city laid up in heaven, which is ideal precisely because it is ruled by the philosopher, remains one that the philosopher is *compelled* to rule, in some sense contrary to his natural inclination. Because Hegel rejects transcendence as necessarily abstract, absolute spirit as philosophy collapses back either into mere objectivity (the institutionalized state) or mere subjectivity (the purely inward grasp of and assent to that objectivity).

We have discussed art and philosophy; there remains only religion. As is well known, Hegel ultimately subordinates religion to philosophy since it represents for him a "lower-order" form of the same absolute content, namely, a form that retains a certain degree of otherness insofar as "*Vorstellung*" does not yet imply the total transparency that knowledge does. But we wish to propose that it is precisely this "residue" of otherness that offers the possibility of resolving the contradiction into which Hegel appears to fall here, the possibility of transcending objective spirit. It is interesting to note that the only thing Hegel discusses in the PR that would seem to represent a genuine challenge to the absolute substantiality of the state is the *church*. It is true that, in a footnote, Hegel maintains that things like art and *Wissenschaft* are also distinct from the state to the extent that they, like religion in the church, have an external existence [*Dasein*] of their own,[201] and in fact observes that if the church claims the spiritual as its property, "*science* and cognition in general are also represented in this province and, like a Church, develop into a totality with its own distinct principle which may consider itself as occupying the same position as the Church, but with even greater justification."[202] But in fact science, for Hegel, turns out to converge with the state precisely to the extent that it is true (i.e., truly rational) so that, as he explains, to the extent that it resists the state it must be seen as resisting its own truth and falling back instead

---

201. Ibid., §270Afn. (GW.14-1.214fn.). Hegel says there is no room to develop this point, and insists that, nevertheless, the principles of the state would continue to apply even to these relative communities.

202. Ibid., §270A (GW.14-1.219). Hegel says that this would allow science an even greater claim to independence from the state than the church has. However, he does not say this in order to argue for the independence of science, but rather to undermine the church's claim. This is evident because of the fact that he does not elaborate what that independence might mean, he argues in general in his treatment of the state against any principles of independence over against its substantiality, and, later in this remark, as we indicate above, he reduces science in its truth to the state, so that anything in science that resists this reduction resists in fact science's own truth.

The Perfection of Freedom

into mere *subjective opinion*.[203] In this case, the actualization of philosophy is in the end nothing other than the state.

But religion has its actualization in something that Hegel recognizes, so to speak, as difficult for the state to digest. George Kelly has claimed that the question of the relationship between church and state is the "strategic hinge" of the PR.[204] The reason for this is that the point of objective spirit as a whole is to develop a notion of the state as absolute substance, and there is nothing that more directly challenges this absolute status than the existence of the church. We wish to suggest that, because religion represents a kind of non-reducible otherness in its form, it, more than philosophy, stands as the paradigm of absolute spirit to the extent that absolute spirit ought to be defined as non-reducibly other with respect to both subjective and objective spirit.[205] The relevance of absolute spirit for objective spirit thus comes to expression most directly in the church-state relation. This means, finally, that if the reality of absolute spirit is the way to avoid the either-or of the totalitarian state and the formalistic freedom of liberalism, then the key issue for the integration of freedom and form in general is how to understand the relationship between church and state so as to do justice to both. Thus, the theme that occupied Hegel when he began his philosophical writing, namely, the relationship between the religious and the political order, remains the most important question for him at the end—even if it is no longer in the form that he posed, but in a form that *we* are now as it were going to put to *him*.

Hegel's goal in the long remark on the problem of the church-state relation, §270A, is to articulate that relation in such a way that the state retains its absoluteness. To be able to do so, Hegel insists, requires a proper concept of religion, which for him is given only in Protestant Christianity, ultimately because, for him, this is the religion of freedom.[206] One's

---

203. PR, §270A (GW.14-1.214–16). Hegel refers in this context to his discussion of the essentially *subjective* form of consciousness in morality, in the long remark to §140.

204. See Kelly, *Hegel's Retreat from Eleusis*, 120.

205. Hegel in fact himself says that the "supreme sphere" of absolute spirit may be "generally designated," not as philosophy or science, but as *religion*: E (1830), §554 (GW.20.542).

206. Boyle observes that this adherence to a particular religious tradition—specifically, that of Lutheranism—undermines Hegel's attempt to claim for his political philosophy a universality based on reason: Boyle, *Who Are We Now?*, 168. While there is certainly a profound truth in it, Boyle's observation presupposes an opposition between rational universality and religious particularity, which Hegel of course rejects. A criticism of Hegel on this point would require criticism specifically of Lutheranism's conception of basic realities (God, the world, and the self). Boyle gestures in this

politics, he claims, will only ever be as good as one's concept of God.[207] Protestantism has a privileged status for Hegel because in Protestantism, as Hegel understands it, God is not an unknown, abstract "beyond," but rather *essentially* reveals himself, which means becomes wholly actual. Actuality, however, is real, i.e., objective, determination. It follows that God, properly understood, communicates himself, in one respect, wholly into the form of knowledge, and in another respect, wholly into the form of ethical life. This concept of God allows us to affirm both the unity *and* the difference between religion, philosophy, and the state. For Hegel, they all have essentially the same content—this is their unity—but they have that content according to different forms: the state is the whole as objective totality, philosophy is the whole in thought, and religion is the whole in feeling.

It is this conception of their relations that allows him to interpret what he calls a common opinion, namely, that the state ought to be founded on religion. For Hegel, this cannot mean that the state is dependent on something higher than itself, because, insofar as the state is actualized rationality, this would make it depend on the unstable, irrational chaos of subjective feeling. Such a conception would assume for Hegel an abstract notion of God, because it does not allow God to be fully actualized or disclosed. If, by contrast, we recognize that religion develops by its own nature into science we will likewise see that it unfolds naturally into the reality of the state. In other words, Hegel says that religion is the foundation, but "it is at the same time only a *foundation*," which means its purpose is to support what is founded upon it. In this respect, religion proves to be the inward "feeling, representational thought, and faith" ultimately that the state is an "earthly divinity," i.e., the "spirit which is present in the world," and thus, Hegel claims that "[i]t is within this relationship [to religion] that the state, laws, and duties all receive their highest endorsement as far as the consciousness is concerned, and becomes supremely binding upon it, for even the state, laws, and duties are in their actuality something determinate which passes over into the higher sphere as that in which its foundation lies."[208]

Notice, the transition from objective spirit to absolute spirit, which one might have expected to be a movement toward "what lies above," as it

---

direction: "It is a Lutheran vision, and the self, and so the state, which it envisages is too enclosed and too solitary."

207. "A people that has a bad concept of God has also a bad state, bad government, and bad laws" (LPR, 452) (V.3.340).

208. PR, §270A (GW.14-1.214).

were, is in reality toward "what lies below." What prevents the affirmation that the state is founded in religion from degenerating into what Hegel calls fanaticism is the subordination of feeling to reason, or in other words, a recognition that the subjective sphere of religion does not possess its truth except in the reality of ethical life: "The truth, however—as opposed to this [pseudo-religious] truth which veils itself in the subjectivity of feeling and representational thinking—is the momentous transition of the inner to the outer, that incorporation [*Einbildung*] of reason into reality which the whole of world history has worked to achieve."[209] Protestantism is the *perfect* religion in this regard because "Protestantism requires that human beings should believe only what they know."[210] In this case, we do not absolutize feeling and faith, but may nevertheless retain them with respect to what reason grasps explicitly *as* a kind of subjective adherence or assent; if religion is the belief that the state has a divine foundation, reason is the knowledge both *that* and *how* this is the case; it is the articulation of what is implicit in religion, and it is ordered, with religion, to actualization "in the world."

Hegel does not mean, by this, that religion does not have any "expression of its own" in the world apart from the state, but only that this expression, precisely to the extent that it enters into the sphere of objectivity, must take the substantiality of the state as its measure. There will thus be religious communities that engage in distinctive public acts, possess property, and profess their own doctrines. If, in all of this, religion does indeed accept the state's measure, religious practice ought not only to be *permitted* by the state, but actively encouraged and supported, and indeed even required (so long as no *particular* practice is obliged), because "religion is that moment which integrates the state at the deepest level of the disposition [of its citizens]."[211] So we can acknowledge that Hegel does allow religion to have a "being in and for itself," which for that reason places it beyond the sphere of the state: "When the content which has being in and for itself appears in the shape of religion as a particular content, as the doctrines peculiar to the Church as a religious community, they remain outside the domain of the state."[212] It would seem here that Hegel is indeed affirming the transcendence of religion with respect to the state, but we must be clear about what he means. The church lies legitimately

---

209. Ibid. (GW.14-1.215).
210. LPR, 456 (V.3.344).
211. PR, §270A (GW.14-1.216).
212. Ibid. (GW.14-1.220).

outside of the state in its objective being only insofar as that being concerns its *particularity*, and, as we have seen, what defines the particularity of religion is its subjective form (feeling, *Vorstellung*, faith, and so forth). In other words, religion is allowed to be actual only as the objectification of subjectivity *as* subjectivity, which means only in a form analogous to civil society (meaning the universal is subordinate to particularity) and specifically *not* in a truly substantial form. And just as the state comprehends wholly within itself the relative ethical wholes of the corporations, so too it comprehends religion within itself. Religion either remains purely inward (as a devotion that strengthens the absolute status of the state) or it is actualized in a particularized form already contained by the universality of the state; it is thus either merely subjective spirit or merely objective spirit, but no longer absolute.

We may thus understand why Hegel is deeply critical of the actualization of religion one finds in Catholicism.[213] The problem he sees in Catholicism is not only that it understands the church as a subject/substance existing in and for itself and having a real authority other than the political sovereign, but also more subtly that it institutionalizes the "abstraction" of transcendence in the vows of chastity, poverty, and obedience, which represent for Hegel precise *substitutes* for the actuality of spirit in *Sittlichkeit*: marriage, civil society, and the state.[214] For Hegel, there can be no objective authority—authority that pertains to matters other than those that are acknowledged as subjective and therefore as particular—that is separate from the authority of the state. The reason that Hegel claims the fragmentation of Christianity in the sixteenth century is a blessing is that it undermined the credibility of such an authority, and thereby, in his eyes, made the concrete realization of freedom possible. Hegel's ultimate purpose in rejecting the notion that the church should have a genuinely substantial

---

213. See Weil, *Hegel and the State*, 50–51fn12. Cf., Franco, *Hegel's Philosophy of Freedom*, 303. According to Bernard Bourgeois, Hegel became increasingly wary of what he took to be the inherent irrationality of Catholicism in the last years of his life; Catholicism, in his view, was simply incompatible with freedom: *La Pensée Politique de Hegel*, 141–45. Our argument, here, is that Hegel's hostility toward Catholicism is a symptom of his ultimate failure to affirm genuine otherness in his understanding of freedom.

214. Hegel, "The Relationship of Religion to the State According to the Lectures of 1831," in LPR, 454–56 (V.3.342–43). Hegel observes that, "In this way [i.e., in the monastic vows] a religious ideal is set up, a heaven on earth, i.e., the abstraction of spirit over against the substantial [world] of actuality; renunciation of actuality is the basic vocation that emerges, and with it conflict and flight. Something else that is supposed to be more exalted is set in opposition to the substantial foundation, to what is genuine."

unity in and for itself is that it would effectively divide up the realm of actuality into two separate spheres; in this case, that of the church would be occupied with the (infinite) world beyond, and that of the state with the (finite) world below. The problem here is that *Sittlichkeit*, and therefore freedom in its concrete reality, would dissolve altogether: spirit would lose substance because it would have its real reality in the abstract heaven, and the substantiality of the state would be deprived of spirit, since it would devolve into the mere mechanical means of protecting individual property. If we recall our discussion at the beginning of the previous chapter, we see that this split would reduce spirit to a purely subjective form, since the "beyond" can exist in reality only in individual minds. In the end, then, Hegel rejects both an undifferentiated unity of church and state, which he says we find in the Oriental state, in which the ruler *is* God, since this form would lack all subjective freedom, and he rejects an "un-unified" separation, which would fragment subjective freedom and objective actuality. What is left is the unity in difference of a religion that understands itself as the subjective *foundation* of the state, which thus represents in turn the church's objective *realization*.

But although this way of conceiving the relation does indeed manage to preserve the substantiality of the state, it does so at the cost of generating the fundamental contradiction we mentioned above. By making the state the realization of religion, Hegel *absolutizes the objective instead of absolutizing the absolute*. Or more precisely by resolving the tension between church and state on the side of the state rather than on the side of the church, and thus by failing to allow absolute spirit *to be actual precisely as absolute*, Hegel is forced to collapse absolute spirit back into objective spirit, on the one hand, or subjective spirit, on the other. The only way to resist such a collapse would be to resolve the tension between church and state on the side of the church, which would mean subordinating the state in some respect to the church.

What form this subordination would have to take is, of course, a delicate question, which we cannot address in any detail here, but we ought to point out at least that it may not take the form of what is generally understood as "theocracy": this would collapse absolute and objective spirit once again by merging religion and politics. Instead, the church would have to be present as a substantiality that comprehends the objective sphere (and the subjective sphere as well) without becoming itself simply a political entity. The key to a proper view of the church-state relation that protected the integrity of both the objective and the subjective dimensions of spirit would, in other words, accord the church an actuality that nevertheless remained "supra-political." As we have seen, Hegel rejected a subordination of the state to religion essentially for two reasons: it would seem to subordinate reason, on the one hand, to feeling and, on the other hand, to an extrinsic authority. But this rejection takes for granted the very collapse we are attempting to avoid, insofar as it assumes that religion belongs essentially to (merely subjective) feeling and that its objective actualization can occur only in a merely external form. The problem here becomes evident when we consider Hegel's portrayal of the "externalities" of Catholicism—the physical reality of the sacraments, for example, and the authoritative office of the clergy—as slavish. Hegel criticized the objection to law and authority in the political order as betraying a formalistic, and therefore subjectivistic, conception of freedom, but Hegel betrays just this conception of freedom in relation to absolute spirit, which means he ultimately has a subjectivistic conception of religion.

The heart of the problem seems to be the following: Hegel assumes that the "otherness" that is proper to the religious order is an essential imperfection, an obstacle to complete actualization, so that the explicit and self-conscious appropriation of that otherness represents *nothing but* a further advance. In other words, he affirms the goodness of otherness, but always as a function of the selfhood it serves to perfect rather than as a perfection in itself to which the self would remain in some respect subordinate. If we challenge this assumption, and affirm the preservation of otherness to be a distinct and non-reducible perfection in its own right (an affirmation that Schelling makes, for example, in his criticism of Fichte, as we saw in our third chapter), then religion would no longer be simply subordinated to philosophy, and so absolute spirit would no longer be subordinated to objective spirit.[215] But this means that philosophy would have to be subordinate to religion *in order to resist philosophy's subordination to the state*. Moreover, if absolute spirit has a genuine reality in itself, there is room for a substantial conception of *Sittlichkeit* that does not absorb the "absolute" reality of individuals into the whole. In this case, the spheres of objective and subjective spirit can reciprocally exceed one another in a non-dualistic way because they are embraced by a higher unity. In short, the transcendence of religion is necessary for a conception of freedom *as social form*, and a conception of social form that is genuinely *free*.

The affirmation of abiding otherness as a perfection, of course, would entail a sea-change in Hegel's philosophy more generally. Whether the change is so total as to require the outright rejection of Hegel's thought is

---

215. As we pointed out in footnote 205, Hegel proposes "religion" as the general name for the sphere of absolute spirit. See Wallace, *Reality, Freedom, and God*, 309.

debatable, but it would seem to represent an internal criticism of the sort we discussed in the beginning of our treatment of Hegel in the previous chapter: though it is a radical criticism, it is one that stems from a contradiction that arises from *within* his philosophy, rather than one that comes about from an external standpoint. Throughout our discussion of Hegel in these two chapters, we have attempted to give a generous as possible reading of the note of "otherness" that runs through his thought on spirit and freedom, but it should be clear—and has been to many commentators—that otherness has a sort of "precarious" status in Hegel. If absolute spirit is allowed to collapse in the way we have suggested, the ambiguity will tend to resolve itself in the direction of unilateral assimilation. If, by contrast, we re-weight this ultimate dimension, it would reinforce this note and liberate new dimensions of Hegel's thought. However that may be, the implications of this change for Hegel's basic notions open up well beyond the present context, and while we cannot follow them up, we will reflect on what it entails for the meaning of actuality in our concluding chapter, and close this one with a brief observation regarding the implications of this point for Hegel's concrete definition of freedom.

William Desmond has pointed out that, for all of Hegel's references to the other, he always makes these references from the perspective of the self. In other words, the other is always the other *of the self*.[216] But if spirit is absolute, it transcends both, which ought also to imply a reference to the self specifically from the perspective *of the other*. Robert Spaemann makes a pertinent observation in reflecting on the nature of personhood.[217] He recalls a bumper sticker he once saw, which read: "Remember your wife and drive safely!" This means, think not only of what your wife means to you, but of what you mean to your wife. In other words, it appeals to one's capacity to think of oneself as a part of the life of the other, rather than merely thinking of the other as a part of one's own life. This is a simple, ordinary act, but it reveals the extraordinary transcendence that spirit is capable of; a transcendence greater than Hegel generally allows. Nevertheless, it brings to even clearer expression what Hegel himself indicates is the essence of spirit: an "I" that is "We" and a "We" that is "I"—even if it does suggest a reformulation of his definition of freedom: freedom in its most concrete sense is not simply being at home with oneself *in* the other (*bei-sich-Sein-im-Anderen*), but also, more generously, being at home *with* the other (*bei-dem-Anderen-Sein*) and offering the other a home in oneself.

216. Desmond, *Hegel's God*, 4, 38.
217. Spaemann, "Wirklichkeit als Anthropomorphismus," 20.

7

A Dramatic Conclusion: Opening Up Actual Possibility

IN HIS CLASSIC STUDY on Hegel, Charles Taylor identified two trends in late modern German thought that arose in reaction to the Enlightenment.[1] The first he called "expressivism," which he described as the drive to see human life as a whole, a work of art, each aspect of which unfolded from a central core. This trend, he explained, sought among other things to recover the unity between body and soul, the real and the ideal, that the Enlightenment had fractured. The second was the emergence of a radical notion of freedom that soared sovereignly over the "mere" objectivity of the natural world. According to Taylor, there were some thinkers—especially Schelling and Hegel, but most successfully the latter—who attempted to bring these apparently opposed trends together in a synthesis.

Our study confirms Taylor's characterization of this synthesis, which we have expressed as the integration of freedom and form, but it also suggests a qualification of his formulation that has far reaching implications. While form includes "expressivism," it places the emphasis, not first on the act, but on the actuality. In other words, it makes primary the completed whole rather than any of the particular elements, such as the power to achieve it, even while it comprehends all of these. To speak of expressivism leads one to focus most basically on the subject that communicates itself, while the language of form highlights the encompassing order within

---

1. Taylor, *Hegel and Modern Society*, 1–14.

The Perfection of Freedom

which the subject acts.[2] Now, it is precisely the centrality of form that we have claimed is the genuine distinctiveness of the conceptions of freedom offered by Schiller, Schelling, and Hegel; it is what most decisively prevents the notion of freedom from collapsing into individual agency, what thus expands freedom beyond the constraints of mere subjectivity, and so what ought to make these Germans particularly attractive to an age that has grown increasingly dissatisfied with the conventional notion. Because of the complexity of these thinkers, it is good, here at the end, to retrace our itinerary in broad strokes before offering a concluding reflection on a central problem that emerged over its course.

The key to the enrichment of our understanding of freedom lies in the "breakthrough beyond subjectivity" that Hegel attributed to Schiller, for it is here that *substance* is given to freedom in its integration with form. If Kant restricted freedom from the phenomenal world because that world is subject to a mechanical determinism incompatible with it, Schiller described freedom precisely as *aesthetic*, which means as something that achieves itself phenomenally. On the other hand, this objective turn did not entail, for Schiller, a new naturalism; though freedom *appears* as beauty, it is not exhausted by the appearance, but remains transcendent. Schiller finds the paradigm of this paradox in the spirit of nobility: one subordinates oneself to others in one's outward manifestation—which Schiller interprets according to his own experience as the devotion of self-gift—but precisely in so doing one reveals one's sovereignty. Freedom is both in and over form. Schiller discovered an analogy of this paradox in what he called the "beautiful style" in prose: the determinative concept, and the necessity it entails, remains implicit within free expression. The more perfect it is in itself, the more present it is in the appearance, and *at the same time*, the more independent the appearance becomes from the concept.

The implication of this simultaneity is three-fold. First, we have a *direct* relationship between freedom and form, so that, because each implies the other, they increase in tandem. By virtue of this relationship, limitation becomes liberation, and the more completely I embrace my determination ("heautonomy"), the freer I am, just as the increase in freedom enables my self-limitation. Second, insofar as the perfection of one's self coincides with the subordination to appearance, which is, as it were, a "being-for-others," the freedom of the self is essentially tied to the liberation of the

---

2. As we pointed out in chapter 5, Taylor himself exhibits just this tendency in his contrast between absolute freedom and situated freedom (p. 286–87, fn. 143).

other. As Schiller put it, a noble soul by definition ennobles everyone, and indeed every*thing*, he comes in contact with, which is another way of saying he sets them free. Finally, because of the simultaneity of transcendence and immanence, perfect freedom means at the very same time a harmony between body and soul and an elevation of the soul, so to speak, above the body. In other words, a free person has both grace *and* dignity, and both are due to the very same cause. Far from opposing these features, Schiller is able to see them as flip sides, so to speak, of the very same coin, because of his rich notion of freedom. What most commentators on Schiller have taken to be a confusion is due, instead, to Schiller's offering a genuine alternative to our typical understanding of freedom.

But Schiller's integration of freedom and form is precarious. We described him as identifying freedom with form's reaching all the way to the center of one's being. This is possible only to the extent that nature is apt for form, or, to put it another way, is apt to receive freedom. Without this, freedom would not be able to manifest itself *in* appearance (which is how Schiller defined beauty), but only *through* appearance in a way that makes the appearance a merely extrinsic vehicle of expression. But this would mean that freedom never *really* appears. To sustain Schiller's "breakthrough beyond subjectivity" thus requires a view of nature other than that which is presented in the system of Newton's mechanics and Kant's appropriation of that system. Schiller's philosophical interests, and perhaps his philosophical talents, did not reach quite far enough to engage this task. There remains therefore, in the end, a tendency in him to make merely metaphorical what would otherwise be a genuine analogy to freedom in nature, and thus to render beauty superficial by definition. To the extent that this occurs, and his notion of freedom collapses back into the mere subjectivity from which he had, so to speak, liberated it, his notion likewise loses its essentially generous relatedness to the *other*. Although the drift of his thinking moves in a different direction, the danger of Schiller's conception is to degrade into a bourgeois aestheticism, the effete fragility of what Hegel, borrowing Schiller's own term, criticized as the "beautiful soul." Nobility, here, is replaced by nothing more than gentile manners.

One of the first tasks to which Schelling devotes himself in the service of philosophy, which he characterizes as having its beginning and end in freedom, is just what was lacking in Schiller, namely, a *philosophy of nature*. The breakthrough beyond subjectivity demands, as a complement, a reinterpretation of objectivity that brings to light its primordial relation and ultimate ordination to the subject. As we saw in chapter 3, Schelling engaged this reinterpretation as a systematic critique of the mechanism of modern physics, which marginalized the internal teleology of organism, and indeed transformed it into an accidental arrangement of what was inherently dead. For Schelling, the objective correlate of a philosophy of freedom is a recovery of the centrality of organism in the natural world, and the consequent relativizing of mechanics to this center. What is at stake here for Schelling, in other words, is not merely how we understand the natural world itself, but how we understand the whole human reality, as we saw in our discussion of Schelling's lectures on academic studies. A mechanistic physics entails an impoverishment of the spiritual/intellectual life of human beings, and therefore an impoverishment of the core of that life, namely, of freedom.

To accomplish his task involved understanding subjectivity and objectivity in terms of each other from the very beginning, without ever reducing either to the other. This entailed an appropriation of Spinoza's distinction between *natura naturans* and *natura naturata* in a fundamentally organic context that Schelling felt was missing in Spinoza. In Schelling's thought, these two principles became a spontaneous life principle (which he called at one point the "world soul") and its endlessly varied productions—"essence" (*Wesen*, which Schelling interpreted, before Heidegger, as a verb) and "form." At the peak of his insight into nature, Schelling affirmed a coincidence of these two aspects in the organism, in which a being's inner life and external expression are inseparable. Organic form is the physical expression of freedom. Thus understood, freedom in turn reveals itself to have an inherently objective dimension, which we see in the production of beauty and in the unconscious accomplishment of providential ends; that is, ends that benefit the whole beyond one's own subjectivity. But the success of his project was continually frustrated for two reasons. On the one hand, his desire to rescue the life of nature by "subjectifying" it in its depths paradoxically eclipsed the significance of objectivity as such, and so eclipsed precisely that which makes the real different from the ideal. On the other hand, this eclipse was itself due to his connecting of subjectivity and objectivity only through the unity of a higher indifference, which left the two essentially external to one another. As a result, while Schiller had substantialized freedom as "living form," Schelling was unable to avoid continually dissolving form *into* life.

As we then argued, the late positive philosophy in which his "protean" thinking culminated was not a simple break from his early thinking as many scholars assume but arose from his discovering a new path to resolve essentially the same problem, namely, a recovering of the significance of the real in the face of the ideal precisely as a way of giving genuine substance to the ideal. The real reveals its significance, for Schelling, in its resistance to the ideal, a resistance that produces the tension that he claimed gives life to personality. As Schelling saw it, a reduction of the real to the ideal at any level, however ultimate, would entail the dissolution of this life-giving tension, and so he endeavored to rethink God specifically as *person*, and thus as including tension within his unity. Schelling found an impetus for his conceptual interpretation of the *living* God above all in Christianity, and specifically in its doctrines of the Trinity and the salvation-historical incarnation, doctrines that he thus appropriated within the sphere of philosophy. But because he never overcame the extrinsicism in his attempt to integrate freedom and form, we argued that he ended up conceding an essentially possibilistic conception of freedom, equally capable of good and evil, order and disorder. Freedom, then, is redeemed, restored to order, not through an internal integration with form, but only through the post hoc advent of a *deus ex machina*.

Hegel followed a path that led in essentially the opposite direction from Schelling's, though he ended covering similar ground. In contrast to Schelling's reduction of freedom to possibility, he interpreted it, more than any other thinker in history, precisely as actuality. It is just this that is required, finally, to sustain Schiller's breakthrough. As actuality, and not just power to act, freedom in its wholeness includes a basic reference to the other: in Hegel's words, the most adequate definition of freedom is "being at home with oneself in the other." We argued in chapter 5 that an understanding of this view of freedom is necessary properly to interpret what Hegel meant by his notorious identification of the rational and real in the preface to the *Philosophy of Right*. Freedom *is* the actualization of spirit, the locus of which is the political order in history. In this case, we can no longer view the will, to which freedom belongs as its essence, simply as the faculty of an individual agent. Instead, individual ability comes to be seen as a constitutive element of will in its complete sense, which is a concrete, and thus objective, whole. In the introduction to the *Philosophy of Religion*, Hegel spells out his view of the will in terms of both form and content. Formally, the will has three moments, the indeterminate self, the determination of choice, and the identity of the two as a concrete infinity. But even this self-determination is still only the *abstract formal* sense of the will, though many people mistakenly assume it to be Hegel's definition of freedom. In fact, this formal sense itself requires content for its actualization, a content that he sketches broadly in the introduction and then through various levels of concreteness over the course of the rest of the book. It is thus not the case that Hegel articulates his notion of the will and freedom in the introduction and then in the body of the text discusses various applications of that freedom in the political order; rather, the book as a whole is a statement of what Hegel means by will, and therefore freedom.

The interpretation of freedom as actuality entails an identification of freedom, in the end, with *social form*. In chapter 6, we rooted Hegel's novel philosophy of the will more generally in his understanding of spirit specifically as manifestation. As we saw there, such an understanding, according to Hegel, requires an essentially trinitarian notion of spirit, in which the "'I' is 'We' and the 'We' is 'I.'" If Schiller's aesthetic form and Schelling's organic form were both constituted by a mutual dependence between parts and the whole, the social form, in Hegel, at its highest level consists of a perfect reciprocal inherence, so that the parts and whole ultimately become in a basic respect identical. For Hegel, only *Geist* is capable of such transparency. This social form—which he names *Sittlichkeit*, ethical life—is achieved above all in the moments of family, in which two human beings become one and transcend themselves in a third; in civil society, in which particularity is set loose and yet contained within a complex system of social interaction; and, finally, in the state, which unites the two moments in a concrete universal. Precisely because it brings together the most perfect human unity with the furthest extremes of individuality, the state represents for Hegel the most complete actualization of spirit and so the final realization of freedom.

While this conception provides an unprecedented substance to freedom, we argued that, for a number of reasons, Hegel interprets objectivity too exclusively in political terms, so that, in the end, he divests spirit of any *specifically* supra-political actuality. This becomes manifest most clearly, we suggested, in Hegel's radical subordination of the church to the state, which wholly subjectivizes absolute spirit as religion, and so eliminates in principle any substantial ground for the objective actuality of absolute spirit more generally. This is another way of saying it undermines a specifically absolute form of freedom that would transcend subjectivity and objectivity and so have "room" for them both. Thus, if Hegel restores the substance to freedom that Schelling lost, it is only ultimately by, we might say, removing freedom from substance. This leaves us with a dilemma, which we will reflect on as a final conclusion.

The dilemma can be most succinctly formulated in terms of the relationship between possibility and actuality. As we saw, Schelling ultimately interpreted freedom as the "capacity for good and evil," which makes *possibility* freedom's essential note. What is gained in this conception, among other things, is a ground for radical novelty and therefore radical otherness. The new interpretation that Schelling offers of freedom coincides with the development of his positive philosophy, at the center of which lies a God whom Schelling claims to be the first to interpret in a systematic, philosophical way as *personal*—which means, as *free*, as an ever new beginning. Even God, for Schelling, has a future, which means that divine eternity does not simply eclipse time. However disconcerting the claim may appear to be, the reason Schelling insists on it is evident: to have freedom is to stand before an order that can change by virtue of one's act, and so, to have a future. If God were not free, then there would be no such thing as freedom anywhere. It is significant that Schelling criticizes the traditional view of God as *actus purissimus*, and instead reconceives him precisely as a relationship of *Potencies*, which we may translate in the present context as "possibilities."[3] Now, the notion of novelty, and therefore possibility, is no doubt indispensable to a concept of freedom, but we saw in our criticism of Schelling what his conception entails: ultimately, it implies the destruction of form, and the restoration of it only as an absolutized dis-order. If we identify freedom with the "yet to be," it comes most immediately to expression in the negativity of the *not* yet, a negativity that has no room for the essential (*das* Wesen*tliche*) because it has no room for what "has been" (*gewesen sein*).[4] We might say that Schelling's view of freedom implies an openness that gapes so wide it cannot contain anything. Freedom interpreted primarily as possibility is thus devoid of content.

Hegel's philosophy of freedom responds perfectly to this problem, for it is so to speak all about the essential. As we have indicated, his interpretation of freedom as actuality, and so as an always already articulated whole, offers the enormous advantage of filling freedom with content,

3. "If God has his *prius* in *actus*, then he will have his divinity in potency, in that he is the *potentia universalis*, and as this is that which is above being, the *Lord* of being," GPP, 202 (W.6E.160).

4. The term Aristotle coined for what was later translated as *essentia*, namely, *to ti ēn einai* (literally, 'being what a thing was being'—the imperfect "*ēn*" indicating the past progressive), likewise has a direct reference to the past.

giving it substance, and so making it something genuinely meaning-full. As such, freedom for Hegel is not only compatible with order, but in fact it is in the end perfectly co-extensive with order. Order, for Hegel, is after all the order *of spirit*, and freedom is spirit's fullest actuality, its truth. Hegel's conception thus gets us beyond the dualism that haunts the modern mind, and continues to haunt Schelling in the end, namely, a dualism that thinks of order most essentially in mechanistic, deterministic, rationalistic terms, and so forces freedom to take a ghostly, unreal, shape, however contrary this may be to one's intentions. But if Hegel thus redeems Schelling's failure, he does so only by surrendering the very contribution Schelling made that we have called indispensable: Hegel's view eliminates all novelty in principle. Whatever *is* not already disappears for him into the im-potence of the "ought," which implies an order to be given merely in the *future*. But there is no future for Hegel in the strict sense. As we saw, history, for him, is not in any sense a movement into an unknown novelty, but rather the gradual illumination of our ignorance about what always already has been from the beginning. To achieve a *concrete* sense of freedom, Hegel *closes* the form of spirit, and in so doing shuts it off from anything truly new. It is interesting to note that Hegel subordinates the transcendence of the church to the actuality of the state, while Schelling, in perfect contrast, affirms the ultimate dissolution of the state into the church (though, revealingly, this absorption is deferred to the eschaton).[5] Both of these represent a failure to integrate freedom and form.

In its sharpest terms, our dilemma can be put thus: either we embrace a conception of freedom as possibility, and therefore novelty, and accept the disorder, emptiness, and irrationality it implies, or we conceive of freedom as *meaningful* actuality, and thereby lose transcendence, otherness, and therefore novelty.

As with most dilemmas, an adequate response requires challenging the meaning of the terms that produce it. As it turns out, Schiller's dramatic notion of form offers a way out of the problems presented by Schelling and Hegel that at the same time would allow us in principle to preserve the essential contribution that each makes. As we saw in our second chapter, Schiller has an essentially *analogous* sense of form. It is not only the logical concept of a thing, but also the inner principle that "overcomes" the logical concept. This, we recall, was the basis of his distinction between autonomy and heautonomy. In relation to our present dilemma, we may interpret this analogous concept as the ground of novelty, which is nevertheless not

---

5. See Schelling, *Phil of Rev*, 321.

irrational (i.e., contrary to the logical form) because it is always the novelty specifically *of* form.

Let us look at this point more closely, recalling what we said above. Something is beautiful, for Schiller, when it has expressed itself, that is, manifested its inner being, in an outward form, but in such a way that it is not *constrained* in that expression. A thing of beauty shows that it remains, so to speak, "more" than it actually is. There is in Schiller's conception, therefore, an implicit response to both Schelling and Hegel. For Schelling, there is invariably an *opposition* between a thing's potential and its actuality: if we use the terms of his philosophy of nature, the inner essence (the *natura naturans*) always remains above any particular accomplished form (*natura naturata*), which ends up making it a kind of blind force that looks back on form, so to speak, as something it has always already left behind. For Hegel, the outward expression is ultimately *identical* with the internal concept, so that potentiality is exhausted in that external form.[6] In this case, there is nothing "more" to being than what it has already given. Schiller's dramatic notion of form differs from both of these, insofar as he affirms a genuine *unity* between the inner being and the outward form, which nevertheless preserves an abiding difference—and this is the meaning of analogy. The "more" of a being, and therefore its "reserves" or potential, do not lie above and beyond, but rather precisely *within* its actuality. This is the very mystery of beauty as a specifically *objective* quality that Schelling sought to capture in the *Kalliasbriefe*.

There are many examples of this inwardly open form in Schiller's aesthetic writings; we will consider two of them that bear directly on the problem we have set into relief in Schelling and Hegel. First, as we saw in our initial chapter, Schiller presents poetry as an illustration of a *free form*. Why is it free? Not because the form is loose, or unfinished. Precisely to the contrary, such an "open-endedness" would represent for Schiller a lack of freedom. The freedom comes to expression, rather, in the *perfection*, the *completeness*, of the form. But it is just this completeness that liberates, so to speak, an infinite possibility of meaning. One never finishes interpreting a poem, not because one can always continue to manipulate it and make

---

6. It bears repeating here that this formulation of Schelling's and Hegel's position is an oversimplification. As we have suggested all along the way, the matter is essentially ambiguous in both cases; the formulation given here represents the direction in which the drift of these two philosophies tends to resolve the ambiguities by virtue of the logic of foundational assumptions. What we are proposing here is that, among other things, a retrieval of Schiller's original insight would allow us to resolve each in a more fruitful direction.

it say whatever one arbitrarily wishes, but because its perfection creates an inner source that is inexhaustible. The key to this particular conception of freedom, as we saw, is precisely that the concept is, in one respect, *not* explicit, but remains within, even while, in another respect, the outward expression, when perfectly achieved, is transparent to the concept, which makes it explicit indeed. Here, both Hegel's and Schelling's concerns are met: there is a unity between the inner and the outer, which is how Hegel defined actuality, but at the same time there remains, as Schelling required, an infinite potential for more.

We might sum up the integration of freedom and form that we have been seeking by borrowing a text that was loved by Schelling's and Hegel's old roommate and one of Schiller's young admirers and associates, who like Schiller felt caught in some sense between poetry and philosophy, namely, Hölderlin. The text is what is popularly known (erroneously as it turns out) as the *"Grabschrift"* of Ignatius of Loyola, and was used as the epigraph for Hölderlin's poetic novel, *Hyperion*: "*non coerceri maximo, contineri tamen a minimo, divinum est*" (unable to be circumscribed by what is greatest, and yet contained by what is smallest: this is divine)—or we might say, "*libertas est*" (this is freedom).

The second is what Schiller referred to as the "aesthetic state," and which he described—in terms Hegel himself often used—as a "filled infinity" in distinction from the "empty infinity" represented by sheer indeterminacy, i.e., the sheer potential to be determined. This "filled infinity" is the expression, he says, of an "inner abundance." As filled, it is in a sense wholly determined, but at the same time is not in the least limited by this determination. Again like Hegel, Schiller insists that beauty is infinite "not in the *exclusion of certain realities*, but in the *absolute inclusion of all realities*."[7] But Schiller differs from Hegel in interpreting this inclusion not as an actuality that has always-already been accomplished, but rather as a kind of inward, implicit completion, a "super-actuality," that comes to expression as a readiness for anything that may come, i.e., for any novelty. One who has been aesthetically educated, Schiller argued, is one who we might say is disposed to any particular possibility: he is equally ready for physical activity, for contemplative thought, for creative work, for a sublime moral deed, equally ready to enjoy and to sacrifice. Given this description, we may perhaps formulate the proper disposition of freedom, which is both open and closed, both determinate and determinable, both actual and full of possibility, and indeed both concrete (Hegel) and

---

7. Schiller, AEM, XVIII, 125 (SW.8.364).

indifferent (Schelling), thus by defining it as *perfect readiness*. As *perfect*, it is complete in itself, an end to be aimed at, an ideal, a place to rest; and as *readiness* it is at the same time ordered to what is "more," open to a future, poised in responsiveness to a genuine other.

To make this notion of freedom as perfect readiness concrete, let us rethink what Hegel presented as the paradigm of *Sittlichkeit*, namely, marriage. And let us do so all the while holding onto Schelling's characterization of love, which is a unity of two that preserves their uniqueness and individuality with respect to one another. Hegel's notion of marriage would seem to pose a threat to just this liberation of uniqueness precisely as a result of his particular conception of actuality. As he affirmed in his *Lectures on the Philosophy of Religion*, a revealed God no longer contains any mystery; by extension, we may say that, to the extent that a couple has become actual as an ethical whole, to the extent that they have thus fully disclosed themselves to one another in the consummation of the total self-gift in the vows, they would therefore have nothing more to reveal to one another. But this fails to do justice, at least to the best marriages, which as such most clearly represent the meaning of marriage. Marriage is not the end of personal disclosure, but rather provides in its completeness a space for the development of intimacy, for the mutual self-manifestation of one person to another over time and in principle without end. But this temporal unfolding is not simply the bad infinity of an open and so aimless possibility. In taking vows, the couple has already *implicitly* realized the whole. When one pledges oneself, one hands over not simply one's present being, but in the very same act one includes both one's past and one's future. The future is, so to speak, anticipated in advance and so taken into spirit and given form. But this embrace of the whole *a priori* does not replace the future; it does not eliminate the graduality of time. Instead, it is a pledge precisely to live out that future in all of its temporal *Unvordenklichkeit*. In this case, we have a filled infinity, a form that is closed, and indeed perfectly, exclusively closed, but which for that very reason is now "ready for anything." The American writer Wendell Berry is right to compare the form of marriage with poetic form: there is, indeed, a powerful analogy here.[8] Just as the closed form of poetry gives it an inexhaustible

---

8. See Berry, "Poetry and Marriage," 92–105. Berry here explains that what characterizes the forms of both poetry and marriage is, on the one hand, a restriction, and on the other hand, a new openness. This second "is an opening, a generosity, toward possibility. The forms acknowledge that good is possible; they hope for it, await it, and prepare its welcome—though they dare not *require* it. These two aspects are inseparable. To forsake the way is to forsake the possibility. To give up the form is to abandon the hope," 93.

wealth of meaning, a depth of possibility that would be lacking in simply the aimless jotting down of thoughts, so too the ethical form of marriage opens up an endless source of personal gift, an infinite potential of spirit. In this case, insofar as it represents a super-actuality that embraces but does not exhaust possibility, we may point to marriage once again as a paradigm of freedom.

It is perhaps not an accident that stories often end with a marriage, since this provides a specifically *dramatic* conclusion that serves to gather together the infinite opposition of personalities into a single form. The fact that those who marry in so many traditional fairy tales disappear from the narrative into an implicit "happily ever after" perhaps betrays a sense deeply rooted in human culture that freedom and form belong together. Dostoevsky once observed that stories should *not* end this way, but should rather *begin* with marriage, because it is then that things become interesting and the real adventure starts. But, indeed, that may be just why it makes the perfect ending.

Bibliography

Works by Johann Christoph Friedrich von Schiller

German Edition:

Schiller, Johann Christoph Friedrich von. *Sämtliche Werke*. Edited by Hans-Günther Thalheimer et al. 10 vols. Berlin: Aufbau, 2005.

English Translations Used:

Schiller, Johann Christoph Friedrich von. *Essays*. Edited by Walter Hinderer and Daniel O. Dahlstrom. New York: Continuum, 2001.
———. "'Kallias' or Concerning Beauty: Letters to Gottfried Körner." In *Classic and Romantic German Aesthetics*, Edited by J. M. Bernstein, 145–83. Cambridge: Cambridge University Press, 2003.
———. *On the Aesthetic Education of Man: In a Series of Letters*. Edited by Elizabeth Wilkinson and L. A. Willhoughby. Oxford: Clarendon, 1982.
———. *On the Aesthetic Education of Man*. Edited by Reginald Snell. Mineola, NY: Dover, 2004.
———. *Schiller's "On Grace and Dignity" in Its Cultural Context*. Edited by Jane Curran and Christophe Fricker. Rochester, NY: Camden House, 2005.

Works by Friedrich Wilhelm Joseph von Schelling

German Editions:

Schelling, Friedrich Wilhelm Joseph von. *Grundlegung der positiven Philosophie*. Edited by Horst Fuhrmans. Torino: Bottega d'Erasmo, 1972.
———. *Historisch-Kritische Ausgabe*. Im Auftrag der Schelling-Kommission der Bayerischen Akademie der Wissenschaften begründet von Hans Michael Baumgartner†, Wilhelm G. Jacobs, Jörg Jantzen, Hermann Krings†, Francesco Moiso† und Hermann Zeltner†. Edited by Jörg Jantzen et al., 40 volumes (planned). Stuttgart: Frommann-Holzboog, 1976–.
———. *Philosophie der Offenbarung (Paulus-Nachschrift)*. Edited by Manfred Frank. 3rd ed. Frankfurt: Suhrkamp, 1995.

Bibliography

———. *Philosophische Untersuchungen über das Wesen der menschlichen Freiheit und die damit zusammenhängended Gegenstände*. Edited by Thomas Buchheim. Hamburg: Meiner, 1997.

———. *Sämmtliche Werke*. Nach der Original Ausgabe in neuer Anordnung [in a new arrangement]. 6 vols. and 6 supplementary vols. Edited by Manfred Schroter. Munich: Beck and Oldenbourg, 1927–59.

———. *Der System der Weltalter: Münchener Vorlesung 1827/28 in einer Nachschrift von Ernst von Lasaulx*. Edited by Siegbert Peetz. Frankfurt am Main: Klostermann, 1991.

———. *"Timaeus" (1794)*. Edited by H. Buchner. Stuttgart-Bad Cannstatt: Frommann Holzboog, 1994.

English Translations Used:

Schelling, Friedrich Wilhelm Joseph von. *Ages of the World*. 1813 draft. Translated by Judith Norman. *The Abyss of Freedom: Ages of the World*. Ann Arbor: University of Michigan Press, 1997.

———. *Ages of the World*. 1815 draft. Translated and edited by Jason Wirth. Albany: SUNY Press, 2000.

———. *Bruno: or, On the Natural and Divine Principle of Things*. Translated and edited by Michael. G. Vater. Albany: SUNY Press, 1984.

———. "Concerning the Relation of the Plastic Arts to Nature." Translated by Michael Bullock. In *The True Voice of Feeling*, edited by Herbert Read, 321–64. New York: Pantheon, 1953.

———. *The Grounding of Positive Philosophy: The Berlin Lectures*. Translated by Bruce Mathews. Albany: SUNY Press, 2007.

———. *Historical-Critical Introduction to the Philosophy of Mythology*. Translated by Mason Richey and Markus Zisselberger. Albany: SUNY Press, 2007.

———. *Ideas on a Philosophy of Nature as an Introduction to the Study of This Science, 1803*. Translated by Priscilla Hayden-Roy. In *The Philosophy of German Idealism*, edited by Ernst Behler, 167–202. New York: Continuum, 1987.

———. *On the History of Modern Philosophy*. Translated by Andrew Bowie. Cambridge: Cambridge University Press, 1994.

———. *The Philosophy of Art*. Translated and edited by Douglas W. Stott. Minneapolis: University of Minnesota Press, 1988.

———. "Schelling's Aphorisms of 1805." Translated by Michael G. Vater. *Idealistic Studies* 14 (1984) 237–58.

———. "Stuttgart Seminars (1810)." Translated by Thomas Pfau. In *Idealism and the Endgame of Theory: Three Essays by F. W. J. Schelling*, edited by Thomas Pfau, 195–268. Albany: SUNY Press, 1993.

———. "System of Philosophy in General and of the Philosophy of Nature in Particular (1804)." Translated by Thomas Pfau. In *Idealism and the Endgame of Theory: Three Essays by F. W. J. Schelling*, edited by Thomas Pfau, 139–94. Albany: SUNY Press, 1993.

———. *System of Transcendental Idealism*. Translated by Peter Heath. Charlottesville: University of Virginia Press, 1978.

Bibliography

Works by Georg Wilhelm Friedrich Hegel

German Editions:

Hegel, Georg Wilhelm Friedrich. *Gesammelte Werke*. 31 planned vols. Edited by the Rheinisch-Westfälische Akademie der Wissenschaften. Hamburg: Meiner, 1968–.
———. *Grundlinien der Philosophie des Rechts oder Naturrecht und Staatswissenschaft im Grundrisse*. Edited by Hermann Klenner. Berlin: Akademie, 1981.
———. *Phänomenologie des Geistes*. Edited by Wolfgang Bonsiepen. Hamburg: Meiner, 1980.
———. *Sämtliche Werke: Jubiläumsausgabe*. 20 vols. Stuttgart: Frommann, 1927–40.
———. *Vorlesungen*. 17 vols. Hamburg: Meiner, 1983–2007.
———. *Vorlesungen über Rechtsphilosophie*. 4 vols. Edited by Ilting. Stuttgart: Frommann-Holzboog, 1973–74.

English Translations Used:

Hegel, Georg Wilhelm Friedrich. *The Difference between Fichte's and Schelling's System of Philosophy*. Translated by Walter Cerf and H. S. Harris. Albany, NY: SUNY Press, 1977.
———. *Elements of the Philosophy of Right*. Edited by Allen Wood. Translated by H. B. Nisbet. Cambridge: Cambridge University Press, 1991.
———. *The Encyclopedia Logic*. Translated by Theodore Geraets, W. A. Suchting, and H. S. Harris. Indianapolis, IN: Hackett, 1991.
———. *Hegel: The Letters*. Translated by Clark Butler and Christiane Seiler. Bloomington: Indiana University Press, 1984.
———. *Introduction to the Philosophy of History*. Translated by Leo Rauch. Indianapolis, IN: Hackett, 1988.
———. *Lectures on the History of Philosophy*. Translated by E. S. Haldane. 3 vols. Lincoln: University of Nebraska Press, 1995.
———. *Lectures on the Philosophy of Religion*. Edited by Peter Hodgson. 3 vols. Berkeley: University of California Press, 1996–98.
———. *Miscellaneous Writings of G. W. F. Hegel*. Edited by Jon Stewart. Evanston, IL: Northwestern University Press, 2002.
———. *On Art, Religion, and the History of Philosophy*. Edited by J. Glenn Gray. Indianapolis, IN: Hackett, 2004.
———. *On Christianity*. Translated by T. M. Knox. New York: Harper Torchbooks, 1961.
———. *The Phenomenology of Spirit*. Translated by A. V. Miller. Oxford: Oxford University Press, 1977.
———. *Philosophy of Mind*. Translated by William Wallace and A. V. Miller. Oxford: Oxford University Press, 1971.
———. *Philosophy of Nature*. Translated by A. V. Miller. Oxford: Oxford University Press, 2008.
———. *Political Writings*. Translated by H. B. Nisbet. Cambridge: Cambridge University Press, 1999.

Bibliography

———. *The Science of Logic*. Translated by A. V. Miller. Oxford: Oxford University Press, 1977.

Other works cited

Adler, Mortimer. *The Idea of Freedom: A Dialectical Examination of the Concept of Freedom*. Garden City, NY: Doubleday, 1958.
Adolphi, Rainer. "Warum ist überhaupt Zeit und nicht vielmehr ewiges Sein und Wahrheit? Schellings spekulative Theorie der Zeit und ihre antiken Bezüge— eine Skizze." In *Das antike Denken in der Philosophie Schellings*, edited by Rainer Adolphi and Jörg Jantzen, 355–95. Stuttgart: Frommann-Holzboog, 2004.
Aquinas, Thomas. *De ente et essentia*. In *Opuscula Philosophica*. Volume 1. Edited by R. Spiazzi. Turin and Rome: Editori di San Tommaso, 1979.
———. *Quaestiones disputatae de veritate*. Volume 22, parts 1–3 of *Sancti Thomae Aquinatis opera omnia*. Leonine Edition. Rome: Editori di San Tommaso, 1975–76.
———. *Summa theologiae*. Volumes 4–12 of *Sancti Thomae Aquinatis opera omnia*. Leonine Edition. Rome: Editori di San Tommaso, 1888–1906.
Aristotle. *The Basic Works of Aristotle*. Edited by Richard McKeon. New York: Modern Library, 2001.
Augustine. *The City of God against the Pagans*. Edited by R. W. Dyson. Cambridge: Cambridge University Press, 1998.
———. *The Enchiridion on Faith, Hope, and Love*. Translated by J. B. Shaw. Washington, DC: Regnery, 1961.
Avineri, Shlomo. *Hegel's Theory of the Modern State*. Cambridge: Cambridge University Press, 1972.
Bach, Thomas. *Biologie und Philosophie bei C. F. Kielmeyer und F. W. J. Schelling*. Stuttgart: Frommann-Holzboog, 2001.
Balthasar, Hans Urs von. *The Glory of the Lord*. Volume 5: *The Realm of Metaphysics in the Modern Age*. San Francisco: Ignatius, 1991.
Barnouw, Jeffrey. "'Freiheit zu geben durch Freiheit': Ästhetischer Zustand–Ästhetischer Staat." In *Friedrich Schiller: Kunst, Humanität und Politik in der späten Aufklärung*, edited by Wolfgang Willkowski, 138–61. Tübingen: Niemeyer, 1982.
Baum, Manfred. "Die Anfänge der Schellingian Naturphilosophie." In *Schelling: zwischen Fichte und Hegel*, edited by Christoph Asmuth et al., 95–112. Philadelphia: Grünner, 2000.
Baumgartner, H. M., and H. Korten. *Friedrich Wilhelm Joseph Schelling*. Munich: Beck, 1996.
Baxter, Anne Margaret. "The Beautiful Soul and the Autocratic Agent." *Journal of the History of Philosophy* 41.4 (2003) 493–514.
———. "Pleasure, Freedom, and Grace: Schiller's 'Completion' of Kant's Ethics." *Inquiry* 51.1 (2008) 1–15.
Beach, Edward. "The Later Schelling's Concept of Dialectical Method, in Contradistinction to Hegel's." *Owl of Minerva* 22.1 (1990) 35–54.
———. *The Potencies of God(s) Schelling's Philosophy of Mythology*. Albany: SUNY Press, 1994.
Beiser, Frederick. *The Fate of Reason: German Philosophy from Kant to Fichte*. Cambridge, MA: Harvard University Press, 1987.

———. "Hegel and the Problem of Metaphysics." In *The Cambridge Companion to Hegel*, edited by Frederick Beiser, 1–24. Cambridge: Cambridge University Press, 1993.
———. "Kant and *Naturphilosophie*." In *Kantian Legacy in 19th Century Science*, edited by Michael Friedmann and Alfred Nordmann, 7–26. Cambridge: MIT Press, 2006.
———. *Schiller as Philosopher: A Re-Examination*. Oxford: Clarendon, 2005.
———. "Schiller as Philosopher: A Reply to My Critics." *Inquiry* 51:1 (2008) 63–78.
Bensussan, Gérard. "La vie comme contradiction: de Hegel à Schelling." In *Das Leben denken: Hegel-Jahrbuch 2007*, 133–36. Berlin: Akademie, 2007.
Berger, Karl. *Die Entwicklung von Schillers Ästhetik*. Weimar: Böhlan, 1894.
Bernstein, J. M., ed. *Classic and Romantic German Aesthetics*. Cambridge: Cambridge University Press, 2003.
Berry, Wendell. "Poetry and Marriage." In *Standing by Words: Essays*, 92–105. Berkeley, CA: Counterpoint, 2005.
Bieler, Martin. *Freiheit als Gabe: Ein schöpfungstheologischer Entwurf*. Freiburg: Herder, 1991.
Bonsiepen, Wolfgang. *Die Begründung einer Naturphilosophie bei Kant, Schelling, Fries and Hegel*. Frankfurt am Main: Klostermann, 1997.
Borchmeyer, Dieter. "Rhetorische und ästhetische Revolutionsdialektik: Edmund Burke und Schiller." In *Die Weimar Klassik als historisches Ereignis und Herausforderung im Kulturgeschichtlichen Prozess*, edited by Karl Richter and Jörg Schönert, 56–80. Stuttgart: Metzler, 1983.
Bourgeois, Bernard. *La Pensée Politique de Hegel*. Paris: Presses Universitaires de France, 1969.
Bowie, Andrew. *Schelling and Modern European Philosophy*. London: Routledge, 1993.
Boyle, Nicholas. *Who Are We Now? Christian Humanism and the Global Market from Hegel to Heaney*. Notre Dame: University of Notre Dame Press, 1998.
Brito, Emilio. "La création chez Hegel et Schelling." *Revue Thomiste* 87.2 (1987) 260–79.
———. "Schelling et la Bonté de la Création." *Nouvelle Revue Theologique* 108 (1986) 499–516.
Brod, Harry. *Hegel's Philosophy of Politics: Idealism, Identity, and Modernity*. Boulder, CO: Westview, 1992.
Brown, Robert. *The Later Philosophy of Schelling*. Lewisburg, PA: Bucknell University Press, 1977.
Buchheim, Thomas. *Eins von Allem: Die Selbstbescheidung des Idealismus in Schellings Spätphilosophie*. Hamburg: Meiner, 1992.
———. "Grundlinien von Schellings Personbegriff." In *"Alle Persönlichkeit ruht auf einem dunkeln Grunde". Schellings Philosophie der Personalität*, edited by T. Buchheim and F. Hermanni, 11–34. Berlin: Akademie, 2004.
———. "Das 'objektive Denken' in Schellings *Naturphilosophie*." *Kant-Studien* 81 (1990) 321–38.
———. *Unser Verlangen nach Freiheit: Kein Traum, sondern Drama mit Zukunft*. Hamburg: Meiner, 2006.
———. "Zur Unterscheidung von negativer und positiver Philosophie beim späten Schelling." In *Berliner Schelling-Studien 2*, edited by E. Hahn, 125–45. Berlin: Total, 2001.
Buchheim, Thomas, and F. Hermanni, eds. *"Alle Persönlichkeit ruht auf einem dunkeln Grunde": Schellings Philosophie der Personalität*. Berlin: Akademie, 2004.

Bibliography

Burschell, Friedrich. *Friedrich Schiller in Selbstzeugnissen und Bilddokumenten.* Hamburg: Rowohlt Taschenbuch, 1958.

Burtt, E. A., ed. *The English Philosophers from Bacon to Mill.* New York: Modern Library, 1939.

———. *The Metaphysical Foundations of Modern Science.* Garden City, NJ: Doubleday, 1954.

Carrier, Martin. "Kants Theorie der Materie und ihre Wirkung auf die zeitgenössische Chemie." *Kant-Studien* 81 (1990) 170–210.

Carter, Curtis. *Art and Logic in Hegel's Philosophy.* Brighton: Harvester, 1980.

Cassirer, Ernst. *Gesammelte Werke.* Volume 7. Edited by Reinold Schmücker. Hamburg: Meiner, 1998.

———. *The Myth of the State.* New Haven, CT: Yale University Press, 1946.

Cervantes, Miguel de. *Don Quixote.* Translated by John Rutherford. New York: Penguin, 2003.

Constant, Benjamin. *Political Writings.* Translated and edited by Biancamaria Fontana. Cambridge: Cambridge University Press, 1988.

Courtine, Jean-François. "Temporalité et Révélation." In *Le Dernier Schelling: Raison et Positivité*, edited by Jean-François Courtine and Jean-François Marquet, 9–30. Paris: Vrin, 1994.

Curran, Jane. "Schiller's Essay 'Über Anmut und Würde' as Rhetorical Philosophy." In *Schiller's "On Grace and Dignity" in Its Cultural Context*, edited by Jane Curran and Christophe Fricker, 21–36. Rochester, NY: Camden House, 2005.

Danz, Christian. "Christologie als endliche Freiheit." In *Schelling: zwischen Fichte und Hegel*, edited by Christoph Asmuth et al., 265–86. Philadelphia: Grünner, 2000.

———. "Die Philosophie der Offenbarung." In *F. W. J. Schelling*, edited by Hans Jörg Sandkühler, 169–89. Stuttgart: Metzler, 1998.

Danzel, Theodor. "Schillers Briefwechsel mit Körner." *Wiener Jahrbücher der Literatur* 121 (1848) 1–25.

Derrida, Jacques. *The Gift of Death.* Chicago: University of Chicago Press, 1996.

Desmond, William. *Art and the Absolute: A Study of Hegel's Aesthetics.* Albany: SUNY Press, 1986.

———. *Hegel's God: A Counterfeit Double.* Burlington, VT: Ashgate, 2002.

Dionysius the Areopagite. *The Divine Names and the Mystical Theology.* Translated by C. E. Rolt. New York: Cossimo, 2007.

Douglas, Mary. *Natural Symbols: Explorations in Cosmology.* 3rd ed. London: Routledge, 2003.

Dudley, Will. *Hegel, Nietzsche, and Philosophy.* Cambridge: Cambridge University Press, 2002.

Eckermann, Johann Peter. *Gespräche mit Goethe.* Wiesbaden: Brockhaus, 1949.

Ehrhardt, Walter E. "Nur ein Schelling." *Studi Urbinati de storia, filosofia e letteratura* 51, new series B.1–2 (1977) 111–22.

Ellis, John M. *Schiller's Kalliasbriefe and the Study of His Aesthetic Theory.* The Hague: Mouton, 1969.

Esposito, Joseph. L. *Schelling's Idealism and the Philosophy of Nature.* Cranbury, NJ: Associated University Presses, 1977.

Ferrarin, Alfredo. *Hegel and Aristotle.* Cambridge: Cambridge University Press, 2001.

Findlay, John. *Hegel: A Re-Examination.* New York: Collier, 1962.

Fischer, Kuno. *Schiller als Philosoph.* Frankfurt am Main: Hermann, 1858.

Bibliography

Franco, Paul. *Hegel's Philosophy of Freedom*. New Haven, CT: Yale University Press, 2002.

Franz, M. *Schellings Tübinger Platon-Studien*. Göttingen: Vandenhoek and Ruprecht, 1996.

Freydberg, Bernard. *Schelling's Dialogical Freedom Essay: Provocative Philosophy Then and Now*. Albany: SUNY Press, 2008.

Friedmann, Michael. "Kant-*Naturphilosophie*-Electromagnetism." In *Kantian Legacy in 19th Century Science*, edited by Michael Friedmann and Alfred Nordmann, 51–80. Cambridge: MIT Press, 2006.

Gadamer, Hans-Georg. *Truth and Method*, 2nd ed. New York: Continuum, 2002.

Gilson, Etienne. *Introduction à l'étude de Saint Augustin*. Paris: Vrin, 1949.

Goethe, Johann Woldgang von. *The Collected Works*. Vol. 12: *Scientific Studies*. Princeton: Princeton University Press, 1988.

Gräb, Wilhelm. "Anerkannte Kontingenz: Schellings existentiale Interpretation des Johannesprologs in der *Philosophie der Offenbarung*." In *Biblical Interpretation: History, Context, and Reality*, edited by Christine Helmer and Taylor Petrey, 141–54. Atlanta: Society of Biblical Literature, 2005.

Grant, Iain Hamilton. *Philosophies of Nature after Schelling*. New York: Continuum, 2006.

Gregg, Samuel. *On Ordered Liberty: A Treatise on the Free Society*. Lanham, MD: Lexington, 2003.

Gregory of Nyssa. *The Life of Moses*. Translated by Abraham Malherbe and Everett Ferguson. New York: Paulist, 1978.

Hamburger, Kate. "Schillers Fragment 'Der Menschenfeind' und die Idee der Kalokagathia." *Deutsche Vierteljahrsschrift* 30 (1956) 367–400.

Hart, David Bentley. *Atheist Delusions: The Christian Revolution and its Fashionable Enemies*. New Haven, CT: Yale University Press, 2010.

Heidegger, Martin. *Being and Time*. Translated by John Macquarrie. Oxford: Blackwell, 1962.

———. *Die Metaphysik des deutschen Idealismus. Zur erneuten Auslegung von Schelling: Philosophische Untersuchungen über das Wesen der menschlichen Freiheit und die damit zusammenhängenden Gegenstände (1809) (1941)*. Edited by Günther Seubold. Frankfurt am Main: Klostermann, 1991.

———. *Schelling: Vom Wesen der menschlichen Freiheit (1809)*. Edited by I. Schüssler. Frankfurt am Main: Klostermann, 1988.

———. *Übungen für Anfänger: Schillers Briefe über die ästhetische Erziehung des Menschen*, edited by Ulrich von Bülow. Marbach: Deutsche Schillergesellschaft, 2005.

Henig, Robin Marantz. "Taking Play Seriously." *New York Time Magazine*, February 17, 2008. No pages. Online: http://www.nytimes.com/2008/02/17/magazine/17play.html.

Henrich, Dieter. "Fichte's Original Insight." *Contemporary German Philosophy* 1 (1982) 15–53.

Heuser-Kessler, Marie-Luise. *Die Produktivität der Natur: Schellings Naturphilosophie und das neue Paradigma der Selbstorganization in den Naturwissenschaften*. Berlin: Duncker & Humblot, 1986.

———. "Schellings Organismusbegriff und seine Kritik des Mechanismus und Vitalismus." *Allgemeine Zeitschrift für Philosophie* 14 (1989) 17–36.

Bibliography

Hobbes, Thomas. *Leviathan: or the Matter, Form, and Power of a Commonwealth Ecclesiastical and Civil*. In *The English Philosophers from Bacon to Mill*, edited by E. Burtt, 129–234. New York: Modern Library, 1939.

Höffe, Otfried. "'Gerne dien ich den Freunden, doch tue ich es leider mit Neigung...'— Überwindet Schillers Gedanke der schönen Seele Kants Gegensatz von Pflicht und Neigung?" *Zeitschrift für philosophische Forschung* 10 (2006) 1–20.

Hoffheimer, Michael. "The Influence of Schiller's Theory of Nature on Hegel's Philosophical Development." *The Journal of the History of Ideas* 46 (1985) 231–44.

Hoffmeyer, John F. *The Advent of Freedom: The Presence of the Future in Hegel's Logic*. London: Associated University Press, 1994.

Houlgate, Stephen. "Hegel, Rawls, and the Rational State." In *Beyond Liberalism and Communitarianism*, edited by Robert Williams, 249–74. Albany: SUNY Press, 2001.

———. *An Introduction to the Philosophy of Hegel: Freedom, Truth, and History*. 2nd ed. Hoboken, NJ: Wiley-Blackwell, 2005.

———. *The Opening of Hegel's Logic*. Lafayette, IN: Purdue University Press, 2006.

Hoy, Joyce Beck. "Hegel's Critique of Rawls." *Clio* 10.4 (1981) 407–22.

Huizinga, Johan. *Homo ludens: Vom Ursprung der Kultur im Spiel*. Amsterdam: Patheon Akademische, 1939.

Humboldt, Wilhelm von. *Über Schiller und den Gang seiner Geistesentwicklung*. Leipzig: Insel, 1913.

Husserl, Edmund. *Gesammelte Schriften*. Volume 8: *Cartesianische Meditationen*. Hamburg: Meiner, 1992.

Ilting, Karl-Heinz. "The Structure of Hegel's *Philosophy of Right*." In *Hegel's Political Philosophy: Problems and Perspectives*, edited by Z. Pelczynski, 90–110. Cambridge: Cambridge University Press, 1971.

Inwood, Michael J. *A Hegel Dictionary*. Cambridge: Blackwell, 1992.

———. "Hegel, Plato and Greek *Sittlichkeit*." In *The State and Civil Society: Studies in Hegel's Political Philosophy*, edited by Z. Pelczynski, 40–51. Cambridge: Cambridge University Press, 1984.

Jaeger, Stephen. *The Envy of Angels: Cathedral Schools and Social Ideals in Medieval Europe 950–1200*. Philadelphia: University of Pennsylvania Press, 2000.

Jörg Jantzen. "Die Philosophie der Natur." In *F. W. J. Schelling*, edited by Hans Jörg Sandkühler, 82–108. Stuttgart: Metzler, 1998.

Jonas, Hans. *The Phenomenon of Life: Toward a Philosophical Biology*. Evanston, IL: Northwestern University Press, 2001.

———. *Philosophical Essays*. Engelwood Cliffs, NJ: Prentice-Hall, 1974.

Jürgensen, Sven. "Schellings logisches Prinzip: Der Unterschied in der Identität. " In *Schelling: zwischen Fichte und Hegel*, edited by Christoph Asmuth et al., 113–43. Philadelphia: Grünner, 2000.

Kahn, Charles. *The Art and Thought of Heraclitus*. Cambridge: Cambridge University Press, 1979.

Kaiser, Gerhard. *Vergötterung und Tod: Die thematische Einheit von Schillers Werk*. Stuttgart: Metzler, 1967.

Kane, Robert, ed. *Oxford Handbook of Free Will*. Oxford: Oxford University Press, 2005.

———. "Some Neglected Pathways in the Free Will Labyrinth." In *Oxford Handbook of Free Will*, edited by Robert Kane, 406–37. Cambridge: Cambridge University Press, 2005.

Bibliography

Kant, Immanuel. *Critique of Judgment*. Translated by Werner S. Pluhar. Indianapolis, IN: Hackett, 1987.
——. *Critique of Practical Reason*. Translated by Lewis White Beck. Indianapolis, IN: Bobbs-Merrill, 1956.
——. *Critique of Pure Reason*. Translated by Norman Kemp-Smith. New York: St. Martin's, 1965.
——. *Metaphysischen Anfangsgründe der Naturwissenschaft*. In the *Werke in sechs Bänden*. Volume V, edited by Wilhelm Weischedel, 9–135. Darmstadt: Insel, 1957.
Kaufmann, Walter. *Hegel: A Reinterpretation*. Notre Dame: University of Notre Dame Press, 1988.
——, ed. *Hegel's Political Philosophy*. New York: Atherton, 1970.
——. "Introduction." In *Hegel's Political Philosophy*, 1–9, edited by W. Kaufmann. New York: Atherton, 1970.
Kelly, George Armstrong. *Hegel's Retreat from Eleusis: Studies in Political Thought*. Princeton: Princeton University Press, 1978.
Kerry, S. S. *Schiller's Writings on Aesthetics*. Manchester: The University of Manchester Press, 1961.
Kierkegaard, Søren. *The Concept of Irony with Continual Reference to Socrates*. Edited by Howard and Edna Hong. Princeton: Princeton University Press, 1989.
——. *Sickness Unto Death: A Christian Psychological Exposition of Edification and Awakening by Anti-Climacus*. Translated by Alastair Hannay. New York: Penguin, 1989.
Kirchhoff, Jochen. *Friedrich Wilhelm Joseph von Schelling in Selbstzeugnissen und Bilddokumenten*. Hamburg: Rowohlt, 1982.
Koch, Franz. *Schillers philosophische Schriften und Plotin*. Leipzig: Weber, 1926.
Kohler, Georg. "Selbstbezug, Selbsttranszendenz, und die Nichtigkeit der Freiheit." *Studia Philosophica* 52 (1993) 67–79.
Kolb, David. *Critique of Pure Modernity: Hegel, Heidegger, and After*. Chicago: University of Chicago Press, 1986.
Kontje, Tod Curtis. *Constructing Reality: A Rhetorical Analysis of Friedrich Schiller's Letters on the Aesthetic Education of Man*. New York: Lang, 1988.
Kratzsch, Irmgard. *Friedrich Schiller und die Naturforschende Gesellschaft zu Jena*. Jena: Universitätsbibliothek, 1984.
Krings, Hermann. "Natur als Subjekt: Eine Gründung der spekulativen physik Schellings." In *Natur und Subjektivität*, edited by Heckmann and Krings, 111–28. Stuttgart: Frommann-Holzboog, 1985.
Kroner, Richard. *Von Kant bis Hegel*. 2 vols. Tübingen: Mohr, 1961.
Küppers, Bernd Olaf. *Natur als Organismus: Schellings frühe Naturphilosophie und ihre Bedeutung für moderne Biologie*. Frankfurt am Main: Klostermann, 1992.
Landes, Joan. "Hegel's Conception of the Family." *Polity* 14 (1981) 5–28.
Laughland, John. *Schelling versus Hegel: From German Idealism to Christian Metaphysics*. Burlington, VT: Ashgate, 2007.
Lawrence, Joseph. *Schellings Philosophie des ewigen Anfangs*. Würzburg: Königshausen und Neumann, 1989.
Lear, Jonathan. *Aristotle: The Desire to Understand*. Cambridge: Cambridge University Press, 1989.
Leibniz, Gottfried. *Philosophical Essays*. Translated by Roger Ariew and Daniel Garber. Indianapolis, IN: Hackett, 1989.

Bibliography

Léonard, André. "Le primat du négatif et l'interprétation spéculative de la religion: Un exemple: la reprise hégélienne du dogme christologique de Chalcédoine." In *Hegels Logik der Philosophie: Religion und Philosophie in der Theorie des absoluten Geistes*, edited by Henrich and Horstmann, 160–71. Stuttgart: Klett-Cotta, 1984.

Levinas, Emmanuel. *En découvrant l'existence avec Husserl et Heidegger*. Paris: Vrin, 1994.

Lewis, Thomas A. *Freedom and Tradition in Hegel: Reconsidering Anthropology, Ethics, and Religion*. Notre Dame: University of Notre Dame Press, 2005.

Liebruck, Bruno. "Recht, Moralität und Sittlichkeit bei Hegel." In *Materialen zu Hegels Rechtsphilosophie*, vol. 2, edited by Manfred Riedel, 13–51. Frankfurt am Main: Suhrkamp, 1975.

Lindner, Margit. "Zur philosophischen Leistung Friedrich Schillers." *Deutsche Zeitschrift für Philosophie* 32 (1984) 865–73.

Locke, John. *Essay Concerning Human Understanding*. 2 vols. Edited by Alexander Campbell Fraser. New York: Dover, 1959.

———. *Second Treatise on Government*. In *The English Philosophers from Bacon to Mill*, edited by E. Burtt, 403–503. New York: Modern Library, 1939.

Losurdo, Domenico. *Hegel and the Freedom of the Moderns*. Durham, NC: Duke University Press, 2004.

Lutz, Hans. *Schillers Anschauungen von Kultur und Natur*. Berlin: Ebering, 1928.

MacIntyre, Alasdair. *After Virtue: A Study in Moral Theory*. 2nd ed. Notre Dame: University of Notre Dame Press, 1985.

Maletz, Donald J. "Hegel on Right as Actualized Will." *Political Theory* 17 (1989) 33–50.

Man, Paul de. *Aesthetic Ideology*. Minneapolis: University of Minnesota Press, 1996.

Maritain, Jacques. *Creative Intuition in Art and Poetry*. New York: Meridian, 1955.

Marx, Werner. *The Philosophy of F. W. J. Schelling: History, System, and Freedom*. Bloomington: Indiana University Press, 1984.

———. *Schelling: Geschichte, System, Freiheit*. Munich: Albert, 1977.

Matter, Jacques. *Schelling et la philosophie de la nature*. Paris: Challamel, 1842.

Meyer, Hermann. "Schillers philosophische Rhetorik." In *Zarte Empirie: Studien zur Literaturgeschichte*, 337–89. Stuttgart: Metzler, 1963.

Miller, R. D. *Schiller and the Ideal of Freedom*. Oxford: Oxford University Press, 1970.

Muehleck-Müller, Cathleen. *Schönheit als Freiheit: Die Vollendung der Moderne in der Kunst: Kant–Schiller*. Würzburg: Königshausen und Neumann, 1989.

Mueller, Gustav Emil. *Hegel: The Man, His Vision and Work*. New York: Pageant, 1968.

Murdoch, Iris. *The Sovereignty of Good*. London: Routledge and Kegan Paul, 1970.

Mutschler, Hans-Dieter. *Spekulative und empirische Physik: Aktualität und Grenzen der Naturphilosophie Schellings*. Stuttgart: Kohlhammer, 1990.

Neuhouser, Frederick. *Foundations of Hegel's Social Theory: Actualizing Freedom*. Cambridge, MA: Harvard University Press, 2003.

Nietzsche, Friedrich. *The Portable Nietzsche*. Edited by Walter Kaufmann. New York: Penguin, 1982.

Oesterreich, Peter L. "'Der umgekehrte Gott': Augustinus' Einfluß auf Schellings Rede vom Bösen." In *Das antike Denken in der Philosophie Schellings*, edited by Rainer Adolphi and Jörg Jantzen, 483–95. Stuttgart: Frommann-Holzboog, 2004.

Onians, Richard. *The Origins of European Thought about the Body, the Mind, the Soul, the World, Time, and Fate*. Cambridge: Cambridge University Press, 1951.

O'Regan, Cyril. *Gnostic Apocalypse: Jacob Boehme's Haunted Narrative.* Albany: SUNY Press, 2002.
Pannenberg, Wolfhart. "Der Geist und sein Anderes." In *Hegels Logik der Philosophie: Religion und Philosophie in der Theorie des absoluten Geistes*, edited by Dieter Henrich and Rolf-Peter Horstmann, 151–59. Stuttgart: Klett-Cotta, 1984.
Pascal, David. *Le vocabulaire de Schelling.* Paris: Ellipses, 2001.
Patten, Alan. "Social Contract Theory and the Politics of Recognition in Hegel's Political Philosophy." In *Beyond Liberalism and Communitarianism: Studies in Hegel's Philosophy of Right*, edited by Robert. R. Williams, 167–84. Albany: SUNY Press, 2001.
Peetz, Siegbert. "Die Philosophie der Mythologie." In *F. W. J. Schelling*, edited by Hans Jörg Sandkühler, 150–68. Stuttgart: Metzler, 1998.
Pelczynski, Zbigniew. *Conceptions of Liberty in Political Philosophy.* Edited by Z. Pelczynski. New York: Palgrave Macmillan, 1985.
———. "Freedom in Hegel." In *Conceptions of Liberty in Political Philosophy*, edited by Z. Pelczynski, 150–81. New York: Palgrave Macmillan, 1985.
———. "Political Community and Individual Freedom in Hegel's Philosophy of State." In *The State and Civil Society*, edited by Z. Pelczynski, 55–76. Cambridge: Cambridge University Press, 1984.
———. "The Significance of Hegel's Separation of the State and Civil Society." In *The State and Civil Society*, edited by Z. Pelczynski, 1–13. Cambridge: Cambridge University Press, 1984.
———, ed. *The State and Civil Society: Studies in Hegel's Political Philosophy.* Cambridge: Cambridge University Press, 1984.
Peperzak, Adriaan. *Modern Freedom: Hegel's Legal, Moral and Political Philosophy.* Dordrecht: Kluwer, 2001.
———. *Philosophy and Politics: A Commentary on the Preface to Hegel's Philosophy of Right.* Dordrecht: Nijhoff, 1987.
Perl, Eric. *Theophany: The Neoplatonic Philosophy of Dionysius the Areopagite.* Albany: SUNY Press, 2007.
Piché, Claude. "Fichte et la première philosophie de la nature de Schelling." *Dialogue: Canadian Philosophical Association* 43 (2004) 211–37.
Pinckaers, Servais O.P. *The Sources of Christian Ethics.* Washington, DC: The Catholic University of America Press, 1995.
Pinkard, Terry. *Hegel: A Biography.* Cambridge: Cambridge University Press, 2001.
Pippin, Robert. "The Rose and the Owl: Some Remarks on the Theory-Praxis Problem in Hegel." *The Independent Journal of Philosophy* 3 (1979) 7–16.
Plamenatz, John. "History as the Realization of Freedom." In *Hegel's Political Philosophy: Problems and Perspectives*, edited by Z. Pelczynski, 30–51. Cambridge: Cambridge University Press, 1971.
Plato. *The Complete Works.* Edited by John M. Cooper. Indianapolis: Hackett, 1997.
Potyka, Klaus Karl. *Naturvorstellungen in ausgewählten philosophischen Schriften Friedrich Schillers.* Berlin: Lang, 1994.
Pugh, David. *Dialectic of Love: Platonism in Schiller's Aesthetics.* Montreal: McGill-Queens, 1997.
———. "Schiller as Citizen of His Time." In *Schiller's "On Grace and Dignity" in Its Cultural Context*, edited by Jane Curran and Christophe Fricker, 37–54. Rochester, NY: Camden House, 2005.
Rahner, Hugo. *Der spielende Mensch.* Einsiedeln: Johannes, 1952.

Bibliography

Rawls, John. *Justice as Fairness: A Restatement*. Cambridge: Harvard University Press, 2001.

Richard of St. Victor. *De Trinitate*. Available in English as *Richard of Saint Victor, On the Trinity: English Translation and Commentary*. Translated by Ruben Angelici. Eugene, OR: Cascade Books, 2011.

Richards, Robert. *The Romantic Conception of Life: Science and Philosophy in the Age of Goethe*. Chicago: University of Chicago Press, 2002.

Riedel, Manfred. *Between Tradition and Revolution: The Hegelian Transformation of Political Philosophy*. Cambridge: Cambridge University Press, 1984.

———. "Nature and Freedom in Hegel's *Philosophy of Right*." In *Hegel's Political Philosophy: Problems and Perspectives*, edited by Z. Pelczynski, 136–50. Cambridge: Cambridge University Press, 1971.

Riedel, Wolfgang. *Die Anthropologie des jungen Schiller*. Würzburg: Königshausen und Neumann, 1985.

———. *Jacob Friedrich Abel: Eine Quellenedition zum Philosophieunterricht an der Stuttgarter Karlsschule (1773–1782)*. Würzburg: Königshausen und Neumann, 1995.

Röhr, Sabine. "Freedom and Autonomy in Schiller." *Journal of the History of Ideas* 64 (2003) 119–34.

Römpp, Georg. "Schönheit als Erfahrung der Freiheit: Zur transzendentallogischen Bedeutung des Schönen in Schillers Ästhetik." *Kant-Studien* 89 (1998) 428–45.

Rosen, Stanley. *The Limits of Analysis*. South Bend, IN: Saint Augustine's, 2000.

Rousseau, Jean-Jacques. *Du Contrat social*. Paris: Frères, 1962.

Ruskin, John. *Modern Painters*. Volume 2: *Of the Imaginative and Theoretical Faculties*. Boston: Adamant Media Corporation, 2000.

Safranski, Rüdiger. *Schiller oder die Erfindung deutschen Idealismus*. Munich: Hanswer, 2004.

Sandel, Michael. *Democracy's Discontent: America in Search of a Public Philosophy*. Cambridge, MA: Harvard University Press, 1998.

Sandkaulen-Bock, Birgit. *Ausgang vom Unbedingten: Über den Anfang in der Philosophie Schellings*. Göttingen: Vandenhoeck und Ruprecht, 1990.

Sandkühler, Hans Jörg. "F. W. J. Schelling—ein Werk im Werden." In *F. W. J. Schelling*, edited by Hans Jörg Sandkühler, 1–39. Stuttgart: Metzler, 1998.

Sayce, Olive. "Das Problem der Vieldeutigkeit in Schillers ästhetischer Terminologie." *Jahrbuch der deutschen Schillergesellschaft* 6 (1962) 149–77.

Schacht, Richard. "Hegel on Freedom." In *Hegel: A Collection of Critical Essays*, edited by Alasdair MacIntyre, 289–328. Garden City, NY: Doubleday, 1972.

Schaper, Eva. "Schiller's Kant: A Chapter in the History of a Creative Misunderstanding." In *Studies in Kant's Aesthetics*, 99–117. Edinburgh: Edinburgh University Press, 1979.

Schindler, D. C. "Freedom beyond Our Choosing: Augustine on the Will and Its Objects." In *Augustine and Politics*, edited by John Doody, et al., 67–96. Lanham, MD: Lexington, 2005.

———. "Homer's Truth: The Rise of Radiant Form." *Existentia: An International Journal of Philosophy* 16.3–4 (2006) 161–82.

———. *Plato's Critique of Impure Reason: On Goodness and Truth in the Republic*. Washington, DC: The Catholic University of America Press, 2008.

———. "What's the Difference? On the Metaphysics of Participation in Plato, Plotinus, and Aquinas." *Nova et Vetera* 5 (2007) 583–618.
Schmitz, Kenneth. "The Geography of the Human Person." *Communio* 13 (1986) 27–48.
Schulz, Walter. *Die Vollendung des deutschen Idealismus in der Spätphilosophie Schellings*. Stuttgart: Kohlhammer, 1955.
Shakespeare, William. *Corialanus*. 2nd rev. ed. Edited by Sylvan Barnet and Reuben Brower. New York: Signet, 2002.
Sharpe, Lesley. *Friedrich Schiller: Drama, Thought and Politics*. Cambridge: Cambridge University Press, 1991.
———. *Schiller's Aesthetic Essays: Two Centuries of Criticism*. Columbia, SC: Camden House, 1995.
Shklar, Judith. "Hegel's *Phenomenology*: An Elegy for Hellas." In *Hegel's Political Philosophy: Problems and Perspectives*, edited by Z. Pelczynski, 73–89. Cambridge: Cambridge University Press, 1971.
Smith, Steven. *Hegel's Critique of Liberalism: Rights in Context*. Chicago: University of Chicago Press, 1989.
Snell, Reginald. "Introduction." In *On the Aesthetic Education of Man*, by Friedrich Schiller, 1–20. Mineola, NY: Dover, 2004.
Snow, Dale. "The Evolution of Schelling's Concept of Freedom." In *Schelling: zwischen Fichte und Hegel*, edited by Christoph Asmuth et al., 317–32. Philadelphia: Grünner, 2000.
Spaemann, Robert. *Natürliche Ziele: Geschichte und Wiederentdeckung des teleologischen Denkens*. Stuttgart: Klett-Cotta, 2005.
———. "Was heißt: 'Die Kunst ahmet die Natur nach'?" *Philosophisches Jahrbuch* 114 (2007) 247–64.
———. "Wirklichkeit als Anthropomorphismus." In *Was Heisst 'Wirklich'? Unsere Erkenntnis zwischen Wahrnehmung und Wissenschaft*, 13–35. Waakirchen-Schaftlach: Oreos, 2000.
Spinoza, Baruch. *Ethics: Treatise on the Emendation of the Intellect*. Indianapolis, IN: Hackett, 1991.
Steinberger, Peter. *Logic and Politics: Hegel's Philosophy of Right*. New Haven, CT: Yale University Press, 1988.
Sturma, Dieter. "Präreflexive Freiheit und menschliche Selbstbestimmung." In *F. W. J. Schelling: Über das Wesen der menschlichen Freiheit*, edited by Otfried Höffe and Annemarie Pieper, 146–69. Berlin: Akademie, 1995.
Suter, Jean-François. "Burke, Hegel, and the French Revolution." In *Hegel's Political Philosophy: Problems and Perspectives*, edited by Z. Pelczynski, 52–72. Cambridge: Cambridge University Press, 1971.
Taminiaux, Jacques. *La nostalgie de la Grèce à l'aube de l'idéalisme Allemand: Kant et les Grecs dans l'itinéraire de Schiller, de Hölderlin et de Hegel*. La Hague: Nijhoff, 1967.
Taylor, Charles. *The Ethics of Authenticity*. Cambridge, MA: Harvard University Press, 1992.
———. *Hegel*. Cambridge: Cambridge University Press, 1977.
———. *Hegel and Modern Society*. Cambridge: Cambridge University Press, 1979.
Tilliette, Xavier. "Une philosophie en deux." In *Le Dernier Schelling: Raison et Positivité*, edited by Jean-François Courtine and Jean-François Marquet, 55–70. Paris: Vrin, 1994.
———. *Une philosophie en devenir*. Paris: Vrin, 1992.

Tunick, Mark. *Hegel's Political Philosophy*. Princeton: Princeton University Press, 1992.
Ulrich, Ferdinand. *Der Gegenwart der Freiheit*. Einsiedeln: Johannes, 1974.
———. *Homo Abyssus*. 2nd ed. Einsiedeln: Johannes, 1998.
———. *Der Mensch als Anfang: Zur philosophischen Anthropologie der Kindheit*. Einsiedeln: Johannes, 1970.
Vater, Michael G. "Intellectual Intuition in Schelling's Philosophy of Identity 1801–1804." In *Schelling: zwischen Fichte und Hegel*, edited by Christoph Asmuth et al., 213–34. Philadelphia: Grünner, 2000.
———. "Introduction." In *Bruno: or, On the Natural and Divine Principle of Things*, translated and edited by Michael. G. Vater, 3–108. Albany, NY: SUNY Press, 1984.
Varela, Francisco, Evan Thompson, and Eleanor Rosch. *The Embodied Mind: Cognitive Science and Human Experience*. Cambridge: MIT Press, 1992.
Vaysse, Jean-Marie. "Schelling contra Hegel." In *Schelling: zwischen Fichte und Hegel*, edited by Christoph Asmuth et al., 363–77. Philadelphia: Grünner, 2000.
Veatch, Henry B. *Two Logics: The Conflict between Classical and Neo-Analytic Philosophy*. Evanston, IL: Northwestern University Press, 1969.
Velkley, Richard. "Realizing Nature in the Self: Schelling on Art and Intellectual Intuition." In *Figuring the Self: Subject, Absolute, and Others in Classical German Philosophy*, edited by David E. Glemm and Günther Zöller, 148–68. Albany: SUNY Press, 1997.
Viganó, Federica. "Schelling liest Platons '*Timaeus*': Die Erneuerung zwischen Platon und Kant." In *Das antike Denken in der Philosophie Schellings*, edited by Rainer Adolphi and J. Jantzen, 227–35. Stuttgart-Bad Cannstatt: Holzboog, 2004.
Voegelin, Eric. *Science, Politics, and Gnosticism*. Washington, DC: Regnery, 1968.
Wallace, Robert M. *Hegel's Philosophy of Reality, Freedom, and God*. Cambridge: Cambridge University Press, 2005.
Weil, Eric. *Hegel and the State*. Baltimore: Johns Hopkins University Press, 1998.
Wessell, Leonard. "The Aesthetics of Living Form in Schiller and Marx." *The Journal of Aesthetics and Art Criticism* 37 (1978) 189–201.
Westphal, Kenneth. "The Basic Context and Structure of Hegel's *Philosophy of Right*." In *The Cambridge Companion to Hegel*, edited by Frederick Beiser, 234–69. Cambridge: Cambridge University Press, 1993.
Westphal, Merold. "Hegel's Radical Idealism: Family and State as Ethical Communities." In *The State and Civil Society: Studies in Hegel's Political Philosophy*, edited by Z. Pelczynski, 77–92. Cambridge: Cambridge University Press, 1984.
White, Alan. *The End of Philosophy*. PhD diss., Penn State University, 1980.
———. *Schelling: An Introduction to the System of Freedom*. New Haven, CT: Yale University Press, 1983.
Whitehead, Alfred North. *Science and the Modern World*. New York: Free Press, 1997.
Wieland, Wolfgang. "Die Anfänge der Philosophie Schellings und die Frage nach der Natur." In *Natur und Geschichte: Karl Löwith zum 70. Geburtstag*, edited by Hermann Braun and Manfred Riedel, 406–40. Stuttgart: Kohlhammer, 1967.
Wiese, Benno von. *Friedrich Schiller*. Stuttgart: Metzler, 1959.
Wilcox, Kenneth Parmelee. *Anmut und Würde: Die Dialektik der menschlichen Vollendung bei Schiller*. Berlin: Lang, 1981.
Wilkinson, Elizabeth, and L. A. Willoughby. "Introduction." In *On the Aesthetic Education of Man: In a Series of Letters*, by Johann Christoph Friedrich von Schiller, xi–cxcvi. Oxford: Clarendon, 1982.

———. *Models of Wholeness: Some Attitudes to Language, Art and Life in the Age of Goethe*. New York: Lang, 2002.

Wilkinson, Elizabeth. *Schiller: Poet or Philosopher?* Oxford: Clarendon, 1961.

Wirth, Jason. *The Conspiracy of Life: Meditations on Schelling and His Time*. Albany: SUNY Press, 2003.

———, ed. *Schelling Now: Contemporary Readings*. Bloomington: Indiana University Press, 2005.

Wood, Allen. *Hegel's Ethical Thought*. Cambridge: Cambridge University Press, 1990.

———. "Hegel's Ethics." In *The Cambridge Companion to Hegel*, edited by Frederick Beiser, 211–33. Cambridge: Cambridge University Press, 1993.

Zaborowski, Holger. "Geschichte, Freiheit, Schöpfung und die Herrlichkeit Gottes: Die 'System der Freiheit' und die unaufhebbare Ambivalenz der Philosophie Schellings." In *System-Freiheit-Geschichte*, edited by Holger Zaborowski and Alfred Denker, 26–47. Stuttgart: Frommann und Holzboog, 2004.

Žižek, Slavoj. "The Abyss of Freedom." In *The Abyss of Freedom / Ages of the World*, 1–104. Ann Arbor: University of Michigan, 1997.

———. *The Indivisible Remainder: On Schelling and Related Matters*. London: Verso, 1996.

Index

Abel, Jacob Friedrich, 5
Absolute, the,
    as actuality, 211n139
    and being/existence, 210–14
    "derivative absolute," freedom
        as, 132n75, 174, 176, 190
    divine ideas, 180–81, 184,
        191–92, 195
    freedom of, 205–6, 213–14,
        215–17, 233
    ground and existence,
        distinction within, 192–95,
        203–4
    and history, 198, 205
    as living, 192, 194–95
    and necessity, 205–6
    ontological argument for, 210
    and the organism, 167–68
    as origin of the world, 173–74,
        190–92, 195
    as personal, 113, 194–95, 203–4,
        217, 224, 379
    potencies of, 212–14, 216
    as self-revealing, 273–75, 367
    as simple, 192–93
    as Trinity, 217–26, 236–37,
        274–75, 319–20
    see also infinite, and the finite;
        pantheism
Acton, John Emirich Dalberg, xv
actuality, 266–83
    freedom as, xvii–xviii, xxv,
        49–51, 89–91, 234, 239–40,
        242, 295–300, 333, 337, 354,
        377–84
    as manifestation, 265, 311

    and mystery, 361–63
    and potency, xvii–xviii, xxv,
        49–51, 211–14, 233, 264–65,
        277–79, 285, 286–87, 361–
        62, 379–84
    and the rational, 245–46, 258–
        60, 261–63
    as unity of essence and
        existence, 262–64
Adler, Mortimer, 239n4, 239n7
ambiguity, 22–23, 45–46, 54
appearance, 11–12, 35, 37, 39, 99–
    100, 182, 339–40, 374, 375
    and form, 11–12, 18–19, 23,
        38–41, 54–55, 85
    see also manifestation
Aquinas, Thomas, 73n81, 81n101,
    147n123, 210n136, 279n125
Aristotle,
    and Hegel, 270–73, 278–79,
        283, 284, 321, 322n61, 354,
        361n188, 364
    and Schelling, 138–39, 147–48,
        379n4
    and Schiller, 53–54, 57, 60, 63,
        66, 68, 69n70
art, 14n43, 141n94, 148n127, 163,
    166–67, 171, 263, 363–64
Augustine of Hippo, 235
autonomy,
    and evil, 196
    freedom as, 53, 61, 227, 239–40,
        299–300
    and heautonomy, 66–68, 70–71,
        84, 105, 200, 380

Index

autonomy (*continued*)
    of the world vis-à-vis God, 192, 195
Avineri, Shlomo, 251n43, 302, 356, 359
Bacon, Francis, 256
Balthasar, Hans Urs von, 186n68, 227n194
Barnouw, Jeffrey, 103n168
Baum, Manfred, 149n128
Baumgartner, H. M., and Korten, H., 113n11
Beach, Edward, 126n56, 177n20, 224n185, 230n201
beautiful style, 10–28, 35, 37, 40, 43–44, 82, 374
beauty,
    danger of, 15, 20–21, 24, 45, 98, 99
    and form, 294, 381
    as "form of form," 39, 53, 56, 91
    and freedom, 11–13, 18–21, 39–40, 49–51, 53, 60–71, 76, 92
    as "freedom in appearance," 50, 53, 60–71
    and morality, 59–60, 67, 105–6
    and truth, 9–16, 24–26, 44–47, 55–56
    and unity, 58–59, 86–88, 381
    as unity of reason and the senses, 10, 15–16, 50, 86–87
Beiser, Friedrich, 1n4, 42–47, 52n13, 58n34, 67n67, 71n74, 145n112, 151n133
Berlin, Isaiah, xv, 327n80
Berry, Wendell, 383
Bieler, Martin, 236n213
body, and soul, 61, 78n90, 80–81, 122, 299, 375; *see also* reason, and the senses
Boehme, Jacob, 206, 272n108, 319
Bonsiepen, Wolfgang, 143n101, 144, 151n134, 186n68
Bourgeois, Bernard, 369n213
Bowie, Andrew, 199n108
Boyle, Nicholas, 366n206
Brito, Emil, 216, 222n182

Brod, Harry, 356n172
Brown, Robert, 194n92
Bruno, Giordanno, 126n57
Buchheim, Thomas, 62n47, 177n20, 193, 197, 206–7, 222n183, 230n201, 278n123
Burtt, E.A., 159n175
Cassirer, Ernst, xxin17, 29, 31, 66n61, 359
choice, freedom as, xiii–xvii, xixn11, xxv, 49, 89–91, 198–99, 291, 296–97, 337
Christ, 220–24, 232, 274
Christianity, 208, 219–24, 257–58, 272–76, 377
church, and state, 276, 304, 365–71, 378, 380
community; *see* individual, and community
concept, 27, 64, 67, 178n21, 264
    and external expression/image, 18–21, 22–23, 25, 37, 40–41, 109, 165, 381
    form as, 54, 56
Constant, Benjamin, xviii-xx
Courtine, Jean-François, 310n28
creation, 147n123, 201, 214–17, 224–25, 231, 236
creativity, 13–14, 15–16, 37–38, 139–40, 164; *see also* receptivity, and spontaneity
Danz, Christian, 214n150, 220
Darwin, Charles, 156n159
democracy, 326, 355–56
Derrida, Jacques, 314n37
Descartes, René, 119–20, 122, 126n57, 180
Desmond, William, 263n74, 272n108, 362, 363n197, 372
determinacy; *see* form, as limit/determination; necessity, interior vs. exterior
difference; *see* identity, and difference; unity, and difference/distinction
Douglas, Mary, 96n150
drama, 28–38, 94, 164
    form as dramatic, 380–81

402

Index

unity as dramatic, 30–33, 35, 37–38, 46, 55, 80–85, 86–88, 106, 381
drives (*Triebe*), 31–32, 36, 78, 80–83, 91, 92, 290–91
dualism; *see* body, and soul; subject-object relation
Dudley, Will, 242n12, 327n80, 361n187
duties, and rights, xv, 326–30, 353; *see also* liberalism
dynamism; *see* nature, as dynamic
education, 15–16, 26, 94n146, 108, 138–43, 290, 294, 344–45, 352
Ellis, John M., 2n6
empiricism, 119, 120–26, 136, 142, 169; *see also* mechanism
end,
  freedom as, xvii–xviii, 69, 72, 76; *see also* actuality, freedom as
  and means, xiv, xxv, 19–20, 33, 65, 76, 94n146, 95, 98, 108, 333, 340–41
Engel, Carl, 63n50
Engels, Friedrich, 263n71
Eugen, Karl, 5–6
evil,
  defined, 195–96
  and difference, 314
  and freedom, 174–76, 189, 195–97, 218–24, 234–36
  and God, 203–5, 216, 219–25
  as privation, 197
family, and marriage, 330–38, 346–47, 350–51, 383–84
Ferrarin, Alfredo, 272, 360n185
Fichte, Johann Gottlieb,
  and Hegel, 243n17, 249n35, 267, 353n164
  and Schelling, 119, 125, 132–36, 151n135, 161, 185–86, 227, 228, 267
  and Schiller, 8–9, 10n32, 11n34, 23, 42n117, 43, 44
Findlay, John, 260n62, 316n42
Fischer, Kuno, 2n7, 29, 48, 55

form,
  and appearance, 11–12, 18–19, 23, 38–41, 54–55, 85
  as concept, 54, 56
  and content, 4, 15–16, 18–22, 23, 38–41, 44, 259, 265–66, 289–95, 310, 381
  as dramatic, 380–81
  and freedom, xvii–xviii, xxi, xxv, 18–21, 25, 38–41, 47, 53, 73–76, 88–91, 97, 164–70, 175–76, 180, 186, 228, 231, 233–34, 235–36, 291–95, 334–38, 344–45, 373–84
  as interior principle of organization, 54–55, 63–66, 70, 76
  as limit/determination, xviii, 39–41, 73–76, 88–91, 166–67, 179, 231
  and matter, 57–59, 83–85, 107, 127–31, 148–49, 157–58
  as self-manifestation, 56–59
Franco, Paul, 240n9, 314n38
Frank, Manfred, 208n129
French revolution, 1, 6n21, 79, 286
Freud, Sigmund, 194
Freydberg, Bernard, 202n116, 204n120
Fries, Jacob Friedrich, 245, 250–54
Gadamer, Hans-Georg, 14n43, 98–101
Gestalt (form), xviii, 53–54, 85, 91–93, 104–105, 180, 295
  lebende Gestalt (living form), xxi, 8n26, 63n51, 84–85, 87, 89, 91, 93–98, 109–110, 164–65, 266–67, 307
gift of self, 16–22, 28, 37–38, 41, 267, 310, 314, 333–34, 350–51, 374, 383–84
Gilson, Etienne, 235n211
God; *see* Absolute, the
Goethe, Johann Wolfgang von, xxii–xxiii
  and Hegel, 254, 267–69
  and Schelling, 131, 215

Goethe, Johann Wolfgang von (*cont.*)
and Schiller, 1, 7, 8n26, 8n27, 34, 52n13, 54, 65nn57–59, 85, 91, 104n169, 269
good, the,
and freedom, xiii–xvi, 189, 196–97, 235–36
as instrumental vs. intrinsic, xiv, 64n55, 95, 98; *see also* instrumentalism
Grant, Iain Hamilton, 114n19, 124
Gregory of Nyssa, 362n191
Haller, Karl Ludwig von, 262n65, 364
Hanby, Michael, 148n123
heautonomy, 66–71, 92, 95, 285
and autonomy, 66–68, 70–71, 84, 105, 200, 380
and heteronomy, 71–76, 109–10; *see also* self, and other
Hegel, Georg Wilhelm Friedrich, xixnn13–14, xxi–xxii, xxiii, xxiv, 238–372, 377–83
and Schelling, xxi, 111–12, 131n70, 133n76, 144n104, 178, 187n73, 188n76, 214, 223n185, 224n187, 228, 229, 237, 241, 243n17, 247, 259, 265, 267, 271n99, 276, 282, 285, 288, 292, 297–98, 299, 305–7, 310n28, 319n53, 353, 363, 371, 378, 379–83
and Schiller, xxi, 25n68, 26n70, 37, 41, 42n117, 49–50, 71, 88, 92, 95n148, 240, 244, 259, 266–67, 269, 277, 285, 288n146, 291n156, 294–95, 307, 310, 321, 343n130, 348, 352, 378–83
Heidegger, Martin, 114, 126n57, 160, 172n6, 189n77, 206n124, 291n155
Henig, Robin Marantz, 93n142
Heraclitus, 24n67
Heuser-Kessler, Marie-Luise, 147n121, 155, 156n159
history, 136–38, 162–63, 189–90, 201–3

and God, 198, 205
see also time, and eternity
Hobbes, Thomas, 327–28
Höffe, Otfried, 17n53, 60, 93
Hoffmeyer, John F., 362n194
Hölderlin, Johann Christian Friedrich, 382
Houlgate, Stephen, 260n62, 280n126, 282n131, 346n139, 355n170
Hoy, Joyce Beck, 346n139
Humboldt, Wilhelm von, 4, 37, 46, 47n135, 104n171
Husserl, Edmund, 179n25
idealism, 119, 125–26, 131–38, 174, 189
ideas, divine, 180–81, 184, 191–92, 195; *see also* concept, and external expression/image
identity,
and difference, 179n27, 181–82, 187–88, 305–6; *see also* indifference; unity, and difference/distinction
law of, 190
Ilting, Karl-Heinz, 241n11
imagination, 10, 12–13, 15, 39, 41
indifference, 187–88, 206–7, 227n194, 234, 236, 305
individual, and community, 250–51, 252–53, 294–95, 303, 309, 322–26, 331–32, 334n100, 340–45, 348–56, 378; *see also* self, and other
infinite, the,
"filled infinity," 88–91, 294, 382–83
and the finite, 88–89, 156, 173–74, 179, 181–86, 221–23, 292–94, 315–17
instrumentalization, of freedom, xiv, xv–xvii, xxv; *see also* end, and means; good, as instrumental vs. intrinsic
Inwood, M.J., 257n56
Jacobi, Friedrich Heinrich, 209n134
Jaeger, Stephen, 96n150
Joachim of Floris, 219n171

Index

Jonas, Hans, 116n28, 130n67, 299
Jürgensen, Sven, 179n27, 224n188
Kahn, Charles, 24n67
Kaiser, Gerhard, 88n119, 99n158
Kant, Immanuel, xxii–xxiii
   and Hegel, 259, 260n62, 267, 291–92, 295, 353
   and Schelling, 116n29, 119, 123, 132, 144–45, 146–52, 154, 156, 158, 210n136, 227
   and Schiller, 7, 11, 41, 49, 51–52, 55–56, 57n31, 60–67, 78n91, 83, 91, 99–100, 102–5, 259, 374
Kaufmann, Walter, xxiiin21, 302
Kelly, George, 366
Kerry, S. S., 29, 33, 91n131
Kierkegaard, Søren, 112
Kohler, Georg, 234n208
Kolb, David, 290n154, 356n172
Krug, William Traugott, 262
Küppers, Bernd-Olaf, 146n117, 147n121, 156n159
Lacan, Jacques, xxiv
Landes, Joan, 334n100
Laughland, John, 215n153, 223n184
law, and freedom, 324–30
Lawrence, Joseph, 125n56, 144n106, 147n122
Le Sage, George-Louis, 120
Leibniz, Gottfried Wilhelm, 66n61, 71n74, 116n29, 145
Lessing, Gotthold Ephraim, 94n144
Levinas, Emmanuel, 239
Lewis, Thomas, 288n147, 334n99
liberalism, xiv–xv, 241–42, 287, 329n85, 345, 356n172, 358–59; *see also* rights, and duties
Liebruck, Bruno, 242n14
Locke, John, 292n159, 329n86
Losurdo, Domenico, xixn14, 241n11
love, 185, 204–7, 223–25, 234–37, 330–38, 363, 383
Lutz, Hans, 2n7
Maletz, Donald J., 297n170
Man, Paul de, 32

manifestation,
   actuality as, 265, 311
   form as, 56–59
   of God, 273–75, 367
   spirit as, 309–10, 378
   see also appearance
Marcel, Gabriel, 49
Marcion of Sinope, 219n171
Maritain, Jacques, 17n53
marriage, and family, 330–38, 346–47, 350–51, 383–84
Marx, Karl, 361
Marx, Werner, 175n17, 211n142, 224n187
matter,
   and form, 57–59, 83–85, 107, 127–31, 148–49, 157–58
   materialism, 78n91, 124, 127–31
   origin of, 173–74; *see also* Absolute, as origin of the world
   as pure externality, 121–22, 125, 129
   and spirit, 308, 312
   see also mechanism
means, and end; *see* end, and means
mechanism, 19–20, 65–66, 75–76, 79, 95, 117, 120, 123–31, 146, 150–52, 183, 186, 341, 376; *see also* empiricism
Mill, John Stuart, xv
Miller, R. D., 75
morality, and beauty, 59–60, 67, 105–6; *see also* duties, and rights; *Sittlichkeit*
Moser, Pfarrer, 5
Muehleck-Müller, Cathleen, 105n172
Mueller, Gustav, 268
Mugdan, Bertha, 66n61
Murdoch, Iris, 65n58
Mutschler, Hans-Dieter, 181
nature,
   as dynamic, 154–58, 166, 178–81, 186
   and form, 63

Index

nature (*continued*)
  and freedom, 60–71, 91, 96–97, 103–4, 115–17, 130n67, 135–38, 155, 158–64, 169, 172, 176, 200, 298–99, 375–76
  and heautonomy, 68
  as origin, 193
  and person, 194–95, 231, 290–91
  as self-limiting, 155–56, 166–67; *see also* form, as limit/determination
  and spirit, 114, 279n126, 280
  as teleological, 63–66, 135, 149–51, 278–79
  and "world," 154–55, 181
  see also organism
necessity,
  in God, 205–6
  and freedom, 11–13, 18–21, 35, 39–40, 57–60, 70–71, 73, 88–91, 199–201
  internal vs. external, 11–13, 18–21, 23, 35, 39, 57–58, 69–70, 73, 89, 92–93
  and truth, 11–12, 14, 19–21
Neuhouser, Friedrich, 240, 251n43, 260n62, 283, 304, 358n180
Newton, Isaac, 130–31, 159, 213n146, 268
Nietzsche, Friedrich, 126n57, 256
Onians, Richard, 338n109
order, and freedom, xv–xvi, xviii, 38, 235, 380; *see also* form, and freedom; law, and freedom; necessity, and freedom
organism, 122–24, 129, 143–58, 159–60, 167–69, 183–84, 226–27, 259, 308, 354, 376
other, the; *see* self, and other
Pannenberg, Wolfhart, 274n112
pantheism, 145n112, 168, 183–85, 190–92, 212–13, 217, 225
particular, and universal; *see* universal, and particular
parts, and whole, 19–20, 22–23, 27–28, 30–33, 35–36, 46, 72–76, 79–80, 86–88, 95, 106–8, 140, 146–47, 149, 227, 250–51, 307–8, 350–51, 354–55, 378; *see also* unity
Peetz, Siegbert, 223n185
Pelczynski, Zbigniew, 238n2, 327n79, 348n148
Peperzak, Adriaan, 260n62, 285, 290n153, 297n170, 359
person, 33–34, 62, 80–82, 91, 203–4, 257–58, 383–84
  God as, 113, 194–95, 203–204, 217, 224, 379
  and nature, 194–95, 231, 290–91
philosophy,
  and faith, 208–9, 273, 320, 365
  and poetry, 3–4, 41–48, 140, 263
  and politics, 246–50, 255–57, 260–61, 272, 364–65
  and the sciences, 138–43, 229
Piché, Claude, 151n135
Pinkard, Terry, 289n150
Pippin, Robert, 246n25
Plamenetz, John, 280n128
Plato,
  and Hegel, 253, 255, 257–59, 269–70, 273, 292n160, 340, 347n144, 365
  and Schelling, 126n57, 127, 129, 144, 156, 184n53, 201n114, 209
  and Schiller, 25, 43, 53–54, 68, 83, 98, 102–4
play, 17n53, 92–98, 108
Plotinus, 58n35, 126n57, 130n69, 297
poetry, 3–4, 13, 38, 41–48, 140, 141, 263, 381–82, 383–84
politics,
  and freedom, xiv–xv, 96, 244; *see also* law, and freedom; liberalism
  and philosophy, 246–50, 255–57, 260–61, 272, 364–65
  and truth, 246–48
  see also state
potency; *see under* actuality

Pugh, David, 76n86, 89n124, 102–4, 107
Quintilian, Marcus Fabius, 45
Rawls, John, xiv–xv, 345
reason,
    and actuality, 245–46, 258–60, 261–63
    and faith, 208–9, 273, 320, 365
    and the irrational, xxiv, 199n108, 247–48
    and politics, 255–61; *see also* philosophy, and politics
    rationalism, 255–60
    and the senses, 10, 14–15, 35, 50, 61, 83, 92, 93, 97, 101, 108, 121–22; *see also* body, and soul
    and sentiment, 249, 253–54, 330–31, 332–33, 351–52
    and will, 284
receptivity, and spontaneity, 16, 17n53, 19, 85, 139–40, 227; *see also* creativity
religion; *see* church, and state; reason, and faith
revelation; *see* Absolute, as self-revealing; appearance; manifestation
Richard of St. Victor, 236
Richards, Robert, 123n50
Riedel, Manfred, 279n126
Rieff, Philip, 298
rights, and duties, xv, 326–30, 353; *see also* liberalism
Rosen, Stanley, 361
Rousseau, Jean-Jacques, 244, 251n43, 289, 299–300, 325–26, 330, 340n117, 348–49
Ruskin, John, 99n156
Safranski, Rüdiger, 4n15, 48n137, 65n58
Schact, Richard, 239n5
Schelling, Friedrich Wilhelm Joseph von, xxi–xxii, xxiii, xxiv, 111–237, 375–77, 379–83
    and Hegel, xxi, 111–12, 131n70, 133n76, 144n104, 178, 187n73, 188n76, 214, 223n185, 224n187, 228, 229, 237, 241, 243n17, 247, 259, 265, 267, 271n99, 276, 282, 285, 288, 292, 297–98, 299, 305–7, 310n28, 319n53, 353, 363, 371, 378, 379–83
    and Schiller, 100n59, 114, 115, 122n42, 139, 151, 159, 164–67, 199–200, 203n117, 259, 376, 379–83
Schiller, Johann Christoph Friedrich von, xxi–xxii, xxiii, 1–110, 374–75, 378–83
    and Hegel, xxi, 25n68, 26n70, 37, 41, 42n117, 49–50, 71, 88, 92, 95n148, 240, 244, 259, 266–67, 269, 277, 285, 288n146, 291n156, 294–95, 307, 310, 321, 343n130, 348, 352, 378–83
    and Schelling, 100n59, 114, 115, 122n42, 139, 151, 159, 164–67, 199–200, 203n117, 259, 376, 379–83
Schmitz, Kenneth, 34n97
Schulz, Walter, 199n108, 225
science, modern; *see* empiricism; philosophy, and the sciences
self, and other, 71–76, 109–10, 134–36, 177n20, 287, 300, 306–7, 310, 317–19, 333–34, 338, 340–41, 371–72; *see also* individual, and community
self-consciousness, 158, 161–62, 301, 307, 311, 313, 323–35, 352–53, 364
self-determination or self-possession, 61–63, 68–71, 75–76, 85, 105, 200–203, 242n12, 285–90, 297–99, 337–38
self-gift; *see* gift of self
sentiment, and reason, 249, 253–54, 330–31, 332–33, 351–52
Shakespeare, William, 251n41
Sharpe, Lesley, 63n50, 77n86, 101n164

407

Sittlichkeit (ethical substance),
    241, 257, 295, 303, 320–56,
    369–70, 378
  defined, 320n57
Smith, Adam, 352
Smith, Steven, xv, 329n85
Snell, Reginald, 25n68, 101n162
Snow, Dale, 146n117, 200n111
society, civil, 338–46, 348–51, 356
soul; *see* body, and soul
Spaemann, Robert, 62n46, 65n58,
    372
Spinoza, Baruch, 70–71, 73, 145,
    154, 165, 173n9, 183–84,
    189, 200, 210, 225, 282, 376
spirit, xxi, xxii, 280–81, 283–84
  as absolute, 273–75, 305, 359–72
  as common or communal,
    251–53, 305–20
  as manifestation, 273–75,
    309–10, 378
  and matter, 308, 312
  and nature, 114, 279n126, 280;
    see also nature, and freedom
  as objective, xxiv, 243–44,
    304–5, 321–22, 324, 359–61,
    364–68
  tripartite structure of, 214n150,
    284
spontaneity; *see* receptivity, and
    spontaneity
state, 301–5, 346–56, 357–71
  and church, 276, 304, 365–71,
    378, 380
  and civil society, 348–51, 356
  and family, 347–48
Steinberger, Peter, 245n23
Sturma, Dieter, 153n142, 173
style,
  beautiful, 10–28, 35, 37, 40,
    43–44, 82, 374
  free, 38–41, 52–53, 96
  popular, 10, 12, 14, 18
  scientific, 10, 11–12, 14, 19–20,
    43
subject-object relation, 114, 119–20,
    125–26, 134–36, 144–46,
    161–64, 165, 177, 183, 186,
    228, 242, 267, 297–98, 376
Taminiaux, Jacques, 53n23, 57n31,
    62n49, 100n159
Taylor, Charles, xxi, 286n143,
    361n190, 373
teleology, 63–66, 135, 149–51,
    278–79
Tilliette, Xavier, 143n101, 208n129,
    230n201
time, and eternity, 23–24, 26–27,
    34–35, 80, 93, 96–97, 113,
    200–203, 379; *see also*
    history
Tocqueville, Alexis de, 356
Trinity, the, 217–26, 236–37, 274–
    75, 319–20
truth
  and abstraction, 10–11, 15–16,
    22, 84
  and beauty, 9–16, 24–26, 44–47,
    55–56
  and freedom, 11–16
  and mystery, 361–63
  and necessity, 11–12, 14, 19–21
  and politics, 246–48
  see also concept
Tunick, Mark, 253n45, 288n147,
    289n151
Ulrich, Ferdinand, 92n132,
    147n123, 275n115
unity
  appearance of, 253–54
  and beauty, 58–59, 86–88, 381
  and difference/distinction, 22–
    23, 27, 32, 46, 82–83, 86–88,
    106–7, 153, 193–94, 197,
    206–7, 218, 220, 227–31,
    234, 236, 312, 314–15, 331,
    350, 383
  as dramatic, 30–33, 35, 37–38,
    46, 55, 80–85, 86–88, 106,
    381
  as event, 153–54, 271
  and freedom, 53, 68–69
  internal, vs. external, 73,
    314–15; *see also* form,
    as interior principle of

organization; necessity,
internal vs. external; unity,
as mechanical
and love, 335
as mechanical, 19–20, 31, 75–76,
79, 95, 97
see also identity, and difference
universal, and particular, 184,
196, 258–59, 276, 282–83,
313–14, 343–44, 347–48,
351, 354
Unvordenklichkeit
("unprethinkability"), xxiv,
113, 177, 209, 210, 224, 233,
383
Vater, Michael G., 178n23
Vaysse, Jean-Marie, 208n130
Veatch, Henry, 137n83
Vico, Giovanni Battista, 45
Voegelin, Eric, 248n31
Wallace, Robert M., 242n13
Wechselwirkung (reciprocal
causality), 21, 27, 31, 35, 37,
41, 83, 88, 100; see also unity,
and difference/distinction;
unity, as dramatic
Weil, Eric, 246n25

Westphal, Kenneth, 323n66,
326n78, 343n132
Westphal, Merold, 337n107,
351n153
White, Alan, 183n51
Whitehead, Alfred North, 299n177
whole, and parts; see parts, and
whole
Wieland, Wolfgang, 116n26
Wiese, Benno von, 5n15, 24, 29, 40,
53n23, 92
Wilcox, Kenneth Parmelee, 22n63,
103n168
Wilkinson, Elizabeth, 23, 27, 29,
30n85
Wilkinson, Elizabeth and
Willoughby, L. A., 3n10,
24n67, 51n10, 53n23
will, 172, 244, 283–95, 325–26,
377–78
Wirth, Jason, xxivn24, 113n12,
196n98
Wood, Allen, 291n157, 302, 327n80
Zaborowski, Holger, 164n192,
199n108
Žižek, Slavoj, xxiv

Index

Centre of Theology and Philosophy

www.theologyphilosophycentre.co.uk

Every doctrine which does not reach the one thing necessary, every separated philosophy, will remain deceived by false appearances. It will be a doctrine, it will not be Philosophy. —Maurice Blondel, 1861–1949

This book series is the product of the work carried out at the Centre of Theology and Philosophy, at the University of Nottingham.

The COTP is a research-led institution organized at the interstices of theology and philosophy. It is founded on the conviction that these two disciplines cannot be adequately understood or further developed, save with reference to each other. This is true in historical terms, since we cannot comprehend our Western cultural legacy unless we acknowledge the interaction of the Hebraic and Hellenic traditions. It is also true conceptually, since reasoning is not fully separable from faith and hope, or conceptual reflection from revelatory disclosure. The reverse also holds, in either case.

The Centre is concerned with:

- The historical interaction between theology and philosophy
- The current relation between the two disciplines
- Attempts to overcome the Analytic/Continental divide in philosophy
- The question of the status of "metaphysics." Is the term used equivocally? Is it now at an end? Or have twentieth-century attempts to have a post-metaphysical philosophy themselves come to an end?
- The construction of a rich Catholic humanism

"I am very glad to be associated with the endeavors of this extremely important Centre that helps to further work of enormous importance. Among its concerns is the question whether modernity is more an interim than a completion—an interim between a pre-modernity in which the porosity between theology and philosophy was granted, perhaps taken for granted, and a post-modernity where their porosity must be unclogged and enacted anew. Through the work of leading theologians of international stature and philosophers whose writings bear on this porosity, the Centre offers an exciting forum to advance in diverse ways this challenging and entirely needful, and cutting-edge work."

—Professor William Desmond (University of Leuven)

"I am absolutely delighted to participate in the activities of the Centre of Theology and Philosophy. The Centre offers new insights on patristic and medieval thought: rather than limiting itself to historical research, it explores the contemporary relevance of these traditions. As such, the Centre dedicates itself to the real functions of both philosophy and theology: a work of extension and reasoning, as well as a reflection in dialogue with the history of the Western tradition as a whole. This combination of historical inquiry and speculative thought is a unique opportunity in contemporary research."

—Professor Olivier Boulnois (Ecole Pratique des Hautes Etudes, University of Paris Sorbonne)

"The amazing amount of activities—conferences, books, seminars, lectures—organized by the Centre of Theology and Philosophy is testament to its creativity, adventurousness, and proves the vitality of its theological paradigm of thought in addressing the major challenges of both our modern and post-modern culture. There is no other Centre quite like it."

—Professor Rudi te Velde (University of Tilburg)

"The Centre provides the most exciting and deep engagement of contemporary European theory, philosophy of religion and theology in the UK and Europe today. Its work combines careful and critical examination of modern theory alongside some of the most far reaching, sensitive and thoughtful positions in contemporary religion."

—Professor James Williams (University of Dundee)

"The separation between theology, philosophy, and science that has come to mark modern thought has led to all sorts of fundamentalisms: fundamentalism in science that has become anti-humanistic and anti-religious;

fundamentalism in religion that has become anti-scientific and anti-philosophical; and fundamentalism in philosophy in a retrenchment into linguistic analysis or phenomenology that has become exclusive of both science and religion. By bringing these three disciplines back together, to interface with one another in dealing with problems we face in our postmodern world of globalization, the Centre for Theology and Philosophy is not only restoring the ancient orthodox view that once saw them as complementing one another, but also performing an important, crucial service for these three intellectual disciplines themselves in need of rejoining with one another for the good of humanity, which is at once scientific, philosophical and theological. I am happy to be associated with this work as a philosopher mediating between science and religion through metaphysics."

—Professor Oliva Blanchette (Boston College)

www.ingramcontent.com/pod-product-compliance
Lightning Source LLC
Chambersburg PA
CBHW021928290426
44108CB00012B/755